DETAILS OF CLASSIC BOAT CONSTRUCTION

DETAILS OF CLASSIC BOAT CONSTRUCTION

THE HULL

LARRY PARDEY

SECOND EDITION
PHOTOGRAPHS AND DRAWINGS BY THE AUTHOR

PARDEY BOOKS
Arcata, California, USA

AN IMPRINT OF AIRLIFE PUBLISHING LTD
Shrewsbury U.K.

Original Edition – W. W. Norton New York and London
Revised Edition 1999 Pardey Books
Library of Congress Cataloging-in-Publication Data

Pardey, Larry.
  Details of classic boat construction : the hull / Larry Pardey ;
photographs and drawings by the author.
        p.   cm.
  Includes bibliographical references.
    1. Hulls (Naval architecture)—Pictorial works.   2. Wooden boats—
Design and construction—Pictorial works.   3. Taleisin (Yacht)—
Pictorial works.   4. Wooden boats—New Zealand—Design and
construction—Pictorial works.   5. Yacht building—Pictorial works.
6. Yacht building—New Zealand—Pictorial works.   I. Title.
VM321.P25   1991
623.8'123—dc20   90-30677

ISBN 0 964 6036-8-3

Pardey Books and Videos
Distributed by Paradise Cay Publishing, P.O. Box 29, Arcata, California 95518-0029 USA
Telephone: 1-800-736-4509
Outside USA: 1-707-822-9063
Fax: 707-822-9163
Note: All of the Pardey books and videos are available from Paradise Cay Publications
Or in the U.K. from Waterline Books, 101 Longden Road, Shrewsbury SY3 9EB
Telephone: 01743 235651
U.K. video distributor Biograph, Yelverton Business Park, Yelverton, Devon PL20 7PE
Telephone: 01822 855582

3   4   5   6   7   8   9   0

To LIN, my full-on partner.
She has walked beside me,
enthusiastically, all the way.

CONTENTS

ACKNOWLEDGMENTS

Below is a chronological catalog of the boatbuilders and boat repairmen who have influenced me and ultimately this book. I am afraid the list is incomplete, as it is impossible to remember the names of every craftsman who shared his time with me, told me why he was fitting one piece before another, or explained the purpose of a particular tool. I thank them and all the men on this list for their time, patience, and willingness to share.

Canada: Peter Rook, Ralph Vittery, Derrick Cove, Mike DeRitter, Frank Fredette, Greg Foster, John Guzzwell. United States: the late Bob Sloan, the late Art Clark, Albert Longtin, Tom Ditmar, Hale Field, Tom Don Carswell, Raleigh Kalayjian, Roy Wildman, the late Bob Ayou, the late Harding Edkins, Yann Egasse, Jay Greer, the late Ted Howard, Les Crawford, Bob Dorris, Frank Mann, Rudy Shackleford, Arno Day, Wayne Ettles, Walt Posten. Mexico: Don José Abaroa and his seven sons. Costa Rica: Sammy Manley. England: Jack and John at Cobb's Quay, Landamore's crew at Wroxham. Gibraltar: John at the Marina Boat Shop. Denmark: A. Walsted, Jr. Switzerland: François Graeser. Italy: Carlos Craglietto, Carlos Sciarelli. New Zealand: John Salthouse, Maury Speight, John Lidgard, Robin Harris, Lindsey Stewart.

Lyle Hess, designer of *Taleisin* and *Seraffyn*, deserves special mention—not only because he provided the plans included in this book, but also because over the years he has taught me the bulk of what I know about building boats. Thanks again, Lyle.

Another group of people who helped in the creation of this book were also craftsmen and professionals in their own right, and I appreciated their assistance. Eric Swenson, editor and vice chairman of W.W. Norton, my publisher, encouraged this project from the beginning and suggested I make it practical by dividing the subject into two volumes—the first on hulls and a second one on decks, interiors, and fitting out. Diane O'Connor has been a tower of strength and source of sanity in the confusion of keeping this manuscript moving toward book form. Doug Logan and Kathleen Brandes did an enthusiastic and scrupulous job of editing. Thom Riedle helped me with hints on setting up a darkroom. He gave me a very helpful timer, which I used for enlarging and cropping the photographs in this book. He also helped improve the quality of those photographs. The late Eric Hiscock gave me his Leitz enlarger, a fine instrument that is the veteran of several illustrated sailing books. Will Thompson, my high school woodworking teacher, got me started on a track that has given me a lot of pleasure over the years. He pragmatically told me that it would take me two and a half years to build the 23-foot Atkin cutter about which I was dreaming. At the age of eighteen, that sounded like a lifetime, so I went out and learned to fix boats and sail them. When I did build my own first boat seven years later, I was prepared for the scope of the project. Bob Jacobson took the excellent photograph that is used as photo 8.12. Nick Peale redrew the lines plan to show the 14-inch centers I actually used for lofting and construction.

During the construction of *Taleisin*, several people helped us with the loan of equipment or tools, with their encouragement, or with labor when we needed an extra hand. They included Jim Crow, Walter Methner, Jim Moore, Jim Newhouse, Doug Schmuck, Harry Vega, Dean Wixom, Allen Zatkin, and the late Sam Zatkin.

The research and organization of the appendix on adhesives was done by my wife, Lin. She was encouraged by Scott Earnshaw, the chemist for Dimet Pty. Ltd. here in New Zealand. Brian Boult, a fellow of construction materials engineering at the University of Auckland, verified the information on using adhesives properly. Our thanks to the Ciba-Geigy Company, High Modulus Fabrics, *Sail* magazine, and *WoodenBoat* magazine for their financial support for the final laboratory-controlled adhesive testing developed for this book.

W. P. Jackson of Lloyd's Register of Shipping, Auckland, New Zealand, and R. J. Rymill, general manager of the Yacht and Small Craft Services, Lloyd's Register, in London, helped us with access to the rule requirements used by their company as a guide to wooden yacht construction. The copyrighted material printed as part of Appendix B is used with the permission of Lloyd's Register of Shipping.

Finally, I would like to thank the people who have asked me about various aspects of boatbuilding—people such as Bill Eisenlohr, Mike Anderson, Linda Smith, Kit Cooney, Fenton Hamlin, Tony Davis, Bob Ramirez, Bertram Levy, and David King. Their questions are the ones I have tried to answer as I wrote this book.

Many people helped us as we updated this book for the second edition. Among them are Mary Baldwin, John Guzzwell, Peter Legnos and Micheal Masculine, Matt and Jim Morehouse and Oscar Lind. Charles Vick of the USDA department of Forestry research labs provided his time and resources for the section on wood and adhesives. Micheal Heine provided legal consul and reviewed the new appendix on adhesives to help us avoid the threat of litigation. Our thanks to each of you and to the many readers who have encouraged us to write another volume on boat building.

AUTHOR'S NOTE: Much of my work has been done in countries where British boatbuilding terms are commonly used, and some readers may be unfamiliar with the American terms often used, so I have tried to use the terms or words that I feel most closely describe an actual part or action of boatbuilding. Wherever confusion could occur, I try to give both the English and the American terms. A case in point would be the fashion timber, which could also be called the transom framing.

INTRODUCTION

The photographs that make up the majority of this book were part of our *Taleisin* boat-building project from the beginning. Therefore, I feel they come as close as possible to providing a videolike view of the skills that some present-day boatbuilders say are "lost forever." I don't believe that these classic construction skills and methods were ever lost, nor that they are difficult to learn. But I do agree that some of the skills have become obscure because they are next to impossible to describe in words. How do you write down the procedures for shaping a carvel plank? Or, for that matter, how do you describe, in conversation, the simple tricks for squaring-up big timbers?

Diagrams help, but I think these photographs showing *Taleisin*'s construction may prove to be more efficient because, in addition to being believable, they show shop details and clamping methods and generally set the scene at a glance. They may also provide answers to questions I never thought to address. In each photographic section I have tried to show sequences that I felt would help potential builders feel more comfortable about working with classic boatbuilding methods. When I thought it might be useful, I supplied step-by-step details of how to fit the different types of joints used in building carvel-planked hulls. For some builders, these detailed discussions may seem unnecessary, but if even a handful of people learn a few tricks that produce better-fitting, stronger joints, the space these sequences occupy will have been worthwhile.

At the end of each photographic section I have listed the hours Lin and I spent on the various sections of *Taleisin*'s hull. Lin kept an accurate diary of each day's work. And even though these hours include some time for photography, they were within the normal building-hour range for a vessel of this displacement finished to yacht-quality standards.

Over the years, Lin and I have discussed the question of yachtbuilding time with people such as Gerry Driscoll in San Diego, California; Carlo Sciarelli in Trieste, Italy; Craglietto Boat Builders in Italy; Lyle Hess in Fullerton, California; John Lidgard in New Zealand. And we have corresponded with Rod Stephens of Sparkman and Stephens in New York. They all agreed regarding the number of hours required to build and outfit a quality, custom-built, one-off yacht under 50 feet in length using wood, steel, glass, or aluminum. For a one-off, moderate-to-heavy-displacement yacht of any material, built to the quality you would expect from a yard like Nevins of City Island, New York, Abeking & Rasmussen of Germany, or Lidgard's of New Zealand, a builder will spend about 800 hours per 2,000-pound ton. For a light-displacement hull, the hours will increase toward 1,000 per ton as the scantlings become lighter and the construction methods more scientific.

Taleisin weighs 17,400 pounds at two-thirds loaded displacement. To finish her to launch-ready sailing condition took the two of us 7,182 hours. It took another 1,500 hours to finish her to full offshore cruising condition, including building a wind vane, a sailing rig, and chocks for the dinghy, heating stove, and other items we wanted for long-distance voyaging. The 4,726 hours we recorded in this book include the setup of a shop and the building of specialized tools and jigs for a onetime project, plus acquisition and milling of timber. A builder in an established shop—with jigs, a supply of timber, and specialized tools—could probably reduce these times somewhat. Furthermore, I built this boat purely to do it the way I wanted. So if it took another two hours to get the lofting to fair up perfectly, or to get a plank to fit just right, or to find a better-looking piece of timber, I took that extra time. If a professional builder spent this extra time, he might enjoy the job more, but the customer would not be pleased when presented with the bill.

I believe a novice could come close to building a fine boat within our time range if he or she already had skills with hand tools and had already built a successful rowing or sailing dinghy. Some professional builders will say they have built boats faster than the times suggested here, but to give a fair comparison of hours, it is necessary to compare the finished products. I have seen contract-price boatbuilders suggest changing the construction methods recommended by the designer in order to accommodate the builder's personal speed tricks, the materials he already had on hand, methods that let him use less-skilled help, and jigs that were already set up—the contract builder knows that time is money. But rarely have I seen these shortcuts produce a better boat for the owner/user/sailor, nor make his boat easier to maintain or more valuable at resale time.

The discussion sections at the ends of most chapters include methods I have seen used successfully to reinforce potential trouble areas—in other words, ways to engineer better stress-spreading structures into the boat during construction. Although I have never owned a boat that leaked, I have had to sail on and repair ones that did. Rarely were the leaks due to rough-and-ready workmanship or less-than-perfect fits at joints or seams. The leaks could be traced to problems caused by poor engineering of the basic structure of the boat or of the design of the joints used to build it. It is this poor engineering—combined at times with poor choice of materials—that has given wooden boats in general a bad name. It is these poorly built boats that are always on the market for the low prices that attract unwary or unknowledgeable buyers. Well-engineered, finely built yachts rarely seem to come on the open market. Instead, they are passed from private owner to private owner, just like a beautiful waterfront home or a unique classic car.

Another area I discuss at the end of each chapter is the repairability and the "survey-ability" of various construction methods. Determining a boat's condition and fixing dam-age as a boat is used are the problems of the owner and user. If a boat is built to be repaired and surveyed easily, it will be easier to maintain throughout its life.

One of the greatest problems facing a first-time builder is making choices. What type of wood should he use? What fastenings? What method of construction best fits his situa-tion and the design he is using? These choices can only be made if he compares the facts and options in some logical manner. In the "pro" and "con" sections of this book, I have attempted to be unprejudiced in showing the advantages and disadvantages of various choices.

There is no such thing as a comprehensive book on any type of boatbuilding. Howard Chapelle's book *Boatbuilding* (see Bibliography) comes as close as any I have seen. I used his book when I built *Seraffyn* and found that even though various methods of construc-tion were well covered, hands-on boatbuilder skills were, in the main, left out. Other books I read covered some details, but, in trying to be complete boatbuilding guides, they did not have room to discuss the specific details new builders most often require. So in writing this book, I have decided to accept that it could not be complete. Instead, I have tried to concentrate on giving details of construction and information about the skills that are not found in the books available on boatbuilding.

Many of the skills and ideas I learned and have shown in this book came from listen-ing to generous, patient craftsmen who would often set down a plane or chisel, light a pipe and answer my seemingly endless list of basic questions. My other teachers were the boats I sailed, maintained, and repaired. The repair work was an especially good teacher. I found that one of the best ways to compare boatbuilding methods and engineering ideas was to work in boatyards specializing in general repairs. Poor construction methods often cause problems that do not appear for ten or fifteen years after a boat is built. Studying these problems and thinking of how to repair them—and how the problems could have been prevented—taught me about proper engineering. Voyaging in my own yachts also was a learning experience. Maintaining and refitting my boats reminded me that you can build time-consuming problems into a boat.

Over the past thirty years, I have owned four carvel-planked yachts. I've raced them and taken them voyaging. I've delivered and sailed yachts over 150,000 miles of oceans and built and repaired boats in several different countries. I firmly believe that, as a con-struction material, wood has *fewer compromises* for the end user than any other boatbuilding material, including steel, aluminum, or fiberglass. Eric and Susan Hiscock confirmed this when they told us that their all-time favorite after fifty years of voyaging on five different *Wanderers* was the 30-foot *Wanderer III*, carvel-planked with iroko over oak frames. She carried them through two and a half circumnavigations. Their next boat was a 49-foot steel yacht that they came to dislike because of several drawbacks directly related to the construction material. Their final yacht, the one on which this particular conversation took place late in 1986, was *Wanderer V,* a 39-foot, three-skinned, kauri-pine hull built in New Zealand. This boat, though not perfect, served them for seven years, and they were "delighted to be back in wood again."

Their observations, my experience, and the experience of friends who have built or acquired a good wooden boat make me believe that classic wooden yachts are a valuable and rewarding proposition. I am fully confident that the present generation of potential builders can learn anything the old-timers knew about classic boatbuilding and, with just a bit of encouragement, can build a first-class oceangoing vessel using that most fascinating of mediums—that beautiful, durable, fatigue-resistant, self-reproducing resource—*wood.*

INTRODUCTION TO THE SECOND EDITION

I've had the pleasure of meeting many of the readers of the first edition of this book as we voyaged and visited wooden-boat festivals in several different countries. My only disappointment is that those builders, though telling me of lots of different ideas they gained from *Details of Classic Boat Construction*, rarely mentioned the appendix on adhesives.

One of the reasons I wrote this book was to get real information, not advertising hype, out to boat builders and designers. Epoxy adhesives have not lived up to their early promises (and many of the promises still being made). Every time I visit a marina I see newer boats with lots of woodwork delaminations. This is not confined to wooden boats. It is obvious wherever exterior wood has been joined using "modern epoxy" adhesives. It breaks my heart to see people investing their man-hours, our planet's valuable timber resources, only to have their project spoiled by a few dollars' worth of glue. So *please, please* take the time to read the updated appendix on more user-friendly, extreme exposure adhesives. The message it contains may not be one people wish to hear, but it is vital to both the wooden-boat movement and the production-boat industry.

Although I have corrected some minor errors in numbering and spelling in the original pages, I have made only one other noticeable change. At the request of several boat-building schools, this book now has a more shop-friendly plastic-coated cover, one that can be wiped clean when grease or paint smudges appear on it.

As more people become involved in computer technology, skilled craftsmen—people who can build things using their own hands—are more in demand. That has made the profession of boat building more valuable. For anyone who can build or repair a boat, can build almost anything, be it in wood, glass, or metal. In the years since I wrote the introduction to the first edition, the actual number of wooden boats out sailing has increased, the number of schools teaching boat building skills has doubled. The debate on the best building methods, timbers, designs continues unabated. The one thing that cannot be debated is that the pleasure and satisfaction of building in wood surpasses that of working in any other medium. I hope this book encourages you to try it.

Larry Pardey, Yeocomico River, Virginia, 1999

1. LOFTING

In order to build an irregularly shaped structure like a boat or a plane, you need full-size three-dimensional drawings, since you cannot simply scale up from 1 inch on the plans to 1 foot to get the actual dimensions of the object you are building—as you would for square-cornered structures. This need to loft full-size, then build in three dimensions, is why I feel the fully shaped wineglass sailboat hull is one of the ultimate challenges available for a woodworker.

I have lofted four boats by following the step-by-step description in Howard I. Chapelle's book *Boatbuilding*. The procedures he recommends are logical and relatively easy to understand. The results in each case were satisfying. I am in complete accord with the reasons he gives for fully lofting any boat you intend to build:

> Lofting the plans, that is, drawing them full size, is the foundation of good workmanship in building a boat. Because this is usually a tedious task and because the builder is impatient to see the hull take shape, lofting is often scimped, even by professional builders who know better. Making the full-sized drawings avoids much "trying and fitting," which represents a great saving in time and labor. In the lofting of the plans the builder has an opportunity to preview the details of building before setting up the hull and this aids greatly in planning the required sequence of operations. Too often only the lines of the boat are "laid down" full size; this enables the molds and backbone to be shaped according to the design, it is true, but leaves much timber to be shaped by trial and error when actual construction starts. By lofting part of the construction and joiner plans as well as the lines, this can be avoided. Mistakes made in the full-sized plan can be easily corrected, which is not true of the full-sized hull; very often what appeared to be a serious problem when studying the plans becomes self-explanatory when drawn full size. Sometimes errors are found in the plans, designers being human, and lofting will expose and correct them. While making the full-sized plans, the builder should build the boat mentally, to get the full advantage of the operation. Plenty of time must be allowed for the task and it should be borne in mind that there was never a boat built in which too much lofting had been done.

The comments in this chapter will, I hope, add to Chapelle's lofting description and clarify some points for those of you who are struggling with lines, battens, and offsets for the first time. In later chapters, I have illustrated how the loft-floor measurements are referred to time and again to give quickly and accurately the correct dimensions and shapes you need during various stages of hull construction.

1.1

1.2

1.3

Photo 1.1   The loft floor was the first construction project in our boatyard. I built it 36 feet long and 10 feet wide, using construction-grade 2 x 4s on 24-inch centers. The leveled framework ewas covered with low-cost ½-inch exterior-grade plywood laid good side up. The diagonal (corner-to-corner) measurements of the framework were equal in order to produce a rectangular floor with 90-degree corners.

Photo 1.2   Both ends of the 36-foot-long framework had a 2-foot-by-10-foot section without a plywood cover. These ends were simply supports for the ends of my longitudinal lofting battens. A ½-inch-thick piece of wood, tacked onto the top edge of the 2 x 4 framing, leveled the ends of the plywood floor. This maneuver saved me a whole sheet of plywood.

Once the floor was built, I worked on lofting in the mornings, when it was cool, and began building the boatshed in the afternoons. I like to have alternative projects in case the primary job (in this case, lofting) is halted because of weather or lack of materials. I jot down a list of these projects—e.g., build boatshed, workbenches, sawhorses, connect machinery. With this list available, I can accumulate the materials I need and be ready for those times when work otherwise would grind to a halt.

Photo 1.3   The shed was sited in the shade of eucalyptus (gum) trees to help keep the temperature down and humidity up during the California summers. At the end of this chapter are some further comments on loft floors, but right now I'll get into some of the things I have learned about lofting that I hope will supplement Howard Chapelle's *Boatbuilding* (see Bibliography).

Photo 1.4 The use of staffs is an accurate method of recording and transferring measurements from one part of the loft floor to another, and eventually to the keel timbers. Staffs also make life easier later when you are correcting and fairing your lines. Tom Don Carswell of Costa Mesa, California, a professional loftsman, uses four different-colored felt pens: one color for diagonals, one for waterlines, one for buttocks, and the fourth for body sections. He uses both sides of his staffs as well as each end. (This divides the number of staffs he needs by four.) In diagram 1.1, all of the half-breadths of waterline 1A (the one above the LWL) are on this side and end of the staff. In the photograph, you can see how I butt the right-hand end of the waterline staff against the plywood straightedge that is secured on the centerline of the body plan.

1.4

Diagram 1.1

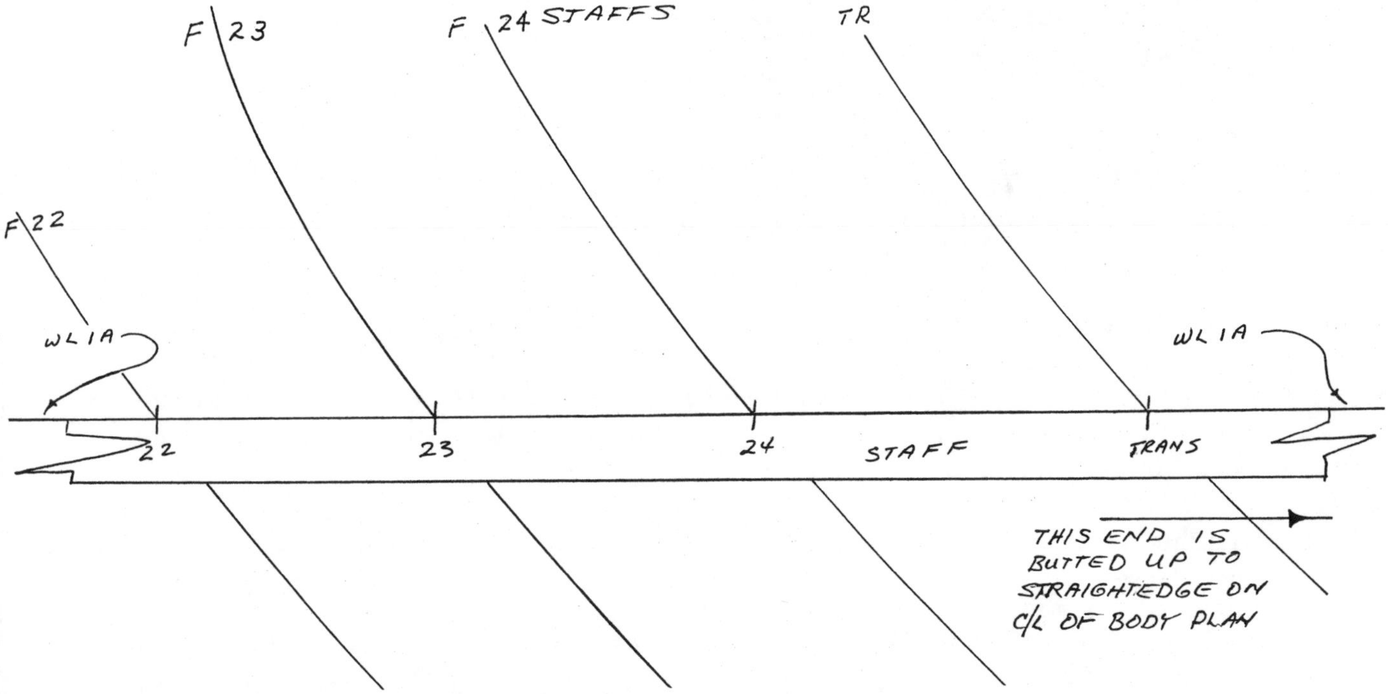

F 23   F 24 STAFFS   TR

F 22

F 22

WL 1A   WL 1A

22   23   24   STAFF   TRANS

THIS END IS BUTTED UP TO STRAIGHTEDGE ON C/L OF BODY PLAN

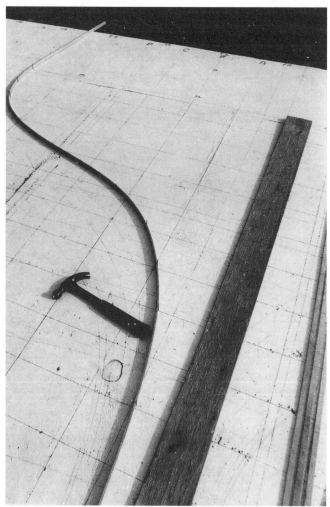

Photo 1.5 Pine or cedar makes good battens for laying down the body sections. The batten in this photo is ¼-inch-by-¾-inch pine. As you cut your battens, select the ones that have the straightest grain for lofting the body plan so they will have less tendency to break when you bend them. Use the reject battens for staffs.

1.5

I used a fiberglass batten for lofting the longitudinal lines on *Taleisin* and was delighted with it. This batten, 5/16 inch by 1¼ inches, was made by Polytrusion of Santa Ana, California, and came in lengths of up to 100 feet. It cost about $1.00 a foot in 1980. You can't break it and it is perfectly fair, since it has no joints. To store it, you can roll the batten into a 6-foot-diameter circle. You can use it on edge or on the flat and it will probably last a lifetime.

These fiberglass battens do have one flaw, however. If you leave them in the sun for long periods or hit them with metal objects, they can develop tiny glass slivers that will irritate or cut your hands.

You will notice in the photographs here, and throughout the book, that I cut my straightedges from plywood. I check them for accuracy occasionally by drawing a line with the straightedge, then flipping it over. If it lines up perfectly on the other side of the line, it is still straight.

One lesson I learned from Lyle Hess* was that a builder should not be overly concerned with the table of offsets provided by the designer. They are only a convenience. If you think there is an error in the offsets, scale the same measurement off the lines plan with a pair of dividers and a scale rule. If there is a discrepancy, use the measurement you scaled from the lines plan. Your full-size lines on the loft floor should eventually look like the smaller version on the lines-plan print. You could take measurements of all of the half-breadths, waterlines, and so on, from these prints and make your own table of offsets. Then you would find how tedious and exacting the job is. For this reason, some clerical errors are to be expected in the table of offsets, even from the most experienced of designers.

As you fair up the lines, expect to do a lot of laying down, then erasing. This is normal; and it gets a lot easier when you loft your second boat. On *Taleisin*, I found the buttock lines needed to be adjusted up to ⅜ inch to align with the waterlines and diagonals. It took me a lot of time to fair up the tuck where the sternpost and transom meet because buttock A, waterline 1A, diagonal II, frame section 24, and the transom line all come together in the same 6-inch square (diagram 1.2.)

I added an extra diagonal, diagonal IV, to ensure that the area near the garboards and floors was fair and accurate. I decided to do this because I found some minor discrepancies in this area after I had built in the floors on *Seraffyn*. I then had to spend a lot of time chiseling the endgrain to get the garboards to lie fairly. You can add diagonals anywhere you wish as you loft to achieve this increased accuracy. Diagonals are, in my opinion, the most important lines produced on the loft floor. They follow almost the same curve as the planks, so if your lofted diagonals are all fair, your hull framework will also be fair—which means your hull will be easy to plank.

I decided to loft outdoors because of the fine weather usually associated with southern California. However, for the first time in eleven years, it rained 35 days out of 50. The paint on the floor started to peel, the plywood began to warp and delaminate, and I had to rush to get my patterns made while the lines were still visible. So I would advise lofting under cover if at all possible.

It took 91 hours to loft this 30-footer, complete with extra body sections on 14-inch centers so I could make patterns for each sawn frame, plus the backbone, keel timbers, and the expanded transom. (This total did not include picking up the frame bevels or the ply-wood patterns for the sawn frames.)

I found this boat to be extremely time-consuming to loft because Lyle drew waterlines every 6 inches. This meant 50 percent more lofting work, but it gave 50 percent more accuracy than a lofting with waterlines 9 inches apart. I compounded the problem by lofting the intermediate sections for each of 24 sawn frames instead of doing body sections on 33-inch centers, as I would have done had I been using intermediate bent frames. But I was rewarded with very tight shape control and eventually a smooth, fair framework. When I planked, I only had to dub 1/16 inch of wood off a few of the frames to get them faired in to accept the planks.

---

* Lyle C. Hess, 5911 East Spring St, #360 Long Beach, California 90808 Telephone 562 595-7923 was the designer of both *Seraffyn* and *Taleisin*. *Seraffyn* was 24 feet 4 inches and similar to *Taleisin*, the boat shown throughout this book.

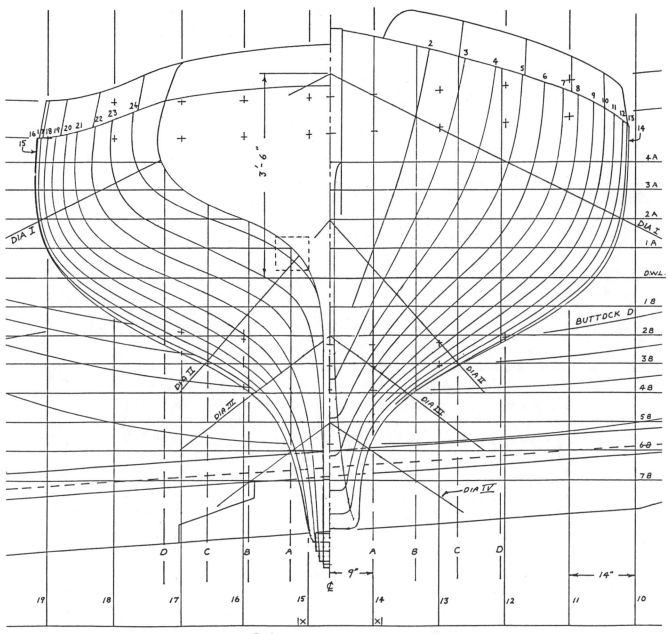

Diagram 1.2

NOTE THE LOWER PARTS OF SECTION LINES 2,4, 6, ETC., HAVE BEEN DELETED
TO MAKE THE DIAGRAM LESS CONFUSING.

CONSTRUCTION TIMES FOR CHAPTER 1

Larry: Building loft floor and lofting	113 hours
Building boatshed, foundations, sides, and roof, including drainage for spring found under the corner of the building site	147 hours
Lin: Scraping, painting, and restoring thickness planer; shopping for materials; painting loft floor; acting as construction assistant	41 hours
Totals to date: Larry	260 hours
Lin	41 hours

DISCUSSION
More on Loft Floors and Lofting

On my next boat, I definitely want to loft under cover, so I plan to build the boatshed first —complete with roof and three sides covered with plywood and windows. The fourth side would only be framed out. I would then do the complete lofting procedure on a loft floor built under the cover of the shed. Next I would pick up patterns, then nail the plywood loft-floor panels onto the inside wall of the shop. This would let me refer to the lofted lines during construction and save the cost of plywood for that final wall. A shop with the traditional mold loft above the workshop would be even handier for any full-time boatbuilder.

One California boatbuilder, Bob Sloan, bought good-quality plywood for his loft floor, then later reused it as the subdeck under a layer of teak on his 36-foot schooner. The nail holes made by lofting on the plywood were covered by the teak, and the unnailed side faced onto the deckbeams. This could also work if you were using a canvas deck covering.

I used the 1969 edition of Chapelle's *Boatbuilding* for reference as I built *Taleisin*. There are a few lofting facts that I would like to expand upon. The first is that to loft a boat well, you must be confident you can distinguish a fair line from a lumpy one. This is as basic to boatbuilding as knowing the wind direction is to sailing.

Look at a french curve. Every line on it is fair. Not one is lumpy or irregular. Lines A and C in diagram 1.3 are fair lines, the rest are not. Recognizing this fairness is a developed skill. A boatbuilder who has a "good eye" always ends up with a more artistic, professional-looking, easier-to-plank boat.

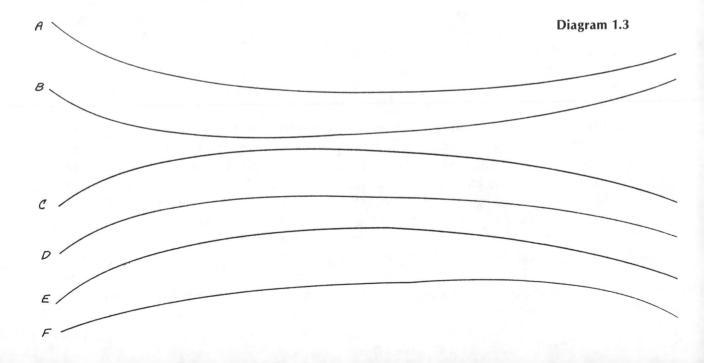

Diagram 1.3

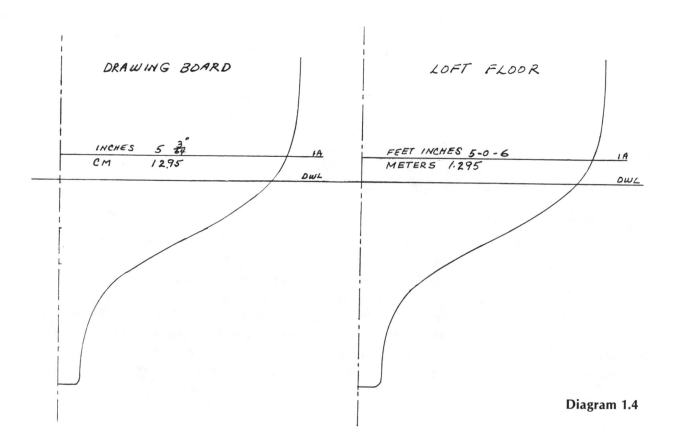

Diagram 1.4

Most first-time boatbuilders find lofting the most intimidating part of the whole project. I know I did. And to shake my confidence further, I found a 1-inch error in the offset measurements for the first line I laid down. But I doggedly followed Chapelle's description and eventually the lofting did work out. I later learned that problems such as I encountered are caused by two types of errors.

The first type of error that commonly creeps into offset tables is caused by expansion. The ink lines drawn by the designer on his plans are 12 times larger than the lines laid down full-size on the loft floor (1-inch-equals-1-foot scale). In other words, if you took your lines-plan sheet and enlarged it on a proportional copier until it was full-size, the ink lines, which are about ¹⁄₆₄ inch thick on the plans, could appear as ³⁄₁₆-inch-thick lines on the full-size copy. If the designer places the point of his dividers on one side or the other of his line, instead of exactly in the center, as he is picking up his measurements, you could end up with an unfair line. Thus, on the full-size loft floor, you have 12 times more accuracy than the designer has when he is using the same pencil line on his plans.

Inaccuracies also occur in the transfer of measurements from plans to offset tables because of clerical errors in the conversion from inches to feet and inches, as shown in diagram 1.4. A few American designers produce their plans and offset with metric measurements to avoid this problem. The metric system simplifies picking up the numbers for a table of offsets because the designer does not need a special scale rule to do the job; he can simply scale up from 1 to 10 by moving a decimal point.

Some of my friends have borrowed a set of patterns and molds made by another builder who has already completed a hull they like. This saves them having to loft their own hull. But, as with any decision you make when you are building a boat, this has advantages and disadvantages:

PRO	Con
Lofting time is eliminated.	The lofting might not be as good as you expected. You have to trust the original loftsman.
Pattern and loft floor materials, plus storage space, are saved.	
Might give a first-time builder the confidence to start a boat project.	You don't have a full-size lofting to refer to for additional measurements and patterns during construction.
It may be possible to go for a trial sail on the first boat built from the plans—i.e., you can be sure it is a successful design before you build one like it.	You do not have the intimate knowledge of the shapes with which you will be working.
	If you hope to turn professional, you are shortchanging your career if you are tempted by existing patterns and molds.

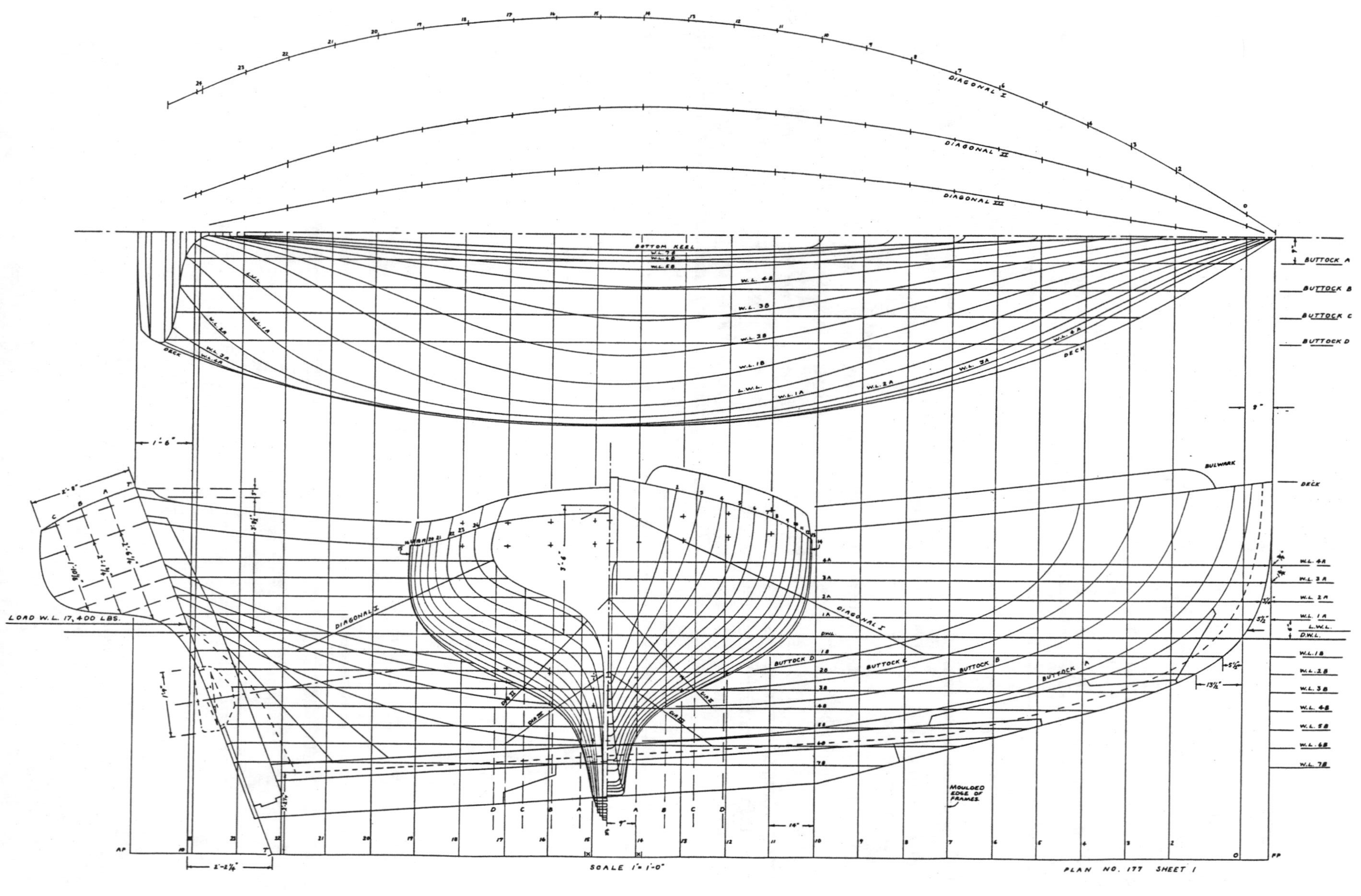
DIAGONAL I
DIAGONAL II
DIAGONAL III
BOTTOM KEEL
BUTTOCK A
BUTTOCK B
BUTTOCK C
BUTTOCK D
DECK
BULWARK
LOAD W.L. 17,400 LBS.
MOULDED EDGE OF FRAMES
SCALE 1" = 1'-0"
PLAN NO. 177 SHEET 1
AP
FP

Diagram 2.1

2. CUTTING
THE BACKBONE TIMBERS

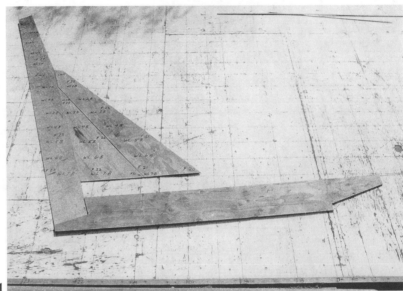

2.1

Photo 2.1 After I finished transferring the backbone profile from the construction drawings (diagram 2.1) to the loft floor, I fitted and nailed the plywood patterns for each timber directly onto the floor. Then I transferred the waterlines, sections, and rabbet lines onto the patterns, using a straightedge for waterlines and sections and the appropriate staff for the rabbet line. The joints between the patterns should fit. I used a felt pen to circle the holddown holes on the pattern so I could reuse those same holes for refitting or checking.

Photo 2.2 The faying edges for the joints on the patterns should be dead straight, as this will make it easier to fit the timbers. Angle the nib ends of the stem knee, as shown in the photos, to facilitate fitting the timbers later. (In chapter 3, I will discuss fitting the nib ends.) If possible, I cut the plywood pattern so the grain runs in the direction of maximum strength for each part of the backbone assembly. This makes the pattern stronger and indicates how I should place it on the timbers. The grain should always run lengthwise on knee, stem, forefoot, and transom knees.

2.2

2.3

2.4

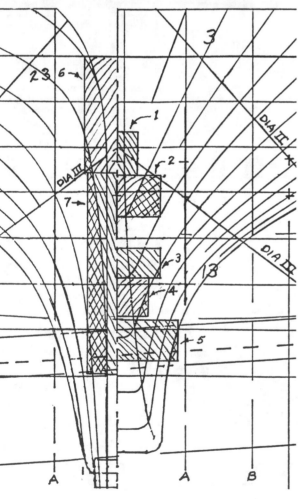

Diagram 2.2

Photo 2.3 These patterns give only a side view of the backbone parts. The cross-sectional views of the timbers, the views that will give you the third dimension (diagram 2.2), must be drawn on the loft floor separately so that you can later take measurements to shape the outside of the backbone timbers. These sectional drawings show you where wood will be removed from each timber as you shape it (see cross-hatching on diagram 2.2).

Photo 2.4 On your plywood patterns, indicate the areas to be removed, so that when you lay them on your timbers, you can plan to have the poorest corners of your timbers face downward. Most of the defects then are likely to be adzed off.

2.6

2.5

Photo 2.5 At this stage I slow down, think, turn over my timber, think, and turn it again. I check the location of any heartwood, knots, and splits and then use a felt pen to circle any hard-to-spot defects in the timber. If necessary, clean the timbers with a hand or electric plane in order to clarify the grain or spot any defects. If the heart is hollow, poke a rod up both ends of it to determine the length of the hole. Use only tight hearts, and keep even these to a minimum.

Photo 2.6 All of the timbers for my project were teak with boxed hearts. I was able to cut the stem, stem knee, and keel timber to eliminate the heartwood. With the other parts, I felt comfortable about the boxed hearts, since they were tight and teak is very rot-resistant. The bonus for all of my measuring, turning, and checking was that I was left with a piece of timber just large enough for the mast step.

Use the marks on your patterns to check whether the rabbet line is going to run through any knots or defects. This is important, as a knot or seasoning check in the caulking surface of the rabbet makes the rabbet hard to cut or chisel, and it could cause leaks later.

Before you start sawing, be sure you have selected a piece of timber for each backbone part.

2.7

2.8

2.9

Photos 2.7, 2.8 I hope you can find straight, square timbers for your project; I never have. So I true them up before I scribe the pattern shape onto the wood. This surface had a crown or rise to it, so I planed the timber until the two carpenter's squares sat flat and parallel on opposite ends of the timber. By sighting along the two squares, I could see if they were indeed parallel. Then I nailed a straightedge to just touch both squares (photo 2.8). I scribed the timber with a knife and repeated the procedure on the other side. Then I planed down to the scribe lines.

Photo 2.9 At this stage, the timber had one side that was straight, flat, and parallel. Using this first side as a guide, you can square and true up the sides to fit your patterns.

2.10

2.11

2.12

Photo 2.10 This is the inside forward piece of the stern knee. The face next to my leg must be square so that floor timbers that land here will not be cocked either to port or to starboard. I tacked the pattern down to the squared edge and scribed around it with a knife.

Photo 2.11 I transferred the pattern marks to the timber with a small square. At the same time, I penciled these lines onto the edge of the plywood pattern, turned over the timber and flopped the pattern to the corresponding side, and aligned the pattern using the squared marks I had just penciled on its edge, along wth the lines across the timber. Then I marked all of the waterlines and sections on the second side of the timber.

Photo 2.12 If your timbers are quite old, with some seasoning checks, expect distortion when you cut. This is caused by unequal moisture content and internal stresses. This photo shows what can happen to a straight saw cut. A change like this might not affect the shape of the part, but it is safest to make the final cut ¼ or ⅜ inch oversize so that if the part is warped, you can use this extra wood to rescribe it.

Photo 2.13 I use a Skilsaw to make the first cut. It pays to check the squareness of the blade before every cut.

2.13

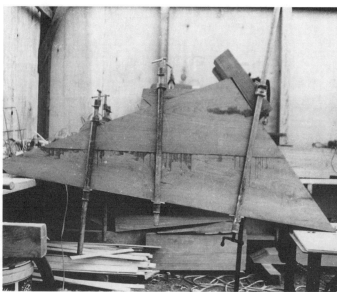

2.14   2.16

2.15

Photo 2.14 Next I used a Makita 6½-inch-depth (14-inch blade) beam saw and followed the first cut. I repeated this procedure on the other side of the timber.

Photo 2.15 The only way to avoid damaging the nib at the end of the forefoot scarf is to use a handsaw for the last bit of the cut.

Photo 2.16 I glued together the two pieces of the transom knee with resorcinol. This made it easier to plane and square them. Since this member of the backbone assembly resolves the angle of the transom, it should be dead square and straight on the jointing surfaces, and it should match the lofted pattern exactly.

Photo 2.17 After I cut all of the parts, I planed or chiseled each one down to the marks scribed from the patterns. Here, the stem piece is set up for planing.

Photo 2.18 Cast-iron planes usually have sharp edges on the forward end of the sole. I round them off so they don't nick or dent the corners of the joints.

2.17

2.18

Photo 2.19 These three classic Stanley (formerly Bailey) planes are numbers 4, 5, and 10. Numbers 4 and 5 have grooved soles to create less friction. If you are working with pitchy wood, you can brush kerosene into the groove. It will leach off and keep pitch and shavings from sticking to the plane. I prefer these iron planes for 95 percent of my boatbuilding work, since they are quicker to sharpen and easier to adjust than wood planes. The micrometerlike screw and lever arm allows minute blade adjustments. But be aware that cast-iron planes will break if they are dropped on a concrete floor. Also, you cannot change the shape of the sole to fit convex or concave shapes, as you can with wood planes. When we cruised on *Seraffyn*, I carried only the number 4 and the number 10, plus a small block plane and a bullnose plane. They were all I needed to earn a living doing boat repairs and renovation work.

2.19

2.20

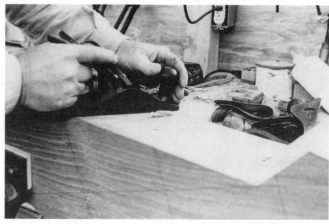

2.23

2.21

2.22

Photo 2.20 I worked this joint on the stem exactly square to the side. The elongated worm hole will be adzed off when the cutwater is shaped. The knots and most of the checking will eventually be under the planking, just clear of the rabbet line. I was able to plan for this with the information I transferred from the loft floor onto my plywood pattern.

Photo 2.21 This jointing surface affects the upright angle of the stem, so it must be dead straight.

You can see the Dolfinite bedding compound I put into the seasoning checks. This reduces the flow of air into checks and minimizes drying and therefore further checking.

Photo 2.22 The side of a plane makes a handy straightedge. You can use it when you are working down to the lines you scribed with your knife. I like to plane a scant 1/64-inch (.015 inch) hollow on each of these jointing surfaces. The outer sides of the timbers always seem to shrink at least that much as they dry out.

Photo 2.23 On wide joints, I usually plane across the grain or at a 45-degree angle, slowly working down to the center of the scribed cut.

2.24

2.25

2.26

Photo 2.24 A rabbet plane such as the Stanley number 10 is the perfect tool for working close in, next to the inside corner of the nib.

Photo 2.25 To move wood in a hurry, I use a 3-pound hammer and a wide, heavy-duty chisel with a metal band on its handle. I only cut to within ⅛ inch of my scribed mark at the nibs during the first fitting so I can adjust them later to align the waterline and section marks on all of the timbers.

Photo 2.26 I chose to laminate the teak deadwood. This is the most shapely part of the backbone, so I would have lost a lot of valuable time and wood by adzing it from 14 inches across at the forward end to only 2½ inches at the aft end. After transferring the measurements to the individual pieces, I bandsawed them out, then stacked and glued them together, using pipe clamps. When you glue up a large timber like this, leave extra wood along the length and width to allow for misalignments, which can easily occur as you are clamping.

To get the measurements for the individual pieces, I went to the loft floor and drew the heights of the top and bottom of the deadwood onto the body plan (see (A) and (B) in diagram 2.3). This gave the correct half-breadths for the top and bottom of the deadwood at station 19. I repeated this procedure for the other deadwood sections. Once the basic measurements for the pattern were complete, I deducted 1¼ inches along the bottom. When the lead keel was in position, I fit a sacrificial worm shoe to make up the 1¼-inch difference. (I will discuss the fitting of this shoe, and the reasons for it, in chapter 19.)

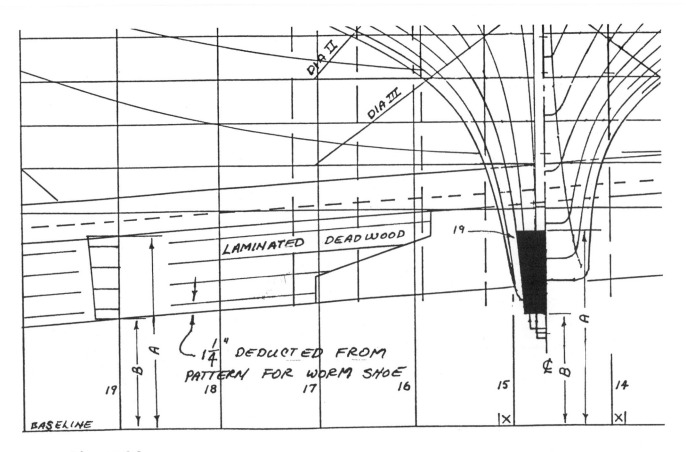

LAMINATED DEADWOOD

DIA II

DIA III

19

1¼" DEDUCTED FROM
PATTERN FOR WORM SHOE

19   18   17   16   15   14

BASELINE

Diagram 2.3

2.27

2.28

2.29

Photo 2.27 I laid out the pattern for the dead-wood parallel to the centerline, along the shaped side. If you lay the pattern directly on the shaped side of the deadwood, it will give you a slightly shorter deadwood than you should have. Remember that the backbone patterns you take from the lofted profile represent the centerline of the boat. If your timber was parallel and not tapered, you could lay the pattern directly on it and transfer your measurements accurately.

Photo 2.28 The deadwood is now shown upside down, with the marks for the sectional half-breadths in place and the batten sprung on and checked for fairness. The line penciled next to the batten represents the port side of the bottom of the deadwood.

Photo 2.29 This scarf joint on the forward end of the deadwood mates up with the ballast keel. First I used a Skilsaw to cut within ¼ inch of my mark, then a large chisel and a hammer to remove the heavy excess wood. This usually is faster than using an adze when you are sawing on a flat surface.

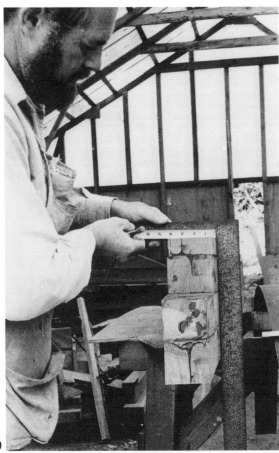

2.30

2.31

2.32

Photo 2.30 When the sides of the deadwood are shaped, be sure the centerline of the part is dead square to the top faying surface. If not, the deadwood will be cocked to port or starboard, which will cause fitting problems later with the sternpost and the ballast keel. I find it easier to shape this piece while it rests on sawhorses. Other builders prefer to attach the roughed-out piece to the keel timbers and then adze it down later.

Photo 2.31 These two timbers come from a 16-inch-by-16-inch-by-21-foot-long teak timber. The one on the left came off the resaw badly curved. So I laid out the other part of the timber with a chalkline and cut 1½ inches off with the Skilsaw and beam saws, ending up with two 1½-inch-by-6½-inch-by-21-foot-long offcuts—plus a timber that had no twist and was dead straight.

Photo 2.32 To make adzing easier, I notched the heartwood that was left over. Once this side was trued up and flat, I sized the timber to the correct thickness on my planer.

2.33

Photo 2.33 I turned the keel timber over and over until I was satisfied I had worked around as many of the defects as possible. I was able to avoid the knot in the lower right-hand corner by angling the keel on the timber. This is the bottom of the keel; the two grub holes next to me

were filled with fungicidal Dolfinite and faced down to the lead ballast keel. The top side of the keel was the better face and is almost perfectly clear.

It is not necessary to make a plywood pattern for your keel timber. Instead, lay out the top and bottom centerlines on your timber and square them to each other at the ends. Then use a long staff to pick up the frame spacings for the top of the keel. Diagram 2.4 (sections 5 to 21) shows why section spacings should be picked up from the loft floor with a long batten and not just measured onto the keel at 14-inch intervals. Since the keel is angled, the distance indicated by the angled line A is longer than the horizontal line B. It is very important to end up with the correct frame spacings on the top of the keel timber. The accumulation of error could make the keel timber come out short.

Next I lofted the top and bottom heights of the keel timber from the profile onto the body plan. I transposed the rabbet line to the body plan also, then took a piece of wood the thickness of my planking and lofted in the end view of the bearding and ghost lines (the top, inner, and lower inner corners of the planking), as in diagram 2.5. I picked up the half-breadths from the bottom of the keel, then the half-breadths from the widest part of the keel timber.

The widest part of the top of the keel is usually at the rabbet line, but do not take this for granted. Draw every keel section before you saw, in case your keel sections are wider at the bearding line than at the rabbet line. (In diagram 2.5, keel section 7 is wider at the top of the keel at the bearding line (note vertical dotted lines); section 14 is wider at the rabbet.)

I picked up the bearding-line and rabbet-line measurements, transferred them to the section lines marked on the timber, and clamped my batten to line up with these marks. Since the batten was fair, I had one more confirmation that the lofting was correct. (You can't afford more than a 1/16-inch (plus or minus) error in this expensive, labor-intensive piece of timber.) After I had done the final marking on the keel timber, I spent the rest of the day doing something else. The next morning, when I was fresh, I checked all of the measurements a final time.

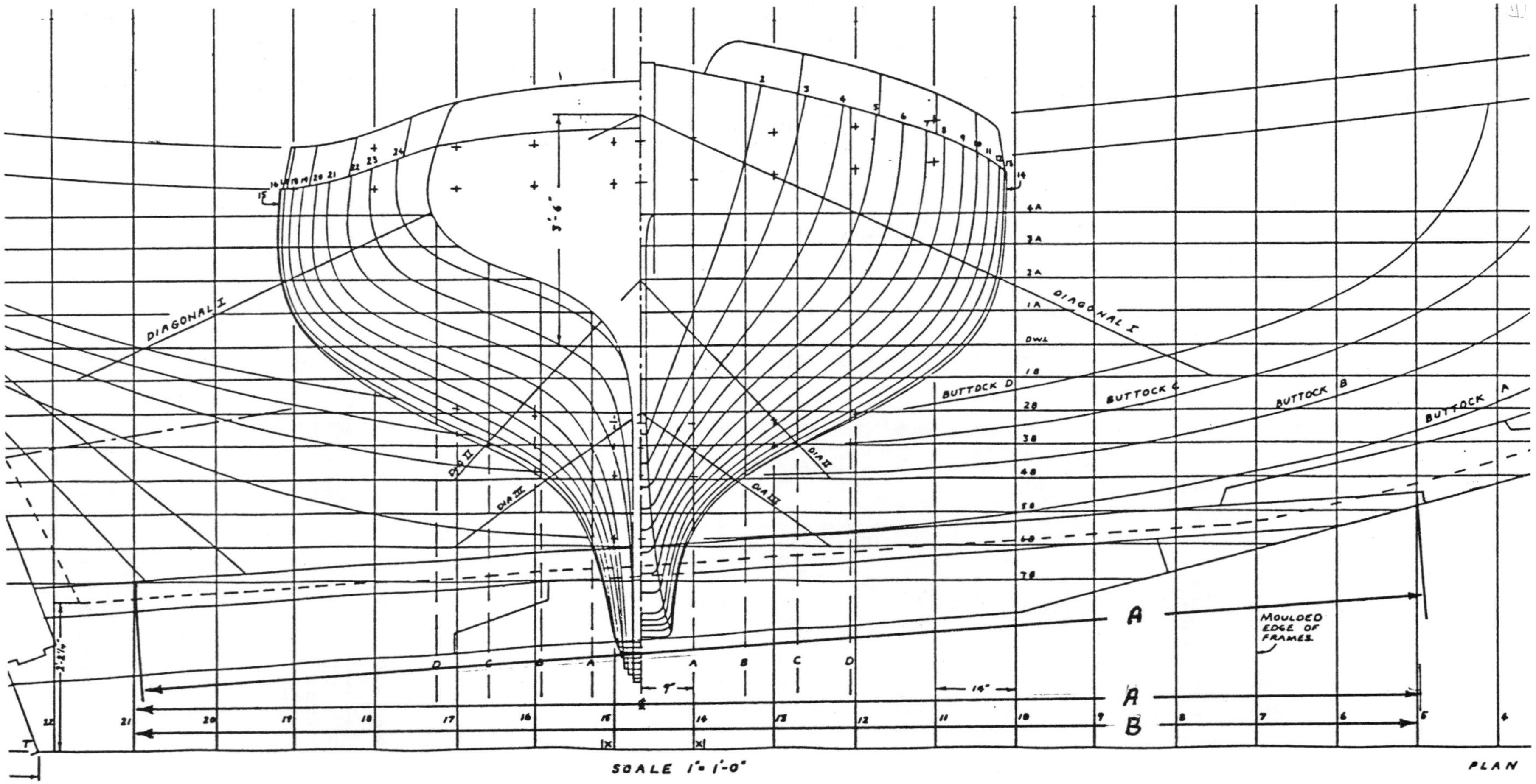
DIAGONAL I
DIAGONAL I
BUTTOCK D
BUTTOCK C
BUTTOCK B
BUTTOCK A
DIA II
DIA III
DIA II
DIA III
4A
3A
2A
1A
DWL
1B
2B
3B
4B
5B
6B
7B
3'-6"
A
A
B
MOULDED EDGE OF FRAMES
14"
SCALE 1" = 1'-0"
PLAN

Diagram 2.4

2.34

Photo 2.34 I cut the timber ⅛ inch oversize with the Skilsaw, then followed along this cut with the beam saw.

Photo 2.35 The keel timber is shown roughed out and ready to accept stern parts.

2.35

Diagram 2.5

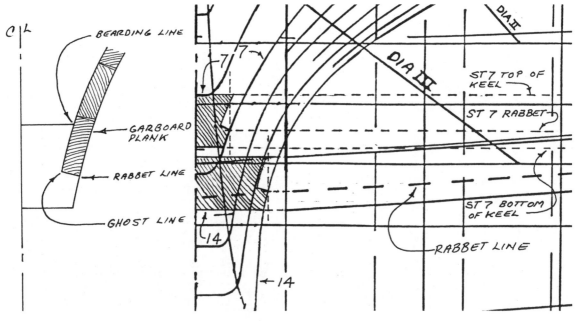

CONSTRUCTION TIMES FOR CHAPTER 2

Larry: Final construction on boatshed; wiring machinery; installing motors on thickness
planer · 117 hours

Milling planking stock before stacking it in storage shed	23
Lofting backbone timbers and rabbet; making patterns	18
Cutting and shaping timbers	128
	286 hours

Lin: Helping with boatshed construction; shopping for materials; arranging supplies in
boatshed · 33 hours

Totals to date (including previous chapters):	Larry	546 hours
	Lin	74 hours

DISCUSSION
Some General Comments on Backbone Construction Choices

We used solid teak timbers for our backbone because we owned a small business that imported boatbuilding teak, so I was able to select what I needed from an inventory of square timbers. This very stable, well-seasoned timber cost us about the same as American white oak.

Timbers of pitch pine, white oak, Alaskan yellow cedar, and tight-grained fir (in order of preference) are all used for backbones in North America. In England, oak and iroko are frequent choices; in New Zealand, kauri pine is a favorite; in the Philippines, hard mahoganies such as geho and apitong are used. Before you make your decisions, talk to local boatbuilders about what is available. The main considerations should be: (1) the availability of seasoned stock, (2) strength and rot resistance, (3) price. Don't be too easily discouraged from using solid timbers. There is a lot of good timber available in Canada and the United States. Talk to local farmers, boatbuilders, sawmill owners. Then, if satisfactory timbers are not available, lamination will be necessary.

A secondary reason for our choice of solid timbers was that they could be cut and assembled singlehandedly. Large laminations require assistants. In many situations, such helpers may be difficult to find.

For this hull, the designer drew the timbers so the planking could be fastened to a wide landing area (rabbet). That meant some of the timbers had to be quite large (diagram 2.6). Any ballasted sailboat will be stronger if it has a wide rabbet, since that will give a stronger connection between planking and keel timbers.

The solid-timber backbone parts for this design are purposely massive, especially at the waterline forward, to absorb the shock of groundings and collisions. These husky timbers can also make a fair amount of natural defects structurally unimportant.

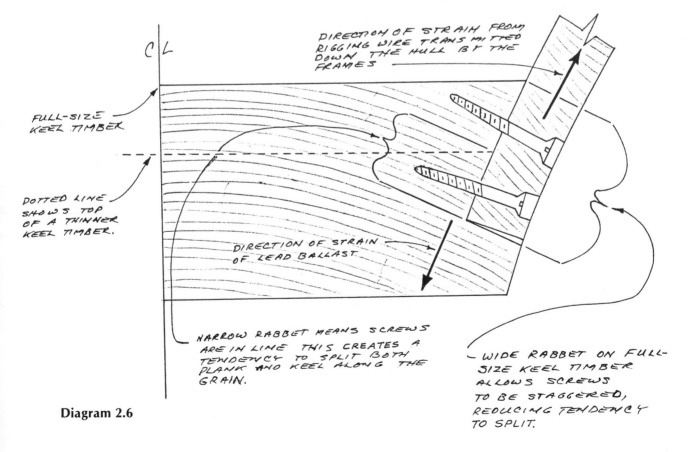

Diagram 2.6

If you are not an experienced boatbuilder, you can inadvertently buy the wrong species of timber, especially among oak or fir species. This kind of mistake can come back to haunt you throughout the whole project. Be wary of oak grown on the west coast of North America (live oak), or red oak from the east coast. Live oak tends to shrink and twist far more than white oak. Its resistance to rot is also questionable. Some types of red oak seem to last quite well when they are used for boat timbers; others start rotting immediately. The old cliche—oak lasts either eight or eighty years—seems to be true with red-oak varieties. Some boatbuilders trust their local red oak, others don't. I would avoid it rather than risk potential rot.

Second-growth fir is also a poor choice for keel timbers. The open grain is soft, pithy, and prone to rot. If first-growth fir is available, fir that has tight grain (twelve annual rings per inch is on the open side, sixteen is quite tight) and a slight pitchy smell, this can make strong, durable backbone timbers.

When I bought timber for *Seraffyn*, our 24-foot Hess-designed cutter, I purchased Appalachian white oak graded to car-liner stock specifications. Car-liner stock is used for flooring in railway cars and trucks. It is a grade down from clear timbers and has some wane (the area right next to the bark) and small knots on one side. Because of its commercial applications, it is usually available for backbone timbers. I was lucky because an experienced timber merchant with a soft spot for boatbuilders had stored these rough-sawn timbers in a damp, cool shed, where they had been completely protected from the sun. He stacked them with 2 x 4s separating each timber, then covered them with rock salt to attract moisture. The endgrain was sealed with wax. All of these precautions worked to minimize shrinking, checking, and splitting. These efforts were reflected in top prices, which were worth paying, since I was building in a low-humidity area of southern California, where poorly seasoned timbers would split and crack faster than they would in a place like Maine or Seattle.

Timbers can be seasoned in various ways. Teak is normally ringed—i.e., a strip of bark and sapwood are cut off right around the tree, which slowly kills the tree—then it is left standing in the forest three to five years before it is felled, so it seasons slowly in the Burmese or Thai rain forests. Oak timbers can be left in a saltwater pond or mud bath. But the most common seasoning methods use time, salt, wax, shade, and high humidity.

After you buy your timbers, store them near—but not on—the bare earth. (If they are directly on the ground, they will pick up bacteria and insects and start to rot.) If you plan to build in a damp climate, eight to twelve months of drying time would probably be sufficient for a 6-inch-by-12-inch oak timber. In California, which is at the other end of the humidity scale, the same size of salted, sealed timber should set for about twelve to fourteen months from the time it is felled until you begin construction. If you can season your timbers longer, do it; you'll have less shrinkage as you build.

Buy your timbers rough-sawn and slightly larger and longer than needed. It is tempting to want to size them to their final dimensions on the timber yard's thickness planer, but resist it. Your timbers could shrink and possibly twist or curve slightly between when you buy them and when you bolt them together, so measuring and alignment problems could plague you during the rest of the building project. That is why I suggest waiting until the last possible moment before sizing your timbers.

Some backbone checking will probably occur as you build. Keep these checks filled with fungicidal Dolfinite or soft linseed-oil putty. Paint, varnish, or oil will also help centerline timbers hold their moisture. Don't use a hardening putty or wood wedges to fill any checks during construction. As soon as the boat is launched, the timbers will absorb moisture from the outside and the checks will close. If you have put a hard substance in the checks, it will act like a wedge and split the original checks deeper toward the center of the timber as it absorbs moisture.

Don't be too concerned about these longitudinal checks. They are quite common, even in the finest of yachts. If they are in deadwood timbers, they rarely present a structural problem. If they run through the rabbet area, they can be a nuisance, but generally, if they do not run deeper than one-fifth of the way through a 6-inch-by-12-inch timber, even in dry areas like California, they will swell shut a few weeks after launching.

Straight pieces of timber are normally used for stems and forefoot sections (gripe), but a grown or natural crook could be used to create a one-piece stem and forefoot with appropriately curved grain. This grown part, which is then scarfed and bolted to the straight keel timber, is the best of all possible worlds. It provides the strength of a laminated timber without the worry about glue failures, plus the ease of assembly and savings on construction time without the waste of sawn timbers. The catch is that a log with the exact curvature you need is about as easy to find as a fifty-carat diamond.

For *Seraffyn*, we laminated the stem and forefoot as a one-piece structure, and it worked fine in the long run. But if I had known it was acceptable boatbuilding practice to glue on sections as shown in diagram 2.7, I could have bolted together *Seraffyn*'s stem and forefoot just as I did the rest of her backbone assembly. Instead, since I couldn't find appropriate timbers for these parts, I spent a lot of time making a bending jig on the loft floor, resawing and planing oak strips (with a considerable loss of wood), and borrowing

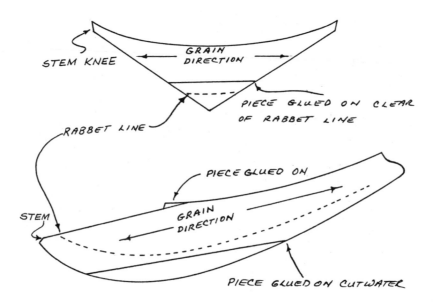

Diagram 2.7

SOLID BACKBONE TIMBERS

Pro

A built-up backbone fastened with through-bolts is long-lasting and a well-proven method of construction.

Less chance of problems, i.e., no glue-failure concerns.

Work can progress on project in spite of temperature and humidity changes.

Few clamps are necessary.

Fast assembly with a minimum of shop setup time or capital investment.

Work can be done by one person.

Con

Large, well-seasoned timbers can be hard to find.

Silicon-bronze through-bolt stock can be expensive.

Special drills needed for long bolt holes.

Heavy-duty saws (beam or bandsaw) needed to cut out individual pieces.

More tendency to check, crack, or rot.

Timbers are hard to transport to boatyard.

Not practical for light-displacement hulls.

LAMINATED BACKBONE ASSEMBLY

Pro

A strong, light assembly, is possible.

The backbone for a fin-and-skeg hull can be glued up right on the molds.

Smaller pieces of easily purchased, well-seasoned timber can be used.

If standard thickness wood veneers are available, less board footage of timber needed.

Errors in individual parts can be covered by adding more laminations.

Little chance of serious checking in larger parts if wood is well seasoned.

Con

Labor-intensive.

Requires heated shop for glue control, jigs, lots of clamps.

Fully laminated backbone will be stronger than necessary on a heavy-displacement yacht.

Laminating stock for hard bends must be clear of knots and have straight grain so it won't break when it is bent onto jig.

Wood costs can be high if resawing and planing are necessary to produce laminating strips.

Glue costs are high and much is wasted.

Glue mixing and cleanup take extra time.

It's hard to repair damaged areas if backbone timbers are wet, i.e., when glue can't be used.

Laminating is great if everything goes right. The boat is worthless if the glue fails a few years after it is launched. (I have seen this happen all too often.)

fifty 12-inch clamps from local boatyards. The day we finally had everything assembled, including two helpers, the thermometer topped 90 degrees. So we had to roll the glue on as quickly as possible with a paint roller and clamp up as fast as we could or we would have lost two gallons of glue and all our work. Planning, dry runs, and the actual glue-up took three people most of one day. The laminations had to be overbent so that the stem-piece would be close to the mold-loft patterns when it came off the jig. We used about 1½ inches of extra lamination thickness to allow for springback. Later this had to be sawn off and discarded, along with almost a gallon of expensive glue that squeezed out as we clamped up.

The comparison of cost, time, and wastage between *Seraffyn*'s laminated stem and *Taleisin*'s sawn one convinced me that for a medium- or heavy-displacement boat, the built-up method is easier, faster, and maybe even cheaper. For a light-displacement boat, you have little choice. You usually have to laminate to keep down the backbone weight.

Although you must find and purchase large pieces of timber in order to saw a solid stem, the wood for laminating the stem has to be of higher-quality, clear, straight-grained stock with only very small knots and as little grain runoff as possible. Otherwise, it can break as you bend it around the jig. For this reason, I would expect the materials costs for both methods to be similar.

If you laminated the whole backbone assembly on this boat, it could be reduced in size by about one-third and thus save approximately 300 pounds in weight. But a lamination of this size and complexity requires professional laminating experience to ensure that it comes out right the *first* time. In my estimation, the time spent laminating a keel timber in a one-man boatbuilding shop might be triple that needed to build a pieced-together backbone. Not only do you lose the time spent building a jig, gathering clamps, producing a warm-enough gluing environment, then cutting and surfacing laminating stock, but you also lose the time spent clamping the whole assembly together (without glue) to test the strength of your bending jig, to make sure your laminations fit tightly, and to see if you have everything you need ready for the final glue-up. Once the laminated part is glued together, you still have to shape and finish it, just as you would a solid part.

One other reason I am reluctant to endorse laminations for the small one-off, boat-building operation is that I have seen several glue failures, even among professionally built boats—failures caused by poor choices of adhesive, improper humidity, poor heat control, or possibly incorrect mixing. When this happens, you lose all of your labor and glue as well as some or even all of your laminating timber. If the delamination occurs a month or two later, as has happened to two builders we know who used epoxy, you will have to dis-assemble about two months' work to repair the problem.

On the other hand, laminated backbone parts are very strong. The grain follows the rabbet line, which makes it easier to chisel and plane the rabbet. For laminated keel timbers, I prefer resorcinol glues. (See Appendix C for information on gap-filling, low-temperature resorcinol.) Full-time boatbuilders find that laminating, especially for lighter-displacement hulls, is cost- and labor-effective because they can use the same shop setup to produce parts for subsequent hulls of the same or similar design.

You can end up with a fine keel assembly by using either method. The list that follows shows the pros and cons of both. But before you decide to build differently than your designer shows on his construction drawings, contact him. He could have made the choices he did for a specific reason.

It is quite common for experienced builders to relocate the backbone joints to accommodate the existing timbers or a change in construction methods. I did that on the forefoot-to-keel-timber joint for this hull, lengthening the aft end of the forefoot joint 9½ inches (see photo 2.4). That way, the floor at F8 could bear on the aft end of the forefoot. (I wanted this for reasons explained in chapter 13, on mast steps.)

3. ASSEMBLING
THE BACKBONE TIMBERS

Now comes the fun part—fitting and bolting together the individual pieces. I generally leave the timbers flat on their starboard and port faces. These unshaped sides make measuring, clamping, and aligning easier. The excess timber can be removed with confidence later, when the parts are bolted together securely. There is no hard-and-fast rule, however, about when you should shape your timbers.

Photo 3.1 I chose to bolt the forefoot onto the keel timber first. This joint is relatively easy to fit because there is only one nib. As you work at each new stage on your boat, you will evolve methods to simplify clamping, aligning, fitting, and fastening. So if you perfect these moves on the simplest parts first, assembly of the more difficult ones will go along more smoothly.

The plywood pads shown glued to the faces of the pipe clamps protect the timbers from clamp marks.

3.1

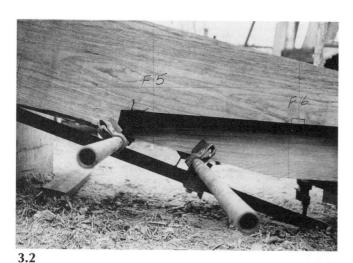

3.2

Photo 3.2 Here are two different clamping methods for aligning and holding timbers. (No protective pads are used here because any scarring or crush marks will be cut off when the sides of these timbers are shaped.) The clamp on the left adjusts the nib athwartships by having the fixed foot of the clamp (visible) turned and resting on the corner of the forefoot; the other foot, with the adjusting screw, is resting on the far side of the keel timber. Thus, the centerline marks on the bottom face of the nib can be adjusted easily and accurately.

The clamp on the right is simply acting as a base for the long fore-and-aft clamp. It is used to pull together tightly the nib between the forefoot and the keel timber. (You can see this longitudinal clamp better in photo 3.1.)

The vertical station marks (F5 and F6) are perfectly aligned in this photo. F6 looks wrong only because the excess forefoot material overhangs the keel. When this is clamped and fitted accurately, I look along the centerline of the keel timber to make sure it looks straight and in line with the centerline of the forefoot. Then I carefully roll the keel and forefoot on to its side and double-check alignment. With a brace and bit, I counterbore for the nut and washer from what will be the outside of the boat. The counterbore hole is made deep enough to take the nut and washer plus a ⁵⁄₁₆-inch-deep plug. The screw hole left in the bottom of the counterbore hole by the auger screw will automatically center the ½-inch drill bit as I drill through both timbers.

Try to drill as close as possible to 90 degrees to the scarf jointing line. This helps keep the joint from creeping and opening at the nib as the through-bolts are tightened. This slipping can also be stopped by cutting a mortise hole at F6 so that the rectangular hole is exactly 1 inch each side of the line at F6. Two wedges that fit the mortise hole can then be driven in from either side to lock the joint and prevent the nib from opening (diagram 3.1). The mortise with its double-wedge tenon should be near the middle of the scarf. The locking wedges should be set in waterproof glue and positioned either above or below the caulking seam of the rabbet. (I would only go to this extra work if I were having problems keeping this nib tight.)

I used ½-inch silicon-bronze rod for the bolts and threaded both ends of the rod with a national-coarse (NC) die. If you make these bolts right on the job, you save both time and money. They can be made in lengths of up to 12 feet, the standard rolled-rod length. The one disadvantage of this type of bolt is that the nut-and-washer-type head requires that a large-diameter counterbore hole be cut in the cutwater of the stem or forefoot. If the design of your boat calls for a narrow flat, or a sharp cutwater face, you can order long carriage bolts, or you can fabricate hammerhead bolts in your shop, as shown in diagram 3.2. This type of hammerhead bolt must be set deep enough into the stem face to clear the sharp entry; a graving piece can be fitted and glued in place later.

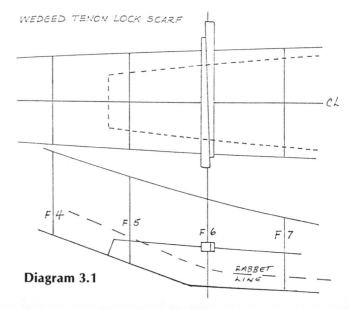

Diagram 3.1

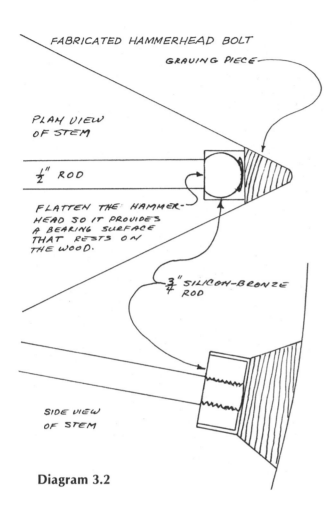

FABRICATED HAMMERHEAD BOLT

GRAVING PIECE

PLAN VIEW
OF STEM

½" ROD

FLATTEN THE HAMMER-
HEAD SO IT PROVIDES
A BEARING SURFACE
THAT RESTS ON
THE WOOD.

¾" SILICON-BRONZE
ROD

SIDE VIEW
OF STEM

Diagram 3.2

Photo 3.3 The stem knee is shown resting on the forefoot with the centerlines aligned. The knee is about ⁵⁄₁₆ inch forward of the section marks (F2 and F3). The nib end of the knee has purposely been left oversize.

Photo 3.4 I adjusted the scribe (a compass) to pick up the fore-and-aft difference between the section lines. Then I marked (scribed) this measurement around the nib end of the knee.

Photo 3.5 Since this measurement is a fore-and-aft one, I was careful to hold the points of the scribe exactly in a fore-and-aft direction as I marked the nib. This scribe mark shows the exact amount of wood to be removed from the nib end so that the stem knee can be slid aft to fit perfectly. Next I chiseled and planed the nib end and checked the fit.

3.3

3.4

3.5

3.6

3.7

3.8

Photo 3.6 If the knee is still slightly forward, I clamp the timbers so the vertical station marks are separated, equal to the kerf of my bench saw. I then recheck the centerline marks and simply saw down through the nib-end joint for a tight fit.

Photo 3.7 Now two ½-inch bolts are in place, drawing the stem knee onto the keel timber and squeezing the Dolfinite out of the joint. This bedding compound is ideal for use between big timbers, which have a tendency to shrink and swell during construction. Glue is not practical with large timbers because shrinkage will cause glue separation along the joint.

Photo 3.8 The pipe clamps at the stem-to-fore-foot-nib connection support a piece of 2 x 4. This provides a shoulder that holds the lower end of the stem while I swing it into place. The tackle used in conjunction with the 2 x 4 shoulder makes it easier to position and then remove the stem for fitting. I first fitted the flat, straight area between the nibs on the stem. Once this was done, I clamped the stem where it meets the knee. Then I supported it above with the tackle while I checked for fit and alignment. To ensure that the stem and knee were in line with the centerline of the backbone, I laid a straightedge along the waterline marks on the side of the knee. Both timbers should be parallel to the straightedge.

3.9

3.10

Photo 3.10 As I drilled for the through-bolts, I kept the holes parallel to the sides of the stem by sighting first along the drill shank and then along the side of the stem.

Photo 3.11 Now aft to the deadwood: The centerline marks on the bottom of the keel timbers were aligned with the centerline marks on the fore-and-aft nib ends of the deadwood. The vertical frame sections should also align.

The four pipe clamps were placed so they were forward of the eventual position of the transom knee. This let me put the transom knee in place later and fit it without unclamping the deadwood from the keel timber.

The safest way to drill the three long holes that go through the deadwood, keel timber, and stern knee is to do them in two stages. I counterbored, then drilled through the deadwood-and-keel-timber assembly.

3.11

Photo 3.9 Notice the incline of both stem nib ends. This angle or slope helps you get tight-fitting nibs. When the alignment and fit of the whole joint was correct, I clamped the timbers together with two pieces of ⅛-inch flat metal between the stem and forefoot, then drilled the bolt holes. This way, the stempiece is held slightly below its waterline marks (the wedges lower the shoulder block). When the flat metal pieces are removed and the bolts are tightened, the stem moves toward the knee and down the slight incline of the nib ends, jamming the nibs together tightly. This "squeeze play" stops the nib ends from opening when the joint is slippery with Dolfinite. If you don't get a tight fit with this method, you might have to resort to the double-wedge device described earlier in this chapter. If your plans call for a hook scarf joint, I would use a mortise-and-wedge scarf instead. It is easier to make, usually fits better, and provides a more positive lock for the joint.

3.12

Diagram 3.3

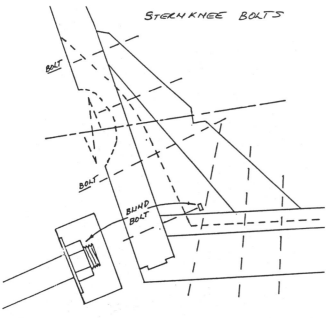

STERN KNEE BOLTS

BOLT

BOLT

BLIND
BOLT

(SEE CHAPT 13 FOR MORE ON BLIND BOLTS.)

Photo 3.12 I clamped and aligned the transom knee using a jig made from a 2-inch-by-8-inch plank secured to the forward face of the knee with six duplex (double-headed) nails. I sited the nails so that floor timbers eventually would cover the holes. I planned the notches on the cleat so they would work now as well as later, when I was ready to clamp the sternpost in place.

Next, I measured the depth of the holes through the deadwood and keel and added ½-inch. I placed a piece of tape on the drill bit to mark this depth and ran the drill through the three separate holes until it reached the tape. This left a ½-inch hole that became a pilot hole so the stern knee could be drilled easily and accurately as a separate piece. Before separating the pieces, I penciled a line parallel to the drill bit to indicate the hole direction across the stern knee.

Before you drill for these long bolts, be sure the location of your prop-shaft alley is marked so you can drill the shaft hole later without fouling any through-bolts. If necessary, you can use blind bolts to clear the shaft hole (diagram 3.3).

Photo 3.13   After removing the stern knee from the keel assembly and laying it on its side, I laid a straightedge along the premarked drill line. Lin lined up the drill bit and the straightedge to keep them parallel horizontally. I kept the drill in line with the premarked line. If the pilot holes on the jointing surface of the transom knee are off-center, the drill can be angled relative to the straightedge so the drill will come out close to the centerline of the knee.

Every inch or so, I withdraw the drill completely and clear the sawdust. This helps straighten the hole on each return and minimizes the grain deflection. Most boatbuilders are satisfied if the nut and washer end up in the middle third of the inside face of the backbone.

Once the holes are through all three parts, I reclamp the knee onto the keel. If a 1/64-inch oversize extended drill is not available, I run a reamer (like the one described in the discussion at the end of the chapter) through the holes to increase the diameter.

Any bolt longer than 18 inches usually will jam

3.13

up when you try to drive it through a hole the same size as the bolt stock, even if you use grease to lubricate both bolt and hole. A bent bolt is a time-waster and hard to remove. Diagram 3.4 shows one way this can be done; Chapelle suggests other methods on page 212 of *Boatbuilding* (see Bibliography), as well as tips on what to do if you cannot remove the bolt.

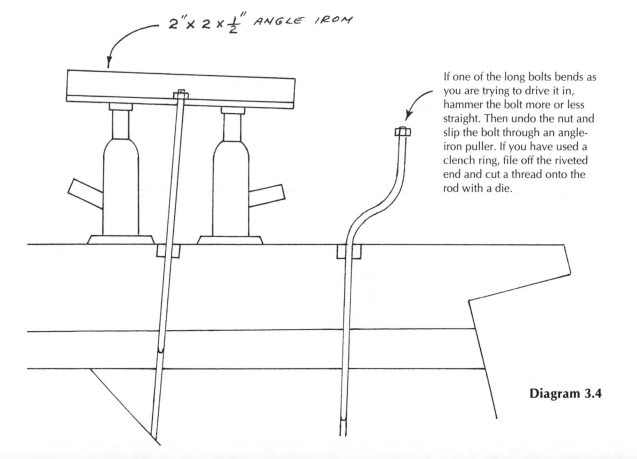

2" x 2 x 1/2" ANGLE IRON

If one of the long bolts bends as you are trying to drive it in, hammer the bolt more or less straight. Then undo the nut and slip the bolt through an angle-iron puller. If you have used a clench ring, file off the riveted end and cut a thread onto the rod with a die.

Diagram 3.4

3.14

Photo 3.14 I took the keel assembly apart and applied Dolfinite to the faying surfaces.

Photo 3.15 The top edge of the knee now has to have a small area chiseled flat, square to the hole, to accept the nut and washer. Once this was done, I drove the bolt with its nut and washer most of the way through. Then I clove-hitched four or five turns of caulking cotton under the washer and drove home the bolts. If one turn of thread is left proud of the nut on the lower end of the bolt, the hammering will rivet the metal over and lock the nut in place.

Once the main keel-timber parts are in place, the keel assembly can be set upright again.

3.15

Photo 3.16 The ends of all timbers, the tops of the stem and sternpost, the ends of the keel, and deadwoods should be left oversize as long as possible so that minor measuring errors and/or endgrain checking can be removed with the off-cuts. In order to fit the sternpost, the aft end of the keel timber now has to be cut off flush with the deadwood and the transom knee.

Photo 3.17 A mortise-and-tenon joint should be cut to lock the sternpost to the deadwood. Some builders put in a dovetail, as shown in diagram 3.5. This dovetail joint (a) will not be as effective in stopping the twisting as a mortise and tenon. On larger boats, fishplates (b) are often let into the timbers and then riveted through both. Or a gudgeon (c) is designed and built to fit over and reinforce both joints. During long offshore passages, the rudder constantly works against the sternpost so the post's lower aft end needs to be securely locked to the keel assembly.

Photo 3.18 You can remove most of the wood in the mortise with a twist drill fitted with a stop to limit the depth of the holes. You need to chisel athwartships, as shown, to clean up this mortise. If you try to chisel forward, the grain will split downward, deeper than intended.

3.16

3.17

3.18

Diagram 3.5

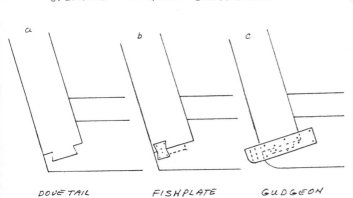

STERNPOST - TO-KEEL CONNECTIONS

a   b   c

DOVETAIL   FISHPLATE   GUDGEON

3.19

Photo 3.19 The sternpost is now ready for fitting.

3.20

Photo 3.20 With a block-and-tackle, hoisting the sternpost into position can be a single-handed job.

The clamping jig used previously is now ren-ailed to the stern knee to clamp the sternpost into place.

3.21

Photo 3.21 The waterline marks across the sternpost line up with marks on the back edge of the transom knee.

Photo 3.22 The top three bolts go through both sternpost and knee. The fourth fastening is a drift bolt that is short enough to miss the aft, vertical stern-knee bolt.

3.22

Photo 3.23 The centerline timbers are all bolted together. This is the moment of truth. I check the measurement from the inside of the sternpost to the inside of the stem on WL4A against the corresponding measurement on the loft floor. If the keel timber is straight and the joints are all aligned correctly, the measurements will be the same. If the keel timber has a little sheer curve to it and the WL4A measurement is ½ inch shy, this could be corrected when the backbone is set upright. The weight of the stem and stern assembly could straighten the keel timber this much. If not, you can rig a wire from the top of the stem forward to a metal pipe in the ground, do the same at the sternpost, and then fit turnbuckles to pull the ends away from each other to straighten the keel. (Chapter 8 shows how to straighten a keel timber that has some sag in the ends.)

The shaft hole on a boat like this is fairly easy to drill, as it has to go through only 21 inches of timber from the propeller aperture (cut into the sternpost) to the inboard face of the transom knee. (In diagram 3.3, note the aperture and the notch for the stuffing box in the knee.) *Taleisin* has no engine, so there is no aperture and no notch.

One word of warning: Take care when you are lifting or lowering the backbone assembly. Be sure to pull evenly on both stem and sternpost tackles so you don't rack or twist the assembly.

CONSTRUCTION TIMES FOR CHAPTER 3

Larry: Fitting and fastening timbers		65 hours
Lin: Assisting with drilling; shopping for parts; arranging shop		10 hours
	Totals to date: Larry	611 hours
	Lin	84 hours

DISCUSSION
Extended Drills, Reamers, and Fastening Choices

Here is the recipe for the most successful long drills I have made: Use a ¼64-inch, oversize, high-speed, extra-long, fluted, hard-steel drill bit with a soft shank. If you can easily file the shank end of the drill, it isn't hardened and should be welded to a mild-steel extension rod to produce a strong, nonbrittle connection. (These 8-inch bits are available through Jamestown Distributors; see chapter 23.) The extension rod should be smaller than the drill so it has enough clearance in the hole to minimize friction.

To get the drill and rod welded together center to center, first wrap some plastic tape around the extension rod, 6 inches from the weld end, until the taped rod equals the diameter of the drill. Put a second band of tape 8 inches away. Now place the rod and drill inside a 2-foot piece of angle iron and clamp them snugly into the V. This aligns and holds the drill and rod for the welder while he uses oxygen and acetylene gas to make the weld. Gas welding gives a more flexible, nonbrittle weld than electric welding. (If a drill breaks off inside your timbers, it can be a major pain.)

Bolt Size	Recommended Drill Size	Extension Rod Size
1/2''	33/64''	7/16''
3/8''	25/64''	5/16''
5/16''	21/64''	1/4''
1/4''	17/64''	1/4''*
3/16''	13/64''	3/16''

* 1/64 inch is enough hole clearance on small extended drills.

Test the weld by clamping the fluted part of the bit into the wooden jaws of your vise. Connect up the drill motor you will be using and give the bit a torque test—repeated, short bursts of drill twisting power—to see if the weld will hold even when the rod twists and torques considerably. Now loosen the chuck just enough so the bit will slip if the drill binds up on a screw, nail, or knot. Do not worry if you see some wobble as you use your new extended drill bit; it doesn't seem to cause any problems.

Drilling long holes is always a bit challenging. Even a brand-new drill bit will have a tendency to be deflected by the wood-grain angle. To get straight holes, first, if at all possible, use an extra-long, fluted drill bit to make your extension drill. The longer flutes of the drill tend to wander less than shorter flutes. You may have to special-order these drills, but it is well worthwhile. I have had better results with these than with bell hangers (long drills with short flutes) or barefoot augers with a single cutter (*Boatbuilding*, page 148—see Bibliography). Bob Dorris, a well-known California boatbuilder, swears by a multi-spurred electrician's bit for large propeller-shaft holes.

Diagram 3.6 shows how grain can deflect a sharply pointed twist drill. You can counteract this deflection by grinding your drill as shown in diagram 3.7. This drill is

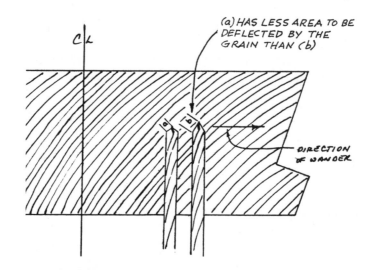

(a) HAS LESS AREA TO BE DEFLECTED BY THE GRAIN THAN (b)

DIRECTION OF WANDER

Diagram 3.6

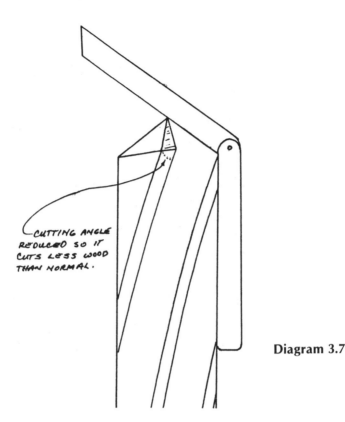

CUTTING ANGLE
REDUCED SO IT
CUTS LESS WOOD
THAN NORMAL.

Diagram 3.7

ground about right for long holes going through hardwoods. I don't believe you can sharpen these long drills on a drill grinding tool. You probably will have to do them by eye. A bevel gauge will help you get the point equal, side to side, but I have found that perfection is not absolutely necessary. Estimating both of the cutting angles by eye as you regrind them seems to work. Try out your extended drill on a scrap of timber to prove it works well. Sight through your test hole to see the amount of wander. Look at the grain of the wood and try to figure out what is causing any deflection. If there is a lot of wander, try angling the drill just a few degrees off true and drill another test hole. All this testing will be worthwhile if it keeps your drill from appearing out of the side of your stern knee instead of near the desired centerline.

The same test holes can be used to check bolt fit. Again, I recommend drilling 1/64 inch oversize for any holes 18 inches or longer. The timbers will swell up around the bolts once you launch and the holes will become watertight. The holes should be just enough oversize so that the bolt will drive through easily but cannot be pushed in by hand.

If your long drill bits are not oversize, you can make a reamer to clear the holes (diagram 3.8). Chuck the reamer into your drill and run it through the long holes once or twice, but be careful not to overdo it. If the holes become too big, water could enter into the deadwood-to-keel-timber joint and travel up the loose bolt hole to leak onto the top of the transom knee.

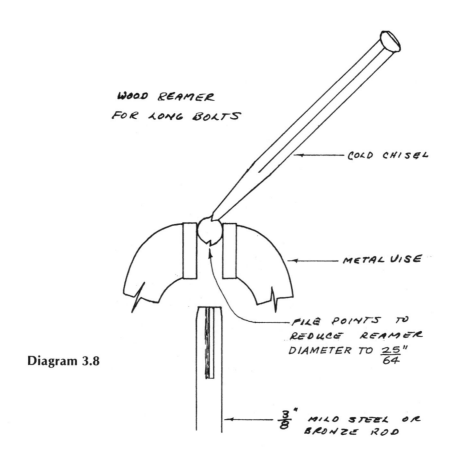

WOOD REAMER
FOR LONG BOLTS

— COLD CHISEL

— METAL VISE

— FILE POINTS TO
REDUCE REAMER
DIAMETER TO $\frac{25"}{64}$

$\frac{3}{8}"$ MILD STEEL OR
BRONZE ROD

Diagram 3.8

Fastening Choices

The fastening metal you choose should be compatible with the quality of your hull materials. If you build with a lead ballast keel, hardwood backbone, and hardwood planking, it would be a resale and maintenance folly to fasten with galvanized bolts and screws. The reverse is true of a hull that will be built to fishboat specifications with iron or iron-and-concrete ballast, less durable softwood timbers, and softwood planking. The cost of bronze and copper would not be justified and the fastenings would long outlast the cheaper hull materials.

The cost of fastenings for our two mechanically fastened boats,[*] *Seraffyn* and *Taleisin*, which both had lead keels and hardwood hulls, was only about 5 percent of the total cost of materials for the finished boat. On boats around 30 feet, built like *Taleisin*, the copper

---

[*] The type of construction shown in the photographs in this book is what I call "mechanically fastened." It relies on bolts, screws, and rivets. Laminated, three-skinned, and strip-planked hulls are what I call "chemically fastened." The latter rely heavily on adhesives to keep them intact and watertight.

rivets, wood screws, and silicon-bronze through-bolts will last at least fifty years. If the same 30-foot boat were fastened with hot-dipped galvanized fastenings, the useful life of the fastenings would be about eighteen to twenty-five years. Rusting and topside bleeding can start within three years of launching and will cause these relatively small fastenings to decay quite quickly, especially along the threads and heads of wood screws fastening the plank ends to the backrabbet. If you are building a relatively small hull, the use of galvanized fastenings would save you only about 2½ percent of your materials cost.

On the other hand, galvanized fastenings will last longer, up to thirty or forty years, on 50- to 60-foot boats simply because the fastenings are larger in diameter. In other words, after twenty-five years of rusting in salt water, a ½-inch bolt could be totally dissolved; a 1-inch bolt probably would have a fair amount—say, about two-thirds—of its metal left.

Whatever its size, the resale value of a galvanized-fastened boat is lower than that of a bronze-fastened one, especially when the boat is fifteen to twenty-five years old. I have done refastening jobs on iron-fastened yachts and usually found it impossible to cure the bleeding. The rust has soaked into the wood, so even with a new bolt in the hole, the red runs out and streaks the hull. These "bleeders" are death to resale values.

Another problem with choosing galvanized fastenings is availability. Electroplated (zinc-plated) bolts and screws, which look silver-colored and smooth, are being substituted for the far superior hot-dipped galvanized fastenings, which are gray in color and rough to the touch. Nuts for galvanized bolts are quite often cleaned out with an oversize tap so they will fit the threads of the hot-dipped bolt (usually about .003 inch oversize). This removes the galvanizing inside the nuts, and corrosion and bleeding are likely to start soon after launching.

To bolt the backbone together with galvanized rod, you have to cut the rod stock to your required lengths. This, plus cutting the threads on both ends of the rod, removes the protective galvanizing. It is possible to make up the bolts and then have all of the parts galvanized, but then you have to wait for the bolts to come back from the galvanizer.

Galvanized clench rings can be used with galvanized rod to produce strong through-fastenings. This rivet-type fastening is superior to double-nutted fastenings because the rod is not reduced in diameter by threading and the galvanizing is marred only on the riveted head. Be sure to get cast-steel clench rings; they are tougher and less brittle than cast-iron ones.

Unless you exercise extreme care, galvanized nails and spikes lose the galvanizing from their heads while they are being hammered in. Lumps of galvanizing quite often lodge in screw slots. These can cause your screwdriver blade to slip out, and this will shear the galvanizing from the slot. Robert Steward, in his *Boatbuilding Manual* (see Bibliography), writes, "In the case of the smaller sized hot-dipped galvanized wood screws, the threads are frequently clogged with zinc when they are dipped, and when driven, they tear the wood around the hole, reducing holding power."

The corrosion caused by damaging the galvanizing on fastenings can be minimized by careful coating with epoxies and paints.

I would stay away from stainless-steel fastenings, especially for boats with oak frames or backbone timbers. I have seen serious bleeding and corrosion on stainless-steel fastenings used with these timbers. The bleeding may have been caused by a reaction to the tannic acid in the oak. In one case, I removed a ¼-inch-diameter stainless bolt that had been holding a lifeline stanchion onto the oak bulwark of a five-year-old boat and found that the fastening was reduced to about ⅛ inch in diameter. On the other hand, I removed stainless-steel screws that were used to refasten the underwater planking on an older schooner after they had been in use for five years and found the screws in perfect condition. This disparity may have been caused by different alloy choices. But since I can't look at a screw or bolt and tell whether it is 304 stainless or the more durable 316, I would feel uncomfortable using stainless-steel fastenings on a new hull. (You can buy an acid test kit to distinguish different grades of stainless steel, but this testing is not commonly done in most boatyards.) Finally, stainless steel is difficult to drill, tap, or cut with a hacksaw.

Bronze and copper fastenings have long lives, don't bleed, and are easy to work. Availability is good in the United States, not so good elsewhere. (For sources, see chapter 23.) A silicon-bronze screw (Everdur 655 or 657) or bolt can be recognized easily by its reddish copper color. Any gold or yellow bolts and screws usually are types of brass or naval bronze and are not as reliable as silicon bronze, although there are special uses for these bronzes and brasses.

One way to identify the bronze- or brass-alloy fastenings used in an older boat is to note the color change caused by contact with salt water. Copper and silicon bronze (90 percent or more copper content) turn a distinct green color soon after contact with salt water. The yellow metals do not. Manganese bronze (in reality, a dezincification-resistant high-strength brass) turns dull yellow, with occasional tiny spots of red. The red (rust) is caused by the one percent iron content. Less noble brasses turn slightly green with yellow, others turn gray or grayish. The higher the zinc content, the grayer they become. Brass fastenings, especially ones with less than 57 percent copper content, usually suffer from dezincification—the zinc dissolves and leaves a porous reddish residue (the leftover copper).

We have fastened both of the boats mentioned throughout this book with copper and silicon-bronze rod and cast-manganese-bronze clench rings, and we have had no fastening problems.

4. SHAPING THE BACKBONE AND CUTTING THE RABBET

The photographs and diagrams in this chapter explain first how to loft and shape these timbers, then how to loft and cut the rabbet. A full-time boatbuilder would probably loft both the backbone sections and the rabbet in one step, but I recommend the step-by-step method for anyone else, as it is less confusing, even though a bit more time consuming.

Photo 4.1 Now the backbone, timbers are shaped. The first step is to loft the actual dimensions of the stem timber onto the plan view of the waterlines (diagram 4.1). Draw the length and the half-width of the stem at WL1A, as shown, then at each of the rest of the waterlines from 4A to DWL. Note the intersection points at (a) and (b). The wood between these two points has to be removed to give the correct stem (cutwater) shape. I then loft the rest of the stem timbers and forefoot timbers at each waterline and frame section to obtain points (a) and (b). Transfer these points to the stem and forefoot assembly.

4.1

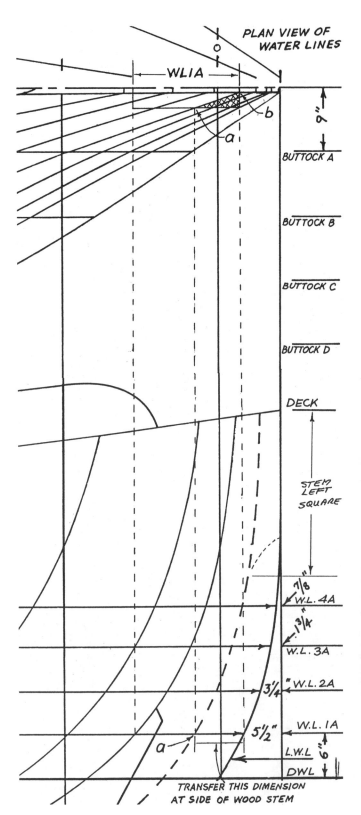

Diagram 4.1

Photo 4.2 The cutwater is relatively easy to shape, as there usually is little or no hollow on its side.

4.2

4.3

Photo 4.3 The area where the forefoot joins the keel appears on the body plan at F5 as two separate timbers (diagram 4.2). Point (a) is on the side of the forefoot timber and point (b) is on the bottom of the keel timber.

Photo 4.4 The stem and forefoot, between line (a) and line (b), are finished to the outside lines of the hull. The upper part of the stem for this boat was left square to make building and fitting the gammon iron (bowsprit stemhead band) simpler.

Diagram 4.2

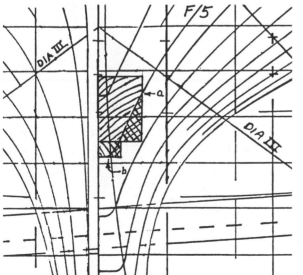

4.4

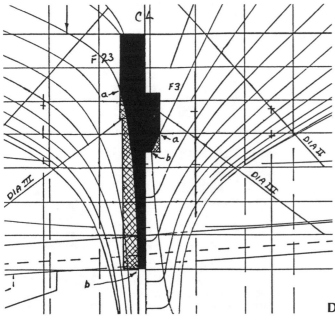

4.5

Photo 4.5 Now the transom-knee area has to be shaped down. The cross-hatching in diagram 4.3 at F23 shows the wood that is being adzed off here and in photo 4.6.

An adze is a quick, efficient tool for removing a lot of wood from a hollow, shaped timber. It can cut off up to 1½ inches of wood at a stroke. The two adzes shown are Casterline lipped adzes. The one on the right is a lining adze, used to cut the trenches (i.e., line out) so the regular, wider-lipped adze can more easily chop down the remaining wood.

Diagram 4.3

Photo 4.6 An adze works better for this job than an electric plane, which can only take a ⅛-inch cut on each pass, and, with its long, flat base, cannot get into hollow sections such as at F23. If you do not have a lining adze, you can use a Skilsaw. Make cuts every few inches, then remove the wood between them with a lipped adze.

Photo 4.7 Be sure your Skilsaw cuts are shallower than the final depth of the wood you want to remove. Be particularly careful in the areas such as where WL2B and WL3B intersect with F23 just below my hand as there is little wood to be removed here. This plywood pattern for F23 shows the exact shape of the outside of the hull between (a) and (b). It is *not* reduced for planking thickness.

4.6

4.7

4.8

Photo 4.8   I made similar patterns for F20, F21, and F22, then shaped the areas at each section down to the net marks. (Net equals the lofted curve of the plywood pattern, which equals the shape of the outside of the finished hull.) At this stage, the excess wood between the net marks can be removed and the backbone timbers faired up fore and aft using a slick (a large hand chisel), scrub planes with convex soles, and battens. If a slick is not available, you can work down the convex areas, though more slowly, with two convex (scrub) planes. One plane should have about a 1/16-inch curve to its blade, the other a 1/8-inch curve.

The Rabbet

Once both sides of the keel assembly were shaped to (a) and (b), which represented the outside of the hull, I went back to the loft floor to draw the rabbet onto the individual backbone sections. The rabbet intersection, or (c), lay between (a) and (b) on the backbone sections (diagram 4.4). Using a staff to measure from the baseline to the designer's rabbet line, I transferred the heights of the rabbet line at each section to the body plan from the lofted profile (see F21 in diagram 4.4). This gives the points that will be connected to become the rabbet line (c), which is the outside of the garboard seam.

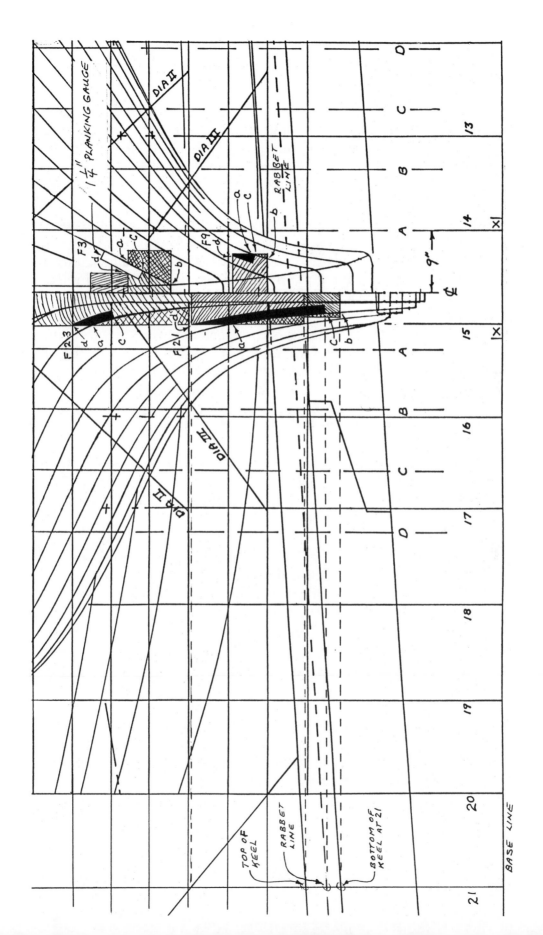

Diagram 4.4

Then I took a staff and measured from (b) to (c) at each station and from (b) to (c) at each waterline of the stem I transferred these measurements to the wooden keel assembly. I sprung a batten along these points (c) to represent the rabbet line as it is shown on the loft floor. It looked like the drawings and was fair, so I tacked a batten in place above the marks (c) and penciled in the rabbet line. (The batten nail holes were removed when I cut the actual rabbet.)

I made a square-cornered block of wood 2 inches by 6 inches the same thickness as the planking (in my case, 1¼ inches) and marked it "PLANK PATTERN." I positioned the block on the loft-floor body plan inside the line between (c) and (a) at each section. I then drew a line around the planking pattern (see F3 in diagram 4.4). This line represents the inside of the planking (rabbet area). The upper corner at the inside of the hull (d) is the bearding line.

To transfer the bearding line to the timbers, I measured vertically from the top of the outside starboard corner of the stem to (d) on the body plan. I then transferred this to the keel assembly, as shown at F3. Farther aft, such as at station F9, the bearding line is on top of the keel timber instead of on the side. So (d) is measured horizontally from the center-line of the keel timbers. All stations from F8 to F19 that lie along the keel timber can be measured this way. (The bearding line drawn on the plan view of the construction plan for this boat appears in diagram 5.1.)

Right aft, near section F23 in diagram 4.4, (d) has to be measured from the top out-side corner down along the stern timbers.

I connected the bearding-line points on the backbone with a batten and penciled in the line. The bearding line wanders from the side of the stem to the top of the forefoot and keel and back again to the side of the stern knee and the sternpost.

Once both the rabbet and the bearding line are on, it is time to start cutting the rab-bet. Instead of cutting the rabbet net, I feel that it pays to leave ¼ inch of extra wood in the rabbet and then chisel and plane off the excess wood as I fit ribbands and planks. There are several ways minor inaccuracies can creep into this area; one of the most common is that planks can vary in thickness if they are scrubbed (hollowed or rounded to fit the curved frames). This occurred in the forefoot area near station F6. If I had cut the rabbet net, the planking would have been below the intended outside of the hull. But since I left the ¼ inch of extra wood until I planked, I was able to keep the planking flush to the out-side of the hull. (This is described in more detail in chapter 17.)

The easiest way to start notching out the rabbet is to use a Skilsaw set ¼ inch shal-lower than the planking depth. Make the first cut ¼ inch inside the rabbet line (c). Leav-ing the extra ¼ inch along the edge of the rabbet line will simplify drilling for stopwaters, as is discussed in detail in chapter 12.

Photo 4.9 The key to running the saw cut accurately along the rabbet line is to fasten a piece of ¼-inch-thick plywood to the bottom of the Skilsaw so that it can rest on the outside face of the stem at b—c (diagram 4.5) and the keel and stern knee without touching any part of the keel assembly other than what is right next to the intended cut.

Photo 4.10 I made a 1-inch-deep saw cut ¼ inch above the rabbet line at 90 degrees to the outside face of the backbone timbers.

4.9

4.10

Diagram 4.5

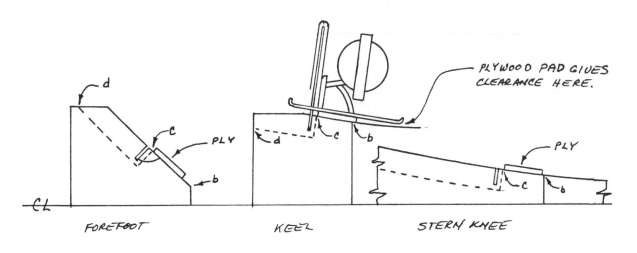

FORETOOT   KEEL   STERN KNEE

Photo 4.11 I made the first cut between F20 and F21. To start the cut, I had to drop the Skilsaw down from the front edge, slowly lowering the back part as the blade started to cut (plunge cut). To gain confidence, you can practice this method an inch above the rabbet line in a relatively easy area on your backbone. When you are comfortable doing it, cut along all of the straight parts of the rabbet first, then progress to the curved lines at the sternpost and finally to the stem rabbet line.

At the top right-hand corner of this photo, where the stern tapers into the sternpost, the rabbet face narrows dramatically. Great care is needed here to make sure that the Skilsaw's metal base clears the sternpost. Otherwise, it could tip the saw blade, cut through the rabbet line, and mess up the caulking seam. If I had not been confident about using the Skilsaw, I would have roughed out this narrow area with a chisel and hammer.

At the other end of the rabbet, the Skilsaw worked fine until I reached the upper part of the stem, where the cutwater is left square. This upper 2 feet of the stem rabbet has to be hand-chiseled for accuracy (see photo 4.17).

Photo 4.12 Next I fitted a limiting depth stop to a regular twist drill and drilled down into the rabbet area the exact depth of the planking thickness (in my case, 1¼ inches). I drilled these holes square (by eye) to the rabbet area between (a) and (c).

Photo 4.13 The holes served as my depth guide. I adzed down only until the hole began to taper toward what had been the point of the drill. This left about ¼ inch of wood on the backrabbet.

4.14

4.15

Photo 4.14 Notice that I used a barrier of wood to protect the rabbet line as I removed the wood quickly with the adze in this area. I chiseled off the barrier last. In flat sections, I removed almost all of the excess wood from the rabbet, leaving visible only the impression of the drill points. In areas where there would be some hollow, I left a full ¼ inch of extra wood to allow for plank scrubbing.

Photo 4.15 Notches representing the eventual rabbet were cut at each frame station along the keel timber (diagram 4.6).

Photo 4.16 I used a 1-inch-wide chisel to cut and gauge the notches and a 1 ¾-inch chisel to rough out the excess wood between stations. I prefer socket chisels with a metal band around the wooden handles; they can stand the heavy blows from a 4-pound "speed" hammer.

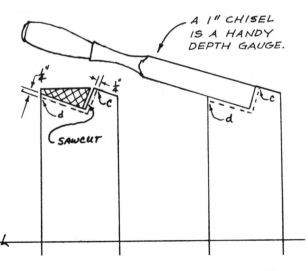

A 1" CHISEL IS A HANDY DEPTH GAUGE.

SAWCUT

Diagram 4.6

4.16

4.17

STOP

TOP OF DECK

Photo 4.17 I stopped the rabbet at the underside of the deck (or bottom of what will be the covering board). This simplified fitting and caulking the deck/covering board later on. The rabbet near the stemhead on this boat must be chiseled by hand because the Skilsaw cannot accurately make the transition from resting on the cutwater face to resting on the square part of the stemhead.

CONSTRUCTION TIMES FOR CHAPTER 4

Larry: Shaping the keel assembly; cutting the rabbet, port and starboard   96 hours

Lin: Making shelves and drawers for workbenches; arranging shop and cleanup   19 hours

Totals to date: Larry   690 hours

Lin   103 hours

5. FLOOR TIMBERS

Once the rabbet is roughed out, the backbone can be set upright, ready to accept floors. These floors are, in my opinion, the single most critical structural member in an outside-ballasted sailboat. Compromises cannot be made in floor timbers without risking leaking at the planking-to-rabbet (garboard) connection.

Taleisin is built with double-sawn frames at each station. Each frame fits flush against the arms of the floors because both the floor and the frame are square to the centerline of the vessel (diagram 5.1—construction plan). We chose to use bronze floors for reasons that are explained at the end of this chapter. But most of the steps and decisions discussed in this section will be the same as those you would have to go through if you built laminated or solid timber floors.

Photo 5.1 These plywood foundry patterns were used to cast the floors in manganese bronze. In order to design and build these patterns, I had to decide where to position the floors relative to the frame stations. One of the main factors that affected this decision was that the floors from F9 aft to F21 would all have a 1½-inch-wide flange that was to be fastened to the keel. By placing the floors on the forward side of the frame, the flange could be beveled to accommodate the angle between the frame and the raked keel timber (diagram 5.2).

5.1

Diagram 5.1

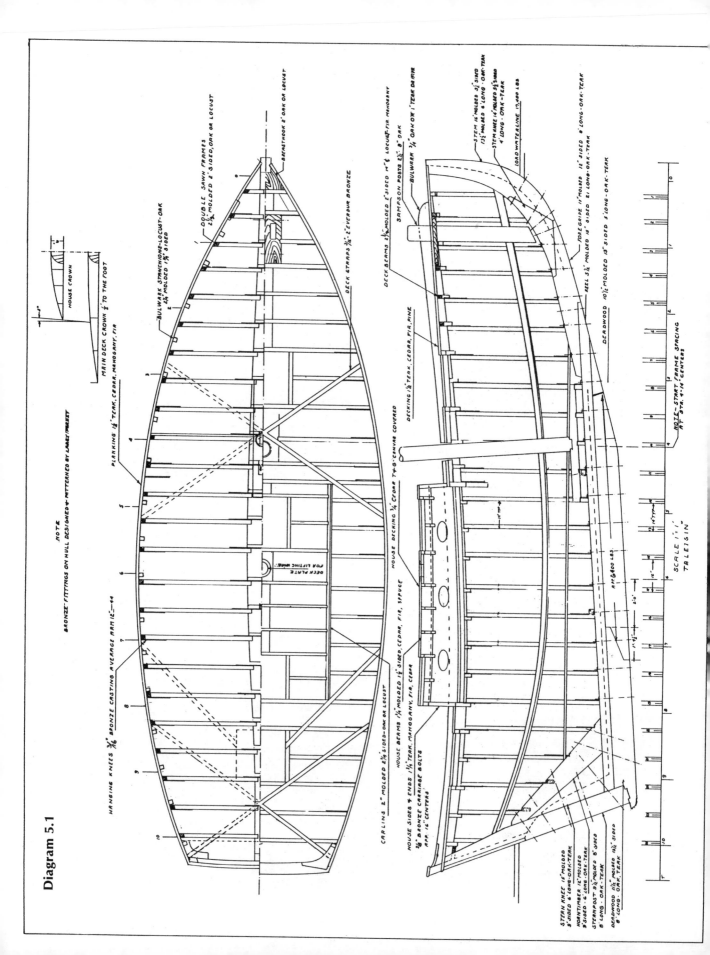

HOUSE CROWN

MAIN DECK CROWN ⅛" TO THE FOOT

NOTE
BRONZE FITTINGS ON HULL DESIGNED & PATTERNED BY LARRY PARDEY

HANGING KNEES ⅜" BRONZE CASTING AVERAGE PART 12"—44

PLANKING 1½" TEAK, CEDAR, MAHOGANY, FIR

BULWARK STANCHIONS-LOCUST-OAK 2½" MOLDED 1¾" SIDED

DOUBLE SAWN FRAMES 2½" MOLDED 2" SIDED, OAK OR LOCUST

BREASTHOOK 2" OAK OR LOCUST

DECK STRAPS ⅜" × 2" EVERDUR BRONZE

DECK BEAMS 2⅛" MOLDED 2" SIDED N° ⅙ LOCUST-FIR MAHOGANY

SAMPSON POSTS 2½" × 8" OAK

BULWARK ¾" OAK OR 1" TEAK OR FIR

STEM 14" MOLDED 9½" SIDED 12½" MOLDED 6" LONG - OAK - TEAK

STEM KNEE 14" MOLDED 8½" SIDED 4" LONG - OAK - TEAK

LOAD WATERLINE 10,400 LBS

FORE GRIPE 11" MOLDED 8½" SIDED 8" LONG-OAK-TEAK

KEEL 3½" MOLDED 14" SIDED 14" LONG-OAK-TEAK

DEADWOOD 10½" MOLDED 13" SIDED 5" LONG-OAK-TEAK

NOTE—START FRAME SPACING AT STA. 4-14" CENTERS

CARLINS 2" MOLDED 2⅛" SIDED-OAK OR LOCUST

HOUSE DECKING ¼" CEDAR + ⅛"-6" CANVAS COVERED

DECKING ⅝" TEAK, CEDAR, FIR, PINE

HOUSE BEAMS 1¾" MOLDED 1⅝" SIDED, CEDAR, FIR, SPRUCE

HOUSE SIDES + ENDS 1⅜" TEAK, MAHOGANY, FIR, CEDAR
¾" BRONZE CARRIAGE BOLTS APX. 16" CENTERS

DECK PLATE FOR LIFTING WING

SCALE 1"=1'
TALEISIN

AM. 6,400 LBS

STERN KNEE 16" MOLDED 5" SIDED 6" LONG-OAK-TEAK

MORTIMER 16" MOLDED 5" SIDED 6" LONG-OAK-TEAK

STERNPOST 9½" MOLDED 8" SIDED 8" LONG - OAK - TEAK

DEADWOOD 11½" MOLDED 13½" SIDED 8" LONG-OAK-TEAK

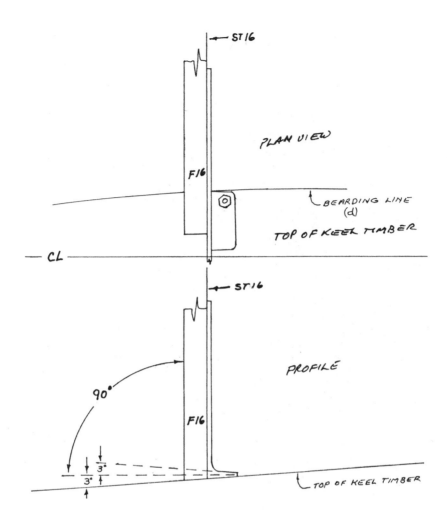

ST 16

PLAN VIEW

F 16

BEARDING LINE
(d)

TOP OF KEEL TIMBER

— CL —

ST 16

90°

PROFILE

F 16

3°

3°

TOP OF KEEL TIMBER

Diagram 5.2

5.2

Photo 5.2 The flanges on floors F9 to F19 sit flat on the keel timber. The 3-degree angle on the flange gives a perfect fit to the keel timber and at the same time creates the draft that allows the wood pattern to pull out easily from the foundryman's sand mold. If the sides of the flange were parallel, it would pull the sand with it, spoiling the sand mold. In this photo, Bill Allen, who did our foundry work, is removing a floor pattern from the sand mold at his foundry.

5.3

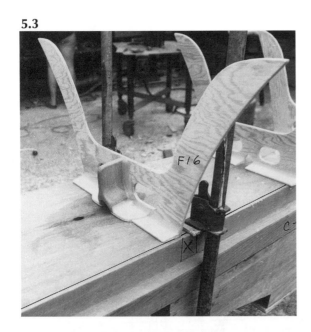

Photo 5.3 The aft side of the floor pattern is lined up with the frame station mark at F16. The sawn frame itself will fit on the aft side of the floor. The lifting eye on floor F16 was an option I built onto the pattern to save space in the bilge between the floors. (The construction drawings, diagram 5.1, show the position of the second lifting eye for this boat at F11.)

Photo 5.4 The floor-pattern shapes from F15 to F21 are on station, so they are exactly the same shape as the lofted body plan minus the thickness of the planking (diagram 5.3). To make these patterns, I nailed the straight lower edge of a piece of ¼-inch plywood to the top of the lofted-in keel section at the frame station. I marked the body-plan centerline on the plywood, plus waterlines 3B, 4B, 5B, and 6B. I but-

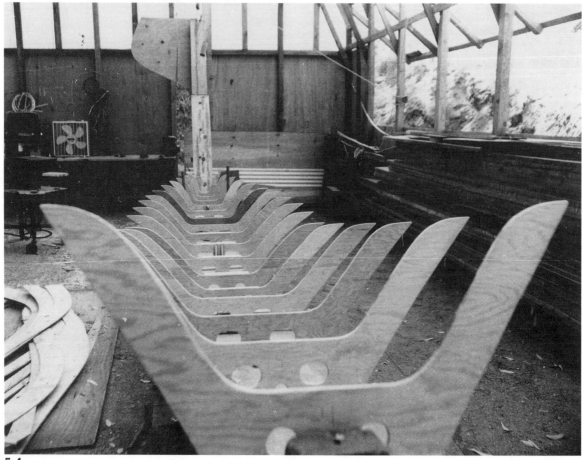

5.4

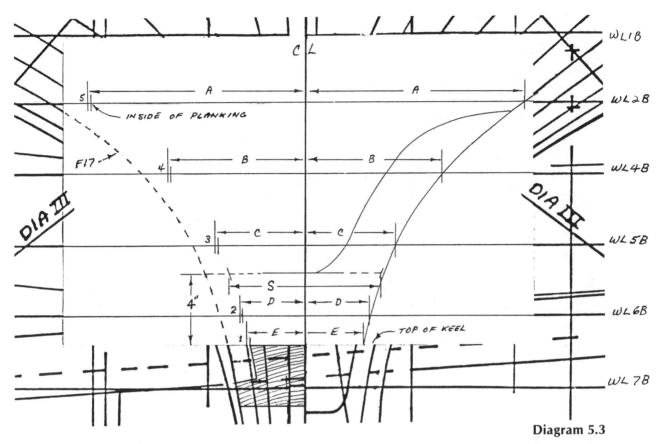

Diagram 5.3

ted the F17 staff to the centerline to give the half-breadth of the top of the keel from the centerline to the bearding line (E), then the half-breadth of 6B, 5B, 4B, and 3B. Then I deducted the thickness of the planking. (Deducting for the planking thickness is discussed in detail in chapter 6.)

Next I determined the shrinkage factor for the metal alloy that the foundryman would use to cast the floors. Manganese-bronze castings, such as we used, will shrink 3/16 inch per foot. This factor must be added to the wood pattern; otherwise, the final casting will be smaller than expected. To make the correction, I measured the width of the proposed pattern at dimension S in diagram 5.3. This is the part of the pattern that will shrink. If the width of S equals 12 inches, for example, I need to add 3/16 inch, which means increasing the half-breadths at 1, 2, 3, 4, and 5 by 3/32 inch, or half of the shrink factor. I did all of the calculations for planking

reduction and shrinkage on the port arm of these patterns, then transferred the corrected half-breadths to the starboard arm. Then I sprung a batten through both sides and penciled in the shape. (Although I have given exact figures for the shrinkage factors, in practice I just estimated these figures, then added the estimate plus 1/16 inch extra to each side of the pattern as shown.) These floors can be trimmed easily with the bandsaw for their final fitting to the frames, so I tended to be a bit generous in my shrinkage-factor additions.

Next, I figured the length for the floor arms. According to Herreshoff's Rules (Appendix B), "The arms should be long enough to lap the timbers from 6 to 9 times the (sided) size of the timbers." *Taleisin's* frames are sided 2 inches times nine, which means an arm length of 18 inches. This ratio gives a strong connection between the floor and the frame, with space for three well-positioned floor-to-frame bolts.

5.5

Photo 5.5 As this later photo shows, I used a factor of 9:1 for the arms on all the floors that were above the lead ballast keel. Forward from F2 to F6 and aft at F18 to F23—areas that receive less-direct strains from the rigging and ballast—I shortened down to a factor of 6:1 or 7:1.

The width of the floor arm is the same as the molded frame width, 2 ½ inches in our case. The vertical web height of all these floors is 4 inches, measured from the keel. I made two standardized curve patterns, one for the end of the arms, the other for the arm-to-web transition.

When all of the plywood shapes have been picked up, they can be sawn out on the bandsaw. The saw is set with a 2-degree angle so the edge of the plywood all around the pattern, including the lightening and limber holes, will pull out of the foundry sand easily and cleanly. All of the corners on the flange side of the pattern are slightly rounded or radiused for cleaner pulling (diagram 5.4).

The material for the tapered flange is cut on the table saw to get the 3-degree taper on both sides, as shown in diagram 5.5.

I made one complete floor pattern (F14) before I went ahead with all of the patterns because I wanted Bill Allen to see it so I could build the rest of the patterns to his specifications. He took a quick look and said, "It will pull okay. No need to paint them—saves you a lot of work." He cast F14 for me and I checked it against the loft floor. My shrink-factor calculations were correct, so I had the technical confidence to assembly-line produce the rest of the patterns.

After picking up the patterns for the floors from F15 to F19, which are exactly on station, I began making patterns for the floors from F14 forward. (Diagram 5.6) These are slightly more difficult to figure than the aft floors because they are 2 inches (the frame thickness) forward of the frame stations. After lofting one of these floors, I realized that for most of the floor positions, the slight narrowing of the hull, plus the rise of the keel timber forward, decreased the width of the floor about equal to the ³⁄₁₆-inch-per-foot

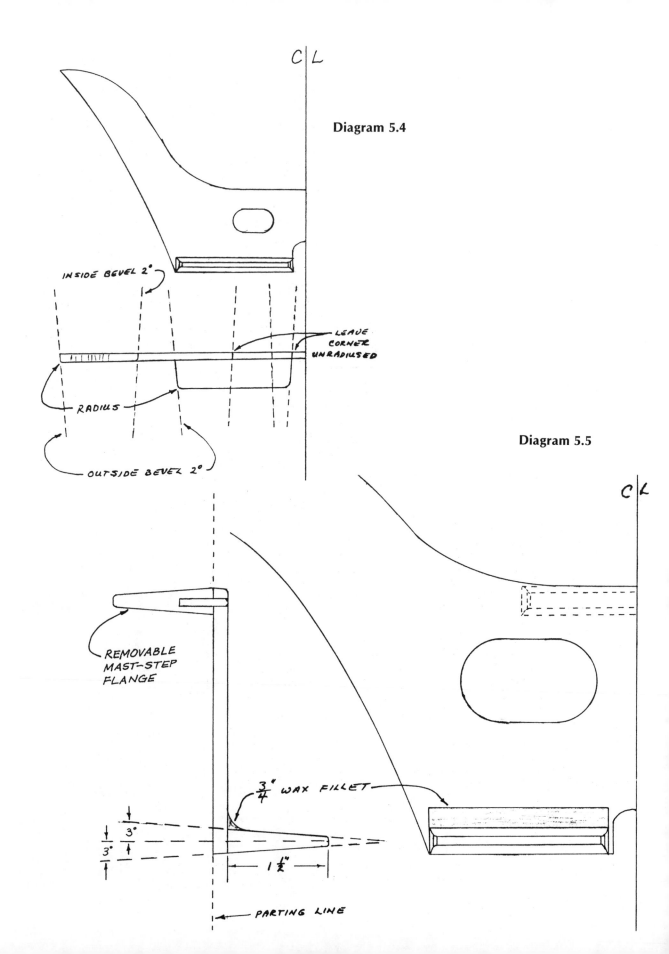

C L

Diagram 5.4

INSIDE BEVEL 2°

LEAVE CORNER UNRADIUSED

RADIUS

Diagram 5.5

OUTSIDE BEVEL 2°

C L

REMOVABLE MAST-STEP FLANGE

$\frac{3}{4}$" WAX FILLET

3°

3°

1 $\frac{1}{2}$"

PARTING LINE

shrinkage. So I built the floor patterns for F12 to F8 directly off the loft floor, on station as I had with F15 to F19, except I didn't add the shrinkage factor. Forward of F8, up to F4, this hull narrows quickly and the floors rise dramatically along the forefoot and stem, so I checked the waterlines to determine the amount of change from each station to the actual floor position 2 inches forward. The differences I found convinced me to loft each of these floors completely before I made the patterns.

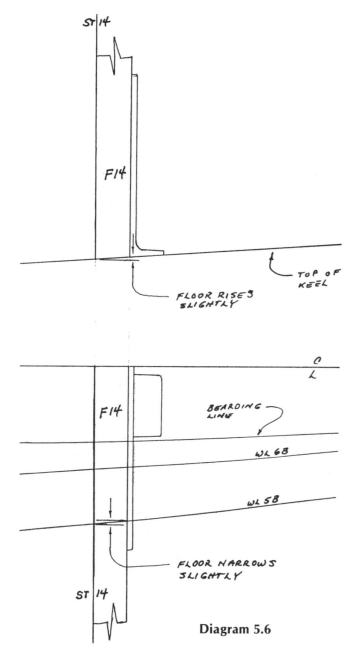

Diagram 5.6

Photo 5.6 This is a "flash forward" showing the mast step being fitted. I attached an extra flange on the backs of floors F8 to F12 to give the mast step a good, wide bearing surface (diagram 5.5). The mast-step flange is left about 1 inch shy of the frame. This way, the flange can be let into the bottom face of the mast step to stop fore-and-aft and sideways movement.

The pattern for this mast-step flange should be attached to the main pattern with dowels so that it is removable. This simplifies the molding for the foundryman.

5.6

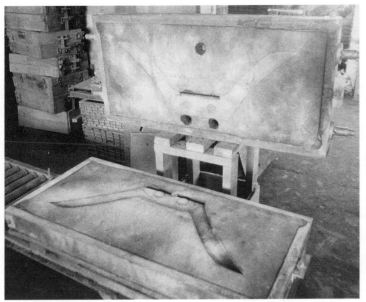

5.7

5.8

Photo 5.7 This foundry photo shows the impression of the plywood floor pattern in the lower flask (cope) and the impression of the mast-step flange in the upper flask (drag), which is standing on edge. The parting line is where the two sand molds fit together.

Photo 5.8 Note where floor F8 is notched into the forefoot, which ends just under the mast-step. Notches have to be cut into the backbone timbers for floors F8 to F4 so they neatly fit the rise of the forefoot.

An addition has to be made to the patterns for the floors aft at F20 to F21, which are also set on notches cut into the stern knee. Although they are positioned on station, they are lower than the frame (diagram 5.7).

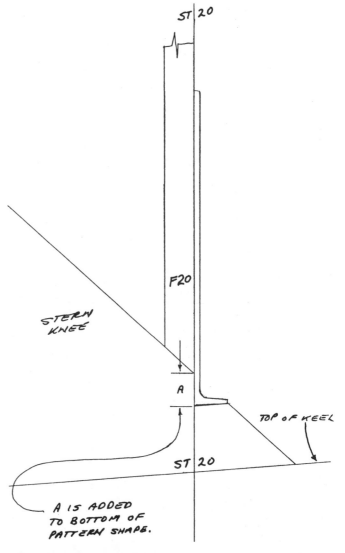

Diagram 5.7

Photo 5.9 The floor patterns for F2 and F3, and F22 and F23, do not need to be lofted. It is easier to fit and build them later when the frames are in place. These single-arm patterns are flanged to the side of the stern knee and the side of the stem. They are fastened to the backbone with a single ⅜-inch bolt, sandwiching the stern knee or stem between the flanges of the bronze floor timbers.

5.9

It is important to use a good, flat piece of ¼-inch plywood for these patterns. Curvature in the final pattern will give the foundryman fits. The plywood should be sanded both sides and have few center-core voids, or you will have to spend a lot of time puttying the edges. I used fir plywood for this project, and it was a mistake. The grain transferred to the castings, and I spent extra time belt-sanding the floors to make them fairly smooth. A tight-grain plywood like maple or good mahogany would have been a better choice. I used only one and a half sheets of plywood altogether, so cost was not a big factor. I used mahogany plywood for all later patterns. To get the most out of the sheet of plywood, I started on the longest-armed floor first, making the next shorter one from the offcut between the arms of the larger pattern.

The solid-pine flange pieces were half-nailed in place with steel finishing nails, then pulled apart and glued (five-minute epoxy is fast for pattern work). Then the nails were driven home.

Between the main plywood web on the floor pattern and the flanges is a ¾-inch-radius wax fillet. This radius is vital in transferring the strain from the floor arms to the flange. The ¾-inch fillet wax, which can be bought in a patternmaker's supply shop, is a great time-saver. Professional patternmakers use a heating iron to stick the wax to inside corners. I simply used a little white glue and rubbed the wax in with a rounded stick. I chiseled numbers onto the forward (drag) side of each floor pattern to simplify identification.

We made sure all of the edges and faces of the patterns felt smooth to the touch, using 150-grit sandpaper for the final work. We sent them to the foundry unpainted. Although these patterns were built originally for only one use, they have since been shellacked and used for six other boats of this type, so the simple construction was strong enough to withstand repeated use.

CONSTRUCTION TIMES FOR CHAPTER 5

Larry: Picking up patterns for floors; making foundry patterns   34 hours

Lin: Buying materials; sanding and numbering foundry patterns   10 hours

Totals to date: Larry   724 hours

Lin   113 hours

DISCUSSION
Floor-Material Choices: Metal, Laminated, or Sawn

Well-engineered floors, be they metal, laminated, or sawn, can each produce a strong hull with a dry bilge. I have owned two boats with wood floors and two with metal ones, and none of them leaked near or at the garboard seams. But it is interesting to look at the displacement-to-ballast numbers for each of these boats. The two with wooden floors had, respectively, 28 percent and 26 percent ballast-to-displacement ratios. The metal-floored boats had 50 percent and 36 percent ballast-to-displacement ratios. I guess the message here is that if you build a heavily ballasted boat (more than 33 percent of displacement), it might be prudent to use metal floors to get the 9:1 floor arm length recommended by Herreshoff, plus the direct through-bolts from the floors to the ballast keel. The critical arm-connection length on wooden floors is often shorter, so it is hard to get a strong floor-to-frame connection. If the strains of the rigging cause the frame to slide slightly upward beside the floor, the garboard will leak. If the bolts holding the floor to the wood keel loosen, the floor timber rises and the garboard leaks. (*Never* use drift bolts to fasten floor timbers that are positioned above or near the ballast keel. Blind bolts create more work, but they are infinitely better if for some reason you cannot use through-bolts.)

Metal floors are simple to loft because you don't have to pick up or make special mold-loft patterns. You can pick up the foundry pattern directly from the loft floor. The metal floors need little or no bevel lofting because the metal is only ¼ inch thick—compared to that on a 2-inch-thick wood floor. If your metal floors should come out ⅛ inch too small, they will not give you any weaker structure or cause any future problem. But if your wooden floors do not fit, the gap between them and the planking could be a perfect spot for endgrain rot to start. With metal floors, you use shorter bolts, for both the frame-to-floor-arm connection and the floor-to-backbone connection (diagram 5.8). The bolts that go through the metal floor can have larger diameters without weakening the floor. If you use metal floors as shown here, the floor-to-backbone and backbone-to-keel bolts can be the same. You cannot put a keelbolt through a sawn wooden floor unless you increase the sided dimensions of the floor by the diameter of the bolt. In other words, a 1-inch keelbolt drilled through a 2-inch floor timber will weaken the wood part by about 50 percent.

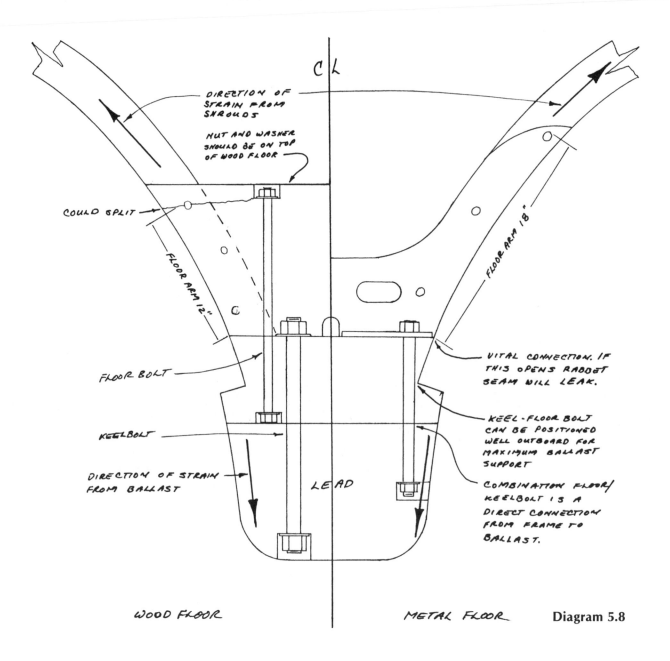

CL

DIRECTION OF STRAIN FROM SHROUDS

NUT AND WASHER SHOULD BE ON TOP OF WOOD FLOOR

COULD SPLIT

FLOOR ARM 12"

FLOOR ARM 18"

FLOOR BOLT

KEELBOLT

DIRECTION OF STRAIN FROM BALLAST

LEAD

VITAL CONNECTION. IF THIS OPENS RABBET SEAM WILL LEAK.

KEEL-FLOOR BOLT CAN BE POSITIONED WELL OUTBOARD FOR MAXIMUM BALLAST SUPPORT

COMBINATION FLOOR/ KEELBOLT IS A DIRECT CONNECTION FROM FRAME TO BALLAST.

WOOD FLOOR

METAL FLOOR

Diagram 5.8

Although the prime reason here for choosing metal floors was structural strength, we have come to appreciate the advantage of space in the bilge for water tanks, chain storage, and wine storage. And the whole bilge is wide open fore and aft for good ventilation. The lightening holes cast into the floors are handy for running plumbing and wiring from one end of the ship to the other. If a limber hole should become plugged, water still will move freely aft to the sump as soon as it rises an inch up the floor.

Another major advantage of the metal floors is that they let you lower the height of the mast step. This adds to the cabin headroom and is achieved without loss of strength or loss of floor-arm length. On the other hand, you can achieve almost the same low profile by using laminated wood floors. These U-shaped floors can provide most of the structural advantages offered by metal floors, but they require longer bolts, take more space in the bilge, and are harder to loft and build.

METAL FLOORS (FIRST CHOICE)

Pro	**Con**
More bilge storage space.	Material cost of bronze.
Water tanks can be in bilge.	Good foundry people can be hard to find.
Fewer and shorter bolts and fastenings.	Delays occur as you wait for castings.
Lowers cabin sole.	Harder to use with steam-bent frames.
Less drilling labor.	Breaks any rum bottles not stored carefully in the bilge.
Long, strong floor arms.	
Direct connection to lead ballast.	
Light weight.	
Less chance of rot.	
Fitting and lofting floors easier.	
No shrinkage or swelling.	
No chance of delamination.	
No painting or finishing necessary.	
Metal flange makes a large washer for keelbolts.	
Floors can be removed easily for repairs and renovations.	
Easy to position keelbolts well outboard, where they are strongest.	
Through-bolts into the frame can be very close to the top edge of the floor arm.	

LAMINATED FLOORS (SECOND CHOICE)

Pro	**Con**
Long, strong arms or even a one-piece frame, floor, and deckbeam is possible.	Takes up more space than metal floors.
Grain all runs in most advantageous direction.	Needs longer bolts than do metal floors.
No foundry work necessary.	More labor-intensive than metal or sawn floors.
Good availability of materials.	Possible glue failures in damp and wet conditions in bilges.
Few shrinking and swelling problems.	Need lots of clamps and a gluing jig. Need high-tech shop with temperature control for gluing.
Easy to add on material for fitting.	Need finishing and painting; should be completely coated or painted.
Less chance of rot in endgrain.	Shortens planking butt blocks in bilge area.
Planks can be fastened directly to the floor.	Through-bolts at top of floor arm into frame must be at least 2 inches from arm end to resist splitting. (Arms must be nine times frame siding plus 2 inches.)

SOLID TIMBER FLOORS (THIRD CHOICE)

Pro	Con
Material is easy to get and not as expensive.	Need finishing and painting.
Many floors can be cut from the same 2-inch-by-12-inch board by opposing the patterns.	Rot can penetrate endgrain if fit is not good.
Strong connection if arm length is long enough.	Shortens butt blocks in bilge area.
Most builders are comfortable and familiar with this straightforward type of construction.	Harder to loft.
	Harder to cut bevels accurately.
Planks can be screwed directly to endgrain.	Hard to fair up endgrain once floors are fastened to keel timber.
Can be built in a simple, unheated shop.	Long floor bolts cost extra.
No foundrywork necessary.	Extra separate keelbolts usually required.
	Extra labor drilling longer holes plus keelbolt holes.
	High, wide floors can shrink and swell considerably.
	Maximum loss of bilge storage.
	Difficult to vent bilges and run wires or plumbing.
	Harder to get headroom with wide, long-armed floors.
	Mast step is higher, which raises cabin sole.
	Fore-and-aft through-bolts from floor into frame at top of arm must be at least 1½ inches from floor top to resist splitting (see diagram 5.8).

We saved 293 pounds of construction weight on *Taleisin* by using metal floors instead of sawn wooden ones. (If we had used laminated wood floors, we would have saved about 100 pounds over sawn wooden ones.)

Lin, the boatyard accountant, calculated the difference in materials costs, figuring the bronze for the floors at $4.50 a pound cast weight, the wood for floors at $2.00 a board foot, and stock for silicon-bronze bolts at $4.90 a pound. She found that the metal floors cost only $350 more than timber ones (1983 U.S. prices). We decided the extra money was a good overall investment, as it represented only 1 percent of the total materials costs projected for the boat.

One limitation of bronze floors is the size of the foundryman's largest sand flask. If your floor arms are too long for his flask, you will have to weld on pieces to lengthen the arms. At that point, laminated floors might be more practical, at least for some of the wider floors amidships.

6. PICKING UP PATTERNS, PLANKING DEDUCTIONS, AND FRAME BEVELS

To build *Taleisin*'s sawn frames, I needed a pattern for each section to transfer the correct body-plan shape from the loft floor to my framing material. I also used these patterns to transfer the bevels, plus the locations of the waterlines and buttocks, to the frames after they were glued together.

Photo 6.1 If you start with the smallest frame first (F24) and proceed to the larger ones, you can pick up several patterns on one sheet of plywood. Here, the pattern for F24 is lying next to my layout work for F23. The method I used was basically the same as what I used to pick up the floor patterns in chapter 5, except that here there is no shrinkage-factor deduction.

My first step was to draw the waterlines, buttocks, and diagonals plus decksheer onto the plywood. The second step was to transfer the outside-of-the-hull measurement points onto the plywood. I used the F23 lofting staff to do this. In the final step, I deducted the planking thickness from the lofted, or outside-of-the-hull, reference points. Diagram 6.1 shows how I determined this deduction. (Other methods are discussed throughout this chapter.)

If you look at F23 at WL2A in the inset on diagram 6.1, you will see where I have drawn in the actual planking thickness. The correct reduction for the planking as it will actually lie across each frame is indicated by (d). In other words, this is the sectional thickness of the planking when looked at in a 'thwartship direction.

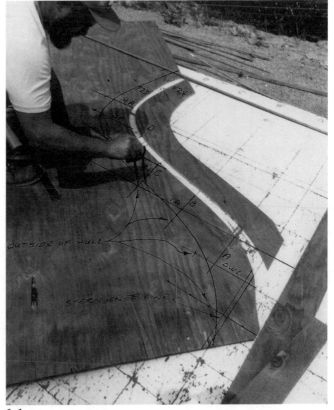

6.1

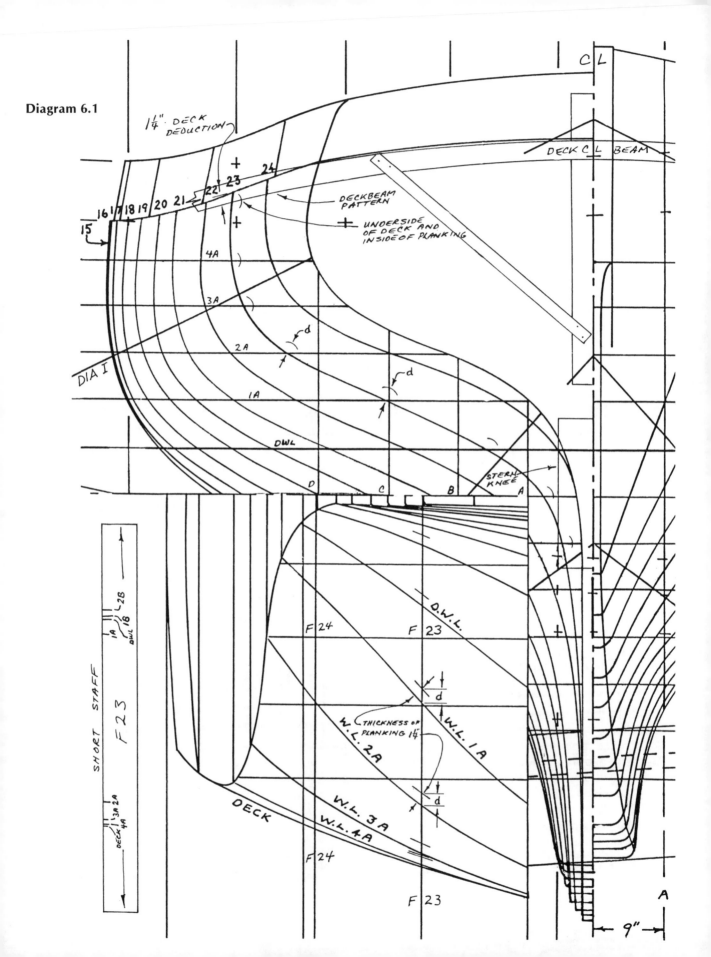

Diagram 6.1

6.2

I marked each waterline with my 1¼-inch planking gauge. Then I used a short staff to pick up all of the sectional planking-thickness measurements (d) and, with a scribe, transferred them to F23 on the plywood pattern material. I bent a light batten to the arcs and scribed the planking-deducted hull shape onto pattern F23.

Next I deducted the thickness of the deck (1¼ inches) from the decksheer. (This is shown on diagram 6.1 at F23 on the body plan.) To make it easier to align the deckbeam angle at each sheer point, I made a deckbeam pattern and triangulated it to a straightedge as shown, so it would slide up and down the centerline of the body plan. This way I could accurately mark the deck angle and curve at each frame head.

Photo 6.2 The F3 pattern lines up with its aft side to F3, WL2B, and the top of the stem marks on the backbone timbers.

Photo 6.3 The aft side of the pattern I am holding here represents the aft side of the starboard frame. The outer edge of the frame angles (bevels) toward the stem. If you take the same pattern and flop it over to the port side of the timbers, the other side of the pattern is aft and the bevels still point to the stem.

6.3

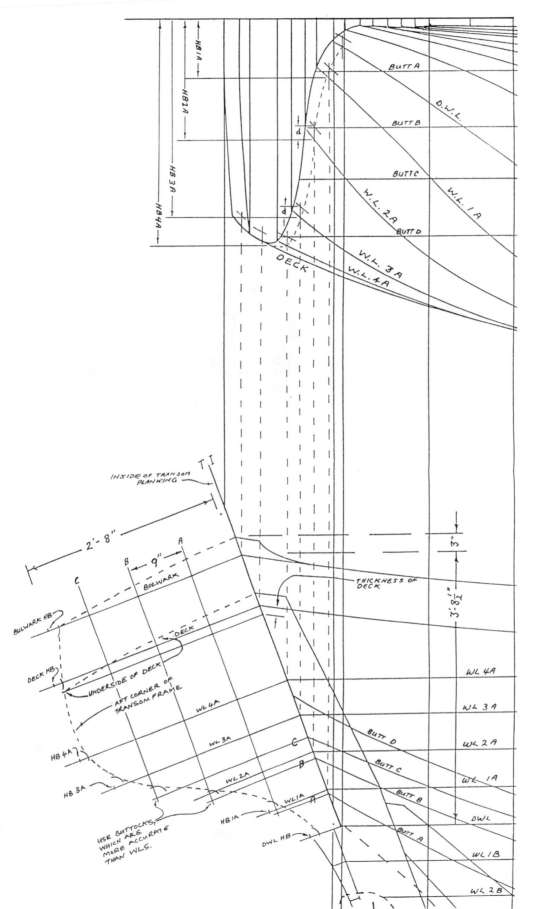

Diagram 6.2

Photo 6.4 The transom pattern tacked onto the sternpost in this photo is picked up by placing plywood over the designer's expanded-transom plan on the loft floor. The straight line on the plywood represented by TI on diagram 6.2 should line up with the inside of the transom planking on the loft profile. I project each waterline and buttock line, plus deck and bulwark lines, onto the plywood pattern at right angles to TI. Then I transfer the waterline, deck, and bulwark marks from the profile on the loft floor up to the plan view (straight dashed lines on this diagram). This shows where the inside of the transom lines (transom minus its planking) cross the plan view of the waterlines and the deck and bulwark lines. Then I can pick up the half-breadths of the inside of the transom from the plan view and transfer them to the lines on the transom pattern. The hull-planking sectional thickness (d) can now be deducted from the half-breadth points using the same method as used for the frame patterns. For this pattern to be correct, it is necessary to deduct not only the transom-planking thickness but also the thicknesses of the hull planking and the deck.

6.4

All of the waterlines plus the curved underside of the deck should line up perfectly when the pattern is tacked to the sternpost.

When all of the frame patterns have been picked up and checked to make sure that they align with their marks on the backbone, the bevels for the frames need to be lifted from the body plan and marked on the patterns (in degrees).

The maximum beam on *Taleisin* is between F14 and F15 (see diagram 5.1). The frames from F14 to the bow are set on the forward side of the station line. From F15 to the stern, they are aft of the station line. The planking face of the forward frames angle (bevel) toward the *bow*; aft, they angle toward the *stern*. These bevels can be picked up with a high degree of accuracy by utilizing local diagonals.

At F6 on waterline 1A in diagram 6.3, a local diagonal represented by the line from (A) to (B) to (C) is penciled in at 90 degrees to the outside of the hull. This local-diagonal line can be diagramed as a triangle with (A) to (C) (1 + 2) as the height of the triangle, the distance between the two frame sections as the baseline, and the outside planking curve of the hull as the hypotenuse (see lower portion of diagram 6.3). The baseline represents a fore-and-aft line at right angles to the body plan at point A, parallel to the centerline of the vessel. The diagonal height of 1 is transferred from the body plan to station 6 on the grid base (point B). The local-diagonal height of 1 + 2 is transferred to the grid at station 7 (point C). A batten is sprung through A-B-C. The angle between station 6 and the batten is the bevel at WL1A for F6. This bevel can now be measured in degrees and transferred to 1A on the pattern.

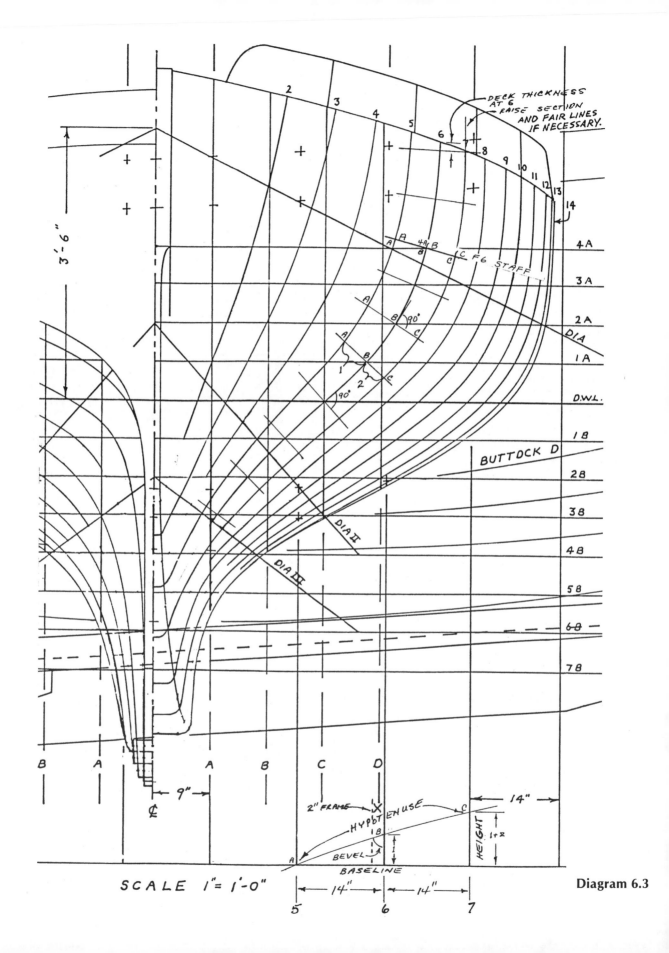

DECK THICKNESS
AT 6
RAISE SECTION
AND FAIR LINES
IF NECESSARY.

BUTTOCK D

DIA II

DIA III

3'-6"

SCALE 1"= 1'-0"

2" FRAME

HYPOTENUSE

BEVEL

HEIGHT

BASELINE

9"

14"

14"

14"

Diagram 6.3

Photo 6.5 For picking up frame bevels, I used a plywood grid board set on sawhorses and modified a metal protractor by adding an L-shaped arm. I used a short staff to pick up A-B-C at WL4B on frame 6. I flipped the staff over and picked up A-B-C at WL3B, then used the other end and both sides so I could transfer four bevels to the grid board at one time. I lofted the bevels, then marked the bevel for each waterline on my plywood pattern. Then I rubbed the A-B-C marks off the staff and returned to the loft floor for four more.

After the bevels are marked onto the pattern, the intermediate bevels can be estimated and marked. In diagram 6.4 at F6, the bevel at WL3B is 8 degrees and at WL2B it is 10. So halfway between is 9 degrees. Farther up the frame at WL1A, it is 17½ degrees; at WL2A, it is 20 degrees. I divided this area into five ½-degree sections—17½, 18, 18½. Halfway between 4A and the decksheer, I lofted in an extra local diagonal because there were no waterlines.

6.5

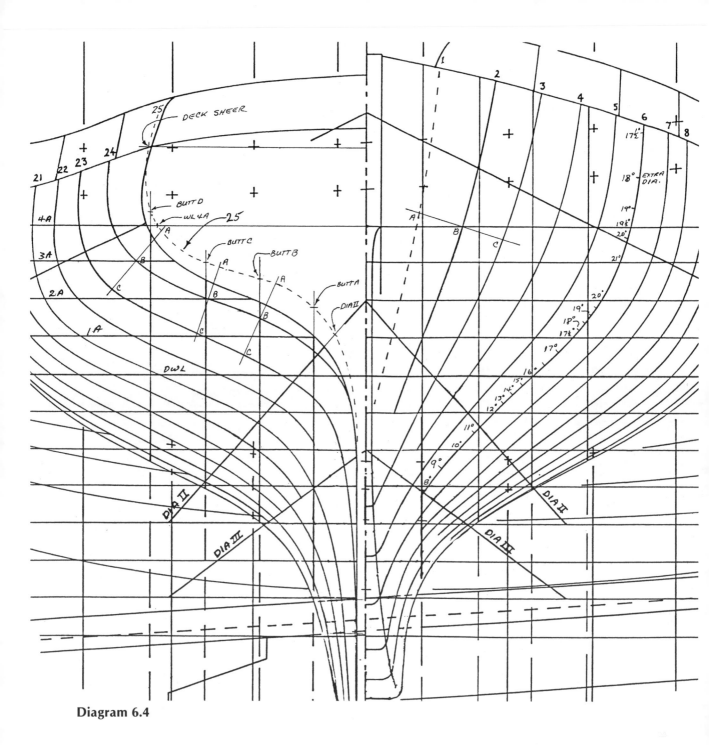

Diagram 6.4

To pick up bevels at F2, I had to loft in a non-existent station, "F1." To do this, I went back to the profile and lofted in a section 14 inches forward of F2. I picked up the F1 half-breadths and transferred them to the body plan (dotted line on diagram 6.4). Then I picked up the local F2 diagonals in the usual way.

A similar procedure can also be used to pick up bevels at F24. A station "F25" can be pen-ciled onto the profile, then the appropriate waterlines, buttocks, and diagonals can be extended aft and faired to F25. From this, half-breadth information for F25 can be lofted, as represented by the dotted line in diagram 6.4, to give reference points for (A) so the bevels for F24 can be picked up.

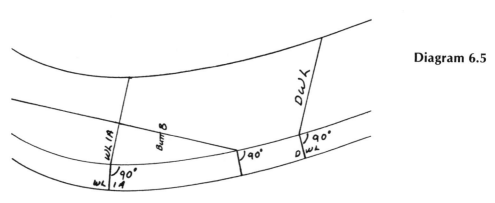

Diagram 6.5

The simplest way to pick up transom bevels, and the one I used, is shown in chapter 9.

It will be convenient to have the bevels written on both sides of the pattern. So I square the edges of the pattern as shown in diagram 6.5 and transfer the information to the opposite side of the pattern. It is not necessary to put all of the lines on the opposite side; I just pencil in "DWL" or "Butt A," and the appropriate bevel next to the squared marks. I save time and confusion by clearly marking both sides of the frame patterns from F14 to the bow: "starboard side—looking forward," or "port side—looking forward." On the frame patterns from F15 aft, I marked "port—looking aft," and "starboard—looking aft."

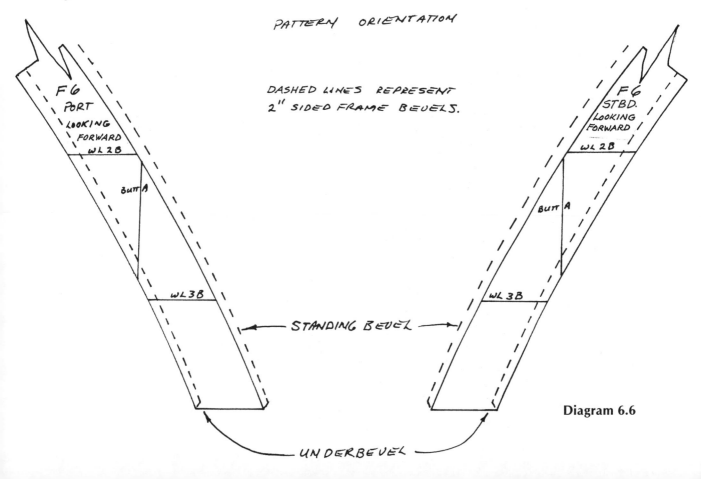

Diagram 6.6

In diagram 6.6, the dashed lines represent the standing bevel on the insides of both frames and the underbevel on the planking side of the pattern. By using these markings, I can look at a pattern and know, for example, that it is for the starboard frame, looking forward, with both bevels angling toward the stem. When this information is transferred to the frame material, I can again look at the frame markings before I saw the bevels to be sure they angle in the correct direction. A friend of mine who built a *Seraffyn*-type hull cut two sets of starboard beveled frames and no port ones because he didn't mark his patterns to indicate which ones were looking forward and which ones were looking aft.

CONSTRUCTION TIMES FOR CHAPTER 6

Larry: Picking up patterns for 23 sawn frames, plus transom; picking up bevels for frames   53 hours

Lin: Making large wooden plugs; shop maintenance   10 hours

Totals to date:	Larry	777 hours
	Lin	123 hours

DISCUSSION
More Thoughts on Bevels and Alternative Ways to Determine Planking Thickness Deductions

If you pick up your bevels using the local-diagonal batten method I described, your deduction for planking thickness can be measured on the batten grid as shown in diagram 6.7. The planking deduction is represented by (d). Before you make your pattern, the bevels can be penciled onto the loft floor; the plank deduction can be picked up and the plywood placed over the frame section. You can then use your staff to transfer the planking deduction to the pattern. Your bevels can be transferred from the loft floor to the plywood pattern when the pattern is removed from the body plan.

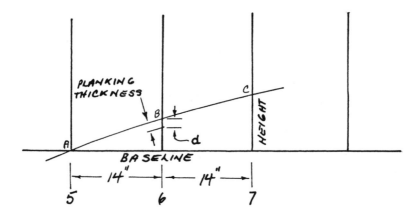

Diagram 6.7

You can also pick up the planking deduction as you pick up your bevels by using a bevel stick (degree ruler). This method is faster than using local diagonals, but it is not quite as accurate. At the lower left-hand side of diagram 6.8, you can see a bevel stick laid out on the 14-inch station grid. (Each bevel stick is special to its own loft-floor station spacings.) The line from corner to corner of the 14-inch square equals 45 degrees. Take your protractor and straightedge and mark the degrees accurately on the edge of an L-shaped piece of 1¼-inch-wide-by-⅛-inch-thick plywood, as shown.

This bevel stick simply measures the height of (1) from (A) to (B) on the body plan, as shown in diagram 6.8. This gives you a bevel of about 17 degrees at F22, LWL at (B). This system is accurate to within ½ degree on frames under 1½-inch sided dimension. If you are building a vessel with heavier frames, you should use the local-diagonal batten method, which is accurate to within a pencil line, because it actually lofts the curve of the planking at each point B.

The bevel-stick width in diagram 6.8 was made the same as the planking thickness for this boat, or 1¼ inches. The planking deduction for any area of the frame that has a 17-degree bevel is simply the angled distance across the 1¼-inch-wide ruler at (d), or 1⁵⁄₁₆ inches (see the right-hand side of diagram 6.8). This bevel stick will not work for a raked transom because the baselines change for every transom waterline.

There are four basic methods for deducting the planking thickness from your patterns. On hulls with planking under ¾ inch, many builders don't bother with any correction at all. They just take ¾ inch off the pattern parallel to the body-plan section line. This gives only about a ¹⁄₁₆-inch error on the average hull.

For thicker planking (up to 1½ inches), picking up the planking deductions from the waterlines is a more accurate method and reasonably quick (diagram 6.1).

The third method (diagram 6.7) is the most accurate and positive method that I have yet discovered. The disadvantages are that it is slower and the bevels have to be lofted from the body plan before you can get the planking deduction for the pattern. This means an extra step—i.e., writing the bevel degrees onto the loft floor and recording the planking deductions on a staff, then transferring this information to the pattern later. In spite of this extra work, however, this method should be used for all high-class yachts with planking thicker than 1½ inches, or for any vessel that requires a thick deduction for molds, stringers, or building jigs.

The bevel-stick method of getting frame bevels is the one used by most professionals and is the quickest way to obtain planking-thickness deductions with a high degree of accuracy. But this method also requires an extra step, as you must first get the bevels before you make your pattern so that you can determine the planking deduction.

When I built *Seraffyn* back in 1965, few people picked up frame bevels, because most boats were built with steamed frames bent inside ribbands, which were wrapped around temporary molds. The molds didn't need bevels, since the ribbands only touched at the one corner that represented the lofted station line. But *Seraffyn* had sawn frames every third frame, so I needed bevels. Fortunately, I met Tom Don Carswell, a loftsman who showed me the local-diagonal method described in this chapter. My bevels came out

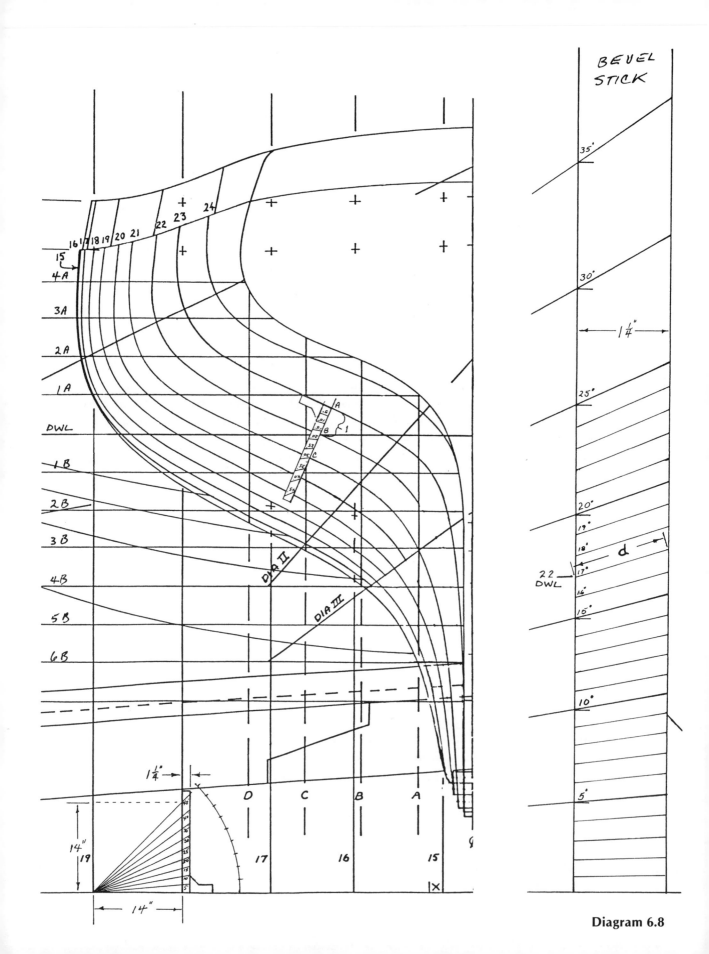

Diagram 6.8

nearly perfect. Only one frame in the bilge area had to be dubbed off ⅛ inch.

Many modern hulls are constructed with three skins and have ring frames. The bevels for these can be picked up right from the floor so the ring frame drops inside the three-skinned (cold-molded) hull and fits the keel and the inside of the planking and also lines up perfectly at the decksheer with the bevel on the top of the integral deckbeam perfect. At this point, it's ready for decking if you use the diagonal method for getting bevels.

I have spent a lot of time discussing bevels here because although most professional boatbuilders and many determined home builders do a fair job of lofting to the *outside* of their hull, many make extra work for themselves by rushing the pattern and bevel procedures. As a result, their wood parts quite often end up under- or oversized. A prime example is a 117-foot schooner that was built and launched in southern California in 1984. It was built with all vertically laminated frames. One of the builders who showed me around the almost-finished hull mentioned that the whole crew of ten spent two weeks fairing up the frames so that the planking would fit. In some cases, the frames forward and aft lost one-third of their molded dimensions as they were hacked down to fair. The errors occurred because of inaccurate bevel pickup and poor lofting. A competent boatbuilder-loftsman could have lofted and picked up the bevels for the whole ship correctly with about 120 to 160 man-hours of labor. Instead, that crew spent almost 800 man-hours at backbreaking, frame-weakening, wasted labor.

A Few Comments on Picking Up Patterns

Plywood was designed for patterns. It holds its shape, has an even thickness, and is strong for its size. If at all possible, use plywood for your patterns. If you look around a bit, you probably can get dunnage plywood that is good enough for patterns at no cost. Try construction companies that install large windows, dockyards where cars arrive from overseas, or railway yards that receive plywood shipments.

There are many other methods of transferring your pattern information to your plywood. Some loftsmen use plasterboard nail heads lying on their sides, or drive nails into the loft floor and cut off the heads, or use various kinds of pickup pointers that go over the wood pattern. But since I already had the half-breadth staffs from the original lofting procedure, I found this method to be faster and more accurate, and it let me utilize my plywood efficiently.

7. FRAMING THE HULL

Now it is time to lay patterns on timber, cut out frames and futtocks, fasten everything together, and, as the old-timers used to say, "get her arms up in the air."

Photo 7.1 Here are the ingredients for producing sawn frames. On the left is locust framing timber. The frame patterns plus my 20-inch Davis-Wells bandsaw are on the right. Outside the shop is a Faye and Egan 24-inch-by-7-inch thickness planer (circa 1912). Next to the planer is a stack of locust. I sorted this stack as I ran each piece through the planer. Next to the backbone I laid out the 2-inch-thick natural crooks that could be cut into full-length frames. I set aside pieces with long curves to be used to make deckbeams later. The pieces in the stack near the planer are not as curved so will be used later for the double-sawn frames.

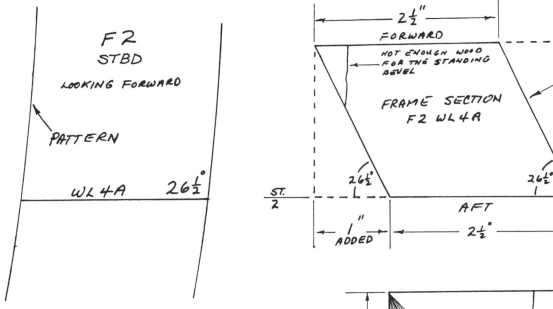

Diagram 7.1

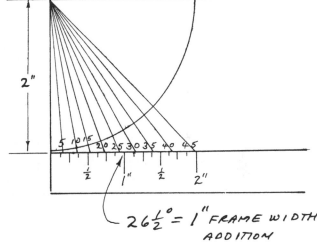

$26\frac{1}{2}° = 1''$ FRAME WIDTH ADDITION

When I cut the trees for this framing, I chose as many as I could get with curved trunks for a maximum of natural curved flitches.* The second plank lying to the left of the backbone was from a nicely S-curved log. Unfortunately, the sawyer snipped off the curved ends, because this made it easier for him to set the timber on his carriage to begin cutting the timber. Fortunately, I caught him on the first log, before he made all of my natural curves into parallel-edged boards.

To start building the frames, I laid my patterns on flitches that had appropriate curves, then roughed out a port and a starboard frame. The plank shown next to the backbone has a split along the heart, certain indication of stress in the wood. When I cut it through the heart to let it relax, it changed shape about ⅜ inch to ½ inch in its 8-foot length. It is safest to rough-cut frames a bit oversize to allow for this unpredictable springback.

As I laid the pattern onto a curved flitch, I had to approximate the bevel offcut for the inside of the frame. In the lower corner of diagram 7.1 is a simple bevel stick I made to help convert the degrees into inches, across a 2-inch-thick frame.

As this shows, for a 2-inch sided frame, 26½ degrees equals 1 inch. So 1 inch needs to be added to the inside of the molded width of the 2½-inch-wide frame. Therefore, a 3½-inch-wide flitch is necessary at F2, WL4A. It was only when the wood futtock I wanted to use seemed a bit narrow that I got out the frame bevel gauge to be sure there was enough material so that there would be no corners missing when I beveled the insides of the frames.

* A piece of timber that is slabbed off a log with the sapwood and bark left intact.

7.2

7.3

Photo 7.2   The first sawn frame (F2) is being cut. A pointer on the inside of the bandsaw table radiuses up the throat of the bandsaw, along a bevel gauge. Lin can read the degrees as she operates the table's tilt handle. The table clamping device is tightened so there is a bit of drag on the tilt mechanism, but it still moves smoothly. The table should not move by itself even if Lin lets go of the handle.

I have added a tilting table extension to this bandsaw. This should be made of coarse-grained plywood to minimize the tendency of wood to slide downhill. The 1-inch-wide blade of the saw also helps keep the wood from slipping. With larger timbers, you might need another person for this job.

Photo 7.3   These two forward frames are the easiest places to start because they have the least molded shape. They also butt to the vertical face of the stem knee, which makes them easy to fasten in place. A C-clamp secures two short pieces of 2 x 2 stock to the stem knee at the heel of F3. The frame heel can be clamped to the 2 x 2 for perfect alignment with F3's station line on the top of the stem and with WL2B on the side of the stem. A single 2½-inch number 14 bronze wood screw secures the frame heels for F2 and F3 until the bronze floors are fitted later.

The 2 x 4 cross spall that supports the frame heads is bolted in place with double-nutted threaded rod. Each cross spall is secured to its neighbor with battens and a 2-inch double-headed nail. To see whether the bevels were about right before cutting out the rest of the frames, I tacked a light batten from the bearding line on the stem along the sides of these two frames.

Photo 7.4 The block-and-tackle is rigged to a fore-and-aft 4 x 4 in the rafters.

Photo 7.5 The bronze floor for F4 is notched into the forefoot. The holes in the floor flange are drilled to 3/8 inch for the final fastening. Until the frames are horned in, the floors are temporarily fastened with 1 1/2-inch-by-5/16-inch-diameter lagbolts. The 5/16-inch lagbolt in the 3/8-inch hole allows convenient floor alignment of F4 to the station line and the forefoot centerline.* The wooden clamps holding the frame heels to the bronze floor are made from locust offcuts and threaded rod. These are put on each set of frames to secure them temporarily. (These clamps are needed again for planking.)

I used the keyhole hacksaw to remove 1/32 inch of wood from the bottom of the frame heel so that the frame waterlines are at the correct height relative to the waterlines on the stem and backbone assembly. The brass plate lying on the backbone restricts the saw cut to the frame heel. Fungicidal Dolfinite eventually is applied between the frame heel and the backbone to protect the frame heel from checking and from rot.

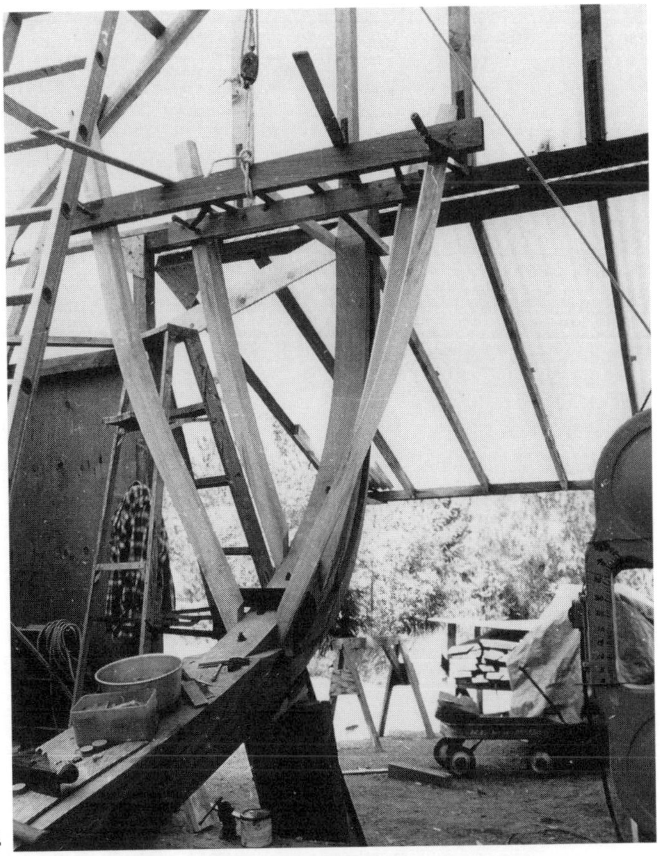

7.4

7.5

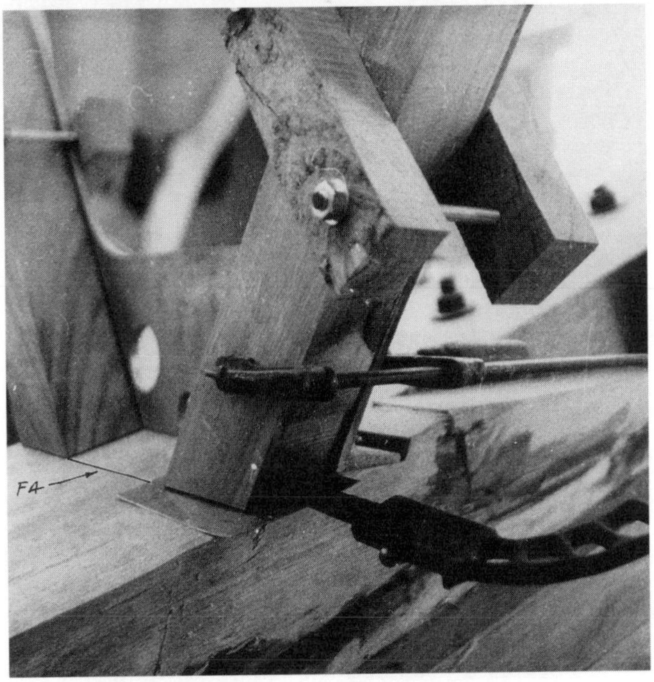

* The floors on the forefoot and the transom knee are blind-fastened with 3/8-inch-diameter bolts. The floors over the ballast keel are fastened with 5/8-inch-diameter combination floor-keel bolts. Temporary 3/8-inch-diameter lagbolts were used there to provide alignment.

7.6

Photo 7.6 The first three frames are one-piece natural curves. I was able to lay out and saw three sets in one day. I had only a limited number of curved flitches, so the next frames aft were a combination of solid natural crooks from the frame heel to the curve of the bilge, where 1-inch-thick futtocks were scarfed onto the lower solid part of the frame. From the turn of the bilge up to the deck the frames were double-sawn. These combination frames took approximately a day per pair to lay out, glue, and bevel.

Photo 7.7 The frames in this picture have natural-crook lower sections. The upper part of each natural curve was halved on the table saw to accept the first futtock. On frame A, the first fut-

tock was scarfed into the halved part of the grown lower section. On frame B, the next futtock was scarfed to the end of the grown frame and glued to the first futtock.

7.7

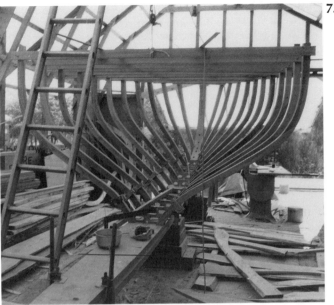

7.8

7.9

Photo 7.8 The combination frames continue to the aft end of the mast step at F12. All the frames from F13 aft to F24 were double-sawn because of a lack of natural crooks.

Photo 7.9 To build double-sawn frames, I first lay the pattern on a 1¹⁄₁₆-inch-thick locust flitch. The two rulers indicate the proposed scarfs of the first futtock piece. The futtock was sawn out oversize to allow sufficient width for the standing bevel, as discussed for diagram 7.1.

Photo 7.10 The first futtock for the starboard frame was used as a pattern for the port frame. I placed it on various potential framing flitches until I found one with the correct grain and least wastage, then I penciled around it and cut out the port futtock.

7.10

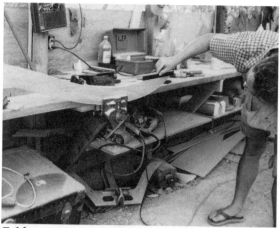

7.11

Photo 7.11 Here I am checking the scarf end of the futtocks to be sure it has been planed square and straight. This makes it easy to fit the next futtock to this scarf joint. I also check across the gluing surface of the futtock. A bit of concave or hollow (1/64 inch or less) will be flattened with the clamps, but a convex curve will not flatten and the glue line then will be wide at both edges.

Photo 7.12 Locust is as hard as marble when it is fully seasoned, so a belt sander is an absolute must for flattening futtocks.

Photo 7.13 The second futtocks are shorter than the first to provide a scarf overlap. These scarfs should be at least 15 inches from point to point. The futtock overlap on the aft frames near F23 and F24 in the topsides can be shorter because of the tight radius of the frames. The sapwood on the right-hand futtock is removed with the offcut of the underbevel.

7.12

7.13

7.14

7.15

7.16

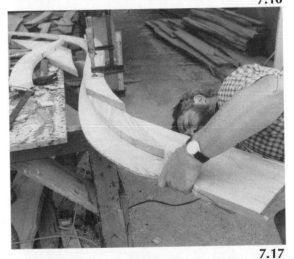

7.17

Photo 7.14 The second futtock is temporarily secured to the first with double-headed nails. The two nailed parts were then clamped to the pattern. The diameter of the nails used here was the same as or slightly smaller than the fore-and-aft rivets I put in after the glue was dry. Note that the frame material overlaps the pattern by ⅛ inch.

Photo 7.15 The wood for the third futtock is shown clamped to the scarfed end of the first futtock. I then adjusted the third futtock so that it overlapped the outside curvature of the pattern by ⅛ inch. I penciled the scarf line onto the bottom of the third futtock. This scarf line was then cut off and planed square and true.

Photo 7.16 Here I am checking the third futtock for fit at the scarf. When it fits, the outside curve of the pattern is penciled onto the futtock itself. Then the third futtock is cut out to width.

Photo 7.17 The fourth futtock has been roughed out, and now the scarf angle is transferred to it.

7.18

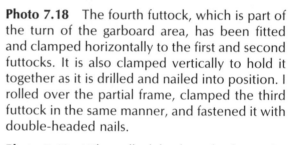

7.19

7.20

Photo 7.18 The fourth futtock, which is part of the turn of the garboard area, has been fitted and clamped horizontally to the first and second futtocks. It is also clamped vertically to hold it together as it is drilled and nailed into position. I rolled over the partial frame, clamped the third futtock in the same manner, and fastened it with double-headed nails.

Photo 7.19 When all of the futtocks that make up the port and starboard frames are nailed together, it is time to glue up. The clamps are laid out, along with 2-inch-by-2-inch plywood protection pads, which will minimize sanding later.

The scarfs on the first futtock were penciled to show where glue was required. The nails on the second futtock in my left hand protruded about ½ inch to facilitate alignment with the holes in the first futtock.

Photo 7.20 The aligning nails are the key to building these double-sawn frames. They should be positioned about 2½ inches from the scarf joints and close to the sectional centerline, as shown in diagram 7.2. This centers the rivet that will be put in later, relative to the inside and outside bevels of the frame.

Naturally this nail alignment is not a big factor on frames with less than 10 degrees of bevel. But the placement of these holes should be systematic and neat so that they will look good on the inside of the hull.

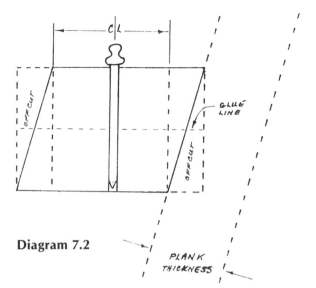

Diagram 7.2

7.21

7.22

7.23

Photo 7.21 I hate using glue. It sticks my fingers together, hassles me with a time limit (at 90 degrees Fahrenheit, we had only 15 minutes' working time), gets all over my clamps and tools, and drips off the frames onto my toes. But glue increases the strength of a double-sawn frame, so it is about three times stronger than the traditional, unglued, butt-jointed, fore-and-aft-bolted sawn frame.

When the glued futtocks are all nailed together, I put half a dozen semitight clamps on the frame, then clamp the scarf joint tightly on a horizontal plane before putting on and tightening the rest of the vertical clamps.

Photo 7.22 When the glue is dry, I rough-sand both sides of the frame. This makes it slide smoothly and level on the saw table and also lets me pencil the pattern shape neatly and easily onto the frame side. If possible, I leave an extra ⅛ inch of wood as I pencil in the exact outside shape of the frame. The excess wood will help, as I saw to the line.

These glued double-sawn frames are very stable. None of ours changed their "S" shape even a fraction of an inch after the clamps were removed.

Photo 7.23 To get the molded width of the frame, I simply measure 2½ inches from the outside pattern line, pencil in marks about every 4 inches on the tighter radiuses, and every 6 inches near the flatter sections. Then the frame pattern is used like a large french curve to connect and fair the inside frame line. (Before you cut the bevels, refer to the bevel orientation discussion in chapter 6 at diagram 6.6.)

Photo 7.24 This frame is part double-sawn, part natural crook. I cut the bevels on the lower part before I glued on the double-sawn upper section. Now the outside bevel is being cut onto the upper section. As I cut around the curved part of the frame, the heel starts to swing off the extension table. This is when it becomes hard to hold the frame flat on the table. Just before the frame got to this awkward position, Lin would reach out and support it with one hand and keep her other hand on the table handle.

Photo 7.25 I could then slip around behind Lin and continue cutting the frame-head section. This way, I could hold on to the center of the frame and keep it flat on the metal saw table.

7.24

7.25

Photo 7.26 These inside bevels are the same as the outside ones. The degree indicator on the saw reads 8 degrees for both bevels. These inside bevels should not be cut until after the outside ones are finished, in case something goes wrong. If I accidentally overcut the line on the outside bevel, the pattern could be shifted slightly inboard toward the inside bevel offcut area to cure the problem.

Cutting the inside bevel the same as for the planking makes it easier to clamp the planking to the frames. It is nicer looking, lighter in weight than unbeveled inner frame edges, and it is easier to fit longitudinal members such as bilge stringers, sheer clamps, and the ceiling next to bunks. It gives a professional-looking finish to the inside of a boat.

7.26

Photo 7.27 Next the outside beveled edges of the frame are sanded. The sander here is a 3-inch-by-21-inch high-speed Skil model. It worked fine for all but the most concave areas of the frame.

It is not necessary to remove all of the band-saw marks after fairing the high spots off the planking side of the frame because the planking will cover this face.

Photo 7.28 The inside of the frames had to be smoothed up in keeping with the quality of the rest of the boat. I borrowed this extra-short sander and fitted it with a curved wooden sole that I screwed in place to approximate the average inside curve of the frame. The sander has to be kept moving back and forth on the frame to prevent dips and hollows. I found that a half-used-up 60-grit belt gave a good, varnishable surface on our frames. I used a belt sander because opposing grains make it almost impossible to clean up the edges of double-sawn frames with planes or spokeshaves.

At this point, I transferred the waterline marks, the buttocks, decksheer marks, and so on, from my pattern to the planking edge of the frame. (These pencil marks, like the saw marks, eventually are covered by planking.)

When the frames were freshly sanded, Lin covered them with one coat of thinned spar varnish to protect the clean wood. This saved us untold hours of sanding later, when we would have had to remove finger marks and stains.

We usually built about three or four frames, port and starboard, going through the whole process, including lifting them up onto the backbone. It was encouraging to see a group of frames go up every seven to ten days, and this made the work less repetitive. Besides, sometimes we found slightly more efficient ways to build or assemble the next set of frames.

7.27

7.28

7.29

7.30

The flat nailheads of the rivets should be on station (see F14 and F15 in this photo). The forward frames have the nailheads on the aft side of the frame and the frames from F15 aft have the nailheads on the forward side of the frame. It is easier to fasten bulkheads (partitions) to the aft side of the forward frames, particularly close to the bow, than it is to get a drill and screwdriver into the enclosed angle of the forward side. This fitting problem is even worse if the sawn frames in a hull are through-fastened with carriage bolts. Then one side will have a raised oval head and the other a nut and washer to get in the way of joinerwork.

Photo 7.30 The locust I used was so hard I could not set these nailheads flush using just a hammer, so I modified a ½-inch-diameter counterbore and adapted it to fit onto a 9/32-inch drill. I countersank into the locust just enough to make the nailhead flush. The 1/16-inch nylon sheet shown in my left hand is used to protect the frame from hammer marks as I rivet.

Photo 7.29 These frames were riveted fore-and-aft through their sided thickness, using the same holes I used for the double-headed aligning nails. The rivets were almost unnecessary, since I used a completely reliable glue, but if there ever was a total glue failure, the boat would have a fallback of mechanical fasteners.

Photo 7.31 Now I have to cut off the frame heels to fit the backbone. It is best to do this on the bandsaw and have a helper hold the other end of the frame. But if you have no helper, clamp the frame to the workbench. Pick up the bevel of the frame heel where it meets the backbone on the loft floor, set the Skilsaw to the bevel, and cut off the heel. Then, if necessary, hand-plane to your pencil line to get the perfect bevel angle.

7.31

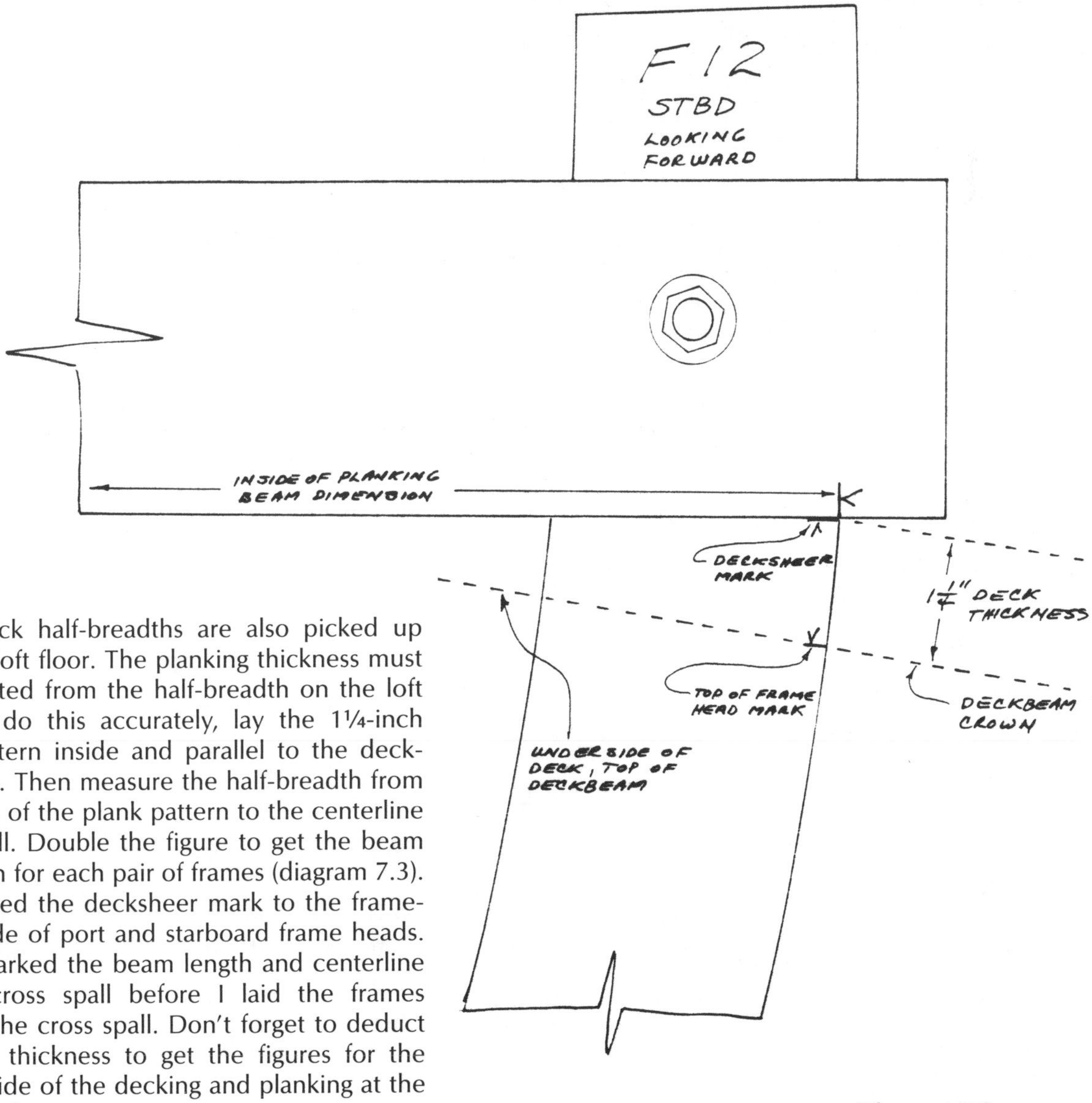

The deck half-breadths are also picked up from the loft floor. The planking thickness must be deducted from the half-breadth on the loft floor. To do this accurately, lay the 1¼-inch plank pattern inside and parallel to the deck-sheer line. Then measure the half-breadth from the inside of the plank pattern to the centerline of the hull. Double the figure to get the beam dimension for each pair of frames (diagram 7.3). I transferred the decksheer mark to the frame-station side of port and starboard frame heads. Then I marked the beam length and centerline on the cross spall before I laid the frames beneath the cross spall. Don't forget to deduct the deck thickness to get the figures for the actual inside of the decking and planking at the frame head.

F 12
STBD
LOOKING FORWARD

INSIDE OF PLANKING
BEAM DIMENSION

DECKSHEER MARK

1¼" DECK THICKNESS

TOP OF FRAME HEAD MARK

DECKBEAM CROWN

UNDERSIDE OF DECK, TOP OF DECKBEAM

Diagram 7.3

7.32

7.33

7.34

Photo 7.32 The long drill not only clears the clamp when I have to drill close to it, but it also saves me from having to kneel down to work.

Photo 7.33 A temporary 2 x 2 handhold is clamped to the lower portion of the pair of frames to stabilize the assembly as we move it.

Photo 7.34 The frame for F19 is hoisted onto the backbone, clamped to the lagbolted floor arms, and then secured to its neighboring frames with battens. Another set of arms is up in the air.

Photo 7.35 With twenty-two pairs of frames built, finish-sanded, primed with a coat of varnish, and secured in place, I can finally admire the boat's three-dimensional shape.

7.35

CONSTRUCTION TIMES FOR CHAPTER 7

Larry: Cutting, gluing, shaping, and finishing frames; cleaning and drilling bronze floors; setting floors and frames in place   683 hours

Lin: Assisting with glue-up, beveling, and sanding of frames; varnishing; shop maintenance; shopping for supplies   114 hours

Totals to date: Larry 1460 hours

Lin   237 hours

DISCUSSION
Frame Choices

There are basically four kinds of sawn frames: (1) natural-crook frames; (2) traditional sawn and bolted or riveted frames with butt joints; (3) double-sawn frames fastened and glued with scarf joints; and (4) laminated frames. My first choice, if I could find the materials, would be to go with all natural crooks.

To build the frames like the one shown in diagram 7.4, I would have to use two curved crooks or futtocks, since S-shaped crooks are rare. In this case, the curved futtocks would overlap in the flattish area of the hull at the middle of the frame (WL2B). This is a good place to have the frame doubled up. The extra thickness stiffens the potentially flexible flattish section of the frame and gives a wide landing area for the bilge stringer.

The only differences in layout between this method and the one described earlier in the chapter are that the lower futtock is forward of the lofted station line and the upper futtock is aft of the station line.

I once had the pleasure of watching as Portuguese builders framed 85-foot fishboats right on the gravel beach and hand-cut the frame bevels using a buck saw. The futtocks for their oak frames were simply bolted together at the overlap.

Diagram 7.4

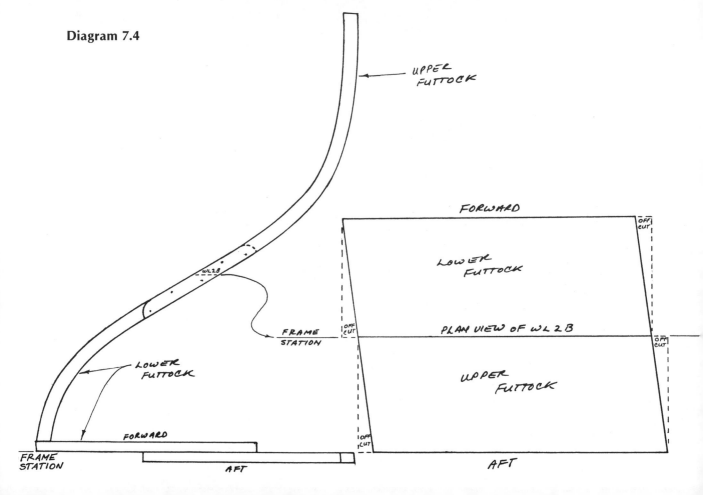

Natural-crook frames probably will be chosen only by patient people who can search out and season their own wood. In fact, from the reaction I get when I talk to friends about crooks, I have almost come to believe that such preplanning is unnatural in our modern society. But the wood to do this is available, especially in the Pacific Northwest and the eastern parts of North America. Check with loggers cutting oak or larch (*Larix laricina*—hackmatack or tamarack; the European variety of larch is *Larix decidua*).

One of the greatest satisfactions of building *Taleisin* came from finding a framing method that would make use of the timber I had cut in Virginia seven years before I had even decided to build myself another boat. The combination of natural crooks and double-sawn frames made good use of the black-locust flitches I had received courtesy of Virgil Gill, a farmer in Urbanna, Virginia. It had been seasoning and waiting for us in his old barn. Black locust is exceptionally strong and rot-resistant, but it is rarely found in clear, long lengths.* A lot of the flitches we already had looked like poor-quality boatbuilding timber because they had various defects ranging from knots to heart rot. But the double-sawn method I used meant I could cut off or around defects.

By using glue and scarfed joints, I built stable, nondistorting frames that are stronger than the traditional butt-jointed double-sawn frames. The butt-jointed sawn frame is only as strong as the single futtock next to each butt joint. This was well illustrated to me on our previous boat, *Seraffyn*. She had a double-sawn frame every third frame. The frames were glued and butt-jointed and worked well except in three instances when the solid futtocks broke right next to a butt joint. In each case, when I replaced the broken futtock, I found there was a planking rivet right next to and parallel to the butt joint. The rivet hole had weakened the solid part of the futtock, causing it to crack on either side of the rivet. Had the rivet been an inch or two either side of the joint of the two futtocks, this probably would not have happened. But this potential futtock breakage problem was solved on *Taleisin*'s double-sawn frames because at the angled joints, the planking rivets fasten through the scarf and help hold the joint together.

Frames that are built up of strips of laminated wood running lengthwise are very strong. This method would be my second choice if natural crooks were not available. In fact, this will produce a frame that is as strong as a perfectly parallel-grained natural-crook frame of the same dimension. This laminated, bent frame could be reduced in size compared to a double-sawn one. For example, a 1½-inch-by-1¾-inch laminated frame could be as strong as or maybe stronger than a double-sawn frame 2 inches by 2½ inches. So the laminated frame would save 1½ inches of interior space throughout the hull (¾ inch on each side) and decrease the final hull construction weight.

---

*L. Francis Herreshoff discusses this in his book *The Common Sense of Yacht Design* (see Bibliography):

Locust (Robinia Pseudoacacia) is a most amazing wood. While it is growing it rots quite freely and the worms and ants eat it, but once it is seasoned it will resist rot the most of any North American wood that I know. Locust is one of our strongest and hardest woods; yes it is even stronger and harder than most hickory. It weighs about fifty-one pounds per cubic foot. Locust has always been the favorite wood for trunnels; it is the best wood for rail stanchions which set through the covering board and thus are apt to rot. It makes the most reliable tiller of all woods, for it will not rot out at the socket. Locust is fine for cleats, belaying pins or any deck trim; it is a safe wood to use in any part of a yacht. The only thing that locust needs is a little advertising.

On the other hand, laminated frames sometimes delaminate, and after repairing so many of them in others' boats, I've become a bit leery of them. I find it not only discouraging to discover frames that are coming apart near the heels, but also hard to find a solution that will give a good-looking, economical, full-strength repair. I have seen glue failures in boats from the best of professional yards and feel it is a possibility with any adhesive.

You need a bending jig of some sort to form and clamp the laminations for this type of frame. The neatest one I have seen was in Denmark at the Walsted shipyard. The jig was built with a 3-foot-by-12-foot-long metal plate about ⅜ inch thick. There were slotted ½-inch holes running across the plate every 6 inches. Half-inch carriage bolts fit in the slots, with the square part of the bolt in the slot and the threaded part pointing upward. These bolts secured 4-inch-by-5-inch, 5-inch-high angle irons to the base plate. A speed handle and socket was used to tighten the nuts and secure the angle irons along the slotted holes, as shown in diagram 7.5. The 5-inch-high angle-iron brackets let workmen clamp up port and starboard frames at the same time, one on top of the other. They could also make one frame that was twice as thick in the fore-and-aft sided dimension, then resaw it to produce both a port and a starboard frame.

The Walsted yard had two of these jigs on casters set on a long, wide workbench. When a pair of frames was glued and clamped up in the jig, it was rolled along the workbench into a temperature- and humidity-controlled oven that would cure a set of frames in one hour. With this system, one man could be clamping up another set of frames while the first set was being cured. Mr. Walsted noted that a skilled man could make eight port and starboard frames in eight hours—sixteen separate frames in one day!

The one part of this job that requires real experience is estimating the eventual springback of each frame and adding enough extra wood strips so that there is sufficient offcut wood for the standing bevel (inside), just the same as for double-sawn frames. The dashed line in diagram 7.5 shows the shape of the frame pattern chalked onto the jig face.

Diagram 7.5

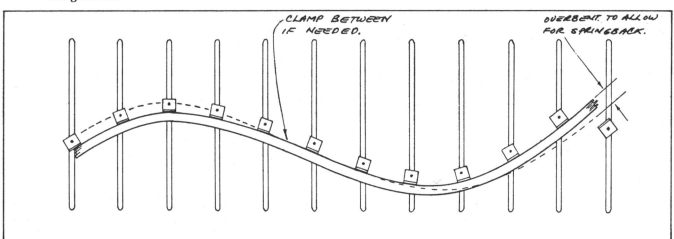

The adjustable angle irons are slightly off this line to allow for frame springback. If you use a jig like this and start laminating the straightest frames first, you will observe the gradual increase of springback as you work aft to the more shapely frames. On these first few frames, you can add an extra strip or two of laminating wood after you remove the frame from the jig if you find you have underestimated the springback. Use wax paper between the jig and the frame and also between the two frames to simplify separating them and to make jig cleanup easier. The fore-and-aft sides of these frames can be cleaned up quite easily on the thickness planer. The inside and outside of the frame can be planed easily after the bevels are cut, as the grain all runs the same way.

A professional laminating jig like the one at Walsted's could also be used for laminating deck and cabin beams, floors, and knees. A cheaper wood jig could possibly be made of 1-inch plywood with a 2-inch-by-3-inch frame around it for stiffening. The problems that would be caused by excess glue sticking to the jig could be avoided by covering the plywood with a thin sheet of metal. It is hard to improve upon the adjustable angle irons Walsted used.

Laminated frames require almost perfect, straight-grained stock so that the individual pieces don't break as you bend them around the jig. A knot, a check, or grain runoff can cause a major hangup when you are clamping up. If the strip breaks when you are gluing, you will have to work quickly to remove the broken pieces and substitute another strip.

Steam-Bent Frames

Although I prefer sawn frames for a boat such as ours, steam-bent frames can be a good choice for certain types of hulls. They are ideal for lapstrake dinghies, U-shaped fin-keel racers, and deep-keeled hulls with little recurve to the garboard. Steamed frames can also work well on the easier curves amidships on more shapely hulls. I would prefer, however, to saw the fairly straight frames in the forward end of a shapely hull so they would fit flush to the floors. Aft, at any sections where the steamed frames threaten to fracture as they are bent in place, I would consider sawn frames or else invest the time to steam-bend two or three laminations into the ribbands, remove them when they have set and dried, and then glue and refasten them in place with lots of clamps between the ribbands. In no case would I use a steamed frame and split the frame heel to get it to bend around a difficult curve—or, as some builders do, simply bend in all or most of the frames in two pieces. I am not at all comfortable with these two glueless solutions, as it is difficult to guarantee that wood preservative will get into the rot-prone crevices between the two layers. Furthermore, if a 1¾-inch-by-1¾-inch bent frame is sawn in half to ease it into place, the heel will be cut into two layers that are only ¹³⁄₁₆ inch thick. If the floor-to-frame-heel bolt size specified is ⅜ inch, there will be only ⁷⁄₁₆ inch of solid wood left on each split frame heel, or ⁷⁄₃₂ inch of wood on either side of the ⅜-inch-diameter bolt. Therefore, this important connection will be too weak to meet the basic scantling rules. (See Nathanael Herreshoff's Rules, Appendix B, for correct sizes of frame heel bolts.)

From the problems I have seen as I repaired and surveyed boats, I have come to agree completely with L. Francis Herreshoff when he says in *Common Sense of Yacht Design* (page 77): "One of the commonest mistakes made with frames is to box them in to the keel (that is, set them into a chiseled-out cavity in the keel). This is very bad practice, for the chiseled-out cavities in the keel weaken the part where the garboard fastenings come and very much encourage rot. The whole strength of the frames should be transferred to the floor timbers by proper bolting or riveting, so it is not of much consequence if the frames do not even touch the keel." (Diagram 8.3 shows the far better Herreshoffian method—also shown on page 74 of Herreshoff's book—which eases the sharp bend of steamed frames at the garboard so that there will be far less tendency for them to fracture. I used this method on *Seraffyn* with excellent long-term results.) I feel that socketed frame heels are used by builders who do not want to spend the time to loft and then pick up the patterns and bevels for floor timbers on the body plan. With socketed frame heels, the frames are steamed in, the heels are nailed into the socket, and then the material for the eventual floors is laid alongside the frames to trace the floor shape and pick up bevels directly from the frames.

In Europe, carvel-planked yachts usually are built with longitudinally laminated sawn frames. Some Portuguese, Italian, and Greek yards still build fishing boats with natural-crook oak frames. Steam-bent frames are commonly used to build carvel-planked boats in the United States. In Britain, carvel-planked boats quite often have sawn (grown) frames for the molds with two steam bent-ones in between (*Seraffyn* was built this way). New Zealanders, in a tradition that goes back to 1890, use three skins riveted over longitudinal stringers. The more modern New Zealand boats have complete ring frames at the mast area. Any of these methods can be used to build a strong, tight boat. In the end, the boat is held together by the integrity and skill of the boatbuilder.

To help you consider which method best suits your design, your skills, your shop setup, and the materials you can easily acquire, below is a pro-and-con list for the framing methods that could be used to build a boat similar to *Taleisin*.

STEAM-BENT FRAMES

Pro

Less lofting required; molds and ribbands can be adjusted with wedges or by shaving molds to fair up ribbands.

Easy to bend into hulls without S-turn at garboard.

Flexible and strong longitudinally.

They don't delaminate.

Steaming cures, hardens, and seasons the wood.

Steam-bending parties are fun, especially with hot buttered rum warming on the steam box.

Frames can all be bent in during one short period.

You can drill 1-inch-diameter holes 3 inches deep into the excess wood at the frame heads above the sheer, then top up these holes regularly with wood preservative. After three months, the poison will drip out the endgrain at the heels to give a rotproof frame.

Con

Difficult to use on shapely hulls with S-shaped frame sections.

High-quality, straight-grained green timber needed for bending.

Strong framework of molds and ribbands required. Ribbands and molds will be discarded after frames are in place.

Steam box setup required.

High degree of steam-bending expertise needed to minimize breakage while bending, especially with frames larger than 1½ inches by 1½ inches.

As the boat is used, cracks quite often develop where planking screws enter the bent outside face of the frame.

Three or four people are needed to steam and clamp frames to ribbands.

Breakage often occurs at garboard area during bending and also years later.

Slitting heels or cutting frames in two to make sharp bends compromises strength of the heel area.

Fore-and-aft holes drilled to take the frame-to-floor-timber bolts weaken the split heel disproportionately.

Unless slit or split frames are glued, rot can develop.

Bulkheads, floors, and joinery are hard to fit as frames are square to planking, not to the centerline of the hull.

Ribbands sometimes pull away under bending pressure. Frames then end up unfair and must be dubbed later.

Hard to repair. Usual choice is sister frame, which will be obvious.

SAWN FRAMES

(includes natural crooks as well as double-sawn and fully laminated frames)

Pro

Sawn frames are building molds, so no need to buy mold material or heavy ribbands.

'Thwartship members such as floor timbers, bulkheads, hanging knees, and deckbeams, plus interior joinery, fit flat and easily to sawn frames. (In my opinion, this is the single most important advantage.)

Frames hold their shape well; less tendency to hog later in life.

S-curved frame shapes are produced without stress, bending, or breakage problems.

Natural-crook and laminated frames are very strong for their size.

Timber with some defects can be used for double-sawn frames.

Less outside help needed in comparison to bent frames.

Positive control of hull shape (most accurate of all methods).

Any single damaged futtock on a double-sawn frame can be removed and replaced to look like original.

Only a few light ribbands are needed for fairing and alignment of frames.

Con

Careful lofting of bevels needed.

Sixteen-inch or larger bandsaw with adjustable table is required.

Pattern necessary for each pair of frames.

Double-sawn and glued frames, such as used on *Taleisin*, must be larger than bent or laminated frames so are heavier and take up more interior space.

To build longitudinally laminated frames, you need a jig.

Longitudinally laminated sawn frames require high-quality laminating strips.

Except with completely grown frames, requires the use of adhesives and subsequent cleanup.

COMBINATION OF SAWN AND STEAM-BENT FRAMES

Pro

Sawn frames become building molds.

Most bulkheads fit sawn frames with no shimming or dubbing.

Produces two types of framing—rigid, shape-holding sawn frames and flexible, steam-bent frames that have exceptional longitudinal strength.

Double-sawn futtocks can be removed if they are damaged and replaced to look as original.

Con

Bevel lofting required for sawn frames.

Need at least 16-inch bandsaw with tilting table.

Large, strong ribbands needed to steam intermediate frames in place.

Spacers have to be fitted onto the thinner steamed frames so that clamps and stringers can be through-bolted (see diagram 7.6).

Steam-bent frames do not fit easily to floor timbers, bulkheads, or joinery.

Difficult to bend large-sized frames, especially ones over 1¾ inches square.

Steam-bent frames are hard to replace or repair. Sister frames produce an obvious patch job.

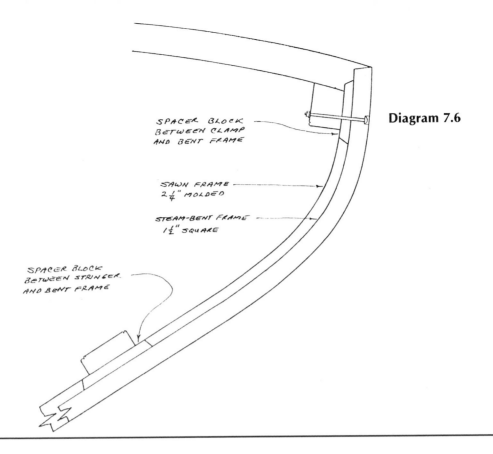

SPACER BLOCK
BETWEEN CLAMP
AND BENT FRAME

SAWN FRAME
2¼" MOLDED

STEAM-BENT FRAME
1¼" SQUARE

SPACER BLOCK
BETWEEN STRINGER
AND BENT FRAME

Diagram 7.6

LONGITUDINAL FRAMING, OR STRINGERS, WITH SAWN RING FRAMES

This framing method is usually used with multiskin construction on sailboats. Motorboats are quite often built with a combination of sawn frames and stringers that are notched into the frames. These hulls are then carvel-planked. This would not be the easiest method for framing a boat like Taleisin, but it does develop a strong, light framework inside the planking, which is ideal for high-speed motor launches and lightweight racing sailboats.

Pro

High strength-to-weight ratio.

Less lofting—you only need to loft the backbone; molds can be made from the designer's offsets.

When the fore-and-aft stringers are notched into the molds, the stringers can be adjusted by driving wedges between the mold and the stringers to fair up the framework.

Floors and ring frames generally are necessary only near the mast area. Since these land on the stringers, with space between the planking and ring frame, bulkheads can be fitted easily.

Planking is simpler.

Few large timbers are necessary for framing.

No ribbands required.

Con

Best suited to fin-keeled hulls.

Difficult to build wineglass-shaped hulls this way.

Stringers trap any water on the top edges so it travels horizontally through lockers and does not drain into the bilge.

Usually there is no sump area that allows bilge water to slop up into lockers and run along the stringers and under bunks—making a mess far out of proportion to the volume of water that accidentally entered the boat.

Stringers trap dust and dirt.

Difficult to fit joinery to the hull around the stringers.

Stringers are difficult to repair or replace.

8. HORNING IN THE FRAMES AND LAYING ON THE RIBBANDS

After the frames have been set up on the backbone, the whole structure must be plumbed and measured until it corresponds accurately with the master plan, the loft floor. To achieve this accuracy, I try to get the plumb bob points to center on each pencil line. If most of the frames are absolutely square and plumb, any inaccurate ones will show up when the ribbands go on. So if the ribbanded framework looks fair, the horning in (setup) is correct, just as the lofting is correct when all of the lines on it look fair.

Photo 8.1 The frames from F2 to F23 have been set up on the backbone close to their final positions. (The transom and F24 are discussed in detail in chapter 9.)

The first step toward horning in is to level the backbone in a fore-and-aft direction. I use a line level strung between hooks screwed inside the centerline of the stem at WL4A and inside the centerline of the sternpost at WL4A. I tension the line tightly and attach a line level at the middle. I jack the backbone up or down, forward or aft, until the level bubble is centered. Then I remove the level and turn it 180 degrees. If the level is accurate, it should read the same.

8.1

8.2

Next I attach two plumb bobs to the fore-and-aft level line. The plumb bobs should be near the ends of the keel-timber centerline. Now I adjust the backbone assembly athwartships until both plumb bobs are in line with the centerline.

When the backbone is level to WL4A and vertical to the centerline, I block the keel timbers securely and attach semipermanent supports from the stemhead and the top of the sternpost to the studs of the building. Then I hang a plumb bob on the forward side of the stem. The string of the plumb bob is lined up with the centerline on the front of the stem. I leave this in place all during construction to allow me to check the plumbness of the backbone at a glance.

8.3

Photo 8.2 The 1-inch-by-8-inch strongback is attached firmly to the stem with a 2 x 2 frame. This board is nailed to each of the frame cross spalls to hold the frames plumb over the centerline and on station.

Photo 8.3 The strongback is slightly to one side or the other of the centerlines on each cross spall so I can attach the plumb bob at the centerline marks as I horn in each frame. The wire and turnbuckle are used to pull the stem and the sternpost together to guarantee that the keel timber stays straight. If left unsupported, it can develop a bit of sag. I tightened the wire until the measurement from the stem and sternpost at WL4A equaled this measurement on the loft floor.

Photo 8.4 I scarfed together some fir to make two full-length ruler-ribbands, one for each side of the hull. These ruler-ribbands and the subsequent unscarfed ribbands for the rest of the hull can be fairly small on a completely sawn-framed hull because they are used only to locate the frames and to prove that they are fair and beveled correctly. The ribbands for *Taleisin* were 1 inch by 1½ inches, but they could have been as small as ¾ inch by 1¼ inches. I run the scarfed ribbands through the thickness planer until they are of equal thickness and width all along their length. This way, they are more likely to bend completely fair along the joint.

8.4

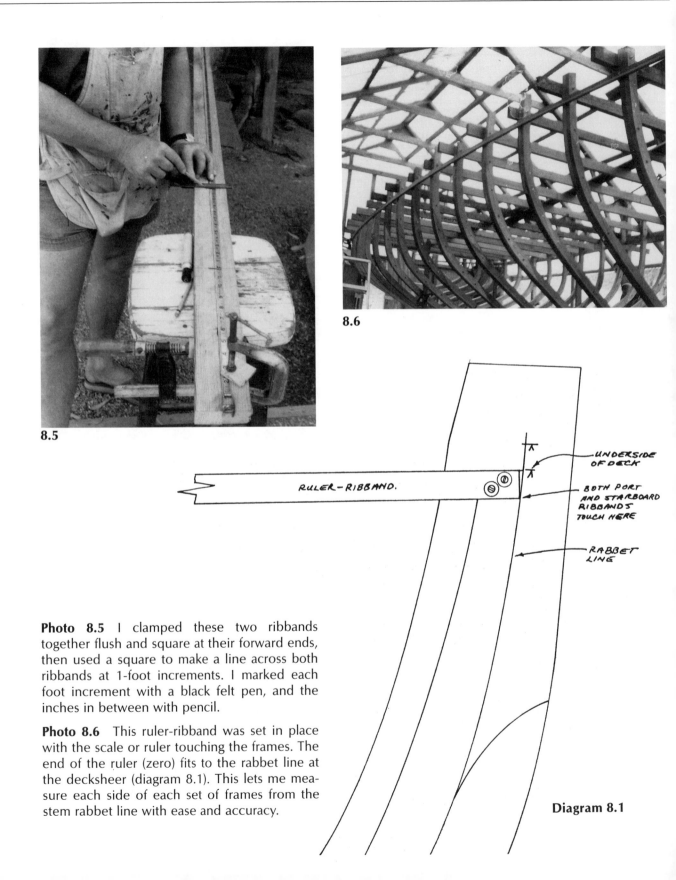

8.5

8.6

RULER – RIBBAND.

UNDERSIDE OF DECK

BOTH PORT AND STARBOARD RIBBANDS TOUCH HERE

RABBET LINE

Photo 8.5 I clamped these two ribbands together flush and square at their forward ends, then used a square to make a line across both ribbands at 1-foot increments. I marked each foot increment with a black felt pen, and the inches in between with pencil.

Photo 8.6 This ruler-ribband was set in place with the scale or ruler touching the frames. The end of the ruler (zero) fits to the rabbet line at the decksheer (diagram 8.1). This lets me measure each side of each set of frames from the stem rabbet line with ease and accuracy.

Diagram 8.1

8.8

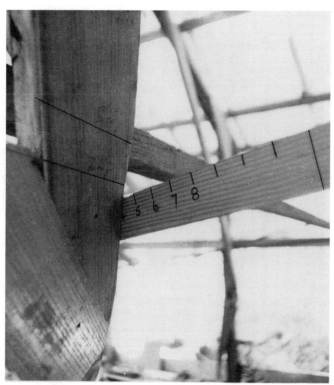

8.7

8.9

Photo 8.7 The after face of the transom frame bisects the ruler at 30 feet 4⅜ inches. Both sides should read the same.

The ruler-ribband is about ½ inch below the top of the deckbeam top mark at this station. It was difficult to spring the sheer curve into it, so I just let it be a bit low for convenience. But I did make sure that both ribbands were the same distance below the marks.

Photo 8.8 The best fastenings for attaching ribbands to frames are sheet-metal screws (self-tappers), which are extremely tough. It is rare to have one break off in the frame if you use an ordinary electric screwdriver drill. I used a combination of these screws and 2-inch double-headed nails for the ribbands. (I had to drill for the screws and nails because the locust frames were as hard as marble.)

Photo 8.9 After the forward end of the ribband ruler was screwed to the rabbet, it was clamped to the underside of the deck marks (the top of the deckbeam mark) at each frame. The straight piece of 2 x 4 under the cross spall at F11 was used to correct any fore-and-aft curvature of the cross spall.

The plumb bob is attached to the forward centerline mark on the cross spall for F11 (on the frame station) so it will hang down near the intersection of the backbone centerline and the F11 station mark on the keel timber.

The C-clamp at the strongback can be used to adjust the frame until the plumb bob is on the centerline of the keel and in line with the F11 frame station line across the keel timber.

8.10

8.11

Photo 8.10 Next I adjust the clamps holding the frame heads to the ruler-ribband so they are equidistant from the stem rabbet. If the plumb bob is still on its backbone marks, I measure from the F11 cross spall parallel to the keel centerline and at the waterlines to the aft side of frame F10. Both sides should be 14 inches between frame heads. If all of these measurements check, the plumb bob is still in line, and the frame heels are equidistant to the keel centerline, I nail the strongback to the cross spall and screw the ruler-ribband to the frame heads.

I find that this procedure is easiest if I start from the bow with F2 and horn in each pair of frames as I proceed aft, checking each time that the frame heads are 14 inches apart from station side to station side, measured horizontally and parallel to the centerline of the hull.

Photo 8.11 When all of the frames are horned in at the sheer, it is time to attach the rest of the ribbands. If you are working alone—as I was 65

percent of the time—loop a line around a ribband that has already been secured in place and use this to support the far end of the ribband. This makes it far easier to clamp the ribbands to the frames.

Once all of the ribbands were in place, I checked the middle of each frame for any fore-and-aft warping. I looked for any spots where the frame bevels did not lie neatly against the ribbands. In any area where the frame was warped, I removed the ribband fastenings above and below the warp and pulled the frame back into alignment with clamps (diagram 8.2). I then checked the frame against its neighbors to see if it was 14 inches away at all points—and again I measured parallel to the centerline of the hull. When I was satisfied, I refastened the straightened frame to the ribbands.

The intermediate ribbands do not need to be scarfed; they can just overlap, edge to edge, across two frames. The overlapped parts of the ribbands are clamped together and then edge-fastened with screws or nails so they are fair.

Photo 8.12 The reward for all of the care and time spent lofting and then computing frame bevels comes when the fairing battens or ribbands are wrapped into place. These ribbands will show immediately whether the frames are as fair as the lines on the loft floor. They also show how well the planking will fit onto its structural framework.

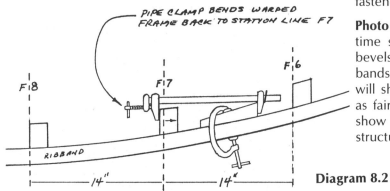

PIPE CLAMP BENDS WARPED FRAME BACK TO STATION LINE F7

F18   F17   F16   RIBBAND   14"   14"

Diagram 8.2

8.12

CONSTRUCTION TIMES FOR CHAPTER 8

Larry: Making ruler-ribbands; cutting ribband stock; fairing frames (horning in); putting ribbands on hull; truing in the frames; fastening the ribbands	101 hours
Lin: Holding ends of tape measure or ribbands	9 hours

Totals to date: Larry 1561 hours

Lin   246 hours

DISCUSSION

These ribbands were a piece of cake to install compared to the ones we needed on *Seraffyn*. In order to shape *Seraffyn*'s steam-bent frames, I had to use ribbands that were approximately 1⅝ inches by 1⅝ inches. To be sure I had enough places to clamp to and enough support to keep the bent frames the correct shape, I had to use twice as many ribbands per side as I did on *Taleisin*. This is one of many reasons I chose to use all sawn frames for this boat. I also remembered the problems that I had with *Seraffyn* in the after sections, where the tightly radiused frames near the bilge forced the ribbands away from and outboard of the sawn frames that were acting as her molds. This left a few of the steam-bent frames in the bilge area sticking out, so I had to hack them down in order to fair up for the planking. A quarter inch of wood had to be dubbed from these 1½-inch square frames. This loss of shape control was a blow to my technical pride, and I vowed to build my next boat with stable shape-holding sawn frames.

Ribbands for Hulls with All Steam-Bent Frames or with Sawn Frames with Intermediate Steam-Bent Frames

To ensure that your hull will be fair, the ribbands for a 30-foot boat being built with steamed frames should be about 1⅞ inches by 1⅞ inches. The ribbands on the topsides should be bent on and attached to the molds so they run parallel to the diagonals marked on the molds, and 6 to 8 inches apart center to center. At the turn of the garboards, the ribbands should be spaced with 4- to 6-inch centers, as shown in diagram 8.3. These lower ribbands should lie into the reverse garboard turn parallel to the tuck plank, as shown in chapter 16. If they do not follow the lines shown, there will be too much twist in the path they have to follow. This twist makes it hard to bend strong, effective ribbands into place. Some builders try to keep their ribbands horizontal all along the hull. Since the lower ribbands become difficult to bend into position, these builders usually end up reducing the ribband dimensions. But undersize ribbands are less stable and more likely to shift or stretch as frames are bent against them. This movement in turn leads to inaccuracies that cost you time when you have to dub or shim the frames to get the planking to lie fair.

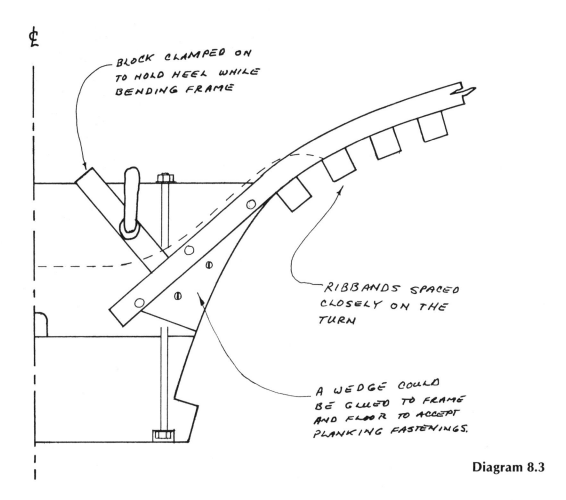

BLOCK CLAMPED ON
TO HOLD HEEL WHILE
BENDING FRAME

RIBBANDS SPACED
CLOSELY ON THE
TURN

A WEDGE COULD
BE GLUED TO FRAME
AND FLOOR TO ACCEPT
PLANKING FASTENINGS.

Diagram 8.3

An excellent way to reduce ribband strains in the garboard area as you are bending on steamed frames is to let the frame heels lie beside the floor timber, as shown in diagram 8.3. This way, the steam-bent frame itself is less likely to break or cause the ribbands to distort, because the radius of the frame heel is reduced. The planking lands on the beveled edge of the lofted floor timber. Most of the long screws that fasten the planking to the floor lie diagonally across the endgrain, so they hold well. Laminated floors could also work well with this method, as the planking screws would go into the laminated floor at right angles to the grain and the glue lines. The dotted line in diagram 8.3 represents an optional laminated floor. For a metal floor, the wedge shown in the diagram would be mandatory.

9. THE FASHION TIMBERS

The fashion timber, or transom frame, is the most technically challenging job a hull builder faces. It is an exercise in boatbuilding skill and patience to do the lofting, deck-thickness reduction, planking-thickness reduction, patternmaking, bevel calculation, and finally the building of the frame itself.

Normally the most experienced boatbuilder in a shipyard is assigned to loft and build the transom frame. No matter how many time I studied the books I bought to build *Seraffyn*, most of the methods for lofting and picking up bevels on a raked transom seemed difficult to understand. I ended up with some minor inaccuracies on her fashion timber. Other boatbuilders made me feel better when they said they had also used these methods and ended up with inaccuracies. For *Taleisin* I settled on a method of doing this job without lofting—a method that is, I think, accurate, easy, and quite straightforward.

Photo 9.1 The forward side of the transom pattern represents the joint between the inside of the transom planking and the aft side of the transom frame. When this transom pattern is nailed flat to the sternpost, at right angles to the centerline, you can prop the ribbands up to the forward edge of the transom pattern, check that the ribbands are fair, and simply pick up the bevel.

This same method can also be used for a curved transom. Temporary horizontally curved beams can be fastened to the back of your plywood pattern to hold it to the proper curve. The pattern can then be attached to the sternpost, and the bevels can be picked up as described for the flat transom. In fact, you could eliminate the transom expansion procedure by making a curved plywood pattern a bit larger than the expanded half-transom shown on your lines plan. After nailing it in place square to the centerline and notching the plywood edge with a sabersaw until the individual ribbands faired up on the starboard half-pattern, you could then pick up the bevels from the ribbands. You thus would have lofted the starboard side of the curved transom in position, and I am sure it could be done far faster and probably more accurately than on the loft floor.

Instead of trying for extreme accuracy as you make the final fashion-timber pattern and compute the bevels, leave about ¼ inch of extra wood on the transom frame. That way, you can be sure of good fits as you put on the planking.

9.1

9.2

9.3

9.4

9.5

Photo 9.2 The aft side of your pattern should be beveled slightly so the ribband is touching the transom pattern at the lofted corner of the transom frame (see arrows in photo).

Photo 9.3 I use a bevel gauge to convert the bevel picked up between the ribband and the transom pattern. Then I write the bevels on the pattern where the ribbands touch.

Photo 9.4 The bevels can be averaged between the ribbands so that the degree changes are regular. If the degrees change radically between the ribbands, as mine did from the sheer to the second ribband, you can clamp temporary intermediate ribbands to the frames and pattern in order to measure bevels at three or four points. I have left out frame 24 so that I would have room to pick up these bevels.

Photo 9.5 It is much easier to fit frame 24 once the fashion timbers and ribbands are in place. It fits to the forward face of the transom frame, the side of the sternpost, and the two upper ribbands. This sounds like a tricky fit, but in reality it was quite easy.

9.6

9.7

Photo 9.6 The transom frame was built with the lower part solid timber and the upper part double-sawn, similar to the forward frames. The futtock you see angled at the deck level makes a hanging knee to triangulate the frame-to-deck-beam connection. The notches in the starboard transom knee are cut so the knee can be clamped tight to the adjoining futtocks during gluing. The 2½-inch molded transom frames are beveled on the inside like the rest of the frames so that the bilge stringer will fit easily. Beveling the transom frame also allows fresh water to drain off at any point along the frame. If any water does collect at the transom-frame-to-tran-som-planking joint, rot could start and infect the whole area, including the sternpost.

Photo 9.7 The transom pattern includes the shape of the bulwark stanchion above the deck level. I built the stanchion as an extension of the fashion timber because this makes a strong, uni-fied cornerpost to connect the bulwark rail and the taffrail to the fashion timber. A transom frame with this bulwark stanchion extension should be made of a rot-resistant timber such as locust, teak, pitch pine, or yellow cedar. If rot gets into the endgrain of the bulwark stanchion and travels belowdecks into the transom frame, you will have a very difficult repair job.

9.8

Photo 9.8 The transom frame is clamped to two straightedges. The vertical one represents the centerline, the horizontal one represents the under-deck mark. The transom half-breadth, taken from the transom pattern, will give the correct half-breadth at the deck. The framing square lying along the two straightedges trues them so the two halves of the fashion timber are square to its centerline. Check buttock A at the lower section of the transom; it should be 9 inches from the centerline straightedge. Buttock C should be 27 inches from the centerline (dia-gram 9.1).

Diagram 9.1

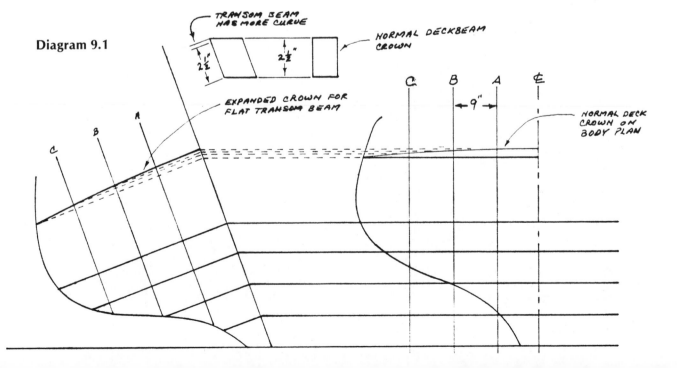

9.9

Photo 9.9   The two vertical lines at the heels of the transom frame are exactly 8 inches apart, the width of the sternpost. The fashion timbers are cut dead square to these lines to fit flat to the sternpost. The deckbeam for the transom is now fitted and half-lapped to the hanging knee. This is one place where many builders, including me, screw up. The raked transom beam has a bit more crown than the normal vertically oriented deckbeams (diagram 9.1). The curve for the aft top edge of the raked transom beam should be taken off the transom expansion at the buttocks.

9.10

9.11

9.12

Photo 9.10 These 1½-inch-by-1½-inch vertical frames are let into the transom frame and beam to stiffen the whole framework vertically and give the 1⅛-inch-thick transom planks some fastening points between the sternpost and the fashion timber. I clamp the vertical frames into position and scribe them to the aft face of the transom frame with a sharp knife. In the photo, I am holding a 1½-inch block and a 12-inch ruler to measure and mark the 1½-inch depth of the frame where it will be let into the beveled aft face of the fashion timber. I do the same to the other end of the frame at the transom deckbeam, using just the block, as the bevel angles in the opposite direction here. Then I scribe along both sides of the frame to mark both the transom beam and the fashion timber.

9.13

Photo 9.11 The let-in scarf joint tapers from 1½ inches at the inside to only ¼ inch when it is within ½ inch of the top of the beam.

Photo 9.12 The lower inside transom frame joint is angled parallel to the lofted transom edge. To get this right-hand corner of the joint and work out the last bit of wood, I use a sniped chisel with about a 15-degree angle at the blade end.

Photo 9.13 These vertical frames—which are jointed, glued, and eventually riveted in place—strengthen the whole transom assembly. When the transom planking is fastened across the 8-inch-wide sternpost and to the various elements of the transom frame, it ties together the whole structure.

The vertical frames have been left 1/32 inch proud just in case anything moves or is slightly awry. This excess will be planed off after the transom is hung on the sternpost.

Photo 9.14 The transom frame is set up on the workbench so the glue will dry quickly in the heat of the morning sun. The inside of the bulwark extension is purposely left oversize and will be trimmed later when the taffrail is fitted.

9.14

9.15

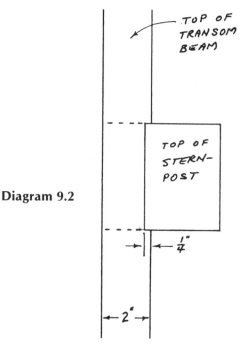

Diagram 9.2

TOP OF TRANSOM BEAM

TOP OF STERN-POST

$\frac{1}{4}"$

$2"$

Photo 9.15   The lower joints where the fashion timbers fit to the sternpost are simply butted and screwed to the post. The horizontal transom-plank fastenings secure this part, and also the rest of the transom frame, firmly to the sternpost.

The upper part of the sternpost is notched out 1¾ inches so that the transom beam fits flush at the aft face. The 2-inch transom beam is notched ¼ inch on its forward face to lock the joint athwartships (diagram 9.2).

I again use soft bedding compound in these large joints because timbers like the 8-inch-wide, 6-inch-thick sternpost could swell as much as ¼ inch after launching. If the joint were glued, it would tear itself apart. Then water could get into the cracks and cause rot.

Photo 9.16   Two temporary bolts are put through the transom beam and sternpost. (The ⅜-inch copper rod I needed for permanent bolts was back-ordered. When it arrived, I replaced the temporary bolts with copper rod riveted over clench rings on both ends.) The plywood straightedge is being used to check that all of the vertical areas of the transom framing are exactly flush.

9.16

Photo 9.17 Then I do the same with a horizontal straightedge along the transom assembly. The square, 1/32-inch-proud vertical frames are now planed down flush to the sternpost and fashion timbers. The ruler-ribband automatically locates the port and starboard quarters of the transom frame. The sheer ribbands have been faired and fitted into the excess wood I left on the planking edge of the fashion timbers. Next, each ribband below the sheer is notched into the excess wood. When they are all fair and fastened in place, the fashion timber is completed.

The final step in the frame sequence is to fit F24 to the ribbands, and the fashion timbers then fasten it in place.

9.17

CONSTRUCTION TIMES FOR CHAPTER 9

Larry: Picking up bevels for the fashion timbers; building transom frame; installing frame
and beam; fastening F24 in place — 50 hours

Lin: Assisting in glue-up and shop maintenance — 6 hours

Totals to date: Larry 1611 hours

Lin 252 hours

DISCUSSION

Taleisin's transom frame could have been built double-sawn, including the transom deckbeam, if large pieces of timber were not available. Since the transom beam is supported vertically by the transom planking, a solid beam is not necessary. The whole frame is simply a corner cleat for attaching the deck, hull, and transom planking together. The transom framing should not be overbuilt, as this is not a high-load area of the hull compared to, for example, the mast area on a ballasted sailboat. Loads will be well distributed here. The boomkin will be bolted through the deckbeams so the backstay strains will be spread forward horizontally through the whole deck. The boomkin stays, which are attached to the outside of the hull, will spread their strains forward through the planking. If this boat did not have a boomkin, the backstay chainplate would be bolted through the top part of the super-strong sternpost. So, in either case, few sailing strains would be transmitted to the fashion timbers unless running backstays were led right to the transom quarters.

I have seen yachts and workboats up to 30 feet in length built without fashion timbers. A solid-timber transom as thick as 2¾ inches is glued and splined together just as is done for the transom of a small rowing boat. Hull and deck planking is simply screwed onto the edge of the thick transom planks. The major disadvantage of this method is that the topside planks are being screwed into the endgrain of the transom planks, so the screws do not hold as well as they could. Another problem is that these large timbers, which need to be well seasoned, are expensive and hard to find. A solid-timber transom has no structural advantages, and the extra weight is a disadvantage on any boat. It would be better to save weight in the transom construction and add it to the lead keel, where it could increase the boat's stability.

10. FASTENING THE BRONZE FLOORS IN PLACE

The next step toward unifying the hull framework was to fit and fasten the metal floors to the sawn frames and the backbone. To do this, I clamped each frame heel so it was on station with its outside lower corner aligned to the bearding line on top of the backbone. I then clamped the frame heel to the temporarily fastened floor.

Photo 10.1 Most of the floors were cast about ⅛ inch oversize, so when the frame heels were properly aligned, I scribed the metal arm next to the frame with a scratch awl and trimmed the excess metal. I have found that ¼-inch-thick manganese bronze can be trimmed easily on a medium-speed woodcutting bandsaw fitted with a metal cutting blade.

I used the drill press to make the holes for bolts in the floor arms, and then hammered a squaring broach through each hole so that the square of my carriage bolt fit snugly into the bronze floor. This way, the round shank of the bolt fit tightly into the wooden frame heel. If I had inserted the carriage bolt from the opposite direction, the threaded part of the bolt would have ended up where the metal floor joints to the frame heel. This has two disadvantages: (1) the weaker, threaded part of the bolt is taking the initial shear strain between the frame and the floor, and (2) some movement can occur when the threaded part of the bolt crushes into the wood of the frame.

Another good fastener for this joint is a hexagonal-headed bolt with a solid shank. You could also make your own bolts from rod stock and use double nuts and washers. In hindsight, I would have chosen hex-headed bolts for this job. They would have been faster to use. But I had the carriage bolts in stock and I also had the broach to square the holes. The carriage bolts have had the advantage that the rounded head does not chafe the flexible water tanks I store in the bilge.

10.1

10.2

Photo 10.2 The floor shown in the extreme right-hand side of this photo has been fastened and bedded permanently in place. The one on the left has been adjusted with clamps so that it is aligned to the centerline of the keel, the port and starboard bearding lines, and the 14-inch spacing of the frame section lines. The ⅜-inch lagbolts, which temporarily hold the floor to the keel, let me adjust the floors slightly fore and aft and athwartships because the floor has ⅝-inch holes in its flange.

When each floor is clamped in place, I double-check along the frames with a batten to make sure it will fair up with the frames forward and aft before I drill for the floor-arm bolts. When I am sure everything is lined up, I drill and fasten the floor to the frame. A short drill motor was a necessity for this job because there was only 11½ inches between each frame.

Photo 10.3 The metal floors have to be let into the inclined stern knee to obtain a secure landing place. If you instead bevel the bottom of the floor (be it wood or metal) to the same angle as the stern knee, the floor will have a tendency to slide downhill as you tighten the vertical floor-timber bolts, and it will end up forward of the correct station position.

10.3

Photo 10.4 When these floors were lofted, additional floor height was added to account for the depth of the notch, the distance shown between the arrows. The floors on the stern knee are all bolted in place. F21 and F22 are blind-bolted to a depth of 5 and 6 inches, respectively. You can see the square holes where the nut and washer are inserted from the side of the stern knee. (This blind-bolting procedure is described in chapter 13.)

The last two frames in the hull, F23 and F24, are connected to the stern knee by separate (two-piece) single-arm floors. These floors are fastened athwartships, through the side-mounted flanges, with a single ⅜-inch bolt.

The floor on F23 is the only one located on the aft side of a frame. There just wasn't enough room on the transom knee forward of the frame to attach the floor flange yet still clear the limber hole at the heel of the frame. All three of the aft frame heels have been relieved at least ¾ inch so water will drain down beside the stern knee. F21 has its limber hole on the centerline of the floor because the planking here fits flush to both the frame and the stern knee.

10.4

CONSTRUCTION TIMES FOR CHAPTER 10

Larry: Trimming bronze floors; bolting floor arms to frames; setting floors into sternpost and onto stem — 57 hours

Lin: Varnishing frames; oiling keel timbers; assisting with alignment — 21 hours

Totals to date: Larry 1668 hours

Lin 273 hours

DISCUSSION

Floor-Timber Bolts

My first choice for every floor-timber-to-backbone fastening is a through-bolt because of the tremendous strains exerted on this floor-to-keel connection on a ballasted sailboat—especially on an offshore cruising or racing boat. Diagram 10.1 shows the forces on these

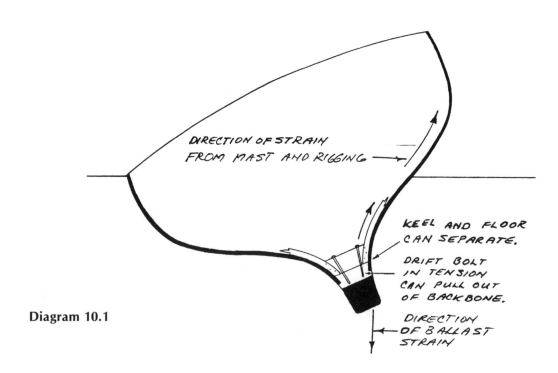

Diagram 10.1

bolts over the ballast keel. But other forces are at work forward and aft of the keel area, and I think those who use drift bolts in the stem and stern areas are forgetting about the tremendous vertical strains taken on these floors when the boat is going to windward. There is even more strain if that same boat is being powered directly into a head sea. The bow of the boat is coming down and slamming the seas with terrific force, while the anchor chain piled on top of the stem adds a sledgehammerlike effect that can loosen anything not fastened with a through-bolt. This problem is exaggerated if your boat's bow has a tendency to pound while sailing to windward. Aft, the engine beds, which usually are attached directly to the floors, are transmitting the vibrations of the powerful diesel engine to the floor-timber bolts. This vibration can be magnified by poor propeller-shaft alignment and/or a slightly bent propeller blade. So, in my opinion, through-bolts are needed to hold every floor in the boat to the backbone.

11. BILGE STRINGERS

The purpose of a bilge stringer is to stiffen and support the almost-flat sections of the boat's frames between the turn of the bilge and the top of the floor timber. It is easier to install this structural timber before you start planking.

Photo 11.1 On the left, lying on the frames above the wider spiling batten, is my fiberglass lofting batten. In order to locate my bilge stringer, I slipped the batten through the open transom and then sprung and clamped it in the middle of the flattish part of the frames between the floor arm and the turn of the bilge. I had to edge-set this batten about 5 inches to get it to lie where I eventually wanted the bilge stringer to lie. Once it was in place, I marked each frame on its inboard face to indicate this fair line.

Here I am using the 4-inch-wide spiling batten to pick up my edge curve so that I know what shape (curve) my stringer will need to be in order to conform to my batten marks. (See discussion of spiling in chapter 17.)

Photo 11.2 I originally planned to use teak for my bilge stringer, but, as you can see here, it couldn't take the twist from F2 aft to F9. So I had to get some white oak, which I knew from experience would bend and twist in easily.

11.1

11.2

11.3

Photo 11.3 There is about 6 inches of spiling (curve) in this 32-foot-long stringer. If I'd simply

cut out the stringer, I would have needed a board 9½ inches wide and 32 feet long. The thin, tapered offcuts would have been wasted. So I picked out four pieces of oak 2 x 4, each 18 feet long. Then I scarfed them together in the slightly offset fashion shown in diagram 11.1 to get the spiled and tapered stringers with very little wastage. The stringers are 1½ inches by 3½ inches, with 3½-foot-long scarfs. I prefer to edge-scarf stringers so that the glue joint is in shear rather than in tension. A scarf is in tension when it is bent to the hull's shape, as shown in the top part of diagram 11.2. The feather edge of the scarf then has a tendency to pull away from the glue when you bend it. The feather edges of the scarf can be planed straight and square if they rest on the end of a board as shown.

Diagram 11.1

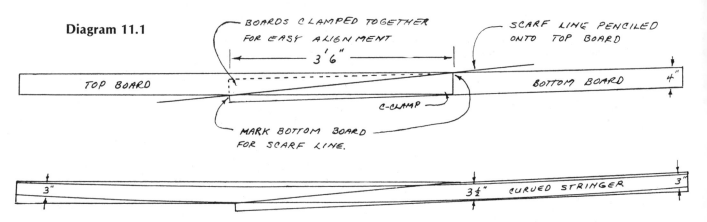

Diagram 11.2

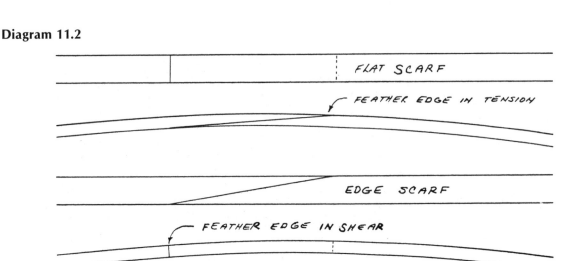

11.4

11.5

Photo 11.4 When the joints were dry-clamped I drilled the pilot holes for these duplex locating nails. The nails simplified the gluing assembly, and I was able to use the same holes later for edge rivets that I added as backup mechanical fasteners.

Photo 11.5 In order to pick up the stem angles, I clamped a 6-foot-long, 1½-inch-by-3-inch piece of timber in the stringer position. I figured the angles, transferred them to the stringer, and removed the offcut with a handsaw. With this method, the end should fit the first time.

Photo 11.6 The starboard stringer is now fitted. If I had been dissatisfied with the fit on the first try, I would have scribed around the end, unclamped the stringer, and planed it down to my scribe marks.

To fasten the end of the stringer in place, I simply toed two 4-inch number-16 wood screws through the bilge stringer and into the stem. (I have never seen a breasthook connecting bilge stringers to the stem on any yacht. Only large workboats need them.)

11.6

Photo 11.7 The molded dimension of my frames is 2½ inches. The fashion timber is the same. The bilge stringer will fit nicely to all of the inside frame bevels and stick out through the still-open transom. The time I previously spent sawing the inside frame bevels is beginning to pay off by giving me easy fits. The aft end is easily sawn off and planed flush to the fashion timber.

These stringers will be fastened with temporary 3-inch-long sheet-metal screws. Later, during the planking process, permanent rivets will be fastened through plank, frame, and stringer.

11.7

CONSTRUCTION TIMES FOR CHAPTER 11

Larry: Scarfing and installing teak bilge stringers, removing the wreckage; installing oak stringers		47 hours
Lin: Varnishing and cleanup work; drilling and countersinking clench rings		15 hours
	Totals to date: Larry	1715
	Lin	288

DISCUSSION

I originally wanted to eliminate these bilge stringers to simplify interior joinery, as L. Francis Herreshoff did with most of his designs. But when I mentioned this to Lyle Hess, he explained the difference between Herreshoff's narrower, easy hulls and his (Lyle's) beamy, firm-bilged ones. Herreshoff's hulls usually didn't have long, flat sections in their frames. Most of his drawings show frames with more curves and less unsupported distance between the turn of the bilge and the top of the floor arm. Besides, L. F. Herreshoff was one of the few designers who regularly recommended completely eliminating bilge stringers. His father, Nathanael Herreshoff, in his widely used rules for wooden-boat construction (see Appendix B), recommended extensive ceiling for all yachts as a substitute for bilge stringers. Henry Nevins's rules for boat construction state that all wooden vessels must have full ceiling or bilge stringers.

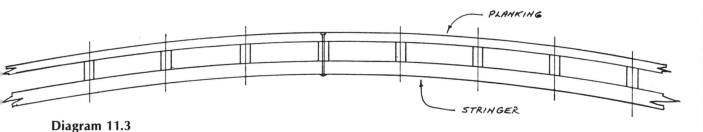

Diagram 11.3

Lyle showed me that the curved box girder formed by the bilge stringers, frames, and planking can be a great stiffener, especially for a boat with sawn frames (diagram 11.3). These sawn frames are much more rigid and hold their shape better than the smaller-dimensioned steam-bent frames.

If I were building a steam-bent-framed hull, I would prefer to add strength below the turn of the bilges by using multiple light stringers (partial ceiling) instead of a single, locally stiff bilge stringer. I have frequently had to sister steam-bent frames. They quite often break where the bilge-stringer fastening is bolted to the somewhat small-dimension bent frame, as in diagram 11.4. The multiple-stringer option in the drawing would spread the loads over a wider area and stiffen the hull without the need for large through-fastening holes, holes that steal strength from bent frames.

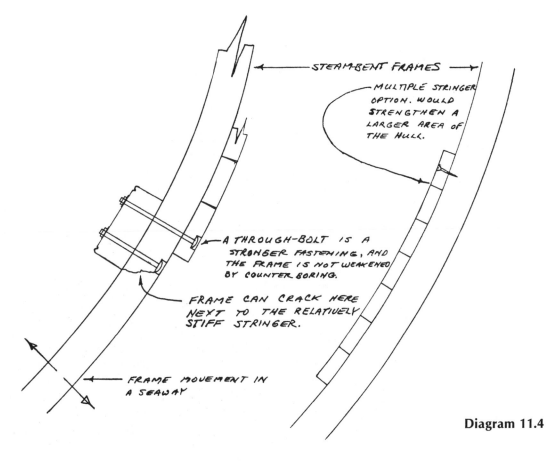

Diagram 11.4

On the other hand, I don't like full ceiling on a yacht, even though it adds a lot of strength to the hull. Here are the reasons for and against this option:

Pro	Con
Adds strength to a large area of the hull.	Difficult to inspect, repair, paint, or clean frames, planking, or butt blocks without removing ceiling.
Easy to bend and fasten in place.	
Can use small-dimension timber for ceiling pieces.	Poor workmanship or poor materials can be hidden behind ceiling.
Bulkheads and joinery are easier to fit to the smooth surface of the ceiling.	Cannot be inspected, so it is very difficult to locate leaks from inside the hull.
The ceiled inside of the hull is easy to paint or varnish.	Rot can start surreptitiously behind ceiling.
Keeps bilgewater out of lockers.	Bulkheads and joinery cannot be fastened as securely or as easily as if they were attached to a frame.
	Large holes must be cut for installation of all through-hull fittings.
	Ventilation is not very positive.
	A leak from a collision cannot be located from inside the hull.*

*The last reason for *not* having ceiling is especially important to me because Peter Tangvald lost his cutter *Dorothea* when he hit a log at sea and could not get behind the ceiling to reach the hole. He also could not get to the hole from outside the boat because of the jagged edges of the hull's copper sheathing, which was torn loose in the collision.

Whether you choose a single bilge stringer or multiple ones, it is not absolutely necessary to scarf them as I did. Before the advent of waterproof resorcinol, bilge stringers were edge-scarfed, painted on the faying surface, and then bolted. The ends were nibbed as shown in diagram 11.5a. This tended to lock the nibs as the timber was bent into place, especially if the nibs fit tightly.

For workboat hulls, it is considered acceptable to overlap stringers instead of scarfing them, as shown in diagram 11.5b. This is a strong alternative, especially in difficult repair situations. Large workboats were built with three or more stringers, and quite often the joints were simply staggered and butted on the frames.

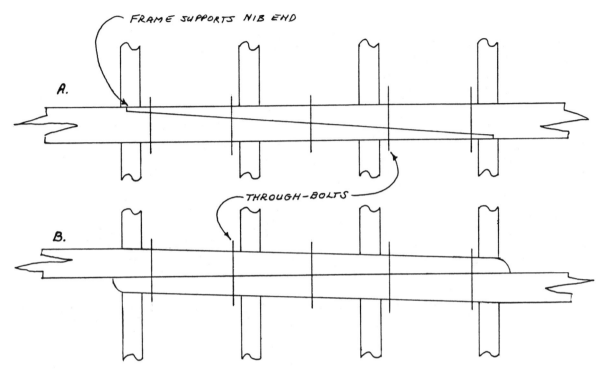

FRAME SUPPORTS NIB END

A.

THROUGH-BOLTS

B.

Diagram 11.5

12. STOPWATERS

Stopwaters should be fitted before you plank. These softwood dowels are driven into close-fitting holes that are at the intersection of the rabbet line and the backbone joints. After launching, the softwood swells up and keeps water from traveling fore and aft along the joints.

Photo 12.1 This is the stopwater at the forefoot-to-stem-knee joint (arrow).

Photo 12.2 The arrow indicates the stopwater at the keel-to-transom-knee joint. It is easier to start your drill bit accurately on the rabbet line if, as I recommended in chapter 4, you leave ¼ inch of excess wood inside the rabbet line. The hard part of this job is drilling the hole so that it is square to the timber and comes out at the same spot on the opposite side of the joint/rabbet line. The drill should have a tendency to follow the joint between the two timbers, but don't rely on this too much.

Photo 12.3 For accuracy, you need two people to drill for stopwaters. Here I am lining up the extended ⅜-inch drill parallel to a plywood straightedge that is flush to the frame section on the forefoot. Meanwhile, Lin is sighting the drill horizontally, keeping it parallel to the carpenter's level. Be careful not to put too much pressure on the drill as it exits the hole; it could tear the rabbet-line joint.

Any softwood is fine for stopwaters, but I prefer cedar over white pine, as it is more rot-resistant. I make sure to use dry stock, which will swell and seal the joint tightly. Don't glue

12.1

12.2

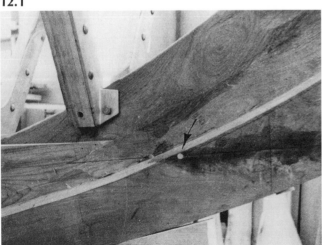

the stopwater into the hole. This would retard moisture absorption into the stopwater. If your timbers have shrunk during construction, quick-swelling stopwaters could make your launching day less traumatic (or less wet).

You can make stopwaters in your own shop by using a ½-inch variable-speed drill motor and a dowel cutter that you can make from a ¾-inch-square-by-1½-inch-long piece of mild steel. I went to the trouble of making this dowel cutter because I knew there would be numerous other applications for stopwaters and dowels during the rest of the boat's construction (diagram 12.1).

12.3

STEP 1. HAMMER THE END TO RADIUS IT.

STEP 2. DRILL $\frac{25}{64}$" HOLE, LEAVING ABOUT $\frac{1}{4}$" UNDRILLED.

STEP 3. FINISH THE HOLE WITH A $\frac{3}{8}$" DRILL. THE $\frac{1}{64}$" OVERSIZE HOLE REDUCES DRAG ON THE CUT DOWEL.

STEP 4. HACKSAW CUTTER SLOTS.

STEP 5. FILE DOWN SHADED AREA TO LEAVE CUTTER EDGE PROUD.

STEP 6. FILE CUTTING EDGES SHARP IN THE SLOTS WITH A FINE, THIN FILE.

DOWEL CUTTER (MILD STEEL)

RIGHT-HAND CUTTER

Diagram 12.1

12.4

Photo 12.4 A square of straight-grained cedar, slightly larger than the eventual finished size of the dowel, is chucked up in my drill. The end of the square stock has been pointed with a file or plane until it has a slight taper so that it will start easily in the cutter. I start the variable-speed drill very slowly and increase the speed when the dowel starts through the cutter. If you do not accelerate slowly, the square stock will oscillate and break, especially if you are cutting ¼-inch or smaller dowels.

CONSTRUCTION TIMES FOR CHAPTER 12

Larry: Making dowel cutter; making and installing stopwaters   3 hours

Lin: Sighting for stopwater holes; cleanup   3 hours

Totals to date: Larry 1718 hours

Lin   291 hours

DISCUSSION

Although it is better to put in stopwaters before you plank any boat, if you do happen to forget them, you can successfully install them later, as shown in diagram 12.2. The length of the seam between the "afterthought" stopwater and the rabbet should be about as long as your narrowest caulking-tool blade, or 2 to 3 inches. If the joint is quite tight, you will need a number 0 crease iron (thin iron) plus a dumb iron or a wide chisel to widen the seam and make enough of a V to accept caulking cotton. This can also be a handy repair trick if you suspect that the stopwaters on an older boat are leaking or nonexistent.

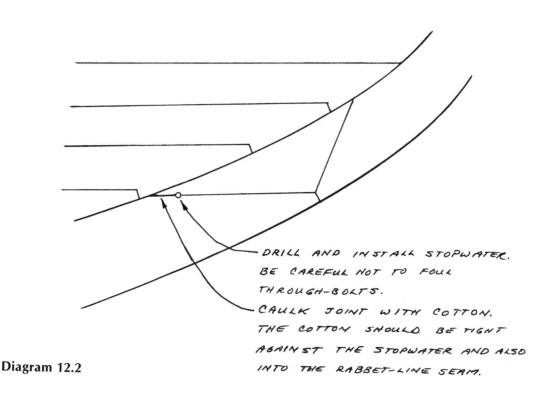

DRILL AND INSTALL STOPWATER.
BE CAREFUL NOT TO FOUL
THROUGH-BOLTS.
CAULK JOINT WITH COTTON.
THE COTTON SHOULD BE TIGHT
AGAINST THE STOPWATER AND ALSO
INTO THE RABBET-LINE SEAM.

Diagram 12.2

13. THE BALLAST KEEL

My next major project was casting the lead ballast keel, then fitting it in place. I chose to do it at this time because it is easier to drill and measure for the keelbolts before the hull is planked.

There are a number of reasons why I prefer casting my own lead keel as close to the hull as fire safety precautions permit. First, I can buy my own lead at (usually) bargain prices instead of paying the going price at a foundry. We paid 35 American cents for unreprocessed clean scrap lead—6,200 pounds at 35 cents, or $2,170. The foundry would have charged us 55 cents per pound for the reprocessed scrap lead they used, plus an additional casting fee of 10 cents a pound, (for a total of $4,030), plus the additional cost of shipping the pattern to the foundry and delivering the lead casting back to our boatyard, a distance of 75 miles. So I cut my cash outlay by about half on this large purchase. If the savings had been only about 10 or 15 cents a pound, I would have had the foundry cast the keel, because it took almost 95 hours of my time plus 20 hours of Lin's time to do it. If you deduct about 20 hours of my time for the pattern I would have had to make for the foundry, that means I made close to $29 an hour by doing my own casting (at price difference at that time). On the other hand, I had a relatively easy keel to cast, so before you make this decision, see the further discussion at the end of this chapter.

Photo 13.1 The keel has a low-aspect section, so I could build a simple plywood female pattern that was also the mold. But there were two considerations I had to keep in mind: First, the profile drawing on the loft floor shows the centerline of the lead keel, not the slightly longer sides. (This same problem was detailed in the section on the deadwood in chapter 3.) Second, lead shrinks about ⅛ inch per foot as it cools, so the mold should be increased in all dimensions to allow for this (diagram 13.1). Many builders ignore the shrinkage factor and their lead keel ends up smaller and lighter than the designer calculated, and the casting becomes narrower than the keel timber. After the boat has been in the water for a year or two, the wide keel timber will take on water and swell. (As much as ¼ inch is not uncommon.) This will exaggerate the

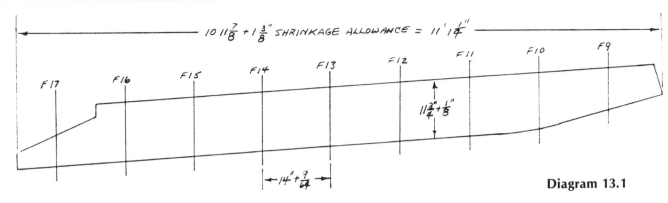

$10\,11\frac{7}{8}" + 1\frac{3}{8}"$ SHRINKAGE ALLOWANCE $= 11'1\frac{1}{4}"$

F17 F16 F15 F14 F13 F12 F11 F10 F9

$11\frac{3}{4}" + \frac{1}{8}"$

$14" + \frac{9}{64}"$

Diagram 13.1

13.1

Photo 13.2 I transferred the frame section bevels for the bottom of the keel from the loft floor to the bottom edge of the plywood mold. This resulted in a running bevel that I planed along the lower edge of the side. For future reference, I indicated the degrees for these bevels on the outside of the mold.

error. To complicate matters, I have observed that when bare plywood is used as a mold,* it will char when the molten lead pours in. This effectively increases the casting width by 1/8 to 5/32 inch and the depth by 1/16 to 3/32 inch, but it is better to have the lead keel slightly larger rather than undersize.

---

* Howard Chapelle (see Bibliography) recommends painting the mold with waterglass (sodium silicate), but I have found this to be a mistake. The sodium silicate will bubble as the hot lead touches it and create thousands of tiny craters on the surface of the lead keel.

13.2

13.3

Photo **13.3** The plywood side has been clamped onto the plywood bottom. Notice how the bevel changes from almost vertical aft to flared forward. The plywood cleats align the sides to the correct bottom of the keel half-breadths, which include my shrink-factor additions.

Photo **13.4** Because the bottom of the keel is flat, the centerline corresponds directly to the lead keel's profile on the loft floor. So it is accurate and simple just to add the shrinkage factor to the length of each section. If you align the shrinkage-allowance section lines on the curved sides of the pattern as you bend it to fit the bottom section lines, they should all line up like F11.

Photo **13.5** The sides of the mold—which are made of three layers of ½-inch plywood with staggered butts—are glued and then nailed after the glue is set. The inclined forefoot section of the bottom is simply butted to the bottom and glued in place.

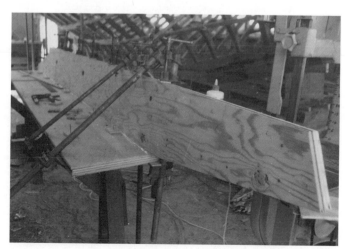

13.4

13.5

13.6

13.7

Photo 13.6 I have fastened 1½-inch-by-1½-inch vertical stiffeners to the sides of the mold. Horizontal spreaders, ¾ inch by 1½ inches, are nailed between these stiffeners to secure the correct beam dimension at each station. The clamp at the bottom right-hand corner of the mold is holding a radiused pine fillet, which will give the finished keel its rounded corners.

Photo 13.7 This fillet can be made quite easily on the table saw. First clamp a temporary wood fence at an angle to the saw blade. By changing the angle of this fence in relation to the angle of the blade, you can increase or decrease the size of the radius cut into the wood. Start the first pass on a scrap piece of wood with the saw blade no more than ⅛ inch high. Check that the radius is correct and that the cut is in the middle of the board. If it isn't, and you have to center the saw cut across the face of the board, use a felt pen to mark the position of the wooden fence on the metal saw table. Then adjust the wood fence so it is parallel to your pen line at all times. This keeps the radius the same but moves the centerline of the cut. When you are satisfied that the radius is correct and the board is centered, radius all of your pine pieces, one after the other, without changing the saw-blade setting. I ran four pieces of pine through the ⅛-inch-high saw blade. For the next four passes, I raised the blade ⅛ inch at a time. For large radiuses, or with hardwood, take a proportionately smaller bite. Don't try for more than a ⅛-inch cut at a time or the saw might jam and mess up your wood.

Photo 13.8 After the radius is sawn, the fillets have to be cut to fit the corners of the mold. First saw the side that fits to the bottom of the mold. The angle here is 45 degrees. The other side has a running bevel that is the same as the bevel previously planed onto the edge of the plywood mold sides. These running bevels can be cut into the fillet with the bandsaw.

13.8

13.9

Photo 13.9 The scarf joint on the aft end of my mold needed a lid and two small bulkheads for the nibs that would match up with the dead-wood timbers.

Photo 13.10 This is the underside of the lid. The two holes were drilled a little smaller than a 1¼-inch galvanized pipe so that two riser pipes could be threaded into the plywood to vent the gases formed by the molten lead trapped under the lid. The grooves in the lid angle upward to help the gases move toward the vents. These vents did not prove totally successful: I ended up with a shrink hole about the size of my first in the top of the scarf joint. But this was an improvement over the nib end on *Seraffyn's* keel: I didn't put riser pipes in her mold and ended up with a shrink hole the size of an 8-inch-diameter ball. To repair these defects, I heated some extra lead and poured it into the hole after the keel had cooled.

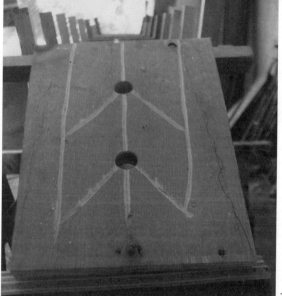

13.10

Photo 13.11 The mold is settled in the ground with dry sand tamped around it for extra support. The wire Spanish windlasses across each section also help keep the mold from bulging. The two pieces of 2 x 4 clamped to either end of the mold are to correct a ¼-inch twist that developed during construction. I inserted two 3-foot-long threaded rods into the ground so I could tighten nuts on the outboard end of the 2 x 4 to adjust the twist out of the mold and get it completely level.

13.11

13.12

Photo 13.12 The lead for *Seraffyn*'s 1½-ton keel was melted in one bathtub. But this keel weighed 3 tons. I figured that a single tub with 6,200 pounds of lead in it would be three-fourths full. This would raise the center of gravity of the tub to the point where it could easily tip over. It also worried me that the only cast-iron tubs I could find had rounded bottoms. So . . . along with four legs made up of firebricks, I added four pipes to steady the lips of each of two tubs. Just for insurance, I added an angle iron, which I bolted to the lips of both tubs and then in turn bolted to the 4 x 4 stud post of the boatshed.

The lead shown piled up on the right side of the photo was telephone cable sheathing, which was clean and slag-free. I had 5 percent extra on hand just in case there was a miscalculation, or if for some reason the 6,200 pounds did not fill the mold completely.

Photo 13.13 A major problem was keeping our cat out of the mold. The two long mold-filling pipes had brass gas valves to control the lead flow. These valves were a hassle. When we were pouring the lead, the handle on one of the valves twisted off as if it had been soft cheese. In order to get the lead to pour, we had to improvise a sheet-metal trough under the 90-degree elbow that was welded to the bottom of the tub. I then unscrewed the fill pipe and valve from the elbow and the lead flowed unchecked into the mold.

13.13

13.14

13.15

Photo 13.14   This is a more reliable way to pour lead (no valves). The chain holds up the pipe as you heat the lead. When you want to pour, use the chain to lower the pipe until the pipe end is in the middle of the mold.

Photo 13.15   The 90-degree elbow should be electric welded to the bottom of the tub. If you bolt a pipe flange to the outlet, as I did once, the heat and lead pressure will stretch the bolts and there will be a puddle of lead all over the yard. After you have the elbow welded onto the tub, screw a pipe plug tightly into the outlet, then put a gallon of gasoline in the tub to check the welds for leaks. If the tub holds gas, it will hold lead. One of our tubs did leak at the weld, so I had to load it back into our pickup and take it back to the welder.

Photo 13.16   We leaned sheets of plywood against the boat and the walls of the boatshed, then had four large CO_2 fire extinguishers handy before we started the fires burning under the tubs. The scrap-metal signs shown leaning against the tub were to retain the heat and reduce the fire danger.

It took about half a cord of firewood to melt all of the lead. Fortunately, we had lots of scrap wood around the yard. We had to stoke the fires for just under 5 hours before all of the lead was melted. Several friends helped with this. (If we had not had the scrap wood, we could have rented propane burners.)

13.16

13.17

13.18

13.19

Photo 13.17 The longish pipes had to be heated with an oxyacetylene torch to get the lead to run through the pipe and valves. (This heating usually is not necessary with the valveless chain-and-pipe method.) Anyway, we finally got the lead in the mold and Lin and I will be forever grateful to the dozen friends who just showed up to help us—complete with the ingredients for a picnic lunch.

Photo 13.18 I had to wait until the keel was fully cooled—two and a half days in this case. Then I dug under the ends and jacked it up, one end at a time.

Photo 13.19 Lead is definitely the best material for a ballast keel: You can cast it yourself; you can hand-plane or chisel it, power-plane or drill it; woodscrews screw into it and Bondo Car-body putty was designed to stick to it. And, yes, it is also very heavy yet relatively inexpensive. Substituting less dense materials such as cast iron, lead shot in resin, or, worst of all, concrete and boiler punchings, will make your boat more tender and lower its resale value.

I trued the top of the keel with an electric plane and a straightedge.

13.20   **13.21**

Photo 13.20 I used this plywood pattern to check that both sides of the deadwood scarf were exactly the same so I would get a good fit on the first try. This is faster than jacking the keel in and out of place two or three times to get a fit.

Photo 13.21 It was quite easy to roll the keel under the boat with pipe rollers and a 2 x 4 lever.

13.22

Photo 13.22 The fabric on top of the ballast keel is Irish felt impregnated with creosote. (You could substitute roofing felt or canvas.) This method of insulating the keel is time-proven and allows the keel timbers to swell and move when they absorb moisture. I wouldn't use any glue or adhesive between the timber and the lead, because, as the timber swells, it will cause stresses that can crack and disturb the connection. The bonded keel would also be difficult to remove for adjustments if it didn't fit perfectly on the first try. Finally, if modifications to the keel were ever necessary, it would be very hard to take off the lead without having the adhesive tear hunks of the keel timber with it.

I also creosoted the faying surfaces of the wood keel and deadwood to keep worms from getting into the timbers.

Photo 13.23 Here I am jacking the lead up one end at a time, checking the keel's stability as I go.

13.23

13.24

Photo 13.24   The lead has been jacked up and blocked and wedged into its final home, and it is time for the floor-to-keel bolts to be installed. (See the discussion at the end of this chapter for reasons I chose to drill for keelbolts rather than cast the bolts into the lead.)

Diagram 13.2

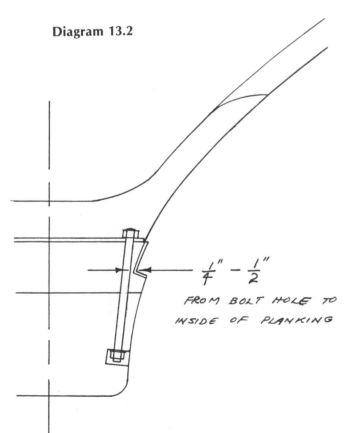

13.25

Photo 13.25   The bolt holes should be drilled so that they are close to the inner rabbet line. About ¼ to ½ inch is best (diagram 13.2). These bolts give a stronger, more direct connection from frame to ballast if they are set as close to the rabbet as practical. It is fairly simple to eyeball your drill as you work to keep the hole clear of the rabbet.

Lead drills as easily as wood if you use a cooling substance. Drilling the lead without a coolant causes it to heat the drill bit, which then melts the lead, which effectively tries to solder the bit into the lead keel.

My cruising friend Gordon Yates came by to visit and was put to work squirting acetone into each hole as I drilled. The acetone cooled the bit and the lead peeled out of the hole in long, beautiful shavings.

The ⅝-inch twist drill is marked with masking tape and provides a handy depth gauge for drilling all of the holes exactly 6 inches into the lead. (See the discussion section at the end of this chapter.)

13.27

13.26

Photo 13.26 I then stuck a piece of ⅝-inch rod into the hole to indicate the exact direction of the bolt holes. I used this as a guide to get a parallel pencil line on the outside of the wood and the lead keel.

Photo 13.27 Depth measurement is marked on the side of the keel, bisecting the vertical pencil line that represents the center of the bolt hole.

Photo 13.28 With my other drill motor and a ¾-inch twist drill, I drilled two holes, side by side.

13.28

13.29

13.30

Photo 13.29   When the ¾-inch side holes were drilled deep enough (about 2½ inches), I chiseled a flat on the upper side, making a D-shaped blind nut hole. This straight surface provided a landing for the washer to bear against when the bolt was tightened up.

Photo 13.30   Here I am putting my tape measure in the bolt hole and hooking the end of it to the flat of the D-shaped hole to get the exact length of the keel-to-floor bolt. I then added enough length for two nuts and one washer. A washer is not needed on the metal floor flange, but some caulking cotton should be clove-

hitched between the nut and the floor flange to stop potential leaks. A little grease on the nut threads will slow corrosion and make bolt removal easier if repairs are ever needed.

These bolts were made from silicon-bronze ⅝-inch rolled rod stock. I used a fine thread for the nuts, since this leaves more bolt diameter intact than a coarse thread. The upper end of each bolt had an extra ¹⁄₁₆ to ³⁄₃₂ inch of threads standing proud above the nut. Before I put each bolt into the keel, I held it in the vise and peened the exposed threads onto the nut until I had, in effect, a long cap bolt. I then inserted the bolt into the hole so that three or four threads showed through the washer flat in the blind (D-shaped) hole. To insert the nut and washer, I used a pair of needle-nosed pliers that were ground to hold the hex nuts (diagram 13.3). I again greased the threads of this nut and also put some grease between nut and washer, since this tended to hold the washer to the top of the nut, making it easier to get them both in place.

As I turned the bolt from the top with a socket wrench, the nut started threading onto the bolt. When the nut was well started, I inserted a large, heavy-duty screwdriver beside the flat of the nut and the side of the hole in the lead. This wedged the nut and held it as I tightened the bolt with the socket wrench.

When the floor-to-keel bolts were done, I through-bolted the lifting eyes that were cast into floors 11 and 16.

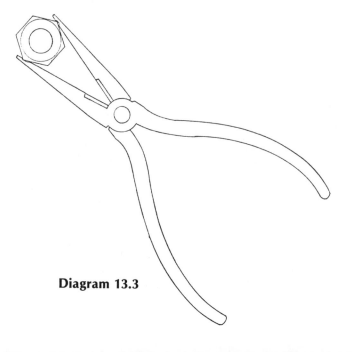

Diagram 13.3

13.31

13.32

Photo 13.31 I used a 4 x 4 drilling jig to get the holes for the lifting-eye bolts drilled square to the top of the floor flange. This provided a flat, square landing face for the nut. I made the jig on the drill press. The 3½-degree drilling angle was set on the tilting table of the press. This provided an accurate hole angled correctly to the backbone and automatically made the hole square athwartships.

Photo 13.32 The drill in the jig is being checked for squareness to the top of the floor flange.

Photo 13.33 These are two ¾-inch fine threaded through-bolts that will fasten one of the lifting eyes to the bottom of the lead keel. The plate on the bottom is ⅞ inch thick and 3-inch-by-6-inch cast manganese bronze; it is drilled and tapped to accept the bolts. The plate will be countersunk into the bottom of the lead to give a wide, load-distributing area on the somewhat soft lead keel. (In his *Common Sense of Yacht Design* (page 74), L. F. Herreshoff states that lead with 3 percent antimony has about the same hardness as white oak.)

13.33

13.34

Photo 13.34 Lying under the keel, wearing safety goggles, and cursing, I hand-chiseled the rectangular countersink hole for these nut plates and made it 1⅛ inches deep. The top of the plate was then bedded in Bondo to guarantee a flush, square fit between the 3 x 6 plate and the lead keel.

It is important to take the time to ensure that these bolts are aligned perfectly in their holes so that no unusual or indirect strains are placed on them when they are used. Keep in mind that these bolts some day will be lifting the whole boat.

The D-shaped holes on the sides of the keel were eventually plugged with slightly tapered lead plugs that Lin bandsawed out of a ¾-inch slab of lead. (She kept a can of kerosene and a brush handy to lubricate the saw blade so lead did not build up on the rubber wheels and derail it.) These plugs were then hammered in, with epoxy as a bonding agent. Most boatyards simply would have plugged the holes with Bondo.

CONSTRUCTION TIMES FOR CHAPTER 13

Larry: Building mold for lead ballast keel; setting up for lead pour; lifting keel out of ground, cleaning and fairing it; bolting keel onto hull; filling and leveling boatyard floor.

149 hours

Lin: Transporting lead; arranging safety equipment; assisting in pour setup and during pour; filling blind bolt holes; doing final fairing of sides of keel

40 hours

Totals to date: Larry 1867 hours

Lin   331 hours

DISCUSSION

Casting your own keel is a technical challenge. Some people would resent the time and labor spent here, but others would revel in the complexity of it all. The former should probably have their keels cast at a professional foundry if the cost difference is not substantial. The latter will be able to save some money, but the decision to do it at your own boatyard should be weighed against the complexity and size of the keel mold needed for

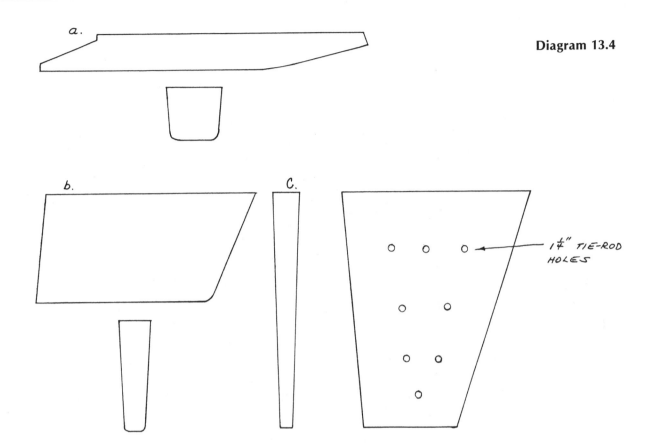

Diagram 13.4

a.

b.   c.

1¼" TIE-ROD HOLES

the job. *Taleisin's* lead keel is about the easiest shape you can cast (diagram 13.4a). The only easier keel shape would be one that had a straight-sided, parallel box mold that is rectangular in section. A long, low profile keel, such as *Taleisin's*, not only gets the weight of the lead as low as possible on the boat, it also simplifies mold-building problems. The pressures in a mold such as this are relatively small compared to those of a high-aspect, short-length fin keel for a fin-and-skeg type of hull. Most of these fin keels are also airfoil-shaped and usually weigh about 50 percent of the yacht's total displacement. The mold has to be made extremely strong to take the downward (columnar) pressure of the molten lead. For large fin keels of this type, ones of 12 tons or more (diagram 13.4c), professional foundrymen use 1¼-inch-diameter iron tie-rods through-fastened from side to side of the mold to stop the sides from swelling outward as the lead is poured. These bolts have to be quite large; otherwise, the heat of the lead will soften them and cause them to stretch. The holes left by the bolts are filled after the lead has cooled. Because of technical problems such as this one, a moderate fin keel, with proportions such as in diagram 13.4b, would be all I would attempt in a boatyard.

I used the plywood female-mold method described here because it eliminated the need for both a pattern and a mold, thus saving materials and labor. A mold such as this one can be made of plywood, solid planks, or—if your keel is complex and fully shaped—strip planks.

If you want to cast your keel in sand or concrete, you first have to build a male pattern to give the mold its shape. This pattern can be made of solid or laminated pine. It can even be shaped from a block of Styrofoam. I am not very familiar with the advantages and/or disadvantages of a concrete or sand mold over the method I used, but after having success with three keels cast this way, I feel it is the least labor intensive.

I prefer to cast with the mold buried in the ground, instead of above ground, for the following reasons:

1. If the mold leaks slightly, the lead seepage will solidify in the ground and stop the leak.
2. The buried mold is lower, relative to the melting tub. This lets you keep the tub as low as possible so it is easier to support and safer to work around.
3. With the lower setup, the lead does not have to be lifted as high to get it into the tub.
4. The in-ground mold does not have to be as strongly built or as well supported as an aboveground mold.

A final warning to those who are casting their own keels: Keep both the lead scrap and the keel mold perfectly dry. Any moisture in the mold will turn rapidly to steam as your pour the lead. Molten lead will blow all over your shop. This would be an extra problem with a concrete mold, as the concrete can take a long time to dry and cure completely.

Keelbolts—Methods, Materials, and Placement

The blind-bolt method I used to fasten this keel sounds complicated, but it is easier than through-bolting. I made all eighteen floor-to-keel bolts with a hand die and a hacksaw and installed them using 18 hours of labor. With through-bolts, not only do you have to drill longer holes through the lead, but you then have to counterskink the nuts and washers into the bottom of the keel. If the ballast keel is close to the ground, it's hard to get a drill motor underneath it to countersink for the nut and washer. You have to roll the keel out and turn it over. We had to do this on *Seraffyn's* ballast keel, and I remember that it took at least an extra day. The blind-bolt method, with its shorter bolts, also saves expensive rod stock.

If you are putting a lead keel on a fiberglass or cold-molded hull, the blind-bolt method is more difficult because you cannot drill the keelbolt holes before the planking goes on. So people building these types of hulls usually cast their bolts into the lead keel. They use a pattern to locate and hold the bolts in position while the lead is poured. After the lead has cooled, the pattern is used to check that the bolts have stayed in position. If it can slide easily on and off the embedded keelbolts; the same pattern can then be tacked underneath the wood keel, where it serves as a guide as you drill up into the keel timber and/or floor timbers. A variation on this method is to drill the holes for the bolts after the keel is cast, make a pattern, insert the keelbolts into their holes, and then use the pattern to drill through the wooden keel on the hull.

If you use either of these methods, make sure before you drill that the top side of the pattern faces up to the keel timber. If you accidentally reverse the pattern, you will end up with bolt misalignment (in some cases, this can be quite severe). I have seen this happen twice—once to a pro and the second time to an amateur. The pro now marks his keelbolt pattern with huge red letters indicating which side faces up to the wooden keel.

I used a fine thread for both ends of these bolts. A fine thread leaves a stronger, larger bolt diameter intact after the threads are cut. I am aware that some builders worry about fine threads because they are affected by corrosion more quickly than coarse threads, but I feel that if the threads are greased, corrosion should be minimized.

Bolt material should be matched to your type of construction and your ballast material: bronze bolts for lead-ballasted wooden hulls; stainless steel bolts for fiberglass hulls with lead ballast; iron bolts (galvanized steel) for wood or fiberglass hulls with cast-iron keels.

Stainless steel generally is not used on wood boats because the acid in some woods (especially oak), combined with salt water, seems to cause stainless steel to pit and corrode faster than would ordinary galvanized mild steel.

We saved a considerable amount of money on *Seraffyn*'s keelbolts by buying second-hand, slightly bent 1-inch bronze propeller shafts.

Some boatbuilders in New Zealand have taken a hint from L. F. Herreshoff (*Common Sense of Yacht Design*, page 74) and simply drilled and tapped and then threaded their bolts into the lead keel according to Herreshoff's instructions: " . . . six or eight times the diameter of the bolt." I personally do not like this method and have heard of failures with such tapped-in keelbolts.

Diagram 13.5

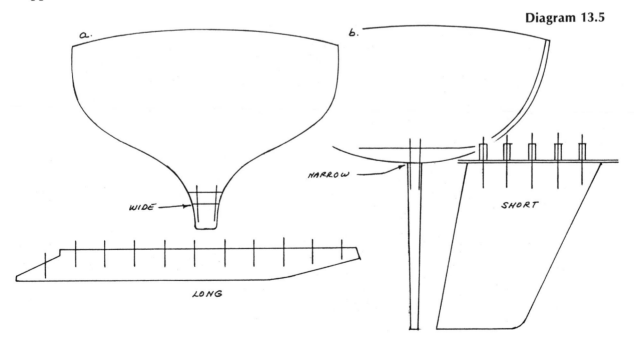

Some keel-casting companies have been using stainless steel fully threaded (all thread) rod, which they bend into a J-shape, or else they weld a bar between two bolts and then cast them right into the lead. In the early 1980s, *Charlie,* a TransPac racer, lost her high-aspect keel on the beat back to the mainland from Hawaii. The keelbolts were under tremendous strains as the boat pounded to windward; pulled the bolts out and let the lead ballast keel fall off. Fortunately, the crew was able to sail the vessel downwind to safety. This problem would have been prevented by nuts and large washers bedded deeply into the keel to secure the bolts.

It is simple to secure a long, low-aspect ballast keel like *Taleisin's* since there is room for eighteen widely spaced keelbolts. Getting the same secure attachment on a boat with a fin keel is much more difficult. The attachment area at the top of the fin keel is much shorter and narrower, so the bolts cannot be widely spaced; nor is there room for as many fasteners. There are fewer floor timbers over the fin keel to spread the loads (diagram 13.5). For this reason, the keelbolts and the bolting arrangement for a fin-keeler should be designed and built with extreme care.

14. THE MAST STEP

In order to spread the mast strains, the mast step must be well secured to the floors so it cannot move fore-and-aft or sideways. To do this, I recessed the bottom of the mast step to form a mortise over the bronze floor flanges.

14.1

Photo 14.1 I shaped the mast-step timber to the designed dimensions, then cut the tapered profile angle for the forward lower face. You can use one of two methods to obtain the shape of this incline; you can loft it on the loft floor, or, as I did, you can pick up a profile pattern directly from the floors that are in place on the backbone.

When the timber has been shaped, it is necessary to settle the mast step flush to all five floors to mark the lower face for the mortises that will have to be cut. The notches shown on the corners of the upside-down mast step are chiseled to clear the frames forward where the hull is narrower.

14.2

Photo 14.2 The clamps are holding the mast step aligned to the centerline of the hull and flush to the floor flanges so that I can scribe around the floor flange for the mortises. I use a knife to scribe any line that I plan to chisel later. The knife indentation automatically aligns the cutting edge of the wide chisel.

The five rectangles I scribed on the lower face of the mast step have to be chiseled or routed down ⅜ inch to fit over and lock onto the floor flanges. This will cause the whole mast step to settle ⅜ inch lower into the hull. So before I unclamped the mast step I measured and scribed the appropriate corners of the step so I could deepen the angled notches where it fits over the frames.

The rectangular hole seen in the aft end of the mast step is cut so that a lifting cable eventually can be attached to the lifting eye cast into floor F11 (see diagram 5.1).

14.3

Photo 14.3 Without the planking in place, it is possible to get under the mast step to scribe and measure for the floor-flange mortises.

When the mortises on the bottom of the step fit the floor flanges and the notches fit the frames correctly, I removed the step and chiseled an additional ⅛ inch of wood out of the middle floor mortise (F10), then removed ¹⁄₁₆ inch of wood from the mortises over F9 and F11. These clearances close up as soon as the mast exerts its compression load on the step. The advantage of doing this is that the load of the mast step is spread more evenly, exerting the first strains on the end floors, then on the floors with ¹⁄₁₆-inch clearance, and finally onto the ⅛-inch-gapped center floor, which has the mast directly above it. It gives what is, in effect, a prestressed mast step that spreads its loads more proportionately over all five floors. This is not common practice, but I feel it is worthwhile; this way, the floors most directly under the downward-pushing mast will not have to take all of the initial strains.

In order to get a perfect flush fit between the crowned mast step and the floor flanges, I brushed varnish (you can use water if you prefer) onto the top of the floor. I then clamped the center floor flange, increasing the pressure on the clamps until they closed the ⅛-inch gap. When I removed the step, I chiseled off the wet (varnished) areas. I repeated the procedure until the wet varnish covered the whole horizontal surface of the recessed mortises.

14.4

Photo 14.4 As mentioned in chapter 2, I varied the design by lengthening the aft part of the forefoot timber by 9½ inches. This longer joint let the floor at F8 bear on the end of the forefoot, which spreads the load of the mast step partially onto the forefoot.* I was able to make this change yet still keep the headroom we needed because of the lower-profile metal floors (4-inch web height), which meant the final location of the top of the mast step was about 9 inches above the keel timber. The top of the mast step in a wood-floor boat built to this design would be about 14 or 15 inches above the wood keel.

* In the construction drawing, the forefoot end is between F7 and F8. This drawing was done for a boat with wooden floors. Lyle Hess drew the shorter stem joint because he was trying to keep the wood floors on the keel timber as deep as possible in order to lengthen the floor arm, yet still keep the cabin sole as low as practical in order to provide headroom above the mast step.

14.5

Photo 14.5 The mast step was through-bolted to the floor flange at both ends. Two more bolts were placed through the mast step and floor flange at the center of the step, clear of the eventual mast mortise needed to tighten up the prestressed crown. To complete the job, I put two 'thwartship rivets through the edge of the mast step just forward and aft of the mast position. These fastenings help the mast step resist splitting.

I wait until the mast is built to cut the mortise into the top of the step. After the deck framing and mast partners are in place and the finished mast with its tenon cut onto the butt end. That way, I can position the mortise correctly so the mast rakes exactly as shown in the sail plan and construction drawings. The exact shape and size of the mortise can then be transferred from the mast tenon by making a plywood pattern that slides onto the tenon. I use the hole in the plywood as a guide to scribe the exact size of the mortise onto the mast step. When the mortise is finished, I drill a ½-inch limber hole through the step at the lowest point in the mortise. This drains any water that might otherwise settle and start rot in the mast step. Before the mast goes in place, a copper coin should be placed in the mast-step mortise—for good luck and also because any salt water that does get into the mortise will produce oxidation on the coin (cuprous oxide and copper oxychloride). Copper oxides will kill the bacteria that start rot.

CONSTRUCTION TIMES FOR CHAPTER 14

Larry: Building and bolting mast step in place   26 hours

Lin: Shopping for supplies; cleaning up Dolfinite   9 hours

Totals to date: Larry 1893 hours

Lin   340 hours

DISCUSSION
Mast-Step Design

The mast step is an extremely important structural member on a ballasted sailboat. If it is properly proportioned and fitted, the step can spread and disperse the compressive loads of the mast over a large area of the backbone timbers. If this strain is not properly distributed, it could force the backbone (directly below the mast) downward so that the garboard seams open and the boat leaks. Larger working vessels, 80 feet and above, usually have a long mast step (keelson) that sits on all of the floors of the straight keel area. More than one mast can be stepped onto this 10- or 12-inch sided timber. This works well for large ships, but it is not necessary or desirable on yachts because the keelson cramps access and storage in the bilges and makes the bilge difficult to clean. Also, the extra timber adds unneeded weight. So for yachts, it is desirable to design a mast step large enough to spread the necessary loads, yet small enough to be as unobtrusive as possible.

The basic problem involved in designing a mast step that will spread strains adequately is calculating these compression loads. A heavily ballasted yacht will develop more compression strains than a lightly ballasted, tender boat. Naturally, a single-masted yacht with a high ballast-to-displacement ratio will develop much greater strains against its mast step than a two-masted yacht with the same ballast ratio. For any sloop or cutter with more than a 30 percent ballast-to-displacement ratio, I recommend a mast step that spans five floor timbers. Sloops and cutters with more than 50 percent ballast should have steps that cover six or seven floors, especially boats longer than 45 feet on deck.

On two-masted vessels like ketches and schooners, the foremast quite often ends up on top of or close to the scarfed forefoot-to-keel joint. If this is the case on a boat you are building, it is important to be sure the mast step will spread the strains over this joint as widely as practical. The arrangement of the mast step, keel, and forefoot area in diagram 14.1a (I sketched this diagram from the plans of a ketch drawn by a well-known designer of wooden boats) unfortunately is weak. In diagram 14.1b, the mast step rests on five floors and there is a longer forefoot-to-keel joint. This arrangement is much stronger than 14.1a and would be less likely to direct strains onto the forefoot joint.

The width of the mast step on any vessel under 45 feet should be two and a half times

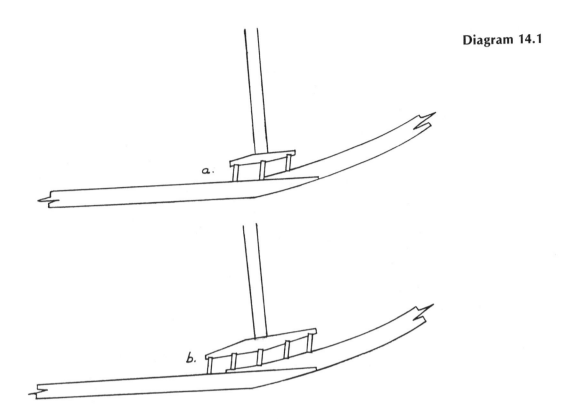

Diagram 14.1

the 'thwartship dimension of the mast tenon. For a 4-inch-wide tenon, you would need a 10-inch-wide mast step. (The 'thwartship dimension of the mast tenon should be between one-half and two-thirds of the diameter of the mast heel.) The vertical thickness of the mast step should be about two-thirds of the sided keel dimensions. The step should be made from a durable, rot-resistant hardwood.

The top edge of the mast step in profile should be at 90 degrees to the centerline of the mast. This makes the eventual mortise and tenon square-ended, and therefore easier to cut and fit.

Some builders find they can add a bit of headroom to the interior of a boat by drawing the mast-step profile on the loft floor so that it is level with the top of the cabin sole. We did this on *Seraffyn* because the wood floor timbers beneath the step raised it until it was about 12 inches above the keel timber. By using the step as part of the cabin sole, we saved 2 inches of headroom.

Deck-Stepped Masts

The masts on some yachts are stepped on deck or onto the cabintop, thus allowing the designer to draw a more open interior. But extra engineering is required to make sure the structures under the mast will take the strains of sailing. A compression post or reinforced bulkhead (or bulkheads) needs to be built to take the compression loads from the mast down to an appropriate floor structure. Some designers draw masts that are stepped onto three or four laminated-wood or fabricated-metal ring frames or tabernacles, with no central compression posts or bulkheads. Most of these boats have a metal T-section structure that spans the reinforced area of the deck under the mast. The mast is then bolted onto the upright flange or set into a metal collar, which acts as an on-deck mast step. Although I have owned and raced a boat with a deck-stepped mast (a Knud Reimers–designed Tumlaren), I prefer to have my mast stepped through mast partners at deck level and onto a mast step set on top of several floors. First, the extra length of mast going through the deck and into the hull supports and stiffens the gooseneck and the spinnaker-pole end of the spar. Second, in the event of a dismasting, the broken spar or even the boom could be restepped and held in place by the step and the mast partners until shrouds could be jury-rigged. This would be much simpler than trying to restep a jury-rigged mast with a deck- or cabin-stepped arrangement.

Rod Stephens, one half of the most successful yacht-design team of this century, confirms my feelings when he writes:

> An unhealthy trend found in many smaller cruising boats is the mast stepped on deck. This is an attempt by designers and marketers to remove the "unsightly" mast from the interior and to save some construction costs. With a deck-stepped mast, if a shroud that terminates on deck breaks or is disconnected, the whole mast will topple over. A proper seagoing yacht must have her mast stepped through the deck and onto a well-engineered mast step that is structurally supported by the keel. In the event of a dismasting there will almost always be a stump of spar left to carry sail.*

---

* *Desirable and Undesirable Characteristics of Offshore Yachts*, CCA Technical Committee (New York: W. W. Norton, 1987).

15. BULKHEADS

The last job I did before planking was to install the main structural bulkhead. I would like to have fitted all of the 'thwartship bulkheads for the interior at this time to save several hours of fitting time. It is simpler to get good fits between the hull skin and bulkhead edges if you install them before you plank or lay on the decking. Since the hull is still an open framework, you can fit each piece of wood for the bulkhead around stringers, sheer clamps, mast steps, and partners with ease and accuracy. Unfortunately, we had not finalized the interior layout for *Taleisin,* so we didn't have the exact positions for nonstructural bulkheads, so I only built the single structural bulkhead shown on the construction plan (diagram 5.1) at this time.

Photo 15.1 To attach this main bulkhead, I first had to install the deckbeams and mast partner that land at the bulkhead station (see chapter 20). The first layer of the bulkhead is made from ½-inch-by-1¾-inch strips of teak. I resawed these strips from shorter pieces of 2-inch-thick teak that had defects. I could usually cut off the defects as I fit the various lengths in place.

I left the inside face of the teak strips rough-sawn for three reasons: (1) They would bond better to the epoxy adhesive* this way; (2) I only needed ⁹⁄₁₆-inch-thick stock to clean up one face so it measured ½ inch thick, whereas if I had planed both sides I would have needed ⅝-inch-thick stock; and (3) I saved the labor of having to run the stock through the planer for a second time.

Using the table saw, I removed the corner on each side of the face of the teak strips. I then sanded the 45-degree-angled corner with the belt sander to produce a V effect. This tongue-and-groove appearance not only is a traditional touch that I find attractive, but it also makes any joint irregularities less apparent. Later, if the varnish on any single strake gets scratched, we only have to revarnish that strake. The V-shaped grooves cut to ¼ inch by ¼ inch assist ventilation and drainage into and through lockers near the bulkheads.

I fastened the individual strips of this first layer into the frame and deckbeam with 1-inch number 6 flathead silicon-bronze wood screws.

15.1

---

* Since we had an unheated shop and were doing this job during the winter at temperatures of approximately 55°F, we chose a well-known epoxy backed up with mechanical fasteners. In retrospect, we would have preferred to use Aerodux winter-grade resorcinol, which is a gap-filling, waterproof-rated, cold-cure (down to 50°F) glue. (See Appendix C for more on adhesives.) We had not learned about this glue at the time.

15.2

15.3

Photo 15.2 The outboard end of this deck-beam is notched into the frame so that the forward face is flush with the forward side of the frame to accommodate the bulkhead.

It is quite easy to fit this first layer, because the bulkhead and sawn frame are both square to the centerline of the hull. I left the ends of each laminated strip ⅛ inch long top and bottom so that the edge of the bulkhead can be planed, flush when the planking is being fitted.

Photo 15.3 This second, or core, lamination is ½-inch-thick Western red cedar, which is quite inexpensive, especially if you buy it as shorts, 6 feet and under. It is also highly rot-resistant and holds glue well. This lamination will triangulate the corner of the deckbeam and frame, just as a hanging knee would.

The fifth piece of cedar from the right was the first strake I fitted. I placed it parallel to the outboard edge of the bilge stringer. This simplifies fitting the next piece, which can then be scribed and fitted to the flat side and edge of the bilge stringer.

Before I fitted each piece of ½-inch cedar, I checked for flatness across the boards. If the board was slightly concave, I fastened it to the first lamination of teak. This way, the temporary screws and clench rings pulled the concave center of the board flat until the glue dried. (I used these clench rings as temporary washers, since they were more convenient than the ⅜-inch-thick, 1½-inch-by-1½-inch plywood pads I normally use for jobs like this.) With this method, I got a snug fit and a flat surface for the next lamination.

Photo 15.4 I used the belt sander to remove the glue runs from the core layer. Then I checked the cedar surface for trueness with a straightedge and planed it where necessary. This ensured that the final layer of vertical teak strakes would bond well, without glue voids.

Photo 15.5 The final lamination was glued and through-fastened with 1-inch number 6 flathead bronze wood screws every 6 inches on each vertical strake. These screws hold all three laminations together, so that if the glue should fail, the fasteners still will be adequate to hold the bulkhead together. To finish off the forward side of the bulkhead, I used ¼-inch-deep, ⅜-inch-diameter wood plugs. The aft side of the bulkhead, which is more obvious, has no wood plugs.

Photo 15.6 This is the forward side of the port bulkhead. It is wider than the starboard side, as the companionway is offset to starboard. To simplify fitting the cedar around the bilge stringer and to the corner of the mast partner, I put in the left-hand piece first. I clamped this to the top edge of the bilge stringer and then scribed and fitted the top into the corner of the mast partner. Next I clamped and fitted two more pieces of cedar before cutting each of the three pieces so they were ⅛ inch overlong. I mixed up a batch of adhesive, used a brush to spread it, and fastened all three pieces in place at the same time. A small roller could speed up this operation of putting glue on both faying surfaces.

15.7

Photo 15.7 This photo was taken after I had finished planking. It shows the bulkhead fastened securely to the frame and deckbeam with ¼-inch rivets spaced 8 to 10 inches apart. These rivets are an important final touch, as they ensure that the bulkhead and framing will be unified.

CONSTRUCTION TIMES FOR CHAPTER 15

Larry: Milling tongue-and-groove material; laying up three layers of bulkhead; cleanup for varnish
50 hours

Lin: Assisting in milling; cleanup of excess glue from between bulkhead strakes; varnishing bulkhead
17 hours

Totals to date: Larry 1943 hours

Lin 357 hours

DISCUSSION

Bulkheads can be divided into two categories—structural and nonstructural. Structural bulkheads are ones that are absolutely necessary to support high-load areas of the hull or deck. To put this in the most basic terms, you couldn't safely sail without these bulkheads or you would risk racking or hogging the boat.

Nonstructural bulkheads are ones that are used only to create dividers or to support interior joinery. Usually designers indicate structural bulkheads on their plans by showing them thicker than other interior joinery. Bulkheads shown as ¾ inch or thicker on hulls over 35 feet would be structural, as would ⅝-inch ones on 30-foot hulls or ½-inch ones on 25-foot hulls. If the bulkhead drawn on your plan is near any large deck openings, such as companionways, cabins, or cockpits, it probably is structural.

The job of a bulkhead is to tie the deckbeam and frame together and unitize high-load areas, to minimize loads that could cause hull distortion, especially near the ballast keel, chainplate, mast-step area. The carlines on many yachts also need the support of partial bulkheads, especially if the carline length is greater than 10 to 12 feet. Structural bulkheads here should be attached to the carline, the short deckbeam, and the hull frame.

Most three-skinned hulls (cold-molded, diagonal-planked) are designed around stringers with bulkheads to reduce flexing. Almost every bulkhead in these boats is a structural one—even the partial bulkheads that appear only to support ends of berths.

The boatbuilder's challenge is to build the bulkheads strongly, reasonably fast (i.e., easy to fit), and inexpensively. If you can attach the bulkheads to sawn frames, you can save a lot of time. Attaching bulkheads to steam-bent frames is slower and more difficult because the frames—which are shaped by being clamped to the ribbands—are square to the inside of the eventual planking, not square to the centerline of the hull (diagram 15.1). Furthermore, it is hard to bend a steamed frame into place so that it is absolutely straight and plumb to your section lines. This means you cannot easily fit bulkheads or joinery directly onto steamed frames, and this is a serious obstacle as you do interior joinery. The

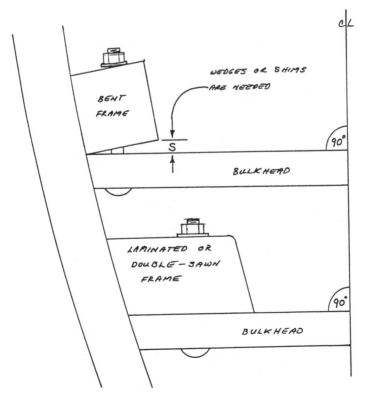

Diagram 15.1

simplicity of fitting joinery and bulkheads tightly and easily to sawn frames is in direct contrast to this and is one of the most satisfying rewards for the extra effort of lofting and figuring the frame bevels for double-sawn or beveled laminated frames.

Special frame cleats (partial frames) can be made for bulkheads that land between the frames or between deckbeams. They are beveled to be square to the centerline of the hull, just like a sawn frame would be. If they are the supports for a structural bulkhead, they also should be riveted or bolted to the planking and decking and should be as strong as the regular frames and beams. For nonstructural bulkheads, however, these cleats can be much lighter and can simply be screwed into place.

The strongest wooden bulkhead you can build is a complete, nonopening one attached to a full-width deckbeam and its corresponding port and starboard frames. This type of bulkhead is quite often used to form a watertight collision bulkhead just aft of the chain locker in larger sailing yachts and some motoryachts. Watertight bulkheads that fit

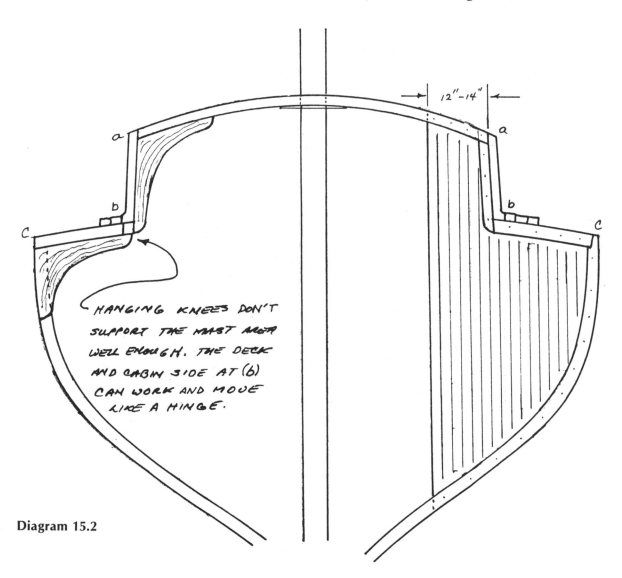

Diagram 15.2

against sawn frames can be bedded to the faying surfaces between deckbeam and floor timber for a continuous seal. You can caulk the bulkhead seams around the bilge stringers and also the sheer clamp and shelf. In order to ensure a good fit, watertight bulkheads should be built before the planking and decking are in place. Naturally, a watertight bulkhead would not have limber holes in it, so the bilge section forward of the bulkhead should have its own independent bilge-pumping system.

Bulkheads that support the mast area are usually easier to build and stronger if they attach to a deck-level beam such as the one on *Taleisin*. This in-line attachment gives direct support to the mast partner, which in turn absorbs the side loads exerted by the mast. This is not the case if the mast is stepped through a deckhouse. The mast partners in the cabintop must spread indirectly any load exerted on them down the cabin beams, by way of the cabinsides. To help this situation, there should be a structural bulkhead as close as possible to the mast partners in the cabintop. This bulkhead should be attached and bolted to the hull framing, short deckbeam, a cleat secured to the cabinside, and finally to the cabintop beam, where it is also firmly attached (diagram 15.2). With this arrangement, the relatively weak corners at the frame-to-deckbeam joint (c), the deckbeam-to-cabinside joint (b), and, finally, the cabinside-to-cabin-beam joint (a), are all interconnected to the stress-spreading bulkhead. If the bulkhead is well fastened to frames, beams, and a cleat on the cabinsides, it will firmly support the through-the-cabin mast area.

The three-layer laminated method I used on *Taleisin's* main bulkhead is about twice as thick as a plywood one, but it would be my first choice for any structural bulkheads. The following list shows the pros and cons of this method:

THREE-LAYER, LAMINATED-IN-PLACE BULKHEAD

Pro	Con
It is easy to fit individual pieces tightly around stringers and clamps	It is difficult to build a laminated-in-place bulkhead less than ¾ inch thick.
Small pieces of offcut wood can be utilized.	Sawn frames and deckbeams set vertical to the bulkhead or special cleats are needed, as you cannot easily laminate a bulkhead to a steam-bent frame.
If a strake is cut incorrectly, it can usually be used where a shorter length is needed.	It is difficult to fit and measure individual strakes if planking and decking are in place.
The outer layer of hardwood can match or contrast with the interior, as you prefer.	
The outer layers are thick enough to be sanded or planed to remove scratches or minor dents.	
Screws set through thicker laminations add a backup mechanical fastener to ensure long-term integrity of the bulkhead.	
It is easy to cap the endgrain of the bulkhead (see diagram 15.3).	

Diagram 15.3

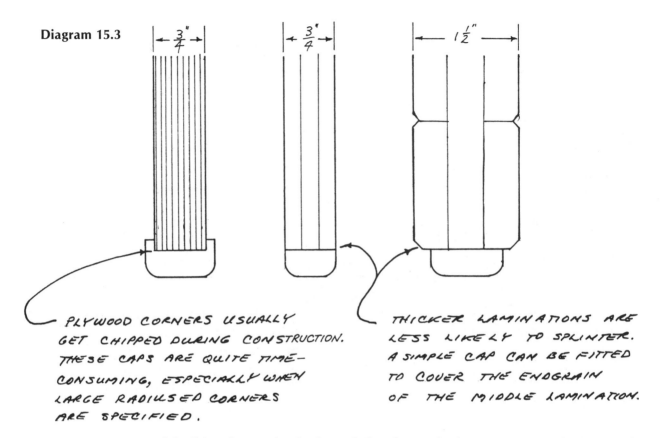

PLYWOOD CORNERS USUALLY GET CHIPPED DURING CONSTRUCTION. THESE CAPS ARE QUITE TIME-CONSUMING, ESPECIALLY WHEN LARGE RADIUSED CORNERS ARE SPECIFIED.

THICKER LAMINATIONS ARE LESS LIKELY TO SPLINTER. A SIMPLE CAP CAN BE FITTED TO COVER THE ENDGRAIN OF THE MIDDLE LAMINATION.

Nonstructural bulkheads can be built and fitted simply by using a single layer of tongue-and-groove stock. The 'thwartship joinery bulkheads on *Taleisin* were later built from ⅝-inch-thick tongue-and-groove stock. The fore-and-aft partition bulkheads were built from ½-inch-thick tongue-and-groove. I cut the material from the offcuts left over from planking, resawed the 1¼-inch offcuts into the proper sizes, then sent everything to a friend who had a spindle shaper and the proper cutters for the final tongue-and-groove configuration. This meant I wasted very little of my teak planking stock and had only the cost of final shaping for all of my interior and bulkhead stock.

In a few places on board, forward and aft sides of the ⅝-inch bulkheads were visible, so for these I grooved all four corners to give a nice-looking finish. (diagram 15.4).

Use a ripping jig on the bandsaw (see chapter 23) to provide accuracy. By keeping my bandsaw blade kerf cut to about 1/16 inch, I cut one piece of ½-inch stock and one piece of ⅝-inch stock from each offcut of 1¼-inch planking, giving me about 1/32 inch of material left to plane off the back of each strake. This means only a ⅛-inch loss of wood. You can set up the ripping jig so anyone can feed the stock through the bandsaw.

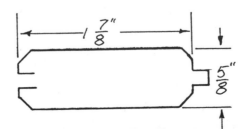

Diagram 15.4

Plywood Bulkheads

Most boatbuilders choose to use plywood for bulkheads because of its high strength-to-weight ratio. Plywood bulkheads also go in quickly, since they start with large single pieces of wood rather than several dozen smaller pieces. For small yachts, especially 18- to 22-footers, ⅜-inch to ½-inch plywood can be used for both structural and nonstructural bulkheads to keep weight down and strength up. For boats over 22 feet, however, plywood might not be the best choice. Below are the pros and cons of using plywood for bulkheads on larger boats.

PLYWOOD BULKHEADS

Pro

There are no joints, so it is easy to sand and finish.

You can cover it with vinyl or ConTact-type paper.

There will be little or no overall swelling movement compared to the tongue-and-groove method.

Con

It is difficult to fit plywood bulkheads tightly to bilge stringers, sheer clamps, and other elements. All edges have to be sealed to reduce the chance of delamination.

Fir-plywood bulkheads, even with exterior glue, quite often delaminate in the bilges because fir is a softwood. It shrinks a lot when dry, swells when wet.

The highest-quality, marine-grade, hardwood-core plywood should be used for bulkheads because it is less prone to this shrink/swell syndrome that stresses glue joints. Marine-grade plywoods, such as Bruynzeel brand, are very expensive.

Large, wide plywood bulkheads have to be scarfed or butted on butt blocks. This means extra labor.

Though plywood bulkheads are quick to fit initially, the later finishing/sealing of endgrain and the capping of raw edges makes these bulkheads as labor-intensive as the build-in-place type.

If you make a major mistake in fitting a plywood bulkhead, you could spoil an expensive sheet of material.

It is hard to get a smooth, nongrainy finish on softwood ply, so you must use the more expensive hardwood or paper-covered grades.

The outside skin on teak- or mahogany-veneered plywood is quite thin (usually about 1/32-inch). You can sand right through this veneer if you have to remove any construction dents or scratches in preparation for a clear finish.

Capping plywood bulkheads is more difficult than capping laminated-in-place ones (diagram 15.3).

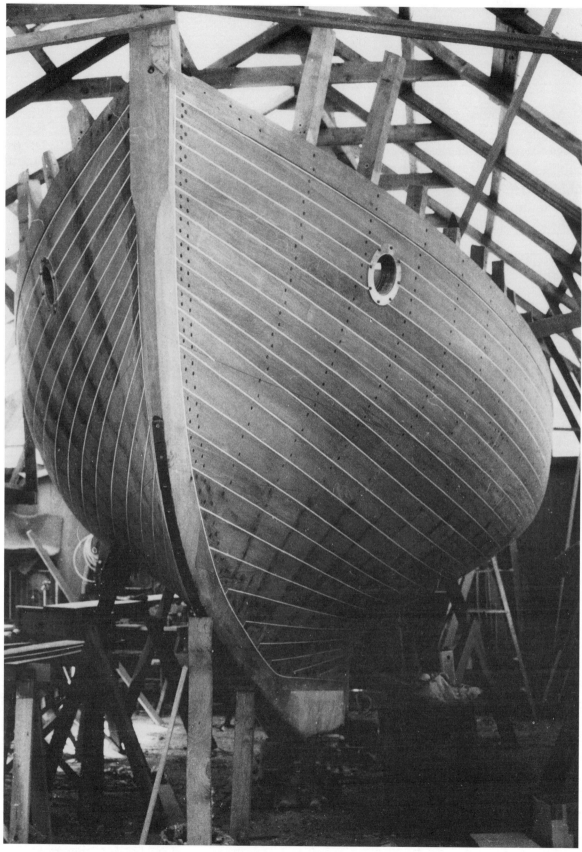

16.1

16. LINING OUT

The term *lining out* is used to describe the process of deciding on the width and location of each plank on a hull before planking commences. A good lining-out job will help you find the least difficult places to position planks so you can minimize twist and the possibility of breakage. It also will reduce the amount of scrubbing (plank hollowing) you will have to do. On hull forms such as this one, proper lining out can eliminate stealers and the need to steam planks. (Even the best lining-out job, however, cannot eliminate the need for steaming planks for the hull of a beamy double-ender, especially if it is lapstrake construction.)

With a good lining-out job, it is possible to have three separate planking crews working simultaneously on an 80-foot vessel—one crew to work the topsides, another to work on the area from the garboards to the tuck of the transom, and the third to fit the strakes between the tuck plank and the topsides.

Photo 16.1 The final bonus of a good lining-out job will be topside planks that fit right, look right, and are of equal widths, tapering proportionately toward the bow and the stern. This procedure is only discussed briefly in the boat-building books I have read, and those authors usually consider it "too difficult for amateurs." I don't agree. Quite often, home builders are more willing to take the time to line out every plank to be sure the final results are of professional quality.

Photo 16.2 The first thing I do as I line out the hull is determine where the pivotal tuck plank naturally lies on the hull. This plank starts aft, where the tuck of the transom, or the reverse curve, joins the sternpost.

16.2

16.3

Photo 16.3 This photo, along with photo 16.2, shows the hull planked up to this tuck strake. Notice that the tuck strake has a gentle, easy twist from forward to aft. It goes in the middle of the lower reverse curves of all the frames. It should be lined out so that the twist from aft to amidships (which in this case is 40 degrees) has as gradual a transition as possible. This gradual twist will make it easier to bend on the planks without steaming or breaking them. As shown in diagram 16.1, the tuck plank follows diagonal III quite closely forward but sweeps up from the diagonal aft.

Diagram 16.1

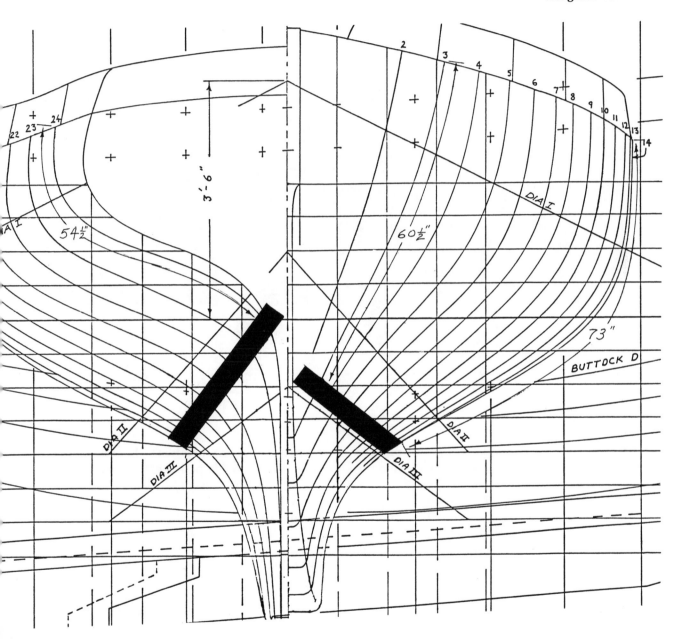

16.4

Photo 16.4 I determined the line of the tuck strake by experimenting with a 4-inch-wide batten and clamped the aft end of the batten in the middle of the tuck curve at the transom. I then adjusted the forward two-thirds of the batten up and down until it lay into the curve near the garboard with a gradual, easy twist and very little edge-set. (Edge-set is discussed in chapter 17.)

As I adjusted the forward part of the batten, I kept checking the girth dimensions (the distance from the decksheer down along the frame to the tuck batten) at F24, F14, and F3. They measured 60½ inches at F3, 73 inches at F14, and 54½ inches at F24. I purposely left the girth at F24 6 inches narrower than at F3. I did this because the plank widths of the topsides along the tight curve of the transom have to be narrowed to 2⅜ inches—for reasons that will be discussed below.

When I was satisfied with the tuck-batten position, I used a felt pen to mark along the batten edge. This provided a future reference point on each of the frames to indicate the eventual top edge of the tuck plank.

Photo 16.5 The next area I lined out was the topsides. I used my fiberglass lofting batten to experiment and find where the topside planks could be fitted most efficiently, keeping in mind that the planks should lie much as the diagonals do. I clamped the batten below the turn of the bilge amidships and below the turn of the transom, then clamped the forward end of the batten up to the stem in a natural sweep. Diagram 16.2 shows the position of this batten. Notice that it looks similar to diagonal I and lays on almost like an intermediate diagonal IA.

16.5

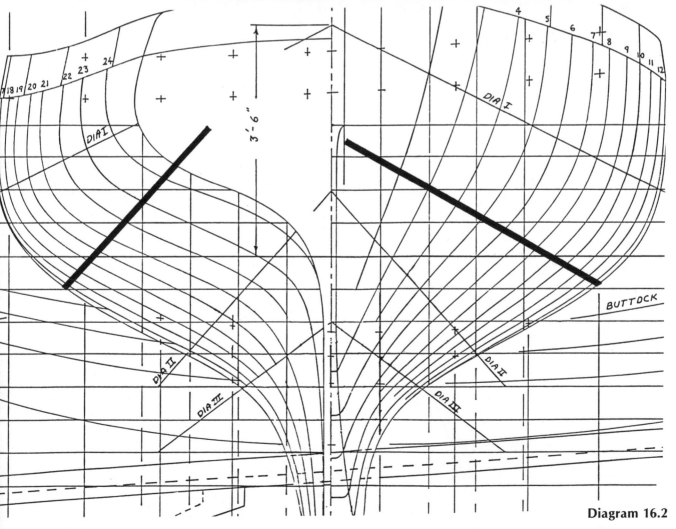

Diagram 16.2

The reason the topside planks are lined out from this batten position is that the turn of the bilge, with its sharp radius, is the hardest area to plank. Compare the topsides on this hull to those on a hard-chined boat, where the flat topside planks fit to flat frame sections. That would be an easy planking job. But since this project means dealing with rounded bilges, it's necessary to think like a barrelmaker. The cooper, like me, has to cope with the all-important problem of scrubbing.

I feel that the maximum amount of wood thickness that should be scrubbed from any plank on any boat is ⅛ inch. There are three reasons for this: (1) deep hollowing of planks is labor-intensive; (2) excessive hollowing reduces plank thickness and strength; (3) by sticking to a ⅛ inch maximum, you can plank the whole boat with the same thickness of stock instead of having a second thickness to allow for areas that require more scrubbing. So, since I was fitting flat boards to these rounded topside frames, the amount of frame curve limited the width of the topside strakes.

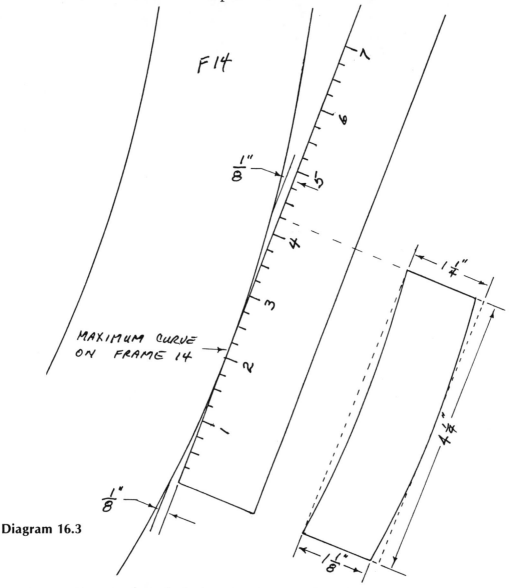

Diagram 16.3

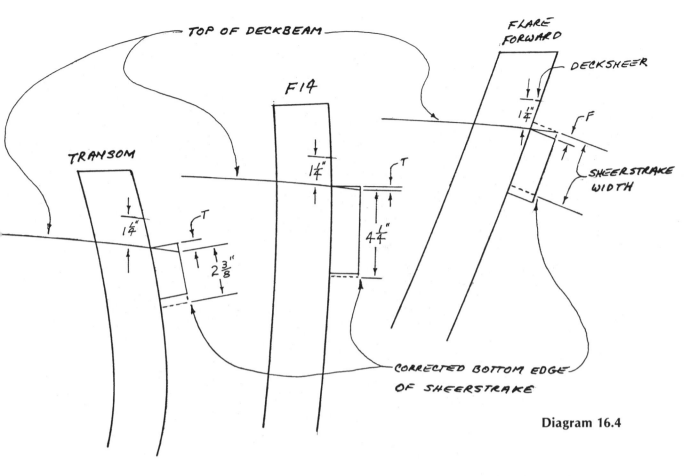

Diagram 16.4

To determine the width of the topside planking, I used a 12-inch ruler as shown in diagram 16.3. I figured which frame had the longest girth measurement and therefore would be the widest point of the topside planks: F14. So I laid the ruler on the roundest part of frame 14, positioning the ruler's lower end so there was a ⅛-inch gap between it and the frame. At 4¼ inches along the ruler, the gap again became ⅛ inch. This meant that at the most curved part of F14, 4¼ inches was the widest plank I could use and still stay within the ⅛-inch scrub limit. Keep in mind that this ⅛ inch of scrubbing is only necessary at the most rounded part of the topsides, near the turn of the bilge. The rest of the topside planks require less hollowing because they go on less curved areas.

I next used this same procedure on the transom frame, laying the ruler on the frame at its roundest area. The greatest planking width possible here with ⅛ inch of scrubbing was 2⅜ inches. (The width of the forward end of the topside planking is not determined by the scrub limit because the sections here are more or less flat and require little scrubbing.)

Next I marked the thickness of the deck down from the decksheer (in this case, 1¼ inches) at F2, F14, and the transom (diagram 16.4). Although each of the topside planks eventually will appear to be the same width at each frame station, it is essential to approach the sheerstrake with care. If the hull you are building has flare or tumblehome, it will affect the bevel on the top edge of the planking where the deck fastens to the sheerstrake. This bevel change varies the width of the sheerstrake, as shown in diagram 16.4.

The top of the deckbeam at the transom has been projected outboard to the top out-board corner of the sheer plank. This corner of the sheer plank eventually will have to be planed off so the covering board will fit flush to the top of the deckbeam and sheerstrake. This cut reduces the outside plank width by the width of the bevel height at T. The dot-ted line below the sheer plank shows the correct "T" addition needed for the lower edge of the sheerstrake to ensure equal-looking widths for all of the topside planks. If there is flare forward on your hull, the problem is reversed, and, as at point F in diagram 16.4, the 90-degree plank edge will end up below the top edge of the deckbeam unless you make an allowance for the bevel. (I have seen a lot of sheerstrakes with wedge-shaped strips glued to the forward top edge to make up for this difference.) On *Taleisin*, the correction at F was about ⅜ inch and at T about ¾ inch. If your hull has more flare or more tumblehome than *Taleisin*, the T and F corrections can become quite large.

The easiest way to compute these corrections is to clamp the lower edge of the deck-beam pattern to the port and starboard frame heads at the underside of the deck mark (i.e., down 1¼ inches from the top of the sheerline). Next clamp a square-edged block—the same thickness as your eventual sheer plank—to the outside edge of the frame so that it touches the bottom edge of the deckbeam pattern. Measure the T and F corrections and write them on the edge of the frame head. It is very important that the flare correction be marked in red pencil above the top of the deckbeam so that when you actually measure (spile) the plank and fasten it in place, the top edge of the plank ends up even with the higher red marks. Otherwise, the flared part of the plank will be shy at the outboard corner and you will need to glue on a wedge to correct for the error. You can compute the T corrections the same way and also penciled them onto the frame edge. This correction eventually will be added to the *bottom edge* of the sheerstrake aft. When you have marked these T and F bevel corrections on all of the frames, you are ready to line out the sheer-strake and then the topsides.

As diagram 16.5 shows, use the plank widths determined by the scrub limit to mark the corrected bottom edge of the sheerstrake onto the frames. Clamp your batten to this set of marks and check carefully to be sure the batten looks fair so that the plank eventu-ally will taper evenly. Then mark the batten position onto the frame edges with a felt pen.

Starting from this corrected bottom-edge mark of the sheerstrake, I scribed arcs 4¼ inches wide at F14 (the maximum possible width within the scrub limit), going down until I was near the batten I had secured under the turn of the bilge. This gave me nine arcs (or nine topside planks) plus a sheer plank. I then adjusted the lining-out batten even with the bottom arc. I used the same procedure at the transom frame. I again started at the lower edge of the corrected sheerstrake and made 2⅜ inch arcs (the widest plank that would fit to the transom with only ⅛ inch of scrubbing) until I again had nine plank widths scribed along the edge of the transom frame, plus the sheer plank with its T cor-rection. I then aligned and clamped the topside lining-out batten to the bottom of the ninth arc.

Forward at the stem rabbet, I lined out nine strakes plus the sheerstrake, using 2⅞-inch arcs down to the topside batten. Although the scrub calculation did not limit the

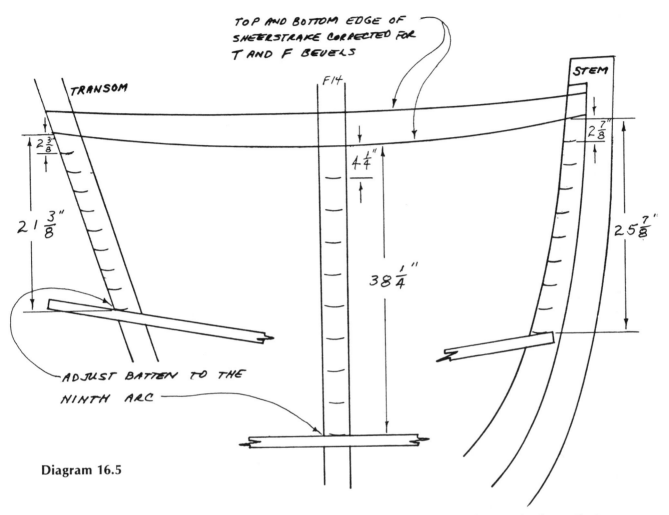

Diagram 16.5

width of planks at the stem, I decided that this plank width not only would fit easily into this area, but also would look nice.

I have found that a nice-looking topside plank generally tapers about 25 to 30 percent from amidships to the forward rabbet and a bit more aft. But it is important to remember that plank ends should not be much narrower than twice their thickness; otherwise, you will not have room for two well-spaced fastenings near the plank end.

At this point I sighted along the topside lining-out batten at the turn of the bilge to see if excessive edge-set had developed. The fiberglass batten curved upward about 4 inches. I felt this was an acceptable amount of edge-set because the downward curve of the sheer amidships is about 4 or 5 inches. (These plank curves diminish as they approach diagonal I in the middle of the topsides.) If, on the other hand, I had found more than 5 inches of edge-set, I would have readjusted the lining out of my plank widths because I would not have been able to spile the topside planks out of boards less than 12 inches wide. So, as a rule of thumb, if your topside lining-out batten is straight and has no edge-set, fine. If it is edge-set no more than 4 or 5 inches up or down, don't worry, as this variance can be taken up in the planks below the topsides. If it has more than 4 or 5 inches of edge-set, rescribe the width of the topside planks to reduce it. If you plan to fit a shutter plank, try to keep the batten free of edge-set. A shutter is easier to spile if the lower edge of the lower topside plank is straight (see chapter 17).

If you reduce the width of each plank aft by ¼ inch, you could raise the girth at the aft end of the batten by 2¼ inches (¼ inch times nine planks). The girth at the bow could be reduced 3⅜ inches by reducing each plank ⅜ inch. This would reduce the 'midship, upward edge-set of the lining-out batten to bring it within the acceptable limit of a 3- or 4-inch curve. Always keep in mind that the planks at F14 and the Transom are made as wide as practical, while incorporating the ⅛ inch scrub limit. The planks on these shapely sections can be reduced in width to suit the lining-out maneuvers as long as they remain close to twice their thickness, but they cannot be made wider or else deep scrubbing will be required to get the planks to fit the frame curves.

Diagram 16.6

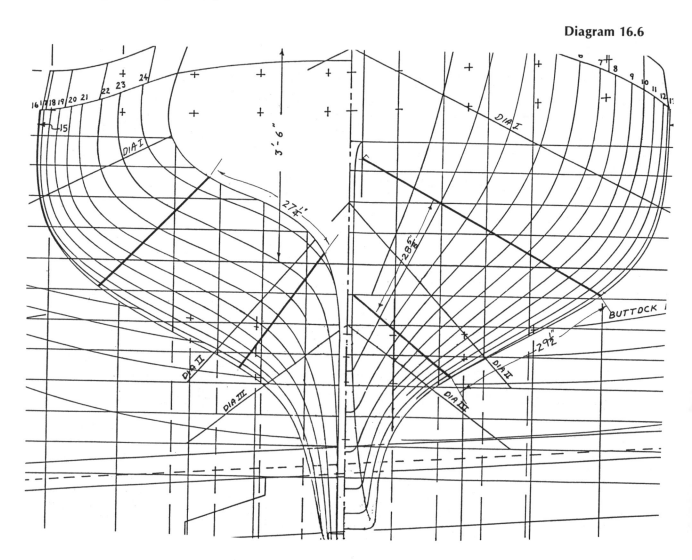

Diagram 16.6 shows the topside batten marked in, with an acceptable amount of edge-set and a fair look to it. The tuck plank is marked on the frames. In this diagram, all that is left to consider before starting to plank is the section between these two areas. This is usually the easiest area to plank on a hull of this type because it has relatively flat sections. The only area with any amount of frame curve is just above the tuck of the transom. When I measured the girths for this area, they were as follows: transom, 27¼ inches; F14, 29½ inches; and F3, 28⅝ inches. So I knew the planking for this area would be almost parallel and about as easy to lay on as the boards on a fence (when compared to the topside or garboard area). They would have little edge-set and could be cut out of relatively narrow boards. This had been my goal when I previously adjusted the forward end of the tuck-plank batten to make sure the girth at F3 was 6 inches longer than the transom-girth measurement (diagram 16.1). This batten maneuver accounted for the fact that the planks in the topsides at the transom would be narrower than the forward end of the topside planks.

When you are lining out for the planks in the middle area of a hull, keep in mind the ⅛ inch scrub limit. If you wish, planks below the waterline can be an inch or two wider than the topside planking and parallel all along their width, because they stay wet and swollen. In contrast, the topside planking should be kept fairly narrow to give extra caulking seams that can compensate for any shrinkage or swelling caused by changing humidity. The following table gives the maximum recommended widths for planking at various areas on various hull lengths.

RECOMMENDED PLANKING WIDTHS (IN INCHES)

	25-Foot Hull	30-Foot Hull	40-Foot Hull
Topsides	3½	4½	5
Flat sections below waterline	4½	5½	6
Garboards—broads or stealers	12	14	16
Sheerstrake, including deck thickness	4½	6	6½

I decided to plank *Taleisin* from the garboards up to the sheerstrake, eliminating a shutter plank. The reasons for this are discussed in chapter 17. The more usual method—and possibly the easiest progression for the inexperienced builder—is to plank the topsides first, then the garboards, working upward to place a shutter plank between the topsides and the bottom in the flattest (minimum-twist) area of the hull. If you decide to do the topsides first, I suggest you go to the trouble of lining out each plank, then check each line with a full-length batten to guarantee fairness. This is more lining-out work than an old pro would bother to do, but it will give you topsides that look good (remember that these seam lines are what most dockside bystanders see first). It also will guarantee that you do not have excessive edge-set, so you can cut your planking from boards of reasonable width.

As you do this extra lining out, look carefully at the batten from all angles and from as many different heights as possible. Get a ladder and place it as far away as possible from the hull to sight along the batten. If you are not satisfied with the fairness, adjust the batten until it looks right. You may have to rescribe some of the topside frame girths a couple of times, but the adjustments will rarely be more than ⅛ inch per plank spacing. Work from top to bottom and continue fairing up and marking each plank onto the frames on each side of the hull. When you get down to the tenth and last topside plank, if the batten looks fair and the scrub limits discussed earlier have been met, you are ready to cut the first plank.

If, on the other hand, you feel comfortable about planking without lining out each topside strake, it is still important to transfer to the other side of the hull the locations of the top of the tuck strake and the bottom of the topside planking.

I worked the starboard side of the hull first because I had more room on this side of the boat and so could stand farther back to check for fairness. After I was satisfied with my lining out, I transferred the reference marks to the port side by measuring the girths for each point at the stem, at F14, and at the transom. That way, I could be sure that inaccuracies did not creep into the port-side planking as work progressed.

CONSTRUCTION TIMES FOR CHAPTER 16

Larry: Lining out hull	17 hours
Lin: Assisting with hull line-out	3 hours
Totals to date: Larry	1960 hours
Lin	360 hours

17. PLANKING

Section 1: Garboards

After I had lined the hull into three separate planking areas, my next step was to line out the individual planks from the garboard up to the tuck line. As diagram 17.1 shows, the girth measurement for this area at F21 is 30¾ inches more than the girth measurement at F3. Some builders prefer to use stealers to equalize this difference in girth measurements, but I prefer using triangular planks that are wider aft than forward. They are not only easier to install than stealers but also stronger, as the following photo sequence shows.

17.1

Photo 17.1 Once again, I like to wrap my 4-inch-wide spiling batten into various positions in the area I will be planking in order to observe the twist and bend necessary for each plank. The narrower lower batten in this photo represents the top edge of the garboard plank, which I have decided will be 13 inches wide aft, tapering to a 1¼-inch-wide nib (hood end). The garboard plank therefore will be about 10 feet 3 inches long.

The wider batten is at the approximate top edge of the third plank, or what is called the second broad. Both the garboard and the two broads are wider at their aft ends so that as I plank up to the tuck line, the top edge of each plank becomes closer and closer to parallel to the tuck line.

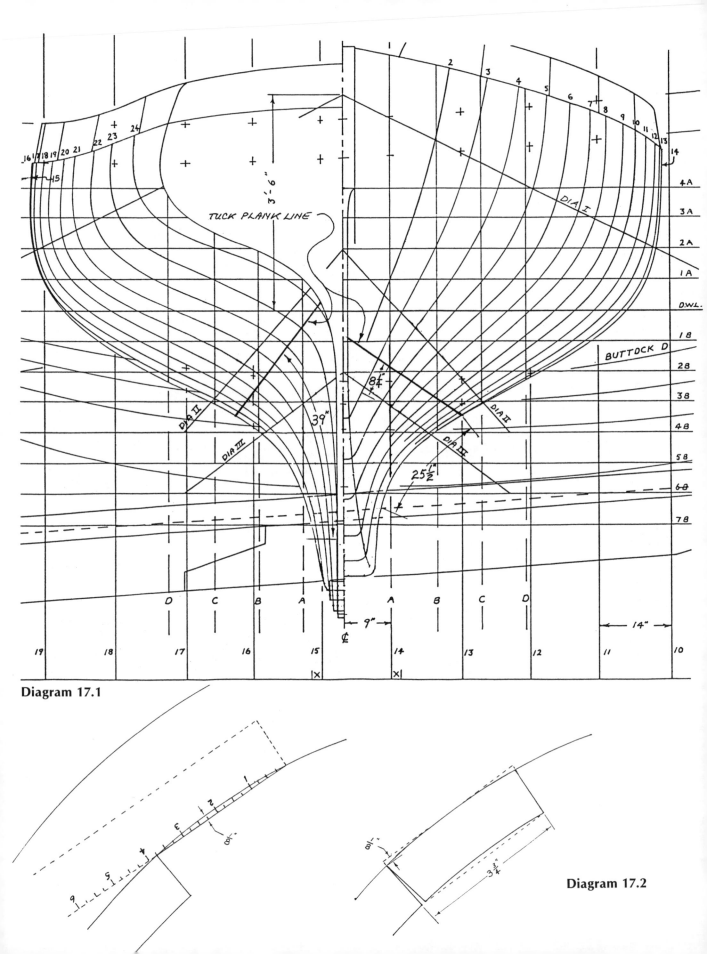

Diagram 17.1

Diagram 17.2

17.2

17.3

Photo 17.2 I am measuring the girth from the tuck line down to the top of the 4-inch broad batten. Since the girths between the wide batten and the tuck line are within an inch or two of parallel, I know that this planking scheme will let me gain most of the 30¾-inch difference in girths before I get near the tuck line. As I near the tuck line, therefore, I can narrow the planks to about 3½ to 4 inches aft.

Photo 17.3 The narrower planks above the garboard and the broads are easier to twist and bend into the lower curves of the hull. The exact width of each of these strakes is governed by the scrub limit, just as with the widths of the topside planks, but here the inside of the plank is rounded, not hollowed, as diagram 17.2 shows.

Once again, an uninitiated builder might like to line out and mark for each plank in this area before going ahead with the garboard.

17.4

17.5

Photo 17.4 After I have planned the locations of lower planks, the rabbet area has to be faired up to the frames so the planks will fit nicely to the faying surfaces of the backrabbet and to the frames. It is also important that the outside of the planking fit flush and even to the keel and transom knee all along the rabbet line. (This is where you could create errors by cutting the rabbet to exact depths before you start to plank.)

The tools I used to fair up the rabbet are all shown in this photo. They include a 2-inch slick; a 1¾-inch chisel; the rabbet plane, which is behind the batten; a ¹⁄₁₆-inch convex-soled wooden scrub plane; the 1¼-inch planking gauge; and a couple of nice, straight ¼-inch-by-1⅛-inch pine battens.

Photo 17.5 The garboard has been lined out so that it is 13 inches wide at the aft end. As diagram 17.3 shows, the vertical curve of the rabbet area is ⅛ inch in 13 inches. I will be rounding the inside of the 1¼-inch-thick plank by ⅛ inch, so some areas of the plank will be only 1⅛ inches thick (diagram 17.3a). The backrabbet on the transom knee must therefore be left ⅛ inch oversize so the scrubbed plank ends up flush with the outside of the deadwood. In diagram 17.3b, the black area denotes the ⅛ inch of wood I had to leave on the backrabbet to make sure that the planks would end up even with the backbone timbers.

The lower section of the rabbet where the garboard fits is cut to 1¼ inches net. This is done because here the garboard fits to sections that are almost flat. So, once again, leave the rabbet ¼ inch oversize until you see if there is any area near it with curvature.

Because of the irregularities caused by scrubbing, I only fair up enough rabbet area to fit each round of planking. It is also less boring to do it bit by bit than to fair up the port and starboard rabbets as one long job. This fairing job near the rabbet went easily on *Taleisin*. I did not need wedges, nor did I have to glue on strips to fair the hull. This was the reward for lofting in the extra diagonal—DIA IV on the body plan—to fair this area.

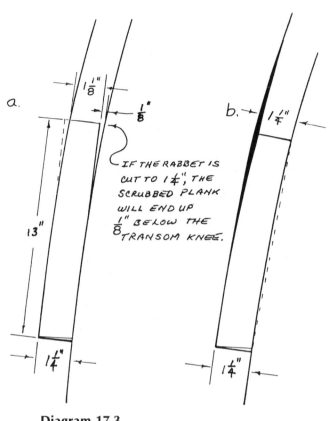

a.

$1\frac{1}{8}"$

$\frac{1}{8}"$

IF THE RABBET IS
CUT TO $1\frac{1}{4}"$, THE
SCRUBBED PLANK
WILL END UP
$\frac{1}{8}"$ BELOW THE
TRANSOM KNEE.

$13"$

$1\frac{1}{4}"$

b.

$1\frac{1}{4}"$

$1\frac{1}{4}"$

Diagram 17.3

17.6

17.7

Photo 17.6 When the batten lies in fair and is at its required depth, I mark a pencil line on the transom-knee backrabbet to indicate that the area is ready for planking. I check and mark for horizontal fairness about every 3 inches.

Photo 17.7 The ¼ inch of wood I left next to the rabbet line can now be planed square to the rabbet line itself. The pointy depth-gauge holes that I used to determine the thickness of the rabbet in this area are now paying off by helping me judge how much wood should be left on the backrabbet to compensate for plank scrubbing. The dotted section in the photograph shows the drill holes where I have left extra wood in the backrabbet to take into account the scrubbing of the top aft corner of the garboard.

17.8

Photo 17.8 My spiling batten is shown tacked in place with a vertical extension nailed to its aft end. The metal pointer of my scribe is resting on the rabbet seam edge. I scribed a penciled arc onto the batten at each frame station and every 6 inches along the rabbet line of the transom knee. The aft lower corner of the batten should have two arcs scribed about 1 inch from the corner, and a couple of more arcs should be drawn at 90 degrees to the rabbet of the stern knee. If you keep the scribe locked at a constant width—in this case, about 1¾ inches—the arcs transferred to the batten will be parallel to the rabbet seam. It pays to record this scribing width somewhere on your batten for reference in case you drop the scribe and break the pencil point or otherwise change this measurement.

Photo 17.9 I removed the spiling batten and placed it on a teak board about 11 feet long and 16 inches wide. Before I lay out a plank, I place a straightedge across the board. If there is more than ¹⁄₃₂ inch of hollow, I use the concave side of the board for the outside of the plank. This hollow, faced the correct way, reduces the amount of rounding that I will have to do to the inside of the plank. Then I consider the possibility of getting another plank out of the offcut part of the board. In this particular case, I found that with a bit of planning, both triangular garboards could be cut from the same plank.

If you look closely at the near end of the board in this photo, you will see some swirly grain, which caused a hollow about ¹⁄₁₆ inch deep. The rest of the plank was flat. The spiling batten, which shows the garboard for the starboard side of the hull, was positioned over the concave area of the board to take advantage of this natural hollow. The width of the garboard was reduced about ⅜ inch to ensure that I could cut the two planks from this single board. I left the grain of the teak running parallel to the top edge of the garboard. With the grain running diagonally to the rabbet seam, there is less chance of the fastenings causing the plank to split along its length (diagram 17.4).

I have drawn a straight line ⅛ inch from the rough-sawn edge at the left-hand side of the board. I wanted to be sure the top edge of the

17.9

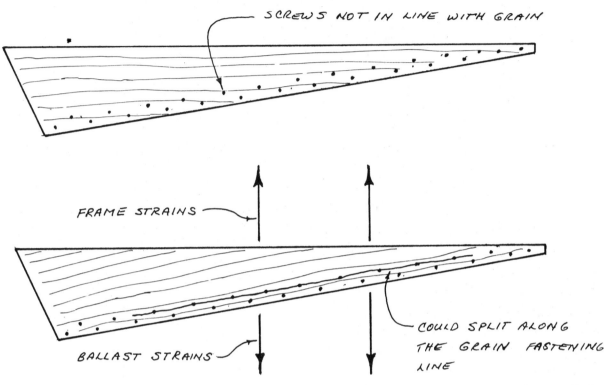

SCREWS NOT IN LINE WITH GRAIN

FRAME STRAINS

BALLAST STRAINS

COULD SPLIT ALONG THE GRAIN FASTENING LINE

Diagram 17.4

garboard plank was straight and square to simplify the spilling of the next plank. So I adjusted my spiling batten to this top-edge line to give me a plank that was, in this case, 13 inches wide aft and 1¼ inches wide at the nib end. To determine the width of the garboard, I measured down from the top-edge line and penciled in a 13-inch mark that aligns with the aftermost arc on the spiling batten. I set the scribe point on the aft arc and slid the batten up and down until the scribe's pencil point was even with the 13-inch mark. Then I clamped the aft end of the spiling batten to the plank. Next I adjusted and clamped the forward end in the same way to give a 1¼-inch-wide nib. After the batten was secured, I could spile the various arcs on the batten to the plank. I removed the spiling batten and connected the arcs on the plank by tacking a narrow batten at the apex of each arc. This gave me a line that is the same shape as the rabbet line where the plank eventually would fit. I

tacked the batten in position with tiny nails, which I placed on the offcut side of the arcs. (I put the nails ⅛ inch from the edge of the batten. That way, the eventual kerf of the saw cut eliminates the nail holes.) I penciled in the line of the plank and sawed it out exactly to the line.

A Skil 77 is my favorite tool for cutting out planks because I can cut them right on the sawhorses. You can also cut planks with a 2 hp, 10-inch table saw or a bandsaw with a 1-inch-wide blade.

After I had cut the first garboard, I planed it to fit the rabbet line at a bevel that would produce a ³⁄₃₂-inch-wide caulking seam. The rule of thumb for planking-seam widths is that you should have an opening of about ¹⁄₁₆ inch per inch of plank thickness. (A detailed, step-by-step photo sequence of fitting a plank and cutting the caulking seam appears in section 3 of this chapter.)

17.10

17.11

Photo 17.10   The short, triangular garboard has several advantages, including the fact that it is easier for one person to handle. It is in effect, a stealer/garboard that helps to achieve parallelism to the tuck strake with the least amount of labor. And, as this photo shows, it fits into a relatively flat area aft with a minimum of bending or twist. Most of the twist in this style of garboard is forward, where the narrower, tapered end will conform more easily than will a wider, longer, more parallel garboard. Remember that you'll save a lot of time and effort if your planks can be fitted without resorting to steam torture.

If, instead of using a short, wide, triangular garboard, you used a full-length one that started at F22 and went up to F6, the plank would have had to twist from almost vertical (3 degrees outboard at F22) to 28 degrees outboard at F6. The triangular board on *Taleisin* only had to twist from 3 degrees at F22 to 18 degrees at F14.

Photo 17.11   I first clamped the plank in place aft, then clamped the more flexible forward nib end. All of the scrubbing adjustments for the garboard have to be made to the inside of the plank, where it fits to curved parts of the dead-wood and to the frames.

Photo 17.12   The width of the nib end of the plank should be no less than the thickness of the planking. This is wide enough so that the nib-end fastening should not have any tendency to split the plank.

The next plank has to have a hood or hook on it to fit to this nib end. In effect, the backrabbet acts as a butt block for this nib and hook. In my experience, this means less work and is an easier technique than putting in a separate stealer above a full-length garboard. The forward end of the stealer would require a butt block, since it is poor practice to have the ends of stealers land on frames. There would be only enough room for a single fastening on the frame at the forward end of the stealer.

Besides eliminating the need for stealers and cutting down the twist in the garboard plank, the lining-out method I used meant that my first three rounds of planking could all be full length.

Before you fasten the garboard in place, trace around it onto the board you have selected for the port garboard. If you forget to do this, you will have to spile separately for each plank for each side of the hull. In my normal

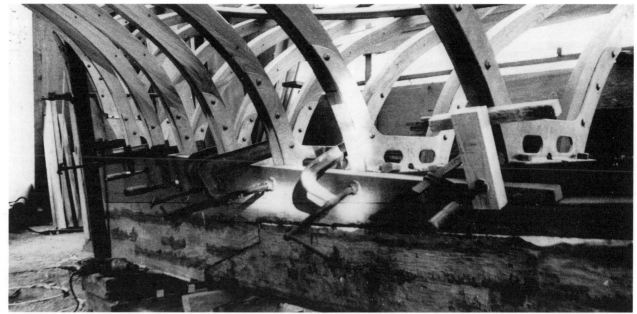

rush to put on the planking, I occasionally forget to do this.

When I was satisfied with the fit of the garboard to the frames, the backbone timber, and the inner edge of the plank, as well as at the rabbet-line caulking face, and once the seam opening was about 3/32 inch wide along the outside of the garboard seam, I was ready to fasten it in place.

Photo 17.13 I used 2¼-inch-long number 14 silicon-bronze flathead wood screws. I like to use number 14 screws for planking on boats from 28 to 40 feet because the screw head is slightly smaller than a ½-inch wood-plug hole. Large-diameter wood-plug holes weaken the outside of a bent plank, and sometimes you will see a fracture starting along a plank face where they have been used. On larger boats—40 to 45 feet—I tend to space these screws closer rather than use a number 16 or 18 screw, which would need a 5/8-inch wood-plug hole. For *Taleisin*, with her 1¼-inch-thick planks, I set the wood plug ¼ inch deep. This allows for up to ⅛ inch of scrubbing as I fair the outside of the hull, yet the remaining plug will still be about 3/32 inch deep, the thinnest-size plug that will stay glued in place. By using a 2¼-inch-long screw with a ¼-inch-deep counterbore hold, the screw is still holding onto 1 inch of the plank thickness and the threads go into the backrabbet 1¼ inches, which is enough to get a good, secure grip.

To make sure I didn't foul any of the through-bolts in the backbone assembly as I drilled for screws, I marked bolt positions along the backbone, outside of the rabbet line, with a felt pen.

The screws holding the garboard to the keel timber should be staggered to minimize in-line splitting of the backrabbet. Space the screws about 4 to 5 inches apart—closer if there is a quick twist to the plank.

The garboards literally fell into place. Fairing up the rabbet, plus cutting, fitting, and fastening both garboards in place, took 14 hours. Clamping the nib ends was easy; in fact, I could tighten the clamps that held it with two fingers, so there was no question of needing the assistance of steam.

17.14

17.15

Section 2: The Broads

Photo 17.14 The next two planks are called broads and are neither remarkable nor difficult to handle. They usually can be made wider than the tuck planks above them. In my lining out, I made *Taleisin*'s two broads wider aft to help equalize the girth measurements relative to the tuck line.

The aft end of the spiling batten is marked to show the location of the inclined rabbet line for the broad. (Note the limber holes cut under the lower outboard corner of F21 and its bronze floor. Before you secure planking in place over frame heels, check to make sure that each frame heel has proper drainage. it is almost impossible to put in good limber holes after the planking is in place.)

Photo 17.15 The hood (hook end) of the first broad is spiled onto the batten with arcs. Be sure that the angled mark on the batten above the hook is projected directly up from the lower end of the garboard nib. If the seam is too wide between the nib and the hood end, the aft end of the plank at the stern rabbet can be planed to close up the nib seam. But careful spiling can minimize these time-consuming adjustments.

The plank width of 4¼ inches just aft of the nib was transferred from the lined-out marks on the frame to the spiling batten. The aft width was also noted on the batten.

Photo 17.16 Once again, I put the broad plank in place by starting to clamp aft, where the plank is widest. A plank may have to be reclamped in place two or three times (and occasionally four) before the fit is satisfactory. Planks for boats that are being built to a contract price usually get one or two fittings maximum. Getting perfect fits to the frame and backrabbet—along with parallel-looking 3/32-inch-wide seams that fit tight inside the hull—may be a bit time-consuming at first. But at the risk of sounding preachy, I'd like to say that if you always start out going for good fits, it becomes a habit and your speed will increase. These fine fits will be a source of satisfaction as you build as well as later, whenever you are cleaning or painting the bilge.

Photo 17.17 Screws are still necessary to fasten this broad into the backrabbet and the transom knee. Farther forward, I used copper nails through the frames with roves to form rivets.

17.17

17.16

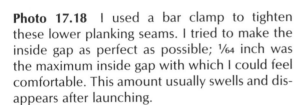

17.18

Photo 17.18 I used a bar clamp to tighten these lower planking seams. I tried to make the inside gap as perfect as possible; 1/64 inch was the maximum inside gap with which I could feel comfortable. This amount usually swells and disappears after launching.

Photo 17.19 Here I am using a Fuller 1/2-inch counterbore on a long twist-drill bit to make pilot holes for the nails. These fastenings should always be staggered as shown to reduce frame splitting. I use the same drill motor for screw and nail pilot holes. I keep the tapered drill bit (with its own counterbore) handy in my apron pouch.

When you clamp the plank in place for the final time, it helps if you reverse the C-clamps so the threaded end is inside the hull and doesn't get in the way of the drill or counterbore.

17.19

17.20

Photo 17.20 Here the next broad is being spiled. I made a tight-fitting pattern for the after angle of this plank, then nailed it to my spiling batten and proceeded as usual.

Photo 17.21 Note the bit of unfairness between the third and fourth planks. I corrected this droop at the nib of the third plank by making the fourth plank about ¼ inch wider in this area. I also compensated by making this fourth plank a bit longer. The top edge of the fourth plank is completely fair.

This bit of unfairness along a seam in the underwater planking is acceptable, but it is visually unacceptable in the topsides. It would have been easier if I had spotted this unfairness before I fastened the third plank in place. I could have simply planed off the lump.

17.21

Photo 17.22 This area, where the keel timber joins the forefoot, is a particularly tricky spot. The backrabbet widens quite dramatically at F8. In the transition between the keel and the forefoot, I had to leave the lower backrabbet ⅛ inch high to account for scrubbing. The nib end of the plank in the photo should be ⅛ inch proud of the keel for about 12 to 14 inches. (This extra wood will be planed off later, when the hull is faired up.)

The fitting of these separate hood ends is easier in the long run than fairing up, fitting, and steaming a long garboard into place. Good fits are more likely when you are fitting the individual hood ends into the lower rabbet. Tight fits minimize movement between the planks and the backrabbet.

The grain where the forefoot joins the keel runs in opposing directions. I slicked, planed, or scraped across the grain at the joint area to fair this section of the backrabbet.

17.22

Photo 17.23 I use the 1¼-inch planking gauge to check the depth at the rabbet line. Once again, extra wood is left on the backrabbet to compensate for scrubbing.

Photo 17.24 The spiling batten is in place, ready to pick up the shape of this butted plank. Two arcs are scribed onto the batten at right angles to the butt end of the existing plank. The hood end of the pattern fits to the nib end of the previous plank.

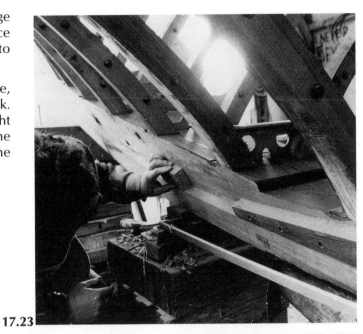

17.23

17.24

17.25

Photo 17.25   There was about a foot between the sawn frames to allow for a long butt block. A long butt block is stronger, just as a long scarf joint is stronger. I have left a ¾-inch limber gap between the ends of the butt block and the two frames so that it is possible to sand and varnish the endgrain of the block as well as the sides of the frames and the planking. Water on the top edge of the butt block drains quickly through these limbers, and they can easily be kept clear of dirt and lint. The block overlaps its two neighboring planks by ⅜ inch so that it is held securely in place. (Measuring and fitting of butt blocks is discussed in section 6 of this chapter.)

Photo 17.26   The first four rounds of planking are now in place. The garboard and two broads are full length. The fourth plank had to have a butt. From here on, each strake was butted at least once; a couple of strakes needed two butts.

17.26

DISCUSSION
Garboards and Broads

Although this method of fitting garboards is not perfect for use on all types of hulls, it usually will work on any that need stealers aft.

If you have an interest in being employed as a boatbuilder, you should learn this method, because if you are assigned to plank a lapstrake (clinker) hull such as the classic 25-foot Folkboat, you could not use stealers and would have to plank from the garboard to the sheer, as this chapter describes. I have spent hundreds of hours prowling around boatyards all over the world when we were off cruising, and I have noted that most of the yachts built in the finest yards in Great Britain and the United States—yards such as Herreshoff, Nevins, Fife, and Nicholson—have been planked with triangular garboard/stealer planks like I used on *Taleisin* and *Seraffyn*.

There is another method you can use to deal with the shim ends on planks below the waterline on a carvel-planked yacht if hook ends seem impractical for some reason. In Landamore's yard in Norfolk, England, I saw planks that were simply nibbed into the stem and forefoot wherever necessary (diagram 17.5). The proportions of the nib were about the same as those used for deck nibs into covering boards or nib strakes. This is a bit more labor-intensive than using hood-ended planks, but it is fine boatbuilding practice. It could be used in a repair situation where you are required to fix damaged shim ends on planks. (You do, however, need a fairly wide cutwater and backrabbet to use this repair trick.)

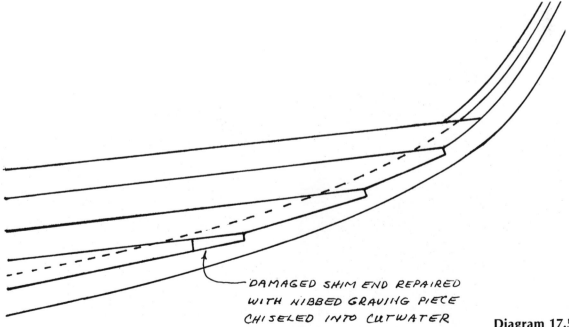

DAMAGED SHIM END REPAIRED
WITH NIBBED GRAVING PIECE
CHISELED INTO CUTWATER

Diagram 17.5

SECTION 3: Fitting the Tuck Plank

Step-by-Step Details of Fitting a Carvel Plank

Fitting a plank to a round-bilged hull with reverse turns below the transom is considered by many to be one of the most difficult tasks of wooden boat building. I feel this is within the skills of anyone who can build a fair framework, but it does require patience and attention to detail. So in order to dispel (I hope) the concerns of potential builders, this section goes into step-by-step detail about the fitting of a single plank. I chose the tuck plank for detailed study because that particular carvel plank was the most challenging one on *Taleisin*: It jointed into the sternpost rabbet for the lower part of its width and mitered into the lowest transom plank above that. It also had as much twist as any other plank on the hull.

17.27

Photo 17.27 It is easier to fit the aft part of the tuck strake first, because you can fit the plank to the transom and sternpost by sliding it slightly aft until it fits. Then you can cut off the butt end midway between the appropriate frames at its forward end.

Once again, leave extra wood on the backrabbet to allow for the scrubbing of the plank.

17.28

Photo 17.28 As shown here, the rabbet line bisects the transom-planking cutout. A scraper is about the only tool that can get into this awkward spot.

Photo 17.29 The rabbet seam is chiseled square to the outside of the sternpost.

Now I have glued and screwed a block to the side of the sternpost to increase the width of the backrabbet where the tuck plank lands. This blocking allows room for a wider pattern of screws to hold the plank firmly into the sternpost. This blocking would be less important if there were no twist in or near the plank end.

My pencil is pointing to the seasoning check that runs along the grain of the sternpost. This check, though relatively long, is quite shallow. It will not affect the caulking seam because the cotton will be driven into the lower third of the seam.

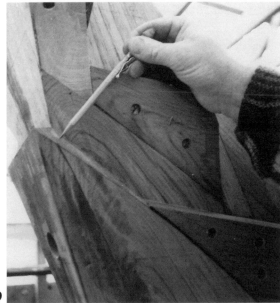

17.29

When the rabbet at the tuck area and all of the frames are faired up, check the previous plank's edge at the butt-block area. Lay a short batten (about 6 feet long) on the top edge of the butt joint to be sure it is fair. If it is unfair, true up the plank edge at the joint with a chisel and a rabbet plane before you spile the tuck plank. This butt area is one spot where small plank humps often develop. They may protrude only 1/16 inch, but they will show and will cause fitting problems later if they are not corrected.

17.30

Photo 17.30 When you lay your spiling batten in place against the frames, it should lie flat. The spiling batten in this photo does not. Its right-hand side is flared away from the frames, which indicates I have let some edge-set creep in as I sprung the batten in place.

17.31

17.32

17.33

Photo 17.31 For accurate spiling, the batten should lie on all of the frames evenly, as it does here.

Photo 17.32 Pencil marks—to indicate the sweep of the previous plank edge—are arced onto the spiling batten. The angled area at the rabbet aft is also indicated by arcs top and bottom. The scribe is held at a 90-degree angle to the caulking seams.

Photo 17.33 After being sure I have made arcs for each frame and the appropriate butt positions, I remove the spiling batten and adjust and clamp it onto the board so that the arcs at both ends and the middle of the batten will lie on the board. I then check to be sure the board is wide enough all along its length to give me the plank I need. Before I transfer my spiling, I inspect the board for end checks and adjust the spiling batten so that these defects eventually will be cut off. Fastenings, especially screws, can wedge open these innocent-looking checks and cause a serious split in the end of the plank. I also inspect for flatness across the board; in this case, the hollow, if any, is on the outboard side of the plank.

17.35

Photo 17.34 Now I transfer my rabbet-seam arcs to indicate the angled cutoff for the rabbet seam.

Photo 17.35 Now a 1¼-inch cedar batten is tacked to the spiling arcs on the lower edge of the plank. The tiny nails are only ⅛ inch from the edge of the batten, so the holes will be eliminated by the saw cut. (It is best to use a cedar or soft-pine batten for this job because the nails will have less tendency to split the softwood.) The line along this batten could end up slightly unfair. *Do not* adjust and fair the batten. It is necessary to stick to the line indicated by your spiling arcs; otherwise, the spiled edge of the plank will not fit the previous plank edge.

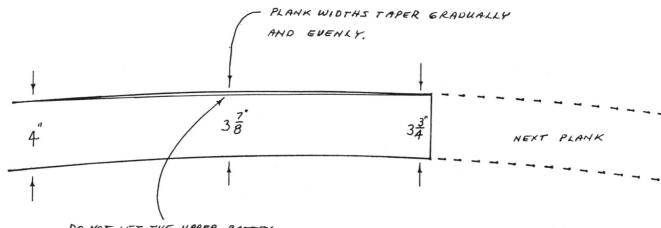

PLANK WIDTHS TAPER GRADUALLY AND EVENLY.

4"

$3\frac{7}{8}$"

$3\frac{3}{4}$"

NEXT PLANK

DO NOT LET THE UPPER BATTEN FLATTEN OUT, OR UNFAIRNESS WILL DEVELOP AT THE BUTT BLOCK

Diagram 17.6

17.36

Photo 17.36 The width of the plank (determined by the lining-out marks on the edges of the frames) is now transferred to the board in three or four places. I spring the batten to these width marks and check for fairness, especially at the butted end of the plank. As diagram 17.6 shows, the batten is sprung beyond the plank so it takes a curve that is a natural continuation of the plank curvature forward of the butt block.

Photo 17.37 When I am satisfied that the lines for the plank are correct, I check the saw for squareness, put on safety glasses, and cut to the line. A carbide blade on a 1½ hp Skil 77 is a must, especially with teak planks. I cut exactly to the spiled plank line without removing any of the pencil marks.

Photo 17.38 The saw marks are removed square to the pencil line so that the spiled line (on the outside of the plank) is transferred accurately to the inside of the plank. This is important, as it is the inside edge of the plank that ultimately must fit snugly to the previous plank's inside edge.

Photo 17.39 I pick up the bevel at each frame and transfer it to the correct spot on the outside of the plank. As I do this, I adjust the bevel to account for the caulking seam. (The bevel gauge was adjusted as shown so that the seam opening was about ¹⁄₁₆ inch for the first fitting.) The wooden part of the bevel gauge rests on the edge of the frame at the tuck-plank felt-pen mark that indicates the width of the plank (where my thumb is in this photo). This gave the plank edge bevel at F21, and from here I could simply go over to the plank, held in the bench

17.37

17.38

17.39

vise, and put the bevel directly onto the F21 frame mark. I usually just estimate the bevel gaps as shown in diagram 17.7 and pencil a mark onto the plank face equal to the bevel gap formed by the gauge. This gives a bevel that is close enough for a first fitting, and, as planking progresses and your skills increase, this will give you a completely accurate bevel. If you under-estimate the bevel, you can always plane a bit more bevel onto the plank edge to open the caulking seam before the final fitting.

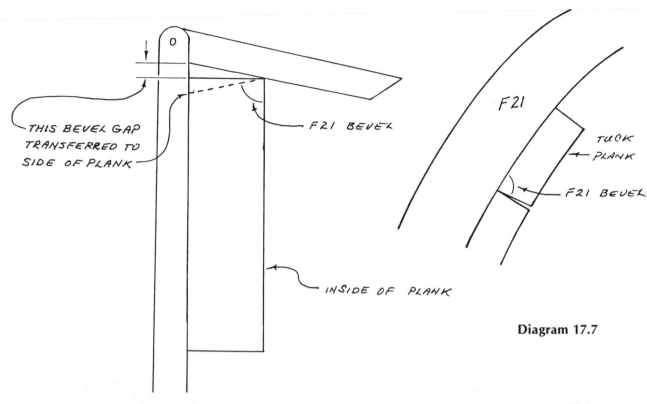

THIS BEVEL GAP TRANSFERRED TO SIDE OF PLANK

F21 BEVEL

INSIDE OF PLANK

F21

TUCK PLANK

F21 BEVEL

Diagram 17.7

17.40

17.41

17.42

17.43

Photo 17.40 Next I rest my middle fingernail on the top edge of the plank and use the nail as a guide for running a pencil line to connect all of the bevel marks. As I move from a wider mark to a narrower one, I gradually adjust the pencil to give a fair transition. With a bit of practice and a bit of erasing, you will get the hang of this sleight-of-hand trick. This is much faster than clamping a batten to the bevel marks on the plank to get the same line.

Photo 17.41 When the bevel line is marked, I also make a ⅛-inch-wide pencil mark all along the spiled edge of the plank at the eventual inside of the seam. This ensures that I don't inadvertently plane off this edge. (The reason for this mark will become apparent soon.) If I need to remove more than ⅛ inch of wood to get the correct bevel, I use a slick, which removes wood faster than a plane.

Photo 17.42 I plane down to the bevel line, as shown in this photo, leaving the ⅛-inch-wide pencil mark untouched at the inboard beveled edge of the plank.

The bevel gauge hanging on the plank is a Lufkin ship's bevel. It has a short brass gauge

arm at one end and a longer arm at the other. It is 12 inches long, so it fits easily into a side pocket on my apron. (Don't put your bevel gauge in your back pocket or you will sit on it accidentally and break the wooden body, as I did with mine.)

You can make a small planking bevel gauge from two old hacksaw blades. Simply rivet the blades together side by side through the existing hole; the bevel arms can be any length you require.

Now, before I hang the plank for the first time, I cut the angled rabbet end and transfer the rabbet-seam bevels to the end of the plank and plane to the bevel line.

Photo 17.43 This is the first fit. I check along the inside seam for spots where daylight shows through. Then I mark any high spots on the outside of the plank to indicate where I will want to plane the edge of the plank when it is back on the bench. I mark the seam opening at the same time, so I can adjust it as required. Diagram 17.8 shows a sample of the pencil marks I put on the outside of the plank.

Diagram 17.8

$\frac{1}{64}$ I $\frac{1}{32}$ I $\frac{1}{64}$ I

$\frac{1}{64}$ O $\frac{1}{32}$ O $\frac{1}{64}$ O

PREVIOUS PLANK SEAM EDGE

17.44

Photo 17.44   I mark the I (inside) and O (outside) adjustments for the rabbet seam aft on the plank.

Photo 17.45   The next notation I make is for the amount of scrubbing (rounding) I will need at each frame. (This photo has the mark 3/32+ near F23—the height of the radius between the middle of the plank and the frame.)

Check the gap at the aft side of the frame. Occasionally the aft side has slightly more or less gap. If so, I record it in pencil on the plank face. It is important to mark these gap dimensions on the plank face next to each side of the frame.

We glued plywood pads to each of our clamps to prevent clamp marks on the frames. This worked far better than using separate pads, even though we had to attach new clamp pads occasionally.

17.45

17.46

Photo 17.46 The first adjustments I make to the plank when it is back on the bench is for the seam corrections. As diagram 17.8 shows, if the inner seam has a high spot that swells from 1/64 inch to 1/32 inch and then back to 1/64 inch, I make a light pencil mark across the high area. A single plane stroke removes the pencil mark—and about 1/64 inch of wood. I then pencil across the area just planed. Next I plane 1/64 inch off the whole high area. A bit of care is needed to finish off both ends of the high spot with a taper—either by taking a thinner cut with the plane or by using a file so no hard spot develops along the plank edge and it remains a fair, constant curve.

When all of the seam high spots are corrected, I repencil the inside of the seam edge with a 1/8-inch-wide pencil mark, as shown in the photo. This wide mark, which we originally put on when the seam was beveled, represents the spiled inner seam where it fits to its adjoining plank. This pencil mark needs to be at least 1/8 inch wide, because some of it will be removed later when the plank is scrubbed.

I then use the same method to correct for the outside seam gap and make the O (outside) adjustments that I marked during the first fitting.

Although this process sounds laborious and slow, it becomes quite simple and quick. I could usually do the first fitting, the marking, and planing (which took 3½ typed pages to describe) in a couple of hours.

Photo 17.47 To round the inner face of the plank, I write the scrub amount in fractions of inches (in this case, 3/32 inch +) on one edge of the plank so I can see the numbers as I plane. Then I make pencil marks on both edges of the plank to indicate this 3/32+ dimension (diagram 17.9). Then I repeat the operation at each frame station. I connect this series of marks along each plank edge using a pencil line with my nail as a guide, just as I did previously for the seam bevel.

17.47

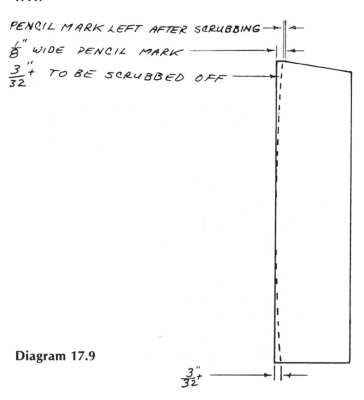

PENCIL MARK LEFT AFTER SCRUBBING

1/8" WIDE PENCIL MARK

3/32"+ TO BE SCRUBBED OFF

Diagram 17.9

3/32"+

17.48

Photo 17.48 A flat-soled jack plane is fine for rounding off planks. I lay my pencil flat in the middle of the board and run a light, full-length mark along the plank. This reminds me not to plane this area, as it should remain net. As I plane off the wood near the edges, I keep checking with a small square to see if the crown is keeping a fair curve, side to side. The scrub dimensions that were marked on the plank edge serve to confirm that I am rounding the plank to the correct scrub dimension.

Photo 17.49 The rabbet-end I and O marks are now planed down and the plank is ready for its second fitting.

Photo 17.50 At this stage, the plank can still be moved slightly forward or aft if required. Even as much as ½ inch of adjustment will not noticeably affect the scrubbing or the seam alignment. I resist cutting the ends off a plank until I am satisfied with all of the other fits.

Photo 17.51 The edge of the plank can be tightened down into position using wedges and our homemade locust clamps to hold together the floors and frames. The ¼-inch-by-1⅜-inch pine batten shown on the edge of the plank protects the caulking seam. The bent nails hold the protective batten in place while I adjust the wedges. I have wrapped the nails with tape to prevent scratches on the inside of the planking. This protective batten should be long enough to rest against two frames. That way, it won't be pushed into the hull as the wedges are driven in.

Photo 17.52 I have driven a second wedge under a planking clamp to tighten a bit of edge-set out of the plank. This wedge goes in a fore-and-aft direction. It is best to cut such wedges out of softwood so they do not damage the sharp corners of your frame. The planking clamps are adjusted with a ratchet and deep socket. When they are not in use, I slide them higher up along the frame and leave them ready for the next plank.

17.49

17.50

17.51

17.52

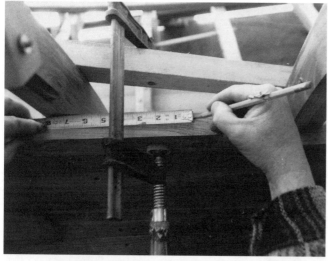

17.53

Photo 17.53 When I feel that the plank fits quite well and needs only minor seam or scrubbing adjustments, I finally mark the butt-block end halfway between the frames—one mark as shown in the photo and another mark equidistant near the lower inside edge of the butt end.

Photo 17.54 For reasons that are discussed in chapter 21, I miter my hull planking to my transom planking. To prepare for this, I now mark the inside of the plank where it first fits to the sternpost.

Photo 17.55 I then lay the 1¼-inch planking gauge flush to the sternpost, the transom frame, and the outboard top corner of the plank. I mark this point on the plank.

Photo 17.56 The next mark is for the lower outboard corner of the plank where it coincides with the top of the transom cutout. I draw a line on the outside of the plank to connect these two marks.

17.54

17.55

17.56

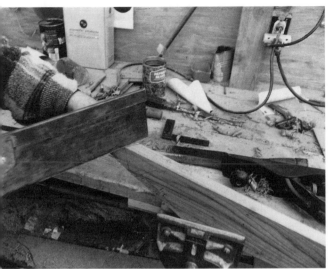

17.57

17.58

17.59

Photo 17.57 Now I remove the plank for the last time, put it in the vise, and make any minor adjustments to the scrubbing or the caulking-seam edges. I finish the aft end of the plank, cutting the pencil line in half if I feel confident that my saw will make a smooth, fair cut. If not, I cut fairly close to the line and then plane or file the end to half of the pencil line. An accurate cut here will simplify fitting the transom planking later.

Photo 17.58 Once again, I halve the pencil line for the butt end of the plank. This end can be square and the seam bevel can be cut onto the end of the plank that will butt up to it.

Photo 17.59 I fair up and square the top edge of the plank, check to be sure all of the scrubbing and seam corrections have been made, then scrape and hand-sand the inside of the plank. (We plan to leave most of the planking visible on the inside of the hull.) It is much easier to sand and clean up the planking while it is on the bench than when it is on the hull.

Finally, I trace the plank shape onto a board for the port-side plank.

Photo 17.60 Now I am ready to fasten the plank in place. The screws that secure the additional rabbet block should be marked so that you can place your planking screws without fouling them. Here I used a 3-inch number 14 screw to fasten through the block and into the sternpost.

17.60

17.61

Photo 17.61 To drive these planking screws, I use a variable-speed, ½-inch chuck drill with a bit made from a round-shank screwdriver. I tighten the chuck only enough so that the bit will slip just before the screw head starts to crush into the wood. This will almost guarantee that you do not twist off or break these screws or split the plank ends by overtightening them. The safest (but slower) way to drive these screws would be to use a brace and screwdriver bit.

17.62

Photo 17.62 These scotch-cut, hard-drawn copper nails (made by Clendenin Brothers—see chapter 23) are designed so they can be driven through a slightly undersize pilot hole without bending. They are about as stiff as a mild steel nail and will drive through a piece of Philippine mahogany without a pilot hole. The nails are square, with slightly rounded corners. Their sides are knurled to increase their grip. The 4-inch-long number 8 nail has a ⅜-inch-wide head (the head size varies just a bit and is slightly ovaled) that drives easily into the ½-inch counterbore hole.

Photo 17.63 The plank is now finished and nailed in place. The knurled nails have enough friction to hold the plank until I finish the whole round of planking. Then I come back and rivet all of the nails at the same time.

If this planking procedure seems unduly difficult, complicated, and time-consuming, keep in mind that I have just finished describing the step-by-step fitting of the most complicated and labor-intensive plank on the whole hull. Most of the other planks will be more straightforward. Many of the moves described here will become almost instinctive as you plank toward the topsides. Your confidence and speed will pick up and you probably will find you can nail or screw most of the planks in place with only two fittings.

17.63

Section 4: Edge-Setting
or
How to Make Narrow Planking Stock Seem Wider

As I spiled planks for the garboard, up toward the beginning of the topsides, I found that the curves I picked up were not extreme. There was rarely more than 2 inches of curve in a 16-foot-long plank. But as I began to plank the topsides, I found that some of the planks had to be quite shapely. Those near the sheerstrake had as much as 4½ to 5 inches of curve in 16 feet. Occasionally I would lay my spiling batten on a beautiful 5-inch-wide, 16-foot-long board and find it was just a bit too narrow to accommodate the spiled curve for the next topside plank (diagram 17.10a). So I would clamp both ends of the spiling batten in place, push gently against the middle of the batten, and edge-bend it into a slight curve. The curved spiling batten let me transfer all of my spiling marks to the board (diagram 17.10b).

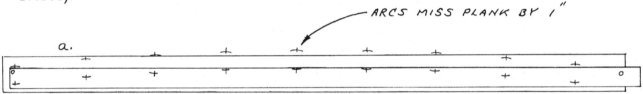

— ARCS MISS PLANK BY 1"

a.

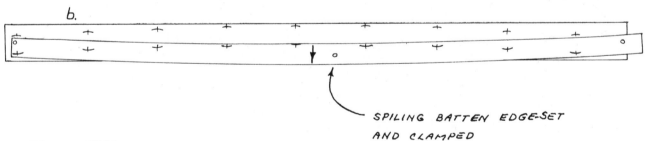

b.

SPILING BATTEN EDGE-SET
AND CLAMPED

Diagram 17.10

Art Clark, a California builder who was seventy-two and had been building boats for fifty-six years, told me that the rule of thumb for edge-setting was ¼ inch in 4 feet of plank length, or 1 inch per 16 feet. This is a good, average, allowable edge-set for 4- to 5-inch-wide planks. Narrower planks (3- or 4-inch maximum width) can be edge-set a bit more—say, 5/16 inch in 4 feet. If you use a spiling batten that is about as wide as your widest topside plank and ¼ inch thick, the reasons for these limits will become apparent as you edge-set the batten. The batten will lie flat on the board until you edge-set it to the limits just mentioned. If you continue edge-setting it, the batten will start to flare up in the middle (diagram 17.11).

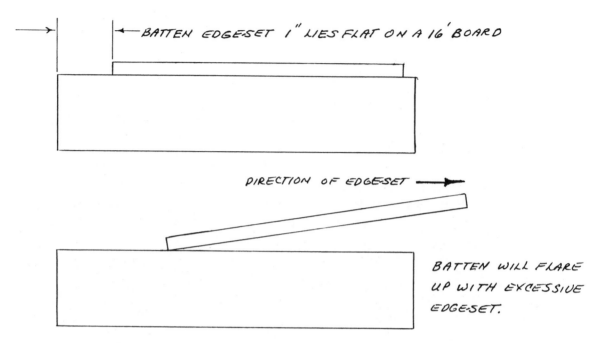

BATTEN EDGE-SET 1" LIES FLAT ON A 16' BOARD

DIRECTION OF EDGE-SET ⟶

BATTEN WILL FLARE UP WITH EXCESSIVE EDGE-SET.

Diagram 17.11

If you spiled a plank from this flared-up, edge-set batten, you would get a plank that wanted to flare away from the frames as it was clamped and forced into position. This flaring would make it hard to hold the edge of the plank flush to the frames. Excessive edge-set creates poor fits between plank and frame. I have also noticed that it is harder to get the seams to fit well on a heavily edge-set plank. Occasionally I have cheated and edge-set my 4-inch-wide spiling batten so that it flared up, away from the board, ½ to ¾ inch on a 16-foot plank. Eventually I was able to get a good fit, but the extra work of clamping, wedging, and seam adjusting made it a labor-intensive job.

Once again, careful lining out will help minimize plank curvature, which in turn minimizes the need for edge-set and the need for excessively wide planking stock with its resultant waste of material.

Section 5: The Forward Tuck Plank

Photo 17.64   To fair the edge of the metal floor and the wood frame next to it, I used my belt sander with a 36-grit production belt. A metal file and a wood plane will also do the job; they are a bit safer to use, but also slower.

The aft nib of the forefoot-to-stem-knee joint created a bit of a water trap, which I fixed by fitting and gluing a graving piece to the nib end so the water from the chain locker would drain aft. I could have gouged a limber hole into the backrabbet below frame 4 to drain the water aft, but I preferred using a graving piece because then the plank ends could be screw-fastened into a wider joint surface at this area.

Photo 17.65   The scraper shown here is a Hyde number 10150. It has an unattractive-looking plastic handle, but that's the only thing wrong with it. The blade can be filed to a convex curve to conform to the curvature of the backrabbet. It also works great for removing scrub-plane marks from a hollow scrubbed plank. I file the scraper edge with a fine file every few minutes as I use it. This gives me maximum cutting efficiency.

The special features of this L.I. and J. White slick include an offset handle and a blade with a fore-and-aft curve. This lifts the handle far enough from the wood so that you don't skin your knuckles as you work. The cutting edge is

17.64

17.65

17.66

17.67

hollow-ground, and its end is round instead of square. The bottom face of the cutting edge is radiused about 1/32 inch so that the corners don't dig in as you slick off wood. The 1/32-inch radiused bottom edge also tends to fit nicely to the slightly curved parts of a backrabbet. If you turn the slick so its blade is upside down, the round nose can work as a shallow gouge.

Photo 17.66 Here is another spiling variation for fitting the end of a plank. Fit a piece of pattern stock to the end of the nib and to the rabbet edge. Then nail it to the spiling batten. Spile the measurements for the rest of the plank from the edge of the previous plank in the normal way.

Photo 17.67 These hood ends are a quite economical use for planking stock. If the plank (which has a 2-inch curve along its length) did not have a hood end, the forward lower part of the board would end up being a fairly wide, wedge-shaped offcut. The hood end utilizes this otherwise-wasted offcut to solve the dilemma of the narrow, shim-ended plank.

Now the batten is adjusted to the board. Once the spiling marks are transferred, I simply trace the pattern to get the correct hood-end shape. The exact length to the butt end of the plank can be determined by marking two horizontal arcs onto the spiling batten. Or you can leave the plank a bit long and cut it off later.

Photo 17.68 Out of about ten wide boards that you rip, one may open up due to internal stress —rather like this one has. One out of a hundred boards will try to do the opposite and close up along the saw cut, causing the plank to split in front of the saw blade. I know of no way to predict when this will happen. This problem will reduce the spiled curve of the plank I am cutting. Usually you can edge-set the plank into place, but if you notice an extensive change as you begin to cut, stop sawing (as I have done in the photo) and respile your plank to the stress-relieved part of the board.

This teak board is an especially long and wide one. By planning and juggling a bit, I was able to lay out both the port and the starboard planks so I could cut them from this single board with almost no waste of material.

Photo 17.69 I sometimes use a bit of plywood to record and transfer the seam bevels to the spiled, squared edge of the plank.

Photo 17.70 A burl like this one, or swirly grain next to a knot, can make the plank edge rip or tear as you plane along the grain. If you plane *across* the grain or *toward* the burl, as shown, you can get most of the wood down to the bevel line. Then you can file or belt-sand the last 1/32 inch exactly to your line.

17.68

17.69

17.70

Once you are sure the nib at the hood end fits nicely, you can overlap the butt end of the plank and clamp it snugly to the previous plank's butt. Then you can mark for the cutoff where the aft end touches. This is the safest way to measure for the length of the plank, but it is a bit slower than marking the butt position directly onto the spiling batten.

Photo 17.72 Each time you fit a port-side plank, check that the girth measurements are working out equal to the starboard side girths. When you trace around the spiled starboard plank to outline the port plank, it tends to come out about two pencil thicknesses wider. Trim off this excess if it accumulates to ⅛ inch, which is just fine for girth measurements.

If you scrutinize the photo, you can see that I have clamped the butt ends of the starboard tuck plank inward about 1⁄16 inch. I do this to help the wood relax so the butt end will have less of a tendency to spring outboard after the plank ends are fastened in place by the butt-block rivets.

Photo 17.71 Fitting planks singlehanded is easier if you rig a line with an adjustable clove-hitch loop. The loop holds the far end of the plank at about the right height so that you can clamp the forward end and then work aft, clamping the rest of the plank into position. (A rolling hitch would be a better knot to use with heavier planking.)

Section 6: Fitting a Pair of Butt Blocks

Butt blocks should be positioned in areas where there is little or no plank twist. If the butt ends of the plank must be twisted by more than $\frac{3}{16}$ inch to get them to fair up, you will find it is damned hard to pull the ends into the butt blocks, even with clamps and bolts. If I have doubts about a butt-block position, I clamp a 6-foot-long, 4-inch-wide batten to the frames and eyeball the amount of local twist. If it looks excessive, I relocate the butt to another, less difficult spot.

Photo 17.73 The plank ends here are ideal: no twist and little bending. The joint doesn't even need a clamp to hold it close to position. Twist, which would show as a misalignment of the plank ends, is the real killer in fitting butt blocks. On *Taleisin*, I had to resort to carriage bolts to pull in a couple of sets of plank ends, and they only had $\frac{1}{8}$ to $\frac{3}{16}$ inch of twist misalignment.

On *Seraffyn*, the frames were on 9-inch centers (average for a steam-framed vessel of her size), which left $7\frac{1}{2}$ inches between the $1\frac{1}{2}$-inch-square steamed frames. It was almost impossible to pull any twist out of the short ($3\frac{3}{4}$ inches) plank ends, even if I did use carriage bolts. The oak butt blocks were 7 inches long, with a $\frac{1}{4}$-inch gap on each side for drainage. This minimal limber gap made it difficult to sand and varnish to protect the endgrain of the butt blocks from rot.

Taleisin had her frames on 14-inch centers, the usual spacing for sawn-framed vessels. This left 12 inches between each of the 2-inch-sided frames. The extra space meant it was easier to pull the plank ends tight to butt blocks, since each plank end was 6 inches from its respective frame. The butt blocks were also easier to fit because they could be $\frac{3}{4}$ inch away from the frames yet still be $10\frac{1}{2}$ inches long.

Butt blocks should be spread out as much as possible. The basic minimum requirement is two (preferably three) planks between butt blocks in the same frame bay. The photo shows the standard fore-and-aft spacing. (See discussion of butt-block placement later in this chapter.) Here I am noting the angle between the frames and the edges of the butted plank, plus the width of the plank.

17.73

17.74

Photo 17.74   The butt blocks for this plank will have final dimensions of 4⅞ inches by 10½ inches. The width includes the 4⅛-inch plank width plus ⅜ inch on each side to allow for the edges to overlap the adjoining planks. I used locust for these butt blocks because of its high strength and resistance to splitting. The material for the butt blocks must be check-free so that the butt will have little or no tendency to split when you drive in the fastenings. Next I lay out the plank-edge-to-frame bevels on each end of the proposed butt blocks. Then I cut out the block, leaving all four edges square.

Photo 17.75   The inside face of the butt block is hollowed 1/16 inch to fit the plank ends.

Photo 17.76   If the grain of the block is swirly and hard to plane, you can use the belt sander to hollow the block up to about 1/16 inch. Tip the sander and gently move it from side to side to hollow the hardwood. The curved-bladed Hyde scraper can take the last 1/64 inch of wood off the concave block.

Photo 17.77   I used the 60-grit belt on the sander to clean up the endgrain and the face side of the block to prepare it for varnish. If the 60-grit belt had left scratches that showed through the varnish, I would have used a finer-grit belt.

17.75

17.76

17.77

17.78

17.79

17.80

Photo 17.78 I rounded the corners to a ⅜-inch radius with my Stanley bullnoser. (Unfortunately, this fine little router is now out of production.)

If the sides are routed first, then the ends, there is less chance that the endgrain will be chipped off at the corner. A well-sharpened router bit also prevents chipped corners.

Photo 17.79 The two butt blocks are finished and ready to be fastened in place. The right-hand block has vertical endgrain and therefore is more likely to split than the left-hand one. If screws rather than rivets had been specified for these blocks, I would have selected and used only flat-grained blocks.

Since the butts will have large limber areas next to the frames, there is no need to bevel the top edges of the blocks for drainage.

Photo 17.80 A robust but small clamp is needed to hold the plank ends in snugly to the butt block during fastening. This heavy-duty machinist's clamp, with its protective plywood pads, is ideal.

17.81

17.82

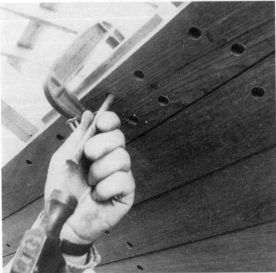

17.83

Photo 17.81 There is no unfairness (birdbeak) along this butt joint because it is in an area with zero twist and little bend. The fit is good and the wood is rot-resistant, so I don't need to put any bedding compound between the planking and the butt block. If I had used Dolfinite, I would have drilled for the fastening holes before I put the bedding compound on the block. Otherwise, it is quite difficult to clamp the slippery block in place.

If there had been twist in this area, I would have used a ¾-inch-by-1-inch-by-5-inch piece of hardwood, placed perpendicularly over the middle of the butt seam so that the clamp would exert equal pressure on both plank ends without damaging them.

Photo 17.82 When the block is positioned ¾ inch away from the frames and overlaps the neighboring planks equally, I drill for the rivets. I use a square-cornered block as a drill guide so that the rivets end up being evenly spaced on the inside of the hull. If you drill these pilot holes without a guide, they usually look like buckshot inside the boat.

When I put a butt block onto a wider strake than this one, I tend to position the two fastenings next to the butt seam farther apart. I then place the two that are away from the butt closer together so that they are not directly in line along the grain of the plank ends.

Photo 17.83 I set these nails with a small, light punch, which I keep handy in my apron.

Photo 17.84 I don't bother to set the nails too hard because my rivet clamp will do that for me. (This is the rivet clamp I developed because I was working alone.)

Photo 17.85 I made this improved helper out of a 10-inch standard clamp. The distance of the throat from the screw center to the clamp body is 3⅝ inches. (A clamp with a deeper throat—5 or 6 inches—would be an improvement.) The round part of the screw was ground to fit into the bung hole.

17.84

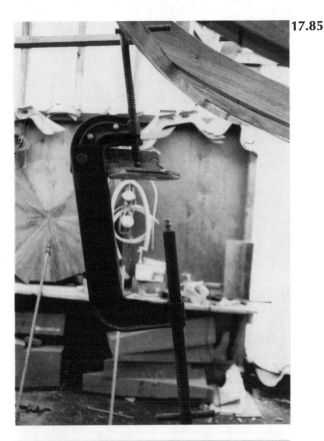

17.85

17.86

The piece of ⁵⁄₁₆-inch-by-2-inch-by-3-inch angle iron that makes the adjustable foot hinges at the ½-inch bolt. Part of a 6-inch clamp was bolted to the foot end. The round part of the upper screw locates itself in a countersink dimple on the 3-inch-wide face of the foot.

Photo 17.86   The foot has a 1½-inch hole near its end. This hole is located over the nail and rove. The foot part of the clamp has to be twisted so that the hole is in line with the end of the large screw. A ⅛-inch plywood protection piece is glued to the foot to protect the frames or butts.

When you tighten the swing foot, the butt block is squeezed tight to the plank and the nail is compressed firmly through both wooden parts. This device is very powerful and probably should be used only on hardwood planking with large flathead nails. The clamp could easily force a nail head right through a 1¼-inch cedar plank.

Once the riveting machine is in place, I drive the rove onto the nail. The rove set is a bit of heavy-walled ½-inch red-brass water pipe countersunk to fit the ⅝-inch copper roves I am using.

Photo 17.87   When the rove is set snug to the block, the excess should be nipped off.

Photo 17.88   I leave about ³⁄₃₂ inch of nail above each rove. This amount will peen over (flare) and tighten the rivet securely. If I left only ¹⁄₁₆ inch, there would not be enough metal to produce a fully mushroomed flare over the rove. On the other hand, if I left the nail too long, the nail could collapse and bend in the hole, allowing the rivet to loosen later. I suggest experimenting to determine this cutoff length by riveting together some scrap wood in the vise. Once you get the hang of it, you'll find it quite fast and simple.

Photo 17.89   I made the hole in the clamp the correct diameter so that the peen head of the hammer could hit not the wood but only the rivet or the clamp hole. This eliminated ugly hammer marks on the wood and made varnish preparation easier.

I rivet the outboard nails first. Then, to do the inboard ones, I adjust the angle of the foot on the clamp downward slightly so it rests equally on the inboard edge of the butt block and the outboard rove. This adjustment only requires a ¼-inch loosening of the outside lower screw on the riveting clamp.

(Normally I left the machinist's clamp in place while I riveted up each butt block, but here I have removed it so I could take photos that were less cluttered and confusing.)

17.90

Photo 17.90 The eight rivets hold the plank ends in tightly. I found it was a good idea to varnish the butt blocks as soon as possible, especially along the endgrain. This kept the blocks from discoloring or checking.

Photo 17.91 There was about ⅛ inch of twist from frame to frame where I had to place the butt block for *Taleisin*'s sheer plank. In order to get the planks to lie in fair, the butt block had to be shaped on its faying surface to align with this twist. To get the shape, I clamped the butt block to the plank ends and marked the approximate twist on the top and bottom edge of the block (diagram 17.12). To add to the difficulty of fitting this particular block, the sheer plank is ¼ inch thicker than the other planks. This made it a bit more difficult than normal to pull in the plank ends to make them lie flat and fair against the blocks. The positions of the clamps and the carriage bolts indicate that I had to apply pressure at opposing corners to pull the proper twist into the plank ends. I final-fastened this block using four rivets plus four ⅜-inch carriage bolts to hold the plank ends in tightly.

17.91

Diagram 17.12

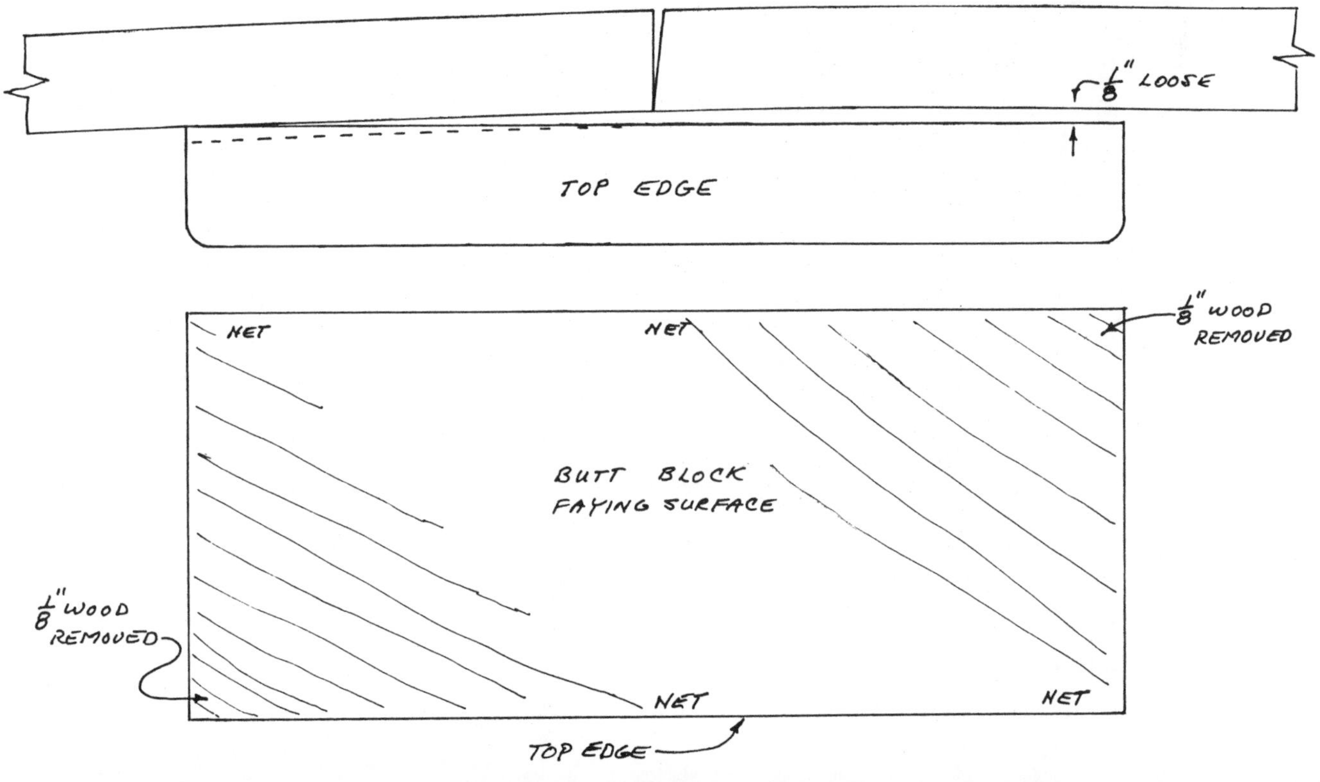

TOP EDGE

$\frac{1}{8}$" *LOOSE*

NET   *NET*

$\frac{1}{8}$" *WOOD REMOVED*

BUTT BLOCK FAYING SURFACE

$\frac{1}{8}$" *WOOD REMOVED*

NET   *NET*

TOP EDGE

DISCUSSION

Butt Blocks, Alternate Methods, and Butt-Block Placement

It is not common to find full-length planks used in boats over 20 feet because there is little advantage to justify going to the extra trouble and expense of purchasing full-length stock just to avoid using butt blocks. Furthermore, full-length planks for boats of this size are unwieldy and difficult for one person to handle. Properly designed and fastened butt blocks will result in a first-class, professional-quality planking job that combines strength with practicality and economy.

The rule of thumb used to determine the length of butt blocks is that they should be six to eight times the thickness of the planking. This allows room for four well-spaced fastenings in each of the plank ends. It also means that the fastening area will be at least as long as the plank-end connection at your stem rabbet—and, in most cases, longer. The width of the butt block will vary with the width of the planks, but the rule of thumb here is that the block should lap onto the adjoining planks by ⅜ to ½ inch. This overlap locks the butt block into line with the two neighboring planks so that the plank ends that land on the butt are held fair to the rest of the hull.

Although butt blocks usually are the same thickness as the planking stock, most builders prefer to make them from wood that is tougher and harder than the planking material. This tougher timber will resist splitting when the fastenings are driven in. For screw-fastened butts, I would make the blocks 20 percent thicker than the planking. This would allow you to use longer screws with more gripping power. This extra thickness would also help the butt block resist the wedgelike splitting effect exerted by wood screws.

My wood choice for butt blocks, in order of preference, would be black locust, hard pitch pine, teak, iroko, white oak, or hard mahogany. On composite-construction boats, galvanized iron or bronze plate is sometimes used for butt blocks. The nails are simply riveted over onto the plate without roves. Carriage bolts are commonly used to fasten galvanized butt blocks.

Even if I were screw-fastening a hull, I would prefer to use rivets or bolts to fasten the butt blocks. Not only would this eliminate the potential splitting effect of screws, but it also could add to the longevity of the joint. Screw fastenings depend for their holding power on the local condition of their thin metal threads and the condition of the wood threads in the butt block. Rivets or bolts, on the other hand, not only are less likely to split the block (since they can be driven through pilot holes of the same or similar diameter) but also will lose little of their holding power if the wood around them softens a bit due to immersion in water. The through-fastening is not totally reliant on the surface condition of the wood in its pilot hole for its holding power. Instead, a large cylindrical section of wood is gripped by the bolt head and its washer and nut. The same holds true for the copper rivet head and its rove. By comparison, the area gripped by a screw head and its threads is quite limited.

As I have mentioned, I don't fit blocks tight to the frames—for several reasons. This fitting is time-consuming, especially between steam-bent frames. Since the steam-bent frames are square to the inside of the planking, they will be toed in slightly toward the inside of the hull, so fitting a butt block tightly between these angle-sided frames is difficult unless you plane a bit of wood off the inboard side of the frame. You will then need some system for draining the water off the top edge of the butt block. One method is to angle off or chamfer the top of the block. This means extra labor and somewhat wider material for the butt blocks, and it will not work in the lower areas of some boats where the frame sections are almost horizontal. Butt blocks in these areas will require more than 45 degrees of chamfering, which is impractical. In such a case, the only other choice is to saw about ¾ inch off the outboard vertical corner of the butt block so the water can drain behind the butt block next to the frames. This limber-hole chamfer adds a bit of labor, but, worse, it is difficult to paint, survey, or clean the rot-prone endgrain of the butt block. The only advantage to the tightly fitted butt block is that it is slightly longer for a given frame spacing.

The one exception I made to nonfitting butt blocks was on the sheerstrake. In *Taleisin*, the 2-inch-sided deckbeams narrowed the bay, leaving only 10 inches from deckbeam to frame side. In order to make the block as long as possible to hold the 1½-inch-thick sheer plank in place, I fitted it to the frame and the deckbeam. Then I left the block high enough above the planking so that it could be planed off later to fit the underside of the deck. Water drainage is not a problem at the sheer-to-deck joint. A good, tight fit protected by Dolfinite should minimize any chance of rot in the butt block.

Although it is unusual, I have seen butt blocks fitted with the grain running vertically, a bit like sister frames. This method was used on one hull that had closely spaced bent frames. There was only about 5 inches between the ¾-inch-by-1½-inch flat steamed frames. The vertical butt blocks, which were about 4½ inches wide and 12 inches long, overlapped one complete plank each side of the butted plank. Fitting these blocks required extra work and time, but they definitely are stronger than a 4½-inch-long horizontal-grained block would be. This vertical butt block could be used to advantage if you had to repair the planking on a boat where the frame bays were cramped and narrowed by bulkheads, sister frames, bulwark stanchions, or wooden floor timbers.

Plank ends should never be butted on steam-bent frames. The fastenings near the plank end could easily cause the planks to split, and there is not enough area on the frame to space fastenings so they will hold the two plank ends securely.

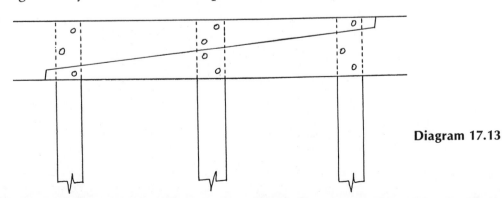

Diagram 17.13

Builders of large workboats—with double-sawn frames that are 8-inch sided or larger—butt their planks onto the frames. I would feel comfortable with this if the butt ends were fastened with carriage bolts that went right through the frame futtocks.

I have seen another butt-blockless plank-joining method that works well for sheer-strakes. The plank ends are nib-scarfed, as shown in diagram 17.13. Because this method eliminates blocking, it makes a joint that can accommodate inside chainplates. You can fasten this joint to the frames and use a caulking seam or you can fit and glue this scarf. It does take more work to fit and glue it tightly.

Some builders use flat scarfs to join their planks and eliminate butt blocks. But this is a case of complete—and not always successful—reliance on the long-term holding power of adhesives. When we were in Costa Rica, I saw an otherwise-beautiful 40-foot Alden sloop on which all of the flat-scarfed butts were delaminating. The outboard feather edges of the scarfs were sticking out on the topsides and bottom like flaps on envelopes. I could not think of a reasonably priced and professionally satisfying way to refasten these butts and pull the feather edges back into place without adding butts and replanking almost half of the hull.

Once you come to the first of your planks that requires a butt, it is a good idea to make a butt-block diagram that will help you space the joints as far apart as possible using the planking you have in stock. (diagram 17.14). As you lay out this plan, try to place butts where there is the least amount of twist in the planking. If the chainplates on your boat are to be secured to the inside of the planking, you will have to avoid locating any butts where the chainplates will attach to the hull. If the chainplates are on the outside of the hull, you can space the butts where you like, as I have found nothing against having an occasional chainplate bolt through a butt block.

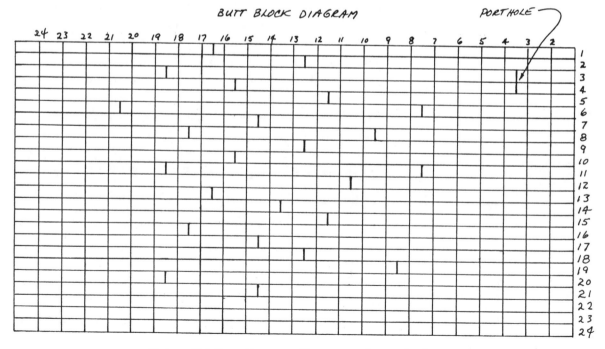

Diagram 17.14   Note: NO BUTTS IN THE FIRST THREE PLANKS

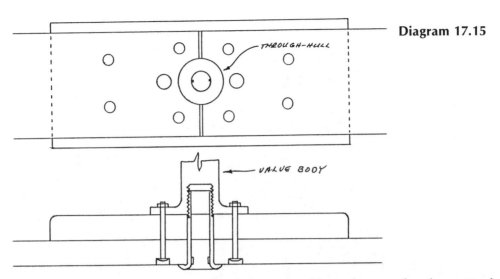

Diagram 17.15

I figured the butt-block layout positions from the second broad up to the sheer. Each time I penciled a butt onto the layout diagram, I checked for twist between the frames in the butt area by laying a ¼-inch-thick, 4-inch-wide-by-6-foot-long batten in place and sighting along it. If the twist looked like more than ⅛ inch between the two frames, I tried to locate the butt elsewhere. As I did this, I double-checked against my planking stock to make sure I had the lengths I would need to correspond with the modified plan.

If you are fortunate enough to be able to purchase some long boards for your planking stock—perhaps 20 to 24 feet—you can space the butts quite easily. You should then be able to have only one butt per plank round instead of needing two to space the butts more widely. This will save a bit of time as well as some butt-block material.

Another way to space out butt blocks is to land some of the butt joints where a through-hull fitting will eventually be located. The through-hull fitting and valve body will hold the plank ends together like a large bolt and washer with a hole in the center (diagram 17.15). Add this to the carriage bolts that hold the valve body to the block and planking and you end up with a super-fastened combination butt block and through-hull backing block.

On this hull, I was able to space out the butts by butting two planks near the bow, one under the other, where we planned to have opening portlights. I cut a 6-inch round hole dead center on the butt joints and then through-bolted the heavily framed bronze ports in place. The portlight and its outside flange ring acted as a butt block for both strakes (see photo 16.1). This let me use two very short strakes on each side forward, then a 16-foot plank and a 20-foot plank amidships, with two shorter planks aft to spread the topside butts over a wider area of the hull.

This placement of through-hulls and portlights takes some careful planning and a general idea of the eventual interior arrangements of the boat. Furthermore, if you are building to Lloyd's Rules or the American Bureau of Shipping Rules, it pays to check whether these less common, but definitely strong, substitutes for butt blocks would meet their requirements.

SECTION 7: Fastening the Planks

Further Details of Singlehanded Riveting

17.92

Photo 17.92   After I finished fastening the butt blocks in place, I had to rivet each round of planking. The friction of the knurled copper nails held the planks until then. If someone had been available to buck up the rivets, I would have waited and done several planks at a time. But since I was riveting singlehanded, and my riveting clamp could only just reach the lower rivet on any single plank, I had to rivet up each round of planking as I fitted it to the hull before starting the next round of planks.

The 12-inch spacing between the frames gave me room to reach through the frames, so I could do most of the riveting without having to get inside the hull. In most cases, the nail cutting, peening, and riveting procedure was the same as described in the butt-block sequence. But the photographs here show some of the variations I used for situations where the regular riveting vise would not fit, or where I needed a different type of fastening.

Photo 17.93   In this case, the reach of the rivet clamp's throat was blocked by the bilge stringer, so I had to devise a long-reach rivet clamp. This is simply a piece of 1 5⁄8-inch-by-3-inch oak with a ½-inch threaded rod secured through it with nuts and washers on each side. The protruding part of the threaded rod is ground until it will fit easily into the ½-inch counterbore holes. A foot pad of 1½-inch-by-2-inch-by-4-inch fir is screwed onto the other end of the long-reach rivet device. The C-clamp, fastened from the bilge stringer onto the middle of the rivet device, pushes the threaded rod against the nail head and holds pressure on it so that I can drive on a rove and rivet the end of the copper nail. To protect the wood around the rivet from possible denting, I have a 2-inch-by-4-inch piece of thick leather with a 1-inch hole that I hold over the rove as I work.

17.93

17.94

Photo 17.94 Before the planking gets any higher, the bulkhead should be fastened to the frame it butts against. (You could do this as soon as you built the bulkhead, but I waited until I had set up for riveting.) If you forget to rivet this before you plank, it will be very difficult to drill the fore-and-aft holes along the edge of the bulkhead and through the frame.

The first step in this process is to drill the pilot holes about 6 inches apart on both port and starboard bulkheads. An extra-long $^{17}/_{64}$-inch twist drill is ideal for this job, as it keeps the drill motor clear of the next frame forward of the bulkhead. I try to drill the holes square to the bulkhead face to make it easier to use the riveting clamp.

Photo 17.95 Once the holes were drilled, I made clench-ring heads for the copper rivets. I clamped the length of ¼-inch copper rod into the vise, leaving about ³/₁₆ inch of the rod sticking through the ¼-inch clench ring. These clench rings (dome-shaped washers) are cast manganese bronze and serve the same purpose as the copper roves, but they can be used with larger rod stock. (See chapter 23 for more on clench rings and making your own patterns.) While the rivet is still in the vise, I peen and mushroom the protruding rod evenly and neatly to get a finished-looking head. This is easier than finishing the rivet head when it is already fastened in the bulkhead.

17.95

17.96

17.98

17.97

Photo 17.96 Since the ¼-inch rod will push easily through the ¹⁷⁄₆₄-inch pilot hole, I put the whole length of copper rod through until the clench ring on the forward side is flush with the bulkhead face. I then cut off the rod, leaving the thickness of another clench ring plus ³⁄₁₆ inch extra on the aft side for peening. Then I take the rod back to the vise and make another rivet. I made the heads for all of the rivets and sawed them off to size before doing all of the riveting. This was faster than measuring individually for each rivet.

Photo 17.97 The rivet clamp has an additional aluminum foot to fit over the end of the screw. This foot is similar to the one usually found on a clamp except that it is made from a ¾-inch-thick piece of 1-inch-diameter aluminum rod. The rod stock has a recess in one end that lets it slide onto the clamp screw end (see chapter 23). The other end of the aluminum rod has a dimple on it that conforms to the clench-ring head of the rivet. This additional foot, which is just barely visible on the forward side of the bulkhead, holds the clench-ring-formed rivet as I peen over the far end.

Photo 17.98 This next plank will be fastened to both the frames and the bilge stringer with ¼-inch rivets to produce the box-girder effect discussed in chapter 11.

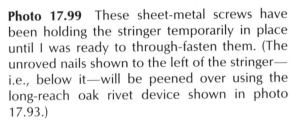

17.99

Photo 17.99 These sheet-metal screws have been holding the stringer temporarily in place until I was ready to through-fasten them. (The unroved nails shown to the left of the stringer— i.e., below it—will be peened over using the long-reach oak rivet device shown in photo 17.93.)

Photo 17.100 After the plank is clamped to the bilge stringer, the sheet-metal screws are removed and the screw holes become pilot holes for the through-bolts. It's crucial to make sure that the drill does not foul a plank seam. If it looks like the drill bit might come out close to a seam, I angle the drill so it comes out at least 1 inch from the seam. In one case, the sheet-metal screw hole was directly above a plank seam, so I refastened the stringer to the frame at that spot with a 4-inch-long number 14 wood screw. A ¼-inch clench ring was countersunk enough to accept the head of the wood screw to provide a washer that looked and acted like the clench ring.

Photo 17.101 After the holes were drilled through the starboard stringer, I bored the outside with a ⅝-inch Fuller counterbore to accept the ⁹⁄₁₆-inch-wide flat head of the rivet. I ground the cutting edges of the counterbore almost flat to make sure the head of the rivet would seat well in these holes. (You can see the flattened shape of the counterbore in photo 17.100.)

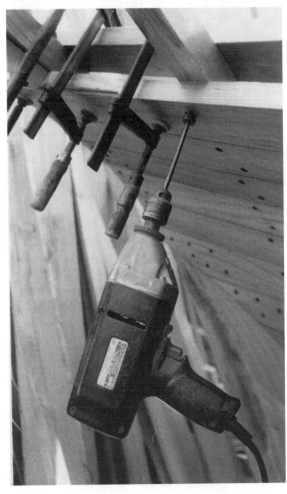

17.101

17.102

17.103

areas onto two sides of the drill-bit shank so that the set screws could grip the flat sections securely. I wrapped the drill-bit shank with a turn or two of plastic tape to shim up the 1/64-inch difference, then tightened the counterbore's Allen screws onto the shank of the drill. I used the slow setting on the drill press to run the drill-bit assembly into the 15/64-inch hole of the die. The material used to make the Fuller counterbore is harder than the mild steel of the die, so it cuts into the face of the angle iron and gives the impression for a good rivet head. (The head should be about 3/32 inch thick next to the rod and about 1/16 inch around its perimeter.)

Photo 17.103 I clamped the rod in the die, leaving about 5/8 inch sticking up above the jaws. (Make sure the end of the rod is cut about square.) Then I hit the protruding rod directly on its end with a 4-pound hammer, which caused the copper to swell evenly until it looked a bit like a tulip bulb. As I continued hammering evenly, this bulb of metal slipped down toward the head recess in the die and began to mushroom out until it filled the depression neatly. When a bit of copper occasionally flared over the edge of the die, I trimmed the edges on a sander until they fit into the 5/8-inch counterbore hole. This hammer forging actually hardens and toughens the copper so that the head is stronger than the original rolled rod.

To ensure that the arms of the die rested flat in the jaws of the vise, I had to put two 1/4-inch metal shims under the horizontal arms. These shims are held in place by the roundhead bolts shown on the top of the die. With a bit of practice, it becomes easy to forge these flat heads for bolts or rivets.

Photo 17.104 I drove the flathead fastenings through the bilge stringer and the plank and riveted them, using either the long-reach device or the metal clamp riveting tool. In the case shown here, the long-reach device was necessary. The wedge between the frame and the foot pad on the tool stabilized it so it rested steadily on the beveled edge of the frame. These rivets were cut off and peened over just as was done with the ones on the bulkhead.

Photo 17.102 I used a mild-steel die to forge 1/4-inch-diameter flathead rivets for the bilge stringer. I made this die on the drill press. The two pieces of 2-inch-by-3-inch-by-5/16-inch mild-steel angle iron were clamped firmly together while I drilled a hole (shown next to my finger) so that half of it ended up on each side of the split. I made this hole 15/64 inch—or 1/64 inch smaller than the 1/4-inch rod—so that it would grip the rod firmly. To make the head imprint in the die, I used the same modified 5/8-inch Fuller counterbore shown in photo 17.100. Since the metal of the eventual die is far harder than wood, the Allen-head screws that tighten the counterbore to the drill had to be locked more securely onto the drill's shank. To be sure they held well, I ground opposing 1/8-inch-wide flat

To finish fastening the plank that is behind the bilge stringer, I used a 2¼-inch number 14 wood screw as the second fastening on each frame. A second through-rivet would have been impractical and unnecessary.

Photo 17.105 The butt block under the bilge stringer cannot be riveted in the normal way. It must be fastened with either screws or bolts. If you choose to use bolts, you could use either ¼-inch silicon-bronze carriage bolts or home-made bolts. The head of a ¼-inch carriage bolt will fit perfectly into a ⅝-inch counterbore hole.

Photo 17.106 If carriage bolts are not readily available, it is possible to make ¼-inch flathead silicon-bronze bolts, as I did. I formed the head in the die using silicon-bronze rod stock whenever I felt the stresses would be more than a copper bolt could take. I heated the silicon-bronze rod until it just began to turn blue. Then I could hammer and forge it into the die quite easily. I used a national-coarse (NC) thread (twenty threads to the inch for ¼-inch stock) for the nut end.

Some builders may argue that copper is not strong enough to make good bolts, but I tested both a copper bolt and a silicon-bronze one made with my die. I overtightened both bolts until I broke them off. They both pulled their washers into the teak and crushed it about the same amount, so I felt comfortable using either one. The copper bolt did twist off sooner than the bronze one did, but for bolting together relatively low-stress wooden parts such as butt blocks, in areas where there is little twist to the hull, the copper bolt is good enough and probably stronger than a regular copper rivet. Those who don't agree can forge bronze ones instead.

Since this butt-jointed plank meets where there is little twist, I chose to use copper bolts. But to ensure that no unnecessary strains went on the individual bolts, I kept the plank ends C-clamped to the butt block until all of the bolts were tightened down evenly.

SECTION 8: The Topside Planks

At this point, you have to decide whether to continue planking *up* to the sheerstrake or whether to start from the sheer and work *down* to finish up with a shutter plank. The final result will be about the same, whichever way you go. I prefer planking up to the sheer because I feel the frames and the frame bevels will have a natural tendency to adjust slightly to fit the planking as I work upward. This could reduce the time I would have to spend final-fairing the frames. (*Taleisin*'s framework has very few ribbands and no sheer clamp attached to the frame heads, so this allows a bit of free-floating alignment of the frames as the planks are clamped and fastened to them.)

By eliminating a shutter plank, you save time because only the lower edge of the sheer plank has to be spiled to fit. With a shutter in the middle of the hull, both edges must fit right the first time. (More on this appears later in this chapter.) It is also easier to rivet each plank if you continue upward. And, having done it both ways, I can say for sure that it is easier to clamp, view, and adjust planks to fit the frames and butt blocks if you can look and work from above the plank. I also found that I could pick out and correct slight bits of unfairness in the top sheered edge of each plank as I worked upward. These irregularities are harder to see on the lower edge of a plank, especially if it is just under or at the turn of the bilge.

The method described here is the only way you can plank a lapstrake hull, because a shutter plank is impractical. If you were building a carvel-planked canoe stern or double-ended hull, this garboard-to-sheer method would work well. It is quite difficult to fit a shutter on a double-ender, because the two planks have to fit both stem and sternpost and be a precise length to join at a butt block. It is possible to get this double-rabbeted strake in place without the aid of clamps, but that is not the easiest way.

Photo 17.107 Here I am measuring the girth from the batten at my left hand down to the existing plank. The batten represents the lower edge of the sheerstrake. This batten looked fair and produced nicely tapered sheer-plank ends. The plank near my right hand is also fair and true. To make sure the topside plank widths stayed correct, I marked every third frame to indicate the plank seams.

Photo 17.108 The divider was set at 4¼ inches (girth at F14 = 38¼ inches ÷ 9 planks) to make a light pencil mark (easy to rub off) on the side of each frame. If the last arced-off plank spacing came out too narrow or too wide, I adjusted the scribe and re-marked the frame girth until all nine were equal. I divided up every third frame on both port and starboard sides of the hull and made sure the pencil marks were easy to refer to while I was fitting the planks to the rest of the

topsides.

If you like, you can clamp your long batten onto each set of scribe marks to check each eventual plank seam for fairness. I did not do this because I was confident that the plank under the turn of the bilge and the sheerstrake batten was fair, so this topside section, when divided equally, logically would produce nine fair topside planks. It worked.

Photo 17.109 The topside planks can be spiled from the inside of the hull. This is slightly more accurate than spiling on the outside of the batten. The arcs transferred to the spiling batten, and later to the eventual plank, actually represent the inside curve of the plank seam. (This system cannot be used if it is difficult to reach into the hull.) Once you are above the bilge stringer, most of the topside planks can be easily spiled this way if you plank up to the sheer.

17.107

17.108

17.109

17.110

17.112

17.111

Photo 17.110 I used two different wooden scrub planes to hollow the planks. One had a ¹/₁₆-inch radius across the sole and the other had about a ⅛-inch radius. The outside edges where the pencil points must be left net. Care is essential, as it is easy to plane off these corners inadvertently. If they do get planed off, the hollowed section of the plank will no longer fit correctly.

Photo 17.111 To prevent the corners from being planed off, I used my forefinger like a plane guide as I scrubbed the planks. That way, the plane would tend to run parallel on the board and not cut down the slightly higher corner. I found it was safer and easier to start planing the center of the plank first and then work gradually toward the edges. As I neared the edges, I left my forefinger against the plank edge at all times to warn me when I was close to the edge. I scraped the last ¹/₆₄ inch of hollow into the plank with the round-edged scraper and then gave the plank a light sanding to remove scraping and planing marks.

Photo 17.112 *Taleisin* has a gammon iron designed to fit to her stemhead. It is far easier to make and fit hardware to a flat-sectioned stemhead than to one that has the cutwater carried all the way to deck level. It is not a bad idea to leave this square on any new boat until you have decided what hardware will be bolted to the stemhead. It can be shaped after all of the hardware is fitted.

17.113

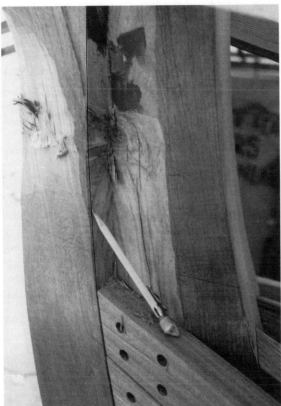

17.114

Photo 17.113 In this photo, my pencil points to a line faired to the outside of the planking, up toward the deck. The pencil point is at the lower aft intersection of the square-headed stem. Once these port and starboard intersection points of the cutwater are faired up with a batten and are of equal height at the rabbet line, the reverse transition curves of the stem can be finished exactly net. (Notice the strong backrabbet area where the plank ends land on the stem. There is room for four well-spaced wood screws to fasten each plank end—especially important here because this end of the boat can bash into things.)

Photo 17.114 It is easier to finish the stem curve net before the planking goes on the rest of the topsides. Notice how the top ribband fits to the rabbet where it stops short of the stemhead. The sheerstrake should fit the same way. The covering board eventually fits to the flat side of the stem directly above the sheer plank.

17.115

Photo 17.115 I made a plywood pattern for the side and for the forward curve to ensure that the port and starboard sides of the stem curve came out exactly the same. If they did not—even if they were only out ¹⁄₃₂ inch—any visiting boatbuilder would notice and shake his head. As you can see, it is best to do this job before the planks are in the way because you can use a chisel, plane, and scraper from almost any angle to work this curve easily down to the pattern marks.

The wide plank shown at the bottom of this photo is the one just below the topside planking. It is 4¹⁄₈ inches wide forward and almost the same width along its whole length. It is below the boottop on this hull so does not affect the visual appearance of the topside planking once the hull is painted. Therefore I made it as wide as I could. Wider planks like this also made better use of the widths I had in my planking stock, so they kept wastage to a minimum.

Photo 17.116 The sheerstrakes are ¹⁄₄ inch thicker than the other planks. Not only do they help strengthen this area to compensate for the fact that this hull has no inside sheer clamp, but the thicker sheerstrake helps give the hull a lower-looking profile. The forward 14 inches of the starboard sheerstrake has been tapered down toward the rabbet line forward so that it becomes flush with the stem rabbet and flush with the next plank. This is done mainly for appearance and to add symmetry to the hull. I used a slick and a rabbet plane to fair in these ends.

The lower edges of the sheerstrakes were bullnosed with a ³⁄₈-inch radius just before the final fitting. The two short planks that butt where the portlights eventually will be installed are held in place with blocks and temporary through-bolts. This helps train the planks into position so they do not want to spring out as much when it comes time to fit the porthole.

17.116

Photo 17.117 The aft end of the sheerstrake is marked with a 1½-inch block to lay out the miter for the transom. The 1¼-inch-thick covering board, which eventually will be fastened to the top edge of the sheerstrake, will increase the visual width of the plank to a pleasing proportion.

Photo 17.118 The whiskey plank (shutter plank) was the starboard aft sheerstrake. When I compared the fitting of this to the work and concerns I had while fitting *Seraffyn*'s under-the-bilge shutter plank, I was tickled that it was so easy. I just fitted the lower edge and forward butt seam, then fastened the plank in place during a whiskey-plank party. (It was a blowout party, complete with 250 friends and lots of Jack Daniel's whiskey in, believe it or not, stone jugs.) I installed the butt blocks a few days after the party and later faired the top edge to accept the covering board.

17.117

17.118

Fitting a Shutter Plank

It is simpler to fit the shutter plank on a new hull if the lower edge of the topside planking is lined out so that it is almost straight (i.e., it has no edge-set). This way, the straight spiling batten can lie easily between the lower topside plank and the upper bottom plank. If this line is not straight, you will have to make a curved spiling batten to fit between the planks and flush to the frames.

Photo 17.107 shows the area where a shutter plank could be fitted on *Taleisin*. Had I not planked her from bottom to sheer, I would have had the shutter where the topmost plank is fastened. This plank has very little twist or edge-set. This is a good place for a shutter plank, as the aft end does not have to fit into the rabbet of the sternpost. Instead, the aft end can be cut off after the plank is final-fitted. If at all possible, avoid fitting a shutter where it will have to rabbet into both the stem and the sternpost. To minimize scrubbing, most builders plan the shutter position so it fits to the flattest sections of the frames. They also look for an area where the butt can lie with the least twist. Fitting and connecting the butt block for the shutter is far easier when there is no twist at all.

To fit the shutter plank, first tack a spiling batten to the forward frames between the topside and bottom planking. Then spile both top and bottom edges of the plank (diagram 17.16). Arc in the stem rabbet in the usual way, then indicate the position of the butt block so it lies between the appropriate frames.

Next lay the shutter spiling batten on a board, set the scribe to the correct arc length, and spile both edges of the plank onto the eventual plank, along with the butt and stem-rabbet locations.

Diagram 17.16

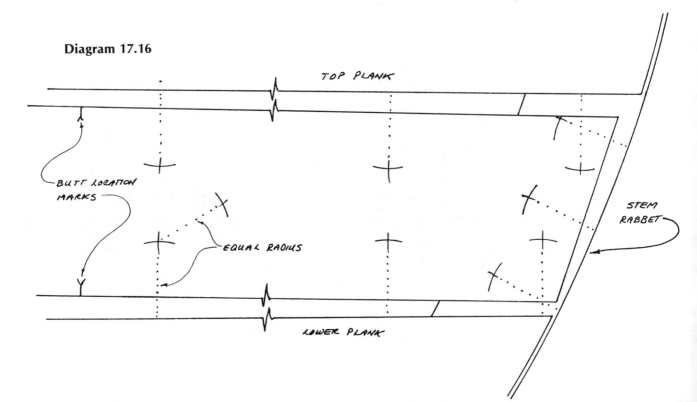

The key to fitting the shutter is to make the plank 1/16 inch wider than the shutter opening in the hull, so add this amount to one edge of your partially spiled plank. Connect the spiling marks with a batten and pencil in the line.

When you are satisfied, cut out the plank and transfer the seam bevels at the plank edges and at the stem rabbet. If the plank needs scrubbing, transfer the frame curvature to the inside of the plank and hollow it as needed. Now bevel the inside sharp corners of the plank just a bit so they don't jam on the existing planks. Finally, before you begin to place the plank on the hull, run some beeswax onto both of the inside edges of the plank to lubricate the wedge of the shutter between the two existing planks.

Start at the stem with a 6-inch-long 4 x 4 block of softwood to serve as a pad that will spread and absorb the hammer blows. Hammer the hood end of the plank into the stem rabbet until it fits up to about the first frame. The plank should lie flush to the planking above and below and hold itself in place. Check all of the fits and the seams, and if everything looks good, screw-fasten the hood end to the backrabbet. Then hammer the plank up to the next frame. Check inside for scrub fits at the backrabbet and the first frame, then work along, a frame at a time, fastening and checking inside fits at each frame until you get to the butt. If you are not too confident that the plank will fit well, fasten it in place with double-headed nails or screws so the plank can be removed. Just pull the fastenings and nudge the plank off from the inside, using a hammer and the softwood pad. Improve the fits and hammer it back in place.

Getting the butt end of the plank to pull into the butt block is the only really tricky part of fitting a shutter plank. If the curvature of the hull at the shutter plank butt area is slight, a 2 x 2 shore and a wedge driven in across the butt end of the plank usually will pull the butt close enough so that you can fasten the plank to the butt block. The butt block for the shutter plank should be cut and shaped before you fit the plank in place. (That is one of the reasons you want this plank to lie in an area with little twist.) It should then be wedged firmly into place between the frames, as shown in diagram 17.17, with the proper amount of overlap onto each adjoining plank. You can use temporary bolts or screws to pull and train the plank ends against the butt block. These bolts can be left in place for a week or two until the timber relaxes and wants to conform to the shape of the hull. Later, the two butt blocks can be permanently riveted or bolted to the plank ends.

The aft shutter plank is fitted and set in place in the same manner as the forward shutter. Hammer in the butt end first and hold it with bolts or screws. Then tap the plank in place, working toward the transom, and clamp the aft end to the transom frame. Check the scrub fits and the seams, then mark the miter for the end of the shutter plank. Remove the aft shutter, cut off the mitered end, and make any small seam or scrubbing adjustments. Then set the plank aside. Fit the two shutter planks on the other side of the hull. Then use whichever aft one you prefer as the last and final one to be fitted. This way, the whiskey plank should go into place without a hitch, even though there is a watching crowd and the Jack Daniel's is flowing freely.

Although many first-time builders feel concerned about fitting shutter planks, I have seen some Costa Rican shrimp-trawler builders use shutter planks to solve a unique local problem. I watched these builders complete a 72-foot trawler from keel timber to launching during a four-month period. They lined out the planking on their double-sawn frames and proceeded to plank from the garboard to the sheer. I watched as the first of the bottom planks went on and was amazed to see the builders skipping every second plank as they worked quickly upward toward the sheer. Sammy Manley, the shipyard owner whose father had been a boatbuilder in England, explained:

> You see, the mahogany we plank with is soaking wet and it is almost impossible to season the amount of timber we use in this rain-forest climate. We build a 72-foot trawler every 120 days or so, and that is a lot of timber to season. We had to develop a method that would take into account what happens when the topsides dry out later. So the alternate shutter planks are each made about a millimeter [1/16 inch] oversize. Then they are driven into place with hammers so that when they do dry out, the hull opens up very little compared to boats we built previously using the normal method of planking.

Lin and I were guests at the launching of this trawler, the *Don Fernando*, and an inspection showed that the inside seams fit as well as those on many yachts I have seen.

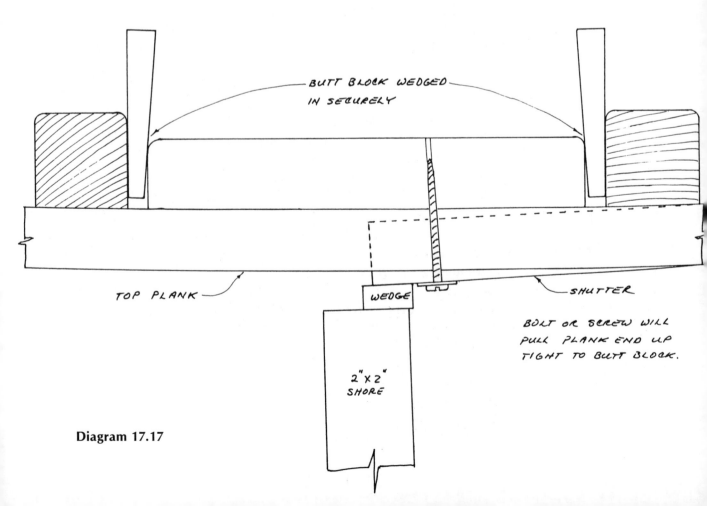

Diagram 17.17

Eliminating Scrubbing

Sammy Manley also showed me another trick for speeding up production on carvel-planked, round-bottomed fishboat hulls. His crew flatted off each frame with an electric hand plane so that the planks did not have to be scrubbed to fit. This flat area was equal in width to the plank that would fasten to that particular frame location. The finished frame ended up with a series of plank-width flats. With large-dimension sawn frames such as were used on the *Don Fernando*, there was very little strength lost by dubbing the frames in this manner. This system served two purposes at once: (1) it was easier and faster than hollowing each plank, and (2) by flatting the frame, the plank-to-frame-bevel fit could be improved as the men worked upward along the frames.

Naturally, a hard-chined boat is the easiest of all types to plank, as the planks will have almost no scrubbing. The Grand Banks motoryachts, designed to be built in series in Singapore by American Marine, were hard-chined. They were designed so they could be planked with *straight* boards of 1⅛-inch-by-4-inch mahogany, which meant that the chine-to-sheer girth measurements had to be parallel from bow to stern. This measurement also had to be worked out to fit the 4-inch-wide boards, a width that was easily available to the builder. In other words, the girth-from-sheer-to-chine measurement had to be a multiple of the desired plank width, such as a 40-inch girth to equal ten 4-inch planks, to make this time- and cost-saving method succeed. I have rarely heard of this being done, but it does show that when a designer or a designer/builder understands plank line outs, he can create a hull shape that will make it easier for the boatshop that will be producing a standard, stock-model hull.

CONSTRUCTION TIMES FOR CHAPTER 17

Larry: Milling planking stock; fairing rabbet; planking hull; riveting bulkhead to frame and bilge stringer to planking   805 hours

Lin: Wood-plugging and varnishing bulkhead; finishing lead keel; varnishing interiors of planking and frames   259 hours

Totals to date: Larry 2765 hours

Lin   619 hours

DISCUSSION
Planking-Method Choices

There are five basic methods you can choose to plank a 20- to 40-foot, round-bilged, wooden hull: (1) carvel over vertical frames; (2) double-skinned carvel with vertical frames; (3) single-layer strip planks over frames; (4) strip planks with two diagonal layers; and (5) three-skinned diagonal with longitudinal stringers.* (In Scandinavia, hulls of this size are sometimes planked lapstrake, but since this is rarely done in other parts of the world, I have not included lapstrake planking in this discussion.) In professional yards where boats are built in series, three-skinned diagonal planking can be laid over a planked mold—one that will be used over and over again. Then the hull can be lifted off and set upright, and vertical frames and floors can be fitted to eliminate stringers. But this discussion is aimed toward the majority of wooden boat builders, those who will be building one-off designs in a shop set up just for this purpose.

Most of my professional boatbuilding work has involved doing boat repairs on a contract basis. I have repaired damaged carvel, clinker, and three-skinned planking, so I have seen which planking systems were easiest to repair and survey, which were longest lived and most user-friendly. Very often, only the convenience and cost of building are considered by either the first-time one-off builder or the professional builder. But after the boat has been launched, planking choices can affect the owner more than almost any other choice he is asked to make (other than the design). If a boat is in a collision (and most boats eventually are), being able to assess the extent of the damage quickly and completely can prevent later problems. I recently repaired a triple-skinned hull that was hit by a ferry and dismasted four years earlier. Other than scratched paint and a shattered spar, there appeared to be little damage at that time. But the insurance surveyors overlooked a tiny fracture in the sheerstrake area. Four years later, water stains began appearing inside the hull coating near the sheer fracture. Unfortunately, the owner could no longer file a claim against the insurance company. Had his boat been more surveyable, he would have been money ahead. The same applies for repairs. If you are planning to take your yacht away from easy access to boatyards and good shop facilities, this factor could be exceptionally important to you.

Between 1980 and 1989, several other hulls identical to the one described in this book were built using three different planking methods. I have been able to glean good information on the merits of each method as they apply to the builder. I visited with Arno Day and Tony Davis in Maine and Jim Callery of Vermont, who built carvel-planked hulls like this using local woods. In California, Kit Cooney built a strip-planked version

---
* Naturally these methods can be mixed and matched to suit special situations. When Wayne Ettles, a builder in California, rebuilt *Lucky Star*, a Schock-designed schooner, he left the bottom as per the original —carvel, single-layered, caulked planking. But he replaced all of the topside planking with two layers of fore-and-aft planks that he glued together. This produced strong, stable, tight-seamed topsides that would help spread the chainplate loads over a larger area of the topsides.

with vertical framing and Linda Smith built a strip-, then double-diagonal-planked hull with multiple bulkheads instead of frames. A comparison of the hours needed to build these four boats—plus the costs involved, the tools needed, and the construction complexity—produced some good information.

Here in New Zealand, I've talked shop with John Lidgard and John Salthouse, owners of two of the best-known boatbuilding yards near Auckland. Both yards have built traditional carvel and multiskinned hulls—Lidgard for more than thirty years, Salthouse for twenty-five years. Multiskinned construction methods have been popular in New Zealand since the 1870s, when immigrant Scottish boatbuilders transplanted triple-skinned construction methods. There are many triple-skinned yachts eighty, ninety, and even a hundred years old that are still going strong. They were built with red lead or red lead and canvas between the skin layers. These hulls quite often were built with full-length stringers and held together with thousands of copper rivets fastened through the stringers and skin, as well as between the stringers to hold the skins together. In more recent years, glued three-skinned construction has been the most popular choice for racing and racer/cruiser hulls in New Zealand. But most of the displacement yachts, powerboats, and fishboats are built with single-layer carvel planking.

The following sections give the pros and cons of each planking method as I see them. I am basing these comments on building one-off hulls in a yard that will be set up just for this one boat project, and I assume that in each case the builder is striving for a yacht-quality interior and exterior finish.

Carvel Planking

Carvel planking has definitely stood the test of centuries. I have owned four yachts between 20 and 30 feet long and all of them were carvel-planked, caulked with cotton, and payed with various seam compounds. Not one of them leaked except after they had been hauled out for the winter. (After four or five months in the yard, some of the underwater planking had dried out and shrunk a bit, so at the spring relaunching, they leaked for a few days.)

One reason I particularly like this type of planking may be that I grew up and learned to sail in the Vancouver (Victoria) area of Canada, where there are a great many drifting logs and deadheads—floating debris that can damage any planking that is not stout and thick. Carvel planking is tough and flexible in this puncture-type blow situation. Carvel planking is also the easiest of all planking to repair. A plank can be refitted in almost any weather—rain, snow, or high wind. I have even seen a couple of quick, sure boatbuilders replace a damaged plank between the tides. Concerns about wood humidity or gluing temperatures will not stop a builder from getting a plank back onto the hull and caulked up quickly so that the owner soon can be back on the water.

This repairability probably explains why a majority of the world's fishboats and workboats are still being built with carvel planking. Carvel workboats (and occasionally yachts) are being built in small yards all over North America, but they rarely advertise, so few people are aware of the number of small, low-overhead, single-shed, low-tech boat-yards turning out carvel-planked boats of various types and varying quality.

If you are interested in being a professional boatbuilder, carvel-planking skills will put you in demand in boat-repair yards worldwide. If you want to work in a shipyard with a slipway, you'll be required to know how to replace or repair carvel planking. It has been my experience as we voyaged that anyone with efficient boatbuilding skills and a knowledge of carvel-planking repairs can find good-paying work worldwide. (In New Zealand boatbuilders are—and have been for a long time—on the top of the labor list for desired immigrants.)

As you use, clean, and maintain a carvel-planked boat, you can easily observe its general condition. Since each plank is one solid piece, there never will be any concern about delamination. Because you can see every joint and almost every fastening, you can do a quick inspection at any time. If you find a weeping butt block or seam, it is simple to repair. Just tighten the cotton or add more cotton the next time you haul out to paint the bottom. If a leak develops anywhere on a multiple-skinned hull, it will be hard to figure out the source of the water. If you see one small bit of delamination anywhere on a glued-up hull, you will wonder if any delamination is starting somewhere else—and if there is, how will you dry the hull sufficiently to reglue the laminations?

This surveyability of carvel-planked boats is also helpful if you are buying a used boat or are negotiating for an insurance policy for the boat you own. Any surveyor will have difficulty assessing the condition of the adhesive that is holding together the inner laminations of a glued hull. With a carvel-planked hull, he (or you) can remove a few fasteners, pull a bit of caulking cotton from between two planks, and assess the hull's general condition. If there are defects, the solutions will be straightforward repair jobs.

If I appear prejudiced, it is because we have been doing some intense studies into adhesives, assisted by Brian Boult, a research fellow at the University of Auckland, plus the research department at Ciba-Geigy chemical company. As Appendix C shows, we have found that adhesives are not always what they claim to be. Furthermore, I dislike working with glue, and carvel planking is the method that uses the least glue. I also think young builders are being unfairly discouraged from trying this method of construction just because some poorly built or poorly maintained older boats leaked. Furthermore, these young builders are discouraged because there are no manufacturers who have anything to gain by suggesting this type of construction, so they advertise that carvel planking is passé. I feel that if people examined finely built carvel hulls, they would see that they can be as dry as any other type of hull. They definitely are not passé, and the skills to build in carvel are not any more difficult to learn than the skills required to build nice cabinetry or good-looking spars.

CARVEL PLANKING

(used for any type of hull—heavy displacement, moderate, even light; for yachts and workboats)

Pro	Con
Strong and flexible in collisions.	Planking adds little vertical strength to hull.
Can be built or repaired in any climate, cold or wet.	Good, fair, strong framing job a must.
Does not require a heated shed to build or repair.	Planks need to be scrubbed so must be ⅛ inch thicker than final hull thickness.
Shipyards worldwide know how to repair it.	Lining out must be done carefully to give nice-looking topsides.
Easy to survey, easy to assess extent of damage after a collision.	Spiling and fitting skills needed.
Can be repaired so that it is impossible to find the replaced plank.	Fitting and refitting of planks seems labor-intensive.
Good for one-off shop, as no special tools or setup are needed.	Supply of large clamps needed.
Built upright, so easier to see fairness of topsides. No need to turn hull over.	Needs to be caulked.
Low-tech materials are available from a small sawmill, or trees can be felled and cut with chainsaw.	Hard to use unskilled helpers to good advantage.
Defects can be cut off as you spile for each plank.	Need some wide and some long boards.
No special milling needed.	A miscut plank seems a disastrous waste of wood.
Offcuts can be used to make framing and tongue-and-groove stock for interior work.	There will always be a bit of seam movement if the boat sails from one climate to another. Movement can cause cracks in the topside paint.
Doesn't need sheathing, so any unfair spots can be planed off and faired, even after launching.	
More thickness of skin to fair up.	
Paint job can be simple sanding and finishing with oil-base paints.	
Glue is not required so there is no messy cleanup inside or out.	
Visible framing structure inside looks good and gives feeling of strength.	

Double-Planked Carvel with Fore-and-Aft Strakes

This planking method was popularized by Nathanael G. Herreshoff, who used it to build many yachts in series. I do not know of any workboats built with this planking method. In its original form, this method used light cotton sheeting set in shellac between the two layers of planking. In recent years, waterproof glue has been adopted to strengthen the hull and seal the two planking layers against water penetration. Many well-known and successful yachts designed by the Herreshoffs and by Sparkman and Stephens have been built this way.

This double-planking method can produce a stronger hull than plain carvel planking. But the hull cannot be much thinner or lighter. The outer layer of the planking must be thick enough so there is sufficient wood to set wood plugs for the fastenings that hold the planks to the frames. It also must be thick enough to give good holding power for the intermediate planking screws that hold together the two layers of the hull. The total thickness of 1⅛ inches, as shown in diagram 17.18, is about average for a 40-foot boat built this way. On hulls under 25 feet, this method doesn't work well, as the two layers of thin planking would be difficult to secure together satisfactorily.

Double planking is more time-consuming to fit than carvel, as it must be done twice. But since the planks are thinner, they will have a tendency to shape to the frames when they are clamped and fastened. This can reduce the amount of scrubbing and hollowing on the parts of the frames with gentle curves.

Butt blocks are usually eliminated with this method of planking. Instead, the planks are butted on the frames, with the butt joints on the inner layer and the outer layer staggered so that they don't land at the same place. Some builders scarf the butts of the outside layers to get a smooth, butt-free appearance. They also tight-fit (i.e., fit the planks with no caulking seam or gaps) and glue each plank to the next to obtain a smooth, seamless-looking hull.

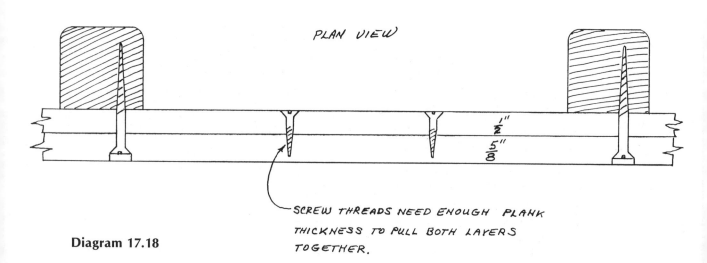

PLAN VIEW

$\frac{1}{2}$"

$\frac{5}{8}$"

SCREW THREADS NEED ENOUGH PLANK THICKNESS TO PULL BOTH LAYERS TOGETHER.

Diagram 17.18

DOUBLE PLANKING

*(used for moderate- to heavy-displacement yachts;
not for fishboats)*

Pro	Con
Vertically strong.	Have to fit planking twice.
Stable, smooth hull if seams are glued.	Harder to replace or repair glued planking.
Less scrubbing of planks.	Edge fits need to be spiled twice.
No butt blocks required.	Many seams to fit.
No caulking required.	Uses more fastenings.
Can produce a stronger hull for the same weight than single carvel planking on hulls over 25 feet.	Plank fastening heads inside hull between frames look unfinished.
No sheathing required.	Glue is expensive and cleanup labor-intensive.
Planks lighter and easier to handle.	Temperature-controlled building shed needed for gluing.
	Difficult to assess extent of damage after a collision.

Strip Planking

At first glance, strip planking seems like a simple, straightforward, and efficient way to plank a boat. But in fact, it is the most labor-intensive method of all. There can be no time saving with the framework, as most strip-planked hulls have not only the original molds but also a normal laminated or solid-timber backbone, a cut-in rabbet, floor timbers, frames, stringers, and clamps. You will have to spend time or money for the extra milling work to produce strips with concave edges. If these strips must be resawn from large boards, the labor and wood wastage can be quite costly.

Strip planking goes far more smoothly if you can do it with a full-time helper who can work inside the hull to clean up excess adhesive before it runs and sets on the planking. Cleaning the inside of a strip-planked hull after the adhesive is set can be very time-consuming. To keep production moving, the helper can also be scarfing strips so they are ready when needed.

Kit Cooney, the builder of the strip-planked *Taleisin*-type hull, works as a joiner, putting custom wood interiors in glass hulls. After completing his strip-planked hull, he told me, "Getting good fits both inside and outside the hull so that I could put a clear finish inside and didn't need to sheath outside, took me more hours than it took you to plank *Taleisin*." If you decide to sheathe the hull, this adds not only hours but materials costs to strip planking.

STRIP PLANKING

*(usually used on medium- to heavy-displacement yachts,
sometimes on workboats)*

Pro	Con
Strong vertically and longitudinally, as it gives a one-piece hull.	Most labor-intensive planking method.
Good puncture resistance.	Obtaining good fits on shapely hull can double the planking time.
Works well for either fin-and-skeg or wineglass-shaped hulls.	Strips need to be scarfed.
Not formidable for a new builder.	Milling of strips can be expensive.
Not wholly dependent on adhesives for strength and longevity.	Glue is expensive and messy.
Can be done by relatively unskilled helpers.	Progress is dependent on speed of strip scarfing.
Can cut defects out of timber and add scarfs to get usable stock.	Long scarfed strips are awkward for one man to handle.
Professional boatshop can use offcuts from carvel hulls for strips.	Hardwood strips require predrilled pilot holes for each edge fastening.
No caulking needed.	Helper needed for efficiency in gluing.
Can be planked right side up.	Rogue nails can stick through side of planking.
Lends itself to coating or sheathing.	Unless glue is waterproof, hull must be sheathed or coated.
Glue joints all visible inside and out for surveying.	Edge fastenings and frame fastenings needed.
Moderately easy to assess extent of damage after collision.	Heated shop needed for gluing.
	Repairing a hole in edge-nailed, strip-planked hull is difficult.
	Planks can bulge away from bulkhead as hull accepts moisture.
	Finished hull hard to hand-plane.
	Less attractive inside than carvel or double planking.

The most disturbing aspect of strip planking—the one that I have seen cause great problems as a boat ages—is that it will absorb moisture, and the strip planks sometimes will bulge away from the bulkheads by as much as 4 inches. This is fairly common on boats that were built with dry, well-seasoned strips. The planking swells and the tightly glued seams cannot absorb any of the expansion of the individual planks. The expanding wood pulls the fastenings out of the bulkheads and can break and separate the frames. There are two possible ways to avoid this problem: (1) sheathe or coat the hull with a moisture-resistant barrier inside and out, or (2) plank during the most humid time of the year.

Both the inside and the outside of a strip-planked hull are hard to smooth up with hand tools or planes because the grain of the narrow strips does not all run in the same direction. Machine-sanding is usually the only alternative. If you are not highly skilled with a disc sander, you will either have to use an orbital sander (a relatively slow method) or hire someone with disc-sanding skills.

I did see a good trick for using a disc sander on both topsides and bottoms with less fear of making circular gouges. A professional finisher in a San Diego boatyard used a soft pad that he modified to be square instead of round. Then he glued on square pieces of sandpaper. The flexible corners of the rotating square pad had little or no tendency to dig in and leave the classic disc marks. The disc-sander operator did say that the square pad was a bit dangerous if it was not handled properly. He recommended starting the sander after laying it up against the hull surface and stopping it before removing it from the work. If the square sander is running and you clip a scaffold plank or frame with it, it can yank the whole machine out of your hands and possibly cause injuries.

Double Diagonal Laid Over Strip Planking

This method of laminated planking is the one I would choose for building a glued-up hull. It is a combination of a layer of fore-and-aft strip planking (either nailed or doweled together) with two additional layers of diagonal planking stapled and glued to the outside of the strips. It eliminates the need for almost all framing other than near the high-stress areas of the rigging and in the bilge over the ballast keel. John Lidgard of Auckland built his own 44-foot fin-and-skeg cutter *Reward*, winner of the first Melbourne-Osaka two-handed race, using a variation of this method. He used 1-inch strip planking with a ¼-inch diagonal layer over it, finishing up with a single layer of unidirectional fiberglass as both a structural layer and a sheathing.

This method of planking means you can use a quite simple set of plywood building molds combined with permanent bulkheads. The strip planks are bent around the molds, edge-nailed to each other, and fastened to bulkheads. The strip layer should be about 50 to 60 percent of the total hull thickness. But it cannot practically be less than ½ inch thick because it will become difficult to fasten or edge-nail together without the nails coming through the side of the lower strips.

If you were trying to build a light hull under 30 feet, this method may not be the best, because to get strength without excessive framing, you would need the inner ½-inch strip layer and three layers of ⅛-inch diagonal on top. This would give a ⅞-inch-thick hull, which would be relatively heavy when you included the weight of adhesives and sheathings. If you chose to use only two outer diagonal layers, you would need more internal framing to keep the boat from flexing.

STRIP PLANKING WITH DOUBLE- OR TRIPLE-DIAGONAL LAYERS ON TOP

(usually used for medium-displacement yachts)

Pro	Con
Good strength in all directions.	Labor-intensive, as there are three or four skins to fit, glue, and fasten.
Less inside framing and no stringers, so hull is easy to finish inside, easy to keep clean.	Usually built upside down, so must be turned over.
Permanent bulkheads can be used as molds and left in place.	Molds must be very accurate, as little fairing can be done to outside of hull after planking.
No rabbet to cut, only a backrabbet.	Strips must be scarfed before use.
No stringers to trap water or dirt.	Heated shop necessary to maintain gluing temperatures.
Does not require sophisticated mold.	
Strips are self-fairing.	Veneers and strips can be expensive and hard to purchase.
Ideal for find-and-skeg designs.	Sheathing or coating, if used, is labor-intensive and expensive.
Little chance of water-absorption bulging compared to regular strip planking.	Repairs to inner strip layer are difficult.
Few expensive screws, rivets, or bolts required.	Difficult to assess extent of damage after a collision.
Strips do not have to be concave or convex.	Hard to survey inner glue laminations.
Repairs to outer layers relatively easy, as there are no fastenings to avoid.	Repairs require heated shop.
	Not practical for boats under 30 feet or with less than 7/8-inch skin thickness.
	Glue failure could mean a total write-off for the hull.

If you build a fin-and-skeg hull with this method, there is no need to concave and convex the strips for the inner skin. Instead, you can use rectangular strips, which fit tightly on the inside at the turn of the bilge. The slight gaps on the outside of the hull will fill up with glue as you set the next lamination of wood in place, then fit and staple it.

Care must be taken to ensure that the lofting for this type of hull is very accurate and the molds are set up correctly and carefully. Otherwise, the thinnish strips will conform to any slight lumps on the molds and bulkheads. This unfairness will show through the diagonal layers after they are fastened on. Remember that there will be little wood thickness that can be planed off later to fair the hull.

The veneer laminating strips for the diagonal layers will be quite expensive, as they have to be sliced (sheared) off square timbers, which are usually number 1 select clear stock, the highest timber rating. If you cannot get sheared veneers, you will have to use veneers that are sawn out and then planed smooth. This is very expensive, since as much wood ends up as sawdust and planer chips as you actually put on the hull. I feel this method of milling laminating veneers verges on the criminal, as it is a waste of good boat-building timber.

Triple Diagonal with Stringers

This can be an efficient way to build a one-off hull, as the fore-and-aft stringers can be bent around temporary molds and permanent bulkheads to form the inside building mold. This method is widely used by builders of lightweight racers and multihulls. I have seen strong, light hulls—from 10 feet to 60 feet—built this way.

Fin-and-skeg-type hulls lend themselves to this method better than do wineglass-shaped hulls. It is difficult to bend and fair the veneers to conform with the tight reverse curves of a wineglass hull. It is also hard for staples to give you the holding power you need to keep the veneers in place in these tight curves.

The stringers for this type of hull must be spaced quite close together if you wish to have an effective mold framework. This is why it can be more difficult and time-consuming to attach, then fair up the inner laminations of this type of hull than it is to fair up the strip-planked or strip-and-diagonal-planked hull.

The work of scribing, fitting, gluing, stapling, glue cleanup, then staple removal for each of three separate skins is quite labor-intensive. But this process appears fast in a professional shop because several men can work on the planking at the same time. In other words, six men can be at work planking a triple-diagonal hull. They will probably require the same number of hours as two men will, but the large crew will make the job look like it is going three times as fast on an elapsed-time basis.

The main problem with this method of construction is the stringers. They will trap water and hold it while it travels most of the length of the boat.

The thin skin produced by triple-diagonal planking can be extremely strong in most ways, but it is not puncture-resistant. A sharp blow that lands between the stringers can hole the hull.

From my own observations and from the comparisons I did with other builders of the same hull, I am convinced that there is no planking method that really saves time. It will take about the same number of working hours for the owner/builder to set up a shop, loft, frame up, plank, then fair up and finish a yacht-quality hull built of any of the five methods just discussed. John Lidgard, who has built all types of wooden yachts, using each of the methods discussed, during his thirty-seven years as a professional builder, confirms this by saying, "All of the methods take about the same number of hours for the first-time builder. It is only when you set up an efficient shop with all of the tools, building molds, with skilled and trained help, that you can build boats using the more modern

TRIPLE DIAGONAL WITH STRINGERS

*(usually used for lightweight racing boats,
both monohulls and multihulls)*

Pro	Con
Ideal for light displacement.	Less puncture-resistant than all other types of wooden hulls.
Thinner skin than other methods to get similar strength.	Fitting, scribing, and fastening three sets of planks is labor-intensive and boring.
Few expensive screws, rivets, or bolts.	Fitting bulkheads to stringers is difficult.
Ideal for a fin-and-skeg hull.	Stringers trap water and dirt.
Good strength in all directions, as it is virtually a one-piece hull.	Repairs require dry, heated conditions.
Only short lengths of planking stock required.	Difficult to fit to hulls with reverse curves.
Less internal framing required than with carvel.	First two layers can be hard to fit and fair, as they are quite flexible.
No caulking.	Considered the most difficult system for the amateur.
Good for production shop; same mold can be reused.	Lofting and mold setup must be very accurate, as thin skins give little thickness for fairing after the hull is built.
Large planking crews can work at same time.	Unless resorcinol is used, hull must be sheathed or coated inside and out.
Repairs relatively easy compared with strip methods, as few fastenings get in the way.	Sheathing materials and expensive and labor-intensive.
	Glue is expensive, messy, and has high wastage.
	Must have heat- and humidity-controlled shop.
	Veneers expensive and delicate to handle.
	Veneers can be hard to obtain.
	Glue failure could mean total write-off for the hull.
	Hard to survey.
	Hard to assess extent of damage after a collision.

laminated methods to gain any substantial time savings." John not only has built more than 100 wooden yachts from 20 feet to 80 feet, he also knows what he is talking about.

There is a tendency for a boatbuilder to be prejudiced toward the type of planking his shop is best set up to do. Boatbuilders—and most boatbuilding writers—will tell you the pros for their favorite methods, the cons for every other. I have tried to give a fair analysis of the pros and cons of each method, but remember that I, too, have my prejudices.

Estimating the Costs of Different Planking Methods

It is very difficult to give an accurate assessment of the costs of different planking systems, as so much depends on your location, your setup, and sometimes just luck. But as you consider this decision, keep the following in mind. To build in carvel, you need only a simple tool shop and shelter for the boatbuilding area, as you will not be using much glue. To build with strip or laminating methods, your shop will have to be more sophisticated (and rainproof), which could be costly if you have to build or rent. You will also need heating if you are laminating in colder climates.

In the end, the machinery that you need for each method will probably cost about the same. For whatever type of boat you build, you need a bandsaw, a table saw, and possibly a thickness planer.

When you are comparing the materials costs for each planking method, remember that freight is one of the biggest expenses you can incur by choosing the wrong method. If you can buy planking stock nearby, where you can run in and get it yourself with a borrowed trailer, you will save up to 25 percent of materials costs. It is also more common to find bargains in carvel planking stock or strip planking stock than it is in high-grade veneer stock for laminated hulls. You can even cut or salvage your own logs for carvel planking and resaw them yourself—or, as a friend here in New Zealand did, get paid by a furniture factory to cart away its offcuts and resaw them into strip planks at home.

To figure the costs with some accuracy, it pays to know the approximate amount of planking stock you will need. To do this, you need to know the square footage of the hull you will be planking. A quick way to compute this is to figure the length of the hull at its longest point and multiply this by the height of the hull (not the girth) at its widest part on the profile, minus the distance from the rabbet to the bottom of the keel. Multiply this by 2. This will give you the number of square feet (within 10 percent) for both sides of the boat. For carvel or strip planking, you need about 30 percent more stock than the skin area. For triple skin, you need about 10 percent more—plus, of course, the multiple for the number of layers you will be using.

Your costs for carvel planking will include the planking stock, rabbet and frame fastenings, cotton and paying compound. For unsheathed strip planking, the costs include planking strips and their milling, edge nails, frame fastenings, adhesives, cleanup materials for adhesives (i.e., any solvents), and adhesive applicators. For laminated planking styles, you will need veneer stock, staples, plank fastenings, adhesives (times the number of layers), solvents, and sheathing materials—plus the fuel for heating the shed if this is necessary to maintain gluing temperatures.

In comparing the three hulls built in southern California by Kit Cooney, Linda Smith, and ourselves, the planking for Linda's sheathed hull came out a bit more expensive than Kit's strip-planked hull. Had we chosen cedar rather than teak, the carvel hull-planking materials would have been less expensive than the others. But the cost savings from any of the three methods would have been less than 4 or 5 percent of the cost of the materials for the finished boat.

Sheathing, Coating, and Underwater Hull Protection

I myself do not like sheathed hulls because of the extra cost involved, the extra labor, and the possibility of sheathing separation once the hull has been in the water for a while. If the sheathing is damaged and has to be repaired or totally replaced, it can be a major shipyard job—first because it is very difficult to sheathe a hull that is right side up, and second because it is hard to get good, dry conditions outside a large shipyard shed to make sure the wood you are resheathing is dry and the adhesives will work. Large timbers like the backbone and deadwood usually swell up after the boat is launched. When this happens, the sheathing will crack and begin to pull away from the hull. I have seen this happen at the garboard seam area and the radiused corners at the stem, forefoot, and deadwood.

Carvel-planked hulls should not be sheathed unless the fabric used is very flexible, such as muslin or light canvas set in paint. Otherwise, the individual planks will shrink and swell and crack a more rigid sheathing.

To protect single- or double-planked and/or a strip-planked hull and guarantee them a trouble-free long life, I would do two things. First, I would choose resorcinol glue for any underwater gluing jobs. Then I would coat the bare wood, from the boottop down, with three coats of creosote to give permanent worm protection. Resorcinol is designed to take the abuse of deep-cycle situations better than other adhesives. As for creosote, it is one-third the cost of epoxies and a hundred times cheaper than a sheathing or coating for the entire hull.

SHEATHING A WOODEN HULL

Pro	Con
Sheathing can add strength, especially if a unidirectional fiberglass cloth is used.	Extra cost of materials.
Hull will be less likely to leak.	Extra labor.
Sheathing stops worms.	Hard to do on an upright hull.
Covers up poor joints.	Additional fairing is difficult once the sheathing is in place.
	Cannot be used over large timbers or the sheathing may crack.
	Hard to repair, patch, or replace.
	Only good on laminated hulls with internal backbone structure, or on hulls on which the keel stub and ballast keel can be bolted in place after sheathing is cured.
	Hull should be well coated inside to assist timber stability.
	Very difficult to survey hull and hull adhesives.

Creosote not only is inexpensive, it also is extremely effective against worms. I have used it on my boats for thirty years. It does not replace antifouling paints; it just keeps tropical worms out of the wood if the paint is rubbed off. The creosote will penetrate and protect up to $1/4$ inch into absorbent woods such as oak, fir, and cedar, or $1/8$ inch into mahoganies. It is compatible with any bottom coatings that use turpentine or nonvinyl bases. It also seems to help the bottom paint adhere to the wood.

If you wish to have a covering other than paints and creosote on your hull, I would recommend covering the hull with several coats of epoxy both inside and out. This coating will be far easier to repair than sheathing. If you want to fair up the boat a bit after you get it out of the boatshed and sight along its topsides in the sunlight for the first time, you can fair up through the coating and just recoat it. Once it is sheathed, you can never fair it again without major costs and a lot of work.

If you do wish to sheathe a hull, the best type of boat would be either one that has a very light backbone structure (like a multihull) or a fin-and-skeg design in which the lead keel can be bolted in place after the hull is sheathed. If the design you are using is for a flat-floored fin-and-skeg hull with a stub piece (deadwood) set in between the hull and the ballast keel, this chunk of wood should be left unsheathed so it can expand and contract as it wishes without threatening the sheathing.

If you laminate your hull with epoxies, all of the manufacturers of this adhesive recommend that it be fully sheathed or coated inside and out with three to five coats of epoxy. This will keep the timbers from moving too quickly as they adjust to the moisture content of life afloat so that the inevitable small amount of swellage does not stress the glue joints. The coatings also will protect the water-resistant epoxy glues, which are not designed for deep-cycle situations.

Timber for Planking

Don't be daunted by the planking-timber specifications written by various experts and boat designers. If you used only the perfect, air-dried, quarter-sawn, high-quality, clear mahogany, teak, or whatever they said was essential, you could double the cost of materials for your hull yet gain very little in value. Many types of wood can be used for planking—be it carvel, strip, or multiple skin. I have seen both yachts and workboats planked successfully with the timbers listed in Appendix A.

When you are choosing the planking stock for a carvel-planked hull, you should look for the type of timber most readily available in your locale, one that is reasonably priced, rot-resistant, bendable, and, *most* important, easy to hand-plane. Choose a timber that you can find in adequate widths and lengths to accommodate spiling and minimize butt blocks. I would prefer to plank a boat with cedar—which is rot-resistant, easy to work, lightweight, and usually available in clear large boards—rather than use a more difficult-to-work timber such as mahogany, unless the hardwood was reasonably priced and available in a good selection of widths and lengths. I used teak on *Taleisin*'s hull because I was able to select and mill my own timbers in the Orient. I ended up paying the same price for this planking stock as I would have paid for good-quality fir or Philippine mahogany. But I did have to work around a considerable amount of defects in many of the boards. Had I been buying timber for this hull in the United States at the time I built the boat, I would have used one of the fine cedars from the Pacific Northwest.

If the species of planking stock specified on your plans is not readily available, you can use any good planking timber that has a similar weight per cubic foot—or choose one that weighs less. But be careful if a very light wood—such as cedar, which weighs about 21 to 27 pounds per cubic foot—is recommended and the most inexpensive, readily available planking stock in your area is pitch pine at 45 pounds a cubic foot. This could present a problem, since the planking on any hull represents about 8 to 10 percent of the total finished displacement of the average sailing yacht. If you double the weight of the planking materials, the planking can become as high as 20 percent and the boat will float low on her lines.

As many of us know, clear or quarter-sawn, perfectly straight-grained boards have rarely found their way into boatyards. Perfect planks are made into such items as pianos, and perfect large timbers are sliced into veneers for furniture and plywood. These top-grade clear planks demand twice the price of timber the next grade down—the grade usually sold as boatbuilding timber. This boatbuilder's grade usually has a few knots or checks, which can be cut out or avoided as you spile your planks.

Air-dried timber is fine, but it is not absolutely necessary for boat or yacht work. Kiln-dried wood is equally as good, but it is important to remember that kiln-dried wood is initially drier and temporarily more brittle when it comes fresh from the ovens. I began acquiring my boatbuilding skills in the high humidity of the Pacific Northwest (Vancouver, British Columbia), where I used both air-dried and kiln-dried stock. I then worked on repairs and built two boats in the low humidity of southern California, using a majority of kiln-dried stock. There I learned the hard way that kiln-dried stock should be allowed to rest for a couple of weeks so it can absorb some moisture and become less brittle. The ideal moisture content for bending timber is about 12 to 16 percent. It is at its strongest and most flexible within these limits. But during the fall and winter in southern California, there are hot, dry, easterly Santa Ana winds, which cause the ambient air humidity to drop to the point where the moisture content of boatyard wood can get as low as 6 percent. Even air-dried stock will fracture if bent during those conditions.

If you are using kiln-dried stock during dry conditions, get out the garden hose and wet down the boards on both sides, then store them with strips in between in the coolest, shadiest part of the yard. If you let the boards rest for several days, the kiln-dried stock will absorb some moisture into its outside surfaces and stabilize. It is these outside surfaces that need to be flexible, because when a board is bent, the inside surface of the bend must compress a bit and the outside must stretch somewhat. For this reason, soaking a dry plank even overnight can make a large difference and help it bend without breaking. This same problem can occur in cold climates, especially ones with heavy snow and below-freezing temperatures over long periods. Add a big, woodburning shop heater to the equation and timbers stacked indoors can become very dry. This is why it pays to buy a simple hygrometer. I found that by keeping the humidity in my shop at about 35 percent, my timber stayed at a nice, workable moisture content and my large timbers developed very little checking during construction. I controlled the humidity during the dry season by running an evaporative cooler and wetting down the dirt floor at dusk each day.

Kiln-dried stock does have some definite advantages over air-dried stock. The first is its lower cost. It is expensive to warehouse wood while it air-dries, and large amounts of capital must be tied up in stacks of timber that cannot be sold for long periods of time. Kiln-dried stock can be sold within a short time of its arrival from the forests.

Kiln-dried stock is usually waterstain free. Air-dried stock often has age stains, water stains, and marks of various kinds. In some cases, a considerable amount of wood has to be removed to make the timber suitable for varnishing. This again costs money because you have to purchase thicker stock to allow for cleanup.

Finally, kiln drying seasons the wood more quickly and cleanly, and this procedure is similar to steaming green, unseasoned oak for bent frames—the steamed oak becomes harder and more fungus-resistant than air-dried stock. It seems that the heat of steaming or kiln drying kills the bacteria that could cause rot in susceptible timbers.

So I would use kiln-dried stock for planking or for any part of the boat, especially if I were building in a humid part of the country.

When you are buying planking stock, check the boards for falling breaks. These almost-imperceptible, across-the-grain cracks happen if a tree falls over another log as it is felled. The blow causes slight fractures, and these cracks will show up in the boards when they are planed smooth. Sometimes you can be unfortunate enough to get a large stack of boards from the same stressed tree, and each board will break as soon as you bend it onto the hull. So check your planed stock for these cross-grain stress fractures. If you find quite a few, take the planks back to your timber dealer and trade them in for good ones. If this isn't possible. Set the boards aside for other uses.

If you buy your planking stock from a small sawmill operator, or if you are cutting planks from your own logs, make sure the sawyer leaves the bark on the edges of each board (flitch cut). These flitch-cut boards will be wider at the butt end. This extra inch or two of width can help considerably when you are spiling curved planks.

Although it is often specified that all planking should be quarter-sawn, if you are using small logs (18 inches in diameter or less), you will have to ask for random grain (plain sawn). An 18-inch-diameter log that is quarter-sawn will yield only narrow boards, and, as we know, wide boards are more useful for planking.

If you are planking with a hardwood, tight-grained cedar, or cypress (sixteen annual rings per inch or closer), it is generally considered fine to use plain-sawn boards. The specification of rift-, edge- or quarter-sawn planking is only important if a more open-grained wood, such as fir or pine, is being used. These slash or flat, open-grained softwood planks will make it more difficult to get a smooth, grain-free yacht finish on the topsides. But these slash-grained planks do bend on more easily and have less tendency to split as they are fastened. It is only the difficulty of getting a smooth finish that causes them to be considered inferior. They will last just as well, and I have been successful 50-year-old fish-boats that were planked with random-grained fir or pine.

One word of caution. If you are using mahogany for planking, *do not* specify edge-grained stock. Edge-grained mahogany has a tendency to tear slightly in either direction when you hand-plane it. This makes it almost impossible to smooth up the outside of the planking and scrub or round the inside with hand tools. You can identify edge-grained mahogany by the ribbonlike grain.

How clear of knots should your planking stock be? Once again, it is a choice between yacht or workboat finish. I've seen workboats and some low-cost yachts planked with juniper (white cedar) that had small, tight knots every 8 or 10 inches. For yacht-quality specs, allow a maximum of two or three small, tight knots per board. These will be only a small cosmetic irritation as you finish the topsides. They will often reappear, rather like ghosts, when the wood absorbs moisture or dries out.

You will find three basic knot shapes in potential planking stock. The pin knot runs edge to edge through the plank, the face knot is like a wood plug that goes right through the thickness of the board, and the diagonal knot runs at an angle through the grain. The pin knot weakens the board more than any other type of knot. I would not use a board with any pin knots because they usually will cause the plank to break as you bend it onto the hull. The small face knot is the least likely to cause the plank to break, but face knots sometimes fall out a week or two after the plank has been fitted to the hull. If this happens, bore or file out the knot hole and fit and glue a slightly tapered wood plug in its place. The diagonal knot, if it is tight and small, is the least likely to fall out or cause a plank to break.

In any case, knots are a problem. They make planing or scrubbing more difficult, so the money you save by using stock with knots spaced 12 inches apart will be eaten up quickly in the extra labor you expend working the gnarly timber. On the other hand, paying double the price for absolutely knot-free planking stock is also economically unsound.

A final consideration that could influence your choice of planking timbers is the quality of the sapwood. The new annual-growth rings of a tree are usually a lighter color than the older inner part (heartwood). Normally, about 10 percent of the diameter of a log will be sapwood. If this sapwood is rot-resistant, it can be incorporated into the spiled, curved planks. This means that a wood like cedar, with durable sapwood, will yield more planks per flitch than a timber with unreliable sapwood. In oak and fir, the sapwood is inferior to the heartwood and should be avoided.

Choosing Fastenings for Carvel Planking

Four common types of metal fastenings are used with carvel planking: bolt, screw, rivet, and nail. All four will have a quite similar shear strength if they are of equal diameter. But their holding power in tension and their effect on the longevity and condition of the boat as a whole will vary. In diagram 17.19, they are shown in the order of my prefer-

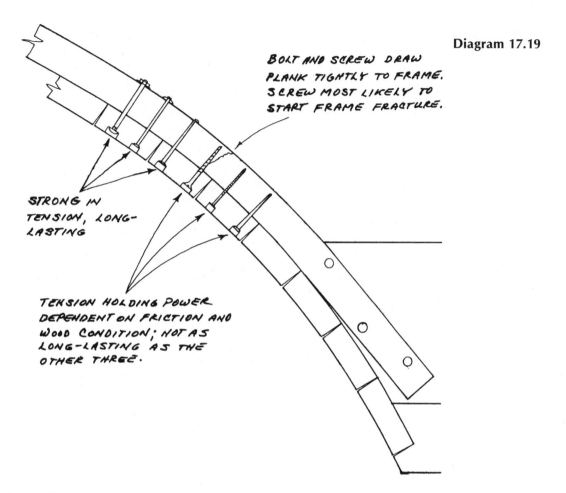

Diagram 17.19

BOLT AND SCREW DRAW
PLANK TIGHTLY TO FRAME.
SCREW MOST LIKELY TO
START FRAME FRACTURE.

STRONG IN
TENSION, LONG-
LASTING

TENSION HOLDING POWER
DEPENDENT ON FRICTION AND
WOOD CONDITION; NOT AS
LONG-LASTING AS THE
OTHER THREE.

ence—which also happens to be in order of tension holding power. The order of cost from most expensive to least would be: bolt, screw, rivet, clout nail, Anchorfast nail, boat nail. (The types of metals used for fastenings are discussed in chapter 3.)

Nails. The holding power of nails in both tension and shear is adequate for keeping planks attached to frames if the nail doesn't corrode and the wood surrounding the nail hole doesn't soften. If you consider the cost, holding power, longevity, and the amount of labor required to install and finish the fastenings, the best all-around plank fastening is probably the copper or galvanized boat nail with a chisel point, which is driven through the frame and then bent (or clenched) over. Many of the fishboats and some yachts built on the west coast of British Columbia were fastened this way. My first boat was. In most cases, I prefer this method over using screws. Unfortunately, however, a bent-over nail is not considered yacht-quality construction. These clench nails are ideal for planks laid over two-layer, steam-bent frames as the nails hold all three pieces together like an economical rivet. Nails with chisel points are very common and easy to purchase in galvanized steel. But copper ones (clout nails) recently have become harder to find.

Some builders use Anchorfast (ringed) nails for planking, but ring nails are hard to drive without using a pilot hole, and most of the smaller ring nails are too skinny, so they tend to bend easily when they are driven in. The hard-drawn, square-cut scotch nails I used are less likely to bend, but the serrations have less holding power than the rings on an Anchorfast nail. Both the round and the square-cut copper nails can be used for rivets.

Wood screws. Flathead wood screws are a common choice for fastening planks. They can have quite good holding power if the metal threads do not corrode and the adjoining wood threads don't soften. If dampness, age, or corrosion of the fastenings causes the wood to soften, the planks will have to be refastened with larger-size screws to grip new, hard wood.

Screws are the best possible fastening for holding plank ends to the backrabbet of any wooden hull, but they are the worst possible fastening to use with steam-bent frames, especially in the high-load area of the reverse turn near the floor timbers. They tend to start cracks in this area of the frame if the boat flexes at all when it is going to windward. The wood screw, which is self-tapped into the frame, exerts a splitting, wedgelike pressure as the threads force their way outside the perimeter of the pilot hole. One of the most common repair jobs I have done is to sister broken steam-bent frames, and the break coincides with a screw hole nine times out of ten.

Screws work quite well on laminated or sawn frames, which have less internal stress than steam-bent ones. They usually are of larger dimension, so they spread the loads of the screw more widely.

Wood screws hold far better than ring nails and are easy to remove when they are new. But they are quite expensive—twice as costly as rivets, three times as much as boat nails. They do not last as long as bolts, rivets, or copper clench nails, as the thin bronze threads can corrode away over a thirty-year period.

Copper rivets. These are the first choice of wooden boat builders in England, New Zealand, Scandinavia, and most other European countries. I have observed that older copper-riveted boats do not need to be refastened, even after fifty to sixty years. The rivets usually will outlast the wood, and they tend to reduce the incidence of broken frames. These fractures are far less common with rivets than with screws, especially on bent frames.

Rivets work like bolts, holding all of the planking and framing together, yet the rivet will give or stretch just enough so that if the wood swells, it can move and not crack. Rivets are long-lived and inexpensive. A copper nail plus its rove will cost less than half the price of a wood screw. The same nail can be used in a variety of situations; all you have to do is cut it to length. With wood screws, you need to have an inventory of different lengths. Rivets are easily surveyable and relatively easy to remove. You can use the same rivet hole if you remove a plank and replace it for some reason. On the other hand, rivets are more labor-intensive to use. They make it harder for the person who will be sanding and varnishing the inside of the frame faces. They also make it harder to fit ceiling inside the hull behind bunks.

Bolts. Bolts can be a good fastening for any wood parts on a boat. They are generally used as planking fastenings only on large vessels with large-dimension frames. But a bolt is the ideal fastener for the butt ends of planks that fit against butt blocks. A bolt is the easiest fastening to remove and replace if you wish to do a repair or a fastening survey. If costs were not the important factor, I would prefer that the planks on any vessel over 50 feet be fastened with silicon-bronze carriage bolts.

The disadvantage of this is that more costs are incurred for the labor involved in sawing off any of the threaded portion of the bolt that is proud of the nut. The nuts will make it difficult to fit interior joinery and ceiling, and the finished fastening will not look as tidy as a rivet looks inside the hull.

Caulking Seams

The first rule for caulking seams is: snug on the inside, open on the outside, so that the cotton wedges into the seam as it is driven with the caulking irons yet can't be pushed through into the hull. The second rule is: the outside opening should be about 1/16 inch for each inch of planking thickness.

The fitting of caulked, carvel-planked seams is usually done in one of three ways (diagram 17.20), all of which will keep the water out of a new hull. The method shown in (a) is the hardest of the three to fit because two-thirds of the seam ideally should have a tight fit. Because the wedge angle of the seam is more acute, the caulking is more likely to crawl out than it is with seam styles (b) and (c).

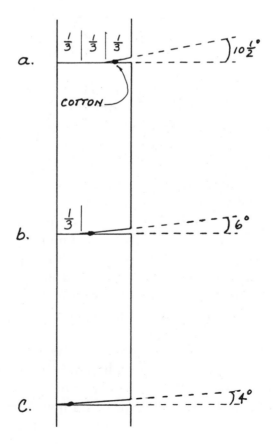

Diagram 17.20

Seam style (b) also requires a good fit for one-third of the seam, but the seam wedge is less acute. Seam (c) is my preference. It is easier to fit each seam because only the inside corners of the plank have to touch to obtain a fit. The seam wedge angle at about 4 degrees is the most advantageous of the three types because the caulking cotton has more of a tendency to stay put. When the boat is launched and the planks begin to absorb water, the outsides of the planks will absorb moisture first. This causes the outside opening of each seam to squeeze in a bit, and the paying compound will pooch out a little. This closing up is great because it locks the cotton into place even more securely. This is the only style of seam I would recommend if you are planking in a low-humidity area such as southern California. If your planking stock is quite dry, the expansion of the planks as they soak up water can break and separate the frames. I have seen cracked frames that were separated by as much as ¼ inch on boats built by well-respected California yards who chose to use seams fitted as in (a) and (b) in the diagram. Philippine mahogany planking is infamous for this determined swelling. Fir, cedar, and teak planking do not seem to develop this unstoppable expansion as often.

Method (c) is the one I used for *Seraffyn*. Her planking was kiln-dried, dark red Philippine mahogany, and she had no frame separation after eleven years and 50,000-plus miles of ocean voyaging. Instead, the inside corners of the plank seams crushed together and raised a slight (1/32 inch) mound of wood along many of the underwater seams. I firmly believe this crushing of the inside corner of the plank relieved the breaking strains on the frames. The teak planking on *Taleisin* showed far less swelling after five years of sailing, and the underwater seams inside the hull do not seem to have moved at all, although the paying has pooched out a little and the seams have narrowed slightly outside below the waterline.

A final advantage to this deep seam is that there is room to add more cotton if a hull develops leaks and requires additional caulking.

The only disadvantage to seam (c) is that it takes a lot more paying compound to fill the remaining seam after it is caulked.

In Canada and England, where the climate usually is cool and humid and the summer sun is not too intense or continual, it is very common for builders to use type (c) seams and set in a strand of cotton. Then, instead of paying the seams, they fit and glue in cedar wedges that just touch the caulking cotton. This method is great in the right climate, as the glue ties the planks together and gives them more horizontal structural strength. The topsides on these boats are easier to finish to a perfect high-gloss, seamless look. But if you take one of these wedge-seamed boats into the tropics, nine times out of ten the topside planking will split at the seams as the relatively damp timber dries out under the intense tropical sun. Naturally, you can minimize the cracking by combining a stable wood such as teak with these wedges.

One other type of carvel seam should be mentioned. Called the Swedish or tight seam, it is common in damper climates such as in Scandinavia. In fact, my second keelboat, *Annalisa*, was built this way—all of the timber from one log, all planks tight-seamed, varnished inside and out. But again, this type of seam will crack and open if the boat is taken

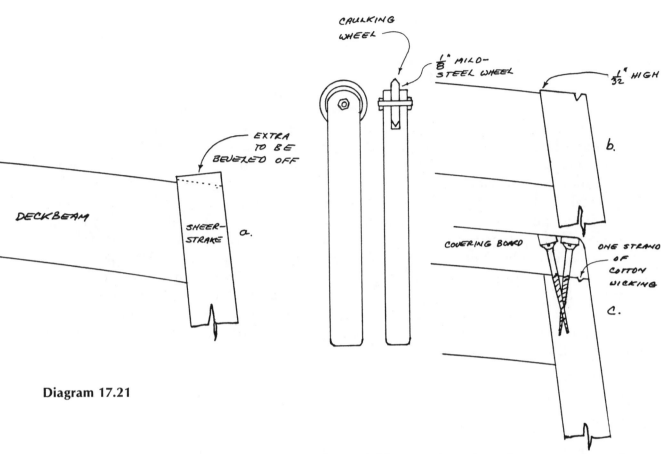

Diagram 17.21

into the tropics. The topside seams on *Annalisa* would open a bit when the summer sun of Canada dried the topside planks. On the other hand, this tight seam is very practical for the top edge of any carvel-planked or strip-planked hull in which, the deck covering board fits against the sheerstrake. Diagram 17.21 shows how to make a Swedish-style tight seam for this use. The top of the sheerstrake is beveled off, leaving 1⁄32 inch of wood above the deckbeam height. A caulking wheel is run along the top outside edge of the sheerstrake to crush a V into the plank. The 1⁄32 inch of extra wood is planed off flush. If water gets into the seam, the crushed V will swell up tightly to the deck covering board and create an automatic seal. I like to add a single strand of cotton wicking, which I hold in place in the V with a bit of shellac as I fasten the covering board. This cotton adds one extra bit of leak-prevention insurance. But if the joint is going to be glued, the cotton is not necessary, as the glue in the V will be pressed upward to seal the joint. On the other hand, since this joint will be well fastened with screws, glue is not absolutely necessary and the cotton-strand method will be effective and faster—cleaning up the excess adhesive from around the frame heads and deckbeams inside the hull is a time-consuming job. The screws that hold the covering board down to the sheerstrake should be about 4 inches apart, staggered and angled, as shown in diagram 17.21 (c), to lock down the covering board.

18. CAULKING

Caulking a new boat is a simple, straightforward procedure, one that can be done easily by any person who can build a boat. In most boatyards, the boatbuilder learns about caulking by doing his own seams. This generally improves the uniformity of the seams. Quite often, a promising young apprentice is given a couple of hours of instruction, then he goes right to it, caulking alongside the builder and doing a good job. On the other hand, a professional caulker is a skilled specialist. It takes several years of experience and common sense to recaulk the seams on older boats, because these seams often are tired, they become uneven, they open on the inside, and their edges become ragged. Naturally, the full-time professional caulker hates to lose the new-boat work—the plum jobs. He will convince you that his services are the only thing that will keep your boat afloat. Fortunately for me, my boatbuilding mentor, Art Clark, told me in no uncertain terms: "Any damn fool can caulk a boat, especially a new one." I have completely caulked two new hulls since Art said that. I have also recaulked sections of several others, old and new. The caulking was successful, so Art must be right.

18.1

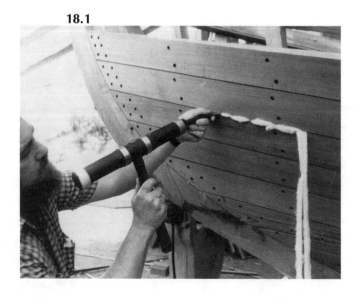

Photo 18.1 I caulked the lower section of the hull when the planking reached the bilge stringer. This was to accommodate Lin, who was varnishing the interior of the boat. Without the caulking, the varnish would have seeped through the seams and run down the outside of the hull. I caulked from the bottom up, but I stopped caulking (as the photo shows) at the second-to-last seam. I stopped here because as you caulk, the forces exerted by the irons can accumulate and wedge the planking slightly sideways. This could have opened up the uppermost seam on the section and left a gap that would show inside the hull. I caulked this last seam when the topsides were completely planked.

18.3

By angling the handle upward slightly, I can scrape the upper edge of the plank. (To scrape the lower edge, I angle the handle downward.) I sharpen the corners of the hook by running a half-round fine file at 90 degrees to the inside curved face of the hook.

This tool works fine on hardwoods such as mahogany, teak, and yellow cedar, and I prefer to use it rather than the dumb iron to open up seams that are too tight. (A dumb iron is a thick, wedge-shaped iron used to open narrow seams. It crushes the plank edges inward and opens them so there is enough room for the cotton. The dumb iron should work better than the raking tool for softwoods such as fir and white cedar. Art told me the dumb iron was named after a planker who couldn't get the seams right.)

I raked out any seams that needed opening, working from the seam between the garboard and the broad upward to shoulder level. Then I caulked this area. Later, when I had set up scaffolding for the upper seams, I raked the topside seams where necessary, then caulked the topsides.

I like to do the butts first and then caulk all of the plank seams, from bottom to top. I then finish up the hull by caulking the rabbet/garboard seam, working from the top of the stem right back to the sternpost at the transom tuck.

Photo 18.2 My rosewood caulking mallet was made for me by Art Clark. The making iron (lying closest to the mallet) is about 1/32 inch thick at its end. The nib iron (also called a spike or butt iron) is about 1/16 inch thick at its end. The hooked raking tool is a piece of 7/16-inch mild steel that I have bent to shape. The rounded end of the hook is 1/16 inch thinner than the curved cutting edges. The hook tapers from 1/8 inch wide to about 1/32 inch at its point.

Photo 18.3 This raking tool is used to open up the seams wherever they are a bit too tight. It will effectively and quite easily scrape a shaving of wood off either the top or the bottom edge of the seam. This tool can also be used to fair up the appearance of topside seams.

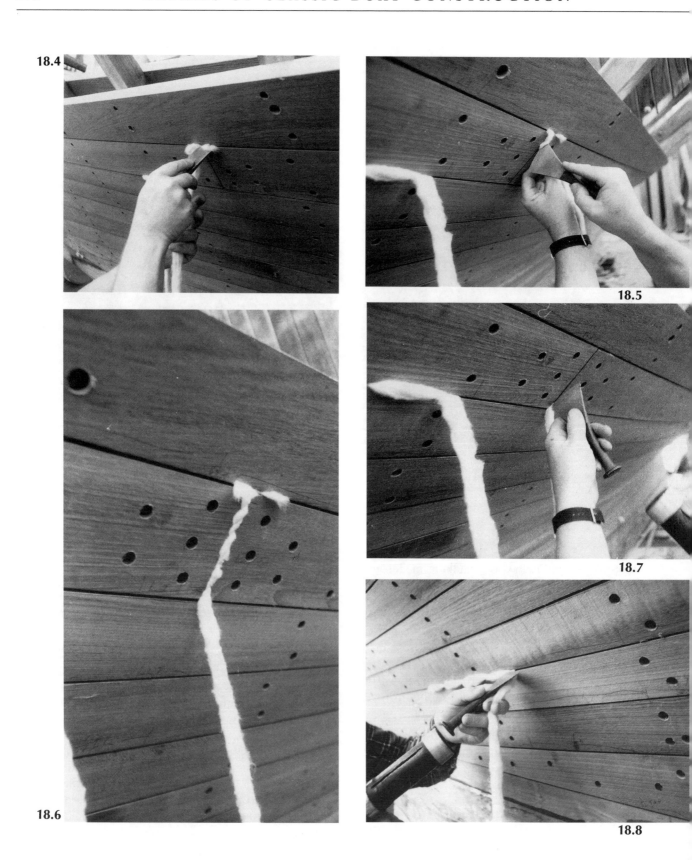

18.4

18.5

18.6

18.7

18.8

Photo 18.4 I divided the end of the cotton in half and pushed the two parts (mustaches) into the plank seam above the butt.

Photo 18.5 Then I tucked the cotton into the seam, using the making iron as shown. If the iron and the seam are the correct size, the iron on its own will slip two-thirds of the way into the seam with ease.

Photo 18.6 When the cotton was tucked (looped) into the butt, I broke it off and made another divided mustache at the lower end.

Photo 18.7 I set the cotton in with the iron and the mallet. I try to keep the mallet blow even so the driving force is the same along all of the caulked area. The force of the blow at butt seams is about the same as I would use to drive a 2-inch common nail into a piece of fir. (Later in this chapter, there is a chart for what I call the "nail scale," or hammering force for caulking various areas of the hull.) Keeping these hammer blows even is the critical factor with caulking, because if they are too heavy, the forces exerted by the cotton can accumulate and have a wedging effect that will build up excessive strains all through the hull.

Photo 18.8 Next I caulked the seams. This is the way I normally hold the iron and the cotton as I tuck it into the seam. I use the iron to shove the tuck of cotton into the seam with a light hammer tap, keeping light pressure on the cotton as I guide it with my middle and forefinger. This lets the cotton slide through as needed as I tuck it into the seam.

Photo 18.9 When several tucks were in place I came back and hardened in the cotton. The tucks of cotton you see here are just the right length for a seam that is 1/16 inch open per inch of planking thickness and tight only on the inside edge. The cotton, when it is driven into the seam, ends up in the lower third. If you look down into the seam, the finished cotton bead will appear to be about 1/32 to 1/16 inch wide.

18.9

Photo 18.10 I started each new seam with a mustache just like at the butt joint. Unfortunately, even with the most careful planking job, seams will vary a little, so the amount of cotton that will be tucked in has to be reduced for a tighter seam; conversely, for a larger-than-ideal seam, slightly more cotton has to be caulked in to fill and seal the seam adequately.

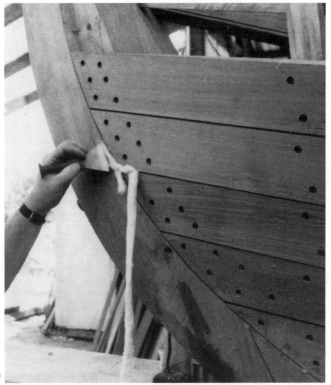

18.10

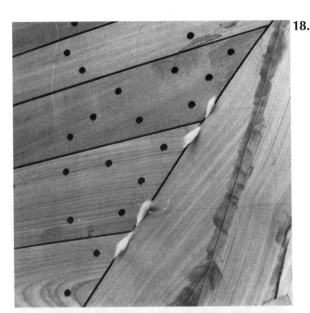

18.12

18.13

18.11

Photo 18.11 Before I put the cotton in this seam, I checked the depth by inserting the bare iron into the seam every 2 or 3 feet along its length. As mentioned earlier, the iron ideally should have gone in about two-thirds of the plank thickness. But in this case, it went in only one-third of the way. So I knew a full strand of cotton would have been too large to drive down into the lower third of the seam. I stripped off about 30 percent of the cotton strand to reduce its bulk. Farther along, when the seam opened up the normal amount, I rejoined and tapered the separated section to make a full strand again.

　　If a seam had been quite open and the bare iron had fit sloppily, I would have needed to loop the cotton so it was hanging down ½ to 1 inch from the seam between each tuck. These loops add cotton so that there is enough to fill the lower third of each seam completely. If the seams are too wide for this to work efficiently, you can also drive in two strands of cotton at the same time, looping both strands enough to fill the seam to the desired depth.

　　Use the same even mallet force no matter which width of seam you are filling—narrow,

normal, or wide. On plank seams, I use less force for each blow than I would on butt seams. The constant-force hammer blow for plank seams should be about the same as you would use to drive a 1½-inch common nail into a piece of fir.

Photo 18.12 I like to leave the mustaches for each seam visible so I know at a glance which seams are caulked.

Photo 18.13 I harden up the nib ends with the same force as I use for butts—i.e., equivalent to driving a 2-inch nail.

18.14

Photo 18.14 I like to caulk the bottom seams first, alternating from side to side on the hull every three or four planks as I work upward. This way, I can set up to do all of the sitting-down work at the same time, then the standing-up work, and finally the scaffold work.

Photo 18.15 The insides of the seams on a newly planked hull can sometimes open up 1/32 inch or even 1/16 inch in dry weather, especially before the hull is sealed with paints or varnishes. (The gap in the seam shown at the top of the photo is about 1/32 inch wide.) Note these gaps as you go along and mark them with chalk or pencil. This will help as you plan your caulking sequence so that you get equal-looking seams on the inside of the planking. For a workboat or a fully ceiled yacht, forget about the gaps. But if you plan to have an unceiled yacht finish inside the hull, take the time to mark the gaps.

18.15

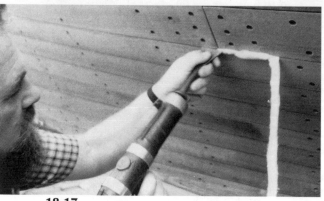

18.17

Photo 18.16 As I caulk, I first harden up the normal, unmarked light-tight parts of each seam. When I come to an area of seam that is marked to indicate that I could see light through it, I only tuck the cotton in lightly. By judiciously caulking the tight seams first, I usually can squeeze together any 1/32-inch gaps until every seam on the hull is more or less tight. I come back and caulk the slightly more open areas last. If you

don't use this method, the open areas will be wedged even wider and will be more exaggerated than necessary.

This photo shows me firmly setting up the fourth seam before going back to set the cotton into the slightly open areas of the lower seams. The slight gaps in the lowest seam will be tightened and closed up a bit when I caulk the garboard seam and drive home the cotton.

This sequence is also used to caulk a leak in an older boat. The seams for the planks two above and two below the leaking seam are hardened up first and the seam with the leak is retightened last. This sequence of seam tightening reduces the wedging-open effect that caulking can have on the inside of a single seam.

Photo 18.17 I like to stretch out the tucks a little as I pass over the mustaches from each butt. Otherwise, the butt mustaches will cause the seam to fill unevenly.

Before I start to caulk each new seam, I check to be sure the amount of cotton in the box is the length of the seam plus about 25 percent. If it is too short, I start a new roll and use the short pieces of cotton elsewhere. That way, I don't have to join the cotton as I work. This saves time and helps keep the cotton even in the seams. On the other hand, you can splice the cotton by rolling it on your knee. If you want to be real fussy, you can put in a 12-inch longsplice similar to the longsplice in a rope.

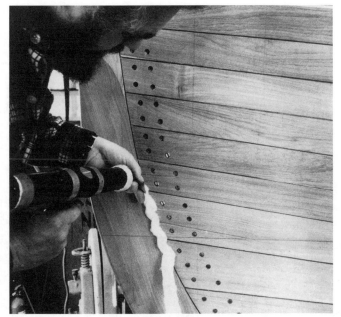

18.18

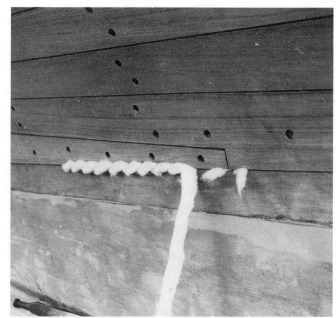

18.19

18.20

Photo 18.18 The final rabbet and garboard seam should be tightened a bit more firmly, using the same blows as for butt seams and nibs. This is because the nibs and butts are staggered throughout the hull, without neighboring seams that can swell and squeeze them tighter once the hull is launched. The horizontal garboard seam needs more caulking pressure because it is the last seam caulked. With the pressure of all of the planks above it to keep it from creeping as it is caulked, it will have no tendency to move. Furthermore, the extra fastenings along the rabbet connection hold the plank above this seam more securely than any other plank. All of the areas where I suggest firmer caulking are backed up by either butt blocks or backrabbets. This ensures that the firmly driven cotton will not bulge through the seam into the hull.

Photo 18.19 The loops of cotton should be spaced closer so that more cotton is driven in here than in a plank-to-plank seam.

All of the mustache ends from nibs and hood ends are tucked neatly under the final strand of cotton along the rabbet seam.

Photo 18.20 Areas where seams run vertically next to large timbers—such as here at the sternpost—should be caulked more tightly because there is more likelihood of the seam's loosening a bit as the wood of the wide backrabbet on the stern knee swells across the grain. Along this vertical area of the rabbet seam, I used pressure equivalent to the blows I would use to drive a 3-inch common nail into a piece of fir.

Fir and oak timbers expand more than teak, so if your boat is built with one of these species, you might have to tighten the caulking in this seam or add a strand of cotton after the boat has been in the water for nine or ten months. The well-seasoned oak knee on *Seraffyn* swelled after she was launched, and this seam opened about 1/16 inch. This caused only a slight weeping, and an extra strand of cotton, driven in firmly, solved the problem to give her an absolutely dry bilge for the next 15 years.

18.21

Photo 18.21   I left the ends of the cotton about 3 inches long at the transom. When I finally caulked the mitered seam from sheer to sheer around the edge of the planked transom, I separated these strands and covered them.

CONSTRUCTION TIMES FOR CHAPTER 18

Larry: Preparing seams and caulking (including transom seam)	34 hours
Lin: Sanding and varnishing interior	13 hours

Totals to date:	Larry	2799 hours
	Lin	632 hours

DISCUSSION

The combination of caulking and carvel planking is the ultimate in practicality. (See chapter 17 for a discussion of the best seam design for a carvel-planked hull.) Caulking can be driven into seams in rain or shine or snow. Any leaks that develop in a caulked hull are simple to locate (assuming you don't have ceiling). You can quite often simply slide a thin steel wire through the damp seam from the inside of the hull so you can tell on the outside where the leak is. This is in direct contrast to the mystery leak in the sheer area of the three-skinned boat I mentioned in the previous chapter. I had a very difficult time locating the source of that leak.

The practicality of caulked planking helps get boats repaired and back to sea quickly. It can be a great time-saver if you hit a log during your two-week summer holiday and spring a leak. You can even tighten the leak under water with iron, mallet, fins, and mask.

The reason caulked seams keep water out of a boat is that both the planks and the cotton swell up when it gets wet. Some people worry that the cotton will fall out of the seams, but if a boat is kept in the water and not allowed to dry out excessively, everything works together to keep the cotton in place. The cotton is also held in by the grip of the paying compound and even the pressure of the water that is supporting the hull and exerting 4 or 5 pounds of inward force per square inch into all of the seams. Of course, the Achilles heel of a caulked boat is the connection between the floors and the frames and the connection of the hood ends of the planks to the backrabbet. The wedging effect of driving the cotton can open up the garboard on an improperly framed hull, and no amount of extra cotton or caulking force will stop a leak in a hull with a poorly engineered garboard area.

Caulked Seams on Launching Day

When launching day approaches, inspect the seams on the hull before you paint the bottom of the boat. If the planks have dried out and shrunk away from the seams by $1/64$ inch or less, simply putty any areas that are open, using soft paying compound, then paint the boat and launch her. But if any seams have opened up more than $1/64$ inch, seal all of the open underwater seams with 1-inch-wide masking tape and then paint the hull. The tape will slow the leaks while the planks swell. Later, when the hull is tight, you can haul out for a few days to remove the tape and put on the next coat of bottom paint.

Do not recaulk the seams if they open up during construction. If you originally caulked the hull using a force equivalent to driving in a $1\frac{1}{2}$-inch nail, and you recaulk it with the same force, you have doubled the caulking force, which will cause excessive strains to be transferred onto the frames and fastenings when the planks eventually swell.

Most caulked hulls will take on a bit of water when they are launched. But in every case, the seams will swell shut within two or three weeks. The seams on a cedar hull sometimes will stop weeping within a few hours of launching. *Seraffyn*, with her Philippine mahogany planking, took on 5 gallons of water before she took up four days after launching. With hardwood planking such as teak, the weeping can continue for two to three weeks. *Taleisin* took on about a pint of water a day at first, and it was two weeks before she became completely tight.

If you are relaunching an older boat, be sure to putty and/or tape all of the open underwater seams if the boat has been out of the water for more than a month or two.

I feel that, if practical, no softwood hull should be left out of the water for more than ten days in a dry climate—or two to three weeks in a humid one. With hardwood planking such as teak, which does not move much, I would still restrict time spent out of the water to two or three weeks in dry climates and a month in humid ones. Also, try to get the hull in a shady spot in the boatyard if at all possible, and shield the bottom from direct sunlight to reduce moisture loss.

If I lived in a cold climate where sheet ice could be a threat to planking, I would cover the boat with a canvas cover and rig a bubble system to stop ice from forming at the waterline—rather than haul the boat for winter storage. If this were not practical, I would copper the waterline about 4 inches above and 3 inches below to protect the hull from the sharp ice. I firmly believe the annual autumn haulout and spring relaunching, which is common in Great Britain and the northeastern United States, creates shrinking and swelling that will age a hull twice as fast as the hull that is left happily stable and supported in its natural wet environment.

Details of Caulking

The caulking forces I have suggested were about average for use on a new, southern California–built hull with 8 to 12 percent plank humidity content. If you planked a boat in Vancouver, British Columbia, during the winter and it was raining much of the time, you would want to caulk the planking a bit tighter because the moisture content of the timber would already be as high as 18 to 20 percent, and the timber would not want to expand as much after the boat was launched. The following table shows the suggested driving forces I would use to caulk a boat up to about 50 feet long when the timber had 14 to 16 percent moisture content.

These forces should be reduced to the next lower driving force if the moisture content of the wood is below 14 percent at the time of caulking; conversely, if the planking material has a higher moisture content, the next higher driving-force range should be used.

If you are unsure of how much force to use as you caulk, remember that too much force is worse than too little—i.e., it is better to undercaulk a boat than to overcaulk it. I have seen professional caulkers who were used to working on large, heavily built workboats ruin lightly built yachts by driving the cotton in too firmly and forcing open the seams on the inside of the hull. This can cause the frames to break as the boat swells and even cause the floors to pull away from the keel timbers. I have seen overcaulking break and split away the inside edges of plank seams. If you undercaulk, the worst that will happen is that you will have to reef (pull) out the paying compound and tighten the cotton in the seams that leak.

THE NAIL SCALE

(This represents the force of a normal claw-hammer blow required to drive a round common nail of a given length into Douglas fir at 14 to 16 percent moisture content.)

Plank Thickness	Softwood Planking Nail Scale		Hardwood Planking Nail Scale	
	Plank Seams	Butt Seams	Plank Seams	Butt Seams
5/8″	3/4″	1¼″	1″	1½″
3/4″	1″	1½″	1¼″	1¾″
1″	1¼″	1¾″	1½″	2″
1¼″	1½″	2″	2″	2½″
1½″	2″	2¾″	2¾″	3½″

Most builders prime a boat's seams before and after they caulk. The primer can be oil-based paint or a mixture of 50 percent beeswax and 50 percent turpentine that is heated until it liquefies. Then it is immediately painted into the seams. The caulking cotton can be driven in while the priming is still damp.

These methods protect the cotton and are time-tested, but they require that you use an oil-based putty to pay the seams, as most modern synthetic compounds are not compatible with beeswax or oil-based paints. I caulked *Taleisin's* seams dry because I wanted to use 3M 5200 sealant for the seam paying compound. Lyle Hess reassured me in this decision by saying that the oil in the teak would help preserve the cotton and give it an increased life span. He said the usual life of cotton that has been primed before and after caulking is thirty-five to forty years. Unprimed cotton can sometimes begin to decay after twelve to fifteen years.

Larger hulls—those with planks 2½ inches or thicker—normally are caulked with oakum. (Oakum is made of Russian or Italian hemp preserved with pine tar.) Because it is coarser in texture, rather like manila, it tends to grip the plank seams with more friction than cotton. For this reason, oakum sometimes is used on small boats to caulk wide or roughed-up seams. But oakum, because of its tar impregnation, has less tendency to swell than cotton, and, because of its coarser texture, it seems to have more of a tendency to let water seep into the hull unless it is driven home quite firmly. On medium-sized vessels, some caulkers caulk first with a strand of cotton and then lay a strand of oakum on top to take advantage of its extra holding power.

The caulkers in some European repair yards—especially those that deal with ancient, oak-planked workboats and barges—have a brutal way of caulking seams that have become too wide and open on the inside (¼ inch and more) to hold cotton or oakum. Their ultimate solution is to jam an appropriate-sized steel rod (usually about ⅜ inch in diameter) two-thirds of the way into the seam. When the steel rusts, it scales, and the scale causes it to expand and seal the leaks in the old bucket for a few more years.

Caulking Tools

The various types of caulking irons often come boxed in a set of ten irons, which include crease and nib irons.

Crease irons (standard making irons) are numbered BB (1/32-inch-thick blade), 0 (1/16-inch-thick blade), 1 (1/8-inch-thick blade), 2 (3/16-inch-thick blade), and 3 (1/4-inch-thick blade). Nib irons (also called spike or butt irons) are packaged in sets with five blade sizes, the same as crease irons.

Crease and nib irons come in bent-iron versions. The bent irons are used to caulk in awkward areas, such as along a motorboat's garboard or along the deck seams or wood stanchions next to a bulwark. Reefing irons, which look like bigger versions of my seam raker, come in various sizes, as do dumb irons, which are used to open up seams that are too tight.

As mentioned earlier, the hooked seam raker can be used to widen tight seams on hardwood planking, but the rake cannot be used on the endgrain of butts or the hood ends of planks. A thick-bladed iron with a little taper (a dumb iron) is the only option if you need to widen these seams. This dumb iron usually is your only choice for widening the seams on a hull planked with softwood.

Most of these irons can be hammered out of some 3/4-inch round mild steel. Heat the steel until it is red hot and hammer it into the shape you need. This is the time-honored approach to caulking irons, as most irons were made right on the job by the boatbuilder when he encountered an awkward corner or seam he had to caulk.

Caulking mallets are somewhat the same. Although some caulkers will demand a mallet with a perfect ring, this may be one more bit of mystery the professional caulker is trying to maintain in order to keep new-boat jobs for himself. My mallet, made of rosewood, has no ring at all. A caulking mallet is designed with a long head and proportionally short handle so that you use short tapping strokes instead of long swinging strokes. This keeps you from delivering too much power with each blow. For 1¼-inch- to 1½-inch-thick planking, grip the mallet about at the middle of the handle. For thinner planking, grip it nearer the head to produce lighter taps. It is only when you are caulking vessels that have planking 2½ inches thick that you should swing the mallet by holding it near the end of the handle.

As with irons, you can make your own mallet. Use live oak or mesquite and band the ends with tempered steel. To get a nice ringing sound, you can cut slots in the round head.

You can even caulk a small boat, 40 feet or under, using an ordinary wood mallet. But do not use a steel mallet on a caulking iron. The metal-to-metal blows are too hard and penetrating, and they could cause additional hammer force that could add up to that sin of all sins, overcaulked seams.

19. FINISHING THE HULL

In the days when wooden boat building yards were far more common than they are today, certain craftsmen specialized in the work of fairing up or smoothing hulls. They were called *outboard joiners*. It was their work that highlighted a fine construction job, because as a boat was pulled from the shed into the harsh light of day for the first time, dockside loungers would sight along the hull, looking for the slightest bit of unfairness. Fairing is not a difficult job, but it is one that will test your patience and the accuracy of your eye. It is a job that must be done for any type of hull that you build—metal, fiberglass, or wood —with the exception of lapstrake wooden hulls. If you are planning to sheathe your hull, fairing must be done correctly before the sheathing goes on. But if you are building an unsheathed carvel hull, such as I show here, you do not have to agonize too much over the fairing. If you happen to find a few high spots on the topsides once your boat comes out of the shop, you can smooth them down later, during the next haulout.

19.1

Photo 19.1 There are four basic axioms for outboard joinery (assuming your framework was fair):

1. The planks are already fair fore and aft.
2. The frames are fair vertically.
3. At the turn of the garboard (bottom planks), the seams must be left untouched—i.e., they are already net so the planks must be hollowed evenly between the seams (diagram 19.1).
4. At the turn of the bilge or topsides, the middle of each plank is already net and fair fore and aft, and only the seam edges of the plank must be rounded of so that they are fair vertically (diagram 19.1).

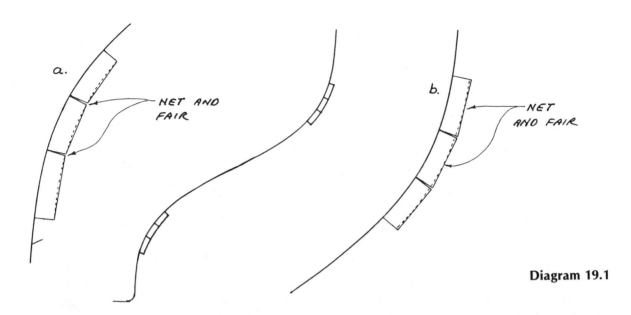

Diagram 19.1

There is a big difference between smoothness and fairness. I have seen a lot of fiberglass hulls that felt very smooth to the touch, yet few of them look perfectly fair. As you sight down the sides of these hulls, bumps and hollows usually appear. Even though these bumps and hollows may be only 1/64 inch or less, they pick up the light and distract your eye. The higher the gloss or the darker the hull finish, the more obvious these blemishes will be. It is these various-sized bumps and hollows that I try to minimize as I scrape, plane, and sand the hull.

Good planking stock will make outboard joinery easier. If the grain is straight and the wood cuts cleanly under the plane iron, this job can be very satisfying. But if the grain of the planking is swirly, if it is full of knots or is ribboned (like edge-grained mahogany can be), the wood will tear under the plane iron and you will lose time and probably your patience as you scrape, sand, and fill these defects.

19.2

Photo 19.2 These tools are the basic ones I needed to smooth up this carvel-planked hull. The five planes are (from right to left): convex block plane, 1/8-inch curved sole; convex block plane, 1/16-inch curved sole; wood-soled smoothing plane, 1/32-inch curved sole; metal-soled smoothing plane, flat sole; and metal-soled jack plane, flat sole.

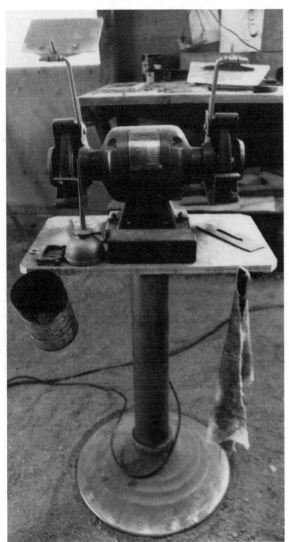

Photo 19.3 I dress my plane irons regularly to keep a razor-sharp, hollow-ground cutting edge at all times. When the hollow begins to diminish from hand-sharpening the irons on the stone, I rehollow each iron on the grinder.

A portable sharpening station comes in handy in any boatyard. The heavy base for this sharpening station is the stand from a second-hand restaurant table.

Photo 19.4 It is a good idea to fair up the aft garboard area first, as the hull is almost flat along there. I faired the deadwood aft, which is below the garboard, before I bolted it to the keel. Since

19.5

19.6

I knew this was not only shaped to the loft floor but also net, it gave me a good guide as I began fairing in the planking. I chalked or penciled along the areas of fore-and-aft planking seams that must be left net, so that they were readily identifiable as a guide.

I find it best to work on two planks at a time along the bottom of the hull. In this case, I started by scrubbing a conservative amount of wood out of both the garboard and the first broad. Being very careful not to scrub too deeply, I kept checking the depth of the scrubbing with a short, thin batten, using the seams (which, as stated above, are net) and the faired-in deadwood as a guide line.

Overscrubbing must be avoided at all costs, as it leaves hollow or flat areas that are below the correct lofted shape of the hull. The hollow then has to be filled with Bondo. The Bondo will not hold paint like the wood around it, nor will it sand the same, so it will cause minor problems throughout the life of the boat. The problem of overscrubbing is most acute on the topsides, as this area is far more visible than the bottom, and the paint on it probably will have a high gloss, which accentuates any dips or hollows.

When I have conservatively scrubbed about 3 feet of two planks, I start the final planing. I rub chalk onto the vertical batten and rub it fore and aft along the scrubbed area to mark any high spots. Then I plane or scrape off these high spots. I modify the scraper blades to fit the vertical hull curves just as I did when I was scrubbing the insides of the topside planks.

I prefer to leave the wood plugs out of the hull until the fairing is finished. If the hull is plugged before it is faired, the edges of the wood plugs can be chipped out by the plane, since the grain of the wood plugs does not always align exactly with the grain on the surface of the planking.

Photo 19.5 I used the ¹⁄₃₂-inch and ¹⁄₁₆-inch convex planes for most of the final fairing. They were set to take a thin cut. The ¹⁄₈-inch convex plane, which I used mainly for preliminary rough scrubbing, was set for a deeper cut. That way, I did not have to keep readjusting the planes.

I fitted the belt sander with a wooden sole that was curved like a 1/16-inch scrub plane (similar to the sole I described in chapter 7). With this modified sander, I could smooth out the concave spots where there the grain was irregular.

I used machine tools as little as possible for fairing the hull, and then only for preliminary scrubbing. A machine sander of any type can overscrub or overhollow very fast and go very deep. Only the most confident professional outboard joiner should attempt to fair a hull with machines, and I would not let anyone within a hundred yards of my boat with a disc sander.

Photo 19.6 As I work up to the flatter sections of the hull (where my left hand is in the photo), I switch from convex planes to flat-soled planes. I grind and oilstone the blades to approximate the slight bit of curve in these sections. From here on up to the sheer, I use only the metal smoothing plane and the jack plane.

Photo 19.7 The topsides present the reverse problem to the bottom. Here the center of the plank is net and fair fore and aft and the seam areas are the high spots that need to be planed

19.7

off. Unlike on the bottom, I work along the whole topsides, planing all along each of the planks for each step of the fairing and rounding. The sheerstrake and the top half of the second plank do not need to be rounded in order to look correct. I only round and taper the ends of the 1/4-inch-thicker sheerstrake. The rest of its length is left flat as a landing for the rubrail, which will be installed later.

To begin fairing the topsides, I plane flats along the hull, with the planking seams exactly in the middle. The width of the flat area should be equal to the width of the area that is left unplaned in the middle of each plank. When I am satisfied that these flat areas all look equal in width to the flat areas above and below them, I chalk the edges of the two seams and the middle of the plank, as these are now net and the chalk will give me a reference point that I know is "right on."

Quite often, as you plane the flat over the seam between two planks, the grains will be opposing. This can cause the wood to tear, whether you plane forward or aft. The solution is to flat off this area by planing it at a 45-degree angle across the seam. Experiment to see which angle direction cuts the cleanest. In very difficult grain situations, this flatting can be done by sanding with a block, a belt sander, or a 2-foot-long flexible plywood sanding board with 60-grit sandpaper bonded to it. This 3- or 4-inch-wide 1/2-inch plywood sanding board should have two comfortable handles attached to its back about a quarter of the way in from the ends.

The next step in fairing the topsides is again to flat off the fore-and-aft ridges created when I made the first flat with the seam in the middle (diagram 19.2). This is similar to the procedure used to round a spar, and it gives equal-width smaller flats on each plank. I again chalk the middle of each intermediate flat to indicate all of the net areas.

Diagram 19.2   TOPSIDE   ROUNDING

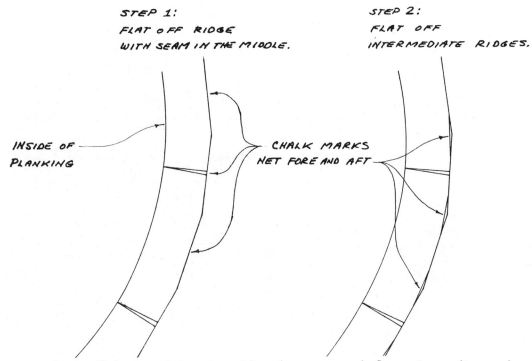

STEP 1:
FLAT OFF RIDGE
WITH SEAM IN THE MIDDLE.

STEP 2:
FLAT OFF
INTERMEDIATE RIDGES.

INSIDE OF
PLANKING

CHALK MARKS
NET FORE AND AFT

I now plane off the remaining tiny ridges between each flat, using a diagonal stroke at 45 degrees across the grain. I use a razor-sharp plane to hit just the high spots and leave the net chalk marks just barely showing. I tend to hold the forward handle of the plane down so it has a tendency to just nick the high spot as I make each stroke.

19.8

Photo 19.8   I kept checking with the chalked, sliding batten. I planed and scraped or stroked the hull with the flexible sanding board until the hull felt fair in a vertical direction both to the batten and to my hand.

I prefer to do my final hand-sanding after the wood plugs and seam paying are finished and the waterline is on the hull. Once the hull feels smooth to the touch, I go on with other aspects of finishing. I did the last bit of fairing and sanding after the transom was planked, although for the sake of continuity, I will discuss painting and final fairing now.

After the wood plugs and graving pieces were in place and the seams were payed, I final-faired the hull to get rid of the last small dents and hollows. I used 60-grit sandpaper, then 100-grit paper for this final sanding.

Although I didn't use an outboard joiner's scraper, it could be helpful, and it is another tool you can make. This 4-inch-by-12-inch scraper can be cut out of the blade of an old handsaw and burnished and filed like a cabinet scraper. To make a handle, rivet two 12-inch-long ¼-inch-by-¾-inch strips of wood along the top edge of the metal blade. The scraper blade is left flexible so it conforms to the rounded topsides. Properly used, it can remove even see-through shavings to fair up any remaining high spots on the hull.

Once the hull is sanded, I apply two coats of paint and then sight along the topsides, holding a 100-watt light below the area I am checking. The indirect light will show up any high or low spots. Although low spots are completely undesirable, if they are only slightly hollow—less than 1/64 inch below the surrounding hull areas—they can be faired out by sanding or scraping around the perimeter of the hollow to make the low area less apparent. As you work, leave the paint untouched in the center of the hollow. These hollows should not occur if you leave a hint of your fore-and-aft chalk lines on the hull as you fair up.

High spots should be faired down with a sanding board until the paint not only comes off the high spot, but also begins to come off all around the area. I sanded off any discrepancies around the hull and repainted the areas wherever the wood showed through, then came back and checked with the "trouble light" the next day.

When we launched the boat, her hull had about five coats of paint, just enough so that she looked bright white and no wood-color shadows showed through. The grain was not completely filled. After the boat had been afloat for six months, several half-moon bumps came out, along with other odd shapes. These obviously were bruises from hammer blows or other accidents to the planking that occurred in storage or during construction. I used sandpaper to fair these until they blended into the hull, then touched up the paint job and, as we voyaged, began working toward an eventual grain-free, high-gloss yacht finish.

Cutting In the Waterline and the Boottop

19.9

19.10

Photo 19.9   The next item on my worklist was to cut in the waterline and the top edge of the bootstripe (boottop). These cut-in lines save time and labor during haulouts. They eliminate the hassle of masking tape, which sometimes pulls fresh paint off the hull. Because you do not need to wait for paint to dry so that you can put tape on top of it, these cut-in lines can turn haulouts into short weekend affairs. To further speed up haulouts, we put antifouling paint right up to the top of the bootstripe. This eliminates the need for a separate color of paint for the bootstripe, with the attendant need for brushes and paint pots. During a weekend haulout, you can scuff the topsides with sandpaper and then paint them quite quickly. The brush can overlap the cut at the top of the bootstripe as you lay on the enamel. The next day, as you apply the antifouling paint, the brush bristles can drop into the sawn groove, making it simple to get a neat, quick line between the bottom paint and the topside paint.

Photo 19.10   If the hull has become out of level, adjust it before striking the waterline by moving the deck level supports until the plumb bob is on center. I erected a straight, horizontal 2 x 4 crossbeam as shown, even with the designed waterline marks on the front face of the cutwater. This mark originally was transferred from the loft floor to the backbone patterns and cut into the stem and sternpost as permanent reference points.

Photo 19.11   The same type of setup is used at the designed waterline (DWL) at the stern of the boat. (Even though it is essential that the hull be level side to side, it is not important that it be level in a fore-and-aft direction, as the uprights that align with the DWL will account for any fore-and-aft discrepancies.) Now the string is stretched between the two DWL straightedges and adjusted until it just touches the hull at its maximum beam. A second string is stretched in

19.11

19.12

the same way on the port side of the hull. When this was done, I checked both horizontal straightedges for level, then measured from the sheer at the maximum beam down to the string on both sides. (If for some reason this measurement is not equal, the hull needs to be adjusted slightly to port or starboard until the topside girth measurements are the same on both sides.) Next I put a ½-inch-long finishing nail through the string where it touched the hull and tapped the nail in lightly for about one-third of its length.

Photo 19.12 An 8- or 10-pound weight attached to the string at both ends kept it tight while Lin slid the string inboard until it touched the planking 4 inches from the first nail. I placed another nail through the string and we kept sliding the string inboard and nailed every 4 inches.

19.13

Photo 19.13 In the bow and stern sections of *Taleisin*, there are hollow sections where the string will not touch the hull. I therefore had to transfer the string height by using a level and an outboard 1 x 2 support, which I clamped to the level. I marked the planking every 12 inches in the hollow areas.

Photo 19.14 I removed the string and tacked a ⅜-inch-by-½-inch batten to line up with the center of the nail holes. Then I stepped back and tried to look at it from all angles to be sure it was straight and pleasing—and fair. It is especially important to have a fair line when seen from the side.

19.14

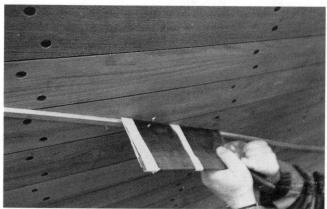

Photo 19.15   I used my bench saw to cut along the top of the batten. I made the cut ¹⁄₁₆ inch, or about the depth of the saw teeth. The tape on the saw corner stops the end from digging into the planking in the hollow areas. The tape on the middle of the saw guides the aft end of the blade nicely in the hollow areas of the hull.

19.15

Now that you know how to cut the waterline, I am going to advise you not to do it in the shipyard if your boat is the first hull of an original design. It seems that very few first-off boats float exactly at their designed waterline. Something always seems to happen to affect this calculated point of flotation. So if there is any doubt about the waterline position, simply scribe the stem and sternpost so that the waterline can be positioned and cut in permanently after the boat has had its sea trials and most of its gear and stores are on board.

The top of the bootstripe, on the other hand, usually can be cut in with no problem at the time of construction. If you have a bootstripe that will be parallel to the waterline, simply raise the straightedges used for the waterline cut-in and repeat the waterline method of layout.

I prefer a bootstripe that has a sheer to it. It looks attractive and seems to suit this type of hull, and it also is practical: It is less likely that weeds and barnacles will adhere to the antifouling paint during long passages when bow and quarter waves keep this area of the hull wet constantly. This sheered waterline is especially nice aft, as it is awkward and hard to scrub any growth off the areas under the aft quarters of the hull from a dinghy.

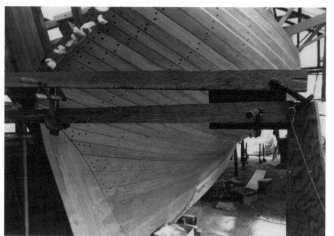

Photo 19.16   To do a sheered bootstripe, clamp a straightedge 6 inches above the right-hand side of the waterline upright, as shown. Then clamp the inboard end 10 inches above the waterline upright. This 4-inch difference between is the amount of sheer I got from amidships to aft. I wanted to have the sheer forward sweep up until it was 12 inches higher than the LWL, so the forward rise was from 6 inches to 12 inches. The string was laid against the maximum beam of the hull amidships and nailed in place, then it was gradually slid up the inclined straightedges fore and aft and nailed against the planking to mark this line in the same way we did the load waterline.

19.16

19.17

Photo 19.17 I decided on the rise of the sheered bootstripe by first drawing it in black on the sail plan. The lower plank of the varnished transom was positioned to the bootstripe marks to create a continuous line of red bottom paint at the bootstripe level. The beaded seam detail on the lower edge of the transom plank became a natural cutting-in line for paint on the flat of the transom.

Photo 19.18 The bootstripe batten was then nailed on and checked for fairness from all angles. I adjusted it slightly until it looked fair, then sawed the line in to a depth of 1/16 inch. (This depth should be adjusted according to the planking thickness. For planks 3/4 inch thick, it should be only about 1/32 inch deep. For planking over 1 1/4 inches, it can be as deep as 1/16 inch. There is little reason to have more than 1/16-inch depth on larger hulls.)

The nail holes made by attaching the string to the hull are eliminated from view by the saw cut. The nail holes made by attaching the saw-guiding batten will fill with creosote and paint.

Before I paint the hull for the first time, I sand the sharp edges of the cut line lightly to remove the hairy edges and give a tiny radius. The bootstripe and waterline cut will be good cutting-in guides until they begin to fill with paint. When this happens, clean out the line with a hacksaw blade. We find we need to do this about every fourth or fifth time we haul. It takes only 20 minutes and ensures that our paint lines continue to look smart and fair.

This cut-in waterline system works fine for any wooden hulls that are not sheathed and are either carvel-planked or have an outside skin of 1/4 inch or more. If the hull is sheathed or coated, this cut-in is impractical, as the cloth and resins would fill it, so for these hulls, you will have to resort to masking tape each time you repaint.

19.18

Photo 19.19 Since we like the look of grooved seams on a hull such as this one, I chamfered the edges off each plank by using a V-shaped block and 60-grit sandpaper. It takes only a few strokes to sand off the corners until the widest part of the V is about 5/16 inch across. I usually judge the width of the V by eye, but if you are not confident, you can make a gauge to keep the V a constant, accurate width. If there was a slight unfairness along any seams in the topsides, I found I could sand a bit more on one seam corner than on the other and fair up the seam.

19.19

Photo 19.20 I taped the planks up to the edge of the V with 1-inch-wide masking tape. This is vital, as the excess 3M 5200 sealant I used is almost impossible to sand or scrape off once it dries. I used a ratchet-type cartridge gun to squeeze the compound into each seam.

To scrape off the excess paying compound, I used a plastic squeegee with a 1/4-inch radiused corner. I then used a putty knife to put the excess paying into the next unpayed seam so it wouldn't be wasted.

19.20

Photo 19.21 I smoothed and rounded the paying compound in the bottom of each V, using a 1/4-inch-diameter copper rod that I bent to form a smooth arc. I wiped the rod clean before each pass and made long sweeps to avoid any bumps along the seams. As soon as the seams were filled and smoothed, I removed the tape. Lin cleaned off any excess 5200 compound that had lapped over onto the wood before it could set and bond to the hull.

When the seam compound was firmly set (I waited about two weeks), I radiused the two corners of the seam slightly so that the topside paint would build up to a good thickness along these wooden corners.

19.21

Some Comments on Seam Compounds

Some manufacturers label paying compounds as caulking compounds, but this is a misnomer, as this term comes from the plumbing world, where these mastics are truly used as caulking. In boatbuilding, caulking is the cotton or oakum that is driven or rolled into each seam. Paying compound refers to the oil, pitch, rubber, or synthetic mastics that cover the cotton and finish off the seam to give a good painting surface.

Do not eliminate the cotton from the seams of any carvel-planked hull or single-thickness laid deck just because a salesman claims he is selling you caulking compound. I have seen too many decks (and even a few hulls) that leaked like a sieve when the cotton was left out. In such cases, the owners had to reef out each seam and then caulk and pay the hull or deck correctly—a labor-intensive and depressing job. If the compound manufacturer insists that his mastic is a substitute for cotton, ask for a written guarantee that will cover both labor and materials if the seams later leak. If you don't get that, and you find water seeping around the edges of the compound, the manufacturer will replace only the paying compound.

When we built *Seraffyn*, the most commonly used seam compound was Kuhl's compound. The British equivalent is Jeffries Marine Glue. This is definitely not a glue. After eight years, we found that the compound had lost its resilience and become brittle. Cracks developed on the outside and it was difficult to keep a good coat of paint on the seams. So we redid the seams with 3M 5200 white sealant at the suggestion of an old-time yacht finisher who had used this compound for ten years. After watching those seams for the next three years, we decided we were satisfied, so we used the same compound for *Taleisin*'s seams. This white compound is rated as a waterproof, flexible adhesive. It does not need to be mixed with a catalyst.

Two-part compounds often form bubbles after they are mixed together. The bubbles form voids in the finished seam. The adhesive qualities of 5200 may add some strength to the hull, as the compound bonds together the planks. On the other hand, it is almost impossible to get it out of the seams once it has set. The only successful method we have found is to use an X-acto knife and cut along each edge of the compound, then pull it out with a seam raker.

Do not use any seam compound that turns hard. The hard paying compound will crack away from the planks when the hull dries out in the summer. Even worse, the hard compound could cause excessive strains on the frames as the planks swell in damper climates or during winter rains.

---

* Formulations of enamel paints have changed during the past few years and I have had problems getting the paint to stick to the 3M 5200 I used on *Seraffyn*. Most recently I have begun using Sika Flex 221. It does seem to hold the paint better. But I still get some paint breakaway and cracking along the seams when *Taleisin* moves from one climatic area to another.

Filling Defects in the Hull—Wood Plugging

Photo 19.22 On a new hull, I like to grave in any defect that is over ¼ inch in diameter. These cosmetic graving pieces (or dutchmen, as they are sometimes called) make it easier to keep the topside paint looking good. Not only do wood patches have grain that closely matches the planking, but they also have the same paint-holding characteristics and the same shrink-and-swell rate as planking. Large Bondo or polyester-filler patches do not blend in well because they are much harder than the wood. When you are sanding, the paint has more of a tendency to come off the Bondo than off the wood.

I have found I can get a neater, faster clean edge for my graving pieces if I use this crystal-type shape. The chisel edge cuts the angled ends more cleanly and has less tendency to crush the wood than if I chiseled straight across the grain. (If you chisel across the grain of softwood planking, it will tear, creating a bad fit between the graving pieces and the plank.)

I cut out the elongated crystal graving piece on the bandsaw with a 2-degree tilt. (This makes the edges of the graving piece taper slightly inward.) Then I held the smaller side of the graver in tightly over the defect and scribed around it with a knife. The graver should be twice as thick as the eventual chiseled depth of the defect in the plank. This way, if the graver ends up slightly loose, the inboard side of the taper can be reduced in thickness so the graver becomes slightly wider and slightly longer and will tighten up in the plank recess.

Photo 19.23 I aligned the chisel into the knife-scribed marks and chiseled in ¹⁄₃₂ inch at 90 degrees to the mark, then backcut at about 45 degrees from the center of the defect toward the ¹⁄₃₂-inch-deep scribe mark. By repeating this procedure of deepening the scribe mark gradually, then chiseling out the wood from the middle toward the scribe until I reach the desired depth for the graving pieces, I can keep my shapes more accurate than if I chiseled right down to the full depth with deep chisel strokes, which creep beyond the scribed marks as the chisel point wedges into the wood and result in a loose fit.

19.22

19.23

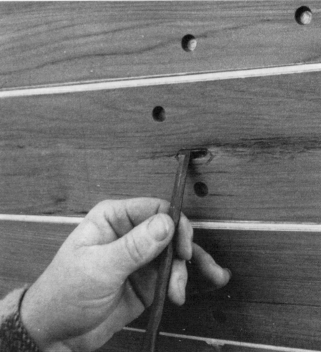

19.24

Photo 19.24   The graver should fit hand-tight. Once it does, I leave it in place until I have fitted all of the graving pieces on the hull. Then I come back and set each one in glue and tap it into place. When the glue sets, I chisel most of the excess wood off each graver, leaving it about 1/32 to 1/64 inch proud. I then block-sand this last bit flush. This hand-sanding of the final fraction guarantees that I do not form a hollow that will show once the hull is finished glossy.

Photo 19.25   Where there are small pin knots, I bore into the planking with a brace and bit and fit 1/4-inch-deep wood plugs.

Photo 19.26   For larger knots—those over 1 inch in diameter—I used an expanding auger to ream out a plug hole. Then I cut a round plug, using a narrow blade on the small bandsaw with 2 degrees of taper.

With a bit of practice, fitting graving pieces can become a very fast job—faster than puttying and then sanding and reputtying shrink defects. I spent less than half a day graving the defects on this hull.

19.25

19.26

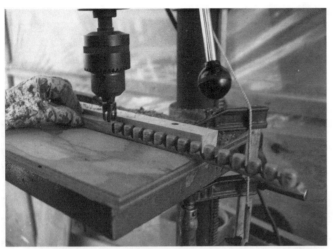

19.27

19.28

19.29

Photo 19.27 Albert Longtin, of Costa Mesa, California, taught me this production method of wood plugging twenty years ago. It is a good way to store and inventory plugs with far less chance of confusing one size for another.

To make ½-inch-diameter wood plugs, the first step is to bandsaw 9/16-inch-by-5/8-inch-wide strips from planking offcuts. (The strips for any size of plugs should be ⅛ inch wider than the

appropriate plug cutter and 1/32 inch thicker than the cutting depth of the plug cutter, including the slight taper in the upper part of the tool.) When you are selecting stock for these wood-plug sticks, look for close-grained offcuts with the grain running straight. If the grain tends to run at an angle along the stick, the wood plugs will split off at an angle below the hull surface when you chisel them off. For varnished work, cut some of the plugs so they end up edge-grained, others so they are flat-grained. Then you can further match the wood plugs to the work you are plugging.

I set up the drill press with a wooden guide so the Fuller plug cutter just touches the upright on the guide and makes a slight depression there. The cutter depth is set to stop 1/32 inch short of the plywood base of the plug-cutting jig. Set the drill press to run at its fastest speed. The plugs are cut so that they are as close together as possible without nicking the previously cut plug.

Photo 19.28 The 1/32-inch wood backing strip that holds the plugs together should break easily by hand and be quite flexible. To use the wood-plug sticks, first pour some glue into a flat dish. Rub a short section of plugs (three or four) in the glue. This effectively places a nice, thick rim of glue around the tapered end of the plug so that it is not necessary to brush glue separately into each plug hole.

Photo 19.29 With the plugs attached to their thin backing, it is easy to determine which way the grain runs, so alignment is fast, simple, and obvious. As the plug is started into its hole by a light hammer tap, the backing should break easily. If the backing is too thick, the next plug will dent the planking slightly.

It is best to use a lightweight hammer or small wooden mallet for setting wood plugs. This keeps them from being crushed when they hit bottom in the counterbore hole.

I prefer to slick off the plugs before the glue dries. The excess plug chisels more easily without hardened glue around it, and the wet glue doesn't dull the chisel. I use a 2-inch-wide slick to take the wood plugs down close to the hull. On the first pass, I snip off all of the plugs in one section, about ⅛ inch above the planking, so I can see which way the grain runs and be sure no plugs break off too deeply. Then I come back and clean the plug down to within ¼64 inch of the hull. Then, when I finally hand-sand the hull for the first coat of paint, this last ¼64 inch will fair in without any chance of depressions or flat spots.

The Worm Shoe and Stemband

As shown in diagram 19.3a, the sacrificial worm shoe is butted up to the aft lower end of the ballast keel. Irish felt or tarred roofing felt is sandwiched between the deadwood and the worm shoe. All of the wood faying surfaces are coated with creosote. The shoe is then fastened onto the bottom of the deadwood with wood screws, and the holes for the wood plugs are set as deep as practical so that the screw heads will not be fouled easily if the boat goes aground on rocks. Worm shoes are extremely important for any wooden parts of a hull that can touch the ground. If the wood is gouged or even slightly damaged in a grounding, worms can get a start. Without a worm shoe, worms could cause extensive damage that could get up into the deadwood and possibly the keel timbers. The screwed-on worm shoe is relatively easy to replace.

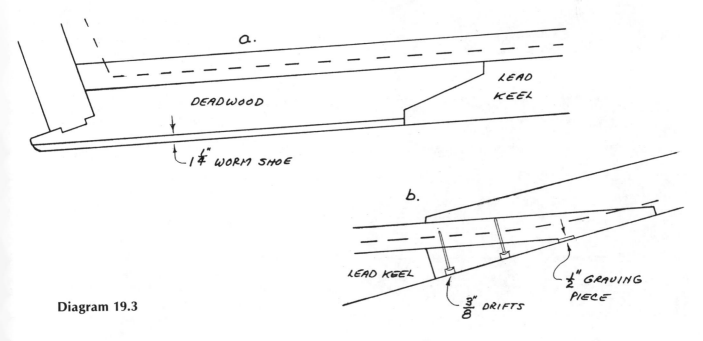

Diagram 19.3

A worm shoe is also a good idea on a sheathed hull. The sacrificial timber protects the sheathing from the damage that even a minor grounding can cause. By keeping the sheathing intact, it protects the keel timbers from moisture expansion.

Diagram 19.3b shows how I finished off the deadwood forward of the lead keel. I cut off the shim end of this deadwood to give a ½-inch-thick nib, then fitted a graving piece into the keel timber. As a result, there was no sharp point or corner to hang up on a lobster pot or line, or to catch the edge of a piece of sandpaper. The grain in this deadwood piece should run parallel to the forefoot line, and it can be drifted on, as it is nonstructural.

19.30

Photo 19.30   At this point, I installed a ¼-inch-thick rolled-copper stemband. This band runs from under the top edge of the bobstay fitting, along the flat area of the stem, aft along all of the stem and forefoot timbers, to overlap the lead keel by about 18 inches. The two ½-inch bolts that will eventually fit through the bobstay fitting pass through the copper band, sandwiching it between the bobstay fitting and the stem. The rest of the stemband is fastened with 2¼-inch-long number 14 silicon-bronze wood screws every 4 inches, including the length along the lead keel. I had to use a slightly larger drill to sink the pilot holes into the lead for the screws. To find the correct hole size, I experimented by increasing the size until a wood screw lubricated with grease would self-tap into the lead with no more than the usual amount of torque.

This stemband transmits the strains of sailing and potential collisions from the bobstay right back to the lead keel. The strap also absorbs and spreads all of the strains that are normally taken by the individual joints of the stem-and-forefoot assembly; it protects the cutwater of the stem and forefoot from driftwood damage; and, finally, it serves as part of the grounding system for lightning protection.

Photo 19.31   Just before priming the topsides, I fit the 6-inch-wide portlights into the bow. I removed the temporary blocks from the two planks butted one above the other, then cut the holes for the ports. The 1½-inch-deep spigot of the bronze portlight connected to a 1½-inch-wide inner flange. The four ends of the planks were clamped between the separate outer flange ring and the inner flange. Eight ¼-inch through-bolts held both flanges firmly together. I bedded the portlights in fungicidal Dolfinite.

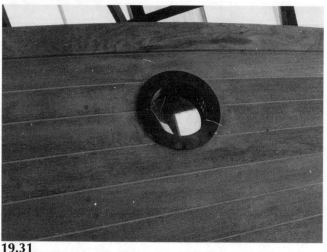

19.31

Final-Finishing the Hull

I did the final sanding of the hull mostly by hand, using 60-grit sandpaper to fair in the slightly proud wood plugs and remove any seam compound that had overlapped the tape. In some of the flat bottom sections I used the belt sander, also with 60-grit sandpaper. This paper produced tiny grooves that the first coats of paint could grip onto. I thinned the first coat of paint, an oil-based glossy enamel, 30 percent so it would soak into the wood, then, only a few hours later, put on a second coat using 15 percent thinner. This gave a bit of sheen to the hull. I used a worklight on an extension cord and looked along the hull for any low or high areas, circled them with a pencil, then went back and sanded them fair. I repainted these areas to get a slight gloss again, then returned a day or two later and checked the hull again, holding the light at various angles to pick out any defects. It took about four passes with the light, sandpaper, and paint to get the hull looking good and ready for the finish coats of paint.

Finishing the Interior of the Hull

Photo 19.32 The seams inside the hull between each frame need a little fairing up with a block plane. In areas of twist, the planks will fit well against the frames, but they can have up to 1/16 inch of misalignment between the frames.

Photo 19.33 I used the scraper to remove minor seam-edge misalignments near the frames. A 1/2-inch-wide chisel can be used to fair up the plank seam between the butt block end and the frame. (I slide my hand up and down the planking to feel for any lumps, and if any seam lumps are 1/32 inch to 1/16 inch high, I use a plane for fairing.) I planned to use varnish for the whole interior of this hull, so the inside fairing job did not have to be as perfect as the outside of the planking. The change in color of the different parts of the wood grain showing through the varnish disguises minor unfair spots that would stand out glaringly if the inside of the hull had a one-color, high-gloss finish like the outside of the hull.

19.32

19.33

19.34

19.35

Photo 19.34 Farther up the hull, where I could not use a plane, fairing had to be done with a scraper or sandpaper. I filed the edge of the blade to fit the concave shape of the planking.

Photo 19.35 To avoid developing chatter marks with the scraper, I angled the blade 20 to 30 degrees for each separate stroke. Without this precaution, chatter ridges will show up after the paint or varnish is applied. Getting rid of ridges caused by constantly scraping at exactly the same angle is a slow job that can be done only with sandpaper.

I scraped across swirly grain at a 45-degree or even 90-degree angle to remove any scrub-plane marks and to prepare for the first coat of varnish.

We chose to varnish the interior of our hull because we enjoy the look of varnished wood and the cool, eye-relaxing feeling it gives in the heat of the tropics. Besides, a varnished finish shows off the quality of the boatbuilding skills that went into the hull. Less-than-perfect fits will not be puttied and hidden under paint. To obtain this clear finish, the builder must work carefully and minimize clamp marks and dents during construction. With varnish, the hull structure—with its rounded corners, interesting wood grain, and graceful curves—becomes beautiful joinery that needs no additional woodwork trim to make it look good. No filling is required to achieve an impressive-looking finish with varnish. For these reasons, most of the top-quality wooden yachts built in Scandinavia, Scotland, and New Zealand have oiled or varnished interiors.

The varnished interior is also an advantage for the boat owner. The quality and condition of the wood inside the hull are evident immediately, and the wood can be inspected or surveyed easily during regular hull-cleaning sessions. With a painted hull, it is difficult to assess the condition of the timber.

If an area of the inside of the hull does become scuffed or damaged, it is easy for the owner to sand, revarnish, and blend in the repair area so that it hardly shows. A touch-up repair inside a painted hull is next to impossible to blend in, as paint tends to fade or discolor with age. Finally, varnish hides dust, fingerprints, and the smudges caused by living aboard far better than light-colored paint, so the boat gives a fresher appearance between annual spring cleanings.

CONSTRUCTION TIMES FOR CHAPTER 19

Larry: Fairing hull; slicking off plugs; making graving pieces; doing seam grooving; applying seam compound; final sanding and paint on topsides; final fairing and preparation for top coat; fairing and final-sanding hull interior from sheer to keel, stem to sternpost for first coat of varnish; making worm shoe and stemband   346 hours

Lin: Cutting wood plugs; plugging hull; painting topsides; varnishing interior (five coats)   180 hours

Totals to date: Larry 3145 hours

Lin   812 hours

20. DECK FRAMING

The method of attaching deckbeams to hull frames with hanging knees to eliminate the need for a sheer clamp can be used only on hulls with sawn or laminated sawn frames. This method, along with hints for using other methods, is discussed at the end of this chapter.

20.1

20.2

Photo 20.1 As mentioned in the planking section, I left the top three strakes off the hull while I put in the deck framing. This facilitated fitting, clamping, drilling, and riveting, and I recommend it if you are fitting either a sheer clamp or hanging knees as I have done.

Photo 20.2 The first piece of deck framing I fitted was the breasthook. This timber should be quite wide (in a fore-and-aft direction) to help connect the deck planking and sheerstrakes securely to the stem. The breasthook literally holds together the bow section of the hull at deck level.

Photo 20.3 I rested the untrimmed breasthook on the temporary plywood ribbands shown here. These located the breasthook, so it was easy to scribe and fit it to the aft side of the stem.

20.3

The V mark on the side of the stem indicates the underside of the deck or top of the deckbeams. Once I properly sited the center of the breasthook in relation to this mark, I fastened it temporarily in place and then shaped it athwartships to the same curve as the deckbeams. Once it was shaped, I lined it up by using a batten from the underdeck mark at the stem to the underdeck mark on frame 2. Then I marked the underside of the breasthook next to the temporary plywood ribband and figured the bevels for its sides, or its flare angles. I picked up these angles from the bottom face of the breasthook and the inside face of the ribband. I took three bevels equidistant along the breasthook. Since these bevels changed slightly from forward to aft, I gradually changed the angle on the bandsaw table as I made the final cut. This meant that almost no planing or chiseling was needed when I fitted the sheerstrake.

20.4

I later fastened the sheerstrake into the rabbet with two 2¼-inch-long number 14 wood screws and five more 3-inch-long screws equally spaced into the side of the breasthook. (The deck strakes eventually will fasten to the breasthook. Then the covering boards fasten into both the breasthook and the edge of the sheerstrake. This gives a multidirectional fastening pattern to connect the deck and hull planking to the breasthook and stem.)

Photo 20.4 The breasthook in turn was bolted through the stem. I heated the silicon-bronze rod for this bolt until it was blue, so it mushroomed quite a bit over the clench ring as I hammered it. The bevels and the beam curve on the breasthook are visible in this photograph.

Photo 20.5 The two quarter knees were resawn from a single 5-inch-thick offcut from the stem timber. I removed the top guide and the thrust bearing from my bandsaw to increase the ripping height to 15 inches. To get accurate resawing, I used a 1-inch-wide blade and cut very slowly.

20.5

Photo 20.6 To fit the 2¼-inch-thick quarter knees, I made a cardboard pattern by tracing along the inside of the hull. The grain on any knee should run diagonally (i.e., from end to end of the knee), never parallel to the joints, or it will have a tendency to split.

I adjusted the pattern until it missed the grub hole indicated by the pencil.

Photo 20.7 The port and starboard knees were cut and fitted at the same time. I clamped the F24 deckbeam to its frame head, 2¼ inches below the underside of the deck mark, to act as an accurate support for the quarter knees while I fitted them. I also removed the screw that held the upper ribband to the frame head. Then I used a pipe clamp to spring the frame head forward about ⅛ inch from the vertical. This let the slightly oversize knee slip between the frame head and the transom frame.

20.7   I picked up and then cut the bevel for the aft edge of the knee, along with the slight jog where the fashion timber is ³⁄₁₆ inch thicker than the transom beam. The aft joint between the fashion timber and the knee must fit before the measuring can be done around frame 24. I left the forward and inboard edges of the knee oversize so I could fit the knee by moving it outboard if necessary.

Photo 20.8 When I was satisfied with the fit to the fashion timbers, I scribed the top and bottom aft faces of the frame heads. On the top, a ⅛-inch scribe was marked as shown. The lower aft face of the knee was scribed to ³⁄₃₂-inch spacing in the same manner. The difference of ¹⁄₃₂ inch in the scribing accounts for the frame head's slight tilt forward. The top and inboard frame edge was also scribed to fit to the knee. I then removed the knees and used the chisel and the rabbet plane to work them down to the scribe marks. I set them back and loosened the pipe clamp to let the frame heads settle back into place. Then I made the final fitting adjustments, and when the joints were satisfactory, I placed the cardboard pattern on both knees to trace the final inboard shapes so that the inside edges of the knees were equidistant from the centerline of the hull.

20.9

20.10

Photo 20.9 The inboard face of the knees was beveled as shown so the flat clench rings would seat neatly to the knee edge. Three copper rivets, ⅜ inch in diameter, fasten the knee to the transom framing. The locust and teak are so rot-resistant that I dispensed with bedding compounds or paints on the faying surfaces.

Photo 20.10 Both inboard nib ends of the knees were cut square and flat but angled out at the top. This angle made it easier to fit the deck doublers between the knee ends and the stern-post. (These doublers, which show well in photo 20.12, provide a landing place for the aft ends of deck strakes.) At the same time, I through-riveted the sternpost to the fashion timber.

Photo 20.11 I laid the straightedge flush to both frame heads and then marked the top and bottom of each knee. I sawed off the knee ends and then planed them straight and flush to both the port and the starboard frame faces. (The outboard edge of the knee was trimmed off when the sheerstrake was fitted.)

20.11

20.12

20.13

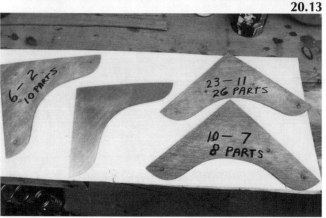

20.14

Photo 20.12 By fitting the quarter knees before the topsides were planked and the deckbeams were installed, this job could be done faster and better fits could be obtained. If the sheerstrake and deckbeams are fitted first, it is very difficult to fit the quarter knees into the box canyon of the fashion timber, sheerstrake, frame head, and after deckbeam face. When I built *Seraffyn,* I finished the planking and then laminated the 2¼-inch-by-4-inch clamp in place. I fitted all of the deckbeams to the sheer clamp with some difficulty because the sheer planks were in the way. I then proceeded to fit breasthook, quarter knees, ten lodging knees, mast partners, and blocking for the bits and for the centerline. All were difficult to fit in between the deckbeams or into boxed-in areas between the beams and the sheerstrake. Good fits are important here, as they reduce the possibility of water traps, which can allow rot to start in the endgrain of knees and beams.

It is far simpler to fit the deckbeams with no planking in the way. The next beam is fit flush to the bronze hanging knee, which in turn is sandwiched between the frame and the stern knee. Two 4-inch-long wood screws fasten the beam through the frame head and knee and into the stern knee.

Photo 20.13 I next drilled and riveted the lower part of the bronze knee to the frame. These cast-bronze knees are ³⁄₁₆ inch thick. They have a 10½-inch arm along the beam and another 10½-inch arm going down the frame. This forms a gusset that triangulates between the beam and the frame to make any movement or racking at this corner of the hull virtually impossible.

Photo 20.14 I used three simple plywood patterns to cast all twenty-three pairs of hanging knees and found this job most satisfying. One pattern produced several almost-finished parts that, with very little extra work, were quickly and easily fastened into the boat. The bronze knees did not have to be varnished or polished; they are strong for their weight, take up little space, and will never rot or split.

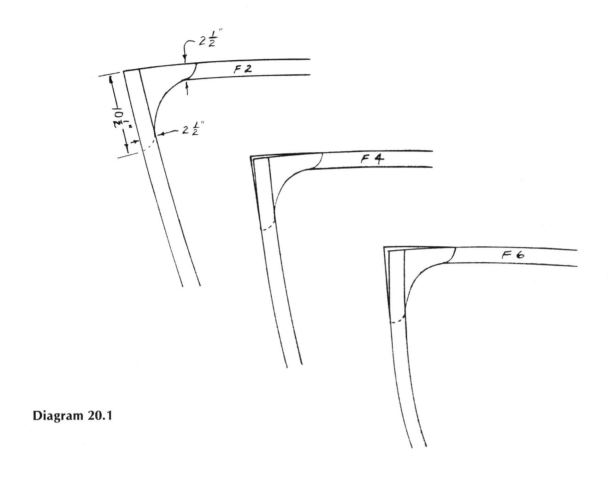

Diagram 20.1

The first pattern (on the left) made the knees for frames 2 to 6 inclusive; the other two patterns (on the right) were for the remaining frame knees, numbers 7 to 23. The unmarked knee shown is a finished casting, ready to be installed.

To make these patterns, I clamped the plywood deckbeam pattern to the frame heads at F2. The angle formed by the top of the deckbeam and the outside of the frame at F2 is the same as that used for the pattern marked 6-2 in this photo (see also diagram 20.1). I then drew a classic-shaped knee, making sure the arms were 2½ inches wide and 10½ inches long.

By trimming the top and outboard edges of the metal knee, the same pattern could be used to fit several frame-to-beam connections, as diagram 20.1 shows, but when the arm widths began to narrow below the 2½-inch molded width of the frame, I had to cast a knee with a different sheer angle. I kept the inner curve and the arm end curve on all three patterns as similar as possible so they would look alike inside the hull (see photo 20.64). I cut a 3-degree angle on the edges of the patterns so they would pull cleanly out of the casting sand. The countersunk holes on the patterns were cut by the foundryman. He screwed these patterns to boards so he could use what is called a "production ram-up" to speed things along.

20.15

20.16

Photo 20.15 I ground and faired the edges of the knee after their final fitting. The corners of the knee were marked to indicate where they lay against the beam and frame. These faying corners were left sharp. I used the drum sander to radius all of the other corners ¹⁄₁₆ inch.

Photo 20.16 The long deckbeams that would be next to hatches or cabin openings (king beams or main beams) were sawn from locust, which had sweeping curved grain, to follow the curve of the beam and thus give the extra support needed for the hatches and deckhouse. I cut as many of the other beams as possible from my curved stock and cut all of the short beams from straight-grained stock.

The pattern for the deckbeams was cut and scarfed to be 11 feet long and 2½ inches wide, the same width as the eventual beams. (Diagram 20.8 shows how to make a deckbeam pattern.) I marked the centerline of the pattern, then placed it on the body plan on the loft floor to pick up the 'thwartship length of each beam. Next to each beam measurement on the pattern, I indicated whether it was port or starboard, looking forward or looking aft. This information came in handy because I could lay the pattern onto a piece of wood and then trace the exact shape and length of the beam.

I cut the long beams about ³⁄₈ inch wider on both edges than their final molded dimensions. Boards with curved grain, such as I was using, quite often change shape as the saw cuts into them. The excess let me re-mark the beams to the correct crown of the pattern.

On a sawn-framed vessel with the beams fastened flat to the frames, every deckbeam has to be individually beveled on the top and the bottom edge. The top-edge bevel fits to the underside of the deck planking; the bevel on the bottom edge has to fit to the sheer clamp or shelf. Although this boat has no shelf or clamp, I beveled the bottom edges of the beams to give a nice look to the overhead inside the boat. I picked up these bevels using the vertical station-line-to-sheer angle, as shown in diagram 20.2. (F8 equals 10 degrees, F7 equals 12 degrees, and F6 equals 15 degrees.) I wrote a list of frame numbers with their correct beam bevel on a piece of wood. Then, as I cut and marked each beam, I wrote the appropriate bevel in degrees onto the beam stock.

Before I cut each beam bevel on the bandsaw, I mentally checked that the bevel was sloping correctly with the sheer. I could have cut these beam bevels with a Skilsaw, but adjusting the Skilsaw bevel takes more time.

The bandsaw marks came off quickly with a belt sander fitted with 60-grit paper. Then Lin put on a first coat of varnish to keep the beams from checking or staining. Though I finished the sides and bottom of each beam completely at this time, I just faired the saw marks on the top edge, leaving some of the marks showing. I have learned that even with the most careful of lofting and planning, some final fairing has to be done before the deck is laid.

Diagram 20.2

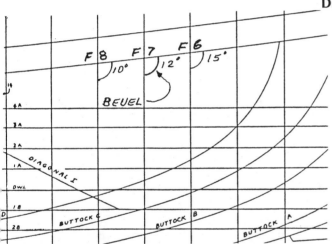

Photo 20.17 My next step was to check the frame heads, because they occasionally twist a bit as they are fastened to the planking.

Photo 20.18 I planed off enough wood on the head of the frame so that the knee arm fit easily. These fits were not time-consuming; in most cases, only one frame out of five needed any planing, and then it was only about $\frac{1}{32}$ inch.

20.17   20.18

20.20

20.21

Photo 20.19 This full-width beam (called an auxiliary or ordinary beam, as it is not a king beam) and its port and starboard knees were clamped into their correct positions. The top of the beam lines up with the faired-up underdeck marks on the outboard frame edge—i.e., 1¼ inches below the decksheer. In the photo you can see the strip of wood I have tacked onto the top edge of the hull planking to protect it from dents.

Photo 20.20 I adjusted the knee between the beam and the frame so that there would be a similar amount of metal trimmed off both top and outboard edges.

Photo 20.21 I marked the top edge of the knee with a scratch awl. (The grain on this particular auxiliary beam is not parallel to the beam curve, but since it is not a main beam, it does not take excessive strain. Furthermore, the bronze knee, which will be fastened 10 inches inboard along the beam, helps to support this less-than-perfect grain structure.)

Photo 20.22 When you are picking up sheer bevels, the bevel gauge must be held parallel to the fore-and-aft centerline of the hull, as shown. This bevel then will be exactly the same as the bevel on the top edge of the deckbeam.

To pick up an accurate bevel for the edge of the knee so it will align with the planking, the bevel gauge must be positioned at 90 degrees to the outside curve of the frame, as shown in diagram 20.3a. These bevels are written directly onto the knee, along with a notation, "underbevel" or "overbevel," to designate which way the bandsaw cut should angle on the knee edge.

Photo 20.23 Here the bevels for the F5 starboard knee are being cut. In this case, they are underbevels. As diagram 20.3b shows, when the bandsaw degree pointer indicates 15 degrees, it is measuring the angle at 90 degrees to the bandsaw blade. Accurate pickup of these bevels will eliminate the need to fair in these metal knees later when the sheer plank and covering board are fitted.

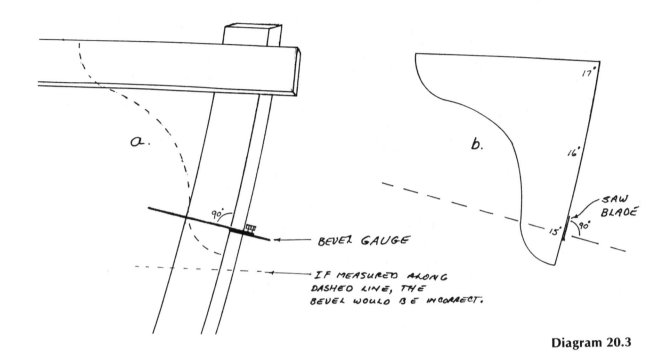

a.

90°

BEVEL GAUGE

IF MEASURED ALONG
DASHED LINE, THE
BEVEL WOULD BE INCORRECT.

b.

17°

16°

15°

SAW
BLADE

90°

Diagram 20.3

20.22

20.23

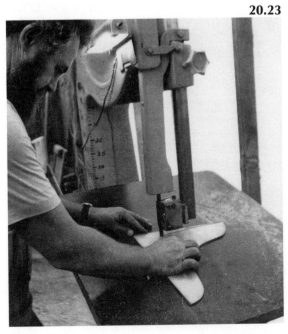

20.24

20.25

20.26

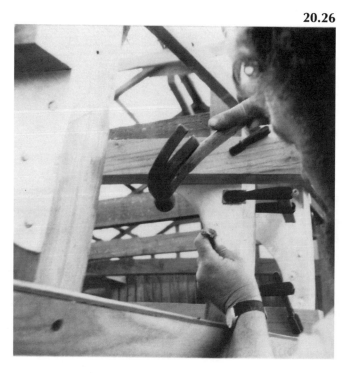

Photo 20.24 After the knees were trimmed, they were clamped into position with the beam. I checked for fit and then marked the beam cutoff line next to the frame head.

Photo 20.25 I also marked the cutoff angle on the bottom and top of the beam at both port and starboard ends of the beam. I cut off the ends, leaving just half of my pencil mark.

Photo 20.26 After I checked that the top of the beam was accurately aligned with the underside of the deck marks, and that the knees were positioned correctly, I center-punched the lower arm of the hanging knee, using a staggered pattern that placed the lowest rivet as far away as practical from the deckbeam. I used the same pattern on each successive knee to give a uniform-looking appearance.

20.27

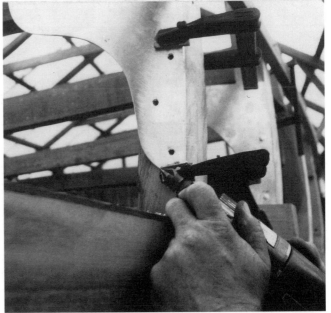

20.28

Photo 20.27 The uppermost rivet—the one that goes through frame, knee, and deckbeam —should be positioned in the lower inboard corner of the frame. This gives a connection that tends to resist splitting in the event of a beam-on collision.

The holes for these rivets should be drilled about parallel to the beveled edge of the frame. A short drill motor, a 90-degree-angle drill, or a 90-degree-angle drill attachment is needed to get into these areas.

Photo 20.28 I countersank the hole about 40 percent of the depth of the metal so the rivet would flare tightly to the metal knee.

Photo 20.29 In order to get the flat surface of the clench ring to lie flush against the frame head, I peened the copper rod until it approximated the angle of the frame bevel. (Later, when I rivet this fastening in place, the clench ring will align to and tighten up flat against the wood face of the frame.) If carriage bolts were used here instead of rivets, it would be difficult to get neat-appearing flush fits between the bolt head or washers and the frames, especially on the forward frames, which have acute bevels.

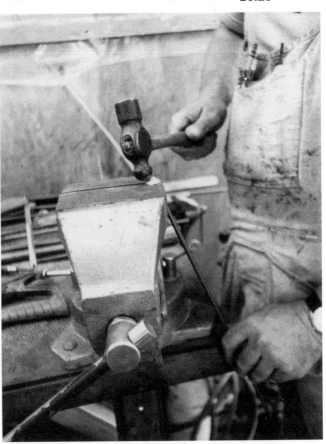

20.29

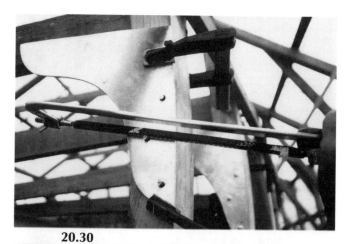

20.30

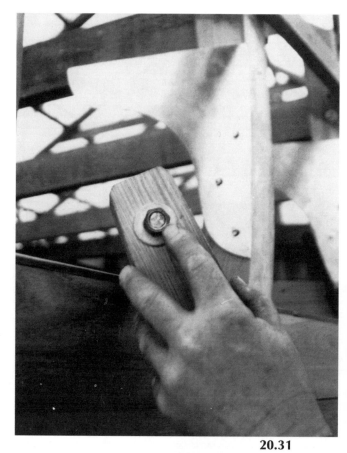

20.31

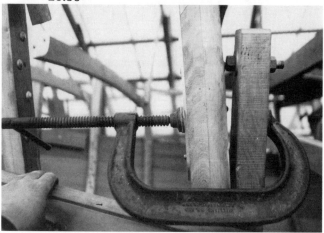

20.32

20.33

20.34

Photo 20.30 The rivet should protrude ³⁄₁₆ inch past the flat surface of the knee so there is enough metal to peen over to a nice, strong, mushroomlike head.

The head of the copper rivet swells as it is hammered and fits tightly not only to the metal knee and clench ring, but also in the ¼-inch hole between the beam, frame, and knee. This helps form a rigid connection that will eliminate any chance of movement or angle change between the knee and the frame. These fastenings are good-looking, especially if you intend to leave the boat's interior unceiled. They are inexpensive, but they do have one fault: They are more labor-intensive than bolts or wood screws.

Photo 20.31 The bucking tool for these rivets can be used on either countersunk holes or clench rings that are laid flush to wood surfaces. One end of the rod was left ¹⁄₁₆ inch lower than the nut to form a depression so the tool would not slip off the clench ring while I was hammering the rivet.

Photo 20.32 The bucking tool is shown in place. The plywood pad on the foot of the clamp protects the knee.

Photo 20.33 The copper flare of the rivet is hardened by the hammer blows. I like the pattern of hammer marks surrounding each rivet. They seem to give a handmade look to these otherwise-stark metal parts. But if you do not have the same feeling, you can use a protective piece of leather or plastic as you rivet.

Photo 20.34 When the lower three rivets were bucked up, I clamped the beam in place. Then I drilled for the long rivet through the beam and the frame. This rivet should be angled so it is parallel to the frame and deck bevels. Once this rivet was in place, I drilled and then riveted along the upper arm of the knee to the deckbeam, again using a staggered rivet pattern.

Photo 20.35 As explained in chapter 15, the mast partner and its two supporting king beams were installed before I planked any of the hull. The half-beam attached to the bulkhead was jointed to the mast partner using a 3½-inch-long scarf at the inboard end. This scarf joint tapered to a ¾-inch blind nib.

20.35

20.36

Photo 20.36 The mast for *Taleisin* was 7 inches in diameter. I shaped it so that it was octagonal from the mast step to 1 inch above the deck; it was round the deck to the masthead. To leave room for the eight ³/₄-inch-thick mast wedges I wanted to use, the octagonal hole in the partner had to be 8¹/₂ inches wide. On *Seraffyn*, the mast and the hole in the partners were round, which meant I had to use concave/convex mast wedges. Not only was this time-consuming, it also was difficult to make the wedges fit well and lie evenly so they looked good inside the boat. The wedges for the octagonal mast were easy to make and easy to fit, and they lay neatly and evenly inside the partners. They took only about an hour to cut and install.

I made the 2-inch-thick mast partner in four pieces to simplify cutting the mast hole and drilling the long holes for the fore-and-aft fastenings. I jointed the timber, clamped it together dry, and marked the octagonal shape onto it, as shown in diagram 20.4. I then unclamped the parts and cut the octagonal half-holes with the bandsaw. I located the two other joints on the mast partner where the through-bolts would be positioned. To make a pilot hole so that drilling for these long bolts would be straightforward, I sawed a ¹/₈-inch-deep-by-¹/₄-inch-wide dado (groove) along the center of both joints. As soon as I had glued and clamped together the four pieces of the eventual mast partner, I ran a ⁷/₃₂-inch-square piece of wood through the pilot holes to clear out the excess glue so the drill would not be deflected. Later, when the glue was dry, I bored through the ¹/₄-inch-by-¹/₄-inch hole with a ²⁵/₆₄-inch-diameter long drill bit. I

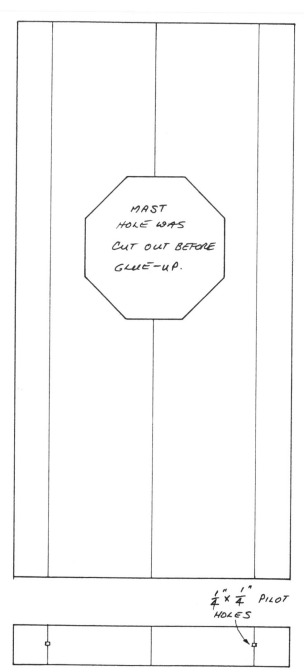

Diagram 20.4

then clamped the partner timber to the forward deckbeam and aligned it so I could drill from aft to forward through the partner and the forward deckbeam. Then I clamped the aft beam into place and ran the drill from forward to aft through that beam. I used ³/₈-inch copper rod with clench rings for these two long fastenings. To complete the connection, I used 4-inch number 14 wood screws, staggered between these rivets at 4-inch intervals. (Copper nails could have been substituted for the screws.)

Photo 20.37 The king beam for the forward end of the deckhouse—which is also the landing for the aft end of the partner—was positioned halfway between frames 11 and 12. It would have been far easier if it had landed right on a frame, but I wanted a minimum of 12 inches of space between the deckhouse and the mast for an on-deck propane locker and a 10-gallon gravity-feed water tank. This king beam was temporarily supported at the outboard ends by the sheer ribbands. Eventually, I fitted a short frame—16 inches long and 2 inches by 2½ inches—directly under the king beam, with a bronze knee fastened to the forward side of both. The short frame was later fastened to the planking.

Once all of the king beams, full-width auxiliary beams, quarter knees, mast partners and various deck blocking were fitted in place, I struck an exact centerline onto the top of the full-length beams by stretching a string from the inside aft face of the stem at breasthook height to the centerline mark at the sternpost. After checking the hull for plumbness, I used a carpenter's level to transfer the line of the string directly down to every third deckbeam. I used a long batten to fair in these centerline marks.

Photo 20.38 The positions of the carlines (also called carlings or headers) were marked onto the deckbeam pattern with their inside and outside limits (sided dimensions).

I fitted the forehatch carlines and the cockpit-hatch carlines first. Since these are short, if I had made a mistake, it would have been less costly than a mistake on a long cabin carline. As I fitted these short carlines, I was reminded of the proper moves to make, since they are fitted and jointed the same as the long cabin carline. The only difference is that the carlines for the cabin must be tilted inward 3 degrees so they line up with the cabinsides, which also must have a 3-degree inward tilt. (If the cabinsides are vertical and parallel to each other instead of tilting inward, they will appear to slant outward because of the optical illusion created by the sloping side decks. The cabinsides also need a sheer curve along their top edges so the deckhouse avoids the humpback look. These small details are important for creating a nice-looking deckhouse. Otherwise, it will look just like what it is—a rectangular box set on top of the deck.)

20.37

20.38

20.39

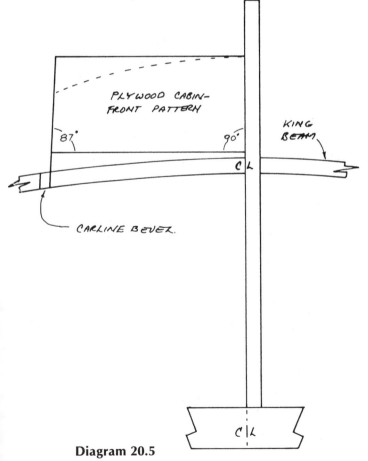

PLYWOOD CABIN-
FRONT PATTERN

87°   90°

KING
BEAM

C L

CARLINE BEVEL.

C L

Diagram 20.5

Photo 20.39 To get the correct fore-and-aft shape for the cabin carline, I clamped the deck-beam pattern halfway between the fore-and-aft king beams, then supported it with a light upright post. I then laid a long batten on top of the deck at the X's that marked the carline position. When the batten lay in a fair, sweet curve —across the deckbeams forward, across the temporarily installed deck pattern amidships, then onto the afterdeck—I laid a piece of ¾-inch-by-6-inch pine alongside it and traced the curve of the batten. (This same pattern will be used for the carline, the cabin sill, and eventually for the bottom and top edges of the cabinsides.)

To determine the 3-degree inward tilt of the carline and cabin with little chance of error, I erected a straightedge from the centerline of the cabin king beam (diagram 20.5). I then cut a plywood pattern to show the half-breadth of the forward end of the cabin with the 3-degree inboard angle on it. I set the cabin pattern in place against the centerline upright and ran a line down from the pattern cabinside onto the king beam to get the correct angle for the inboard tilt I wanted. (This same pattern will give the correct angle plus the width of the cabin at all four corners. It will be used later during installation of the cabinsides.)

Once the angles were laid out for the four carline joints, I was ready to saw the carlines using the fore-and-aft curve on the pine pattern and the carline bevel. (Before I saw out the carlines, I like to check that both are marked port or starboard, forward or aft. The top-edge bevel should be marked "under," the bottom-edge bevel, "over." These two carlines are like port and starboard frames; they are identical except that the bevels are cut in opposite directions. An error in marking can leave you with two port carlines and no starboard one.)

I cut the molded width of the carlines ⅛ inch larger than necessary for their first fitting.

20.40

20.41

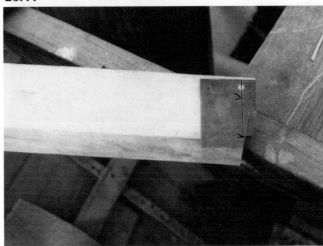

20.42

Photo 20.40 The port-side carline is shown sitting on top of the king beams. I have clamped and ribbanded the two king beams so they remain parallel to each other. When the shaped carline is lying across the king beams at its correct location, I double-check with my plywood pattern to make sure I have the correct inboard tilt. If the carline bevel is slightly out, the extra ⅛-inch thickness will allow for a bit of vertical adjustment.

Photo 20.41 I clamped the carline to the king beams and scribed the inside and outside of the carline. Then I turned the carline over 180 degrees and clamped it to the underside of the king beams. I checked the scribe marks to ensure that the carline was the correct length along its bottom edge.

Photo 20.42 I made a copper template for laying out the carline shoulder step joint. The hole in the template lines up with the scribe line on the side of the carline. The lower part of the template, opposite the hole, should align with the scribe line at the bottom of the beam. I laid out both sides of the joint so they were the same, then cut them out with a handsaw. More details about this layout work appear in the captions that follow.

Photo 20.43 To transfer the overall carline length onto the tops of the king beams, I rolled the carline over and aligned it fore and aft with the scribed marks on top of the king beams. Then I scribed around the beam end to give the correct amount of joint cutout. The 1-inch-by-2-inch ribband shown under my wristwatch is securing the beam so it has no 'thwartship curve and does not shift while I am working on it.

20.43

20.44

20.47

20.45

Photo 20.44 I cut the beam notch and checked it with the template.

Photo 20.45 I left the carline ⅛ inch high and fitted it flush to the bottoms of the beam and the carline. Then I glued the joint and nailed it through the beam into the endgrain of the carline with two 4-inch scotch-cut copper nails.

Photo 20.46 It is simple to fit the half-beams to the carline when there is no sheerstrake in the way. The beams can be left long and adjusted inboard until the step joints fit correctly. The outboard ends of the half-beams then can be cut to length.

First I positioned a clamp and a block of wood to support the half-beam at the correct height and square to the carline. Another clamp secured the outboard end flush to the top edge of the bronze knee. I then scribed the inboard end and cut it off flush with the correct angle so it could lie up against the carline.

Photo 20.47 I scribed along the rule. This gave me the template line (TL). (As you can see by looking at the joint in the foreground, the steel rule is a bit wider than the depth of the beam joint.) The bottom of the plywood tool tray you can see just 3 feet away from me on the forward beams was later covered with carpet to protect the top corners of the faired-up deckbeams from chipping or denting.

20.46

20.48

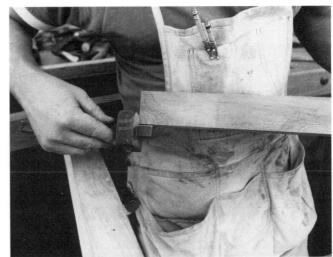

20.49

20.50

Photo 20.48 Then I marked the depth of the joint onto the top edge of the carline.

Photo 20.49 The depth of the joint on the top of the beam is even with the TL side marks.

Photo 20.50 The template hole has a scratch mark on both sides. This mark is lined up with the template line at the top of the beam. The lower edge of the template aligns with the TL at the bottom inboard corner of the beam. Scribe both sides of the beam square to each other.

Photo 20.51 Here my pencil points to the TL (dotted). The line squared across the bottom of the beam should line up with the TL on the opposite side. This squared line is important, since the lower edge of the joint will be obvious inside the hull.

20.51

20.52

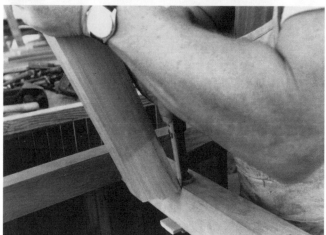

20.53

20.54

20.55

Photo 20.52 The saw blade should be set at exactly 90 degrees. The edge layout mark should line up exactly to the saw blade.

Photo 20.53 After the joint was cut, I checked the width of the top inboard corner and also the bottom marks scribed onto the carline.

Photo 20.54 Then I cut exactly to the center of the scribe mark, down to the lower inside corner of the carline. (I am always careful not to overcut the lower corner of the carline, as a slip here will show forever.)

Photo 20.55 I chiseled out the excess wood, working first from the top and then from the bottom.

20.56

20.57

20.58

20.59

Photo 20.56 Next I marked the height of the shoulder step.

Photo 20.57 The 90-degree end of the template makes a handy square for use inside the joint.

Photo 20.58 As I chiseled down to the shoulder step, I left about ¹⁄₁₆ inch of extra wood on the step to allow for vertical adjustment.

Photo 20.59 I checked the joint depth for uniformity.

20.60

20.61

20.62

Photo 20.60 The 6-inch steel rule and a bull-nose rabbet plane are helpful for trueing up the insides of the joint until they are dead straight.

Photo 20.61 I used the beam to check the fit at the top and bottom of the joint. (If the joint is tight, I lightly plane or scrape the sides of the beam end until the beam pushes snugly into the carline with only the force of my hand.)

Photo 20.62 If the beam is too high, I chisel the appropriate amount off the step in the carline. The step locks this joint and keeps it from moving down. The beam is stopped from separating from the carline by horizontal tie rods that will later fasten through the carline next to each beam and connect to the hull. The cabinsides are in turn edge-bolted down through the carline so these beam ends are held down.

Photo 20.63 The outboard end of the half-beam is being marked and then cut off on the bandsaw. I then glued the shoulder joint in place and let the glue cure completely. Finally, I riveted the hanging knee, half-beam, and frame in place.

20.63

I cut down my time by doing all of the half-beam layout, then sawing the beams and their joints and fitting them all at the same time. Then I glued them all at once. (In order to photograph this sequence, this beam was left unfitted and done step by single step.)

If you are using timber that is not as rot-resistant as locust or teak, coat the outboard endgrain of the beams with some type of rot prevention before the sheerstrake is fastened.

Photo 20.64 These long carlines are among the potentially weakest structures in any boat. Most side-deck carlines on boats of this size are very springy until the cabinsides are bolted onto the carlines. I knew the 10½-inch knees connecting the half-beams to each frame in *Taleisin* would give more support than a clamp or a clamp and shelf because of the longer lever-arm length. I was pleased to find that these carlines were almost rigid as soon as the half-beams were in place. I tested the carlines by jumping on them with all the force of my 180 pounds and found they moved barely ¼ inch, even without the support of the posts I installed later. These posts

—two 1½-inch-by-1½-inch lengths of teak on both port and starboard sides—were mortised and tenoned ¼ inch into the carline and then screw-fastened on top of the bilge stringer. This gave us the confidence to take the boat anywhere we wanted.

Photo 20.65 The hatch carlines were fitted parallel to the vertical centerline of the hull. (If this forehatch had high coamings (over 10 inches), I would have wanted to build in the 3-degree inward tilt I used for the cabinsides.)

When all of the deck framing was in place and secured, I rounded the lower corners with the Stanley bullnose router discussed in chapter 23. Where interior joinery or bulkheads would fit, I left the beam corners unedged so fits and fastening would be easier and neater. When I was in doubt as to whether joinery would be fitted later against a beam or a frame, I left it square and did the radiusing after the interior was completely fitted. Lin then went ahead with varnishing the radiused beams, working to have the deck framing completely varnished before I laid the decking.

20.64

20.65

20.66

20.67

20.68

Photo 20.66 Many boat plans show the king beams thicker than the auxiliary beam in sided dimension. This would be important if the beams were sawn from stock with straight grain, as that would have grain runoff at the ends. Since I was able to cut all of *Taleisin*'s king beams out of curved stock, the grain ran parallel to the curve of the beam, so strength was not a problem. To get a landing for the ends of the deck strakes at the ends of each deck opening, I used doublers laid along the beams.

Photo 20.67 The doublers were glued and riveted in place to give them the strength required to resist the separating effect of caulking the ends of the deck strakes.

Once all the deck framing was in place, but before I did the final fairing or cut off frame heads, I fitted the last three hull planks. Then I caulked and payed the hull.

This photo shows the battens we tacked onto the top edges of all hatch and cabin openings to protect these sharp corners. Eventually these will be joint corners, and if they are not damaged, the deck sill or hatch coamings can be fitted neatly to the carlines and beams. If a good-looking fit is achieved here, you won't incur the extra labor and materials costs of fitting trim to hide a dented or scarred corner.

Photo 20.68 Now the deck framing and planking have been completed.

Photo 20.69 My next job was to fair up the sheerstrake and cut down the extra wood on each frame head. I used a handsaw to cut into the sheerstrake parallel to and ¹⁄₁₆ inch shy of the top edge of the deckbeams.

Photo 20.70 The grain under the socket chisel tapers up toward the saw cut marked A. Near the second saw cut (B), the grain dips down a little. I take care to chisel from the opposite direction to ensure that the chisel does not split the grain below the deckbeam height. The trick is always to watch the grain structure on the outside of the hull and to change the chisel-cutting direction when necessary. If you want to have a line to work to, tack a batten to the excess wood above the sheerline saw cuts and then mark in the sheerline.

20.69

20.70

20.71

Photo 20.71 After the sheerstrake has been chiseled down almost flush, but is still about ¹⁄₃₂ inch above the deckbeam level, saw off the excess on the frame heads.

20.72

20.74

20.73

Photo 20.72 I made the saw cuts into the sheerstrake parallel to the top of the quarter knee. To fair up the sheerstrake and frame head and the top edge of the bronze knee, I used a belt sander with 36-grit belts. (It is a magnificent tool for this area.) I used a hand plane to level off the last 1/32 inch of the sheerstrake and a 12-inch ruler to check my work.

The top edge of the sheer plank and the first 6 inches along the deckbeams should be flat so that the covering boards go on easily. The rest of the beams should have the normal, even curve along their length.

Notice that I added one more rivet to the quarter knee to connect it to the sheer plank.

Photo 20.73 Once the sheer and covering-board area was faired up and net, the rest of the deck framing had to be faired up so the fore-and-aft deck strakes would fit tightly onto all of the beams.

I started by fairing up the hatch openings, king beams, and carlines. These beams should be faired athwartships so the batten laid along each beam fits tightly and fairly. I then faired (in a fore-and-aft direction) along the carlines where they meet the beams. Then I faired the transom framing. Since the sheer was faired first, this meant all of the border areas of the deck framing were fair, so it was a simple job to fair in the rest of the 'thwartship beams and blocking to match these perimeter areas.

An electric plane and a belt sander were the tools I used to remove excess wood from any beams that were a bit high. I hand-planed the last ¹⁄₃₂ inch from the beams and used a stiff, straight-grained fir batten to check the fits regularly, imagining that the batten was a deck strake. As a final check, I laid one of my long 1-inch-by-1½-inch ribbands along the deck in several places. This stiffer ribband/batten provided the acid test: The deck strakes would fit tightly and fairly to the beams.

Photo 20.74 Once the deck was fair, I let in the diagonal strapping flush to the top edges of the beams. This strapping triangulates the deck structure and helps control any hull-twisting forces exerted by the mast as it works in opposition to the righting force of the ballast keel. Straps like these are only practical on the flush areas of the deck, or sometimes across a large deckhouse.

One set of straps was crisscrossed just in front of the mast and passed under the forward corners of the deckhouse. I clamped the ³⁄₁₆-inch-thick, 2-inch-wide straps and scribed next to the ends and edges with a knife.

Photo 20.75 The butt blocks fitted here formed a landing for the eventual joint of the covering boards. I positioned these blocks so that they were clear of the sheerstrake butt block and so that I could cut the individual covering-board pieces from the 12- to 14-inch-wide boards I had available. To determine their positions, I made four pine patterns, which I fitted along the sheer from stem to stern to determine the exact shape and size of the final teak covering boards. These butt blocks then had to be fitted before I laid the straps in place so that if a strap landed on a butt, as it has in the photo, it could be fitted flush into the block face instead of later having to fit the block from below to the frame heads, beam, sheerstrake, and strap all at the same time.

There were four pairs of straps across the framing of this deck. Only two straps had to be landed on covering-board butt blocks. The ends of the others were simply angled to fit against the sheerstrake. Later, when the covering boards were on and the deck was laid, they were all fastened from underneath with wood screws through the straps and up into the covering boards and the deck strakes.

The dotted line indicates the eventual covering-board butt position. The screw-fastening positions for the covering board are marked as O; the fastenings that will go down through the strap into the butt block are marked with an X and positioned so they will be clear of the screws that eventually will hold down the covering-board butt.

20.76

Photo 20.76 I clamped the straps in place and then scribed along the sides and ends. The first strap I fitted at the mast area was set into a dado (rebate) that sweeps down so that where the two straps cross, the top of the upper strap is level with the top of the deckbeams. But to get a uniform appearance inside the hull, the straps were fitted to be flush with the deck at the outer edges of the mast partner.

Photo 20.77 The Skilsaw blade was set to a depth of ³⁄₁₆ inch, then locked. I checked this cutting depth by running the saw over a scrap of wood. I used a new, multitooth carbide blade as insurance against chipping the edges and corners of the beams and blocking pieces. I cut the center passes first, and after that, my skill and courage had improved, so I was able to cut exactly to the scribed lines.

Photo 20.78 I chiseled out the remaining wood, being careful not to chip the beam edges and the edge of the blocking where the metal exited.

Photo 20.79 For the final cut, to make sure the dado or rebate was exactly ³⁄₁₆ inch deep, I used a rabbet plane. I trimmed the edges of the dado with a bullnose rabbet plane. I used an offcut of strapping as a depth and width gauge.

Photo 20.80 The blind end, where the strap fits into the butt block, was cleaned out with a 1³⁄₄-inch chisel. The straps were then laid in place and fastened into the tops of each beam, the partners, and the blocks with 1-inch number 14 flathead wood screws. (As mentioned before, once the deck was laid, I screwed up through the straps into the deck strakes at about 8-inch intervals and fastened them with 1-inch number 14 round-headed screws.)

The deck framing is now finished and faired, ready for its skin of a single thickness of 1½-inch teak strakes.

20.77

20.78

20.79

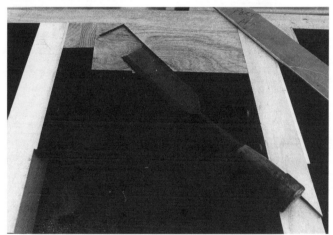

20.80

CONSTRUCTION TIMES FOR CHAPTER 20

Larry: Milling deckbeam material; cutting beams; installing bronze knees, beams, carlines, mast partners, breasthook, and stern knees; fairing sheerstrake; cutting off frame heads; dadoing and fastening bronze cross-strapping; fairing all deck framing to prepare for laying deck strakes; edging underside of deck framing; preparing for varnish   465 hours

Lin: Drilling clench rings; milling materials; varnishing (five coats on deck framing, three coats on upper surface of deck framing)   154 hours

Totals to date: Larry 3610 hours

Lin   966 hours

DISCUSSION

Deck-Frame Stresses

When you are building or designing a deck frame for a yacht, it pays to understand the stresses a deck must withstand. These can be divided into *deckload, twisting,* and *panting.*

Deckload is the most obvious strain. It is caused by someone jumping on the foredeck or by carrying a load of lumber on the side deck. This strain is first absorbed and spread by the deck covering. It then spreads onto the cambered deckbeams, which are in turn supported by being securely connected to the hull frames with a clamp, a clamp-and-shelf combination, bulkheads, or hanging knees. The bulkheads, posts, deck-to-keel bitts, hanging knees, and compression posts used under deck-stepped masts are designed to support the deck structures so the deck does not depress under the strains that can exist when a green sea breaks on board.

Twisting is the strain imposed on a deck when the boat is sailing hard, especially to windward. The ballast keel of the heeled hull is exerting a strain in one direction, while the mast, which usually is positioned near the forward end of the lead keel, is twisting the hull in the opposite direction. The hull on its own, without a deck structure, would twist quite easily. But when a deck is properly laid, the whole structure becomes rigid. It is easy to recognize this strain if you try to twist a 1-inch, thin-walled metal tube. The round tube firmly resists twisting. But hacksaw the same tube in half longitudinally and the U-shaped pieces will twist with relatively little strain. This is why a flush-decked yacht—which resembles the tube—is the ultimate structure to resist twisting, assuming the hatches are kept small. The more openings there are in the deck structure, the more prone to twisting the whole hull becomes. A deck with a long opening for both cabin and cockpit—one with no bridge deck to add structural support—will be weak unless there is some careful design work to resist the strains of twisting.

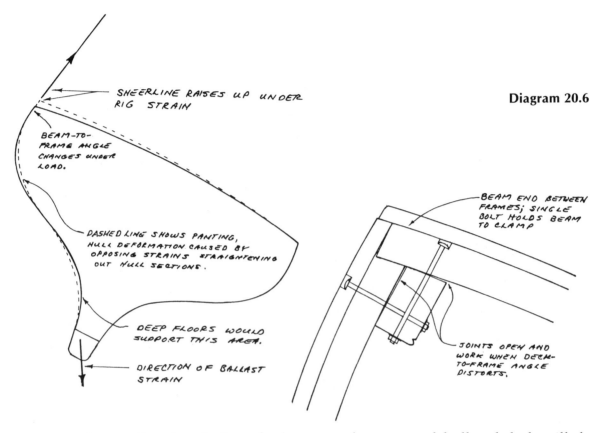

Diagram 20.6

SHEERLINE RAISES UP UNDER RIG STRAIN

BEAM-TO-FRAME ANGLE CHANGES UNDER LOAD.

DASHED LINE SHOWS PANTING, HULL DEFORMATION CAUSED BY OPPOSING STRAINS STRAIGHTENING OUT HULL SECTIONS.

DEEP FLOORS WOULD SUPPORT THIS AREA.

DIRECTION OF BALLAST STRAIN

BEAM END BETWEEN FRAMES; SINGLE BOLT HOLDS BEAM TO CLAMP

JOINTS OPEN AND WORK WHEN DECK-TO-FRAME ANGLE DISTORTS.

Panting is a perfect description of what a poorly structured hull and deck will do when it comes under the strains of hard sailing. The hull will try to change shape amidships under the strains imposed by the rigging and the ballast. The shrouds will try to compress the hull, the deck will try to spring up in the middle, the sides of the boat will try to straighten out, and the joint at the corner of the deck and hull will try to open as the sheer is sprung upward (diagram 20.6). Deep floors and a strong frame-head-to-beam connection are critical in reducing panting.

Over a period of time, the combination of all three strains can cause the hull of a boat with a poorly designed deck structure to rack so that the sheer will rise up into an unnatural curve called "hogging," as shown in diagram 20.7. It is almost impossible to eliminate the panting and twisting stresses in large hulls, but they can be minimized by proper design and construction. On hulls smaller than 40 feet, strains can be virtually eliminated by using deep, long-armed floor timbers, strong cabin-sole beams, well-bolted and strong sheer clamps, hanging knees, or partial bulkheads that are bolted to both the frames and the deckbeams to stop any movement between the deckbeams and the frames. For larger hulls, belt frames, hull strapping, and additional hanging knees become necessary, as shown in Herreshoff's Rules in Appendix B.

A lightly ballasted hull of any size will have less tendency to hog, twist, or pant than a heavily ballasted one. So the higher the ballast ratio on the boat you are building, the stronger the joints and deck structure must be to prevent hull distortion.

Diagram 20.7

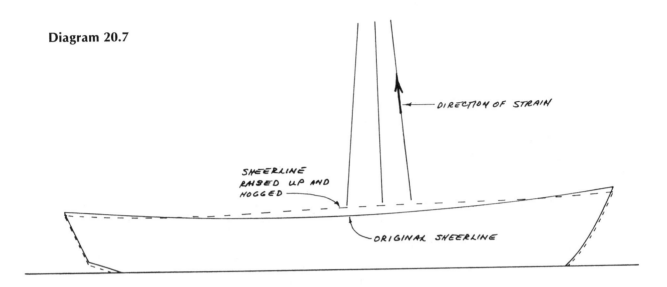

DIRECTION OF STRAIN

SHEERLINE
RAISED UP AND
HOGGED

ORIGINAL SHEERLINE

Decking Choices and Their Effects on Deck-Frame Design

There are four basic methods used to cover the deck of a wooden hull: (1) Tongue-and-groove strakes can be laid in a fore-and-aft direction and covered with canvas; (2) one-layer fore-and-aft deck strakes can be laid, caulked, and payed; (3) a plywood deck can be laid and then painted or covered with canvas, sheathing, or a layer of teak; (4) a cold-molded deck can be built up of three layers of veneer then painted or covered with canvas or sheathing, or the third layer can be teak strakes.

If cost, simplicity of construction, and watertightness are your main considerations, the best all-around method of decking would be 3-inch-wide, ¾-inch-thick, tongue-and-groove cedar laid fore-and-aft and then covered with canvas. This method has little diagonal strength to it, so the deck framing would need to be reinforced with tie-rods at every other half-beam, plus substantial mast partners and either lodging knees or diagonal straps near each end of every deck opening to minimize twist in the deck.

The second decking method—laid decks, such as used on *Taleisin* and *Seraffyn*—is far more costly, as teak usually is the timber of preference. This method requires all of the framing and reinforcing used for the tongue-and-groove deck to resist twisting plus extra tie-rods to resist the accumulated 'thwartship expansion strains exerted during caulking. With a caulked deck, I like to fit a tie-rod next to every half-beam so that the beam-to-carline joint is not separated by the amazingly heavy loads exerted as the cotton is driven into the seams. If a tie-rod does not contain this strain and spread it back across the whole deck and onto the sheer clamp or hull sheer, the joint will open, the deck will leak, and any bunks under or near the carlines will become wet.

Since tie-rods and substantial lodging knees or strapping are necessary, why build a single-layer teak deck? Because just like carvel planking, it is easy to repair (leaks are easy to trace and stop), looks magnificent, and can withstand a lot of use without appearing worn.

Plywood can be used and simply painted and sanded to produce an inexpensive, serviceable workboat deck, or it can be used as a subdeck and covered with canvas or teak strips. Plywood adds a tremendous amount of horizontal strength to the framework of a deck, thus making lodging knees and deck strapping, tie-rods, and large mast partners redundant. The deck framing still needs to be strong enough to withstand deckloads, so breasthook, quarter knees and mast partners are still necessary as landings to secure the decking firmly to the hull ends. Naturally, plywood does not eliminate the need for a substantial clamp, hanging knees and/or well-fastened bulkheads on beams and frames. The Achilles heel of plywood is that unless you select top grades, you can have rot and delamination problems. Fir plywood, even marine grade, is low in rot resistance. It quite often has rot-prone hemlock as its inner core. If rot does get a start in a deck with a teak overlay, you can be facing a major repair job. (This is one of the most frequent repair jobs I have been asked to do.) Furthermore, tracing a leak in this type of deck is far harder than it is in a laid cedar tongue-and-groove deck or a single-layer teak deck. If you do choose to use plywood as a subdeck under teak, use the best grade of hardwood marine plywood available.

Cold-molded decks are simply homemade plywood, laid up something like *Taleisin's* bulkhead in chapter 15. I would prefer these to plywood, as you can use rot-resistant, inexpensive cedar veneers and control voids by filling them with graving pieces and by getting good fits as each layer is glued in place. This decking method can be very strong horizontally, just like a plywood-covered deck, so the same framing parts can be eliminated. It has only a few flaws. It could be difficult to trace leaks; it requires a lot of adhesives; and the thin upper layer of bare teak (usually a ¼-inch-thick veneer is recommended) will wear down substantially after several years of use.

Shaping the Deckbeams

Beam construction can range from the dead-simple, straight 2 x 4 deckbeams I saw on Peter Pye's 30-foot *Moonraker* to the other end of the scale, the sophisticated, crowned, laminated, taper-ended beams I saw used on the Luders 16, a production-built, cold-molded racing sloop. I highly recommend having some crown on a beam, as it makes the beam stronger, increases the headroom below decks, encourages water or seas to clear off the deck quickly, and looks good. The normal crown used for sawn deck beams is about ⅜ inch to ½ inch of rise per foot of beam. The more crown you have on a sawn beam, the more likely it is to split from the grain runoff at the ends—unless the beam can be cut from curved-grain stock. To minimize the chance of splitting low-density woods such as larch or yellow cedar, I would use a crown rise of ⅜ inch to the foot. On harder, stringier woods such as oak, locust, or iroko, I would feel confident with a higher crown of ½ inch to the foot. If your designer suggests more than ½ inch of crown per foot, your beams should be laminated. Or, if stock is available, they should be sawn out of curved-grain planks.

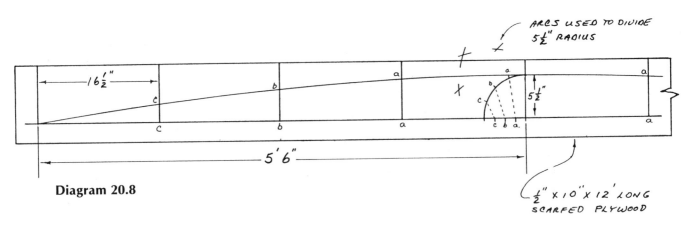

Diagram 20.8

Diagram 20.8 shows the beam-pattern plan I used for *Taleisin*. Her maximum beam is 10 feet 9 inches. To make my computations easier, I figured this to 11 feet. Eleven feet by ½ inch of rise per foot equaled a 5½-inch rise amidships. I laid out a baseline 11 feet long, then put in a perpendicular centerline. I then set my compass at 5½ inches as shown and scribed an arc to the left of the perpendicular. Then I divided the arc into four equal parts along the baseline (a,b,c). Then I divided the arc itself into four equal parts (a,b,c). I next drew three dotted lines from the points at the baseline up to the points on the arc. These three lines show the appropriate rise for the equally divided 16½-inch sections of the 11-foot-long baseline. I transferred these heights and made vertical lines as shown, then bent a batten through the points to get the curve for the pattern. I cut out the plywood pattern and faired the edge, then used a marking gauge set to the molded width of my beams to get the lower edge of the pattern. It is important to use this arc method to get the dimensions for the crown of the deckbeams. If instead you just divided the beam into 1-foot intervals and marked ½ inch more rise at each, the beam would have a far less appealing curve and would be flat toward the ends.

As you are cutting out beams, keep them as close as possible to identical along their top curved edge. Any inaccuracy greater than ¹⁄₃₂ inch along the top edge of the beam will mean much more work when it comes time to fair up the deck framework.

There are three common methods for building deckbeams: (1) sawn beams cut from straight- or curved-grain boards; (2) laminated beams; and (3) steam-bent beams. The sawn beam is the fastest to build and probably uses up the least material (diagram 20.9). It took only four hours to layout and bandsaw all of the white-oak beams for *Seraffyn*. Her beams lay on a sheer clamp, so there was no bevel on the top or bottom edge. The beams

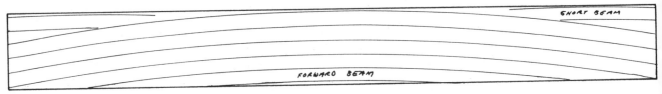

Diagram 20.9

CUTTING SEVERAL BEAMS FROM A STRAIGHT-GRAINED
PIECE 1⅞" X 14" X 10'. SLASH- OR FLAT-GRAINED
STOCK IS BEST, AS IT HAS LESS TENDENCY TO
SPLIT AT THE GRAIN RUNOFF NEAR THE ENDS.

for *Taleisin* took longer. They were cut from curved locust flitches with good sweeping grain, but the top and bottom edges had to be beveled, as they fit flush against the sheer knees and frames. This meant I spent about 8 to 10 hours laying out and cutting all of them.

The one problem with sawn deckbeams is that unless you have stock with good sweeping grain, the beams will have to be fairly wide in the molded dimension to keep the beam from splitting. The curved flitches I had in stock made sawn beams a fine choice.

Laminated beams, as Lloyd's Rules (Appendix B) show, are just as strong as natural, curved-grain sawn beams, but the labor and expense of milling and gluing recur here. One way to save labor and materials if you use laminated beams for your deck structure is to saw out all of the short half-beams, the carlines, and any auxiliary beams that are less than 3½ feet long. All of these parts have little curvature, which means little grain runoff, so no additional strength is gained by laminating them.

Curved deckbeams for smaller hulls can be made from straight-grained wood that is steam-bent and clamped onto a mold. The bending jig should have a bit more curve to it than your deckbeam pattern to correct for the springback of the beam when it is unclamped. If your first steamed beam ends up with too little crown, you will have to put more curve into the jig. Steaming would be a quick and efficient way to shape cabin beams, since they usually have a larger crown than deckbeams. The sectional shape of steamed beams should be square or close to square—say, about 1¼ inches sided by 1⅝ inches molded for a 25-footer—so the beams will bend over the mold without distorting.

Deckbeams can have various shapes to complement the designer's construction plan. But I would avoid the humble, straight beams used on *Moonraker,* as they tend to sag a bit with age, which lets puddles of water settle next to the cabinsides. If cost is a problem when you are having a boat built, it would be preferable to have the builder crown the top of the beams and leave the bottom edge straight. This will give a beam that is heavier than normal, but for fishboats this method is strong, cheap, effective, and quick, as only one curved cut has to be made and faired up.

At the other end of the scale, the deckbeams for a racing yacht should have tapered ends to reduce weight (see Nevins's Scantling Rules, Appendix B). If the tapered beams are to be laminated, the lower-edge lamination strip should not be tapered. The runoff or feather edge caused by tapering the laminated beam should occur at the top edge of the beam. That way, the deck planking and its fastenings will tend to hold down the thin feather edges and the uninterrupted bottom lamination will look neater if the beams are varnished.

To save both time and materials, laminated beams can be glued up of ½-inch-thick-by-10-inch (or 12-inch)-wide layers. The four or five ½-inch layers can be clamped onto the jig with 2 x 2 blocks to spread the clamping pressure equally. When the adhesive has set, beams can be bandsawed to the desired siding, then cleaned up on the thickness planer.

According to Lloyd's Rules (Appendix B), laminated beams can be up to 15 percent smaller in sided dimensions than beams sawn from straight-grained timber, yet still retain the same strength.

When referring to the scantling rules, remember that any full-width beam that does not support a hatch or deck opening is called an ordinary or auxiliary beam. It is these beams that are referred to in the scantling rules. The beams that support hatches and cabins are called king beams (strong beams or main beams), and in most cases these are sided 1¾ times larger than auxiliary beams. Half-beams are any that joint into partners or cabin or hatch carlines. These, along with the short auxiliary beams at the ends of hulls with long overhangs, can be reduced according to the three sets of scantling rules included in Appendix B.

A final word on deckbeams. The wood you select should be rot-resistant. It is extremely difficult to replace a deckbeam if it does rot.

Deckbeam-to-Carline Joints

There are seven basic joints that can be used to make this connection. The following diagram shows these, with some of the advantages and disadvantages listed alongside (diagram 20.10). In making a decision, keep in mind the deck covering you plan to use. Will it strengthen these joints or will it put extra stress on them? In my opinion, none of these joints are very strong unless they have tie-rods to hold them together.

Deckbeam-to-Hull Connections

The standard and most widely used method of connecting beams to hulls is with a sheer clamp or with a combination sheer clamp and shelf. (In Great Britain and New Zealand, these terms are reversed, the sheer clamp being called a beam shelf and the shelf being called a clamp.) If this member is well proportioned and well fastened, it will resist panting and prevent eventual hogging.

L. Francis Herreshoff, in *Common Sense of Yacht Design,* says,
The principal function of the clamp is to make a continuous knee which holds the angle between the side of the yacht and the crown of the deck as designed and supports the deck beams and ties their ends so the yacht cannot spread. In all excepting the smaller yachts (say less than thirty feet W.L.). I use a combination shelf and clamp and believe this arrangement has the following advantages:

1. It is the easiest to spring in.
2. It best supports both the deck beams and frames.
3. It can be made up of short lengths if necessary and the scarphs of each member spread.
4. Two or more fastenings can be used in both beam and frame.

For this clamp-and-shelf method to work well, it has to be designed so it gives a substantial lever arm, as diagram 20.11a shows. The deckbeam ends must also be fastened strongly to the frame heads. If, on the other hand, the beam-to-clamp connection is like that shown in diagram 20.11b, with the beams and frames unconnected, the critical lever arm will be quite short, so it should be strengthened and increased by the addition of hanging knees or a shelf, as shown by the dotted lines in diagram 20.11a.

DECKBEAM-TO-CARLINE JOINTS

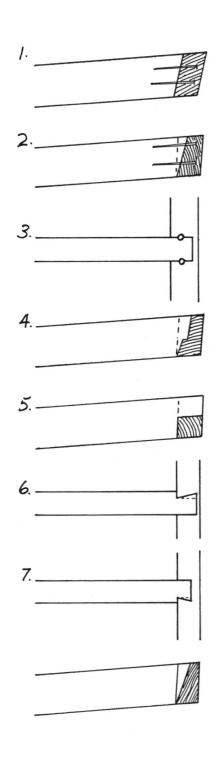

1. BUTT JOINT WORKS BEST WITH WELL-INCLINED CARLINES; NAILS OR SCREWS AND GLUE SECURE BEAM.

2. NOTCHED AND TAPERED; ALSO NEEDS FASTENINGS AND GLUE; MOST COMMON CARLINE JOINT.

3. SIMILAR TO 2, WITH DEEPER NOTCH AND DEEP VERTICAL WOOD DOWELS.

4. STEP LOCKS BEAM FROM SLIDING DOWN. END FASTENINGS NOT REQUIRED IF TIE-RODS AND GLUE ARE USED.

5. THIS IS A POOR CONNECTION. THE BEAM AND THE CARLINE ARE WEAKENED EQUALLY BY THE HALF-LAP.

6. SAME AS 5, BUT WITH HALF-DOVE-TAIL, WHICH CAN EASILY SPLIT ON DASHED LINE

7. TWO VIEWS OF A TAPERED HALF-DOVETAIL BETTER THAN 5 AND 6. DOVETAIL CAN ALSO SPLIT; END FASTENING IS REQUIRED.

Diagram 20.10

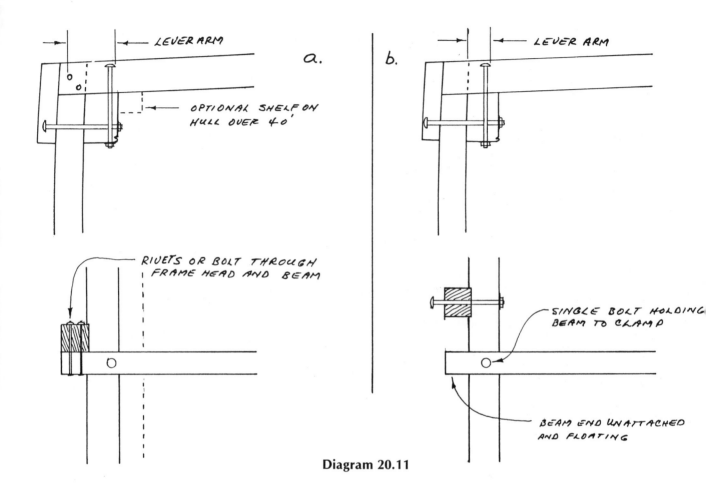

Diagram 20.11

Lloyd's Scantling Rules show another alternative (see Lloyd's section 10.2.2 in Appendix B). This is similar to the method in diagram 20.11a. I would prefer to see this well fastened with bolts instead of screws or nails (dumps). Lloyd's Rules (sections 4.9.6 and 4.10.1) also show methods commonly used for cold-molded hulls. With these methods, there is almost no lever arm to keep the hull from panting. It is definitely necessary to add the lever-arm support of hanging knees or bulkheads to make this joint secure.

For *Taleisin,* I decided to use an alternative method suggested by L.F. Herreshoff in his discussion of sheer clamps: "The shelf and clamp can both be dispensed with perfectly well if there is a knee on each frame and the longitudinal strength of the clamp is transferred to the sheer strake and covering board by making these members thicker."

Nevins and N.G. Herreshoff include this method in their scantling rules on clamps, and I have seen several oceangoing racing yachts during the past years that were built using this method. Their longevity and perfect sheers convinced me that the triangulated connection of the long-armed hanging knees between each beam and frame produced a strong, simple-to-construct joint that would resist panting. Since all of the scantling rules suggest hanging knees in addition to sheer clamps at high-stress points in the hull near partner beams, hatch beams, or at king beams, I felt I would have a stronger deck and hull if I used hanging knees all along the hull to support and triangulate other stress points, such as swept-back intermediate shrouds and genoa sheet-lead connections. So I planned a knee at every frame-to-beam connection except at structural bulkheads, which already are connected to both beam and frame. As Herreshoff suggested, I made up for any longitudinal strength lost by eliminating a clamp and/or shelf: I used a thicker sheerstrake and covering board than normally would be used on a hull of this size. I also added a 2-inch-by-3-inch through-bolted rubrail (belting), which gives additional support for all of the butt joints along the sheerstrake and covering board.

I particularly liked this method, as it eliminated the sheer clamp. A sheer clamp is cumbersome to handle if you are working alone. It can be quite costly, as it usually has to be spiled to fit the sheer curve. For boats over 24 feet in length, sheer clamps almost always need to be scarfed or laminated in place layer by layer.

This hanging-knee method also eliminates the need to joint and fit individual beams to the top edge of the sheer clamp. This is one joint that should fit tight and be well bolted; otherwise, strength will be lost. This method saves weight near deck level and opens up the sheer area for easy maintenance access plus room for bookshelves and storage areas. But the greatest advantage is the additional strength. *Taleisin's* hanging knees triangulate and strengthen this area and give an effective lever-arm support that reaches from the arm-end rivet to the corner rivet. These knees are fastened to each frame and each deckbeam with several rivets that run fore-and-aft and are taking the strains in shear. This is universally accepted as the strongest way to use fastenings. A deckbeam connected to a sheer clamp with one vertical bolt is depending on a single fastening that is in tension.

For the hanging-knee method to work well, the frame heads need to be fairly wide so the frame head will not be weakened by the ¼-inch rivets that will be set through it, and also so the rivets can be well staggered. If the boat were involved in a beam-on collision, the less-staggered fastening pattern and narrower frame heads would be likely to split. For the same reasons, the molded dimension of the deckbeam ends should also be as wide as practical. The minimum frame and deckbeam molded dimension I would consider for use with this type of sandwiched hanging-knee sheer construction would be 1¾ inches.

There are other ways to build these hanging knees. Plywood can be used instead of bronze, and then glued and screwed in place, as shown in diagram 20.12a. This gives a lever arm that is as long as the total knee arm. This method was used on the Sparkman and Stephens–designed 47-foot racer/cruiser *Puffin,* owned and raced successfully by Ed Greeff for many years. I sailed on her in 1982, and after seventeen years of extensive racing and several transatlantic trips, her sheer showed absolutely no sign of hogging, nor of any movement or working inside the hull.

François Graeser, the Swiss designer and builder of *Kion Dee,* a lovely double-ended cruising cutter, developed another variation of this knee-bracket method (diagram 20.12b). He carried one of the upper futtocks of his double-sawn frames inboard to connect with each deckbeam, achieving an effective glued connection and a long lever arm.

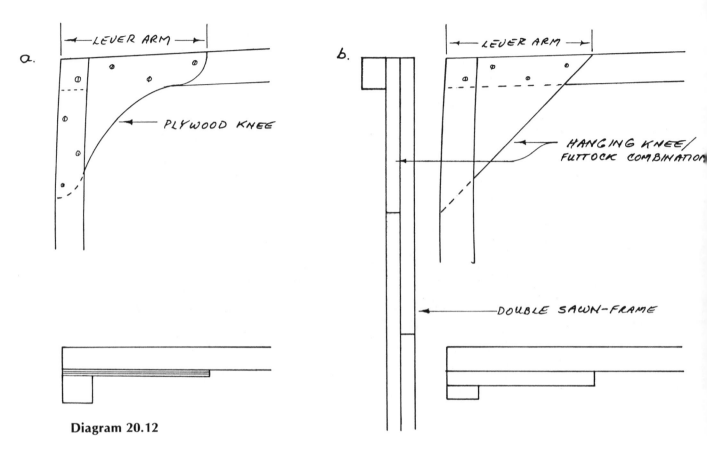

Diagram 20.12

The labor required to use this knee method, or to use a sheer clamp laid along the inside of the frames, is probably about equal if all things are considered. But since there is no need to handle large timbers, this method should be less frustrating for the lone builder.

Mast Partners, Deck Blocking, and Tie-Rods

Herreshoff's Rules state that for all boats the mast partners should be two and a half times longer than the frame spacing (diagram 20.13a). This is a good rule for any marconi-rigged boat with a well-stayed mast, but on boats that are less than 25 feet in length and marconi-rigged, I feel the partners could be reduced somewhat, as shown in diagram 20.13b, to simplify construction. On any gaff-rigged boat, the partners should be at least as long as Herreshoff's recommendations, and possibly a bit wider. A gaff-rigged mast should never be stepped on deck. It should not, in my opinion, be stepped through the cabintop without specially engineered bulkheads to take the extra strains it will impose. The lower two-thirds of a gaff mast (the luff length of the mainsail) is shroudless, so the step and the partners are supporting the mast from deck level to about two-thirds of the way up to the shrouds. With a completely unstayed mast, the partners and mast step are

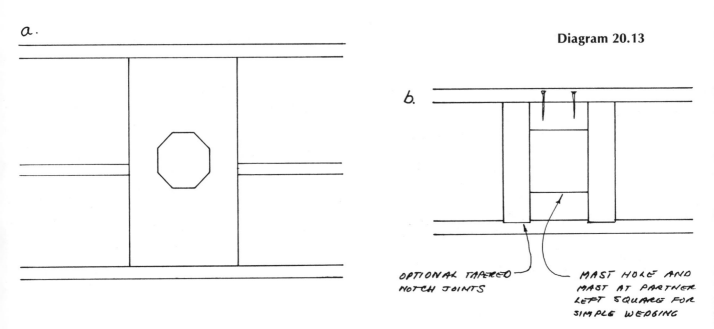

a.

Diagram 20.13

b.

OPTIONAL TAPERED
NOTCH JOINTS

MAST HOLE AND
MAST AT PARTNER
LEFT SQUARE FOR
SIMPLE WEDGING

taking and distributing all of the loads. Therefore, the partners should be even larger than Herreshoff recommends. The larger partners recommended for gaff and unstayed rigs also act as a landing place for eyebolts, sway hooks for halyards, and the pinrail, all of which are through-bolted through deck and partners.

To spread the horizontal mast loads successfully across the whole deck and out to the hull, it is best to attach the mast partners to two full-length deckbeams, so the location of the mast hole relative to the deckbeams and cabin will cut one or two of the deck beams into half-beams, as in diagram 20.13a. If strapping is not used to reinforce this area, lodging knees or plywood decking will be necessary. These should be shown on your plans.

In all cases, a tie-rod that runs from underneath the mast step, through the mast partners and the deck, is necessary to keep the partners and deck from panting upward. If there will be sway hooks, a pinrail, or halyard turning blocks at the base of the mast, this tie-rod becomes doubly important. In *Taleisin,* the tie-rod would have interfered with interior cabinetry, so instead of putting it through the mast step, I made an angled, ½-inch-diameter tie-rod that through-bolted to the deck and fastened to a 10-inch-long, ³/₁₆-inch-thick bronze plate that was screw-fastened to the front of the mast 12 inches below decks. The only disadvantage to this tie-rod method is that the plate has to be removed from the mast in order to unstep it.

Blocking should be fitted between each beam from the mast partners forward to the breasthook to take the compressive loads that will be sent aft from the headstay. If you are

Diagram 20.14

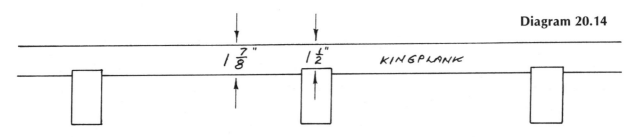

$1\frac{7}{8}$" $1\frac{1}{2}$" KINGPLANK

using a laid deck such as this one, you can spread this load by way of a thicker kingplank that is let down into the beams, as shown in diagram 20.14. This method has the advantage of not needing any extra fastenings that are for blocking alone. I found that the dadoes I had to cut to fit this kingplank/blocking combination took less time and trouble than making individual blocking, and it saved weight.

Carlines

Properly designed and placed carlines can do a lot to help the deck resist twisting. A hull with a cabin that runs well forward of the mast—combined with a large cockpit that has no bridge deck—will be hard to strengthen to prevent twisting. Diagram 20.15a shows this problem We had a similar arrangement on *Seraffyn,* and, after several years of use, there was some evidence of twisting and working caused by hard sailing. Diagram 20.15b shows a bridge-deck arrangement, which, unfortunately, means a shorter cockpit and a longer companionway ladder. Diagram 20.15c shows the strongest possible carline method short of going to a true flush deck. Unfortunately, this means less headroom forward of the mast but far more resistance to twisting. So the length of the carlines basically is a compromise: Long carlines reduce deck working space for sailing the ship but increase room below. They mean the hull will be more likely to twist or work in a seaway. Short carlines mean more deck space and a stronger hull but less interior space and headroom.

On large, flush-decked yachts, carlines are often eliminated completely, even for large skylights as long as 5 feet and as wide as 4 feet. Instead, the deckbeams are carried all of the way across the hull, under the skylight. These full-width deckbeams add substantially to the strength of the deck and only marginally reduce the light and air provided by the skylight.

L.F. Herreshoff designed most of his sailing yachts without carlines. Instead, the half-beams were held in place temporarily with clamps and under-the-deck ribbands until the deck was laid and the cabinsides were fitted. This method is not ideal with laid,

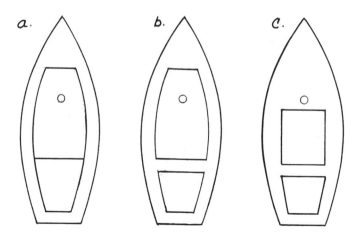

Diagram 20.15

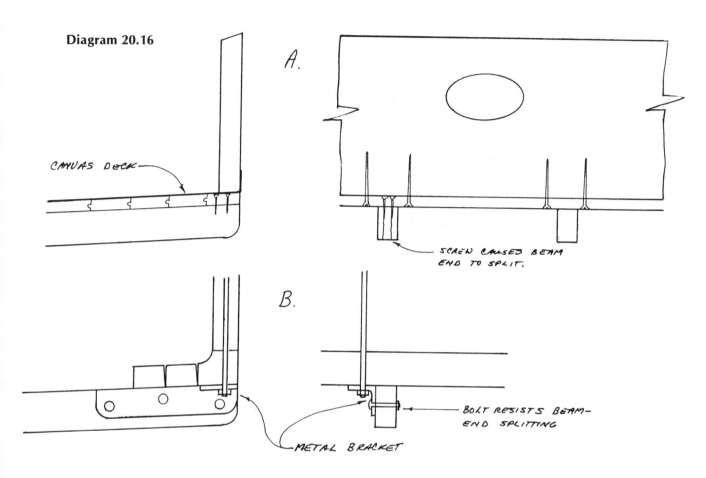

Diagram 20.16

CANVAS DECK

A.

SCREW CAUSES BEAM
END TO SPLIT.

B.

BOLT RESISTS BEAM-
END SPLITTING

METAL BRACKET

caulked decks, as there is no place to land tie-rods. Furthermore, I have seen cracked ends on the beams of some older Herreshoff boats where deck fastenings have split the wood (diagram 20.16a). To use this method for a caulked deck and eliminate the chance of cracked beam ends, I would prefer to add an L-shaped bracket cast from bronze or fabricated from galvanized iron to support the vertical beam-end-to-cabinsides through-bolt and serve as a tie-rod-type connection to spread the loads of caulking back along the whole deckbeam structure (diagram 20.16b). With this addition, I would consider this carlineless, metal-connected, inboard deckbeam end for my next boat. Eliminating the carline would save considerable labor, as there would be fewer time-consuming joints to fit. It would give a bit more headroom over the settee area and also save weight and materials. The cabinsides and deck still are more than sufficient to provide the vertical support needed to hold the side decks in position and control deckloads.

21. PLANKING THE TRANSOM

Few things in my life have provided as much pure joy as building *Taleisin*. One of the most satisfying jobs during this project was mitering and then fitting the splined transom planks to the fashion timbers.

Photo 21.1 The transom on *Taleisin* was simple to plank, as it is flat and the rake of the sternpost is relatively modest. (A curved and heavily raked transom adds technical problems, which are dis-cussed at the end of this chapter.) I started the planking for this transom at the waterline and fit-ted it down into the diminishing miter ends of the side planks.

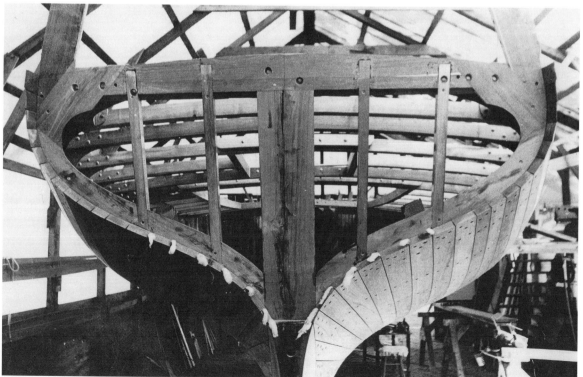

21.1

Photo 21.2 Before I planked the transom, I decided to fit the 1½-inch-thick-by-4-inch-wide teak covering board against which the aft ends of the deck strakes butt. I was fortunate to have a piece of 4 x 6 teak so I could saw out this piece. As a second choice, I would have laminated it from three ½-inch strips, with the top lamination showing edge grain. (Other options are discussed at the end of the chapter.) I used my deckbeam pattern to shape this covering piece. When I laid this covering board temporarily in place—with its aft edge uncut and therefore straight—it emphasized the aft curvature caused by the deckbeam crown intersecting the plane of the flat transom.

This covering board was gradually worked into position and shaped, using the classic diminishing-fit method, until it slid between the horns of the fashion timber. The timber was cut slightly longer than necessary and the ends were adjusted so the covering board could slide slowly aft until it was in line with the flat of the transom.

Once the piece was fitted, I cut a caulking seam between the ends and the inboard edges of the fashion-timber horns.

21.3

Photo 21.3 The covering board, as shown here, is still about ½ inch shy of the middle of the transom beam edge. To fit it, I moved it aft until it was flush with the transom framing amidships. I then marked the bottom edge of the covering board and cut it to the correct curvature and bevel on the bandsaw. If I had not had a piece of timber wide enough for this job, I could have edge-set the covering board aft ½ inch with clamps. This would have given a pleasing curve to its forward edge, where the deck strakes eventually will butt up to it.

Photo 21.4 Once the edge was beveled and the caulking seam ends were fitted, the covering board was glued and screwed to the transom beam to help it resist horizontal caulking strains. I left the covering board 1/32 inch oversize at the aft face and planed it dead flat after the glue was set so I would have a watertight fit to the covering board and transom frame when the top transom plank was finally fastened and glued in place.

21.4

21.5

21.7

21.6

Photo 21.5 I finished up the ends of the cotton caulking by tucking them back into the seam lightly so that they stood slightly proud of the ends of the planks. This left a little hump so that the final caulking in the miter seam could tighten up and seal against each hump.

The planking on the hull is 1¼ inches thick, but the transom planks will be ⅛ inch thinner. This difference is instrumental in making a Baltimore clipper–style mitered seam.

Photo 21.6 The first step toward making this seam is to file the corners of the side planks so they are flush to the 1¼-inch block. This produces the exact outboard miter corner of the faired-in vertical edge of the hull planking (diagram 21.1a).

Photo 21.7 I then worked the ends of the planking down to the correct miter angle with the outboard corner, as in diagram 21.1b. I used a belt sander for much of this job and adjusted the belt so that it was slightly in from the edge of the wheels (¹⁄₁₆-inch inset). That way, the belt would not score the transom frame. Where the plank ends were along an inside curve, I pared them down by cutting across the endgrain with a razor-sharp chisel and a mallet. Then I smoothed them up with a file and sandpaper.

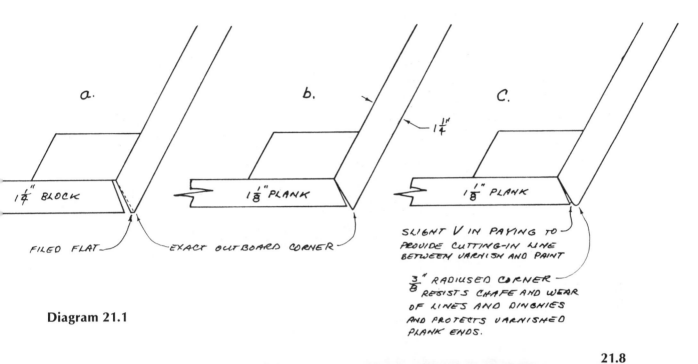

a.

$1\frac{1}{4}''$ BLOCK

FILED FLAT

EXACT OUTBOARD CORNER

b.

$1\frac{1}{4}''$

$1\frac{1}{8}''$ PLANK

c.

$1\frac{1}{8}''$ PLANK

SLIGHT V IN PAYING TO PROVIDE CUTTING-IN LINE BETWEEN VARNISH AND PAINT

$\frac{3}{8}''$ RADIUSED CORNER RESISTS CHAFE AND WEAR OF LINES AND DINGHIES AND PROTECTS VARNISHED PLANK ENDS.

Diagram 21.1

21.8

21.9

Photo 21.8   I lined out the lower portion of the transom planking so that the top edge of the second plank lined up with the cut-in line for the boot top. (The lower seam, at the sternpost, will be caulked.) The seam between the two planks has been fitted tightly and has a loose spline to create the most reliable type of waterproof joint that I know.

Photo 21.9   The clear-plastic straightedge clamped across the top of the transom serves as a horizontal reference line as I plank upward. Its top edge is equidistant above the port and starboard sheer marks. I use this as a guide to check that each plank I fit is horizontal to the deck-sheer marks.

Photo 21.10   The top arc, shown just below the plastic batten on the transom beam, will be the lower edge of the uppermost plank. I laid out the transom planking so that the ends of this plank would be at least 2 inches wide—enough room for appropriate fastenings at the plank ends. This plank will be 5 inches wide at midship to account for the deck crown. I adjusted the dimensions for this plank so the planks between it and the bootstripe plank were 4 inches wide, as this utilized the material I had on hand. I then lined out the rest of the planks by scribing 4-inch arcs along the sternpost.

21.10

21.11

21.12

Photo 21.11 To pick up the seam-miter shape and angle for the end of each transom plank, I used corrugated cardboard. I tapped lightly with the mallet to ''emboss'' the sharp corner onto the cardboard.

Photo 21.12 This pattern, when cut out, gives both the port and the starboard plank-end shapes. To make sure the angles were kept in line, I used the top edge of the previous plank as a horizontal reference guide.

21.13

Photo 21.13 The bevel that must be cut on each plank end has to be reduced by the amount necessary for the caulking-seam opening. So as I measured the angle, I left the bevel-gauge arm about ³⁄₃₂ inch clear of the outer edge of the hull planking. These bevels were picked up at 90 degrees to the eventual bandsaw cut.

Photo 21.14 The bevels were then transferred to the pattern. In the photo, the dark line with two V's marks the upper edge of the proposed plank.

21.14

21.15

21.16

21.17

Photo 21.15 The left-hand end of the ½-inch-by-1¼-inch staff is shown lined up along the top of the existing plank and clamped to mark the length of the lower edge of the next plank.

Photo 21.16 The transom planking was all cut from edge-grained stock and laid out so that any convex curvature in the length of the boards faced forward against the transom framing. (Also, I always placed this convex face against the fence on the table saw so that I could cut in the dado groove with accuracy.) The edge-grained stock planes and scrapes neatly, and the color and grain pattern on the transom looks more even after it is varnished than it would with random-grained planks.

I traced the starboard-end pattern onto the plank, lined up the starboard pencil mark on my plank-length staff, and clamped it as shown. If I had any extra stock, I left the planks a bit wider than 4 inches. That way, if the fit at the ends was not perfect, I could trim the lower edge of the plank slightly, which lowered the plank and tightened up the miters.

Photo 21.17 I then transferred the exact length of the plank to the port end of the planking stock.

21.18

Photo 21.18   I flopped the cardboard pattern to lay out the port end and noted the bevels on the plank.

Photo 21.19   The degrees marked on the inside of the bandsaw throat made it easy to see as I worked on my own. The clamp for the table was adjusted so it had a bit of drag. That way, I could change the bevel by hitting the upper or lower edge of the table with my hand.

I tend to leave the miter ends ¹⁄₃₂ inch oversize, then work them down by hand for a good fit.

21.19

Photo 21.20   Here the plank is shown temporarily in place while I check for fits at the straight lower edge and the mitered ends. As you can see, this plank is wider than the previous ones. I'll cut it to width when I finish the final fitting and detailing.

I counterbored for the fastenings in the quarter knees and transom framing so that the heads of the fastenings were just below the faying surface for the eventual planking. A deeper counterbore with a wood plug would have unnecessarily weakened the framing. The holes are filled with fungicidal Dolfinite as the planking is set in place.

A flashlight helped as I checked the inside fit of the miter, then marked the appropriate I and O indications on the plank ends for fitting adjustments.

21.20

21.21

21.22

21.23

Photo 21.21 A spokeshave and file can be used to trim off up to 1/16 inch of endgrain with little fuss. The plank is still left overwide in case I chip off some endgrain. This cabinetmaker's file (number 50), made by Nicholson File Company, is convenient and accurate, especially for the rounded endgrain areas on these planks.

Photo 21.22 I tend to leave the outside edge of the seam slightly closed until the final fitting. If the inside miter corner does not fit as tightly as I want, I can trim 1/8 inch off the lower edge of the plank and readjust the miters. It is important to fit this miter tightly on the inside of the planking and to have a minimal-width caulking seam on the outside. If, as often happens, the fashion timbers swell after the boat is launched and this seam opens a little, a simple recaulking and repaying will solve the problem but the seam will still not look oversize.

When the plank fit at both ends and was tight along the bottom edge, I measured up 4 inches from the lower edge. Then I measured down from the horizontal straightedge to this 4-inch width mark and noted the measurement. I also marked this measurement on the port side of the transom. This way, the top edge of each seam was kept exactly horizontal and level to the port and starboard decksheer.

Photo 21.23 At the same time, I scribed the desired 3/32-inch-wide caulking seam. I then made a mark 1 inch in from the outer edge of the plank to indicate the eventual ending spot of the beaded seam detail. When all of this was done, I removed the plank and cut the top edge down to the width marks, using a straightedge and the bandsaw.

Photo 21.24 The table saw is shown set up (with two blades separated by a washer) to cut the groove for the spline on the edge of each plank. As I mentioned in the caption for photo 21.16, if there is any lengthwise curve in a plank, the convex side should face up to the table-saw fence so that the dado cut for the spline will align with the dado on the previous plank. If it is faced away, the wooden fingers clamped to the saw table would not be able to keep the wood tight against the fence. The result would be an unparallel dado that would not line up with the dado on the adjoining plank. I like to loose-spline the planks so they can shrink and swell and open a bit without losing their watertight integrity.

Photo 21.25 The cedar spline should be up to 1/32 inch loose in the dado, because it will expand up to 25 percent of its thickness once the boat is launched and moisture works its way into seams. Western red or Port Orford cedar is perfect for this job. They are very gentle in their swelling and cannot create enough force to split the dado grooves. Teak, on the other hand, will not swell much, so this works to create a stable, watertight joint. The spline can also be up to 1/16 inch narrower than the vertical width of the groove to allow for swelling. If you are building in an area with high humidity, the splines should have about 1/64 inch play in the fit.

21.24

21.25

21.26

21.27

21.28

Photo 21.26 The spline ends have been sawn off flush to the miter curve. The exposed corners of the spline were chamfered off by 1/32 inch with a block plane so they slide easily into the dado of the previous plank.

Photo 21.27 The spline ends about 1/16 inch shy of the side planking on the hull. To seal these ends, the seam will be caulked to within 1/4 inch of the outside of the transom.

Photo 21.28 I feel the bead shown here not only looks good but also makes any plank-shrinking movement less obvious. Furthermore, it was fun to do. (I stopped the bead 1 inch short of the transom edge because if it had been carried all the way to the miter, the perimeter of the varnished transom would have looked ragged.)

The beaded-seam detail I used here might not look appropriate on all boats. On more modern hulls, it might be more in keeping to have a standard V-seam similar to that used on tongue-and-groove stock or a tight seam finish. The seam at the top of the bootstripe should have a slight V so it looks similar to the boot-stripe cut-in line and thus simplifies the painting and varnishing of the transom area of the hull.

Photo 21.29 I cut the bead detail on this transom with a fascinatingly simple tool I made by using a 1¼-inch-by-1¾-inch-by-3-inch block of teak and a number 14 flathead wood screw. I drilled the pilot hole for the wood screw dead square to the block, using a drill press. The slot on the screw was then lined up at a right angle to the length of the block, as shown.

Photo 21.30 To make the bead, the block was tipped slightly and pushed so the slot cut at an angle similar to a plane-iron angle. If the grain is running foul, i.e., against the tool, the beading tool can be pulled toward you with the screw slot tipped in the opposite direction. Wherever possible, I select straight, edge-grained hardwood for any strake that will be beaded.

Photo 21.31 To stop the bead short of the plank end, I pressed the screw slot in toward the middle of the plank, starting just at the mark I had penciled when I final-fit the plank. I found that it paid off to have a bit of practice on a scrap of wood with similar grain. After a few practice runs, I could get a neat, even, smooth start to every groove, every time.

21.30

21.29

21.31

21.32

21.33

21.34

Photo 21.32 To get the final detail correct on the bead, I used a file to round the inside and outside edges, then finished it with sandpaper.

Photo 21.33 To sharpen the beading tool, I dressed the slot slightly on all four cutting corners, using a small, fine, flat file. This beading tool works better than a beading plane because it can follow around the curved or radiused end of a board or knee as long as it is used to cut with the grain. (It can be reversed easily to work with the grain whenever the grain changes direction.)

When I was building *Seraffyn,* I bought a special router bit to cut this stopped bead detail. The bit not only was expensive, but also the router was harder to control, so some of the beaded seams turned out less than uniform. Several years later, Frank Fredette, a well-known boatbuilder and designer from Victoria, British Columbia, showed me how to make and use this centuries-old gem of a tool.

Photo 21.34 Before I set each plank in place, I filed and then sanded a ⅛-inch flat onto the top corner of the previous plank. I left the last inch of the seam edge at its outboard corner sharp and square. When the beaded plank is set in place, the radius on the previous plank completes the lower edge of the detail. It is important that all corners of the beaded detail be nicely rounded so the coats of varnish will build up to give a thick protective layer.

21.35

Photo 21.35 The first four planks of this transom are important structural members of the hull. They tie together both the sternpost and the lower sides of the fashion timber, so they are fastened with extra wood screws. I use fewer screws on the upper planks, since they are not as critical.

Photo 21.36 When I was ready to fit the upper transom plan, I fashioned two measuring guides by mitering two pieces of teak that were the same thickness as the sheerstrake and the same sided dimension as the covering board.

21.36

21.37

Photo 21.37 I then clamped these two top corner pieces to the fashion timber to simulate the covering-board thickness and the miter angle. The tops of the covering boards that run along the side of the deck eventually will end up even and flush with the top edge of the transom planking.

The reverse curve at the top of the transom edges (tumblehome) makes the last two planks harder to fit, as they have to be shaped correctly the first time. As I fit these nondiminishing boards, I tend to be conservative and leave 1/16 inch of extra wood on the ends. I carefully work the ends down until the plank fits tight at the inside of the caulking seam and flush against the transom frame.

The deck covering board I fastened at the top of the transom framing serves as a handy cleat for clamping this top strake in place for the final fitting.

Once the plank is fit and a dado is cut on its lower edge for the spline, the plank will have to be angled in to slide onto the spline of the previous plank. To make this possible, the spline should be a full 1/32 inch loose in the groove, and its top corners should be well chamfered for an easy entry.

Photo 21.38 The top plank must be screwed and glued to the fashion timbers to guarantee a waterproof seal between the covering board and the transom planking. I also crushed a V into the aft edge of the covering board about ½ inch down from deck level. To further ensure a waterproof seal, I stuck a single strand of cotton wicking in the V with a bit of shellac.

The plank now has been set on and fastened. To make sure the glue set properly, I set up electric worklights. After the photograph was taken, I made a tent of plastic sheeting and covered this area of the transom to contain the heat for the night. (This top seam can be caulked lightly and payed if you do not wish to use adhesives.)

21.38

The covering boards for the sides of the deck and the top edge of the transom planking at the outboard ends must be flush to each other. They meet at the miter corner, where a smooth caulking seam is filled with white 3M 5200 compound.* The bare teak deck strakes and the covering board across the top of the transom are left ¼ inch higher than the transom planking and the side-deck covering board (diagram 21.2). The decking edge is then rounded with a ⅜-inch radius. Not only does this give a nice cutting-in line for the top of the varnish on the transom, but it also effectively hides the wear on the deck as it is used and scrubbed. With reasonable care, the extra wood should ensure twenty-five to thirty years of hard use before the deck is worn down to the level of the transom edge and the side covering boards.

To finish the transom planking, the top edge is also give a ⅜-inch radius. The miter is caulked and payed and the ends of the hull planking are radiused, as shown in diagram 21.1c, to form a natural paint-to-varnish cut-in line. The transom is then scraped smooth with a cabinet scraper and given several coats of varnish before the name is carved into it.

---

* Since I planned to varnish the transom, I sealed the endgrain of the planks with a coating of epoxy before I caulked and payed the seam.

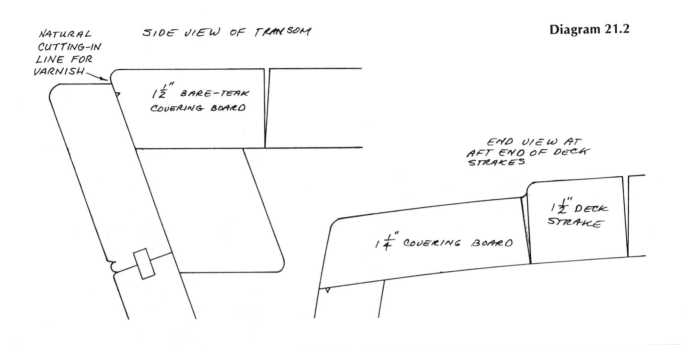

NATURAL CUTTING-IN LINE FOR VARNISH

SIDE VIEW OF TRANSOM

Diagram 21.2

$1\frac{1}{2}''$ BARE-TEAK COVERING BOARD

END VIEW AT AFT END OF DECK STRAKES

$1\frac{1}{2}''$ DECK STRAKE

$1\frac{1}{4}''$ COVERING BOARD

CONSTRUCTION TIMES FOR CHAPTER 21

Larry: Fitting transom covering board; preparing miter; planking and detailing transom; caulking and paying transom seam; preparing for varnish and name carving   31 hours

Lin: Inserting wood plugs on hull and transom; varnishing and finishing transom (nine coats)   29 hours

Totals to date: Larry 3641 hours

Lin   995 hours

DISCUSSION
Stresses on a Transom

Generally speaking, the transom is not a high-load area of a hull, although some strains are transmitted through the transom to the fashion timbers by permanent backstays, running backstays, and the gudgeons and pintles of an outboard rudder. In each case, the fastenings should be attached to the structural framework inside the hull so that no unnecessary strains are put on the relatively weak corner where the transom and fashion timbers meet the hull planking. In other words, the upper gudgeons for the rudder, or the chainplates for the backstay, should be bolted through the planking and then the sternpost. Any running-backstay plates that are led aft should be well attached to the quarter knees and longitudinal members of the hull, or they should have long chainplates led onto the outside of the hull. The actual planking of the transom serves only to tie together the sides of the fashion timber and to keep out the water.

Transom Planking Details

The transom described in this chapter was quite simple to plank. The only simpler transom planking job would be on a completely plumb transom. To make it even easier to plank this hypothetical plumb, flat transom, the planks could be nailed or screwed onto the sternpost and the fashion timbers before the hull was planked. The ends could be cut off flush to the inside of the planking and the hull planking then would cover the end-grain of the transom planks.

Although I try to practice simplicity throughout in my building methods, I have two complaints with this nonmitered transom-planking method: (1) The endgrain of the hull planking is exposed to the weather, which promotes checking and subsequent paint-maintenance problems; and (2) the endgrain border around the transom will not be a consistent width on a raked transom. The border will appear narrower near the top of the transom, wider at the lower edges. This is not as neat as the edge produced by other methods of planking.

A flat, raked transom, such as on *Taleisin,* can be lined out with straight plank seams and they will look fair and correct from astern. But if you did the same on a transom that was not only raked but also curved, the planks would appear to sag in the middle. You can observe this if you nail a 4-inch-wide straightedge across a raked, curved transom frame, then step back and look at the stern as if you were seeing it from a dinghy. This would make all of the planks look banana-shaped, and the top plank would look like a cigar—its lower edge would sag while its top edge would appear to hump up at the curved deckline. Diagram 21.3 shows how to line out the planks for a transom that is curved and raked about 35 degrees. To be certain that the transom seams will look good, line out the planks and then tack ¼-inch-by-¼-inch battens in place to represent each seam. Next step back and view it from astern to make sure the eventual seams will look about level and evenly spaced.

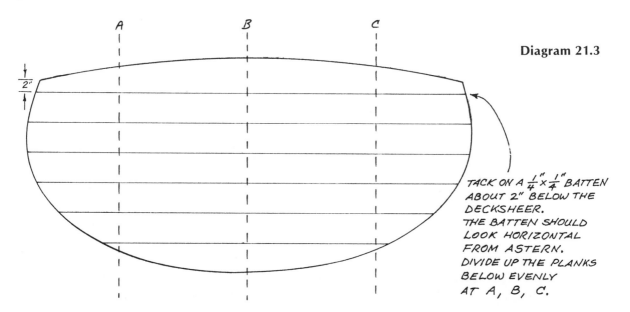

Diagram 21.3

TACK ON A $\frac{1}{4}" \times \frac{1}{4}"$ BATTEN ABOUT 2" BELOW THE DECKSHEER. THE BATTEN SHOULD LOOK HORIZONTAL FROM ASTERN. DIVIDE UP THE PLANKS BELOW EVENLY AT A, B, C.

There are three basic ways to fit the plank seams on a transom. They can be caulked, splined, or tight-fitted with a Swedish seam, as described in chapter 17. The caulked seam is the usual way to deal with a single-thickness transom. If you combine a caulked seam with mitered ends, you have the easiest of all transom planks to remove for repairs. It is important to keep the planks narrow in order to minimize individual plank shrinkage. (I recommend that the planks be between 3½ inches and 4½ inches wide.) A caulked seam looks fine on a painted transom, as the seams will not be obvious.

Splined seams are easiest to use on a flat transom with straight seams, but they can also be used on a curved transom, where the planks have to be spiled and tapered. The only complication here is that you will have to be more careful as you cut or rout the dado into the curved plank edges. These splined seams are very reliable and would leak only if a hull were left out on dry land and exposed to the hot sun for months at a time. Some builders glue the splined seams on a transom, but I feel that this glue presents an unnecessary risk, as it could cause the plank to split at the bottom of the dado if the transom dried out in the sun. Planks on a splined transom can be a bit wider—say, 4 to 5 inches—as a bit of extra plank shrinkage would not let water seep in past the spline. Repairs on a splined-seam transom will be more difficult than they would be on a caulked-seam one. To remove the plank, you would have to Skilsaw alongside the seam, cutting the spline. The dado grooves in the neighboring planks could be graved with square pieces of appropriate timber. Then the new plank could be fitted and caulked using a narrow, shallow seam as shown in diagram 17.21c. This should match the rest of the seam details as closely as possible.

Tight-fitted seams, or Swedish seams, are another alternative for transom planking. I prefer the splined method, as it is more reliable for a boat that must meet ever-changing climatic conditions. If you do choose a Swedish seam, it is best to keep the boat in one locale and insist on a stable wood for the transom planking. Further protection for the wood could come from painting it a light color to reflect the heat of the sun to keep it from drying and moving.

To help you decide whether to use a single layer of planking for the transom or a laminated three-skin system or a plywood subtransom, I have listed what I feel are the pros and cons for each choice:

SOLID PLANKING

Pro	Con
Easily repairable.	Planks will need to be steamed or sawn to fit curved transom.
Leaks can be found easily and caulked.	
Large-diameter fastenings can be used, which resist corrosion longer than many smaller fastenings.	Seams will have a tendency to crack if they
Can be planed or faired without concern about going through finish veneer layer.	are covered by a rigid sheathing or coating.
Only one layer to fit.	
Less chance of rot-prone gaps than with plywood.	
Less endgrain to cover up.	

LAMINATED THREE-SKINNED PLANKING

(two diagonal layers finished with a horizontal layer)

Pro	Con
Thinner, smaller pieces of wood can be utilized (i.e., offcuts from other jobs).	Glued layers harder to repair.
A less-expensive rot-resistant timber, such as cedar, can be used for the inner layers, with only the outer layer being a more expensive, durable hardwood.	Smaller fastenings must be used.
	More labor needed to fit three layers tightly.
	Construction integrity dependent on adhesive.
Less chance of seam shrinkage than with solid planks.	Diagonal appearance less appealing if visible inside hull.
Wood quality can be controlled and gaps eliminated, compared with plywood.	
Outer plank layer can be routed off for repairs.	
Easy to shape and fit individual layers to curved transom frame.	

PLYWOOD SUBTRANSOM WITH A HORIZONTAL FINISH LAYER

Pro	Con
Can use a simple corner joint (as shown in diagram 21.6b) at outside of planking.	Marine-grade hardwood plywood is expensive.
Plywood easy to bend to a curved transom frame.	Voids in plywood are subject to rot or delamination.
Final layer of hardwood is thinner, therefore less expensive.	Repairs due to rot or collision can be a major problem.
Good-quality plywood can be used as mold-loft pattern and then reused as sublayer for transom.	Appearance inside is less appealing.
Less chance of seam movement at glued final layer.	
Fewer seam joints to fit than with a three-skinned transom.	

Transom-Planking-to-Deck-Covering-Board Joints

There are several ways to fit this joint. Diagram 21.4 shows four methods. The joint shown at 21.4a is the one I used on *Taleisin*. (The aft edge of the covering board is hidden by the top transom plank, so a simpler and cheaper covering board could be laminated up as shown in diagram 21.5a and diagram 21.5b.)

The joint in diagram 21.4b is the more usual way to fit a transom covering board for a solid-teak deck. In this case, the transom covering board is put on after the transom is planked. (To look appropriate, this covering board should be either sawn out or jointed together, as in diagram 21.5c.)

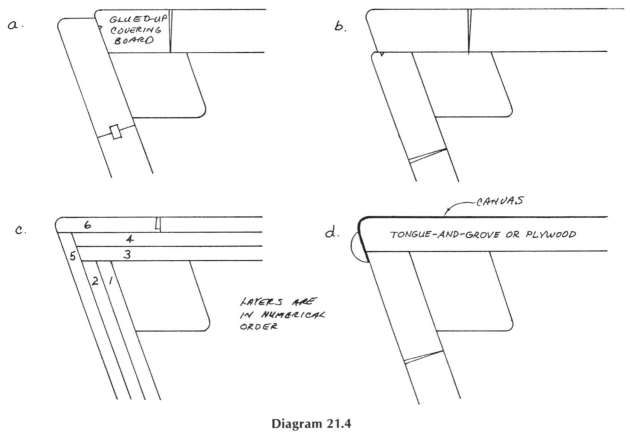

Diagram 21.4

The joint shown at 21.4c is the one used most commonly on plywood or laminated transoms that joint to a laminated deck. In this case, the teak deck layer can either cover the transom edge or vice versa. I think I would prefer having the covering board over the transom laminations to prevent water from seeping downward into the endgrain. But in either case, a tight fit is needed, along with a reliable glue to prevent fresh water from getting into the endgrain of either the transom planking or the deck planking.

The final joint, shown in diagram 21.4d, is simple and effective but used mostly on smaller boats with canvas or sheathed decks. The corner at the top edge of the decking tongue-and-groove stock or the plywood should be well radiused to minimize potential chafe and damage. This radius will also help reduce the chance of corner cracking with fiberglass or epoxy sheathing.

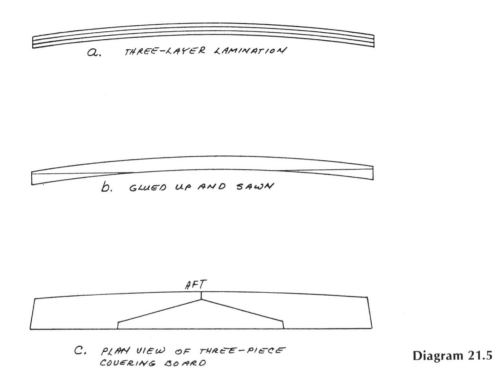

a. THREE-LAYER LAMINATION

b. GLUED UP AND SAWN

AFT

c. PLAN VIEW OF THREE-PIECE
COVERING BOARD

Diagram 21.5

Transom-Planking-to-Topside-Planking Joints

The joint shown in diagram 21.6a is probably the most common one used for boats with solid planking. To use this method, you must plank the transom before planking the topsides. It does expose the endgrain of the hull planking to the weather, but it is the least time-consuming method to use. If I were building a boat for rough service, I would use this method and cover the endgrain of the hull planking with a 1-inch-thick transom margin (dotted line) to protect the plank ends from minor damage.

If the mitered transom planking shown in this chapter does not appeal to you, a single outer layer of carvel planking can be overlapped to cover the hull plank ends, as shown in diagram 21.6b. With this system, the joint on the final transom overlay becomes a critical one, as the leakage here could let fresh water into the endgrain of the topside or transom planking.

Diagram 21.6 PLAN VIEWS

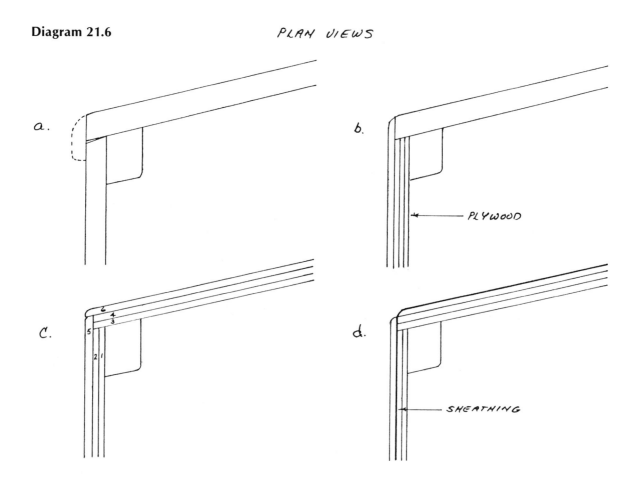

A method commonly used on three-skinned hulls with laminated transom planking is shown in diagram 21.6c. The six layers of the hull and transom would be fitted in the order shown. The final transom plank can be chamfered 1/16 inch to give a cut-in line if the transom is to be left natural or varnished. When this is done, the outside (sixth) layer of hull planking is finally fitted. This gives the same appearance as the beaded miter seam I used on *Taleisin* and covers almost all of the endgrain on both the transom planking and the hull planking.

If you are building a three-skinned hull that is to be sheathed or coated and you still want a varnished transom, you could use the method shown in diagram 21.6d. In this, the first two transom layers are fitted and then all three layers of hull planking are fastened in place. The corner where the transom meets the hull is radiused as shown to reduce the chance of damage or cracking. The hull and transom are covered with sheathing. Then the final transom layer is fitted over the sheathing, ready for varnish and—possibly the real glory of a fine yacht—a carved and gilded name and hailing port. This method does leave the endgrain of the final layer showing, which is a less than perfect solution, but if the edge is kept well varnished, this is a workable and handsome transom solution.

22. BUILDING THE RUDDER

An outboard rudder, such as I used on *Taleisin,* is simpler to build and fit than an inboard rudder with a counter stern. But many of the details will be the same for an inboard rudder as those I show in the photographs that follow.*

Photo 22.1 The finished rudder will be 2½ inches thick at its leading edge and ¾ inch thick at the trailing edge. This means a maximum of ⅞ inch of wood will be removed from each side of the rudder blank to shape the underwater part of the trailing edge. The three pieces of locust shown here have been milled from 3-inch-thick rough timber until they are flat and straight and 2¾ inches thick. Each piece is about 9 inches wide.

After the three pieces were milled, I clamped them together and traced the basic outside dimensions of the rudder onto them, along with the approximate positions of the eventual pintles (within ¼ inch, as will be explained later). I then figured and marked the positions of the drift bolts so they would clear the pintles.

Photo 22.2 I unclamped the pieces and planed and squared the jointing edges, then checked them for fit. The note "L—1/64—L" indicates the high spots on the jointing surface for the strake closest to the bottom of the photograph. These marks show that wood needs to be planed off. I make sure that both jointing surfaces are kept at 90 degrees so the three-piece rudder ends up flat when it is glued together.

22.1

22.2

---

* *The Self-Sufficient Sailor* (see Bibliography) has details that will help you maintain your rudder and propeller shaft.

22.3

22.4

Photo 22.3   The drift positions were laid out at right angles to what would become the leading edge of the rudder. They are spaced about 8 inches apart and eventually will be driven in so they are 1½ inches shy of the trailing edge. These drift-bolt lines also serve as alignment marks for positioning the pieces when they are being glued together.

Photo 22.4   Next I laid out the shape of the rudderhead and bandsawed the curve onto each separate piece. To make clamping easier, I left the lower corner of the rudder unshaped. This angled cut is easy to make with a sabersaw after the rudder blank has been fully glued.

Photo 22.5   Since the trailing edge of the rudder will be only ¾ inch thick when it is fully shaped, the pilot holes for the drift bolts have to be drilled accurately to keep them from poking through the side of the blade. To ensure that they were properly located, I squared and centered the drift locations on the face of the timber that would eventually be the leading edge of the rudder. I drilled a 1-inch-diameter counterbore hole, ½ inch deep, at the position of each eventual drift bolt. This was deep enough so that the clench-ring head for the drift would be ¼ inch below the surface—or just enough so that a wood plug could be glued in to cover it. I then drilled down about ½ inch into the counterbore hole to provide a primary pilot hole for the ⅜-inch bolt holes.

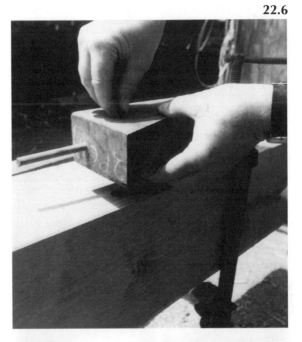

22.6

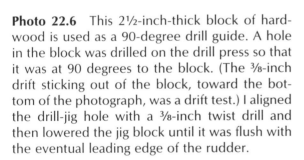

22.5

Photo 22.6 This 2½-inch-thick block of hardwood is used as a 90-degree drill guide. A hole in the block was drilled on the drill press so that it was at 90 degrees to the block. (The ⅜-inch drift sticking out of the block, toward the bottom of the photograph, was a drift test.) I aligned the drill-jig hole with a ⅜-inch twist drill and then lowered the jig block until it was flush with the eventual leading edge of the rudder.

Photo 22.7 I clamped the jig in place, removed the twist drill, and then sighted along the long drill as shown so that it looked parallel to the sides of the plank. I pulled out the drill and cleared the hole every ½ inch to help minimize any hole wandering caused by angled grain deflection.

These pilot holes can also be started square on the drill press. To do this, clamp the plank to a square block on the press table and drill the pilot holes to a depth of 3 or 4 inches. The boards can then be removed from the drill press and the holes drilled right through the rest of the 9-inch-wide plank with a hand-held electric drill.

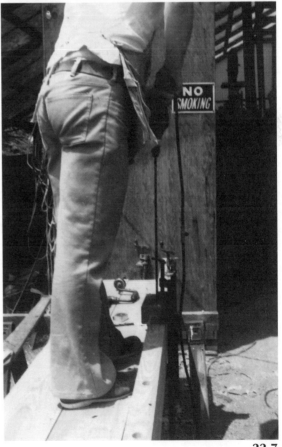

22.7

22.8

22.9

Photo 22.8 The leading-edge plank, shown lying on the right-hand side of this photograph, was lined up and clamped to the middle plank. I then drilled corresponding ½-inch-deep pilot holes into the edge of the next (or middle) piece.

Photo 22.9 The pilot hole shown in the foreground was slightly to the right of the centerline. To correct and realign this hole so that the bolt eventually would run close to the center of the rudder, I placed a 1/64-inch-thick shim (or you can use a thin wedge) under the left side of the drilling jig to angle it slightly and redirect the hole toward the centerline of the plank edge.

Photo 22.10 When all of the drift-bolt holes were drilled, I glued the rudder blank together.

Photo 22.11 When the glue was semihard, I ran a long 5/16-inch drill through to the bottom of the pilot holes to clear out the excess glue. (I used a piece of tape on the drill to mark the correct depth of the pilot hole.)

Before I drove the drifts into the glued-up rudder blank, I drilled an experimental pilot hole into an offcut from the rudder. By doing this, I found that the 3/8-inch silicon-bronze drift would drive into a 3/8-inch hole if I used a firm but steady pressure with a 6-pound hammer. In general, I have found that drifts go into a piece of wood with a high moisture content more easily than they do into one with little moisture. Dry, well-seasoned wood often resists penetration so the drifts may bend when they are partway in.

There will be very little tendency for these drifts to pull out once the rudder is finished. The major force on them will be the bending strain exerted on the rudder blade when it is turned as the boat is being sailed. It is not necessary to roughen or score the surface of the drifts to increase tension holding power; the swelling of the wood and the eventual surface corrosion on the bronze rod will lock the drifts permanently in place.

22.10

22.11

Photo 22.12 Next I ran the whole rudder blank through the planer to take it down to 2½ inches —the thickest part of the rudder. I checked and trued up one side of the blank, using the methods I described in chapter 2. The trued side went down onto the bed of the planer. I then cut ⅛ inch from the top (untrued) side of the blank, flipped it over, and ran it through at exactly 2½ inches. This gave me a dead-straight, flat rudder blank without any twist, which made the next steps in layout quick and easy. If you do not have a planer wide enough to take your complete rudder blank, you can true up each plank separately, then plane each one to the correct thickness before gluing together the rudder blank. This is slower, but it can be just as accurate.

22.12

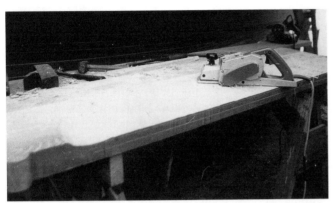

22.13

22.14

Photo 22.13 To lay out the blade taper, I set my marking gauge to ⅞ inch and traced two scribe lines down the trailing edge of the rudder. This left a ¾-inch-wide trailing edge. Before I began the shaping, I marked an exact centerline down the trailing edge of the rudder as a reference point.

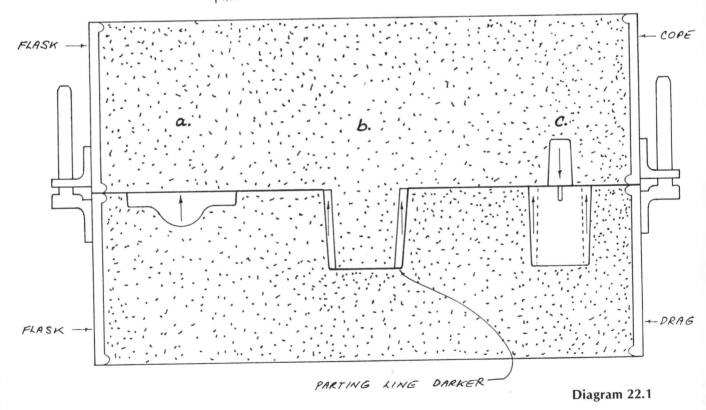

(ARROWS SHOW DIRECTION OF PATTERN REMOVAL)

FLASK →

← COPE

a.

b.

c.

FLASK →

← DRAG

PARTING LINE DARKER

Diagram 22.1

22.15

Photo 22.14 The forward 3 inches of the leading edge of the rudder is left net at 2½ inches. The rough-ended piece of wood lying across the rudder is the pattern for the curve I used to shape the rudder foil and make sure both port and starboard sides were symmetrical. The pattern rested on its edge along the 3-inch flat on the leading edge of the rudder. I shaped the blade curve until the pattern lay flush along the trailing edge. I used a power plane for the first part of this work, then a smoothing plane, and finally the belt sander with 60-grit belts. The semirough finish left by the 60-grit belts provided a good grip for the antifouling paint that we applied just before launching.

Photo 22.15 The four foundry patterns for the gudgeons and pintles were made before I started building the rudder.

The gudgeon that bolts flat to the transom above the waterline is the easiest of the four patterns to make. (The pattern is shown on the left in this photograph.) It is tapered or drafted about 2 degrees from the flat surface on which it rests—the foundryman's parting line. This taper allows the pattern to be pulled out of the sand easily (see diagram 22.1a and chapter 5). The bronze casting made from this pattern is shown at the right. It has a Delrin bushing in the pintle hole. (This is discussed later in the chapter.)

Photo 22.16 The pattern for the middle gudgeon is on the right-hand side in this photo. The final casting, bored for its bearing, is on the left. The pattern for this gudgeon has to be shaped to fit the sternpost, which tapers from the transom down toward the lower part of the keel until it is only 2½ inches wide (photo 22.25 shows this quite well). This means all of the vertical surfaces on the insides of the gudgeon pattern must be tapered to align with the sternpost and to facilitate removal from the foundry sand, as shown in diagram 22.1b.

The lower gudgeon fits to an untapered part of the sternpost, so it is simply drafted like the pintle pattern shown in diagram 22.1c, minus the pin.

22.16

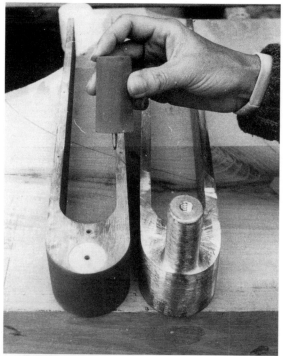

Photo 22.17 The pintle pattern has a removable pin that is held in place by a snug-fitting dowel. The removable pin makes it easier for the foundryman to mold the pintle in the sand (diagram 22.1c). The strap part of the pintle is molded into the drag (upper flask) before the doweled pin is in place. Then the pin is set onto the pattern and the cope (lower flask) is rammed up with sand, which fits around the pin. When the cope and drag are parted, the pattern can be pulled out of the sand in the direction shown by the arrows in the drawing.

22.18

Photo 22.18 The pin on the casting is designed to fit onto a Delrin bushing. I ground the casting taper off the pin with the belt sander and a metal file. Then I coated the hole in the bushing with a black felt pen to locate any high spots on the more-or-less-round pin. I slid the bushing on, ground off highspots indicated by the black ink, and repeated the procedure until the bushing would slide easily onto the pin. In the photo, the inner, top edge of the pin still shows some of the black ink that has transferred from the bushing to mark a high spot.

Photo 22.19 As I removed the taper and trued up the pin, I left about a ⅛-inch radius of metal where the pin joins the solid part of the pintle. This radius will help the fitting resist stresses more than a sharp-cornered pin connection would. To dress the pin until it was smooth and round, I ripped a new 60-grit sander belt into 1-inch-wide strips.

22.19

Photo 22.20 These replaceable, 1¾-inch-long Delrin bushings are 1¹⁄₃₂ inches inside diameter by 1¼ inches outside diameter, with a ³⁄₁₆-inch-thick shoulder. The bushing ensures that the bronze castings do not become galled or worn by the action of two similar metals rubbing against each other. With the bushings, the pin and the gudgeon hole should never oval and could last indefinitely. The Delrin bushing also eliminates the sharp metal-to-metal clicking sound that occurs when you are lying at anchor and a wave disturbs the boat.

The shoulder on these bushings should be left ³⁄₁₆ inch thick to absorb the wear caused by downward load of the rudder head and tiller, which are unsupported by the water.

The bushing should be a push fit into the gudgeon. The Delrin can swell about 1 to 2 percent when it is immersed, so if the bushings fit any tighter, they will be difficult to remove for replacement after the boat has been afloat. The material for these bushings is easy to machine on a metal lathe. I made six bearings while I had access to a friend's lathe, so I had a spare set available when I needed them. These bushings seem to last for about five years of normal usage, or about 20,000 miles of sailing.

I had the holes in the gudgeons bored at a machine shop so they were exactly 1¼ inches in diameter and square to the edges of the strap arms. They were centered athwartships and bored so that the inboard edges of the holes were ⅛ inch away from the sternpost once the gudgeon was installed.

Photo 22.21 The positions of the gudgeons and pintles usually appear on the designer's construction plans. Although the eventual fittings should be close to the recommended positions, they usually can be moved up or down the sternpost by 2 or 3 inches to simplify fitting to the sternpost. In our case, I moved the upper gudgeon about an inch to center it in the middle of one of the beaded transom planks. I located the gudgeons on the sternpost and then picked up their exact locations using a staff, which I butted up to the heel of the deadwood and to the aft side of the sternpost.

22.22

22.24

22.23

Photo 22.22 I then clearly marked the top edges of all three gudgeons on both the sternpost and the staff.

Photo 22.23 The hole in the gudgeon bushing should end up parallel to the aft side of the sternpost. If the bushing is square to the top edge of the gudgeon, as shown in the photograph, it is simple to square and mark the gudgeon dadoes.

Photo 22.24 The dadoes (rebates or grooves) in the sternpost were squared to the aft edge of the sternpost. If for some reason the holes in the gudgeons are not exactly square to the gudgeon arms, the grooves should be cut into the sternpost at whatever angle keeps the bushing hole parallel to the straight edge of the sternpost.

Photo 22.25 You can bend or hammer the straps a bit to fit the shape of the sternpost, but avoid bending the ends of the arms by more than 2 inches.

I roughed out the dadoes, leaving them $1/16$ inch shallow on each side of the sternpost. Then I slowly adjusted them until the tapered gudgeon straps slid into place. All the while, I kept checking the alignment of the gudgeon hole with the centerline on the back edge of the sternpost. Since each of the gudgeons had been bored accurately, they were in line vertically when the holes were equidistant from the sternpost.

22.26

Photo 22.26 I lined up the holes athwartships to the sternpost centerline by chiseling and planing the last 1/16 inch off the inner edges of the dadoes. As I did the final fitting, I put felt-pen ink on the inside of the casting to show up any high spots in the dado.

Photo 22.27 The gudgeons occasionally jammed onto the sternpost as I was fitting them. I found I could easily unjam them by using a piece of pipe and two wedges, as shown here.

To prove that your gudgeon holes are in line, you can use a long piece of shafting or a straight pipe. A string can also be used. But if you keep the holes parallel to the centerline of the sternpost and equidistant from the sternpost, the holes will be in line.

22.25

22.27

22.28

22.29

22.30

Photo 22.28 Before the final fitting, I drilled the holes for rivets in the starboard straps of both lower gudgeons. I clamped the gudgeons so they butted tight to the aft edge of the sternpost and then drilled horizontally through the sternpost and the port strap. I countersank the holes on both sides of the gudgeon straps to a depth of $3/32$ inch and riveted the gudgeons in place using $5/16$-inch copper rod. The fittings were all bedded in place with Dolfinite.

Photo 22.29 Once the gudgeons were in place, I did a final check of their positions with the staff, then clamped the staff to the leading edge of the rudder. I left the lower end of the staff overhanging the bottom of the rudder by $3/8$ inch to give swinging clearance between the rudder toe and the deadwood heel. I transferred the positions of the gudgeons from the staff onto the leading edge of the rudder. The pintles need to be positioned $3/16$ inch above these marks to allow for the thickness of the shoulder on the Delrin bushings.

Each pin is kept equidistant from and parallel to the leading edge of the rudder. The pins' centers are on the centerline marked on the rudder's leading edge. The straps on the pintles overlap the first glue joint on the rudder blade by about 4 inches to provide external strengthening.

22.31

Photo 22.30 I shortened the straps of the top pintle so that they came within ¼ inch of the aft edge of the rudderhead. That way, the aft ends of the straps and their dadoes didn't show or have to be puttied or painted.

The Skilsaw did most of the work of reducing the dadoes, but I took care to leave an extra ¹⁄₁₆ inch of wood on each side of the dadoes for final fitting and alignment of the pintle pins. The pintles are a little easier to fit than the gudgeons, as they can be adjusted forward and aft slightly to line up with the gudgeon holes, but the pins must be dead center and parallel to the rudder centerline.

Photo 22.31 When the three pintles were fitted to the rudder, I clamped the top and bottom ones firmly in place and then drilled and bolted the middle pintle, using a ⁵⁄₁₆-inch threaded rod. I hoisted the rudder into position with a block-and-tackle and checked for pin alignment relative to the two lower gudgeons.

Photo 22.32 The lower pintles can be adjusted slightly forward and aft so that the upper transom gudgeon can be positioned correctly and drilled.

Although it is hard to see in this photo, there is ³⁄₈-inch clearance between the rudder toe and the deadwood heel. I made the mistake of cutting off the deadwood heel before I built the rudder (in fact, almost a year earlier), thus breaking the first rule of boatbuilding: never cut off anything until absolutely necessary. To make up for this, when I later screwed on the 1¼-inch-thick worm shoe (discussed in chapter 19), I glued a rectangular piece to the heel, as shown in diagram 22.2. This heel extension discourages lobster-pot lines and kedging warps from getting in between the rudder and the sternpost.

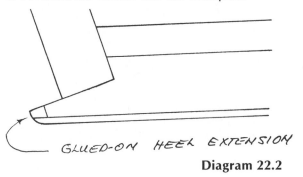

GLUED-ON HEEL EXTENSION

Diagram 22.2

22.32

22.33

Photo 22.33 When the two lower gudgeons and pintles were lined up correctly and fastened, I slid the top gudgeon and its bushing onto the pintle from below. The gudgeon was then held in place by a ⅜-inch retaining bolt and washers, as shown in diagram 22.3. This retaining bolt is a simple way to lock the rudder onto the gudgeon once the boat is afloat. Also, if you are in your dinghy and wish to lift the rudder off the boat while it is in the water, the cap screw is easy to remove.

The wedge shown in the photograph tightened the gudgeon so that it wouldn't rattle as I drilled the ½-inch bolt holes through it and the sternpost. I drilled the port bolt hole, inserted the ½-inch bolt to site the gudgeon, then drilled the second hole. (These two holes were later filed out square so that the carriage bolts would fit with just their radiused heads standing proud.) The bolts for this top gudgeon should be left ½ inch long on the inside of the sternpost because the lower timbers and the lower part of the sternpost on any unsheathed boat will tend to swell across the grain after launching. This swelling moves both lower gudgeons slightly aft, and the rudder will start to bind. At that time, the upper gudgeon will need realignment.

22.34

I launched *Taleisin* with the upper gudgeon attached flat to the transom, as shown. Nine months later, I hauled her out and fitted a 5/16-inch-thick pedestal-like spacer under the top gudgeon so it would line up correctly with the lower ones. When the spacer was fitted, the two bolts still had ¼ inch of thread showing above the nuts on the inside face of the sternpost.

Once the gudgeons and pintles were aligned, holes for the bolts could be drilled. Later, when I removed the rudder, I laid it flat on sawhorses and riveted the pintles permanently in place.

Photo 22.34   Before I unshipped the rudder, I calculated the angles that would allow the tiller to move up and down without interfering with the taffrail or scraping the deck. Then I made a pine pattern for the preliminary tiller shape.

(Here I have clamped the deckbeam pattern in a position that represents the forward lower edge of the taffrail, which eventually will be attached to the fashion-timber horns.)

I tapered the aft end of the tiller pattern in the molded dimension so that the tiller would eventually lift up to a convenient height so I could steer when standing on deck. (This also helps clear the cockpit when you are tacking.)

When the tiller pattern was in the raised position, I marked the rudderhead at the bottom edge of the tiller. This pencil mark shows in photo 22.35.

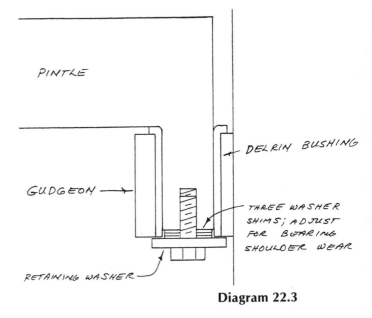

Diagram 22.3

Photo 22.35   Now the tiller is shown at the normal steering height. The top edge of the the tiller is marked on the rudderhead and the lower edge is marked about ¾ inch back from the forward edge of the rudder, as in diagram 22.4. These top and bottom limits determine the profile shape of the tiller socket. I cut out two identical pieces of 3/16-inch-thick bronze plate exactly to this socket shape. These plates prevent wear on the sides of the socket and help with the assembly of the rudderhead.

22.35

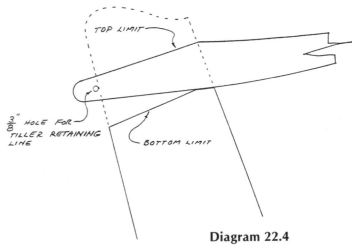

Diagram 22.4

22.38

Photo 22.36 Next I cut off the rudderhead ⅟₁₆ inch below the lower socket-profile marks. The difference was made up with a rot-and-check-preventing plate of ⅟₁₆-inch copper. The plate was fastened in place with 1-inch-long number 6 silicon-bronze wood screws set into the end-grain of the rudder.

Photo 22.37 I shaped the 1¼-inch-thick cheekpieces to fit the rudderhead. (The shaping for the rudder blade has been stopped just below the cheeks to provide a simple, flat joint.) I clamped the two cheeks in place and lined them up, then penciled the profile of the cop-pered rudderhead (lower socket line) onto the inside of each cheek. I lined up the two bronze socket plates with the socket-profile marks and fastened them to the insides of the cheekpieces with 1-inch number 14 silicon-bronze flathead wood screws. I set all of the screws on the cop-per and bronze plates so they were slightly lower than the metal surface. This prevents the screw heads from galling the tiller when it moves up and down in the socket.

Photo 22.38 Before I glued up the cheeks, I clamped them back in place with the bronze plates mating up to the copper plate on the rud-derhead. I then took the block I cut off the rud-derhead and slid it between the cheeks until it was flush to the top of the ³⁄₁₆-inch plates. Then I traced the top shape of the cheeks onto the block. I cut this block to shape and used dou-ble-headed aligning nails to locate the cheeks to the rudder blade and block.

22.36

22.37

Photo 22.39 When the cheeks were glued and riveted, I had a rudderhead socket that was not only strong but also inexpensive and simple to make. This rudderhead required little specialized metalwork. (The small amount it does need can be done easily with a bandsaw and a drill press.) The best feature of this rudder socket is that it allows you to remove the tiller when the boat is at anchor to clear the cockpit for socializing.

The tiller is retained in place for sailing with a 14-inch-long piece of ¼-inch Dacron line, which goes through a hole just behind the rudderhead and has a figure-eight knot tied on either side of the tiller. The sides of the tiller that fit to the socket are protected with ¹⁄₁₆-inch stainless steel plates to resist wear and prevent galling.

When the glue was completely cured, I riveted up the cheeks with ⅜-inch copper rod and clench rings. I positioned four rivets close to each corner of the tiller socket to help hold the cheeks together and strengthen them against the racking strains exerted by the long lever of the tiller when it is pushed hard over in a seaway.

The last job was to cut the forward corners of the cheeks at a 45-degree angle, which allows clearance between the rudder and the transom with its gudgeon when the rudder is hard over. This corner reduction is quite small and thus gives the cheeks almost full strength all along their length. If the rudder had been fitted tightly up to the sternpost, these corners would have had to be reduced far more, which would have weakened the cheeks.

Photo 22.40 With the rudder finished, the major work of building a wooden sailboat hull has been completed.

22.39

22.40

CONSTRUCTION TIMES FOR CHAPTER 22

Larry: Making gudgeon and pintle foundry patterns; building and installing rudder and bushings   63 hours

Lin: Varnishing and plugging   27 hours

Totals to date: Larry 3704 hours

Lin   1022 hours

NOTE: These hours covered completing the hull, ballast keel, deck framing, and rudder up to a ready-to-launch condition, including creosote on the underwater surfaces, paint on the topsides, and varnish on the transom. At this point, the interior of the hull is complete to five coats of varnish on all surfaces (including deck framing) and structural bulkheads are in place, along with the mast step and partners. (Approximately 5 percent of Larry's total hours were spent taking the photographs for this book.)

DISCUSSION

The most common problem with wood rudders is that the blades can warp or cup in a fore-and-aft direction, but you can take some preventive measures as you build. Strapping, which is discussed at the end of this section, can be done either during construction or afterward, to straighten a rudder that has warped.

If you build your rudder of three or four pieces of flat-grained timber, it will have less tendency to warp if the annual rings on each board are alternated, as shown in diagram 22.5a. The same is true if the rudder blade is laminated up of square strips, as in diagram 22.5b. If you alternate the directions of the rings, the individual planks can still warp, but the rudder will have a slightly wavy appearance, not a continuous curve or warp. The ideal solution is to find center-cut boards for all of the rudder laminations, such as is shown in diagram 22.5c. If the annual rings are at 90 degrees to the flat side of the rudder, the rudder should not (in theory) warp.

You can also minimize warping by choosing a wood that absorbs very little moisture. My favorite wood for rudders is an amber-colored, resinous piece of longleaf yellow pine. I used that with complete success on *Seraffyn*'s rudder, and the rudder stayed within ¼ inch of its original shape for fifteen years. My next choice would be a stable, well-seasoned hardwood, such as teak, mahogany, or oak.

The least desirable wood for a rudder is plywood. To keep a plywood rudder stable, it would have to be twice as thick as a solid-wood rudder. Otherwise, it would not only twist quite easily but also flex under the strains of sailing. The twisting motion creates fatigue problems that could cause the individual laminates of the plywood to break down until the rudder became limber and useless.

Diagram 22.5

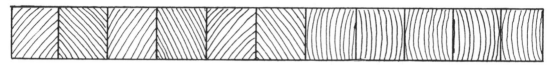

Fastening Together a Rudder Blank

There are four basic ways to fasten together the planks of a rudder (from least effective to most effective): (1) waterproof glue, (2) blind bolts, (3) drift bolts, and (4) port and starboard strapping.

Although I like to use glue to hold together the rudder blank while I shape the blade, experience has taught me that a wide piece of wood will dry out and crack if the boat is hauled out for several months. The cracking weakens the glue joints so dramatically that the glue alone cannot be depended on for long-term strength.

Long, double-nutted blind bolts that go most of the way through the rudder can be a recipe for promoting warping. Unless the holes for these bolts are perfectly centered in the blade, the bolts will not allow the blade to swell across its width and any expansion as the wood swells will cause the blade to warp in one direction or the other.

Drift bolts are the most common way to fasten a rudder blank. If you use a stable hardwood with good grain, the chance of warping will be reduced but not eliminated. The drifts are less likely to cause warping than blind bolts because they allow the swelling wood to expand and shift slightly along the length of the drift rod. This shifting reduces the compressive stresses and therefore the chance of blade warping.

Taleisin's rudder, which was built from green locust only three months out of the log, was glued and drift-bolted together. It warped about an inch to starboard after the boat was in the water for six months. To straighten it, I used a very effective method suggested by Wayne Ettles, a fine, innovative shipwright from southern California. After removing the rudder, I forced it back to the correct shape with timbers and clamps. Then I over-warped it about ¼ inch in the opposite direction. Next I fitted three pairs of straps, about 14 inches apart, from the leading edge to the trailing edge along the warped section of the blade. The straps were ⅛ inch thick and 1¼ inches wide and let into ⅛-inch rabbets. I riveted together the straps with ¼-inch copper rod about every 4 inches. For the next five years, the rudder stayed as true as a die.

Since these straps contain the swelling wood with equal force on each side of the rudder, they discourage the unequal swelling that causes warping. With the next rudder I build, I plan to dispense with drift bolts altogether and simply fit dadoed (rebated) straps to the glued and shaped rudder blade.

External strapping such as this was commonly used on large sailing ships, including the *Cutty Sark,* but her straps were not dadoed (rebated) into the rudder blade; they were left proud.

Rudder Sheathing

Fiberglass or epoxy sheathing is an alternative often suggested to keep a rudder from warping, but I do not recommend it: It is almost impossible in the long term to stop water from entering the encapsulated wood through fastener holes in the rudder blade. When water does enter, the wood expansion will crack a single layer of fiberglass. Unless you are very lucky, the blade then will warp. Three or four layers of glass would help to resist this tendency to crack, but that solution is expensive and time-consuming. It requires not only building and fairing a wooden rudder but also spending an additional two or three days applying glass and resin and then sanding the sheathing smooth.

Rudder Shapes

Diagram 22.6 shows some of the shapes that can be used for the trailing edge of a rudder. Lyle Hess recommends the rudder section shown at 22.6c for his cruising boats, and so do I. It probably has a bit more drag than the airfoil rudder sections shown in 22.6d and 22.6e, but my experience with both types convinces me that the almost-parallel trailing edge gives the rudder better and more positive steering control, especially at low boat speeds. This is particularly important when you are sailing into small harbors or marina berths or picking up a mooring—all times when you need positive rudder control at very low speed.

The modified-airfoil shape shown in 22.6c is probably in the middle of the five shapes as far as drag is concerned. If strapped and riveted on the outside, it would also be about in the middle as far as building complexity.

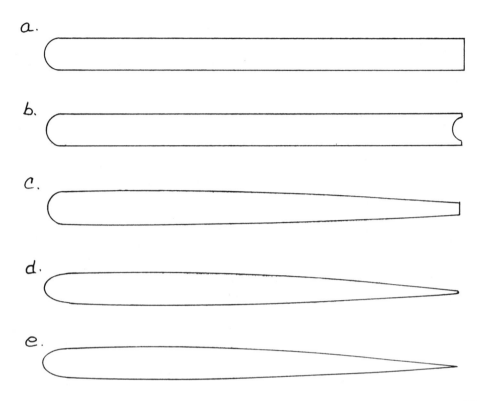

Diagram 22.6

Rudder shapes shown in 22.6a, 22.6b, and 22.6c are those that usually are attached to the sternpost of a long-keeled boat. If the keel sections were fair and airfoil-shaped, these rudders would, in the overall picture, have fairly low drag and would steer well in light winds. The more airfoiled shapes shown in 22.6d and 22.6e would be ideal for balanced spade rudders on fin-and-skeg hulls and would have the least drag of the five types. They would give the most effective steering at speeds above 5 knots. The thinner—and therefore structurally weaker—trailing edges are harder to shape. The thin trailing edge is too small for drift bolts; let-in straps would reduce the thickness of the trailing edge and make it weak, likely to warp, and would be the most difficult to build so that they keep their shape.

Rudder Attachments

If you are building a small centerboard boat, two sets of gudgeons and pintles will be sufficient to support the rudder. But for an outside-ballasted boat from 18 to 30 feet in length, you need at least three sets to take the loads. For boats from 30 to 40 feet, there probably should be four sets of gudgeons and pintles.

Most designers show the rudder set in tight to a concave groove in the sternpost. At most, they will show about ¼ inch clearance between the hull and the rudder. This close attachment makes the rudder and its pintles and gudgeons not only difficult to build but

Diagram 22.7

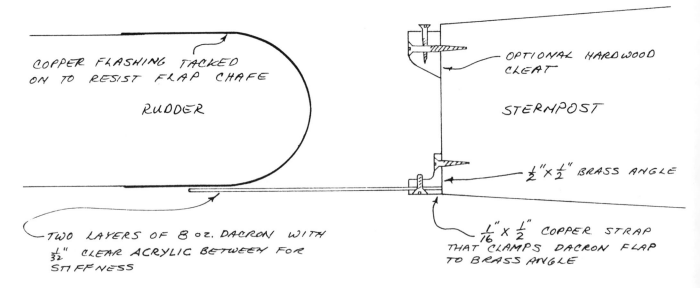

COPPER FLASHING TACKED ON TO RESIST FLAP CHAFE

RUDDER

OPTIONAL HARDWOOD CLEAT

STERNPOST

$\frac{1}{2}"\times\frac{1}{2}"$ BRASS ANGLE

TWO LAYERS OF 8 oz. DACRON WITH $\frac{1}{32}"$ CLEAR ACRYLIC BETWEEN FOR STIFFNESS

$\frac{1}{16}" \times \frac{1}{2}"$ COPPER STRAP THAT CLAMPS DACRON FLAP TO BRASS ANGLE

also harder to maintain. For example, it will be hard to sand and antifoul the back of the sternpost and the front of the rudder. Also, it will be difficult to varnish or paint the transom forward of the rudderhead, and, as mentioned before, the forward edge of the rudder cheeks will have to be angled quite dramatically. After consulting with Lyle Hess, I moved *Taleisin's* rudder aft 2 inches from the position shown on his plans. This meant not only that I could avoid the problems previously mentioned, but also that I could lift off the rudder easily while the boat was afloat without needing to make leading-edge cutouts below each pintle. To fill the space between the rudder and the sternpost so that there would be little turbulence, I fitted two 4½-inch-wide Dacron flaps, which attached flush to the sides of the sternpost and ran the length of the leading edge of the rudder. (This setup is shown in diagram 22.7.) The fabric flaps create less turbulence and are a more effective fairing device than a snug-fitting rudder cuddled up into the sternpost. The fabric flaps can be bent outboard enough so it is possible to inspect, service, and paint the aft edge of the sternpost at each haulout.

Diagram 22.8 shows a simple, homemade method I have seen used for hanging outboard rudders. Copper rudder straps are commonly used in Great Britain and continental Europe. Since no castings are required for this method, it can be cheaper and easier to fabricate than a rudder using cast gudgeons and pintles. A tough hardwood such as locust or oak should be used on the leading edge of this rudder to make the wooden pintles as strong as possible.

Diagram 22.8

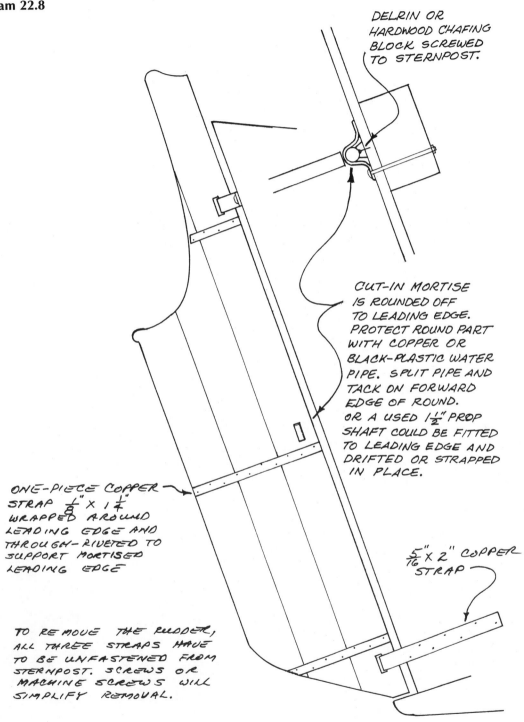

DELRIN OR HARDWOOD CHAFING BLOCK SCREWED TO STERNPOST.

CUT-IN MORTISE IS ROUNDED OFF TO LEADING EDGE. PROTECT ROUND PART WITH COPPER OR BLACK-PLASTIC WATER PIPE. SPLIT PIPE AND TACK ON FORWARD EDGE OF ROUND. OR A USED $1\frac{1}{2}$" PROP SHAFT COULD BE FITTED TO LEADING EDGE AND DRIFTED OR STRAPPED IN PLACE.

ONE-PIECE COPPER STRAP $\frac{1}{8}$" X $1\frac{1}{4}$" WRAPPED AROUND LEADING EDGE AND THROUGH-RIVETED TO SUPPORT MORTISED LEADING EDGE

$\frac{5}{16}$" X 2" COPPER STRAP

TO REMOVE THE RUDDER, ALL THREE STRAPS HAVE TO BE UNFASTENED FROM STERNPOST. SCREWS OR MACHINE SCREWS WILL SIMPLIFY REMOVAL.

23. BOATBUILDING TOOLS

SHARPENING TOOLS

As I have worked with boatbuilders in various countries, I've noticed that the best ones—the ones who accomplished good work in the shortest amount of time—were men who not only made little fuss about keeping their tools sharp but also were willing to modify a tool or build a new one at the drop of a hat. Surprisingly, the best builders often seemed to have the oldest, toughest-looking tools—that is, until you looked at the cutting edges. In the previous chapters, I have shown most of the tools I have gathered over the years. What I haven't shown is how to sharpen them.

While I was building *Seraffyn*, Lyle Hess called and told me that Charlie Weckman, a master boatbuilder, had just died at the age of ninety-one. Charlie had been a ship's carpenter and bosun for several years on the last commercially operated American square-rigged ship, the *Henry B. Hyde*. Lyle had worked with Charlie in the Los Angeles ship-yards during World War II, and he said, "Charlie could align and fit the rudder on a 90-foot tugboat so perfectly that you could push it from lock to lock with one finger." At Lyle's suggestion, I went to see Charlie's widow, Mary, who had complained that her young nephew had been using one of Charlie's adzes for lifting asphalt. Mary Weckman sold me a magnificent set of four L.I. and J. White slicks, two Casterline adzes, a set of long drills, several planes—in fact, most of the specialized boatbuilding tools shown in this book. Each of the tools was oiled and stored in a leather sheath designed to protect its razor-sharp blade. Although I was pleased to have tools that were not only perfect for my work but also collector's items, the real bonus was that now I had examples of how a master shipwright sharpened and cared for his specialized tools. I hope the following sharpening hints, which I inherited indirectly from Charlie, will be helpful.

Photo 23.1 Hollow-ground cutting edges cut more cleanly, have less friction, and are easier and faster to hone on an oilstone. I find that using a 6-inch-diameter grinder creates enough hollow for most tools (diagram 23.1). If I purchase a new tool or blade that has a flat-ground cutting edge, or if I have sharpened out most of the hollow on one of my older tools, I rehollow them as shown, using a square-ended piece of wood clamped onto the blade as a guide. Every five seconds or so, I dip the tool I am grinding in cool water to stop the cutting edge from over-heating and turning blue. If the metal does turn blue, it means some of its hardening has been lost, so it is important to keep the blade as cool as possible.

23.1

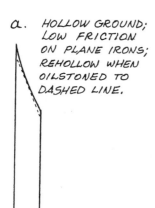

a. HOLLOW GROUND; LOW FRICTION ON PLANE IRONS; REHOLLOW WHEN OILSTONED TO DASHED LINE.

b. GROUND FLAT WITH OILSTONE; THIS EDGE IS OKAY FOR AXES, ADZES AND MACHINE BLADES

c. EDGE ROUNDED WITH OILSTONE; POOR CUTTING RESULTS WITH HAND OR MACHINE TOOLS.

Diagram 23.1

23.2

Photo 23.2 To use the grinder as a tool-sharpening device, I had to grind a notch into the vertical side of the tool support. This gives clearance for the blade guide to slide smoothly in both directions across the grinding wheel.

Photo 23.3 A handy guide for hollow-grinding a plane is the attached chipper. The chipper can be removed from the upper side of the blade and screwed onto the lower face at the proper distance from the blade edge to give the cutting angle you desire. (To loosen or tighten the chipper screw conveniently, use the narrow lower edge of the lever cap.) This neat but surprisingly little-known grinding trick came from my high-school shop teacher, Will Thompson.

If the hollow or curve across a scrub plane (rounded sole) or a spar plane (hollowed sole) is no more than 1/16 inch across a 2-inch-wide blade, you can still use the chipper from a square-nosed plane as a sharpening guide.

The grinding wheel shown in these photographs is quite worn at the edges and has rounded corners. These rounded corners will grind a hollowed spar-plane iron more neatly than could a new, sharp-cornered grinding wheel.

23.3

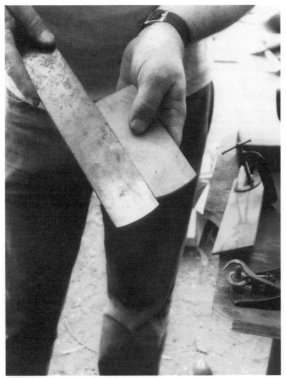

23.4

23.5

23.6

Photo 23.4   This is Charlie Weckman's 2-inch slick. The flat face has about 1/32 inch of rocker across the blade, which gives a slightly hollow cut as you work the wood. This, combined with the rounded and bullnosed end, means the corners of the slick have almost no tendency to dig in and slow or mar your work. The larger, 4-inch-wide slick has about 1/16 inch of rocker across the blade. If you have a new slick with a flat sole, you can grind a bit of rocker into it by using a belt sander with new, 60-grit belts.

The sharpening guide I am holding next to the slick is made from a piece of 1/8-inch pine that I cut to the same end curve as the slick.

Photo 23.5   I clamp the guide onto the slick so that it is aligned parallel to the side of the blade.

Photo 23.6   I tip the slick slowly in toward the wheel and watch along the side to see where it will make contact. I then adjust the guide up or down until the wheel hits accurately at the center of the face I wish to hollow. My aim is to make the cutting angle about as shown in diagram 23.1a, an angle that is about 30 degrees for most tools.

Photo 23.7   I then slide the tool sideways smoothly, keeping light pressure against the grinder support. When the wheel has ground down to the sharp cutting edge of the blade, it will start to throw tiny sparks toward my thumb.

Diagram 23.2

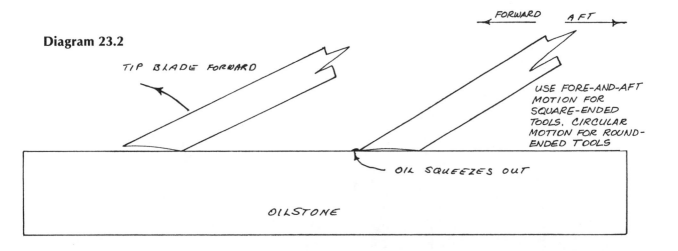

TIP BLADE FORWARD

FORWARD ← → AFT

USE FORE-AND-AFT MOTION FOR SQUARE-ENDED TOOLS. CIRCULAR MOTION FOR ROUND-ENDED TOOLS

OIL SQUEEZES OUT

OILSTONE

I grind across the blade face until these sparks occur evenly all along the cutting edge. I then use an oilstone to smooth off any grinding burrs and hone the cutting edge to a sharp point, as shown in diagram 23.2. I put a 1/32-inch-thick slick of oil on the stone and tip the cutting edge of the blade down until the oil squeezes out. The edge is now at the correct angle and can be honed with a circular or fore-and-aft motion. I turn the blade over and hone the flat side lightly to remove any burrs. This should give a razor-sharp cutting edge.

I use a fore-and-aft motion to hone the blades of square-ended irons, such as those on a rabbet plane. For ones with rounded corners, such as a bullnosed slick, I use a circular motion.

You can purchase special tool attachments that hold an iron at the correct angle to the oilstone, but to save time, it is best to learn the knack of holding a constant angle by hand.

For my smoothing and jack planes, I hone the irons so that the outer corners are reduced in a smooth taper by about 1/64 inch. This taper extends from the outside edge and onto the blade for about 3/8 inch, so I can remove shavings cleanly without the sharp corners of the plane iron gouging into the wood of a wide board. This slight bullnosing and radiusing is all done on the oilstone after the iron has been hollow-ground.

Photo 23.8 A gouge can be ground by using a piece of plastic hose to serve as a guide. The hose is split and the end is cut square. If your gouge is slightly round-nosed, you can trim the hose to have a comparable arc.

23.7

23.8

23.9

23.10

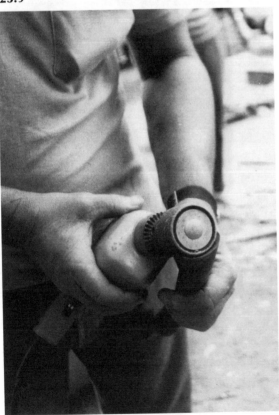

23.11

Photo 23.9 I hold the hose snugly in place with my left hand and roll the gouge against the grinder guide with my right hand. I sharpen the right side first, grinding it until tiny sparks appear over the hollow cutting edge of the gouge. Then I do the left side in the same way. The gouge can be oilstoned on its hollow cutting edge in the normal manner but with a rolling, side-to-side motion.

Photo 23.10 To sharpen the inside edge of a gouge, I use a rubber sanding drum with medium-grit paper on a high-speed drill motor. I use a drum that is either the same radius as the inside of the gouge or slightly smaller.

Photo 23.11 With judicious grinding, a sort of hollow can be approximated by grinding the angled edge with the corners at the end of a sanding drum. Hold the gouge firmly in a vise (not by hand, as I am doing here in order to show the motion I use to get the hollow grind). To dress or hone the inside edges of tools such as this gouge, you need a tapered half-round oilstone.

Photo 23.12 I don't know how to hollow-grind an adze. When I bought my two from Mary Weckman, they were flat-ground—the only tools in the collection that were—so I assume Charlie simply used a method similar to the one I developed to sharpen them. To rough-grind the adze, I clamped it in the vise and used a belt sander with a 60-grit belt. I adjusted the belt so it overlapped the right-hand side of the sander wheels by about ⅛ inch so it could conform slightly to the curved lips as I ground and flattened the straight part of the cutting edge.

I have found that the belt sander is good for grinding tools. I have used it when I did not have access to a grinder to hollow-grind a chisel or a plane iron. Since a sander is turning at a relatively low speed, it will not burn the tool edges blue, as a high-speed grinder can so easily do. The smaller wheel diameter also produces a deeper hollow-ground edge, which generally is a good thing. It is best to hold the sander in a vise while you sharpen smaller tools. The metal frame of the sander next to the rubber back wheel acts as a rest for the guide that is clamped to your chisel or plane iron.

23.12

Photo 23.13 With drill and tapered stone, I grind the edge and lips evenly. I next use the coarse side of my flat oilstone, then the fine side to do the final honing. The finishing of the lips is done with a tapered half-round oilstone. (You can see the copper jaws that protect my Casterline adze.)

Incidentally, the spike on the heel of the adze does have a purpose. It can be driven into the endgrain of large timbers to make a temporary handle that helps you shift or move them.

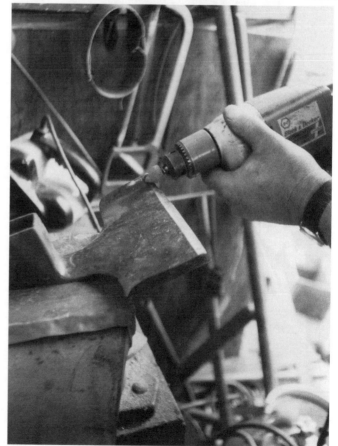

23.13

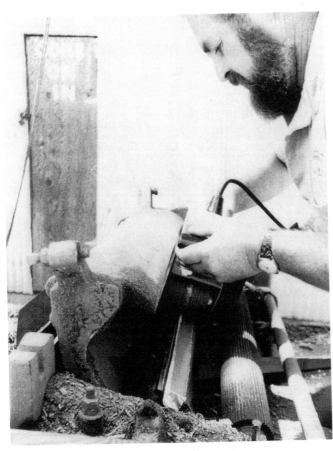

23.14

23.15

Photo 23.14 Some woodworkers would consider this knife-sharpening method highly irregular. But we used a large amount of teak during the construction of this boat, and the teak dulled the planer knives with boring regularity. To remove the knives, send them to a proper sharpening shop, and reset them would take 3 or 4 hours plus a one-week wait for their return, so I needed to find a quicker sharpening method (and, at $50 a crack, a less expensive one). I found that the back edge of the guard and feed-roller scraper, which folded up to give access to the knives, worked as a convenient grinding guide. The frame of the belt sander rested against the back edge of the inside of the guide to hold the sander at constant angle to the flat cutting edge of the knives.

Photo 23.15 I used duct tape to protect the planer head from being scratched by the sander. I locked the head in place by winding the table

up with a piece of wood between the bed and the lower part of the head. I adjusted the head and blade so that the sanding belt hit only the ⅛ inch next to the cutting edge. In the photo, my pencil points this out.) I then used a 60-grit belt that had been worn by use on hardwoods. This gave a good, smooth edge to the high-speed steel. I final-dressed the knives lightly with an oilstone to clean off any metal burrs.

The knives can be sharpened several times with the belt sander, but once the edges become irregular or slightly rounded, remove them and send them out to be trued up and sharpened professionally.

I decided I could not afford to purchase a set of 24-inch-long carbide-steel knives for this thicknesser. In the long run, they might have saved money, but they also are more prone to chipping and more expensive to have sharpened.

Buying Tools for Boatbuilding

I have purchased almost all of my favorite hand tools in secondhand shops, at garage sales, and at swap meets (flea markets) over the past thirty years. I bought my classic Bailey (Stanley) smoothing plane, with rosewood handles, for $1.25 at a southern California swap meet. Three Buck Brothers chisels—⅛ inch, ⅜ inch, and 1 inch—cost me a total of $4.50. They came from the stock of a man who had just finished cleaning out his father-in-law's garage. The brands I would look for in hand tools include:

Chisels and slicks: Buck Brothers, Greenlee, L.I. and J. White (grab these if you see them), Pexto, James Swan, T. H. Witherby, and Marples
Adzes: Campbell and Casterline
Augers: James Swan, Russel-Jennings, and Irwin
Brace-and-bits: Millar Falls
Planes: Bailey (Stanley), Ohio, Marples, Buck Brothers, Millar Falls, and Record

The blades on the older, high-quality tools often have a piece of hard tool steel laminated onto the sharpening edge. Usually you can see this on secondhand tools, as there is a slight color change that differentiates the thin, hardened-steel layer from the rest of the blade. The hardened steel often rusts and pits more than regular steel, so if you notice a definite line of surface rust on the cutting edge, you can be sure it is a laminated blade. If the tool is one you need, buy it even if there is some shallow pitting. Pits up to 1/32 inch deep can be ground off with a belt sander if the hardened-steel layer is thick enough. Cast-iron chisels can also be useful, but from my experience, they are not as good at keeping an edge as tools with laminated blades. My 4-inch L.I. and J. White slick has a laminated blade, my 2-inch one has a cast steel blade. The 2-inch slick needs to be sharpened far more often.

Some older metal planes, such as Bailey/Stanley (the Bailey company was purchased by Stanley many years ago, the tools are the same, and the quality seems to be the same, so I use the names interchangeably), have hard-steel laminated blades. You can recognize these blades by the brand mark, a little heart with SW in the middle. (Keep an eye out for these.) Most older wood planes also have laminated irons. When you see them at a secondhand shop or swap meet, look to see that there is at least ¾ inch of cutting edge left on the iron below the chipper hole. If there is, the iron probably will last you a lifetime.

I tend to use steel-body planes far more than wood planes, as they are easier to adjust. It is also easier to find replacement irons, as most complete hardware stores have them. So if you see a good metal plane without a blade at a swap meet, you are safe in paying a few dollars for it.

Clamps of all types are items I have often found for low prices at swap meets and garage sales. C-clamps often are sold because the articulating foot or button on the threaded end has been lost. Buy these inexpensively and make a simple but very good foot by using 1-inch- or 1¼-inch-diameter aluminum rod, as shown in diagram 23.3.

Diagram 23.3

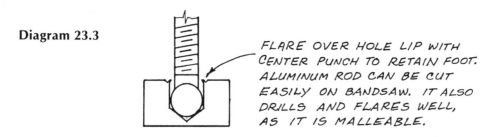

FLARE OVER HOLE LIP WITH
CENTER PUNCH TO RETAIN FOOT.
ALUMINUM ROD CAN BE CUT
EASILY ON BANDSAW. IT ALSO
DRILLS AND FLARES WELL,
AS IT IS MALLEABLE.

Fuller-brand counterboring tools and corresponding wood-plug cutters are vital for boatbuilding. I buy these either direct from the Fuller Company or from Jamestown Distributors (addresses at the end of this chapter). To countersink bronze, brass, or stainless steel, I have a long-lasting uniflute countersink sold by Jamestown Distributors. This fine tool won't chatter, so it cuts a clean, true countersink. The extra-hard metal of the cutting flute can be sharpened with a small, hard oilstone. But take care to remove the same amount of metal from each cutting edge or the countersink will chatter.

Woodworking Machines

The two best investments you can make—even if you are building only one boat—are a top-quality medium-sized secondhand bandsaw (18 inches or larger) and a 20-inch-by-6-inch (or larger) thickness planer. It will pay to buy used equipment up to the value of 2½ or 3 percent of the total completed value of the boat you are going to build. I spent about $2,500 for the used machinery you have seen in this book. I paid about half of the new price for all of them and was able to sell these tools later for at least what I had paid for them. (I'll never sell the thicknesser. It is now here in New Zealand at our home base and repair yard.)

The 24-inch-by-7-inch planer came motorless and rusty looking for $500 from a boatyard in the state of Washington. The babbitt bearings were 10 to 15 thousandths of an inch loose, but there were lots of shims left to adjust them and a good rim of babbitt material left all around the bearing for scraping and refitting. The bed, cutting head, and knives were in good order; the gears all worked and had little tooth wear; and the machine was complete. A few days of hard work, plus a used ¾ hp motor, used 5 hp motor, and the shipping, brought the total cost to $1,200. This thickness planer not only saved us milling time and costs, but it also allowed me to mill material far more accurately for my specific use. I saved money by buying rough-sawn timber and then milling it exactly to my specifications. With the bandsaw, I found I could rip large boards edgewise, then clean them up on the planer, for a 50 percent cost savings. I was able to purchase 2-inch-by-10-inch rough-sawn red cedar and then rip and plane it into three ½-inch boards for our interior shelving and bunkboards instead of having to purchase 1-inch stock that the mill then turned mostly into shavings to give me one piece of ½-inch timber from each 1-inch board.

Another important reason to have a thickness planer is that it helps you build the boat to the correct scantlings. If you have a planer, you will remove that ¼ inch or more of

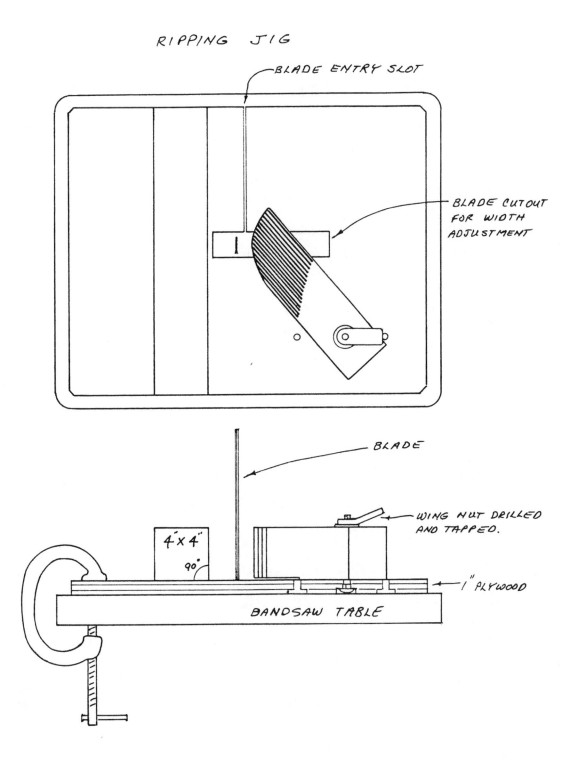

RIPPING JIG

BLADE ENTRY SLOT

BLADE CUTOUT
FOR WIDTH
ADJUSTMENT

BLADE

WING NUT DRILLED
AND TAPPED.

4"x 4"

90°

1" PLYWOOD

BANDSAW TABLE

Diagram 23.4

excess wood; without the planer, you might leave it on rather than remove the wood by hand. I think the lack of a thicknesser is partially the reason for the all-too-common problem of overweight homebuilt boats.

I made a simple ripping jig to fit the table of the bandsaw, as shown in diagram 23.4. A jig like this works great for ripping boards up to 12 inches wide. But to do it, you need at least a 2 hp motor and ¾-inch to 1-inch-wide skip-tooth blade* on your bandsaw. The kerf taken by a bandsaw blade is less than half of that taken by a circular-saw blade. So it pays to use the bandsaw for ripping tongue-and-groove material from leftover planking stock or for cutting expensive 2-inch-thick teak planks into deck strakes. This jig is easy to slip onto the saw. I clamp it lightly into place and then use a hammer to tap the edge of the jig to adjust the distance between the 4 x 4 and the blade. When it is correct and square, I secure the clamps firmly.

If you cannot find secondhand equipment, do not be afraid of less-expensive imports. Although they may not be durable for long-term production work, if you check them over carefully, you will find that these tools can be completely successful even for professional boatyards. Few boatyards use any single piece of machinery full time, eight hours a day, as a production factory will. My grinder, drill press, and large machinist's vise were Japanese or Taiwanese brands. They worked out just fine. I did find, however, that I had the best long-term results with American hand-held driver-drills, especially my powerful, short-bodied, ½-inch-chuck Skil driver-drill.

One tool that I found to be a boatbuilder's treat was the Stanley bullnoser (shown in photograph 17.78). This tool has become hard to purchase, as it no longer is used in the Formica or laminated-plastics business. But keep your eye open for a secondhand one or check with a tool repairman who works on routers. It is invaluable for radiusing the corners of deckbeams, framing, or trim after the wood has been final-fitted and fastened in place. It will neatly radius a deckbeam or cabin beam to within ¾ inch of the carlines to give a nice-looking, stopped-radius detail. These stopped corners make a professional-looking job, reduce the weight of the joinery a bit, and make finishing easier because the rounded corners hold paint or varnish better.

Clench-Ring Patterns

The clench rings shown throughout this book were cast from two foundry patterns I made when I built *Seraffyn*. I took a number of galvanized clench rings—some ¼-inch and some ⅜-inch-diameter—and glued them onto a board, as shown in diagram 23.5. (Each size was on a separate board.) I had the rings cast in manganese bronze, but they can also

---

* I have found that skip-tooth metal cutting blades with four teeth per inch, designed for cutting aluminum, rip wood much faster than multitooth blades and hold their edge better in teak. The only disadvantage with using these metal cutting blades is that you cannot file them yourself; you have to send them out to be machine-ground. I also prefer a slower-running bandsaw. This slower speed seems to cut down on the metal fatigue that causes the blade weld to break, but, more important, with the slower speed you can use the same blade for cutting wood, bronze, or copper. So I have changed the pulleys on the saw to make it run about 30 percent slower than normal.

be cast in silicon bronze or aluminum bronze, since they are used in relatively low-stress areas compared to the nuts and washers used for chainplate, keel, and bobstay bolts.

I found the steel clench rings for my original patterns at a bridgebuilding supply house. If you cannot find them in such a place or at a chandlery, you might have to make individual wood patterns on a wood-turning lathe. Once you have the patterns for the individual rings, it would pay to visit your foundryman to find out what size flask he uses and to plan the runners and gates for your pattern board to conform with his molding and pouring methods. Then you should draw the flask line (dotted line) on your board and lay out the pattern so that all of the parts are at least 1 inch from the outside of the sand mold. Otherwise, the molten metal could burst through the side of the mold.

Ask the foundryman to cut off only his main runners when he takes the castings out of the mold, leaving the small, tapered gate pieces attached to the rings. The attached gate stops the ring from spinning in the drill-press vise as you bore out the hole 1/64 inch over the rod size you intend to use. I have found that the 1/4-inch clench ring, which has an outer diameter of 3/4 inch, can also be used with 5/16-inch copper rod. The 3/8-inch clench ring, with its outer diameter of 1 1/16 inches, is used with 3/8-inch rod and can be pushed for use with 7/16-inch rod.

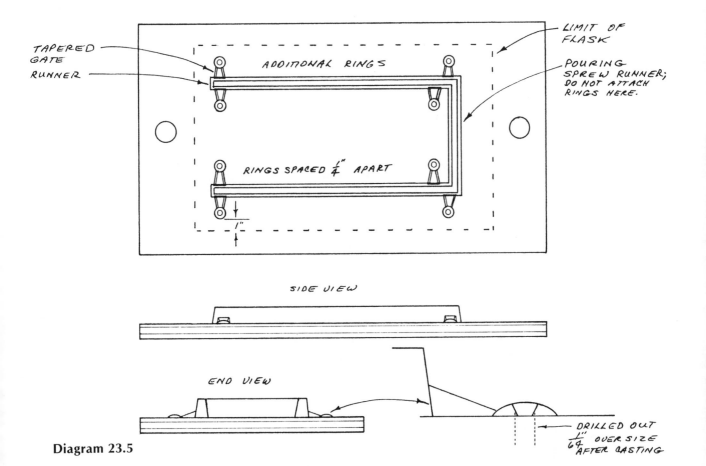

Diagram 23.5

Some Tool Sources

Brookstone Company, 127 Vose Farm Road, Peterborough, NH 03458

Craftsman Wood Service Co., 2727 S. Mary St., Chicago, IL 60608

W.L. Fuller, Inc., P.O. Box 8767, Warwick, RI 02888

Garrett Wade Co., 161 Ave. of the Americas, New York, NY 10013

Jamestown Distributors, 28 Narragansett Ave., Jamestown, RI 02835

Wetzler Clamp Co., 43-15 11th St., Long Island City, NY 11101

Woodcraft Supply, 41 Atlantic Ave., Woburn, MA 01888

Woodworker's Supply of New Mexico, 5604 Alameda Place, NE, Albuquerque, NM 87113

Clendenin Brothers, 4309 Erdman Ave., Baltimore, MD 21213 (scotch-cut copper nails)

For other sources, see the bimonthly issues of *WoodenBoat* magazine (Naskeag Road, Brooklin, ME 04616). Don't overlook the Craftsman tools sold by Sears. They can be very good value, as they are fully guaranteed. We found that Sears immediately replaced any broken tools—even broken putty knives.

APPENDICES

APPENDIX A
BOATBUILDING WOODS

POTENTIAL PLANKING TIMBER

(listed alphabetically)

Common Name	Other Names	Weight (lbs.) per Cubic Foot	Strength Relative to Oak (Oak = 100)
Ash	*Fraxinus americana* *Fraxinus excelsior* *Fraxinus oregona*	42	110
Cedar Port Orford	*Chamaecyparis lawsonia* Lawson cypress	28	65
Spanish	*Juniperus virginiana* pencil cedar	24	60
Western red	*Thuja plicata*	24–27	50
White	*Thuja occidentalis* juniper	21	62
Yellow	*Chamaecyparis nootkatensis* Alaskan cedar	31	65
Cypress	*Taxodium distichum* macracarpa (NZ)	37	79
Elm Canadian rock	*Ulmus americanus*	37	89
English	*Ulmus campestris*	37	85
Fir	*Pseudotsuga menziesi* Douglas fir Oregon pine	37	86
Iroko	*Chlorophora excelsa* kambala tule intuile moreira	46	85
Larch	*Larix decidua* (Europe) hackmatack; tamarack *Larix laricina* (North America)	38	85
Mahogany African	There are more than 171 varieties of mahogany. Generally judged by color, grain, and area of origin.	36–39	90

Rot Resistance	Ease of Bending	Ease of Planing	Comments
fair	easy	easy	Dent-resistant; strongest wood for weight; good for veneers, but stains easily
excellent	easy to fair	easy	Strong for its weight; good, straight grain; works easily
excellent	fair	easy	Hard to purchase; very straight grain
excellent	fair	easy	Inexpensive and available in large boards but soft and relatively low strength; swells substantially, so makes excellent splines
excellent	fair	fair	Absorbs moisture very readily, so must be sealed well; often has small pin knots, so can be difficult to plane by hand
excellent	moderate	easy	Straight-grained; more dent-resistant than other cedars; does not absorb moisture; stable when seasoned; can be difficult to paint; has very little sapwood
excellent	moderate	easy	Termite-resistant; can have strong odor; soaks up water
moderate	easy	moderate	Used as underwater planking on the *Cutty Sark*
moderate	easy	moderate	Does not absorb water readily, so used for underwater planking
moderate	easy	moderate	Very strong when used as planking, but use tight-grained, quarter-sawn boards if possible; hard to paint slash-grained boards
excellent	moderate	fair to difficult	Available in large and wide boards; resistant to termites and teredos; avoid edge (ribbon) grain, as it will be difficult to finish; does not tend to distort or split during seasoning
moderate	moderate	moderate	European-quality yacht planking; very durable; little sapwood
moderate	moderate	fair to difficult	Often available in very large dimensions; ribbon-grain stock hard to plane; stains near metal fastenings

Common Name	Other Names	Weight (lbs.) per Cubic Foot	Strength Relative to Oak (Oak = 100)
Honduras	*Swietenia mahagoni*	39	90
Philippine	tangile; red moranti	38	80
Philippine	lauan	36	75
Pine Huon	*Agathis robusta* (from Australia)	30	65
Kauri	*Agathis australis* (from New Zealand)	30	65
Longleaf yellow	*Pinus palustris* pitch pine	40–45	95
White	*Pinus strobus* hurricane pine	27	60
Teak	*Tectona grandis* Burma teak	42–45	85

Rot Resistance	Ease of Bending	Ease of Planing	Comments
moderate	moderate	fair to difficult	Most beautiful and close-grained of mahoganies; tends to stain black near copper or bronze fastenings; turns gold when exposed to the sun
moderate	moderate	fair to difficult	Fades to gold when exposed to the sun but does not turn black near fastenings; can be a beautiful dark red color (We used it to plank *Seraffyn,* it worked easily, but I specified no ribbon grain.)
fair to poor	fair	fair	Don't use for carvel planking; light tan in color, soft, and can be brittle
moderate	moderate	easy	Similar to kauri; long lengths available
moderate	moderate	easy	Hard to get quality heartwood preferred by boatbuilders; nice to work
excellent	fair	difficult	Does not absorb water; very stable; excellent for underwater planking; need kerosene on tools to work easily
moderate	moderate	easy	Lovely to work; clear stock available in large sizes; good for boats 20 to 40 feet
excellent	moderate	moderate to difficult	Highly resistant to termite and teredos; does not absorb moisture readily; easy to work and polish; weather-resistant but expensive and rarely available in large sizes; not terribly strong for weight; dulls tools but does not shrink and swell as much as other woods; tends to add about 10 percent to resale value

BOATBUILDING WOODS OFTEN USED FOR
NONPLANKING STIUATIONS

Common Name	Other Names	Weight (lbs.) per Cubic Foot	Strength Relative to Oak (Oak = 100)
Butternut	*Juglans cinerea*	25	60
Lignumvitae	*Guaiacum officinale*	78	120
Locust	*Robinia pseudoacacia* black locust	51	135
Oak (white)	*Quercus robur* English oak *Quercus alba* American oak	48	100
Spruce	*Picea* northern white Sitka	26	66

NOTE: Further information on the appropriateness of various woods for specific boatbuilding uses is found in Lloyd's Scantling Rules, Appendix B. Several more woods are listed—woods often used in England and Scotland. Listed here those woods are most commonly used in North America, where I have done the majority of my boatbuilding. Many fine local woods, such as spotted gum, Queensland beech, kaikatea, and totara are used in New Zealand and Australia. So if I were building outside of the United States, before investing in imported woods, I would check with the local boatbuilders to see what they use. Then I would ask the forestry research people in that country for information regarding the durability and workability of various timbers.

As a rule, I have found that the best woods for boatbuilding are usually the hardest to work, with cedars being the major exception. Whenever cost was a factor, I would choose a cedar over any more expensive hardwood.

Although much of the information for the above list came from books listed in the bibliography at the end of this book, I obtained specialized information from: *Timbers of the World* (Timber Research and Development Association, Highenden Valley, High Wycombe, Bucks., England); *A Handbook of Softwoods* (Building Research Establishment Report, Her Majesty's Stationery Office, London, England); and *The MacDonald Encyclopedia of Trees* (Holywell House, Worship Street, London EC3, England).

Rot Resistance	Ease of Bending	Ease of Planing	Comments
moderate	moderate	easy	Does not shrink and swell much; makes nice interior wood; dents easily
excellent	brittle	difficult	Oil-impregnated, making it excellent for stern bearings, block shells, sheaves
excellent	easy	moderate	Hard to find in large, clear boards; rarely available commercially; superb for any part of a boat other than planking, as it is rot- and borer-resistant
fair to moderate; can vary	easy	moderate	Very strong; can be long-lasting but is prone to checking and shrinkage; swells more than other woods; stains easily but very good for difficult bends or planks that require steaming; avoid all sapwood
fair	easy	moderate	Very strong for its weight; glues well; often available in long lengths; superior for spars

APPENDIX B
YACHT CONSTRUCTION
RULES

The following three sets of rules for construction methods and scantlings for wooden yachts were compiled separately by Nathanael G. Herreshoff, Henry B. Nevins, and Lloyd's Register of Shipping. These rules were formulated and effected by the trial-and-error evolution of wooden hull construction. The workable methods were retained and refined, and, naturally, unserviceable methods were deleted. The resulting rules, though formulated by three different sources, appear quite similar, but there are important variations that are interesting to compare. As I use these rules in making building decisions, I like to keep in mind the panting, twisting, and hogging strains that will be exerted on a sailing hull, along with my ultimate aim, which is to produce a boat that will be long-lived and relatively easy to repair should it be damaged.

The first wooden yacht construction and scantling rules included here, compiled by Nathanael G. Herreshoff of Bristol, Rhode Island, in 1927, probably produce the lightest hull of the three. The boats built strictly to this rule—using steam-bent frames, fully ceiled interiors, external keel strapping, and screw fastenings with double-skinned planking—will have a light, strong racing hull. But for a boat slated to be used for some offshore cruising, I would look toward the rules compiled by Henry B. Nevins of City Island, New York, during the mid-1930s. This set of rules produces a hull of more conventional construction that would tend to have slightly heavier scantlings than Herreshoff's. The third scantling rules included are those recommended by Lloyd's Register of Shipping in London. They were updated to 1979 and include not only more detail than the other two scantling rules, but also rules for the use of modern materials, such as adhesives and sheathings that were not common before World War II. Not surprisingly, many of the recommendations are very close to those used by Herreshoff and Nevins.

The Lloyd's Rules read quite differently because they are recommendations to be used in compiling drawings, which are then submitted to the Lloyd's Register (Yacht and Small Craft Services) for approval before construction begins on a hull. The boat is then built under the supervision of a Lloyd's surveyor, who can suggest changes or additions to ensure that the hull is of adequate strength for its intended use and therefore is suitable for certification as "built to Lloyd's specifications and standards."

These three sets of rules were formulated for the types of hulls that are built in the majority of cases—racing boats and racer/cruisers. Many designers increase these scantlings by 15 to 25 percent when a hull is destined for the rough service of offshore cruising. Almost all oceangoing yachts under 40 feet tend to be overloaded and down on their designed waterline at times. We found that 30- to 40-foot boats floating 8 inches below their designed waterline were not uncommon among the offshore fleet. The hundreds of extra pounds that cause this makes the boat far stiffer and harder on its hull and gear. The extra 6 or 8 inches of draft lowers the ballast keel, which also makes the yacht stiffer. This gives it increased sail-carrying ability, which puts even more strains on the rigging, chainplates, bulkheads, frames, and floors. In the case of *Taleisin*, a boat designed for ocean cruising, the design weight was 17,400 pounds. For short inshore race courses, we keep her lighter than that, or about 16,800 pounds. But when she sets off fully loaded for extended passagemaking, her weight is about 18,600 pounds for the first leg of the journey, and she is noticeably stiffer. As the general propositions of Herreshoff's Rules point out, the strains on the framing and planking of a hull increase dramatically as the displacement increases.

To enter both Nevins's tables and Herreshoff's tables, you must know the displacement of the hull in cubic feet. To determine this, divide the loaded displacement in pounds by 64 (the weight of a cubic foot of seawater). In the case of *Taleisin,* designed to displace 17,400 pounds when floating at her designed waterline, the cubic displacement is 272.

In the Lloyd's Rules, depth of hull is measured from the centerline of the main deck to the bottom of the ballast keel. All measurements in this rule are metric.

Herreshoff's Rules
for the Construction of Wooden Yachts (1927)

Captain Nat Herreshoff, known as the Wizard of Bristol, was probably the most innovative and progressive designer/builder the world has ever known. He designed and then built hundreds of yachts in his own shipyard, a yard with its own timber mill, pattern shop, foundry, and sail loft. The Wizard himself controlled every detail of the hull at every step of the construction. The boatyard was set up for production wooden boat building, and many of the construction ideas shown in the following rules reflect this.

Captain Nat designed several different boats for one-design racing, then built dozens of each of these hulls on building molds, so the finished boats were exactly alike in every detail from materials to sails. Thus, he evolved methods that best suited what was in effect a boatbuilding factory. Unfortunately, it would be impractical for someone with a one-man boatbuilding shop to duplicate many of these clever weight- and labor-saving production methods.

General Propositions

Frame Spaces: To be dependent on the displacement of the yacht or boat when at load conditions.   FUNDAMENTAL FACTOR   (I)

Planking: Also Decking, Keel, Clamps, Ceiling, and all other fore and aft members. To be dependent on the displacement of the yacht modified by the ratio of depth to length of hull.   FUNDAMENTAL FACTOR   (II)

Stem Siding: Also Timbers, Floor Timbers, including Plank Floors, etc. To be dependent on the displacement of the yacht.   FUNDAMENTAL FACTOR (III)

Deck Beams: Molded ways to be dependent on the displacement of the yacht modified by the breadth of beam.   FUNDAMENTAL FACTOR (IV)
Sided ways to be dependent on the displacement of the yacht.

                      FUNDAMENTAL FACTOR (III)

House Deck Beams: Molded ways to be dependent on the displacement of the yacht modified by the length of the longest house beam.

                      FUNDAMENTAL FACTOR   (V)

These Fundamental Factors depend upon special formulas developed at Bristol, and involve the practice of the Herreshoff Manufacturing Company during the years from 1878 to 1918. These formulas have been reduced to tabular form, and the resulting tables for finding these factors, directly from the principal dimensions of the yacht, are given below.

Notation and Symbols Used

L.W.L. or l.w.l. Length of water line at load conditions, corresponding to L.W.L. as fixed for Universal Rule by New York Yacht Club in 1913 (same as D.W.L.).

O.a.l. or o.a. Extreme length of hull as measured for Universal Rule—between plumb lines.

L. L.W.L. plus ⅓ of overhangs or $\dfrac{2\text{ L.W.L.} + \text{O.a.l.}}{3}$

B. Extreme breadth of hull, without moldings, taken at 55% of L.W.L. from the fore end of the water line. (Generally called "beam.")

Q.b.l. Quarter beam length as used in Universal Rule.

b. Breadth of hull taken at L.W.L. at 55% of L.W.L. from the fore end of the water line.

d_w or d. Extreme draft of water.

d_h. Depth of hull from top of deck beams to rabbet line taken at 55% of L.W.L. from the fore end of the water line.

b.c.g. Depth of outside ballast from top face to centre of gravity taken at 55% of L.W.L. from the fore end of the water line.

b_b. Breadth at top of outside ballast taken at 55% of L.W.L. from the fore end of the water line.

D. Displacement in cubic feet when in load condition. Corresponding to D in Universal Rule.

S. or S.a. Sail area in square feet. Corresponding to Sail area (S.A.) in Universal Rule.

All data dimensions in feet and decimals

RULES FOR THE USE OF THE TABLES

1. Enter the Table with $\sqrt[3]{D}$ and find at once the values of (I) and (III).
2. Enter the Table with L/d_h and find at once the value of a. Multiply this by (III) to find the value of (II). Formula: (II) = a × (III).
3. Enter the Table with $\sqrt[4]{D \times B}$ (the square root of the square root) and under (III) find at once the value of (IV).
4. Enter the Table with $\sqrt[4]{D \times \text{length of longest house beam}}$ (the square root of the square root) and under (III) find at once the value of (V).

GENERAL RULES AND SPECIFICATIONS

Frame Spaces

The distance between the centers of frames in inches is to be equal to the Factor (I).

Keel

In standard construction, white oak or teak, in as long lengths as possible.

When it is necessary to be in two or more pieces or where connecting to stem or after overhang timber and deadwood, the scarf or lap joint must extend at least

2½ frame spaces, and be well bolted with Navy or Tobin bronze through bolts having head and nut, the nuts being exposed in the inside when possible.

Yachts having the main keel cast in lead and included in the outside ballast, the lead is to be in depth not less than 1½ times the depth required for oak or teak and the casting is to be stiffened by containing not less than 5% or more than 7½% of antimony.

Keels for inside ballasted yachts or power yachts and launches are to be in siding not less than siding of stem and overhang timber, or less than .35 (II). Molded way or depth to be not less than .8 (II); except near ends of vessel it may be reduced to .5 (II).

Tables of the Fundamental Factors

used in connection with

HERRESHOFF'S RULES FOR THE CONSTRUCTION OF WOODEN YACHTS

Enter with	(I)	(III) and (IV) (inches)	a	Enter with	(I)	(III) and (IV) (inches)	a	Enter with	(I)	(III) and (IV) (inches)	a	Enter with	(I)	(III) and (IV) (inches)	a
3.0	5.91	3.35	1.14	6.0	11.03	7.18	1.24	9.0	15.89	11.21	1.31	12.0	20.59	15.38	1.36
.1	6.09	3.47	1.15	.1	11.20	7.31	1.25	.1	16.05	11.35	1.31	.1	20.75	15.53	1.36
.2	6.27	3.59	1.15	.2	11.36	7.44	1.25	.2	16.21	11.49	1.31	.2	20.90	15.67	1.36
.3	6.44	3.72	1.15	.3	11.53	7.57	1.25	.3	16.37	11.62	1.31	.3	21.05	15.81	1.36
.4	6.62	3.84	1.16	.4	11.69	7.70	1.25	.4	16.53	11.76	1.32	.4	21.21	15.95	1.36
.5	6.79	3.97	1.16	.5	11.86	7.84	1.26	.5	16.69	11.90	1.32	.5	21.36	16.09	1.36
.6	6.97	4.09	1.17	.6	12.02	7.97	1.26	.6	16.85	12.04	1.32	.6	21.52	16.23	1.36
.7	7.14	4.22	1.17	.7	12.19	8.10	1.26	.7	17.00	12.17	1.32	.7	21.67	16.38	1.37
.8	7.31	4.34	1.18	.8	12.35	8.24	1.26	.8	17.16	12.31	1.32	.8	21.82	16.52	1.37
3.9	7.49	4.47	1.18	6.9	12.51	8.37	1.27	9.9	17.32	12.45	1.33	12.9	21.98	16.66	1.37
4.0	7.66	4.60	1.18	7.0	12.68	8.50	1.27	10.0	17.48	12.59	1.33	13.0	22.13	16.80	1.37
.1	7.83	4.72	1.19	.1	12.84	8.64	1.27	.1	17.63	12.73	1.33	.1	22.28	16.94	1.37
.2	8.00	4.85	1.19	.2	13.00	8.77	1.27	.2	17.79	12.87	1.33	.2	22.43	17.08	1.37
.3	8.17	4.97	1.19	.3	13.17	8.90	1.28	.3	17.95	13.01	1.33	.3	22.59	17.23	1.37
.4	8.35	5.10	1.20	.4	13.33	9.04	1.28	.4	18.10	13.14	1.33	.4	22.74	17.37	1.37
.5	8.52	5.23	1.20	.5	13.49	9.17	1.28	.5	18.26	13.28	1.33	.5	22.89	17.51	1.37
.6	8.69	5.36	1.20	.6	13.65	9.31	1.28	.6	18.42	13.42	1.34	.6	23.05	17.66	1.38
.7	8.86	5.49	1.21	.7	13.81	9.44	1.28	.7	18.57	13.56	1.34	.7	23.20	17.80	1.38
.8	9.03	5.61	1.21	.8	13.97	9.58	1.29	.8	18.73	13.70	1.34	.8	23.35	17.94	1.38
4.9	9.20	5.74	1.21	7.9	14.13	9.71	1.29	10.9	18.88	13.84	1.34	13.9	23.50	18.08	1.38
5.0	9.36	5.87	1.22	8.0	14.30	9.85	1.29	11.0	19.04	13.98	1.34	14.0	23.65	18.23	1.38
.1	9.53	6.00	1.22	.1	14.46	9.98	1.29	.1	19.20	14.12	1.34	.1	23.81	18.37	1.38
.2	9.70	6.13	1.22	.2	14.62	10.12	1.29	.2	19.35	14.26	1.34	.2	23.96	18.51	1.38
.3	9.87	6.26	1.22	.3	14.78	10.26	1.30	.3	19.51	14.40	1.34	.3	24.11	18.66	1.38
.4	10.04	6.39	1.23	.4	14.94	10.39	1.30	.4	19.66	14.54	1.35	.4	24.26	18.80	1.38
.5	10.20	6.52	1.23	.5	15.10	10.53	1.30	.5	19.82	14.68	1.35	.5	24.41	18.94	1.39
.6	10.37	6.65	1.23	.6	15.26	10.66	1.30	.6	19.97	14.82	1.35	.6	24.57	19.09	1.39
.7	10.54	6.78	1.24	.7	15.42	10.80	1.30	.7	20.13	14.96	1.35	.7	24.72	19.23	1.39
.8	10.70	6.91	1.24	.8	15.58	10.94	1.30	.8	20.28	15.10	1.35	.8	24.87	19.38	1.39
5.9	10.87	7.04	1.24	8.9	15.74	11.07	1.31	11.9	20.44	15.24	1.35	14.9	25.12	19.52	1.39

Keels in rowboats and centerboard sailing yachts to be not less than .35 (II) in depth and not less than .55 (II) plus centerboard slot in width, the ends gradually tapering to match siding of stem and sternpost. In case of centerboard yachts having main keel of lead, the lower pieces of centerboard casing (centerboard logs) and arms to bolt timbers to (floor timbers) are to be cast as part of the keel. The top of lead to be above top of floor timbers to give a clear caulking seam. Planking rabbet to be cast into lead.

Keels in sailing yachts as developed by the Universal Rule, having outside ballast bolted on, to be of flat plank type with planking rabbet worked into edges.

When one piece of proper size is not obtainable, make keel in two pieces butted together amidships and bolted to a deadwood piece underneath—to be steamed and bent to form. The deadwood where butt is made is to be in depth not less than the keel pieces. Butt to be square-ended and made midway between two consecutive floor timbers and fastened with bronze through-bolts, with nuts above a bronze plate covering the joint. Or make the keel in three pieces: the middle one running from forward of the outside ballast to the intersection with the sternpost and laying directly on top of the outside lead casting; the forward section of keel to be scarfed on top of middle section, with its aft end molded deep enough to make scarf, and then running to stem piece, which is scarfed on; the after section to run over deadwood and to transom, with transom knee lying on top.

The middle section of keel may be dispensed with if the outside lead is properly designed with rabbet for garboard planking and satisfactory connection is made with the forward and after overhang pieces and after deadwood. The last plan is preferable in yachts that are hauled out of water for long periods in dry atmosphere.

Stem Piece

Of white oak or teak as standard woods; but in small classes, of not over 150 cubic feet displacement (row and power boats), hackmatac or other tough and lasting wood may be used. Siding to be .5 (III) and molded way over .7 (III) as required. In yachts of over 100 cubic feet displacement, the back rabbet is to be wide enough for double fastening of wood ends of planking.

The stem piece is to lap the keel at least 2½ frame spaces and to be well bolted with not less than 4 through-bolts set up with nuts. There must always be a breast hook piece, well bolted to sheer strakes and clamps and having a good fore-and-aft bolt through stemhead.

Transom

To be white oak or teak plank in yachts of over 500 cubic feet displacement; in smaller ones may be of lighter wood, as mahogany, butternut, etc. To be steamed and bent to form if curved, and to be reinforced at the edges with white oak in larger, and hackmatac in smaller, yachts. Transom to be rabbeted at edge and reinforcement, making back rabbet to receive fastenings of ends of planks.

To be quarter knees and center line knee on to keel, and framing timbers, if necessary. In small yachts, rowboats, etc., without corner reinforcing, transom plank to be not less than .18 (II) and wood-ends of planking exposed.

Timbers or Frames

To be of best quality of white oak selected for ability to bend to required form when steamed. There is comparatively little white oak that has the proper qualities for first-class timbers, but when obtained there is no other wood equal to it for the purpose.

Timbers must be bent over traps or molds and the larger sizes strapped to prevent splitting. They should be square in section, so best side can be selected for bending. This is important. The size to be .2 (III) at head, and in unballasted power boats and yachts and small open boats size to be uniform for full length.

In sailing yachts that are ballasted, timbers are to increase in size below head as follows:

Inside ballasted yachts are to be .22 (III) square and from 7.2 (III) below head are to taper to size at head .2 (III). Taper equal .1 in 36. = $\frac{1}{32}$'' per ft. nearly.

Center-board and moderate draft yachts with ballast close to keel, timbers .23 (III) square and from 7.2 (III) below head are to taper to size at head. Taper .1 in 24. = $\frac{3}{64}$'' per ft. nearly.

Deep draft yachts with ballast well below hull, timbers .24 (III) square and from 7.2 (III) below head to taper to size at head. Taper .1 in 18. = $\frac{1}{16}$'' per ft. nearly.

In any case where the curvature of the bilge is too quick for timbers to bend safely without splitting or upsetting grain, it is best to split the timbers down with a fine saw into equal parts as far as bend extends, and have all planking fastening go through both parts.

In power yachts increase the siding of timbers that come in machinery section, 50% to 75%.

Floor Timbers

To be of white oak or equivalent in strength and lasting qualities. The arms should be long enough to lap the timbers from 6 to 9 times the size of timbers. Thickness of plank floors not less than .185 (III) and not less than 3 times diameter of keel bolts. Knee or crook floors are to be sided not less than .28 (III) with depth in throat not less than .32 (III) and arm ends not less than size of timbers.

There should be not less than 3 timber bolts each side, of diameter $\frac{1}{6}$ to $\frac{1}{8}$ size of timber, passing through timber and floor timber and set up with nuts. Bronze in smaller sizes, but over $\frac{5}{16}$'', good galvanized iron or steel may be used.

Keel bolts should always be bronze if they come in contact with lead ballast. If not, sizes over $\frac{3}{8}$'' may be good galvanized iron or steel. Have two keel bolts whenever possible, in diameter not less than $\frac{1}{5}$ to $\frac{1}{6}$ size of timber, but if only room for one bolt into keel to be larger, depending on character of keel and deadrise of hull section.

When floor timber bolts support outside lead ballast they are to be increased in size. Their diameter in inches is to be not less than the square root of weight of outside lead in tons divided by number of bolts supporting lead,

$$\sqrt{\frac{\text{Tons lead}}{\text{no. bolts}}}$$

If it is desirable to use bolts of different diameters, proper compensation should be made so the total bolt area is not reduced and when bolts are independent of floor timber bolts, their size is to be equivalent in size to the sectional area of adjacent floor timber bolts, as determined above.

Floor timbers over outside ballast are to be increased in size so their thickness is not less than three times diameter of bolts passing through them and length and depth sufficient to receive four timber bolts, each side.

Lead Bolts and Straps

Their diameter to be determined by the size and number of floor timber bolts as explained above. Always have them carefully distributed and as near each edge as possible, and have nuts at their upper end so they can be tightened up when necessary. One or more bolts at each end should pass way through lead. All others may be screwed into the lead and the threads that go into the lead should be similar to those on wood screws and lag screws. The bolts should penetrate the lead 8 diameters and the length threaded 7 diameters. The pitch of threads should be about $\frac{1}{5}$ diameter and depth 1/10 diameter.

All outside lead on wood yachts should have straps extending vertically to connect lead directly with timbers and planking. These straps are to be let in flush and to lap on lead about 5 times their breadth and on to the timbers and above the keel and deadwood about 8 times their breadth.

Tobin bronze appears to be the best material. There are to be 5 to 8 straps each side placed on consecutive timbers in the middle part and on alternate timbers near ends of lead. Their size to be determined by multiplying weight of outside lead in tons by ratio (depth of lead to center of gravity divided by breadth on top), *if over one* and if not, by one. Divide by one and eight-tenths times whole number of straps, which will give sectional area in square inches of each strap.

$$\frac{b.c.g.}{b_b} \times \frac{Tons}{1.8 \ number} \ or \ \frac{Tons}{1.8 \ number}.$$

The breadth to be 4 times and thickness $\frac{1}{4}$ the square root of area.

Diameter of screws and bolts to be $\frac{1}{9}$ breadth of strap and there are to be not less than 8 brass wood screws into lead and not less than 9 bronze through-bolts with nuts through planking and timbers. Countersinking for heads of screws and bolts should not be over $1\frac{3}{4}$ diameter of bolts and the heads worked down flush after being set up.

Outside Planking

The thickness to be not less than .105 (II).

White cedar is the best wood for all small craft under 75 to 100 cu. ft. displacement.

In sizes from 75 to 200 or 250 cu. ft. a somewhat firmer wood is preferable, as Port Orford cedar, Mexican mahogany or Douglas fir. Larger yachts should have planking of woods of still harder texture as Georgia pine, western oak of good quality, teak or mahogany of hard texture.

Small lap streaked boats should have the laps well fastened with copper clinch nails or copper through fastening with bars.

Single planking with square seams should be well and closely fitted and caulked with cotton in small and intermediate sizes. The large sizes with hard wood planking, okum caulking may be used.

When double planked, it is found most practicable to have both layers parallel and the seams about equally lapped. The layers are to be well cemented together. Shellac is found best, but when there is plenty of time (2 or 3 months for setting) white lead is as good, or better in large work. The inner layer should be $\frac{3}{8}$ to $\frac{1}{2}$ of total thickness and softer or lighter wood may be used, as cedar or cypress with Mexican mahogany or Douglas fir outside. Have the layers well screw-fastened from inside between the timbers. It is always best to have garboard and sheer strakes single thickness and a good practice is to have a few strakes above the garboards also single.

The edges to receive double planking should be rabbeted to make a lap joint with one of the layers.

Sheer strakes should be of a hard wood that will well hold drive or screw fastening as white oak, teak, mahogany of hard texture, etc., and to be well seasoned. The molded form is desirable in smaller yachts and the thickness through swell about $1\frac{1}{4}$ times thickness of planking. Extra thickness in larger yachts than thickness of planking is also desirable—to have more wood for the vertical fastening of plank-sheer and rail.

Diagonal Strapping

In small yachts, under 100 cubic feet displacement, it is not necessary. In larger ones strap as follows:

Single planked, 100 to 175 cu. ft. displ. Double " 175 to 300 " " "	2 straps
Single planked, 175 to 300 cu. ft. displ. Double " 300 to 500 " " "	3 straps
Single planked, 300 to 500 cu. ft. displ. Double " 500 to 900 " " "	5 straps
Single planked, 500 to 900 cu. ft. displ. Double " 900 to 1500 " " "	5 diagonal and body strap
Single planked over 900 cu. ft. displ.	7 diagonal and body strap

Yachts over 1,200 cubic feet displacement had better be of composite build. The straps are to be arranged as shown in the diagrams below.

Diagonal strapping

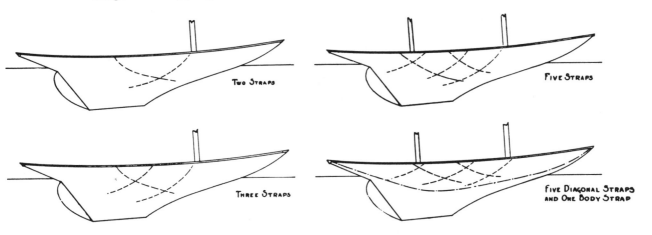

When body straps are used, the diagonal straps are to be fastened to them.

Light draft sailing yachts and power yachts of any considerable size, say over 300 cubic feet displacement, should be diagonally strapped or stiffened in some way. In hulls of from 300 to 500 cubic feet displacement a very good way is to have arched stringers intersected by short bilge stringers of oak or yellow pine, thus

The arched stringers if in two or more lengths to be well secured at the butts, and the bilge stringers well secured to the arch stringers at their ends. All to be well fastened to the inside of the timbers. Larger yachts to have the regular system of diagonal strapping laid on to the outside of the timbers before planking. Their arrangement depends so much on the character of hull and distribution of weights, it is difficult to formulate a rule, but generally, drooping of ends and sagging at position of machinery have to be looked out for.

In the sailing yachts that have body bands, they should be well secured to the stem near its head and run aft under the lower part of body amidships, finally terminating at the quarters where they should be well secured. The lower end of all diagonal straps should terminate at these bands and be well secured to them. Arranged this way straps do not go into the bilge-water and therefore are not subjected to intense corrosion.

The size of straps to be about the same as determined for lead straps, or possibly a little wider and thinner, and body bands about the same thickness but 50% to 75% wider. Screw fastening at each edge into planking and also into timbers. Tobin bronze is standard but in larger sized yachts galvanized steel banding is usual.

Clamps

Clamps for supporting deck beams and making a longitudinal tie should be continuous from breast hook to quarter knees, and if in more than one length avoid if possible having any butt near amidships. The best practice is to have a long length amidship and butted to two shorter ones at ends. Connection to be made by a short filling piece between the clamp and sheer strake between adjacent timbers (the butt being midway of a frame space) and a long butt piece on the inside of clamp covering 5 frame spaces, and well through fastened. This inside piece may be of wood same as clamp or of galvanized steel angle. Bevel clamps at outside so top surface is level and correctly fays to the deck beams, which are to have a level seating. Their size before beveling should be .24 (II) each way and the inner lower corner may be chamfered away about .05 (II) excepting under butt pieces.

In the smaller classes, spruce or other stiff light wood may be used but in larger ones woods of harder texture, as Douglas fir, Georgia pine or oak, and in as long lengths as possible.

In yachts having long cabin trunks, or houses, that cut off the deck beams, it is desirable to have a secondary clamp inside the primary, and well bolted to it.

In many yachts having high topsides and flush decks clamps may be omitted, and the deck beams supported by metallic drop knees or brackets, bolted to deck beam and timber, both being placed in the same plane. If this construction be used longitudinal strength shall then be made up by having a molded or thicker sheer strake and a heavier planksheer or waterway.

Breast Hook and Quarter Knees

There should always be a breast hook to connect the stem, sheer strakes and decking securely together. In the modern sailing yacht it becomes a chunk of wood to receive bolts and fastening, but it should be selected with care for soundness and durability, and it must be well seasoned. There should be a long fore and aft bolt passing through stem and set up with a nut inside. The forward end of clamps should also be bolted to under side of breast hook.

Quarter knees must be fitted to securely connect the sheer strakes, clamps, and transom, and also a ledge piece to receive wood ends of deck. Take particular care that the quarter knees and other pieces in the vicinity are of thoroughly seasoned wood that is not subject to dry rot.

Deck Beams

The most desirable wood is white oak or yellow-bark oak, in the larger sizes. Yellow-bark oak, white ash or chestnut in intermediate sizes, and white ash, chestnut or butternut in smaller. It is recommended they be placed on large side of every frame space, the timbers being on the small, or side towards ends of vessel, excepting at frames where there are hanging knees or when there is no clamp, but knee brackets, then they should be in same plane as timber.

The molded size to be .28 (IV). Camber for both top and bottom sides should be the same, for all beams, and between ⅓″ and ½″ per foot of beam of vessel, or between $\frac{B}{36}$ and $\frac{B}{24}$. The radius of curvature between 9B and 6B. Make the depth of end of all beams .20 (IV), and the under side on level line until intersected by molded or cambered part, as below.

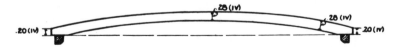

The regular size for siding of deck beams to be .17 (III). Beams each side of mast, and each side of hatches with not more than two beams cut, and at position of belt frames, to be sided .23 (III). At hatches cutting more than two beams, and at breaks of deck, to be sided .30 (III).

Half beams with inboard end supported by hatch coaming or cabin house side may be molded .20 (IV) and sided .17 (III), and there are to be wedge shaped shims between under sides and clamps.

Deck Diagonal Strapping

In yachts over 175 and under 350 cubic feet displacement have one pair running from gunwale to gunwale and crossing near mast partners. Yachts between 300 and 700 cubic feet displacement 2 pairs, and over 700 three or more pairs—all placed where they can best run from gunwale to gunwale and not be cut by hatchways or other deck openings. The angle with center line between 30° and 45°. The size to be about the same as for planking straps. They may be cut into deck beam flush or fairing pieces, thickness of straps placed on top of beams laid in white lead. To be fastened into deck beams and also into deck between beams, with brass screws.

Margin Plank or Planksheer

To run continuously from stemhead over sheerstrakes and deckbeam ends, to and around transom and return on other side. To be worked in long lengths as possible with butts on buttblocks between timbers, and shifted two or more frame spaces from butts of sheerstrakes and clamps. The thickness to be not less than main deck and more is better if deck is bright for holystoning. Breadth to be .38 (II). To be screw fastened into sheerstrake and beam ends. If deck planks are to be laid straight, make breadth .42 (II) to allow nibbing in ends of decking. Best woods are teak, white oak, mahogany of hard texture, in larger; and mahogany, Georgia pine or Douglas fir, in small yachts.

Main Deck

The best wood is clear white pine free from sap and shakes. If a deck is to be canvas covered, which is always recommended in decks less than 1¼″ thick, other light woods are good, as Washington spruce, Port Orford cedar, white cedar, etc.

The best practice is to lay with square seams of thoroughly dry stock and to be tightly caulked with cotton. Bare decks to have seams filled with marine glue after caulking. When canvas covered, seams puttied flush.

In the heavier decks a good practice is to get the stock out square so to be able to select the best side to be up, which must always show edge of grain. Such a deck has one fastening to each beam. For two fastenings, breadth should be from $1\frac{3}{4}$ to $2\frac{1}{2}$ times thickness .185 (II) to .260 (II). Standard thickness to be .105 (II), and if canvas covered, thickness may be reduced to .1 (II)—.05″. If teak is substituted for white pine in the larger sizes, thickness to be .075 (II). It is generally desirable to lay the deck parallel to the margin plank, with ends nibbed into a king plank when approaching center line.

Cabin Trunks, or Houses

If sides are of plank of soft wood, thickness to be .110 (II), and if mahogany, .1 (II), or if teak, .095 (II). The sides should be edge bolted at spacing not over 2 frame spaces.

The house deck beams should be secured to house sides either by a white oak lining strip in width $1\frac{3}{4}$ times molded size of beams and thickness .1 (II). The beams to be dove-tailed into it. Or by metal brackets or clips, securely fastened.

If the sides are framed and with glass or wood panels, frame to be either mahogany or teak .12 (II) in thickness, and glass not less than $\frac{7}{32}$″ thick or .018 (II), and with wood panels, .06 (II).

House deck beams may be dove-tailed into upper rail of framed side provided it is increased in thickness to .175 (II) and not cut through, but leaving not less than .70 (II) of wood at end of beam.

The molded depth of house or trunk deck beams to be .28 (V): where the factor (V) is taken from Table III by entering with $\sqrt[4]{D}$ × length of longest beam. (Square root of the square root); but not less than $\frac{2}{3}$ molded depth of main deck beams. The spacing,—siding of beams and thickness of deck, to be in proportion to corresponding scantling of main deck as the square root of the ratio of length of house to the mean length of hull (L), but not less than $\frac{2}{3}$ of corresponding dimensions of main deck, and to be of equivalent grade of wood. Beams each side of mast hatches, etc., are to be increased as in main deck beams.

Camber to be between 1/24 and 1/36 of length of longest house beam.

House deck to be laid in same manner as main deck, and same allowance of thickness for canvas to be made.

When the house deck extends forward of a mast it must be diagonally strapped as thoroughly as the main deck.

Mast Partners and Steps

At the position of each mast, bitts, capstan, mooring cleats, etc., the deck should be reinforced between deck beams by a well seasoned hardwood plank running thwartships,—in thickness .125 (II) and length equal to $2\frac{1}{2}$ frame spaces, for mast, bitts and main capstan, and not less than $1\frac{1}{2}$ frame spaces for other major deck fittings. Each side of a mast or bitt hole should be edge bolted, passing through adjacent deck beams and set up with nuts.

Mast steps should be of hard wood—white oak is best—and well supported against the intense thrust of the mast. They should rest on 3 or 4 floor timbers of extra size, and in the larger sizes of racing yachts, extra timbers and intermediate timbers or straps connecting with chainplates and passing down under mast step is desirable.

Inside Ceiling

Every wood framed yacht should be ceiled from the cabin sole to within a frame space length of the deck beams, or higher, and for at least ¾ length (¾L) in middle part, but to extend as much farther as is necessary to reach by any sleeping berth. The thickness of ceiling to be .20″ + .025 (II). To be laid in reasonably long lengths, seams close and to be well fastened to timbers. Use cedar in smaller sizes and harder woods in larger, ranging up to Douglas fir or Georgia pine in the largest.

Bilge Stringers

Are not necessary in any yacht that is well ceiled as directed. In cases where a yacht is liable to lay aground and over on her bilge, it is well to have outside protection in the form of one or two or three thick bilge strakes of planking for the middle ⅓ length, or a bilge keel in lieu of it.

Hanging Knees and Belt Frames

In larger sizes of sailing yachts—over 500 cubic feet displacement with outside ballast—they should be strengthened by belt frames and hanging knees. They can generally be placed at frame spaces that will not interfere with berth spaces, and at partitions, and not closer than 6½ to 8 feet apart. Have two on each side on yachts between 500 and 900 cubic feet displacement and 3 or 4 each side on yachts over 900 cubic feet displacement. The belt timber to be .23 (III) square of best white oak, steamed and bent to place. These timbers should be fitted inside the ceiling and *not* cut it, and hanging knees should connect them to the deck beams of same siding as belt frames: have through fastenings of size for lead straps, with heads bunged into outside planking and passing through timber, ceiling, and belt timber, with nuts inside and not over 1 (III) apart.

The lower end of belt frames to be well fastened to face of plank floors, as are the main timbers.

Cabin Floor, or Sole

Should be laid on oak beams, spaced same as main timbers and substantially secured to them, and to be stanchioned to floor timbers where necessary to prevent vibration. Floor may be cedar in small boats, ranging up to Douglas fir and Georgia pine in the largest. The thickness to be .20″ + .035 (II). Beams to be sided .2″ + 0.55 (II) and depth 2½ times siding.

Rudder Stocks

Tobin bronze is standard material for all wood constructed yachts. The diameter in inches for sailing yachts to be not less than .155 times breadth of yacht in feet, (.155B) and also not less than the fourth root of 2/100 times distance of center of area of rudder blade from axis, times area of blade, times mean length of vessel, all in feet. ($\sqrt[4]{.02 \times v \times a \times L}$)

The connection of rudder blade to stock to be by two bronze castings with double arms in the general form as shown. To be fitted and keyed tight to stock, and held to blade by two or three copper rivets.

Proportions:
  If the diameter of the stock A is 1:
    then the other dimensions should be
    B = 1¾   C = 1   D = 1⅛
    E = 4   G = ⅜   K = ¼
    F = ¼ or ⅛ if 3 bolts.
      H and H′ as required for
        the thickness of the blade.
      K is the size of key.

It is difficult to make a close rule for stocks to rudders of power vessels. As a rough rule: When blades are supported by a step or pintles. Diameter in inches not less than .18 (III), and not less than .85 (dia. of propeller shaft).

If blade is pendant, then stock to be not less than .225 (III) and not less than 1.25 (dia. of propeller shaft) and if twin screw, 1.5 (dia. of shafts).

Planking and Deck Fastenings

Brass wood screws are usually used and give good results generally, although occasionally there is trouble from electrolysis, and a different composition than that usually used in wood screws that is not subject to it would be better. For the special purpose, screws that are threaded but six-tenths of length, so the body part will extend into timber to give better sheering resistance, is better. Care should be taken to bore correct sizes for screw end—body and bung, and special bitts that will bore the three sizes at once are desirable. The sizes of screws under No. 10—it is generally more practical to putty or wax the heads instead of bunging, and in that case ⅛ inch longer screws can be used and not counter-bored, but the head set in a short distance.

Table of Sizes of Screws for Planking and Deck Fastenings

Planking Thickness	Approximate Diameter	Screw Gauge Number	Length	Diameter of Bung
3/8″	9/64″	6	3/4″	5/16″
7/16″	5/32″	7	7/8″	5/16″
1/2″	11/64″	8	1″	3/8″
9/16″	3/16″	9	1 1/8″	3/8″
5/8″	3/16″	10	1 1/4″	7/16″
3/4″	7/32″	12	1 1/2″	7/16″
7/8″	1/4″	14	1 3/4″	1/2″
1″	17/64″	16	2″	9/16″
1 1/8″	19/64″	18	2 1/4″	5/8″
1 1/4″	5/16″	20	2 1/2″	11/16″
1 1/2″	11/32″	22	2 3/4″	11/16″ or 3/4″
1 3/4″	3/8″	24	3″	3/4″ or 13/16″
2″	13/32″	26	3 1/2″	13/16″

For double planked yachts use table sizes for inner plank fastening to timbers and same gauge but length as required for fastening between timbers. For outer plank use sizes for total thickness of both inner and outer planking.

Table of Dimensions in Terms of the Fundamental Factors

INCHES AND DECIMALS

	Deep Keel	Moderate Draft, Center-Board: Outside Ballast	Inside Ballast Sailing Yachts: Power-Boats
FRAME SPACES:	(I)	(I)	(I)
KEEL:			
Depth, or thickness at ends:	.28 (II)	.35 (II)	.80 (II)
Width:		.55 (II)	.55 (II)
		+ c. b. slot	+ c. b. slot
STEM PIECE:			
Sided:	.50 (III)	.50 (III)	.50 (III)
Molded:	.70 (III)	.70 (III)	.70 (III)
TRANSOM:			
Thickness:	.095 (II)	.095 (II)	.095 (II)
Reinforcing thickness:	.18 (II)	.18 (II)	.18 (II)
TIMBERS:			
At head (square)	.20 (III)	.20 (III)	.20 (III)
Maximum (square)	.24 (III)	.23 (III)	.22 (III)
Length of taper:	7.20 (III)	7.20 (III)	7.20 (III)
Taper (per foot)	1/16″	3/64″	1/32″
FLOOR TIMBERS:			
Plank Floors: thick	.185 (III)	.185 (III)	.185 (III)
Crook Floors: thick	.28 (III)	.28 (III)	.28 (III)
deep	.32 (III)	.32 (III)	.32 (III)
OUTSIDE PLANKING:			
Thickness:	.105 (II)	.105 (II)	.105 (II)
CLAMPS:			
Before beveling:	.24 (II)	.24 (II)	.24 (II)
Chamfer (not over):	.05 (II)	.05 (II)	.05 (II)

	Deep Keel	Moderate Draft, Centre-Board: Outside Ballast	Inside Ballast Sailing Yachts: Power-Boats
DECK BEAMS:			
Molded: maximum:	.28 (IV)	.28 (IV)	.28 (IV)
at ends:	.20 (IV)	.20 (IV)	.20 (IV)
Sided: regular	.17 (III)	.17 (III)	.17 (III)
at mast & small hatches:	.23 (III)	.23 (III)	.23 (III)
at large hatches:	.30 (III)	.30 (III)	.30 (III)
Half Beams:			
Molded:	.20 (IV)	.20 (IV)	.20 (IV)
Sided:	.17 (III)	.17 (III)	.17 (III)
PLANKSHEER:			
Thickness:	same as deck	same as deck	same as deck
Breadth:			
Curved deck:	.38 (II)	.38 (II)	.38 (II)
Straight deck:	.42 (II)	.42 (II)	.42 (II)
MAIN DECK:			
Thickness: Pine:	.105 (II)	.105 (II)	.105 (II)
Teak:	.075 (II)	.075 (II)	.075 (II)
Canvas:	.100 (II)	.100 (II)	.100 (II)
	—.05″	—.05″	—.05″
CABIN TRUNKS:			
Solid Plank:			
Soft wood:	.110 (II)	.110 (II)	.100 (II)
Mahogany:	.100 (II)	.100 (II)	.100 (II)
Teak:	.095 (II)	.095 (II)	.095 (II)
Glass or paneled:			
Frame (Mahogany or Teak):	.120 (II)	.120 (II)	.120 (II)
Panels	.060 (II)	.060 (II)	.060 (II)
Deck Beams:			
Molded depth:	.28 (V)	.28 (V)	.28 (V)
MAST PARTNERS AND DECK FITTINGS:			
Thickness:	.125 (II)	.125 (II)	.125 (II)
INSIDE CEILING:			
Thickness:	.025 (II)	.025 (II)	.025 (II)
	+.20″	+.20″·	+.20″
BELT TIMBER:			
Square:	.23 (III)	.23 (III)	
CABIN FLOOR, OR SOLE:			
Thickness:	.035 (II)	.035 (II)	.035 (II)
	+.20″	+.20″	·+.20″
Beams:			
Sided:	.055 (II)	.055 (II)	.055 (II)
	+.20″	+.20″	+.20″
Depth:	2.5 × siding	2.5 × siding	2.5 × siding

Nevins's Scantling Rules
for Wooden Yachts

For many years, Henry B. Nevins owned and operated one of the most highly acclaimed boatyards in the United States at City Island, New York. His yachts were known for being not only handsome but also extremely strong. Before and after World War II, his boats earned a reputation as powerful, modern, functional ocean racers. A majority of the boats he built were for and under the supervision of the Sparkman and Stephens design team. The rules he compiled would be more applicable to the man with a small boatyard, because these methods are suited to building one-off hulls, not a whole class of production boats, as Herreshoff often did.

General Clause. The cube root of the displacement in cubic feet, $\sqrt[3]{\text{Disp. cu. ft.}}$, (with the yacht in load condition) is the basis upon which scantlings are calculated.

Keel

Material: White Oak, Teak, or Mahogany.
Molding: Not less than $\sqrt[3]{\text{Disp. cu. ft.}}$ multiplied by .7.
Siding: Not less than double the molding at the widest point of keel.

Stem

Material: White Oak, Teak, or Mahogany.
Molding: Not less than siding.
Siding: At head not less than four times the thickness of the planking. Below head the siding of stem and bow timber shall be gradually increased to siding of keel to provide proper back rabbet.

Sternpost

Material: White Oak, Teak, or Mahogany.
Molding: Not less than siding.
Siding: Not less than four times thickness of plank.

Horn Timber

Material: White Oak, Teak, or Mahogany.
Molding: Not less than twice the thickness of plank.
Siding: Not less than twice the molding.

Frames

Material: White Oak, steam-bent.

Sectional Area: At heel in accordance with table sizes. May be straight-tapered to head to not less than 75% of the heel area. (See below.)

Where untapered frame is used, rule size shall be maintained for ¾ of D.W.L. length. Fore and aft of the ¾ length, the area may be gradually reduced to the ends of the yacht where it may be 15% less than amidships.

Where tapered frame is used, the rule shall be applied to the longest frame in the yacht, establishing thereby a standard taper for all other frames. The head size of the longest frame shall be maintained throughout the yacht, and the established taper applied therefrom to the heel, thereby decreasing the areas at the heel as the frames grow shorter fore and aft of the longest frame.

Spacing: To be in accordance with table. (See below.)

Molding: Optional. Table dimensions are recommended. In no case less than is required to entirely bury the plank fastenings of the length specified for screws.

Siding: Optional. Table dimensions recommended.

Where severe bends are encountered, making it impractical to use a solid frame, it is recommended that the frame be split, in a fore and aft direction, from the end to just beyond the point of extreme bend; or a double frame may be used, one member bent inside the other. In both instances, plank fastenings should extend through outer member well into inner member and the two be drawn tightly together.

If *sawn frames* are to be used, they shall be double, with the members adequately bolted or riveted together. *Sectional Area*—50% heavier than the table size of frames.

Belt Frames

Material: White Oak, steam-bent.

Molding: ¾ that of frames.

Siding: Equal to frames.

Belt frames are to be applied to yachts which are ceiled and there must be at least four on each side. They shall be applied after ceiling is installed.

In the case of single-masted vessels and yawls, one set of belt frames are to be located immediately forward and one immediately aft of main mast, and are to be kneed to heavy partner deck beams.

Belt frames should be used whenever possible, but, should they interfere with any unusual condition inside the yacht, may be omitted, provided the regular frame at that location is doubled in sectional area, or two frames of rule size placed alongside each other and bolted or riveted together. Yachts which are not ceiled are to be fitted with heavy frames having a sectional area of 1¾ times the area of main frames and located in a like manner to the belt frames of ceiled yachts.

In the case of two-masted schooners or ketches, one set of belt frames are to be located immediately forward and one immediately aft of each mast and are to be kneed to heavy partner deck beams.

In the case of three-masted yachts, there shall be 6 pairs of belt frames, one set located immediately forward and one immediately aft of each mast and kneed to heavy partner deck beams.

Planking

Material: Teak, Mahogany, Long Leaf Yellow Pine, and Douglas Fir.

Thickness: In accordance with table. (See below.)

Butts to be shifted so that no two butts shall come on same frame or in same frame space, except there be 3 clear planks between, and in no adjacent plank be nearer than 3 frame spaces.

If teak is used, thickness may be reduced 10%.

Ceiling

Material: Long Leaf Yellow Pine, Douglas Fir, or Spruce.

Thickness: 40% of the table thickness of outside planking. No reduction allowed where teak planking is used.

Ceiling shall be fitted in all yachts having a $\sqrt[3]{\text{Disp. cu. ft.}}$ of over 10, and shall extend for at least the water line length of the vessel and from cabin sole to underside of clamp.

Bilge Stringers

Material: Long Leaf Yellow Pine or Douglas Fir.

Sectional Area: Equal to 3 times the table area of frames for ¾ of D.W.L. length.

Bilge stringers shall be used in all yachts which are not ceiled. There shall be one on each side, to extend from stem to stern wherever possible, and they may be straight-tapered to ends to not less than 50% of the area amidships.

Clamp and Shelf

Material: Long Leaf Yellow Pine or Douglas Fir.

Sectional Area: 3½ times the table area of frames for ¾ of the water line length.

They shall extend the full length of the yacht but may be straight-tapered to the ends to not less than 50% of the area amidships.

A single clamp, or a clamp and shelf of required area, may be used.

Deck Beams

Material: Oak, Chestnut, Douglas Fir, Long Leaf Yellow Pine, Teak, Mahogany, and Ash.

Sectional Area: At center line of boat in accordance with table and may be reduced at ends to 75% of the sectional area at center.

Spacing: Same as table for frames.

Molding: Optional. May be reduced at ends to 75% of the molding at center.

Siding: Optional, but to be not more than 65% of the molded depth at center.

There shall be partner beams and hatch beams whose siding shall be 1¾ times the siding of the main beams.

Half beams and beams beyond the ends of the D.W.L. may be reduced to 75% of the area of the main beams.

Decking

Material: White Pine, Cedar, Spruce, Cypress, or Douglas Fir.

Thickness: Same as outside planking

If teak is used, the thickness may be reduced 10%. If covered with canvas, thickness may be reduced ⅛″.

Floors

Material: White Oak, Teak, Mahogany.

Spacing: One to each pair of frames.

Molding: To be sufficient to allow at least 4 fastenings to heels of frames, whose spacing shall be not less than 1½ times siding of floor, but in no case shall the sectional area over the keel be less than 2 times the sectional area of frames.

In way of lead keel, siding of floors taking keel bolts shall be increased to regular siding, plus the diameter of the keel bolt. Molding to be same as regular floors.

There shall be no concave on top of any floor to show up cross grains at ends.

In any yacht where it is necessary to use the space occupied by wooden floors to install tanks or to meet any special conditions, metal floors—of approved design and of equal weight and strength to the wooden floors—may be used.

Siding: Not less than frame.

Hull Straps

Material: Bronze of not less than 60,000 pounds per square inch of tensile strength.

Width: Twice the planking thickness.

Thickness: .1 the plank thickness. (Other dimensions may be used but shall produce an equal cross-sectional area.)

There shall be 2 diagonal straps on each side at each mast, extending from underside of deck to keel between outside of frame and inside of planking.

Straps shall be fastened at each crossing of frame and between frames to the planking.

Deck Straps

Material, Width, Thickness: Same as hull straps.

Deck to be fitted with 2 diagonal straps at each mast, extending from gunwale to gunwale between top of deck beam and under side of deck and not cut by deck openings.

To be fastened at each beam crossing and between beams into deck.

Hanging Knees

Material: Wood, cast bronze, steel, or bronze plate flanged to frames or deck beams.

Length of Arms: 1.75 times table frame spacing.

Shall be fitted to all belt frames, all extra heavy frames, and partner beams.

Plank Fastenings

Material: Wood screws of noncorrosive metal.

Length: Twice the plank thickness from heel to turn of bilge; from turn of bilge to head may be shortened to suit molding of frame.

Size:

Plank Thickness	Gauge No.	Plank Thickness	Guage No.
5⁄8″	9	1½″	20
¾″	10	1¾″	22
⅞″	12	2″	24
1″	14	2¼″	26
1⅛″	16	2½″	28
1¼″	18		

Should other type of fastening be used—such as bolts, rivets, or drift fasten-ings—they shall be of equal cross-sectional area to those in the table for wood screws, and of suitable length.

Lead Keel Bolts

Material: Bronze, having a tensile strength of not less than 60,000 pounds per square inch.

The number and size to be sufficient to give not less than 1 square inch of sectional area of bolt for 1500 pounds of outside ballast.

Nevins' Table for Size and Spacing of Frames, Deck Beams, and Planking

$\sqrt[3]{Disp.\ cu.\ ft.}$	Planking Thickness In.	FRAMES			Deck Beam Area Sq. In.
		Area Sq. In.	Siding and Molding In.	Spacing In.	
3.8	0.56	0.65	0.81	6.03	0.75
4.0	0.56	0.65	0.81	6.03	0.75
4.2	0.59	0.75	0.87	6.30	0.88
4.4	0.62	0.86	0.93	6.58	1.03
4.6	0.66	1.00	1.00	6.84	1.18
4.8	0.69	1.13	1.07	7.12	1.33
5.0	0.72	1.28	1.13	7.38	1.49
5.2	0.75	1.43	1.20	7.64	1.65
5.4	0.79	1.60	1.27	7.91	1.81
5.6	0.82	1.80	1.34	8.18	1.98
5.8	0.86	1.98	1.41	8.44	2.15
6.0	0.90	2.20	1.48	8.70	2.33
6.2	0.93	2.40	1.55	8.97	2.50
6.4	0.96	2.61	1.62	9.22	2.67
6.6	1.00	2.83	1.69	9.49	2.85
6.8	1.04	3.10	1.76	9.73	3.03
7.0	1.08	3.34	1.83	10.00	3.22
7.2	1.12	3.59	1.90	10.25	3.42
7.4	1.15	3.84	1.96	10.50	3.62
7.6	1.18	4.12	2.03	10.75	3.82
7.8	1.22	4.40	2.10	11.00	4.02
8.0	1.25	4.70	2.17	11.25	4.22

$\sqrt[3]{Disp.\ cu.\ ft.}$	Planking Thickness In.	FRAMES			Deck Beam Area Sq. In.
		Area Sq. In.	Siding and Molding In.	Spacing In.	
8.2	1.29	5.00	2.24	11.50	4.43
8.4	1.32	5.30	2.30	11.75	4.64
8.6	1.36	5.60	2.34	12.00	4.86
8.8	1.40	5.90	2.43	12.25	5.09
9.0	1.43	6.23	2.50	12.50	5.32
9.2	1.46	6.53	2.56	12.75	5.55
9.4	1.50	6.89	2.63	13.00	5.78
9.6	1.53	7.22	2.69	13.23	6.02
9.8	1.56	7.58	2.76	13.47	6.27
10.0	1.60	7.92	2.82	13.72	6.53
10.2	1.63	8.30	2.88	13.95	6.79
10.4	1.66	8.70	2.95	14.20	7.05
10.6	1.70	9.10	3.02	14.44	7.31
10.8	1.73	9.50	3.09	14.68	7.58
11.0	1.76	9.92	3.15	14.92	7.85
11.2	1.80	10.36	3.22	15.16	8.12
11.4	1.83	10.80	3.29	15.40	8.41
11.6	1.86	11.29	3.36	15.63	8.70
11.8	1.90	11.78	3.44	15.88	9.00
12.0	1.93	12.30	3.51	16.12	9.30
12.2	1.96	12.80	3.58	16.35	9.60
12.4	1.99	13.31	3.65	16.60	9.91
12.6	2.02	13.87	3.73	16.83	10.22
12.8	2.05	14.42	3.80	17.07	10.53
13.0	2.09	15.00	3.88	17.31	10.84
13.2	2.12	15.55	3.95	17.55	11.16
13.4	2.15	16.14	4.02	17.80	11.49
13.6	2.18	16.74	4.09	18.03	11.82
13.8	2.22	17.33	4.16	18.28	12.16
14.0	2.25	17.95	4.24	18.50	12.60
14.2	2.28	18.60	4.32	18.75	12.84
14.4	2.31	19.20	4.39	19.00	13.18
14.6	2.34	19.87	4.46	19.22	13.52
14.8	2.37	20.50	4.53	19.45	13.86
15.0	2.40	21.12	4.60	19.70	14.21
15.2	2.43	21.80	4.67	19.95	14.58
15.4	2.46	22.50	4.75	20.18	14.95
15.6	2.50	23.17	4.82	20.42	15.31
15.8	2.53	23.90	4.89	20.65	15.68
16.0	2.55	24.60	4.96	20.88	16.05
16.2	2.58	25.30	5.03	21.12	16.43
16.4	2.60	26.00	5.10	21.36	16.80

Rules and Regulations for the Classification of Yachts and Small Craft
(© Lloyd's Register of Shipping, 1979)

These rules have terms that North American builders may not recognize. For this reason, diagrams are included to help with what is only a translation problem. Many of the timber species mentioned are described in Appendix A.

Wood and Composite

SECTION 1
Materials

1.1   Timber species
1.1.1   The species of timber which may be used for the various constructional members, *see* Figs. 4.1.1 and 4.1.2, are given in Tables 4.1.1 and 4.1.2. A general indication of their known performance in service has been indicated, but in view of the differences in construction methods and in the use of the craft, design considerations may influence the selection of species.

1.1.2   Group A are the species of timber considered to be the most suitable for the purposes set out in Table 4.1.1. Groups B and C are in descending order of preference, but within each group no attempt has been made to list the individual species in order of preference. It is presumed that the designer will relate the known characteristics, e.g. strength, density, bending and working capabilities, of particular species to the constructional design.

1.1.3   The inclusion of a timber in Table 4.1.1 and 4.1.2 does not imply that all material available under the particular name is suitable for the use shown, and care must be exercised to ensure that an appropriate grade is obtained.

1.2   Timber quality
1.2.1   The timber is to be of good quality and properly seasoned and is to be free from heart, sapwood, decay, insect attack, splits, shakes and other imperfections which would adversely affect the efficiency of the material. It is also to be generally free from knots, although an occasional sound intergrown knot would be acceptable.

1.2.2   The timber for the centreline members is to be reasonably seasoned and, where there is a risk of excessive drying-out, it is to be coated with boiled linseed oil or varnish, as soon as erected, to prevent splitting.

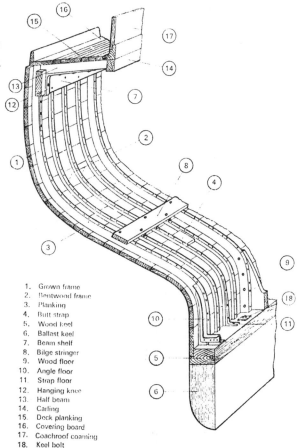

1. Grown frame
2. Bentwood frame
3. Planking
4. Butt strap
5. Wood keel
6. Ballast keel
7. Beam shelf
8. Bilge stringer
9. Wood floor
10. Angle floor
11. Strap floor
12. Hanging knee
13. Half beam
14. Carling
15. Deck planking
16. Covering board
17. Coachroof coaming
18. Keel bolt

Fig. 4.1.1   Midship section of a sailing or auxiliary craft showing terms used in these Rules

Table 4.1.1 Guidance on the selection of timbers for constructional members (*see continuation*)

Timber species	Average density air-dried, kg/m³	Keel and false keel	Dead-wood	Stem	Stern-post	Bilge and chine stringer	Beam shelf, stringer and clamp	Floors	Frames		Hull planking	
									Grown	Bent-wood	Below water-line	Above water-line
Afrormosia	690	B	B	B	B	—	—	B	B	—	—	—
Afzelia	815	B	B	—	B	—	—	—	—	—	B	B
Agba	515	—	—	—	—	—	—	—	B†	—	C	B
Cedar, Western Red	385	—	—	—	—	—	—	—	—	—	—	—
Douglas Fir	530	—	—	—	—	C	C	—	—	—	C	C
Elm, English	545	B	B	B	B	—	—	—	—	—	—	—
Elm, Rock	705	—	—	—	—	B	B	—	—	A*	—	—
Elm, Wych	670	B	B	B	B	—	—	—	—	—	—	—
Guarea	580	—	—	—	—	—	—	—	—	B	B	—
Gurjun	735	C	C	C	C	—	—	C	C	—	—	C
Ipil	720	—	—	—	—	—	—	—	B	A	—	—
Iroko	640	—	—	—	—	—	B	A	A	—	A	A
Kapur	735	B	B	B	B	B	B	B	B	—	B	B
Keruing	735	C	C	C	C	—	—	C	C	—	B	C
Keyaki	625	B	B	B	B	—	—	B	B	—	—	—
Larch	560	—	—	—	—	B	B	—	B†	—	B	C
Mahogany, African	530	C	C	C	C	C	C	C	B†	—	C	B
Mahogany, Honduras	545	B	B	B	B	—	—	B	—	—	B	B
Makore	625	B	B	B	B	—	—	B	B	—	—	—
Oak, American White	770	B	B	B	B	B	B	B	B*	A*	B	B
Oak, English	720	B	B	B	B	—	B	B	B*	A*	C	—
Opepe	735	B	B	B	B	—	—	C	—	—	C	C
Pine, Pitch	705	—	—	—	—	—	B	—	—	—	A	B
Redwood, European	515	—	—	—	—	C	C	—	—	—	C	C
Robinia	720	B	B	B	B	—	—	B	B	B	—	—
Sapele	625	C	C	C	C	C	C	—	C	—	C	C
Spruce, Sitka	450	—	—	—	—	C	C	—	—	—	C	C
Teak	655	A	A	A	A	A	A	A	A	—	A	A
Utile	655	—	—	—	—	—	—	—	—	—	A	A
Yacal	990	B	B	B	B	B	B	B	B	—	—	—
Yang	735	C	C	C	C	—	—	C	C	—	B	C

Beam and frame timbers marked * are suitable in both the natural and laminated form. Those marked † are suitable only when laminated.

Table 4.1.1 Guidance on the selection of timbers for constructional members (*conclusion*)

| Deck planking | Beams and carlings | Knees | | Covering boards, kingplanks and margins | Natural durability | Resistance to impregnation | Ease of gluing | Timber species |
		Hanging	Lodging					
—	B	B	B	B	Very durable	Extremely resistant	Satisfactory	Afrormosia
—	—	—	—	—	Very durable	Extremely resistant	Satisfactory	Afzelia
B	—	—	—	—	Durable	Resistant	Satisfactory	Agba
C	—	—	—	—	Durable	Resistant	Satisfactory	Cedar, Western Red
B	B	—	—	—	Moderately durable	Resistant	Satisfactory	Douglas Fir
—	—	—	—	—	Non-durable	Moderately resistant	Satisfactory	Elm, English
—	—	C	C	—	Non-durable	Resistant	Satisfactory	Elm, Rock
—	—	—	—	—	Non-durable	Resistant	Satisfactory	Elm, Wych
—	—	—	—	—	Durable	Extremely resistant	Satisfactory	Guarea
—	—	—	—	—	Moderately durable	Resistant	Satisfactory	Gurjun
—	—	—	—	—	Moderately durable	Resistant	Satisfactory	Ipil
A	—	—	—	A	Very durable	Extremely resistant	Satisfactory	Iroko
B	B	B	B	B	Very durable	Extremely resistant	Satisfactory	Kapur
—	—	—	—	—	Moderately durable	Resistant	Satisfactory	Keruing
—	—	B	B	—	Durable	Resistant	Satisfactory	Keyaki
—	B	B	B	—	Moderately durable	Resistant	Satisfactory	Larch
B	B†	—	—	C	Moderately durable	Extremely resistant	Satisfactory	Mahogany, African
—	B†	—	—	B	Durable	Extremely resistant	Satisfactory	Mahogany, Honduras
—	B†	—	—	—	Very durable	Extremely resistant	Satisfactory	Makore
—	B*	B	A	B	Durable	Extremely resistant	Satisfactory	Oak, American White
—	B*	B	A	B	Durable	Extremely resistant	Satisfactory	Oak, English
B	—	—	—	C	Very durable	Moderately resistant	Satisfactory	Opepe
B	B	—	—	—	Moderately durable	Moderately resistant	Variable	Pine, Pitch
C	—	—	—	—	Non-durable	Moderately resistant	Satisfactory	Redwood, European
—	—	—	—	—	Durable	Extremely resistant	Satisfactory	Robinia
—	—	—	—	—	Moderately durable	Resistant	Satisfactory	Sapele
C	C*	—	—	—	Non-durable	Resistant	Good	Spruce, Sitka
A	A	A	A	A	Very durable	Extremely resistant	Satisfactory	Teak
A	—	—	—	—	Durable	Extremely resistant	Satisfactory	Utile
—	—	B	B	—	Very durable	Extremely resistant	Satisfactory	Yacal
—	—	—	—	—	Moderately durable	Resistant	Satisfactory	Yang

1.2.3 The material for hull and deck planking is to be generally straight grained and, for deck planking, is to be quarter sawn.

1.3 Timber moisture content

1.3.1 The timber is to be stored under dry conditions and is to have an air-dried moisture content of not more than about 20 per cent before use. Care is to be taken to avoid excessive drying-out during building.

1.3.2 The moisture content of material which is to be glued is to be about 15 per cent. Contents slightly above this value are recommended when resorcinal glues are used, and contents slightly below this value are recommended when phenolic or urea-formaldehyde resins are used. It is recommended that the material to be used in laminating members should be kiln-dried to about 15 per cent.

1.3.3 The moisture content of hull and deck planking which is to be sheathed using synthetic resins is to be as low as practicable, to avoid affecting the efficiency of the sheathing bond.

1.4 Plywood

1.4.1 The plywood used in the hull and deck structure is to be of an approved high grade marine quality with good quality face and core veneers of a durable hardwood species and made with high standards of workmanship in the lay-up and manufacture. The veneers are to be bonded with a **WBP** (water and boil proof) type adhesive, although in special circumstances an adhesive of slightly lesser durability will be considered. Material complying with BS 1088, or other equivalent specification, is acceptable.

1.4.2 Other plywood may also be of quality and standard similar to that of the material in 1.4.1, but may be made from a less durable timber species which has been treated with a wood preservative. The timber is to be of a species which can be satisfactorily treated. The preservative is to be of a tar-oil, waterborne or other suitable type, and is to be applied in accordance with a recognized standard at either the veneer stage or after manufacture. Plywood complying with BS 3842 for treated plywoods for marine use, or equivalent specification, is acceptable. Treatments TO 1, WB 1 and WB 2, or similar, may be used on material of acceptable quality and standard.

1.4.3 Timber species suitable for marine plywood and their durability are given in Table 4.1.3. Timbers of species other than those specified may be used subject to approval.

1.4.4 Plywood sheets are to be stored flat on a level bed and under dry, well ventilated conditions. The moisture content is not to exceed 15 per cent.

1.5 Timber preservatives

1.5.1 Preservatives are to be of suitable types, either from the waterborne fixed salt group such as copper chrome type to BS 3452 and copper-chrome-arsenic types to BS 3453, or from the organic solvent group, such as naphthenates of zinc and copper and pentachlorophenol. Other types of preservatives will be considered.

1.5.2 In the selection of type of preservative, due regard should be paid to the effect on varnish and paint coatings, and on synthetic resins, where sheathing is to be applied.

1.6 Timber adhesives

1.6.1 The glues to be used in the construction and lamination of structural members are to be of a type approved by the Society and of a gap-filling resorcinol or phenolic type, such as those complying with BS 1204 WBP, or other adhesives which have similar durability and can give a WBP bond.

1.6.2 Modified urea-formaldehydes may be used as described in 2.4.2.

1.6.3 The glues are to be mixed and applied in accordance with the manufacturer's instructions with regard to the shop temperature and humidity requirements. Attention is also to be paid to the application techniques for the species of timber being glued, and the manufacturer's advice should be sought in the working of difficult timbers and the effect of preservatives on the adhesive.

1.7 Metal fastenings

1.7.1 The materials used for fastenings are to be a suitable composition of the following metals:—
    Copper
    Gunmetal
    Galvanized iron
    Galvanized steel
    Silicon bronze
    Aluminium bronze
    Stainless steel
    Monel

Table 4.1.2 Suitable timbers for moulded hull construction

Species	Group	Average density air-dried, kg/m³
Agba	B	515
Cedar, Central American	B	485
Cedar, Honduras	A	485
Mahogany, African	A	530
Mahogany, Honduras	A	545
Makore	A	625

NOTES
1. For grouping of timbers, *see* 1.1.2.
2. *See also* Notes to Table 4.1.1.

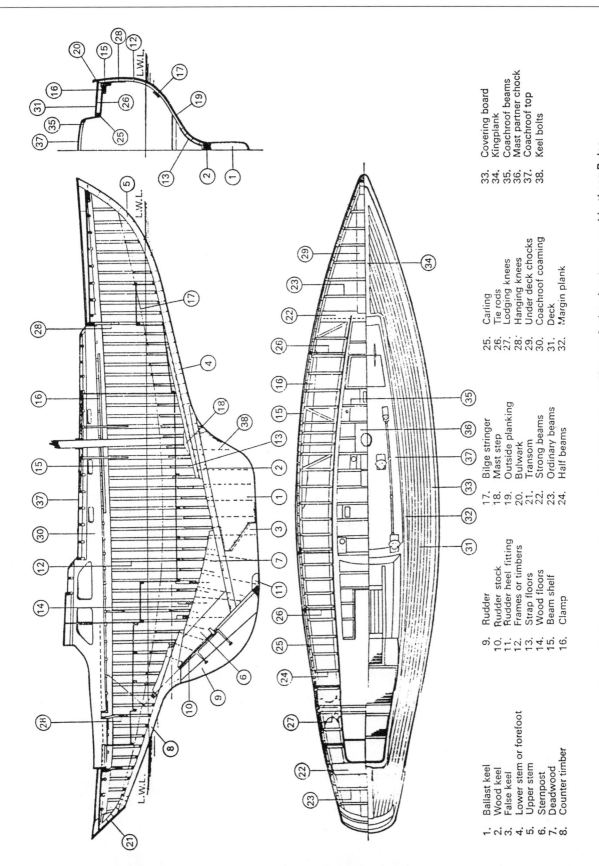

1. Ballast keel
2. Wood keel
3. False keel
4. Lower stem or forefoot
5. Upper stem
6. Sternpost
7. Deadwood
8. Counter timber
9. Rudder
10. Rudder stock
11. Rudder heel fitting
12. Frames or timbers
13. Strap floors
14. Wood floors
15. Beam shelf
16. Clamp
17. Bilge stringer
18. Mast step
19. Outside planking
20. Bulwark
21. Transom
22. Strong beams
23. Ordinary beams
24. Half beams
25. Carling
26. Tie rods
27. Lodging knees
28. Hanging knees
29. Under deck chocks
30. Coachroof coaming
31. Deck
32. Margin plank
33. Covering board
34. Kingplank
35. Coachroof beams
36. Mast partner chock
37. Coachroof top
38. Keel bolts

Fig. 4.1.2   Typical construction profile and deck of an auxiliary craft showing terms used in these Rules

Table 4.1.3 Guidance on the selection of timbers for use in marine plywood

Common name	Botanical name	Density at 15 per cent moisture content, kg/m³	Natural durability of heartwood
Durable hardwood timbers in natural state			
Agba	*Gossweilerodendron balsamiferum*	500	Durable
Gedu Nohor	*Entandrophragma angolense*	540	Moderately durable
Guarea	*Guarea spp.*	580	Durable
Idigbo	*Terminalia ivorensis*	540	Durable
African Mahogany	*Khaya spp.*	500	Moderately durable
Makore	*Mimusops heckelii*	620	Very durable
Omu	*Entandrophragma candollei*	620	Moderately durable
Light Red Meranti Light Red Seraya	*Shorea spp.* (see Note 2)	530	Moderately durable
Sapele	*Entandrophragma cylindricum*	620	Moderately durable
Utile	*Entandrophragma utile*	660	Durable
Timbers requiring preservative treatment			
Douglas Fir	*Pseudotsuga taxifolia*	530	Moderately durable
Gaboon/ Okoume	*Aucomea klaineana*	430	Non-durable

NOTES
1. It should be noted that behaviour towards marine borers and insects, including termites, is not equated to this durability scale.
2. Because of reduced durability, the use of *Shorea spp.* below the density quoted is not recommended unless it is treated with a preservative.

1.7.2   Steel and iron fastenings are to be hot-dipped galvanized, but black iron keel bolts may be coated with a suitable composition. Small screw fastenings below about 20 mm in length which cannot be satisfactorily hot-dipped may be electroplated zinc, provided that the coating is of a reasonable thickness and to an approved specification, such as BS 1706: 1960 Grade Zn 10.

1.7.3   Stainless steel fastenings are to be of a suitable grade of austenitic steel.

1.7.4   Gunmetal fastenings may be used, but where increased strength and corrosion resistance is desired it is recommended that silicon bronze be used. Aluminium bronze may be used, in the larger bolt sizes, where increased strength is desired. Brass fastenings are not to be used for structural purposes.

1.7.5   Ballast keel fastenings are to be in accordance with Ch 6,4.2.

1.8   Other materials

1.8.1   Other materials intended for structural use are to be of good quality, suitable for the purpose intended and to comply with the Society's requirements appropriate to the material. Details of these materials are to be stated on the relevant construction drawings.

1.8.2   Suitable arrangements are to be made to insulate aluminium alloys from timber and dissimilar metals. Paints containing either lead, mercury or copper are not to be used in conjunction with these alloys.

● End of Section

SECTION 2

Construction procedure

2.1   Workshop requirements

2.1.1   The craft is to be suitably protected during the building period from adverse weather and climatic conditions. The minimum protection to be provided is normally a substantial and efficient roof projecting beyond the length and breadth of the craft. Where laminated glued construction is being extensively used, a building shed with controlled temperature and humidity levels may be required.

2.1.2   Workmanship is to be well executed and carried out under adequate supervision throughout the preparation and building of the craft. The various parts of the structure are to be properly faired and fitted.

2.2   Preservative treatment

2.2.1   The faying surfaces of frames, beams, stringers, floors and shelves are to be treated with one of the types of timber preservative indicated in 1.5.

2.2.2   The preservatives are preferably to be applied by dipping and soaking or by pneumatic spray but where these methods are not practicable a liberal application by brush can be used. The timber is to be treated when all work on the member is complete, but where cut or bored after treatment a liberal brush application is to be applied to the exposed timber.

2.3 Plywood

2.3.1 All edges and cut-out areas are to be throughly sealed by glues, varnishes, paints or other suitable compositions to prevent moisture penetrating along the end-grain.

2.4 Gluing process

2.4.1 The timber is to be clean and dry, and the joining surfaces are to be properly prepared and free from dust and grease. The adhesive, complying with 1.6, is to be evenly applied and the joint closed within the manufacturer's recommended closing time in order to obtain a thin and uniform glue line. Sufficient clamps and other pressure devices are to be used and the pressure is not to be released until the joint has set.

2.4.2 Modified urea-formaldehydes may be used in parts of the structure which will not be commonly subjected to continuously wet conditions and will be well ventilated. These parts include the coachroof and superstructures in both wood and plywood craft and internal structural assemblies which are clear of the bilges in plywood craft only. The glue lines in these structures are to be protected by several applications of varnish or paint.

2.4.3 The glues are to be mixed and applied in accordance with the manufacturer's instructions and with due regard to the shop temperature and humidity requirements. Due attention is to be paid to the application techniques for the species of timber being glued and the manufacturer's advice should be sought in the working of difficult timbers and the effect of preservatives on the materials.

2.5 Laminated timbers

2.5.1 The layers forming the lamination are generally to be of the same timber species and are to be of an even moisture content. The grain of the layers is to be approximately parallel to the length of the member, and special attention is to be paid to grain in the selection and assembly of the timber.

2.5.2 Where practicable the layers are to be continuous, and if this is not possible, the layers are to be scarph jointed, the slope of the scarph being not greater than 1 in 10.

2.5.3 Where the layers are bent to produce members of curved form, the thickness of each layer is to be such that the layer will not be unduly stressed in forming, and that a satisfactory interlaminar bond can be achieved.

2.5.4 The glues are to be resorcinol or phenolic resorcinol types complying with 1.6 and are to be applied in accordance with 2.4.

2.6 Fastening practice

2.6.1 Attention is to be paid to the fastenings throughout, particularly the size and disposition. The boring of the timber to receive the fastenings is to be properly executed, according to the density of the timber and the type and material of the fastening.

2.6.2 All hull and deck through-fastenings are to be of a composition similar to that of any metal members they secure. Where this cannot be arranged, suitable insulation is to be fitted to prevent contact between dissimilar metals.

2.6.3 Where craft are sheathed with copper or other non-ferrous metals, iron or steel fastenings are not to be used in way.

2.6.4 Through bolts are to be clenched on rings or washers or are to be fitted with nuts. Nuts, rings or washers are to be of the same material as the bolts.

2.6.5 Short dump or nail fastenings are to be of the same sectional areas as required by Table 4.9.2 for bolt fastenings.

2.6.6 Where bolt fastenings pass through the outside planking or centreline structure, cotton or other suitable grommets are to be fitted under the heads. Keel bolt and centreline fastening holes are to be treated with a suitable composition.

2.6.7 Copper through fastenings are to be clenched on rooves.

2.6.8 Where screw fastenings are used, the thread of the screw must enter the frame or beam a minimum distance equal to the thickness of the hull or deck planking.

2.6.9 Approved countersunk barbed headed nails may be used in lieu of screw fastenings. The size of the nails is to be the same as that required for screws. The Owner's attention must be drawn to the use of these barbed nails in view of difficulties which may arise should it be necessary to withdraw them.

● End of Section

SECTION 3

Determination of scantlings

3.1 General

3.1.1 The scantlings of motor, sailing and auxiliary craft of conventional form and proportions, up to a length of 30 m are to be determined from Tables 4.4.1, 4.5.1, 4.6.1, 4.6.2, 4.7.1, 4.8.1, 4.9.1 to 4.9.4, 4.10.1 to 4.10.3 and 4.12.1 and 4.12.2.

3.1.2 The scantlings will be specially considered where the craft is of unusual design, form or proportions or where either the speed exceeds 20 knots or the length, L, exceeds 30 m.

3.2   Timber density

3.2.1   The scantlings for the timber members shown in Tables 4.4.1, 4.5.1, 4.6.1, 4.7.1, 4.9.1, 4.10.1, 4.12.1 and 4.12.2 are based on the following standard densities, which are for an air-dried condition of about 15 per cent moisture content:—

$$\left.\begin{array}{l}\text{Frames}\\\text{Floors}\end{array}\right\} \quad 720 \text{ kg/m}^3$$

$$\left.\begin{array}{l}\text{Keel}\\\text{Stem}\\\text{Sternpost}\\\text{Deadwood}\\\text{Counter timbers}\end{array}\right\} \quad 640 \text{ kg/m}^3$$

$$\left.\begin{array}{l}\text{Hull planking}\\\text{Shelves and clamps}\\\text{Stringers}\\\text{Beams and knees}\\\text{Coachroof coamings}\end{array}\right\} \quad 560 \text{ kg/m}^3$$

Deck planking 430 kg/m^3

3.2.2   Where the density of the proposed timber differs from the standard density shown in 3.2.1, the tabular siding, s, thickness or modulus, sm^2, is to be increased or decreased by direct proportion in relation to the ratio of the densities, i.e.

Required siding, thickness or modulus =

$$\text{Tabular siding, thickness or modulus} \times \frac{S}{W}$$

where S = the standard density of the timber, in kg/m³
        W = the density of the proposed timber, in kg/m³
        m = the tabular moulding.

The tabular siding or thickness is, however, not to be decreased by more than 6 per cent, except where specifically allowed.

3.2.3   The scantlings of laminate members are to be based on the density of the natural timber and are not to be corrected for the final density in the laminated condition.

3.3   Laminated timber scantlings

3.3.1   Where the centreline assembly, bilge stringers, beam shelves, chines, frames or beams are of glued laminated construction, the scantlings are to be the same as those determined for solid timber, with the exception of frames and beams as indicated in 5.3.1 and 10.1.3, respectively.

● End of Section

SECTION 4
Centreline structure

4.1   Wood keel

4.1.1   The scantlings of wood keels or, for motor craft, the wood keel and hog are given in Table 4.4.1. The Rule moulding is to be maintained throughout but the siding may be tapered towards the ends where it is to be not less than the Rule siding of the stem or sternpost. The scantlings of craft having deep fin keels will be specially considered.

4.1.2   The rabbet for the garboard strake is to have a faying surface not less than twice the thickness of the garboard strake or, for plywood, as given in Table 4.9.3.

4.1.3   When the length, L, does not exceed 10 m the wood keel is to be in one length. In larger craft, the keel should, where possible, be in one length but when a scarph is necessary in the centreline structure it is to have a length, l, not less than 6 times the moulding, m, of the item. The scarph is to be of the hooked or tabled type if bolted (*see* Fig. 4.4.1), or plain type without lips if glued. The depth of the lips is to be about $\frac{1}{4}$ to $\frac{1}{3}$ of the moulding.

4.1.4   Softwood stopwaters are to be fitted in bolted scarphs in keels and other centreline structure, in way of plank back rabbet and in other positions where considered necessary by the Surveyor. For typical details, *see* Figs. 4.4.2 and 4.4.4.

4.1.5   Scarphs in the keel and hog are to be at least 1,5 m apart and the keel scarph, where fitted, is to be clear of engine seating and, if practicable, of the mast step.

4.1.6   Where the keel is cut for a centreboard the siding is to be increased.

4.1.7   Where a mast passes through the deck, the heel is to be supported by a suitable mast step extending well forward and aft. The step is to be adequately fastened to the floors and to the wood keel.

4.1.8   Where a wood false keel is fitted abaft the ballast keel a suitable scarph or tenon is to be arranged. *See* Fig. 4.4.3.

4.1.9   For size of fastenings, *see* Table 4.4.1.

4.1.10   Structural arrangements in way of centreboard casing will be specially considered.

4.1.11   For ballast keel and fitting internal ballast, *see* Ch 6,4.

4.2   Stem

4.2.1   The scantlings of the stem are given in Table 4.4.1 and are to be uniformly tapered from head to heel. The scantlings at the heel may be required to be increased, depending on the shape of the forefoot, to enable an adequate scarph to the keel to be arranged. *See* Fig. 4.4.4.

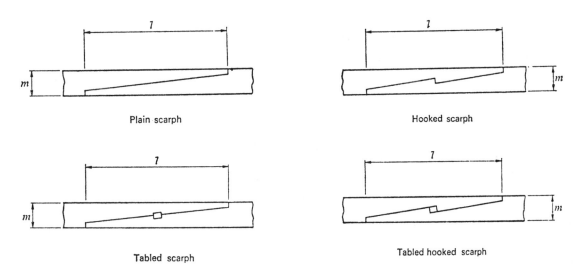

Plain scarph

Hooked scarph

Tabled scarph

Tabled hooked scarph

Fig. 4.4.1 Common types of bolted scarphed joints

Table 4.4.1 Keel, hog, stem, sternpost and fastenings for motor, sailing and auxiliary craft

Length, L, m	Moulding and siding of keel				Siding and moulding of stem at heel, mm		Siding and moulding of stem at head and sternpost, mm		Diameter of bolts, mm, in	
	Sailing and auxiliary		Motor							
	Moulding, mm	Siding, mm	Minimum siding of keel, mm	Sectional area of keel or keel and hog, cm²	Sailing and auxiliary	Motor	Sailing and auxiliary	Motor	Centreline structure	Keel scarph
6	75	150	70	80	90	75	75	75	10	8
8	90	185	80	130	105	90	90	85	10	8
10	110	220	90	190	120	110	100	95	12	8
12	125	255	105	250	140	125	115	105	14	10
14	140	285	115	310	155	140	125	115	14	12
16	160	320	125	380	170	160	140	125	16	12
18	175	355	140	450	190	175	150	140	18	12
20	195	385	150	520	205	195	165	150	20	14
22	210	410	165	600	220	210	175	160	20	14
24	230	435	180	690	240	230	190	170	20	14
26	245	455	190	770	255	245	200	180	20	14
28	260	470	205	860	270	260	215	190	20	16
30	280	480	220	950	290	280	230	200	22	18

NOTES

1. In motor craft, the moulding of the keel is to be not less than the siding, and the moulding of the hog is to be not less than twice the thickness of the outside planking.

2. The Table scantlings are based on a timber having a standard density of 640 kg/m³ and where timber of a different density is to be used the scantlings are to be modified in accordance with 3.2.2.

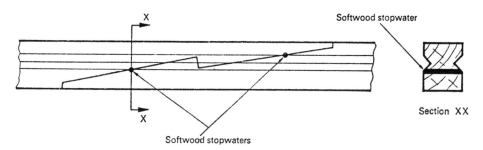

Fig. 4.4.2   Typical hooked keel scarph showing position of stopwaters

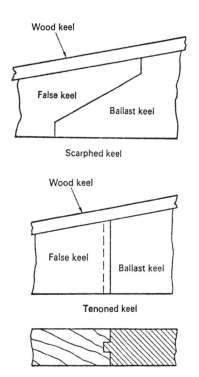

Scarphed keel

Tenoned keel

Fig. 4.4.3   Typical connections of ballast keel to false keel

4.2.2   Where the hull form is such that there is a large radius at the stem head a suitable apron (or fashion pieces) is to be provided to give adequate landing for the outside planking.

4.2.3   For size of fastenings, *see* Table 4.4.1.

4.3   Sternpost
4.3.1   The scantlings of the sternpost are given in Table 4.4.1. The sternpost may be tapered to suit the form of the craft but the siding at the after edge of the back rabbet is to be not less than that required by Table 4.4.1 and care is to be taken to ensure there is adequate material to take the fastenings of the outside planking.

4.3.2   The lower end of the sternpost is to be tenoned or half-lapped to the keel. An inside deadwood or knee is to be fitted and adequately through fastened to the sternpost, and false keel, if fitted. *See* Fig. 4.4.5.

4.3.3   For size of fastenings, *see* Table 4.4.1.

4.4   Counter timber
4.4.1   The area of the counter timber at its forward end is to be not less than the Rule area of the sternpost and may gradually be reduced to 75 per cent of this area at its after end.

4.4.2   The counter timber is to be securely fastened to the sternpost and it is recommended that, where practicable, the sternpost should be tenoned or scarphed to the counter timber and through fastened.

4.4.3   For size of fastenings, *see* Table 4.4.1.

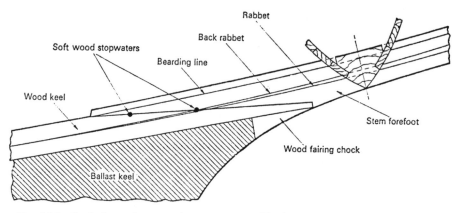

Fig. 4.4.4   Typical scarph connecting stem to wood keel

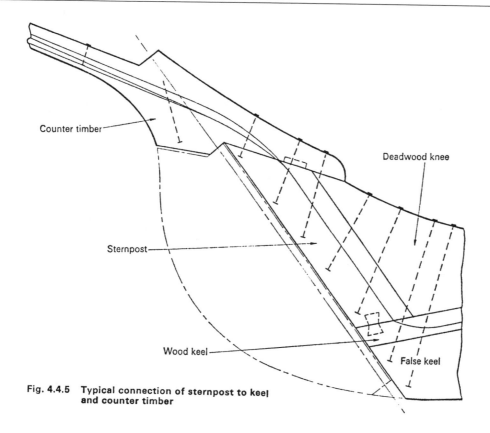

Counter timber

Deadwood knee

Sternpost

Wood keel

False keel

Fig. 4.4.5 Typical connection of sternpost to keel and counter timber

● End of Section

SECTION 5

Framing

5.1 General

5.1.1 The hull is to be provided with an efficient system of side and bottom framing in conjunction with stringers, bulkheads or web frames to provide transverse ridigity.

5.1.2 The framing may be arranged transversely or longitudinally or may be a combination of both.

5.1.3 All frames are to be bevelled or formed to fay closely against the planking.

5.1.4 Where the heels of frames terminate at the centre-line construction members they are to be let into and fastened to them unless floors are fitted at every frame.

5.2 Types of frames

5.2.1 The following types of frames may be used, subject to the limitations given in 5.2.3 and 5.2.4:—

Type 1   Bent frames only

Type 2   Grown frames only

Type 3   Laminated frames only

Type 4   Steel frames only

Type 5   Grown, laminated or steel frames with 1 bent frame between

Type 6   Grown, laminated or steel frames with 2 bent frames between

Type 7   Grown, laminated or steel frames with 3 bent frames between

5.2.2 Alternative framing systems to those in 5.2.1 will be specially considered.

5.2.3 The use of Type 1 is to be confined to craft having a depth, D, not exceeding 3,0 m for sailing and auxiliary or 2,7 m for motor craft, and Types 5, 6 and 7 are to be confined to depths, D, not exceeding 3,6 m and 3,0 m, respectively.

5.2.4 Where the depth, D, exceeds 3,6 m for sailing and auxiliary craft or 3,0 m for motor craft the framing must be Type 2, 3 or 4.

5.3 Scantlings

5.3.1 The scantlings and spacing of the various types of frames are given in Table 4.5.1.

5.3.2 Where the actual frame spacing of timber frames differs from that given in Table 4.5.1 the strength of grown, bent or laminated frames is to be modified in direct proportion, i.e.

$$\text{Actual } (sm^2) = \text{Table } (sm^2) \times \frac{\text{actual spacing}}{\text{Table spacing}}$$

where s and m are the siding and moulding, respectively; the Table siding is to be that after correction for density. *See* 3.2.2.

5.3.3 In no case is the mean moulding of grown, bent or laminated frames to be less than two-thirds of the actual siding except where an increase in the siding is required by 5.3.6. In all cases the siding is to be suitable for the required fastenings.

5.3.4 Where the spacing of steel frames differs from that given in Table 4.5.1 the section modulus is to be modified in direct proportion.

5.3.5 The scantlings determined from Table 4.5.1 are to be maintained for $\frac{3}{8}L$ amidships. Forward of and abaft this region the following reductions may be made:—

Bent or laminated frames	Siding reduced by 10 per cent.
Grown frames	Moulding at heel and siding at head and heel reduced by 20 per cent.
Steel frames	Thickness reduced by 10 per cent.

5.3.6 In sailing and auxiliary craft the framing adjacent to the mast is to be increased each side as given below or equivalent arrangements provided:—

Type 1: Bent frames only — Three grown or laminated frames of Type 2 or 3 scantlings (*see* Table 4.5.1) are to be fitted or, alternatively, the siding of three bent frames increased by 60 per cent.

Type 2: Grown frames only
Type 3: Laminated frames only — The siding of three frames increased by 50 per cent.

Table 4.5.1   Frames for motor, sailing and auxiliary craft (*see continuation*)

Depth, *D*, m		Type 1 Bent wood frames only			Type 2 Grown frames only				Type 3 Laminated frames only		
Motor	Sailing and auxiliary	Siding,	Moulding,	Frame spacing,	Siding,	Moulding, mm at heel	at head	Frame spacing,	Siding,	Moulding,	Frame spacing,
		mm	mm	mm	mm	mm	mm	mm	mm	mm	mm
1,5	1,8	24	19	155	24	31	24	205	25	25	205
1,8	2,1	34	25	170	34	40	31	230	31	34	230
2,1	2,4	40	30	185	42	50	37	255	37	43	255
2,4	2,7	48	36	200	52	61	46	280	43	51	280
2,7	3,0	56	40	215	62	74	55	305	50	61	305
3,0	3,3	65	45	230	72	87	65	330	57	74	330
3,3	3,6	—	—	—	81	100	80	355	62	87	355
3,6	3,9	—	—	—	90	117	98	380	69	105	380
3,9	4,2	—	—	—	100	140	117	405	78	126	405

NOTES

1. For limitation on use of Types 1, 5, 6 and 7, *see* 5.2.3 and 5.2.4.
2. The Table scantlings of timber frames are based on a timber having a standard density of 720 kg/m³, and where timber of a different density is to be used the scantlings are to be modified in accordance with 3.2.2.
3. The frame spacing given in the Table is measured from centre to centre or, for steel frames, from heel to heel of angles.

Type 4:   Steel frames only

Reverse angles or face flats of the size required for plate floors are to be fitted on two frames if *D* does not exceed 3,3 m or on three frames when *D* is 3,3 m or greater.

Types 5, 6 and 7:   Grown, laminated or steel frames with bent frames between

The siding of three grown or laminated frames increased by 50 per cent or reverse angles or face flats fitted to three steel frames.

5.3.7   Where internal ballast is fitted the frames may be required to be increased in strength.

5.4   Grown frames

5.4.1   Grown frames are to be cut to shape from timber having the required curvature of grain.

5.4.2   The siding of each grown frame is to be uniform over its length and the moulding is to be a fair taper from heel to head.

5.4.3   Grown frames may be butted or scarphed. Scarphs are to be glued and have a length not less than 6 times the siding. Where frames are butted, the butts are to be close fitted and side clamps arranged. The clamps are to have a sectional area not less than that of the frame and a length not less than 12 times the frame siding. The clamp is to be through fastened to the frame by not less than three fastenings on each side of the butt and is to fay closely to the planking.

5.5   Bent frames

5.5.1   The siding and moulding of bent frames are to be uniform over the length of the frame. Each frame is to be in one piece from keel to gunwale and, where the form is suitable, may be continuous from gunwale to gunwale.

5.6   Laminated frames

5.6.1   The timber and glue used in laminating frames are to be as required by 2.5.

5.7   Frames for cold moulded laminated hull

5.7.1   Where cold moulded laminated hull construction is adopted and the skin thickness is in accordance with 9.1.4 the spacing of the frames may be increased and the scantlings will be specially considered.

Table 4.5.1   Frames for motor, sailing and auxiliary craft (*conclusion*)

Type 4 Steel frames only			Types 5, 6 and 7 Combinations of grown, laminated and steel frames with intermediate bent wood frames					Depth, *D*, m	
Frame		Frame spacing,	Intermediate bent wood frame		Spacing of grown, laminated or steel frames, mm			Motor	Sailing and auxiliary
Scantling,	Modulus,		Siding,	Moulding,	One bent frame between Type 5	Two bent frames between Type 6	Three bent frames between Type 7		
mm	cm³	mm	mm	mm					
30 × 30 × 3	0,7	205	25	20	365	470	545	1,5	1,8
30 × 30 × 3	0,8	230	31	23	405	505	580	1,8	2,1
35 × 35 × 4	1,2	255	37	26	440	540	620	2,1	2,4
45 × 45 × 4,5	2,0	280	40	29	475	580	655	2,4	2,7
50 × 50 × 5	3,0	305	43	33	515	620	695	2,7	3,0
60 × 60 × 5,5	4,9	330	47	37	565	665	745	3,0	3,3
65 × 65 × 8	7,9	355	50	43	620	725	800	3,3	3,6
75 × 65 × 8,5	11,5	380	—	—	—	—	—	3,6	3,9
85 × 65 × 8,5	14,6	405	—	—	—	—	—	3,9	4,2

4. Where the spacing differs from that given in the Table, the value of *sm²* (or, for steel frames, the section modulus) is to be modified in direct proportion.

5. Where Types 5, 6 and 7 are adopted, the scantlings of the grown, laminated, or steel frames are to be as required for Types 2, 3 or 4, respectively.

● End of Section

SECTION 6
Floors

6.1 General

6.1.1 Wood floors are to be cut from timber having a suitable grain or may be laminated.

6.1.2 Where, at the ends, the frames are continuous across the centreline structure, floors are not required but, where practicable, the frames are to be attached to the centreline structure by two through fastenings.

6.1.3 Limber holes are to be provided in the bottom structure as required for efficient drainage of the craft.

6.2 Type of floors

6.2.1 The type of floor to be fitted is dependent on the frame type adopted as follows:—

Type 1: Bent frames only   (a) Strap floors on every frame within $\frac{3}{5}L$ amidships (on alternates if D does not exceed 2,7 m for sailing and auxiliary craft or 2,4 m for motor craft) and on every third frame forward and aft.

(b) Angle floors spaced as for strap floors in (a).

(c) Where $\frac{3}{5}L$ amidships falls within the waterline length floors are to be on alternates to end of waterline.

(d) The fitting of wood floors in association with bent frames will be specially considered.

Type 2: Grown frames only

Type 3: Laminated frames only

   (a) Wood floors on every frame.

(b) Steel floors on every frame.

(c) Strap floors on every frame.

(d) Angle floors on every frame.

Type 4: Steel frames only   (a) Steel plate floors at every frame.

Types 5 and 6: Grown, laminated or steel frames with 1 or 2 bent frames

   (a) On grown and laminated frames as for Type 2.

(b) On steel frames as for Type 4.

(c) On bent frames as for Type 1 within $\frac{3}{5}L$ amidships. If D does not exceed 2,4 m no floors are required on bent frames outside $\frac{3}{5}L$ amidships.

Type 7: Grown, laminated or steel frames with 3 bent frames

   (a) As for Types 5 and 6 but a floor as required for Type 1 is to be fitted to the middle bent frame.

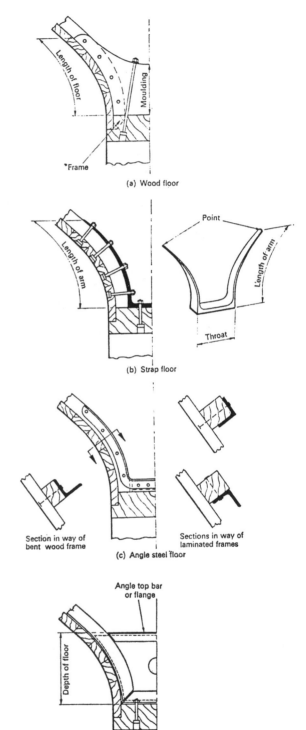

(a) Wood floor

(b) Strap floor

(c) Angle steel floor

Section in way of bent wood frame

Sections in way of laminated frames

(d) Plate floor

Fig. 4.6.1 Typical floors

*To be checked into centreline member where required by 5.1 4.

6.3 Scantlings and construction

6.3.1 The scantlings of floors are to be as given in Table 4.6.1 and the lengths of arms, etc., are to be measured as shown in Fig. 4.6.1. At the ends of the craft the length of arms need not exceed one-third the length of the frame.

6.3.2 The cross-sectional area at the ends of the arms is to be not less than half that given in Table 4.6.1 for the middle line.

6.3.3 Where bolts attaching the ballast keel pass through wood floors, the siding of the floors for the breadth of keel is to be not less than $3\frac{1}{2}$ times the bolt diameter. It may be tapered to the Rule siding at the ends of the floors.

6.3.4 Angle steel floors are to be fitted on top of bent frames and it is recommended that this arrangement be adopted when angle floors are fitted to grown frames.

6.3.5 Where angle floors are fitted to grown frames it is recommended that they be fitted so that the frame fits into the bosom of the angle with a lug fitted to take the throat fastening.

Table 4.6.2 Floor fastenings for motor, sailing and auxiliary craft

Depth, D, m		Diameter of bolts in throat, mm		Diameter of bolts at arms, mm	
Motor	Sailing and auxiliary	Grown, laminated or steel frames	Bent frames	Grown, laminated or steel frames	Bent frames
1,5	1,8	8	6	6	6
1,8	2,1	10	8	8	6
2,1	2,4	12	8	8	6
2,4	2,7	12	10	10	8
2,7	3,0	14	12	12	8
3,0	3,3	18	12	12	10
3,3	3,6	20	12	12	10
3,6	3,9	20	—	14	—
3,9	4,2	20	—	16	—

NOTES

1. Throat to keel: not less than 2 bolts (see 6.4.3).
2. Arms to frames: 3 bolts when arm length does not exceed 250 mm,
   4 bolts when arm length exceeds 250 mm.

6.3.6 Steel plate floors are to be stiffened at the upper edge with a reverse angle, face flat or a flange having the same breadth as the Rule angle. The thickness of flanged floors is to be increased by 10 per cent. The bottom angle in way of the keel is to be 2,5 mm thicker than the floor, and its flange is to be sufficient to take the ballast keel bolts or throat fastenings.

Table 4.6.1 Floors for motor, sailing and auxiliary craft

Depth, D, m		Floors on grown or laminated frames							Floors on bent wood frames				Steel plate floors on grown or steel frames, mm	
		Length of arms, mm		Strap floors, mm		Wood floors at middle line		Steel angle bars, mm	Length of arms, mm	Strap floors, mm		Steel angle bars, mm		
Motor	Sailing and auxiliary	For ¼L amidships	Beyond ¼L amidships	At throat	At point	Moulding, mm	Siding, mm			At throat	At point		For ¼L amidships	At ends beyond ¼L amidships
1,5	1,8	380	250	25×10	20×10	55	25	30×30×5	250	25×6	15×6	25×25×5	150×3	110×3
1,8	2,1	430	300	35×13	30×10	75	35	35×35×5	300	25×9	17×6	25×25×5	190×3	140×3
2,1	2,4	480	350	45×16	40×10	95	45	45×45×5	350	25×12	19×6	30×30×5	230×4	170×4
2,4	2,7	530	390	50×19	45×10	115	55	50×50×5	390	27×12	21×6	35×35×5	260×4	190×4
2,7	3,0	580	430	55×22	50×12	135	62	55×55×6	430	29×15	24×6	40×40×4	280×4	210×4
3,0	3,3	630	480	62×25	53×14	155	70	65×65×7	480	32×16	26×6	40×40×4	300×5	230×4
3,3	3,6	680	530	70×28	56×16	170	80	75×75×7	530	35×17	29×6	40×40×4	320×5	240×4
3,6	3,9	730	570	75×31	60×18	185	90	80×80×7	—	—	—	—	340×6	250×5
3,9	4,2	780	620	80×31	63×20	200	100	90×75×7	—	—	—	—	360×6	260×5

NOTE

1. The Table scantlings of timber floors are based on a timber having a standard density of 720 kg/m³ and where timber of a different density is to be used the scantlings are to be modified in accordance with 3.2.2.

6.3.7   In the machinery space of motor craft, steel plate floors are to be stiffened at the upper edge with a face flat and the thickness of the floors increased by 1 mm above that required by Table 4.6.1.

6.4   Fastenings

6.4.1   The size of the floor fastenings are to be as given in Table 4.6.2.

6.4.2   There are to be not less than three fastenings in each arm where the length of arm does not exceed 250 mm or four when the arm is 250 mm or greater.

6.4.3   The throat is to be attached to the wood keel by not less than two through bolts where practicable.

● End of Section

SECTION 7
Beam shelf and clamp, bilge stringers, breast hooks and bottom girders

7.1   Beam shelf

7.1.1   The cross-sectional area of beam shelf for $\frac{3}{8}L$ amidships is to be as given in Table 4.7.1. Outside this length the area may be gradually reduced to the ends where it may be 25 per cent less than that amidships.

7.1.2   The area of beam shelf determined from Table 4.7.1 is to be that clear of beams; the section removed for the beam end is not to impair the efficiency of the shelf.

7.1.3   Where the beam shelf is not fitted in one length, a plain glued scarph is to be arranged. Scarphs are to be suitably positioned in relation to joints in other longitudinal members and to hanging knees, etc. The face of the scarph is generally to be in the vertical plane.

7.1.4   Where there is a raised deck, it is recommended that the main beam shelf be carried to the ends. Where, however, this is not done suitable arrangements are to be made to maintain the longitudinal continuity of the shelf, and the frame scantlings in way may be required to be increased.

7.1.5   The beam shelf is to be attached to each frame by one through fastening where the moulding of the shelf does not exceed 180 mm and by two through fastenings where the moulding exceeds 180 mm. The size of fastenings is given in Table 4.7.1.

7.1.6   Where the framing is of Type 5, 6 or 7 (see 5.2.1), chocks are to be fitted between the intermediate bent frames and the shelf.

7.1.7   Lugs are to be fitted to steel frames to take the shelf fastenings.

7.1.8   Where steel frames are fitted in association with steel beams, a beam shelf is not required but a deck stringer plate, a sheerstrake and a stringer angle of the scantlings 10.2 are to be fitted. Beam knees are also to be provided in accordance with 10.5.

7.1.9   For size of fastenings, see Table 4.7.1.

7.2   Beam clamp

7.2.1   In way of the mast in sailing and auxiliary craft, a clamp is to be fitted to the inboard side of the shelf with its upper surface faying closely to the under side of the beams. Alternatively the clamp may be fitted below the shelf and it is to fay closely to the shelf and to the frames.

7.2.2   The length of the clamp is generally to be not less than the breadth of the craft in way of the mast, and its cross-sectional area is to be not less than 75 per cent of the beam shelf area at the centre and may be tapered to 50 per cent of this section at the ends.

7.2.3   The clamp is to be through fastened to the beams or frames as appropriate.

7.2.4   Where steel construction is adopted, see 10.5.6.

7.3   Bilge stringer

7.3.1   A bilge stringer is to be fitted where the framing is Type 1 (bent only) or Type 7 (three bents between grown, laminated or steel), or where the length, L, exceeds 9,0 m for Types 2, 3, 5 and 6. For steel construction (Type 4), see 7.3.9.

7.3.2   The cross-sectional area of bilge stringers for $\frac{3}{8}L$ amidships is to be as given in Table 4.7.1. Outside this length the area may be gradually reduced to the ends where it may be 25 per cent less than amidships. The greatest dimension of the stringer is to be fitted against the frames.

7.3.3   Scarphs in the port and starboard stringers are to be staggered and suitably positioned in relation to joints in other members. The face of the scarph in the stringer is to be cut parallel to the frames.

7.3.4   Stringers are to be attached to each frame by one through fastening where the moulding of the stringer does not exceed 180 mm and by two through fastenings when the moulding exceeds 180 mm.

7.3.5   Where the framing is of Type 5, 6 or 7 (see 5.2.1), chocks are to be fitted between the intermediate bent frames and the stringer.

7.3.6   Lugs are to be fitted to steel frames to take the stringer fastenings.

7.3.7   As an alternative to the fitting of a bilge stringer two or more side stringers may be fitted. Where two side stringers are fitted the cross-sectional area of each is to be not less than 60 per cent of the Rule area for the bilge stringer.

Table 4.7.1 Beam shelf and bilge stringer scantlings and fastenings for motor, sailing and auxiliary craft

Length, L, m	Cross-sectional area of beam shelf, cm²		Cross-sectional area of bilge stringer, cm²		Diameter of bolts, mm, in			Steel side keelson and bilge stringer angles, mm
	Sailing and auxiliary	Motor	Sailing and auxiliary	Motor	Arms of breast hooks	Beam shelf stringers	Hanging knees	
6	29	32	25	22	8	6	6	—
8	40	40	32	29	8	6	6	—
10	50	50	40	35	8	6	6	—
12	70	60	50	50	10	8	8	—
14	90	80	65	60	12	8	8	60 × 60 × 4,0
16	110	100	80	70	12	8	8	60 × 60 × 5,5
18	130	110	90	85	12	10	10	65 × 65 × 6,5
20	150	130	105	100	14	12	12	75 × 65 × 5,5
22	170	150	120	110	14	12	12	75 × 65 × 6,5
24	190	170	140	125	14	12	12	75 × 65 × 7,0
26	220	190	160	140	14	12	12	90 × 65 × 5,5
28	250	210	175	150	16	12	12	90 × 65 × 6,0
30	280	240	190	165	18	14	14	90 × 65 × 6,5

NOTE
1. The Table scantlings for the beam shelf and bilge stringer are based on a timber having a standard density of 560 kg/m³ and where timber of a different density is to be used the scantlings are to be modified in accordance with 3.2.2.

7.3.8 For size of fastenings, *see* Table 4.7.1.

7.3.9 For bilge stringers, etc., in steel construction, the arrangements are to be as follows:—
(a) Where the framing is Type 4 (steel frames) a bilge stringer is to be fitted where the depth from top of floor to deck at side amidships exceeds 2,4 m unless a cabin deck is fitted.
(b) A side keelson is to be fitted when the half-breadth at the top of the floor amidships exceeds 2,4 m.
(c) The scantlings of the bilge stringer and side keelson are given in Table 4.7.1. These are to extend as far forward and aft as practicable.
(d) Bilge stringers and side keelsons are to be welded to the frames or attached by frame lugs with not less than two rivets.

7.4 Breast hooks
7.4.1 The beam shelf and stringer ends are to be efficiently attached to the centreline construction. Breast hooks and transom quarter knees are to be fitted as necessary.

7.4.2 The ends of the craft are to be suitably strengthened, and particular attention is to be given to this where there is a large overhang.

7.4.3 For size of fastenings, *see* Table 4.7.1.

7.5 Bottom girders
7.5.1 The engine seatings are to be of substantial construction to suit the power of the machinery.

7.5.2 The longitudinal girders forming the engine seatings are to extend as far forward and aft as practicable and are to be adequately supported by transverse floors and/or brackets.

7.5.3 Additional side girders may be required in the machinery space and in the bottom of the craft forward.

● End of Section

SECTION 8
Bulkheads

8.1 General
8.1.1 Watertight bulkheads are to be provided in accordance with Ch 6,1.2.

8.1.2 The scantlings of wood bulkheads will be specially considered depending on the method of construction.

Table 4.8.1   Bulkhead plating and stiffeners for motor, sailing and auxiliary craft

Bulkhead plating and spacing of stiffeners				Stiffeners with free ends				
Depth of bulkhead at middle line below upper deck, m	Thickness of plating, mm	Spacing of stiffeners, mm	Overall length of stiffener, m	Height of upper deck above top of stiffener, m				
				0	0,6	1,2	1,8	2,4
				Modulus, cm³				
1,5	2,5	300	1,5	2,5	4,6	6,6	8,7	11,0
1,8	3,0	325	1,8	4,8	8,0	11,0	14,0	17,0
2,1	3,5	350	2,1	8,0	13,0	17,0	22,0	27,0
2,4	4,0	375	2,4	13,0	20,0	26,0	33,0	39,0
2,7	4,5	400	2,7	20,0	29,0	37,0	46,0	55,0
3,0	5,0	425	3,0	29,0	40,0	52,0	63,0	75,0
3,3	5,0	450	3,3	40,0	55,0	70,0	85,0	—
3,6	5,5	475	3,6	56,0	75,0	93,0	—	—
3,9	5,5	500	3,9	75,0	98,0	120,0	—	—
4,2	6,0	525	4,2	98,0	125,0	—	—	—
4,5	6,0	550	4,5	125,0	160,0	—	—	—
4,8	6,5	575	4,8	160,0	—	—	—	—

NOTES
1. When the spacing of stiffeners differs from that given in the Table, the thickness of the plating is to be modified at the rate of 0,5 mm for each 100 mm difference in spacing. The modulus of the stiffeners is to be modified in direct proportion to the stiffener spacing.
2. The moduli given in the Table are for unbracketed stiffening sections in association with plating.

3. Where stiffening sections are bracketed at the top and bottom the Table modulus, corrected in accordance with Note 1, is to be multiplied by the factor, F_f, determined from the following formula :—

$$F_f = 0,8 - \frac{h}{3,75(2h + l)}$$

where h = height of upper deck above top of stiffener, in metres.
l = length of stiffener, in metres.

8.1.3   The scantlings of steel watertight bulkheads are given in Table 4.8.1.

8.1.4   In collision bulkheads the spacing of stiffeners is to be not greater than 460 mm.

8.1.5   At the level of the decks below the upper deck, angles or flats are to be suitably attached to the bulkheads for taking the fastenings of the wood deck.

8.1.6   Steel bulkheads are to be attached to wood frames of the size required for grown frames or to a boundary angle of the size required for steel frames.

● End of Section

SECTION 9

Hull planking

9.1   General
9.1.1   The outside planking may be single skin (carvel or clinker), strip, double skin, single skin plywood or cold moulded laminations.

9.1.2   The thickness for single skin carvel or strip construction is to be as given in Table 4.9.1.

9.1.3   Where the frame spacing differs from that given in Table 4.5.1 the thickness of planking determined from Table 4.9.1 is to be modified as follows:—
   Type 1: bent frames   1,5 mm per 25 mm difference
   Other frame types   1,5 mm per 38 mm difference

9.1.4   The thickness determined from Table 4.9.1, after correction for frame spacing and, except for plywood, density of timber, may be reduced for the type of planking as follows:—

Clinker   10 per cent
Diagonal double skin   10 per cent

Cold moulded laminate   The reduction will depend on the framing or stiffening
Single skin plywood   system adopted and will be a maximum of 25 per cent

9.2   Single skin
9.2.1   Butts of the outside planking are to be spaced not less than 1,2 m apart and no butts are to be in the same frame space unless there are three strakes between, see Fig. 4.9.1. The arrangement of butts at the ends of the craft is to be to the Surveyor's satisfaction.

Table 4.9.1   Outside and deck planking for motor, sailing and auxiliary craft

Length, L, m	Basic thickness, mm	Length, L, m	Basic thickness, mm
6	19	20	41.5
8	21.5	22	43.5
10	24	24	45.5
12	28	26	47.5
14	32	28	50
16	36	30	52
18	39		

NOTES

1. The Table thicknesses of outside and deck planking are based on a timber having a standard density of 560 kg/m³ and 430 kg/m³, respectively, and where timber of a different density is to be used the thickness is to be modified in accordance with 3.3.2.

2. For frame and beam spacing corrections, *see* 9.1.3 and 11.1.3, respectively.

3. The basic thicknesses are applicable to single skin carvel or strip outside planking and to a laid deck. For corrections for other types of construction, *see* 9.1.4 for outside planking and 11.1.5, 11.1.6 and 11.1.7 for deck planking.

9.2.2   The butts in the garboard strake are to be kept clear of the keel scarph. Butts in the sheerstrake are to be clear of butts in the covering board.

9.2.3   Butts in the planking are to be strapped or scarphed.

9.2.4   Wood or metal butt straps are to be arranged between the frames but a drainage space is to be left between the strap and the frame. The breadth is to be sufficient to overlap the adjacent planks by about 12 mm.

9.2.5   Wood butt straps are to have the same thickness as the planking. Metal straps are to be not less than ⅛ of the planking thickness, *see* Fig. 4.9.2.

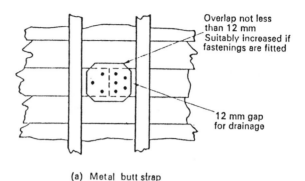

(a) Metal butt strap

(b) Wood butt straps

Fig. 4.9.2   Typical butt straps on single skin hull planking

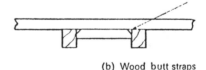

9.2.6   The planking and the straps are to be through fastened. The size of the fastenings is to be as required by

Table 4.9.2 for planking to frames, and the number is to be as follows:—

Width of planking, mm	Number of fastenings in each plank end
Under 100	3
100 and under 200	4
200 and under 250	5

9.2.7   The length of a scarph is to be not less than four times the thickness of the planking. The scarph is to be positioned on the frame, and glued and fastened to it.

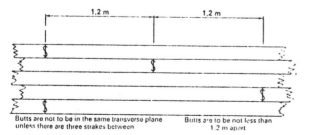

Butts are not to be in the same transverse plane unless there are three strakes between

Butts are to be not less than 1.2 m apart

Fig. 4.9.1   Spacing of butts

Table 4.9.2 Fastenings for outside and deck planking in motor, sailing and auxiliary craft

Planking thickness, mm	Size of fastenings — Outside planking — Grown, laminated or steel frames — Bolts, mm	Wood screws Dia., mm	Wood screws Gauge	Copper boat nails* Size, mm	Copper boat nails* Gauge	Bent frames — Copper boat nails Size, mm	Bent frames Gauge	Deck planking — Wood screws Dia., mm	Deck Wood screws Gauge	Deck Bolts, mm	No. fastenings per plank — Width — Under 100 mm	100 mm and under 150 mm	150 mm and under 180 mm	180 mm and under 205 mm	205 mm and under 225 mm
19	5	5	10	4,5	7	2,5	12	4,5	8	5	2	2	3	3	3
20,5	5	5	10	5	6	3	11	5	10	5	2	2	3	3	3
22	6	5	10	6,5	3	3,5	10	5	10	6	2	2	3	3	3
23,5	6	5	10	6,5	3	3,5	10	5	10	6	2	2	3	3	3
25	6	5,5	12	6,5	3	3,5	9	5	10	6	1	2	2	3	3
26,5	6	5,5	12	6,5	3	3,5	9	5,5	12	6	1	2	2	3	3
28	6	5,5	12	6,5	3	4,5	7	5,5	12	6	1	2	2	3	3
29,5	6	5,5	12	6,5	3	4,5	7	5,5	12	6	1	2	2	3	3
31	8	6,5	14	7,5	1	5	6	5,5	12	6	1	2	2	3	3
32,5	8	6,5	14	7,5	1	5	6	6,5	14	8	1	2	2	3	3
34	8	6,5	14	7,5	1	5,5	5	6,5	14	8	1	2	2	3	3
35,5	8	7	16	7,5	1	5,5	5	6,5	14	8	1	2	2	3	3
37	8	7	16	7,5	1	5,5	5	6,5	14	8	1	2	2	2	3
38,5	8	7	16	7,5	1	5,5	5	7	16	8	1	2	2	2	3
40	10	8	18	9,5	3/0	6	4	7	16	8	1	2	2	2	3
41,5	10	8	18	9,5	3/0	6	4	7	16	8	1	2	2	2	3
43	10	8	18	9,5	3/0	—	—	8	18	10	1	2	2	2	3
44,5	10	8	18	9,5	3/0	—	—	8	18	10	1	2	2	2	3
46	12	8,5	20	11	5/0	—	—	8	18	10	1	2	2	2	3
47,5	12	8,5	20	11	5/0	—	—	8	18	10	1	2	2	2	3
49	12	8,5	20	11	5/0	—	—	8	18	10	1	2	2	2	3
50,5	12	10	24	12,5	7/0	—	—	8,5	20	12	1	2	2	2	3
52	12	10	24	12,5	7/0	—	—	8,5	20	12	1	2	2	2	3

*For grown or laminated frames only.

NOTES

1. The diameter of the wood screws given in the Table is the nominal diameter of the unthreaded shank.

2. The gauge of wood screws given in the Table is British Standard Gauge, and that of copper boat nails is Imperial Standard Wire Gauge.

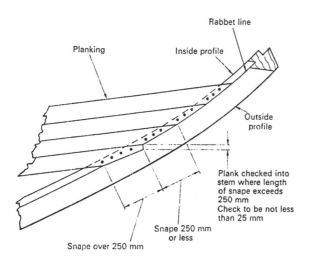

Fig. 4.9.3   Connection of single skin planking to centreline structure (for normal breadth of planking)

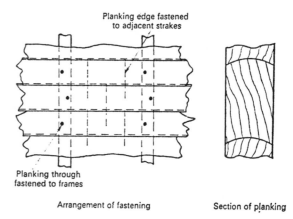

Fig. 4.9.4   Strip planking

9.2.8   In sailing and auxiliary craft, the garboard and adjacent strakes are to be of increased width at the after end to give a reasonable plank run, and the garboard strake is to be in as long a length as possible.

9.2.9   Where, with planks of normal breadth, the length of snaped ends exceeds 250 mm, the planks are to be checked into the centreline structure (see Fig. 4.9.3). The size of the fastenings are to be as for the garboard strake (see 9.2.11).

9.2.10   When strip planking is adopted, the top and bottom edges are to be rounded and hollowed respectively. Each plank is to be glued and edge fastened to the one below with non-ferrous fastenings. See Fig. 4.9.4. Suitable stealer planks may be fitted to suit planking arrangements.

9.2.11   The garboard strakes are to be screw fastened to the keel or hog. The screws are to be of the size required by Table 4.9.2 for outside planking to Type 2 grown frames. They are to be reeled, and are to be spaced not more than twelve diameters apart in each row and are to enter the keel or hog to a depth at least equal to the thickness of the garboard. In way of deadwoods a combination of dumps and screws may be used.

9.2.12   The size and number of fastenings attaching the outside planking to the frames are to be as given in Table 4.9.2. The types of fastenings are dependent on the framing as follows:—

Type 1: Bent frames

Type 2: Grown frames
Type 3: Laminated frames

All through fastenings
Through fastenings to be arranged in way of beam shelf, bilge (or side) stringer, and tuck (in a sailing or auxiliary craft). The remainder may be screws

Type 4: Steel frames   Nut and screw bolts

Types 5, 6 and 7: Grown,   Bent, as for Type 1
   laminated or steel frames   Grown and laminated,
   with bent frames between   as for Types 2 and 3
                                  Steel, as for Type 4

9.2.13   Where frames are increased in way of the mast (see 5.3.6), they are to be through fastened throughout.

9.3   Double skin

9.3.1   Double skin planking may be arranged as follows:—

   (a) Both diagonal,
   (b) Inner diagonal, outer fore and aft,
   (c) Both fore and aft.

9.3.2   The outer skin is to be approximately $\frac{3}{8}$ of the total thickness, and the diagonal planking is to be at approximately 45°.

9.3.3   The inner skin is to be either screw or nail fastened to the frames, and the outer skin is to be through fastened to the frames. In arrangements 9.3.1 (a) and (b) through fastenings are to be fitted at the plank crossings, and in 9.3.1 (c) the inner skin is to be screw fastened to the outer between frames. See Fig. 4.9.5.

9.3.4   In arrangements 9.3.1 (a) and (b) oiled calico dipped in linseed oil or an equivalent membrane is to be laid between the skins, and in 9.3.1 (c) it is recommended that resorcinol glue be used between the skins.

9.3.5   The arrangement at the gunwale is to be such as to ensure that the covering board can be made watertight. Typical methods are shown in Fig. 4.9.6.

9.4   Cold moulded laminate

9.4.1   In view of the importance of maintaining the correct temperature when the skin is constructed as a cold moulded laminate, the Surveyor is to be satisfied that the Builder's premises and facilities are suitable for this type of construction. *See* 2.1.1.

9.4.2   The material may be a suitable marine plywood or one of the timbers given in Table 4.1.2. The use of other timbers will be specially considered.

9.4.3   The breadth and thickness of the individual layers are to be such that they can be readily laid to the form of the craft, and generally are not to exceed 125 mm and 3,5 mm, respectively.

9.4.4   The number of layers is to be such that their combined thickness is not less than that required by Table 4.9.1 reduced in accordance with 9.1.4. The spacing and scantlings of the frames will be specially considered. *See* 5.7.1.

9.5   Plywood planking

9.5.1   Plywood is to be fitted in as large panels as practicable having due regard to the form of the craft. Panel butts are to be staggered between the bottom, side and deck and arranged clear of the mast, ballast keel and engine seating.

9.5.2   The width of longitudinal seam landings on the centreline structure, chine and gunwale members and on any longitudinal stringers is to be not less than that required by Table 4.9.3. Seams are to be glued and fastened with one or two rows of fastenings (*see* Table 4.9.3), and arranged to give maximum spacing of fastenings of 50 mm.

9.5.3   Butts and seams are to be scarphed or strapped where necessary. The length of a scarph is to be not less than 8 times the hull thickness. The scarph is to be glued and, if made *in situ*, fitted with a backing strap of a width not less than 10 times the hull thickness. The strap is to be glued and fastened to the hull with two rows of fastenings of the size given in Table 4.9.4 and spaced about 8 times the hull thickness.

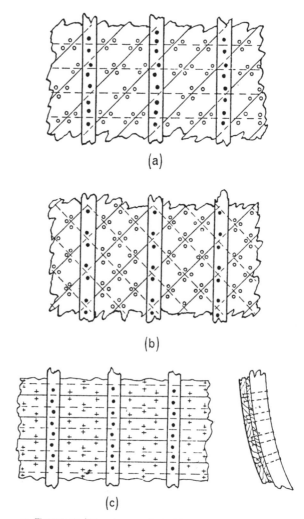

(a)

(b)

(c)

o   Through clenching of outer to inner skin
●   Through fastening of outer skin to frame
+   Screw fastening of inner to outer skin

Fig. 4.9.5   Arrangements of fastenings in double skin hull planking

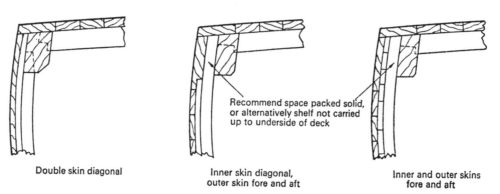

Double skin diagonal

Recommend space packed solid, or alternatively shelf not carried up to underside of deck

Inner skin diagonal, outer skin fore and aft

Inner and outer skins fore and aft

Fig. 4.9.6   Detail of gunwale for double skin planking

Table 4.9.3 Plywood planking: overlaps and fastenings for motor, sailing and auxiliary craft

Plywood planking thickness, mm	Minimum breadth of landing between		Fastenings		
	Hull planking and keel or chine, mm	Hull or deck planking and shelf or longitudinal, mm	Wood screws		Copper boat nails, gauge
			Gauge	Dia., mm	
6	25 ⎫	25 ⎫	8	4,2	10
8	28 ⎬ Single	28 ⎪	10	4,9	10
10	32 ⎭ fastened	32 ⎬	10	4,9	8
13	44 ⎫	35 ⎭	12	5,6	8
16	50 ⎬	44 ⎫	12	5,6	6
19	57 ⎬ Double	50 ⎪	14	6,3	6
22	63 ⎭ fastened	57 ⎬	14	6,3	3
25	63 ⎭	57 ⎭	16	7,0	3

NOTES
1. The gauge of wood screws given in the Table is British Standard Gauge, and that of copper boat nails is Imperial Standard Wire Gauge.
2. The diameter of the wood screw is the nominal diameter of the un-threaded shank.

Table 4.9.4 Plywood planking: butts and butt straps for motor, sailing and auxiliary craft

Plywood planking thickness, mm	Breadth of butt strap, mm		Fastenings		
			Wood screws		Copper boat nails, gauge
			Gauge	Dia., mm	
6		150 ⎫	8	4,2	10
8	Double	175 ⎪	10	4,9	10
10	fastened	200 ⎬	10	4,9	8
13		260 ⎪	12	5,6	8
16		280 ⎭	12	5,6	8
19	Treble	330 ⎫	14	6,3	6
22	fastened	355 ⎬	14	6,3	3
25		380 ⎭	16	7,0	3

NOTES
1. The gauge of wood screws given in the Table is British Standard Gauge, and that of copper boat nails is Imperial Standard Wire Gauge.
2. The diameter of the wood screw is the nominal diameter of the un-threaded shank.

9.5.4 Butt straps are to be of withgiven in Table 4.9.4 and the same thickness as the hull planking. The strap is to be glued and double or treble fastened to the hull planking. The size of fastenings is to be as given in Table 4.9.4.

9.5.5 The hull planking is to be attached to the frames by fastening. The size of fastening is to be as given in generally not more than 75 mm apart.

9.6 Hull sheathing

9.6.1 Whilst it is not a requirement of the Rules that the outside planking be sheathed, if this is done it must be efficiently carried out to the Surveyor's satisfaction.

9.6.2 Copper sheathing should be bedded on bitumastic treated paper or felt. The sheets are to bve dressed to ensure that the sheathing is in close contact with the bedding.

They are to overlap each other by about 22 mm; the vertical laps are to face aft and the horizontal laps are to face upwards. Fastening is to be by coppering nails spaced at not more than 40 mm at the sheet edges. In addition, the panel is to be tack fastened at spacing of not more than 75 mm veritically and 150 mm horizontally. The sheathing is to be stopped short of the rabbet line and a wrapper piece fitted.

9.6.3 Where synthetic sheathing is used, care is to be taken to ensure that the moisture content of the timber is as low as is practicable. All seams and fastening holes to be splined or dowelled or stopped with a compound which is compatible with the manufacturer's recommendations. Wherever possible, the sheathing is to be fitted around the wood keel and deadwood before the ballast keel is fitted.

● End of Section

SECTION 10

Beams

10.1 Scantlings—Timber

10.1.1 The scantlings of ordinary beams, half beams and strong beams are to be not less than those given in Table 4.10.1.

10.1.2 Where the actual beam spacing differs from that given in Table 4.10.1, the strength of ordinary and half beams is to be modified in direct proportion, i.e.

$$\text{Actual } (sm^2) = \text{Table } (sm^2) \times \frac{\text{actual spacing}}{\text{Table spacing}}$$

where s and m are the siding and moulding, respectively; the Table siding is to be that after correction for density. *See* 3.2.2.

10.1.3 Where laminated beams are fitted their siding may be reduced by 15 per cent.

10.1.4 Strong beams are to be fitted at ends of openings when two or more beams are cut. They may also be required to be fitted in way of the mast.

10.2 End attachments

10.2.1 All beams are to be fastened to the shelf by dovetails or dowels. *See* Fig. 4.10.1.

10.2.2 As an alternative to 10.2.1, where a plywood deck is fitted the beams need not be dovetailed or dowelled but may be carried past the shelf and checked over it. The depth of the check is to be about one-quarter of the depth of the beam and the beam is to be screw or dump fastened to the shelf.

10.2.3 Hanging knees are to be fitted as required by Table 4.10.1 and are to be arranged at the mast and other strong beams to give a suitable disposition over the length of the craft.

10.2.4 Hanging knees may be steel straps, flanged plates, angle bar, or grown or laminated timber.

10.2.5 The dimensions of strap hanging knees are given in Table 4.10.1 but at the ends of the craft the length of arms need not exceed one-third of the length of the frame or beam. Angle knees are to have equivalent strength.

Table 4.10.1 Beams and hanging knees for motor, sailing and auxiliary craft (*see continuation*)

Length of beam, m	Spacing of ordinary beams centre to centre, mm	Ordinary beams for ¾L amidships				Ordinary beams beyond ¾L amidships, half beams throughout			
		At middle		At ends		At middle		At ends	
		Siding mm	Moulding mm	Siding mm	Moulding mm	Siding mm	Moulding mm	Siding mm	Moulding mm
1,8	250	30	45	30	30	26	33	26	26
2,1	275	36	53	36	36	32	40	32	32
2,4	300	41	60	41	41	36	45	36	36
2,7	325	46	66	46	46	40	50	40	40
3,0	350	51	72	51	51	43	54	43	43
3,3	375	55	78	55	55	46	58	46	46
3,6	400	59	83	59	59	50	63	50	50
3,9	425	62	88	62	62	53	66	53	53
4,2	450	66	94	66	66	56	70	56	56
4,5	475	69	99	69	69	58	74	58	58
4,8	500	72	103	72	72	61	78	61	61
5,1	525	75	108	75	75	63	82	63	63
5,4	550	79	112	79	79	65	86	65	65
5,7	575	82	117	82	82	67	91	67	67
6,0	600	85	121	85	85	69	96	69	69
6,3	625	88	125	88	88	70	100	70	70
6,6	650	91	130	91	91	71	105	71	71
6,9	675	96	137	96	96	73	112	73	73
7,2	700	102	145	102	102	75	120	75	75

NOTES
1. The length of a wood beam is to be measured amidships to the inside of the beam shelf.
2. The Table scantlings of timber beams are based on a timber having a standard density of 560 kg/m³, and where timber of a

10.2.6 The minimum moulding at the throat of grown or laminated knees is to be 60 or 40 per cent, respectively, greater than that required by Table 4.5.1 for ordinary grown frames at the heel.

10.2.7 Each arm is to be connected to the beam and to the frame by four bolts of the diameter given in Table 4.7.1. The bolts need not pass through the deck or outside planking.

10.2.8 Bulkheads of substantial construction glued and screwed to the beams and frames will be accepted in lieu of hanging knees.

10.2.9 Lodging knees are to be fitted to the beams in way of masts and at ends of deck openings unless a plywood deck is fitted.

10.3 Local reinforcements

10.3.1 The beams and deck are to be suitably strengthened in way of masts, coachroof ends, windlass, cleats, sheet winches, etc. Where a mast is stepped on the deck the structural arrangements will be specially considered.

10.3.2 All deck openings are to be properly framed with carlings fitted to receive the half beams.

10.4 Cabin deck

10.4.1 Where the depth amidships from top of wood keel to top of beam at side amidships is 3 m or greater, cabin deck beams are to be fitted. The strength of these beams is to be at least 60 per cent of that required for upper deck beams, and the beams are to be efficiently attached to the craft's side.

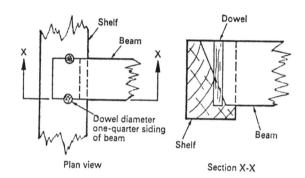

Fig. 4.10.1   Dowel fastening of beam at shelf

Table 4.10.1   Beams and hanging knees for motor, sailing and auxiliary craft (*conclusion*)

| Beams in way of masts and at ends of deck openings | | | | | Strap hanging knees to deck beams | | | | |
| At middle | | At ends | | | Length of arms, mm | | At throat, mm | At point, mm | Length of beam, m |
Siding mm	Moulding mm	Siding mm	Moulding mm	Number on each side	For ⅓L amidships	Beyond ⅓L amidships			
39	55	39	39	3	300	240	22 × 8	19 × 4	1,8
46	65	46	46	4	325	260	22 × 10	22 × 4	2,1
52	74	52	52	4	350	280	25 × 12	22 × 6	2,4
58	83	58	58	5	375	300	30 × 16	25 × 6	2,7
63	90	63	63	5	400	320	34 × 19	30 × 6	3,0
68	97	68	68	6	425	340	38 × 19	35 × 6	3,3
73	104	73	73	6	450	360	42 × 22	40 × 8	3,6
77	110	77	77	7	475	380	46 × 22	40 × 8	3,9
82	117	82	82	7	500	400	50 × 25	45 × 8	4,2
86	124	86	86	8	525	420	52 × 25	45 × 8	4,5
90	129	90	90	8	550	440	55 × 27	50 × 10	4,8
94	135	94	94	9	575	460	58 × 27	50 × 11	5,1
98	140	98	98	9	600	480	61 × 30	50 × 11	5,4
102	146	102	102	10	625	500	64 × 30	52 × 12	5,7
107	151	107	107	10	650	520	67 × 30	52 × 12	6,0
112	156	112	112	11	675	540	70 × 33	54 × 14	6,3
119	163	119	119	11	700	560	72 × 33	54 × 14	6,6
127	172	127	127	12	725	580	74 × 33	57 × 16	6,9
135	180	135	135	12	750	600	78 × 36	57 × 16	7,2

different density is to be used the scantlings are to be modified in accordance with 3.2.2.

3. Where the beam spacing differs from that given in the Table, sm^2 is to be modified in direct proportion. *See* 10.1.2.

4. The siding of a laminated beam may be reduced by 15 per cent.

SECTION 11
Deck planking

11.1 General

11.1.1 Decks may consist of:—

(a) Laid planks,

(b) Plywood,

(c) Plywood sheathed with a laid deck.

11.1.2 The thickness of laid deck is to be as given in Table 4.9.1.

11.1.3 Where the beam spacing differs from that given in Table 4.10.1, the Table thickness is to be modified at the rate of 1,5 mm per 50 mm difference.

11.1.4 Where teak or other approved timber having a density exceeding 720 kg/m³ is used the thickness may be reduced by 12 per cent.

11.1.5 Where plywood is used the thickness may be reduced by 30 per cent.

11.1.6 Where plywood is sheathed with a laid deck the combined thickness may be 30 per cent less than the thickness in Table 4.9.1 provided that:—

(a) the combined density of the plywood and sheathing is not less than 430 kg/m³,

(b) the thickness of the plywood is not less than 30 per cent of the combined thickness and in no case is less than 6 mm, and

(c) where the laid planking is less than 19 mm, the seams are filled with an approved flexible seam compound.

11.1.7 Where the deck is covered with canvas, nylon, glass reinforced plastics or other approved sheathing, the thickness may be reduced by 1,5 mm.

11.1.8 All exposed canvas seams are to be sewn and not overlapped and tacked. Securing of canvas by tacks should be used only where the edges are protected by listings, etc. The canvas is to be suitably bedded to the deck.

11.2 Laid decks

11.2.1 Butts of the deck planking are to be spaced not less than 1,2 m apart and no butts are to be in the same transverse plane unless there are three strakes between. *See* Fig. 4.9.1.

11.2.2 The material for laid decks is to be quarter sawn.

11.2.3 Butts are to be arranged on a beam and are to be of the scarph or caulked lip type unless the siding of the beam is sufficient to allow a caulked square butt to be used. *See* Fig. 4.11.1.

11.2.4 Deck planks are to be attached to the beams by either screw fastenings from above, or side fastening by nails. *See* Fig. 4.11.2.

11.2.5 Where the beam spacing has been increased it may be necessary to fit horizontal dowels in the planking between the beams.

11.2.6 The number and size of screws are to be as given in Table 4.9.2. Deck covering boards are to be screw fastened to the sheerstrake and beams. The screws to the sheerstrake are generally to be spaced not more than 12 diameters apart.

11.2.7 Where steel beams are fitted, the fastenings are to be either nut and screw bolts or round head wood screws fitted from the under side of the beams. The number and size of bolts or screws are to be as given in Table 4.9.2.

11.3 Plywood decks

11.3.1 Plywood decks are to be fitted in panels as large as practicable.

11.3.2 Butts are to be clear of those in the side planking and are not to be placed in the vicinity of the mast. They are to be on a strong beam or are to be strapped.

11.3.3 Seams are to be strapped or scarphed or may be arranged on a longitudinal member having a width sufficient to give a landing of not less than that required by Table 4.9.3. Butts and seams are to be sealed watertight.

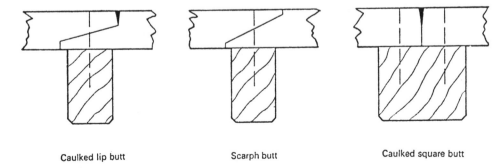

Caulked lip butt   Scarph butt   Caulked square butt

Fig. 4.11.1   Butts of deck planking

11.3.4 Plywood decks are to be glued or bedded to the beams and at the deck edges. They are also to be fastened to the beams and at the edges by screws or barbed nails, as required by Table 4.9.3. The fastenings in seams and butts landing on structural members are to be as required for deck edges. If a strap is fitted, it is to be as required by 9.5.4 for hull plywood planking.

11.3.5 Where plywood decks are laid on steel beams, liners are to be fitted where stringer and tie plates are used. Liners are to be the same width as the beam and the same thickness as the plates.

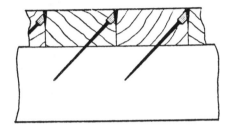

Secret fastening

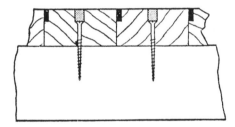

Screw fastening

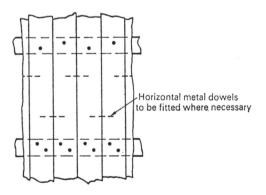

Horizontal metal dowels to be fitted where necessary

Plan view showing arrangement of single or double fastenings

Fig. 4.11.2   Deck fastenings (laid decks)

11.4   Plywood sheathed with laid deck

11.4.1 Plywood decks sheathed with a laid deck are to comply with the requirements of 11.3.1 to 11.3.3.

11.4.2 Where thickness of the laid sheathing on plywood decks exceeds 50 per cent of the total thickness, the requirements of 11.2.1 and 11.2.2 are to be complied with. The sheathing is to be fastened through the plywood to the beams as for a laid deck. *See* 11.2.4 to 11.2.6.

11.4.3 Where the laid sheathing is less than 50 per cent of the total thickness the butts are to be suitably positioned, and the fastenings may pass through the plywood only and are to be in accordance with 11.3.4.

11.4.4 The laid sheathing is to be glued to the plywood with a resorcinol glue.

11.5   Watertightness

11.5.1 Laid decks are to be caulked and payed or an acceptable deck seaming compound, applied in accordance with the manufacturers' recommendations, may be used. Wood dowels are to be glued.

11.5.2 All weather decks are to be hose tested on completion.

11.6   Deck fittings

11.6.1 Fittings fixed to the deck are to be bedded on a suitable mastic compound to maintain the watertightness of the deck.

11.6.2 It is recommended that in way of heavy fittings such as windlasses, winches, fairleads, etc., the deck planking and the fastening holes be coated with a suitable wood preservative prior to the application of the mastic.

11.6.3 Guard rail stanchions are to be bedded on a suitable mastic compound and are to have not less than three fastenings through the palm, one of which is to be a through fastening.

● End of Section

SECTION 12
Coachroofs and deckhouses

12.1   General

12.1.1 Coachroofs and deckhouses are to be substantially constructed and efficiently connected to the carlings and beams.

12.2   Coachroofs

12.2.1 The scantlings of a coachroof are to be as given in Tables 4.12.1 and 4.12.2.

12.2.2 Where the coachroof deck is of plywood the thickness determined from Table 4.12.1 may be reduced by 30 per cent.

12.2.3 Where plywood is sheathed with a laid deck the combined thickness may be 30 per cent less than the thickness in Table 4.12.1 provided that:—

(a) the combined density of the plywood and sheathing is not less than 430 kg/m^3,
(b) the thickness of the plywood is not less than 30 per cent of the combined thickness and in no case is less than 6 mm, and
(c) where the laid planking is less than 19 mm, the seams are filled with an approved flexible seam compound.

12.2.4 If the coachroof deck is covered with canvas or other approved sheathing the thickness determined from Table 4.12.1 may be reduced by 1,5 mm.

12.2.5 Where the coachroof beam spacing differs from that given in Table 4.12.2 the strength of the beams is to be modified in direct proportion and the deck thickness is to be modified at the rate of 1,5 mm per 50 mm difference.

12.2.6 On small coachroofs where it is desired to dispense with beams the deck thickness will be specially considered.

12.2.7 The coachroof and side deck are to be adequately stiffened in way of the mast. Where a mast is stepped on the coachroof the structural arrangements will be specially considered.

12.3 Deckhouses

12.3.1 The scantlings of a deckhouse are dependent on the size of the house but the general standard of strength is to be that required for a coachroof and proposals will be specially considered.

Table 4.12.1 Coachroof coaming and deck thicknesses for motor, sailing and auxiliary craft

Length, L, m	Coaming thickness, mm	Coachroof deck thickness, mm
6	17	13
8	19	15
10	22	17
12	24	19
14	26	22
16	29	24
18	32	26

NOTES
1. The Table thickness of coachroof coamings and deck are based on a timber having a standard density of 560 kg/m^3 and 430 kg/m^3, respectively, and where timber of a different density is to be used the thickness is to be modified in accordance with 3.2.2.
2. Where the coachroof coaming or deck is of plywood the Table thickness may be reduced by 30 per cent.
3. If the deck is covered with canvas or other approved sheathing the Table thickness may be reduced by 1,5 mm.
4. Where the beam spacing differs from that given in Table 4.12.2, the deck thickness is to be modified at the rate of 1,5 mm per 50 mm difference.

Table 4.12.2 Coachroof and deckhouse beams for motor, sailing and auxiliary craft

Length of beam, m	Spacing centre to centre, mm	At middle of beam		At ends of beam	
		Siding, mm	Moulding, mm	Siding, mm	Moulding, mm
1,2	255	28	41	28	28
1,5	280	30	44	30	30
1,8	305	34	48	34	34
2,1	330	38	53	38	38
2,4	355	41	57	41	41
2,7	380	43	60	43	43
3,0	405	44	63	44	44
3,3	430	44	65	44	44
3,6	455	46	68	46	46
3,9	480	48	71	48	48
4,2	505	50	75	50	50

NOTES
1. The Table scantlings are based on a timber having a standard density of 560 kg/m^3 and where timber of a different density is to be used the scantlings are to be modified in accordance with 3.2.2.
2. Where the beam spacing differs from that given in the Table, the strength of the beam is to be modified in direct proportion.

● End of Section

APPENDIX C
SUPERIOR ADHESIVES
FOR THE MILLENNIUM

Could Another Osmosis-Like Disaster Be Brewing?

Let's look at the following photographs with the eye of a surveyor/shipwright. Professionals in both of these fields will tell you that delaminations and the problems they cause form a substantial part of their workload. When I first started repairing boats, the failed glue joints always seemed to have a clear or light-brown glue line (pre-1970). John Guzzwell of *Trekka and Treasure* fame, and Cecil Lange, builder of the Cape George Cutters, two life-long boat builders, agree with me—they have never seen a failure that had the distinctive burgundy glue lines of resorcinol adhesives (page 510, note 23).

Unfortunately, the number of delaminations I see on all types of boats, from wood to fiberglass to metal, seem to have exploded since epoxy was introduced to the professional and home boat-building industry in the late 1970s. I see no signs of this problem decreasing in the near future. Furthermore, my observations of wood to wood epoxy failures raises yet another question: what about the durability of all epoxy composite boat construction, glass to wood, carbon fiber masts, and how durable are epoxy repairs of fiberglass hulls?

Photo 1. When you look at a delamination such as this and see a clean break, with no wood torn away at all, you have a 100 percent glue failure. This is one layer of a laminated winch-mounting pad. The owner of the boat confirmed the pad was glued by a well-known and respected U.S. yacht yard, using a well-known marine epoxy formulation. He was winching his boat away from the dock in a blow when the epoxy let go. The winch shot right past his ear.

We all know this pad and winch should have been bolted through the deck structures. In fact one of the problems with epoxy literature is the suggestion that fastenings can be eliminated in many instances. This has led cost and weight-conscious builders to have more faith in the holding power of epoxy than is warranted. But in any case, as this photo shows, there is no tearing of wood at all. The wood is mahogany. The darker patches are epoxy. These epoxy remnants are $1/32$-inch-thick, which rules out glue-starvation as the cause of failure. This type of catastrophic (i.e. sudden and unexpected) failure is not only potentially dangerous, but expensive, especially if you lose the winch overboard.

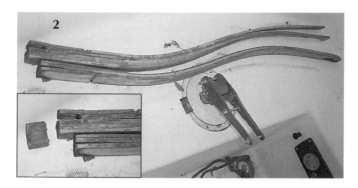

Photo 2. Take a critical look at various glue joints on both wooden and fiberglass production boats that are more than two or three years old. You'll learn a lot about modern adhesives vs. more conservative choices. This photo shows one of the most common delaminations we see when we walk through a marina, especially one in a sunny clime where boats are kept afloat year round. The timber used? Ash and mahogany. The adhesive? epoxy. I was pretty sure when I saw the light-yellow color. The shipyard owner not only confirmed it was a widely advertised epoxy, but offered to show us several more failures just like this one.

Note the close-up view in the inset. As the glue failed, the butt of the tiller wrenched right out of the rudderhead fitting. Hopefully, a steamer was not bearing down on this sailor as the tiller failed.

Screw & washer holding down feather edge of lamination.

Joint opened up ³/16 inch

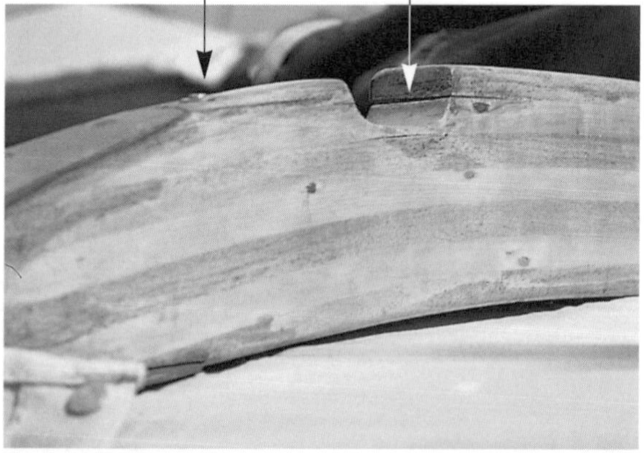

Photo 3. This is another common epoxy failure. Stressed or bent parts such as boom-gallows frames and toerail scarfs often separate as the epoxy warms up in the sun and softens or deflects. (Fig 1, also page 509, no. 13). The epoxy folks call this "creep". The main reasons given for epoxy failing as a wood adhesive are:

(a) It is sensitive to heat (Fig 1); (b) to UV (Fig 2);

(c) to fatigue (Fig 3); and it cannot withstand the "severe stresses of water soaking and drying." (Fig 4).

It is quite likely the heat of the La Paz, Mexico, sun caused the boom gallows on this 40-foot cutter to delaminate. The owner is a master shipwright from New Zealand. He used mahogany and spruce with a well-known epoxy and protected the wood and joints with varnish. When the delaminations began to crack the varnish, it became a vicious cycle: more cracks in the varnish, more shrinking and swelling of wood around the joints, more delamination.

Figure 1.
HEAT DEFORMATION TEMPERATURE (HDT)

That temperature at which a plastic (epoxies are plastics) has lost 30 percent of its strength when tested using ASTM D 648 test methods.

Common Boatbuilding Epoxies have an HDT ranging from 101°F to 123°F (50°C)

Some examples:

At 118°F West System-brand epoxy 105, with 205 hardener has lost 30 percent of its strength *(www. concentric.net/-westsys/phisical.shtml)*

At 123°F (52°C) System Three Epoxy resin has lost 30 percent of its strength (*The Epoxy Book*, by System Three Resins, pub. 1998, page 37).

In each case, the following HDT figures were provided by the technical advisors of the formulators in telephone conversations, June 1999.

EPIGLAS epoxy resin–HDT 118°F (49°C) unless part-cured at elevated temperatures.

POXY-GRIP distributed by Glen-L–HDT 120°F (50°C)

T-88–HDT 101°F (38°C)

If there is no stress at all on the joint, the strength will probably be regained as the epoxy cools and hardens. But testing done at Gougeon Brothers Labs suggests "that wood/epoxy structures may have accelerated fatigue when stressed at higher temperatures." (see page 509 number 13)

Figure 2.

"This epoxy system is formulated to have maximum ultraviolet light resistance consistent with its other properties. However no epoxy resin system is ultimately resistant to degradation by sunlight."

—From *The Epoxy Catalog*, A System Three Resins Publication, January 1999, page 3.

Figure 3.

"Research to date suggests that epoxy-bonded joints will not last as long as the wood being bonded. The reason for this is that the fatigue-trend line for epoxy fails more quickly than that for wood. Wood retains most of its capabilities even after millions of cycles of tension and compression. Millions of cycles of stress are difficult to imagine but they can be translated into operating hours. Boats at sea have been carefully instrumented where cyclic load increases associated with waves were measured once every three seconds. At this rate, after about 833 hours, a hull would experience about a million cycles. The material used in a (wood/epoxy composite) boat would at this time still have about 60 percent of its ultimate strength." (Author's Note—In other words, in about five weeks, your epoxy bond loses 40 percent of its ultimate strength, and keeps on losing more due to fatigue.)

—From *Fatigue Aspects of Wood/Epoxy Composites*, page 32, Gougeon Brothers, Inc. 1987, and *Gougeon Brothers on Boat Construction*, New revised 4th Edition, 1985, page 27.

Figure 4.

"The Forest Products Laboratory (FPL) has received many enquiries over the years about the structural durability of epoxy bonds to wood, usually from builders of wood aircraft and boats, and manufacturers of speciality wood products such as architectural posts and railings. When reporting failures, users invariably have described bonds that delaminated on exposure to water in an exterior environment. Epoxy adhesives do not equal resorcinols in durability of bonds to wood. They develop dry sheer strengths that may exceed the strength of the wood itself, but the bonds fail in delaminations once exposed to the severe stresses of water soaking and drying."

—Charles B. Vick, Research Scientist and E. Arnold Okkonen, Physical Science Technician, USDA Forest Service, Forest Product Lab. *Forest Products Journal* Vol. 47, No. 3, page 71, 1997. *(www.fpl.fs.fed.us/documnts/pdf1997/vicks97c.pdf)*

Photo 4. Here you see a joint that has suffered through years of the worst possible conditions. Constant exposure to the heat and UV of the sun with no coating to protect the adhesive or wood, plus the stress of being bent to conform to the curve of the hull and deck.

These unvarnished toe-rails are built of that oily wood which is known to challenge all adhesives – teak. Yet here they are, 25 or 30 years down the road, perfectly sound and tight, but worn. The wood plugs are, in fact, worn right off. Notice the dark, almost burgundy-colored glue line. It is especially visible at the nibs. This is that rarely-advertised, extreme-exposure adhesive, resorcinol.

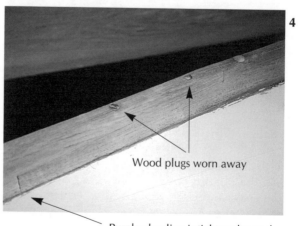

Wood plugs worn away

Purple glue line is tight and sound

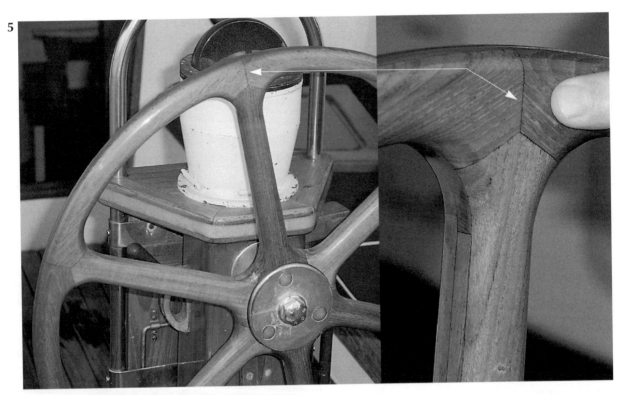

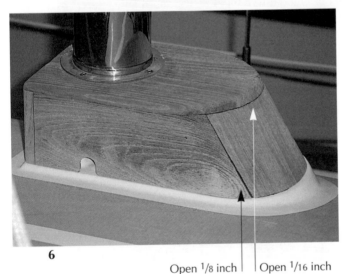

Open 1/8 inch   Open 1/16 inch

Photo 5. After John Guzzwell read the first draft of this appendix, he suggested we take a photo of the laminated teak wheel that has steered *Treasure* through 38 years of tropical and high latitude voyaging. This wheel is made up of 42 separate pieces of teak, glued with Cascophen (U.K.) resorcinol adhesive. It has survived constant exposure to tropical heat, UV rays of the sun, and stress, yet the joints are as solid today as all of the rest of the resorcinol glue joints on *Treasure*.

Photo 6. This Dorade box has no stressed or bent parts. But, the epoxy (yellowish glue line) failed anyway. The craftsmanship of the woodwork shows that the builder cared. The boat was about eight years old and well maintained when I took this photo near Annapolis, Maryland. It has spent its life away from the constant heat and UV of the tropics.

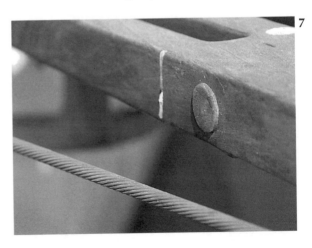

Photo 7. Wood plugs are under minimal stress compared to toerail scarfs. But after I took the photo, I pulled this half-inch-deep, 1¼-inch-diameter wood plug out easily using my fingers. The adhesive? Well known epoxy.

Photo 8. We saw this skylight hatch on a professionally built 36-foot Herreshoff Neria ketch at the Risor Woodenboat Festival in Norway. She is sailed in Norwegian waters and laid up under cover half of the year, so heat and UV from the sun are not a major problem. A sign on the deck of this boat proudly stated its particulars: "Constructed in 1983 with oak and mahogany, teak deck, using -------- brand epoxy." After seeing the open corner joints of the skylight, we also discovered that ALL of the 42 laminated oak frame heels in the bilge had separated and opened up like a fan. This is typical of the delamination problems I have seen on all types of timber in many bilges. After several years, the wet and dry conditions of the bilge stresses glue, and only the best adhesives can survive.

8

Photo 9. Oak, like teak, is a difficult wood to glue. The bitts, (Samson posts), shown here were glued with epoxy and have opened up ³/₁₆ inch. The USDA Forest Service Technical Bulletin No. 1512, page 77, states oak ships, timbers and frames should be glued with resorcinol (*www.fpl.fs.fed.us/documnts/FPLGTR*). Back in 1965, we laminated Seraffyn's backbone from 1 inch by 8 inch planks of white oak. Her sawn frames were laminated from Philippine mahogany. I feel fortunate we chose U.S. plywood brand resorcinol for that job as I am pretty certain (knowing what we know today) epoxy would have failed four or five years later, leaving us in Portugal with a delaminated stem, forefoot, and frames and little possibility of finishing our voyage around the world. Now, 31 years and over 50,000 miles later, the resorcinol structures on *Seraffyn* have been found fully sound in a recent survey.

9

Photo 10. The marine epoxy formulators will say, if you protect the epoxy joint from swelling by sealing it, (encapsulate it) you will solve the problem. You won't convince this boat owner. His whole dreamboat is coming apart. The cabin side on his custom-built 30-foot cutter is delaminating along the deck sill seam and at the lower part of the corner post. This is only one of several failures he pointed out to us during a visit in Southern California. He told us this work was done with a widely advertised epoxy, used by a trained professional two years before we took this photo. The wood was seal coated per the formulator's instructions, using epoxy first, then seven coats of varnish. It was kept well varnished after it was finished. The boat is up for sale.

Photo 11. This boat has delaminated almost completely outside and even inside where it has had minimal weathering. The frames and deckbeams have become structurally unsound. It is leaking so badly it is unseaworthy. Professionally built using a recognized brand of epoxy, this 18-year-old strip-planked mahogany 50-footer was lying in Mexico. The owner said he realized his dream was shattered when he could see light through 30 percent of the topside seams from inside the boat. Now he has been stalled for two years, his life savings tied up in a boat he cannot sell or sail. Are we being alarmist by showing this photo? We don't know, but this is the third major (i.e. whole-boat) disaster we've tripped over in the past four years of traveling. We haven't scoured the world for these delaminations but do wonder how many more are out there.

10

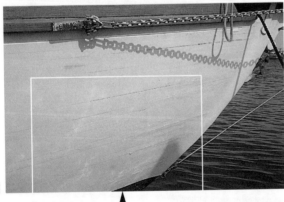

11

Figure 5.

"You will learn to use our products well with practice. . . It's okay to screw up now and then. That's how you learn. Besides, anything you do with our products can be fixed if you make a mistake."

—*The Epoxy Catalog,* System Three Publications, 1999.

Photo 12. The dilemma of the owner of the 50-footer in Photo 11 is a strong reminder to us of what might have happened had we chosen epoxy for *structural* glue joints on *Taleisin*. There was a lot of pressure to do so back in 1980, just as there is today: from formulators, advertisers, other builders, peer pressure. . . As it is, we did choose a well-known epoxy, urged on by the durability promises of its formulator and their technical advisory department. (They did not put these promises in writing.)

This photo shows not only the results, but a perfect comparison between epoxy and resorcinol. When we were making our decisions, we had heard that epoxy could suffer from UV degradation and might not be adequate for extreme exposure (waterproof) usage, so we chose resorcinol for the cabin side-to-deck sill joint as it would be exposed to the sun and salt water outside. But to make clean-up easier around the deckbeams and carlins inside the boat, we used the light-colored epoxy system. The formulators never mentioned *anything* about heat deformation problems. Heat from the stove pipe of our kerosene heater has caused the epoxy to fail. You can see that the 15-year-old spar varnish is still in great shape. It is more heat-resistant than the epoxy. The resorcinol joint, two-and-a-half inches above the delaminated epoxy joint is tight and in perfect condition. The epoxy

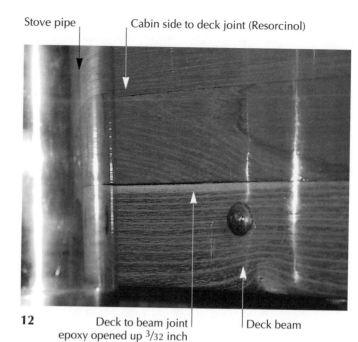

Stove pipe   Cabin side to deck joint (Resorcinol)

12   Deck to beam joint |
          epoxy opened up 3/32 inch | Deck beam

joints on our forehatch and cockpit hatch have also delaminated as has our ash, galley sink drainboard.

The interesting thing is, our spruce ultra-light, barrel-staved spinnaker pole, plus the teak skylight, sliding hatch and cabin beams were also glued with epoxy and are still okay. But now we are worried; when will they come apart?

Now that we have hopefully caught your attention, we would like to help you be an aware buyer instead of one frightened by the caveat "Buyer beware." So, for simplicity and brevity—and hopefully to keep you interested enough to read onward—we have chosen the following question–and–answer format and highlighted some facts that should give you food for thought.

QUESTION – Are you implying that all epoxy-laminated boats are ready to fall apart?

ANSWER – I think any epoxy joint that is exposed to the elements or to hard use could fall apart even if it is sealed with epoxy. One formulator told the owner of the boat in Photo 11: "That batch of epoxy only had about a 20-year lifespan." As I mentioned, the failure rate is not consistent. Not all epoxy joints will come apart, just as not all fiberglass boats will develop osmosis.

When osmosis was finally recognized as a problem, existing fiberglass boats dropped in value dramatically and new boats became suspect. It has been estimated that osmosis concerns increased the cost of new fiberglass boats by 10 to 15 percent, the maintenance cost of older ones by 10 percent. I think the over-enthusiastic use of epoxy will eventually have similar fall-out.

"Some years ago my firm was persuaded to use epoxy in preference to the Casco Glues and resorcinols we had used for more than 50 years. The result was costly: seams split along the glue lines and scarfs delaminated.

I have also seen a bowsprit with a plate stating: 'This bowsprit was built by so-and-so yard in Florida using xx epoxy system. The brass plate looked good—and so did the view through the delaminated seams in the timber. Never again."

—H.R. Spencer, Spencer Thetis Wharf Ltd., Cowes, Isle of Wight, England.

Henry Spencer is a highly respected spar builder/boat builder, and rigger. This letter appeared in *Classic Boat* magazine, U.K., 1997.

Q – If this problem exists, why don't we hear more about it?

A – People are not eager to discuss their delaminations, just as they would be reluctant to discuss their bankruptcy. The people we interviewed in Mexico asked us not to mention their names or boat names. It is about resale value first, pride second.

Q – Do you think there is an actual cover-up?

A – It would seem so. Take a look at Figure 6 and consider the financial impact once people start asking questions about epoxy, especially if they turn to other products. And all companies worry about ongoing litigation. A chemist who was hired as a witness in a suit against one epoxy–formulating company told us the case was settled out of court on the stipulation that

Figure 6.

A FEW OF THE REASONS YOU DO NOT HEAR ABOUT EPOXY FAILURES

1. Would you want to devalue your boat by showing off delaminations?

2. If you call your epoxy formulator's help line and are asked what you did wrong, could you prove you followed all of their directions?

3. If you were an epoxy formulator, marine epoxy salesman, chandler, boatyard store manager, or boat builder who sells epoxy, would you want to discourage people from buying a hot-selling, high-profit item?

4. If you were a boatbuilder, would you risk losing a contract by saying you want to use a less popular adhesive when the competing boatyard would willingly use whatever the customer or designer requests?

5. If you were a builder who had previously used epoxy, would you want to cast doubt on the longevity of the boats you had already built?

6. If you were a publisher or editor, would you want to upset readers, advertisers, or boatbuilders, by discussing problems with such a popular class of products? Would you have the time to do the research and editorial work necessary to cover this subject in a fair and even-handed way?

no party (chemist included) disclose any details of the boat's delamination, glue type, nor the final cash settlement.

Q – Why don't you name brand names?

A – If we name one or two brands, other formulators will jump up and say, "But ours works better." Research with Charles B. Vicks, USDA Forestry Products Research Lab; Brian Boult, University of Auckland Construction Materials Research Dept; Richard Jagels, Professor of Construction Forest Biology, University of Maine, Orono, and others, as shown in the various figures here show that all of the "user-friendly, relatively affordable" marine epoxies have similar shortcomings as a structural wood adhesive.

Figure 7.

CAUTION

Before you decide to purchase any adhesive for structural wooden parts of your boat, ask for written confirmation that the adhesive meets all tests for exterior structural use, as required by the construction industry for use in your area.

In the U.S. the normal specification used to qualify adhesives for structural glued-lamination timbers intended for wet-use exposures under industry standard ANSI/AITCA 190.1 - 1999 (1) is ASTM Specification D 2559. In the UK the standard is BS 1204

"This specification covers adhesives suitable for the bonding of wood, including treated wood, into structural laminated wood products for general construction, for marine use, or for other uses where a high-strength, waterproof adhesive bond is required."

(from *FPL journal* Vol. 47, no. 3, March 1997)

You'll notice we use the term "formulator." None of the epoxy companies actually make anything. They buy epoxy resins, additives, and hardeners from big chemical companies, blend, decant, label and sell them to you (Ref 1, page 508).

Q – What about *Taleisin's* delamination?

A – Showing this in print presented a tough moral decision. We know it will reduce *Taleisin's* value; it might cast doubts on my boatbuilding knowledge. But we've decided to keep the boat indefinitely so price is academic. We are glad our early research encouraged us to confine our use of epoxy to parts that can be replaced relatively easily, not structural components of the boat.

Figure 8.

"The American Institute of Timber Construction (AITC) does not recommend that epoxies be used in design or repair of structural timbers if the bonds are expected to withstand either sheer or tension loading without steel reinforcement."

Q – What are you trying to accomplish with this Appendix?

A – To encourage epoxy formulators to list the limitations of their products on easy-to-understand instruction sheets—use parameters, limitations, problem areas, health restrictions, just as required for most industrial products (or like the info sheets that come with each medication).

2. – Encourage people to speak out about problems they have encountered and help others avoid costly delaminations, while at the same time encouraging a more serious, professional attitude toward the use of adhesives.

3. – Expose the epoxy formulators' systematic and unfounded trashing of resorcinol, the standard against which all other adhesives are tested for exterior structural use. They have inferred in word and cartoons that resorcinol is so difficult to handle that only a few gifted geniuses can use it. They have exaggerated the health problems of resorcinols, and at the same time under-played those associated with epoxy—not only while you are applying it, but later when you are sanding the finished epoxy product. They have even lied about its strength. Witness this patently false statement. . ."Its use is limited to surface where peel and cleavage forces are negligible, and vibration and impact unlikely. . .we also note that resorcinol does not produce reliable joints with oak, especially if subjected to repeated wetting and drying." *A Low Temperature-cure Structural Adhesive*, Gerald Schindler, (president of Chem-tech T-88) *Woodenboat* magazine, issue 4, page 47.

Epoxy resins. . . Their use in wood-to-wood bonding is limited since their permanence has not been adequately established.

—Canadian Plywood Association, 1999. (*www.canply.org/hand5.htm*)

"The lack of structural durability of epoxy bonds to wood has been a continuing frustration to fabricators of adhesive-bonded wood assemblies intended for service in exterior environments."

—*Adhesives Age*, July 1997, Volume 40, Number 8.

"Epoxy resins—Good adhesive to metals, glass, certain plastics and wood products. Permanence in wood joints not adequately established."

—*Wood Handbook: Wood as an Engineering Material*, U.S. Department of Agriculture, pages 9-11.

---

4. – Get people to realize you can laminate the skins on a boat, (three-skin, strip-planked) without epoxy. The Luders 16s were "cold molded" using an early type of resorcinol and are still in fine shape today. Sparkman and Stephens specified resorcinols for many of their 1950 – 1960 designs, which are still going strong. Furthermore, newer resorcinols have gap-filling

abilities, required only close contact, and cure at low temperatures, so work very well for any laminated structures we boat builders can construct.

5. – Get people to open their glue arsenal to include all of the non-colored adhesives that give results as good as or better than epoxy for non-structural uses at far lower prices, with lower health risks. (See following pages.)

Q – So what do you think the consumer and boat builder should be doing?

A – Research, research, research. Distrust heavily advertised products. In 45 years around the boating industry I have found the modestly advertised products are frequently the most satisfying in the long run.

Call the adhesives suppliers, formulators, and chemical companies and ask questions based on the information we have provided.

Demand proof of compliance with industrial standards for marine or exterior use. (Figure 7.)

Q – Why do you call this Appendix Superior Adhesives For the Millennium?

A – With the access provided by the internet today, I feel it is easier to find real information about adhesives than it was in 1980 when we built *Taleisin*. Had the net existed, I would have been able to check information sources right around the world and I would have limited my use of epoxy to sealing, coating, or sheathing.

I feel superior adhesives are ones chosen because they have fine track records throughout all industries, not ones chosen just because they are easiest for the unskilled boat builder to use. I am sure most of you would agree that the job of a structural boat-building adhesive is to guarantee that our boats will have good resale value ten, twenty, or thirty years from now. Just as important is that they will continue to be seaworthy and sail safely well into the millennium.

At the suggestion of our attorney we include the following:

The observations here contain the opinion of the author. In part they are reflective of his experience, and, where expressly indicated in the text, made in reliance upon information which has been supplied from collected sources.

Before embracing a project involving boat construction, I encourage the reader to conduct extensive research on the comparative suitability of alternative adhesives. Further, I encourage the reader, if there is any uncertainty as to the suitability of an adhesive for his intended application, to request express written representations from the manufacturer that the product is suitable for the *precise* use intended.

CHOOSING ADHESIVES

Refer to pages 508-510 for further information where numbers appear.

Saying that there is one perfect adhesive for every bonding job is as simplistic as saying that there is only one perfect wood, or one paint for every job on the inside and outside of your boat. To be a well-versed boatbuilder, you must know the characteristics of a variety of adhesives so you can choose the best one for each situation. You should know about the exposure resistance, heat and fire resistance, waterproofness, pot life, cost, health considerations, ease of use, and the adaptability of each adhesive to the skills you have available and your shop conditions. Your choice then should be based on (1) where the joint will be in the boat, (2) what type of exposure it will get to sunlight, heat, and amazingly corrosive salt water, and (3) how difficult it will be to repair the joint if it does fail. Unfortunately, with the advent of high-profit-margin epoxies[1] has come overenthusiastic advertising,[2] which, in effect, discourages builders from considering other, probably more suitable, adhesives.[3]

I have worked with a wide variety of adhesives and discussed their pros and cons with boatbuilders (including John Guzzwell and Raleigh Kalayjian, to name just two) who have used some of them for up to forty years. I have also corresponded with chemical engineers, including Scott Earnshaw of Dimet Industries, Kern Hendricks of System Three, and Brian Boult, materials engineer and research fellow at the University of Auckland, New Zealand, who organized research for us on how various adhesives react to wet environments.[4] I have spoken to chemists and formulators at Gougeon Brothers Inc., Chem-Tech Inc., and Ciba-Geigy Ltd. Based on this research, I have tried to present a realistic picture of the pros and cons of five types of adhesives used in the construction of *Taleisin*. The adhesives are divided into three groups, starting with water-resistant melamine-urea types; then water-resistant, gap-filling epoxy systems formulated for boatbuilding; and, finally, extreme-exposure, waterproof-rated, gap-filling,* low-temperature resorcinols.

Although you may feel I am being cautious in my assessment of adhesives—and, in fact, in the whole matter of laminations in boatbuilding—I have good reasons. Many of the repairs I have had to deal with during a thirty-year career have involved glue failures (delaminations).

---

* Although gaps filled with glue are acceptable where they are out of sight (such as between multiskin layers or under paint), all joints—and especially varnished or natural (bare) joints—are more professional and more attractive when they are tight. A ¹⁄₁₆-inch or wider glue-filled joint in a cabinside, in a table, or in a varnished caprail is, in my eyes, unacceptable.[5]

Melamine-Urea, Water-Resistant Adhesives

Weldwood and DAP plastic-resin glue, Casco UF 109, and Aerolite 306 and 308 adhesives are inexpensive and relatively easy to use. Cleanup can be done with water. This saves money and eliminates the use of special solvents (e.g., acetone, lacquer thinner), which have high health and fire risks. Each gives full-strength joints with light-colored glue lines that are not affected by elevated temperatures or ultraviolet light. None are suitable for extreme exposure use, nor for long-term deep-cycle situations.*

Weldwood Plastic-Resin Glue

This adhesive is not reliable on woods that contain tannic acid, such as oak. It is only water-resistant and should not be used for structural parts of a boat, such as frames and the backbone. I (and many other builders) have used it successfully for spars, which are kept sealed from moisture by varnish or paint. It is excellent for interior joinery, such as tables, paneling, and wood plugs, as it produces the least-obvious glue line of any adhesive I have used. This is not only because of its color, but also because it can be used to make tight-fitting hairline joints with no loss of strength.

Pro	Con
Almost invisible glue line.	Water-resistant only.
Easy mixing.	Not good for use on oak.
Water-soluable for easy cleanup and lower health risk.	Requires good joint and firm clamping pressure.
No joint-fatigue problems.	Little gap-filling ability—$\frac{1}{32}$ inch maximum.
Not sensitive to high air temperatures or UV light.	Assembly time short at temperatures over 80°F.
Crosshatch sanding not required.	
No gloves or respirator required.	
Can be used at 50°F for full-strength joint.	
Difficult to starve joints.	
Adequate instructions on container.	
Inexpensive.	

---

* Deep-cycle situations exist with such structures as keels, stems, or the bilge end of frames, which will be subjected to constant shrinking and swelling caused by wetting and drying and heat changes.

Casco UF 109

This adhesive has one outstanding feature: The open assembly time and pot life can be controlled by adding more or less of the catalyst powder. We used it with excellent success in 95°F conditions to glue up the spars for *Taleisin.* Although it gives a clear glue line, it is not quite as invisible as plastic-resin glue.

Pro	Con
Controllable assembly time.	Water-resistant only.
Clear glue line.	Little gap-filling ability—$1/32$ inch maximum.
Water cleanup, so lower health risk.	Requires firm clamping pressure.
Not sensitive to high air temperatures or UV light.	Sold only in Canada by Borden Ltd., P.O. Box 58098, Vancouver V6P 6C5 Canada.
No joint-fatigue problems.	
Crosshatch sanding not required.	
Can be used down to 50°F for full-strength joint.	
No respirator or gloves required.	
Difficult to starve joints.	
Easy to measure.	
Inexpensive.	

Aerolite 306 and 308

Aerolite is the most convenient water-resistant glue I have used. The powder component is mixed with water to form a creamy resin. This resin and its attendant hardener can be left in covered glass jars, ready to use. Whenever there is a gluing job, you brush the resin onto one side of the joint, brush the acid-based hardener onto the other side, and then clamp together the two pieces to set up and produce a full-strength joint. For larger jobs, the acid hardener can be mixed directly into the resin. (Brushes with metallic parts should not be left in the hardener because a reaction can stain the wood near joints.) This glue is used in the United States for home-built aircraft. Some English and New Zealand builders use it for the structural parts of boat hulls. Brian Boult's tests[4] showed that Aerolite was more water-resistant than either Weldwood or UF 109, but since it is rated water-resistant only and not for extreme exposure, I feel it is a risky choice in the long run. However, it is excellent for dinghies, interiors, hatches, and any nonstructural woodwork that will be protected by coatings.

Aerolite 308 is a slightly more expensive version of this same adhesive. It is rated as highly water-resistant, to British Government Standards 1204. It is not—as unfortunately designated in some suppliers' catalogs and also in Robert Steward's *Boatbuilding Manual* (see Bibliography)—a waterproof-rated adhesive, nor is it rated for extreme-exposure, deep-cycle situations.

Pro	Con
Convenient to use.	Water-resistant only.
Water cleanup, so lower health risk.	Little gap-filling ability—$1/32$ inch maximum.
Almost clear glue line.	Requires firm clamping pressure.
Can be used at 50°F with no loss of strength.	Available only through mail order in United States (Wicks Aircraft Supply, 410 Pine St., Highland, IL 62249).
No crosshatch sanding required.	
Accurate measuring not essential.	
Not sensitive to high air temperatures or to UV light.	
Difficult to starve joints.	
No joint fatigue problems.	
Adequate instructions on container.	
Inexpensive.	

Epoxy Boatbuilding Adhesives

Epoxies present more of a health risk than the other adhesives I have used. This is due partially to the solvents required for cleanup, partially to the chemical content of the hardeners. They require accurate measurement, are laborious to apply if done according to the manufacturers' recommendations,[6] and, with their required gloves, cleanup solvents, respirators, and safety glasses,[7] more expensive and time-consuming to use than any other boatbuilding adhesive. Information about the correct uses and the limitations is difficult to find, as it rarely is listed on the container labels. Instead, the user must buy a separate technical manual from either the retailer or the formulator. Over the past nine years, Lin and I have studied much of this technical information and found that it often was ambiguous,[8] exaggerated,[9,2,3] couched in legalese, and full of fine print that seems designed to protect the formulators from lawsuits.[10]

If I sound unhappy with epoxy as an adhesive, it is because over the past fifteen years I have tried several different systems and found them unreliable, especially for use in the tropics. I have experienced and seen failures on deck structures, with stressed scarf joints such as on toerails and laminated tillers. Although I once thought these failures happened because epoxies are rated as water-resistant only,[11] I have since learned that epoxy loses strength when it is applied below 65°F[12,8] and when it is subjected to heat[13] and, apparently, to salt spray.[14]

As shown,[13] common boatbuilding epoxies lose strength (deflect, creep) as temperatures rise above 100°F. The most flexible systems, such as T-88, start to lose strength at temp-eratures as low as 101°F; West System epoxy has an HDT (heat deflection temperature) of 118°F; System Three's HDT is 124°F. On an 80°F day, sunlight can cause the temperature of painted white surfaces to raise to 128°F, light blue or aluminium surfaces to 143°F; red surfaces can reach 178°F and black 198°F, according to the West System "Cold Strategy" phamplet. Bare teak decks can reach temperatures above 140°F in the Tropics, as can engine rooms after several hours of powering.

I am uncomfortable with the apparently incomplete testing results available from boatbuilding epoxy formulators.* Brian Boult in 1988 did a worldwide computer search for tests performed to determine how epoxies would perform in deep-cycle marine situations. He found nothing that could apply to boatbuilding.[4] The marine formulators to date have only made available test information related to the fatigue resistance of epoxy structures under dry conditions. The results showed epoxy to be more prone to fatigue than the wood it bonds.[15]

The 3M Company and Dexter Corporation performed tests on room-temperature-cure structural epoxies they formulate for the aerospace industries, which *do relate* to boatbuilding. They subjected adhered aluminum joints to both saltwater spray and tap water at 100 percent humidity. After thirty days, the saltwater-sprayed joints, which initially had a shear strength of over 3100 psi, sheared apart at 500 psi, while those subjected to thirty days of tap water still had a shear strength of 2942 psi.[14] (It is interesting to note that the epoxy-laminated composite boats cited by marine epoxy formulators as long-term successes, such as the trimaran *Adagio,* are kept and sailed on the Great Lakes—fresh water.)

With all of these reservations, where would I choose to use epoxy? It is an effective sealant for endgrain situations and as a base for interior varnish, or for under two-part (reaction lacquer) paints.[16] If you do choose it as an adhesive, its gap-filling ability will be useful and its clear color will facilitate preparation for clear finishes. But since it is labor-intensive, costly, and presents more of a health risk than water-soluble adhesives, I would reserve it for coating jobs or for applying sheathings to the outside of a hull.

---

*More complete testing of polyester resins in the 1960s and 1970s might have eliminated many of the osmosis and blistering problems plaguing fiberglass boat owners today.

Pro	Con
Effective outside seal coat.	Water resistant only.[11]
Clear glue line; easier to clean up inside varnished hull.	High health risk due to solvents, chemicals in hardeners, and fumed silica used as filler.[7]
Effective for bonding sheathing material to hull.	Poor instructions both on label of container and in technical manual—i.e., limitations are not stated clearly.
Widely available.	Loss of joint strength if used below 65°F.[12]
Good gap-filling characteristics when used with fillers.	Joint not as resistant to fatigue as the wood it is bonding.[15]
Helps wood resist rot.	Three steps required to ensure full-strength joint, including crosshatch sanding, before applying two separate coats of epoxy.[17]
	Gloves and safety glasses required for use with all components.[7]
	Respirator required with West System 205 hardeners (and presumably those of others' systems).[7]
	Not reliable on oak, teak, or maple.[18]
	Can lose strength at temperatures above 101°F.[13]
	Regular epoxy is not fire-resistant.[19]
	When properly used, including three recommended seal coats, costs more than twice resorcinol, triple other water-resistant glues.[20]
	Measuring and mixing must be very accurate.[17] Chemists recommend weighing components to ensure accuracy.
	Applying warm epoxy to cold surfaces can cause condensation to settle on the adhesive before parts are mated and will give a low-strength bond.[21]
	Not UV-resistant. If not coated with UV inhibitors, will begin to decay within six months of exposure to sun.[22]
	Firm clamping can starve joint.
	Short pot life—12 minutes at 85°F.

Resorcinol Glues

There are two types of resorcinols. The first, sold by Weldwood, Borden, and DAP in the United States, can be used only at temperatures above 70°F, with close-fitting joints and firm clamping pressure required. (I call this summer-grade resorcinol.) The second, which has been used in Britain, New Zealand, and continental Europe for about twenty years under the name of Aerodux (diagram A), or Cascophen resorcinol, is often called winter-grade resorcinol. It is gap-filling up to 1/16 inch (1.3mm) and can be used to obtain full-strength joints at temperatures as low as 50°F. It requires only close contact while setting and light pressure. On the other hand, it can be used with high clamping pressure to get tight-looking joints with no loss of strength. I feel that this is the best marine adhesive currently available. It passes all government and military specifications, tests for extreme exposure and deep-cycle situations, and is rated waterproof. It has been used successfully since World War II for minesweepers and amphibious aircraft. It comes from the same family of adhesives used to make marine- and exterior-grade plywoods. In thirty years of boat repair work, I have never seen a single glue failure in any structure that had the distinctive purple glue joints of resorcinol. John Guzzwell says the same, and resorcinol is the glue he used to lay up his three-skinned cruising boat *Treasure,* now twenty-seven years old.[23]

Resorcinol is rarely advertised in boating magazines, since this market is minuscule compared with its primary market, industrial construction-materials companies. In that industry it is the standard adhesive for severe-exposure conditions and where fire resistance is important, such as fire doors, and for the structural beams in buildings and bridges.[24] Lloyd's Register of Shipping accepts resorcinol as a standard adhesive for hull construction, and builders need not submit independent test data if they use it on vessels being built under supervision. All of the various epoxy formulations must be reviewed separately and evaluated before Lloyd's will approve their use on a hull. It is interesting to note that Lloyd's Register will not give a 100A1 rating to any laminated hull, no matter what adhesive is used, unless the boat is built in an enclosed shop with temperature and humidity controls. (See appendix B, Lloyd's Rules.)

I particularly like resorcinol because it penetrates the sap cells of the wood. I have seen it go as much as 5/16 inch into the endgrain of an ash scarf joint. This absorption is caused by the capillary action activated by the alcohol in the resin, plus the firm clamping pressure that hydraulically pushes the glue into the cells. This rootlike penetration helps spread the strains that occur in deep-cycle situations. This adhesive works well on any timber, including teak or oak, and it needs no crosshatch sanding or special preparations to give good bonds.[25]

I would recommend the use of resorcinol for any part of a boat, but since it leaves a dark glue line, it would be my second choice for any light-colored woods that will be finished clear and highly visible. It would be my only choice for teak deck structures that are to be left bare (especially in the sunlight) and for any structural hull parts; for outer laminations on a three-skinned hull; for laminated floors and frames; and especially for stems, rudders, and deadwoods.

Pro	Con
Rated waterproof, for extreme-exposure and deep-cycle situations.	Dark glue line.
Water cleanup, so lower health risk.	Excess glue hard to clean up on light-colored woods.
No gloves, glasses, or respirator required, just clean working habits.	Winter grade must be bought by mail order in the United States (Jamestown Distributors, 28 Narragansett Ave., Jamestown, Rhode Island); Or Ciba-Geigy Ltd., Duxford, England; Or Dimet Ltd., P.O. Box 11123, Ellerslie, New Zealand
Test data readily available.	
Helps wood resist rot.	
Time-tested in salt water and on heavy marine structures for more than forty-five years.	U.S.-type summer-grade resorcinol requires 70°F gluing temperatures and firm clamping pressure and is not gap-filling.
Good on all hardwoods, including oak, teak, and maple.	
Fire-retardant.	
No concern about heat distortion.	
Can be used as low as 50°F (10°C).	
Not sensitive to UV light.	
Not affected by boiling water, solvents, acids, molds, or fungi.[25]	
Does not require coatings to encapsulate.[23]	
Can be used on timber with moisture content as high as 25 percent and as low as 6.[25]	
Exact mix ratio can vary by as much as 10 percent.	
Gap-filling to 1.3mm (1/16 inch).[25]	
Long pot life—60 minutes at 86°F.	
Crosshatch sanding not required.[25]	
Difficult to starve joints.	
Moderate cost.	

Aerodux 500

There is now a more user-friendly resorcinol available. Formulated by Dynochem UK for structural use outdoors in the building industry, the resin comes in three grades, fast, medium, and slow. The same hardener is used with each grade. Aerodux 500 has several advantages over the older resorcinols. It can be used as low as 45°F (10°C) and still give full-strength joints that meet all tests set by the British and German governments for extreme-exposure, waterproof, heat-proof, load-bearing structures. It is lighter in color than most resorcinols, giving a reddish-brown glue joint, rather than the purple-black one. With up to 20 percent fillers added, it can be gap-filling up to $1/16$ inch and only requires close contact, not high pressure, while setting to give full-strength joints. The fillers are cheap and easy to handle—wood flour (finely ground sawdust), china clay, or fine chalk. Potlife and clamping time can be varied from as fast as 15 minutes to as long as two hours on a 90°F day. This adhesive will even work on pressure-treated timbers. This is a liquid-to-liquid mix, one-to-one, either by volume or weight. There is latitude for up to 7 percent error in proportions. For a complete review of Aerodux 500 see *Woodenboat* magazine March/April 1999, page 119. For larger quantities contact Dynochem, Ireland Ltd. For quantities of less than 250 kilograms contact B & K Resins, Ashgrove Estate, Ashgrove Road, Bromley, Kent, BR1 4TH, UK. Tel: 44 181-3151207; fax 44 181-3130280.

PVA-Type Adhesives (Gorilla Glue, Wonderbond)

John Guzzwell chose a PVA one-part glue for the skins of a light race boat and commented on the ease of use, relatively low cost and good cosmetic appearance. It is, however, not rated as waterproof to any current standard testing parameters. The chemical manufacturers warn "because of the thermoplastic nature of PVA glues, they are subject to creep under high stress. They should not be used in structural bonding applications." (Bordon Co. specifications.) The Gorilla Glue Comparative Analysis sheet (*www.gorillaglue.com.html*) does state that "resorcinol is a good gap-filling glue, and is a superior adhesive in this regard."

Conclusion

Whichever adhesive you choose, remember first that *all* glue companies are protected by disclaimers. To put it bluntly, no company will accept responsibility for loss of materials or loss of labor in case of glue failure. All you will get from them is some more glue. It will be your own *personal* tragedy if your boat has delaminations caused by poor glue choice or poor technique. I know; it has happened to me. The professional boatbuilder may be less directly affected by adhesive failures, since the boat probably will be out of his shop when they do occur. But in the long run, delaminations could jeopardize his reputation as a knowledgeable builder.

Second, the health risks involved with the use of solvents, hardeners, and any boatbuilding chemicals will be relative to the number of hours you use them, the precautions you take, and the ventilation in your shop. A builder who uses epoxies and their solvents for 20 or 30 hours a week, working indoors in the winter or inside a hull without a respirator, will be exposed to a far-higher risk than a person building in his spare time, especially if he is working in an open shed. But in each case, it pays to check all of the health warnings available both from the formulator and from the Poison Control Center in your state. (Give the center the brand name of the product you are planning to use.) Be cautious, and remember that it took more than forty years for workmen to recognize the dangers of inhaling asbestos and coal dust.

NOTE: The North American distributor for Aerodux 500 and other resorcinol adhesives is:

Custom-Pak Adhesives
11047 Lambs Lane
Newark, Ohio 43055
1-800-454-4583
email: info@custompak.com
www.custompak.com

REFERENCES

[1] "There has been a significant increase in the availability and use of epoxy resin adhesives over the past few years and many 'manufacturers' are now putting products on the market. These firms are not strictly manufacturers as their function is to purchase the basic epoxy resin in bulk from the few large chemical groups like Monsanto, Shell, etc., and then modify it for viscosity and add certain fillers to make the difficult basic epoxy more workable. They then retail the modified resins in small lots, being handsomely rewarded for their efforts.

"Their use is still not so simple and each adhesive has a slightly different handling characteristic and the builder cannot readily change materials without undergoing a further re-learning and familiarization period." A. McInnes, Deputy General Manager, Lloyd's Register—Yacht and Small Craft Services, 71 Fenchurch, London, England—Letter, March 9, 1988.

[2] "Designed to perform without qualification under hostile building conditions. Proven in daily use by boatbuilders working from above the Arctic Circle to right smack on the equator and everywhere in between." Advertisement, System Three Resins, *Small Boat Journal*, April/May 1987.

[3] "The epoxies are excellent bonding agents to a wide variety of surfaces and vastly outperform the earlier resorcinol and urea glues." "The use of West System resins dramatically lowers the cost of bonding and makes laminated construction possible for the home builder." Gougeon Brothers, Inc., Bay City, Michigan, *West System Products Technical Manual*, 1981, page 5.

[4] In 1987 and 1988, Brian F. Boult, M.E. MIPENZ, registered civil engineer, completed comparative tests of different adhesives bonding different timbers subjected to cyclic wetting and drying. Testing paid for by *WoodenBoat* magazine, *Sail* magazine, Lin and Larry Pardey, Ciba-Geigy NZ Ltd., and High Modulus NZ Ltd. Copies of report available from Brian Boult, 7 Edenvale Road, Mt. Eden, Auckland, for $25.

[5] "While West System epoxy can be relied on to fill gaps and span voids, your boat will be lighter, it will look better and it will be cheaper if you work your wood until you have good fits." *The Gougeon Brothers on Boat Construction*, 4th ed., Bay City, Michigan, 1985, page 123.

[6] "Once surface preparation is complete, we recommend applying West System resin-hardener in a two-step process. The first step is to apply a straight resin-hardener (without fillers) to the surfaces to be joined. If the surface has been pre-coated with epoxy and has cured, you should sand the surface lightly before proceeding with the second step. Woods such as balsa and Western red cedar are quite porous and are likely to soak up more of the mixture than other wood species. Therefore they need to be re-coated to maintain enough epoxy at the surface of the wood for maximum adhesion. The end grain of most woods absorbs more than the flat grain, so re-coating may be required in these areas as well. Re-coating is required if the surface starts to take on a dry flat look as the wood absorbs the epoxy mixture. The second step is to modify the resin with the desired fillers to bridge any remaining gaps and provide a dependable bond. The thickened resin can be applied immediately over the surface that has been wet out without waiting for the coating to dry." *West System Products Technical Manual*, Bay City, Michigan, 1987, page 5-4.

[7] Materials safety data sheets, May 1987, System Three Resins, P.O. Box 70436, Seattle, Washington 98107. Materials safety data sheet, 205 and 206 hardeners, 105 resins, March 1, 1986. Gougeon Brothers, Inc., Bay City, Michigan.

See also *The Epoxy Book*, System Three, Seattle, Washington, 1987, page 11; *The Gougeon Brothers on Boat Construction*, chapter 8, pages 51-58.

[8] "Tensile and comprehensive strengths are *more than adequate* [Pardey emphasis] for wooden boat construction. The heat distortion temperature is fully adequate for boats painted light colors, but suggests that dark colored hulls subject to intense sunlight might experience some softening of the epoxy coating." *The Epoxy Book*, page 8.

"We know that our epoxy will work at low temperatures as well as or better than the other brands. The problem is, we also know our product doesn't perform at its best at low temperatures. Neither will anyone else's. Experienced craftsmen know that, even under ideal conditions, they must exercise diligence and great care in their building practices. In cold temperatures, maintaining good quality control of epoxy bonds becomes even more difficult because the chance of joint failure seems to increase as the ambient bonding temperature decreases. . . . Just because an epoxy has set up and become hard, doesn't necessarily mean it has reached a good cure. In fact, it may have only developed a fraction of its required strength. The tough part is that it's really difficult to tell a well-cured joint from a bad one; that is, until it prematurely fails under load, days, weeks or even months later." Advertisement, *WoodenBoat* magazine, January/ February 1987, Gougeon Brothers, Inc., entitled "Should Epoxies Be Used in Cold Conditions?"

[9] "Permanent bonding power—cures as low as 35°F, non-critical 1:1 mix." Advertisement for T-88, *Small Boat Journal,* July 1987, page 108, by Chem-Tech Inc.

"Can be effectively used at 100% humidity. Can be effectively used to 35°F." Advertisement from same issue, page 7, by System Three Resins.

[10] "Has an excellent balance of properties for use with wood . . . where the substrate carries the major portion of the load and the surface temperature is not extreme." *The Epoxy Book,* page 8.

[11] "Works where an application calls for an extremely strong, water resistant adhesive or coating." *West System Products Technical Manual,* page 1-1.

[12] "Epoxies can be made to be forgiving; however we know that they must be used within certain latitudes of application, temperature, humidity, joint fit, surface preparation and cure times. Epoxies rely on an extremely complex chemical reaction to achieve their strength and longevity; and all of these variables can drastically affect, and in many cases compromise, the short and long term performance of epoxy resins. . . . There exists a comprehensive body of fatigue test data that supports wood/epoxy bonding at temperatures of 60°F and above. To our knowledge, no significant body of such test data exists that would suggest 100% bonding effectiveness can be achieved at temperatures as low as 35°F with any epoxy adhesive system." *Strategies for Successful Cold Temperature Bonding and Sealing with Epoxy,* Gougeon Brothers, Inc., Bay City, Michigan, January 1987.

[13] "At about 120°F, common epoxy loses 30% of its strength. At 140°F, it loses another 20%. By the time the temperature reaches 160°F, the temperature at which epoxy begins to soften, it

has retained only 40% of its original strength. The loss of strength is not permanent, lasting only as long as the temperature is elevated. However, testing done at Gougeon Brothers suggests that wood/epoxy structures may have accelerated fatigue when stressed at higher temperatures. This sounds frightening, because a teak deck can certainly hit 120°F in the hot summer sun." Aimé Ontario Fraser, *WoodenBoat* magazine, September/October 1988, page 55.

[14] Initial overlap shear strength after a minimum of five tests, 2500 psi. After environmental aging:

Tap water at 75°F	14 days	3120 psi.
	30 days	2942 psi.
	90 days	2075 psi.
Salt spray at 95°F	14 days	2300 psi.
	30 days	500 psi.
	60 days	300 psi.

From product specification sheet, 2216 B/A Structural Adhesive, revised to January 1980. 3M Company, St. Paul, Minnesota.

"Resists salt spray." From specification sheet, aerospace adhesive EA 93r by Hysol, Division of Dexter Corp., 15051 E. Don Julian Road, Industry, California. (Both of these adhesives are thixotropic epoxy resins with amine curing agents rated as excellent for bonding rubber, metal, wood, most plastics and masonry products. They are commonly used for space-shuttle applications.)

[15] "Research to date suggests that epoxy-bonded joints will not last as long as the wood being bonded. The reason for this is that the fatigue trend line for epoxy falls more quickly than that for wood. At just a few load cycles, epoxy is much stronger in shear than wood, but ultimately at some point the two trend lines will converge and the failure mode will transfer from the wood into the epoxy region of the laminate. This is not necessarily cause for alarm; for most applications, a well-conceived epoxy will last long enough for structural success." *Fatigue Aspects of Wood/Epoxy Composites,* page 32, Gougeon Brothers, Inc., 1987.

"For maximum life, sound wood/epoxy design calls for loading the structure at about 10% of its ultimate strength—as opposed to conventional wood construction, which calls for 20 to 30%." (Pardey note: In other words, to get the same strength over the long haul, you have to increase the scantlings to allow for the possible fatiguing of the epoxy.) Aimé Ontario Fraser, *WoodenBoat* magazine, September/October 1988, page 53.

[16] "If it weren't for the superior sealing aspect of epoxy resins, I doubt that they'd really be used much as boatbuilding glues." Letter from Kern Hendricks, president, System Three Resins, Seattle, Washington, November 14, 1987.

[17] "Disadvantages of Epoxies are—they require far superior cleanliness and preparation prior to gluing and very precise mixing compared with resorcinol or UF-type adhesives. Most joint failures with epoxies relate to poor mixing and/or poor accuracy of measuring resin-hardener; starving of glue line due to excessive clamping pressures; oily timber not being thoroughly degreased, which means the epoxy will not wet surface and therefore does not bond; timber not being crosshatch-sanded to enable epoxy glue to wet out surface." Letter to editor, *Boating New Zealand,* August 1987, from Russell J. Pauling, marine marketing manager, Healing Industries Ltd., Auckland, formulators of marine epoxies.

[18] "Although we have never had any trouble with it, some varieties of teak are notoriously hard to bond. Try some sample joints with teak if you intend to use it before applying it to the deck." *The Gougeon Brothers on Boat Construction,* page 257.

"Epoxy seems to have trouble with oak, but no one knows exactly why." Aimé Ontario Fraser, *WoodenBoat* magazine, September/October 1988, page 52.

[19] "We recommend using 421 (fire-retardant powder) in engine and galley areas where fire hazards may exist. A 421 resin coating is more fire resistant than epoxy alone and it will self-extinguish when the source of flame is removed. It should, however, be considered combustible in a major fire." *The Gougeon Brothers on Boat Construction,* page 45.

[20] "Is it not better to heed the one [sic] limitation of epoxy resin adhesives (prevent from deep-moisture cycling) and use resorcinol where this is a problem?" Letter from Kern Hendricks,

president, System Three Resins, November 14, 1987.

"Wood surfaces should be coated with a minimum of two coats of West System epoxy to provide an effective moisture barrier; three coats should be applied if sanding is to be done." *West System Products Technical Manual,* page 5-1.

[21] "A hull, for example, which is colder than the surrounding air, may experience condensation and result in water contamination to epoxy applied on it." *Strategies for Successful Cold Temperature Bonding and Sealing with Epoxy,* Gougeon Brothers, Inc., page 5.

[22] "Unprotected epoxy resins are not ultimately sunlight resistant. After about six months of exposure to intense sunlight they begin to decay. Additional exposure will induce chalking and eventually the epoxy will disintegrate, losing its mechanical properties." *The Epoxy Book,* page 6.

[23] ". . . but with resorcinol I've never had any glue failures. I've used all the epoxies, but for gluing wood together there's nothing better than resorcinol, in my opinion, especially if the wood is going to be subjected to repeated or continuous water saturation." John Guzzwell, interviewed by Jim Brown, *WoodenBoat* magazine, September/October 1988, page 71.

[24] "Resorcinol and melamine-urea adhesives appear to perform well at high temperatures and the glue laminated timber industries in New Zealand boast about the structural integrity of their material during a fire." Report by Brian Boult (see note 4), page 12.

"Aerodux RL 188 NZ is also suited to the production of heat-resistant composite structures including fire-check doors." Materials safety data sheets, Aerodux RL 188 NZ, March 1986. Available from Dimet Adhesives, P.O. Box 11123, Ellerslie, New Zealand.

[25] Materials safety data sheets, Aerodux RL 186 NZ and RL 188 NZ, March 1986. Available from Dimet Adhesives.

INDEX

BIBLIOGRAPHY

Bingham, Fred P. *Practical Yacht Joinery: Tools, Techniques, Tips.* Camden, ME: International Marine Publishing, 1983.

Chapelle, Howard I. *Boatbuilding.* New York: W.W. Norton, 1941.

The Gougeon Brothers on Boat Construction. 2d ed. Bay City, MI: Gougeon Brothers, Inc., 1980.

Herreshoff, L. Francis. *The Common Sense of Yacht Design.* 2 vols. 1946. Reprint. Jamaica, NY: Caravan Maritime Books.

Herreshoff, L. Francis. *Sensible Cruising Designs.* Camden, ME: International Marine Publishing, 1973.

Jurd, K.H.C. *Yacht Construction.* 3d ed. [originally *Practical Yacht Construction* by C.J. Watts] London: Adlard Coles, Ltd., 1970.

Kinney, Francis S. *Skene's Elements of Yacht Design.* 8th ed. New York: Dodd, Mead, 1973.

McIntosh, David C. ("Bud"). *How to Build a Wooden Boat.* Brooklin, ME: WoodenBoat Publications, 1987.

Pardey, Lin and Larry. *The Self-Sufficient Sailor.* New York: W.W. Norton, 1982.

Pretzer, Roger. *Marine Metals Manual.* Camden, ME: International Marine Publishing, 1975.

Skene, Norman L. *Elements of Yacht Design.* New York: Kennedy Bros., 1927.

Steward, Robert M. *Boatbuilding Manual, 2nd Edition.* Camden, ME: International Marine Publishing, 1980.

ABOUT THE AUTHOR

Larry Pardey spent his teenage years rebuilding several boats ranging from eight to twenty feet in length. As he sold each one, he used his "sweat equity" profits to finance his next project. His largest from-the-keel-up projects have been the two boats he built with his wife Lin; *Seraffyn* the five-ton cutter which took them on an eleven-year east-about circumnavigation, and *Taleisin* the boat shown in this book, which took them west-about over the past fifteen years. As they cruised, Larry put his skills to work earning the majority of his income by repairing and restoring classic boats in fifteen different countries. Many of the ideas he shares in this book were learned form builders he met in the course of his travels.

As Peter Milne, editor of *Classic Boat* magazine commented, "Larry's prime interest might be the building of wooden craft, but he is one of those rare creatures, a builder who has covered a tremendous number of sea miles—more than 150,000—in yachts of his own building as well as other people's. This has given Larry firsthand information about which boat-building techniques work, which don't, out there in the big test-tank, the ocean. With his well-rounded background, Larry has developed a reputation as one of the master craftsmen of the wooden boatbuilding world."

For over 34 years, Lin has worked alongside Larry, doing his purchasing and finish work. Through her efforts as a writer, she financed the building of both *Seraffyn* and *Taleisin*. She also worked as a researcher and editor on this book.

Together Lin and Larry have written nine other books and produced four videos on various sailing subjects. They are currently residing at their homebase in New Zealand where they have a small boat repair facility and work on classic boats.